S0-BYM-410

PRODUCTION AND OPERATIONS MANAGEMENT

PRODUCTION AND OPERATIONS MANAGEMENT

DONALD W. FOGARTY, CFPIM

Southern Illinois University at Edwardsville

THOMAS R. HOFFMANN, CFPIM

University of Minnesota

PETER W. STONEBRAKER, CPIM

DePaul University

APICS

**Published in conjunction with the
American Production & Inventory Control Society**

G12
PUBLISHED BY
SOUTH-WESTERN PUBLISHING CO.
CINCINNATI   WEST CHICAGO, IL   CARROLLTON, TX   LIVERMORE, CA

Copyright © 1989
by South-Western Publishing Co.
Cincinnati, Ohio

ALL RIGHTS RESERVED

The text of this publication, or any part thereof, may not be reproduced or transmitted in any form or by any means, electronic or mechanical, including photocopying, recording, storage in an information retrieval system, or otherwise, without the prior written permission of the publisher.

1 2 3 4 5 6 7 K 4 3 2 1 0 9

Printed in the United States of America

Fogarty, Donald W.
    Production and operations management / Donald W. Fogarty, Thomas
R. Hoffmann, Peter W. Stonebraker.
        p.   cm.
    "Published in conjunction with the American Production & Inventory
Control Society."
    Bibliography.
    Includes index.
    ISBN 0-538-07125-7 :
    1. Production management.   I. Hoffmann, Thomas Russell,
II. Stonebraker, Peter W.   III. American Production and
Inventory Control Society.   IV. Title.
    TS155.F62   1989
    658.5—dc19   88-38136
                                                                    CIP

PREFACE

Production and operations management is one of the most exciting and dynamic areas of business today. Tremendous growth and changes are occurring in the field every day, but the basic concepts and principles are still important.

This text is designed to teach production and operations management on an introductory level. It provides a greater depth of coverage in important areas such as material requirements planning, layout, and forecasting than other texts, yet still maintains a broad perspective. Published in conjunction with the American Production and Inventory Control Society (APICS), it will appeal to instructors in an academic environment as well as to those wishing to provide materials for students seeking APICS certification.

Production and Operations Management examines the concepts, principles, and techniques of production and operations management within a framework of four interrelated characteristics: the time period in which objectives are to be achieved, the resources managed, the major areas affected by the decision, and the management function involved. The text is organized in a logical manner, from long-range planning through medium- and short-range planning to execution, integrating various functional areas of business as they relate to operations management. The systems approach is a core concept throughout the text.

The text allows maximum flexibility of instruction. It is ideal for introductory academic programs of one or two semesters or quarters. Chapters 1–3, 5, 6, 9, 11, 14, 15 and 18-20 can also be used for a one-quarter undergraduate introduction. The book is also suitable for programs conducted by APICS chapters and other practitioner societies.

OVERVIEW

PART I INTRODUCTION defines operations management and emphasizes its relationship to productivity and overall quality of life, as well as the applicability of operations management to manufacturing and service organizations. It answers questions such as: Why study operations management? What do operations managers do? What kind of decisions do they make? What are the differences between manufacturing and service organizations in regards to operations management?

Parts II through V are organized according to long-, medium-, and short-range planning. The text recognizes that decisions are being made in all time frames concurrently with execution and control. It also recognizes that some activities, such as forecasting, take place with regard to more than one time horizon. We feel that studying operations management in relation to planning horizons, execution, and control aids students in understanding the objectives, constraints, and principles of specific decisions by making them aware that these boundaries are not absolute.

Each chapter in Parts II through V contains a description of the decision situations, related management objectives, applicable models, decision techniques and procedures, and information system requirements.

PART II   LONG-RANGE PLANNING introduces a general planning model of the firm, then focuses a series of capacity, location, and process questions that the operations manager must address and ultimately answer in the long, medium, and short range. The planning decisions of the operations manager then are specifically integrated with the criteria for evaluating effectiveness of execution and control. Various qualitative and quantitative methods are used to evaluate location alternatives, and the traditional and emerging process design approaches are analyzed in detail.

We have included these topics in Part II because, for the most part, they involve decisions that do take a long time to implement and are in fact usually strategic in nature. The long-range plan establishes the major definitions of the product or service, the location, and the method of producing. These commitments can not be changed except at great expense and in the long range (a time period that varies tremendously by industry).

PART III   MEDIUM-RANGE PLANNING discusses a variety of critical intermediate decisions. Here some minor adjustments of the product or service are possible; however, redefinitions of the output inconsistent with the long-range plan will again be extremely costly. In the medium range, the operations manager develops the information system to provide a much greater amount of very specific detail pertaining to values of the product, materials, purchases, and human resources, and to the general scheduling of resources for efficiency.

Forecasts are made for events in the distant future (2 to 10 years hence), in the next 12 months, and sometimes in the next few hours, although the methods used may differ for these different situations. Forecasting of customer demand and the aggregate planning of capacity utilization are integrated into an initial "rough cut" schedule, which after numerous reviews becomes a reasonably firm master production schedule. Simultaneously, the layout of the facility and the specific employee functions within that facility are evaluated for organization and efficiency. Layouts may be revised on notice of a day or two, for example, in a storeroom; but most require considerable time for full implementation. We have included the above topics under medium-range planning because most take place 3 to 18 months prior to execution.

PART IV   SHORT-RANGE PLANNING focuses on those decisions that immediately precede execution. Most of the short-range planning in the operations management function involves scheduling. Materials and capacity must be scheduled using inventory management and material requirements planning techniques. Additionally, human resources and specific jobs must be scheduled through capacity management methods. The fundamental plans and methods are established in the medium- and long-range plans. Short-range scheduling is the final evaluation of the production process prior to execution to ensure that the plan will work and that it efficiently uses resources.

PART V   EXECUTION AND CONTROL deals with operations management functions that coincide with the production of the operation's output, including the control of inputs and the distribution of output. The operations manager must simultaneously execute a schedule to produce a good or service and control that process to ensure quality, timing, and delivery specifications.

PART VI   POLICY AND STRATEGY provides a broad overview of the field with emphasis on current developments. Most new students of operations management grasp and understand policy issues better after covering the basic functions of operations management. Although elements of JIT and TQC are integrated into earlier chapters, we include them in this section because their success requires an organizational commitment and broad changes in policy affecting many areas of the firm.

PART VII   TECHNICAL SUPPLEMENTS contains chapters on financial analysis, mathematical programming, simulation, and waiting line theory. They constitute a core of basic technical background material for the rest of the book. These chapters may be covered at any time or they may be used as reference chapters as needed.

FEATURES

Each chapter begins with chapter objectives and a chapter outline, and ends with extensive questions and problems and a list of references. Many of the other features of the text are listed below.

Integration of the principal dimensions of operations management. These include the time period affected, the resource managed, the decision area affected, and the management function.

The time-line orientation. Provides a long-range to short-range planning to execution perspective of operations management.

Service emphasis. Recognizes the rapid growth of services in the economy with several chapters and sections dedicated to service-related topics. Specifically, Chapter 2 differentiates manufacturing and service operations, and chapters 4, 14, 15, 16, 17, 19, and 24 have sections devoted to service-related approaches. Additionally, service industry applications of concepts are discussed throughout the text.

The systems approach. Systems are discussed in Chapter 1 and integrated throughout the book. The information systems requirements of the operations manager are addressed for each topic.

APICS-approved material. The material is specifically consistent with the APICS terminology and doctrine, and the text extensively draws from the rich backdrop of APICS literature. The authors are APICS certified, two at the fellow level.

Currency of topics. Separate chapters are dedicated to MRP, and to JIT, TQC, and OPT. Additionally, CIM is extensively discussed in Chapters 5, 19, and 20. More importantly, all chapters treat the material with emphasis toward these current topics and directions of operations management.

Technical depth. Chapters on technical subjects, such as layout (9), forecasting (6), MRP (12), location (4), work design (10), statistical quality control (18), and independent inventory control (11), among others, have more depth than similar treatments in most other texts.

Extensive and varied end-of-chapter exercises.

The instructor's manual. Contains answers to all end-of-chapter questions and problems. Problem solutions are in large type to facilitate their use as transparency masters. The manual also contains transparency masters of many of the figures in the text.

The Decision Assistant software for the IBM PC. Contains tools to solve many of the end-of-chapter problems and allows students to explore the implications of varying problem parameters.

The Test Bank. Approximately 750 multiple-choice questions. Also available in MicroSWAT II format, South-Western's automated testing package for the IBM PC and compatibles.

ACKNOWLEDGMENTS

We would like to thank the many colleagues who have contributed to this project. In particular we want to thank Yunus Kathawala, Eastern Illinois University; John M. Burnham, Tennessee Technological University; Raman C. Patel, California State University at Chico; and James F. Cox, University of Georgia, for their helpful reviews of drafts of the manuscript. Special thanks go to Patrick J. Devereaux for his assistance with the end-of-chapter exercises and the instructor's manual, and to George J. Foegen, Metropolitan State College, Denver, for the test bank. Finally, we want to thank our many colleagues at APICS, particularly Michael J. Stack, Executive Director, and Charles G. Mertens, Director of Education.

Donald W. Fogarty
Thomas R. Hoffmann
Peter W. Stonebraker

CONTENTS

PART I
INTRODUCTION

CHAPTER 1
Operations Management—A Professional Perspective

CHAPTER 2
Manufacturing and Service Organizations

CHAPTER 1
OPERATIONS MANAGEMENT— A PROFESSIONAL PERSPECTIVE

OBJECTIVES

After completing this chapter, you should be able to

- Give examples of some operations management positions

- Define operations management and describe the functions performed by operations managers

- Indicate and illustrate the diverse influences that have contributed to the field of operations management

- Define a system, explain how organizations may be viewed as systems, and describe how the systems approach might be applied by operations managers

- Define productivity in general and give examples of specific productivity measures; explain how operations management affects productivity and how measures of productivity can be used to evaluate operations management

- Discuss the operations manager's contribution to the organization, the community, and the economy

2

OUTLINE

Introduction
The Operations Function
 Definition of Operations Management
 Examples of Operations Management
History of Operations Management
Systems Concepts and Operations Management
 Definition of a System
 System Elements
 Systems Hierarchy: Suprasystems, Systems, Subsystems
 The Systems Approach
  Systems Analysis
  Management Systems
  Information Systems
Productivity and Operations Management
 Measurement of Productivity
 National Productivity
 Industry Productivity
 Organizational Productivity
  Individual Measures of Productivity
Conclusions
Questions
References

INTRODUCTION

This book examines the concepts, principles, and techniques of operations management, a major functional area of business. An operations manager is concerned with actually operating a business as opposed to financing it or marketing its products. Of course, these functions often overlap, but the focus of this book is on the decisions and actions needed to operate an organization—that is, the functions necessary to produce and deliver the goods and services the organization provides to its clients or customers.

Most of the principles, concepts, and techniques to be examined apply to a variety of products, including manufactured goods, nonmanufactured goods, and a broad array of services. Many students just beginning this course will be more familiar with the operations of service industries, having been customers, than with manufacturing operations. Traditionally, however, operations management has focused primarily on the production of manufactured goods. In recent years the production and delivery of services has assumed an increasingly important role in the economy and become a major priority for operations managers. Throughout this text operations management is applied to both manufacturing and service production, although some concepts are more applicable to one than the other. Chapter 2 highlights some of the special concerns of service operations.

Operations management decisions can be examined within the framework of the following four interrelated characteristics or dimensions:

1. The time period in which the objectives are to be achieved
2. The resources being managed
3. The major operations management areas affected by the decision
4. The basic management function involved

The elements of these characteristics are given in Table 1–1. The interrelationships of these elements are apparent. For example, decisions concerning any resource can affect capacity; planning and control can be performed for all resources and with regard to all areas. Some elements, such as the manage-

Table 1–1   Dimensions of Operations Management Decisions

Time period affected	Resource managed	Area affected	Management function
Long-range	Facilities	Capacity	Planning
Medium-range	Equipment	Materials	Execution
Short-range	Materials	Quality	Control
Present	Labor	Process	Organization
	Information	Personnel	Staffing
	Capital		
	Energy		

ment of capital and personnel, are covered in this text only to the extent that they affect operations management decisions. A more thorough examination of these elements is left to finance or human resource management texts.

THE OPERATIONS FUNCTION

The management activities of most organizations are usually divided into the following major functional areas:

General management
Finance and accounting
Marketing
Product and service design (engineering and research)
Human resources
Operations management
Information systems
Other: legal, insurance, etc.

Their relationship can be illustrated by an organizational chart such as the one shown in Figure 1–1.

Figure 1–1 Chart of a Typical Organization

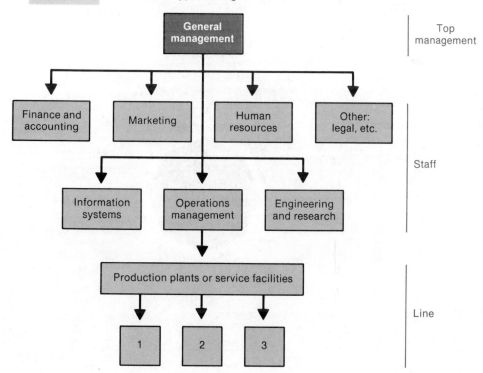

The type of organization, its organizational policies, and the competitive environment in which it operates all affect the organizational structure and the emphasis placed on each of these functions, but each function must be performed. Some organizations traditionally have used different names for some of these functions. For example, in a university the marketing of undergraduate programs is done primarily by the admissions office.

Individual activities and decisions within an organization, while usually supporting one of the major functional areas, must also be in concert in order to achieve the goals of the organization as a whole, as suggested in Figure 1–2. The need to remain competitive and the sensitivity of customer demand require that operations management, marketing, and engineering all participate in decisions concerning a revised product design. In a similar manner, both the kitchen manager and the head chef should be consulted before an item is added to a restaurant's menu.

The proportion of resources allocated to each functional area depends on the type of organization, its policies, and its environment. For example, the advent of the cashless society in the 1960s and 1970s, with its dramatic increase in the number of check and credit card transactions processed by banks and other financial institutions, motivated institutions to pay greater attention to their "back room" operations. They have increased the resources

Figure 1–2   Major Functional Areas

allocated to operations management, including personnel to analyze transaction processing and equipment to perform timely and efficient processing. This increased interest in productivity and allocation of resources to operations management is as pervasive in manufacturing as it is in financial, health care, educational, and other service industries.

Definition of Operations Management

Operations management is a continual process of effectively using management functions to integrate resources efficiently in order to achieve operations goals. Since this definition may seem rather abstract, descriptions of the key terms follow.

Continual process. Operations management is not a single discrete action or behavior. The concerns, issues, and decisions of the operations manager are not one-time actions, but ongoing or continual processes.

Effectively. The effective manager perceives the role of the department as supportive of the organizational goals and gets results by doing those jobs that should be done. Effectiveness is doing the right job well; it is the first criterion of job performance for the operations manager.

Management functions. Operations management functions include the planning, execution (direction), and control of the process; the planning and control of the resources; and the staffing and organization of the operations function itself. Figure 1–3 is a schematic representation of these activities using the systems framework of inputs converted into outputs by a process,

Figure 1–3 Management Functions

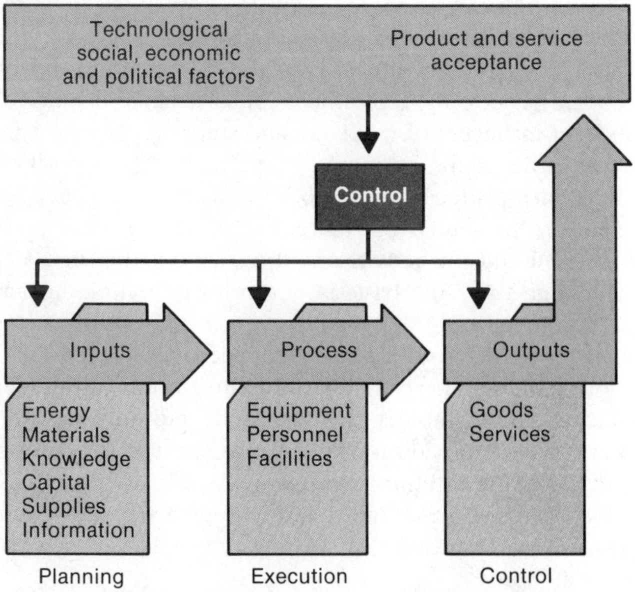

with control attained by feedback that measures the results obtained and the customer reaction to those results. A more detailed description of systems concepts appears later in this chapter.

Integrate resources. A variety of resources, including facilities, materials, capital, equipment, energy, labor, and knowledge, are integrated in the production of manufactured goods or services. Integration involves mixing two or more resources in differing combinations. For example the integration of limestone, iron ore, coal, an electric hearth, and labor produces steel.

Efficiently. The ability to do the job efficiently means making the best use of resources by minimizing waste. Efficiency means doing the job right; it is also the second criterion of job performance for the operations manager.

Operations goals. Operations goals are often measured by such criteria as cost, flexibility, quality, or delivery. In that respect, effectiveness means selecting the best operations goal or objective for the situation and efficiency is optimizing that chosen evaluative measure.

The operations management definition itself is integrated—that is, it depends upon each key word or part to make a whole definition. For example, without goals, there is no need for an operations manager.

Examples of Operations Management

In addition to the factory manager, operations management positions exist in a variety of organizations. Hospital administrators, farm managers, hotel managers, cafeteria managers, airport managers, the director of a regional post office, and the director of a tax return processing office are all operations managers. They manage people, facilities, equipment, and processes to provide a product, a service, or some combination. Inventory managers, purchasing agents, schedulers, designers of statistical quality control processes, methods analysts, individuals involved in designing the physical layouts of offices and processing departments, maintenance planners, shop floor supervisors, and managers of receiving and shipping departments are a few of the many possible examples of operations management positions.

Examples of decisions made by individuals engaged in operations management are presented in Figure 1–4 to give a fuller picture of operations management and the activities of those involved in it.

Although the same basic structure of operations management activities, tasks, problems, and decisions exists in nearly all organizations, the relative importance of decision areas is dependent on the type of organization. For example, although there are important inventory management decisions made in educational institutions, the magnitude and importance of inventory management in such organizations is not as great as it is in most manufacturing organizations. In addition, management of waiting lines is more important in banks, fast-food restaurants, and emergency repair organizations than in a company manufacturing a standard product for distribution from a finished goods warehouse.

Figure 1–4   Typical Operations Management Decisions

1. A plant manager deciding the number of personnel by skill category that will be required to meet production schedules each month during the coming year.
2. A restaurant manager deciding the number of cooks, waiters, and attendants that will be required each shift during the coming week and then scheduling individuals to work those shifts.
3. A college department chairperson (production planner) determining capacity requirements, such as how many sections of accounting courses will be required during the coming year and the number of faculty required to staff them.
4. A process engineer reviewing with design engineering the preliminary design of a part and determining the cost of manufacturing it.
5. A manufacturing quality analyst deciding how the quality of a process should be measured.
6. A facility planner selecting the criteria for evaluating possible plant, warehouse, or retail outlets and then ranking potential sites.
7. A production planner developing preventive maintenance procedures and schedules.
8. A production planner deciding the quantity of materials and purchase parts to order and when to release the orders to meet a production schedule.
9. An operations analyst in a bank studying the processing of customers' cancelled checks, searching for methods of reducing bottlenecks in the operation, reducing flowthrough time, and increasing productivity.
10. A manager of a receiving department studying methods of scheduling arrivals, assigning incoming trucks to docks, unloading trucks, processing the necessary data and information, and moving the items received to their proper location in order to reduce the time required for receiving and moving materials to the point of usage.
11. A hospital materials manager analyzing the decision rules that determine the quantities of items held in individual nursing units and the quantities held in central stores to determine if the inventory investment can be reduced without a negative effect on item availability.
12. A manufacturing control systems analyst evaluating commercially available MRP II software packages.

HISTORY OF OPERATIONS MANAGEMENT

Operations management has existed for eons. Egyptian pyramids, Roman aqueducts, Mayan and Incan temples, and the Great Wall of China supply evidence of enormous feats of operations management as well as engineering. However, historians and operations managers in ancient times left virtually no written descriptions of operations management practices. Although some concepts, principles, and practices were likely passed down by word of mouth,

Figure 1–5   The Foundation of Operations Management Practices

the majority have probably been discovered many times over in many different places. Elements of the body of knowledge and practices that constitute operations management fall into the following categories (see also Figure 1–5):

1. *Applications of knowledge or practices developed in other disciplines, such as economics, finance, the behavioral sciences, and mathematics.* Examples include return-on-investment (ROI) analysis from the finance area and linear and mathematical programming from operations research. These and similar concepts are important in other functional areas, such as marketing and finance, as well as in operations management.

2. *Techniques and concepts that were developed under the rubric of organization and management theory.* There are many schools of management and organizational analysis, including the classical and neoclassical theories of organization, the behavioral approaches, the empirical school, and the decision theory school (Murdick and Ross 1975). Many of these ideas originated during the study of production and factory management, and each has affected operations management, its organization, and the management of personnel.

3. *Technological innovations.* The computer and laser technology are only the latest technological developments to dramatically affect operations management. The development of the printing press, clock mechanisms, the

steam engine, and electricity brought substantial changes in processes and operations management.

4. *Eclectic approaches that are very broad in scope, that incorporate selected elements of many existing approaches, and that promote integrated management activities.* The systems approach is the most prominent example of an eclectic approach. Although total quality control and the just-in-time approach (see Chapter 20) are basic operations management concepts and fall in the category described next, they are also good examples of eclectic approaches.

5. *Concepts that are inherent and essential to operations management.* These constitute the body of knowledge that differentiates operations management from other disciplines such as marketing, finance, economics, management, and operations research. Examples are the independent-dependent demand concept (see Chapter 11), material requirements planning (see Chapter 12), and manufacturing cells.

There have been hundreds, perhaps thousands, of developments, innovations, and improvements arising from many disciplines that have contributed to current operations management practices. The list in Table 1–2 focuses primarily on the developments of the past century. It was during this period that operations management became more than a loose collection of concepts and techniques and took on the semblance of a unified discipline. A few caveats are appropriate while considering the salient developments in operations management. First, the originators of many ideas are unknown; history tends to record the individual who documents (publishes) the concept or technique. This is especially true if the individual is well known and respected in the discipline. For example, the management-by-exception principle probably existed for centuries before Frederick Taylor gave it prominence through his writings. As a result, he frequently receives credit for it. Furthermore, the same solution, conclusion, or new idea often comes to a number of different individuals at roughly the same time; a new approach may be the result of many professionals in different organizations attacking a problem. For example, the current development and refinement of capacity planning concepts and techniques resulted from the work of at least a half dozen leaders in the field.

SYSTEMS CONCEPTS AND OPERATIONS MANAGEMENT

Systems concepts are very helpful in understanding the management process. They provide a framework both for grasping how a decision situation arises and for making decisions. Most importantly, these concepts provide a structure for integrating operations management actions (decisions) with each other and with the primary goals of the organization. Information and decision systems are required for long-, medium-, and short-range planning, execution, and control activities. This section describes the relationship of these activities to systems concepts and information systems.

Table 1–2   Developments in Operations Management

Time Period	Originator	Concept, Principle, or Approach
1490	Shipbuilders of Venice	Assembly line construction
1776	Adam Smith	Specialization of labor
1798	Eli Whitney	Interchangeable parts
1880–1915	Frederick Taylor	Principles of scientific management, exception principle, methods analysis, time study, and standards
1910–1924	Frank Gilbreth	Methods analysis and motion study
1924–1973	Lillian Gilbreth	Fatigue and human factors, selection and training of employees
1890–1919	Henry L. Gantt	Activity scheduling charts, incentive pay systems, humanistic approach to labor
1908	A. K. Erlang	Queuing theory
1913	Henry Ford	Moving assembly line
1917	F. W. Harris	Economic lot size
1925	Czechoslovakia	Group technology
1931	Walter Shewhart, H. F. Dodge, and H. G. Romig	Statistical quality control
1934	Elton Mayo	Participative management, motivation and productivity (The Hawthorne Study)
1934	R. H. Wilson	Statistical order points
1934	L. H. C. Tippitt	Work (activity) sampling
1940	Operations research groups in the United Kingdom	Multidiscipline team analysis of complex problems
1947	George B. Dantzig	Simplex method of linear programming
1951	Ford Dickie	Application of ABC approach
1950	Many individuals	Application of simulation to operations
1959	R. G. Brown	Exponential smoothing forecasting
1959–1961	James E. Kelley, M. Walker, and U. S. Navy Special Project Office	Network project management techniques
1968–1975	Joseph Orlicky, George Plossl, Oliver Wight, and others	Dependent/independent demand concept and material requirements planning (MRP)
1960–present	Japanese manufacturing management and engineers	Japanese manufacturing management approaches
1970	William Skinner	Integrating operations management and organization strategy and policy
1970s	Steve Wozniak and Steve Jobs	Availability of personal computers and networking

Definition of a System

The following definition of a system reveals how an organization, whether it be in a manufacturing or a service industry, can be perceived as a system.

A system is a group of elements such as personnel, machines, energy, and information, working in an integrated fashion toward a set of objectives. This goal-directed activity consists of inputs entering a process and being transformed into outputs.

System Elements

A system consists of six essential elements: inputs, transformation, outputs, feedback, control, and the environment (see Figure 1–6).

Inputs include all the resources that affect or are consumed in the transformation process including personnel, materials, purchased components, facilities, equipment, capital, information, and customers. Since the inputs affect the process, they also affect the output. Examples include raw materials, the technology used in the process (e.g., casting versus forging), the skill of the operators, and the equipment (e.g., computer-controlled versus operator-controlled welding) in manufacturing. Students and faculty are important inputs in the educational process, along with texts and classrooms. The attire and behavior of customers leads many restaurants to establish controls (decision rules) concerning the acceptance of inputs (customers).

Transformation includes all the activities (processes) that take place in achieving the goals of the organization. The machining of parts and the

Figure 1–6 System Elements

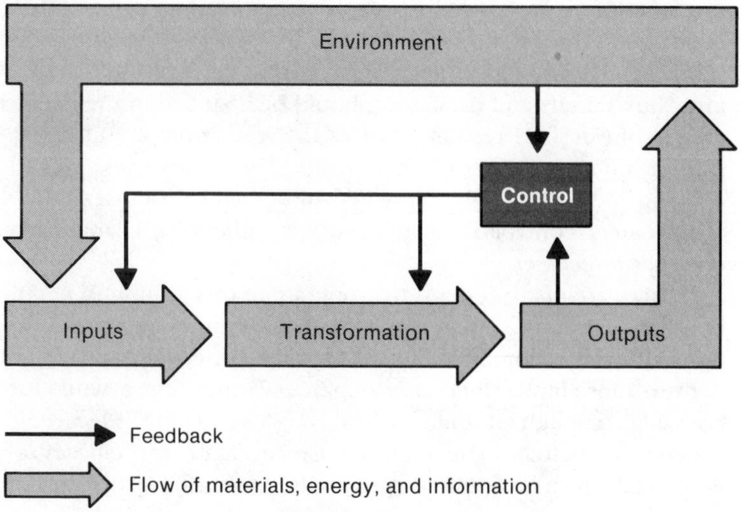

Feedback

Flow of materials, energy, and information

packaging of completed assemblies are examples of manufacturing processes. Registering a guest in a hotel and treating the injury of a patient in a hospital are examples of service processes. But both manufacturing and service organizations perform processes not immediately involved in providing a product or service. These include the recruitment and selection of personnel and the design of the service or manufacturing process. In addition, both manufacturing and service organizations have information systems that record data and convert them into the information required for decision making. Each process is part of a system that must be integrated with the other systems to achieve the organization's overall goals, but it does have its own inputs, outputs, and control.

Outputs are the results produced by the system and exported to the environment. Completed products such as cameras, clothing, new buildings, highways, and fertilizer are examples of manufacturing outputs. Service outputs include many diverse examples such as training received, radio and television programs, medical diagnosis and treatment, financial advice, automotive repairs, and lodging in a hotel.

Control is a three-step activity: (1) measuring actual results, (2) comparing actual results to desired results, and (3) deciding if any changes should be made. **Feedback** is an essential part of control. Feedback includes measuring system performance (determining what the actual output of the system is), transmitting that data to the control unit, and transmitting regulatory directives from the control unit where decisions are made to the individuals or mechanisms that execute the input and process decisions.

The control unit, which may be automatic, such as a thermostat on a furnace, or human, such as a master scheduler or a chef, is the decision-making unit. It receives the measurement of actual results through the feedback channels and then compares the actual results with the desired results. If actual results differ from desired results by more than an acceptable tolerance, the control unit directs that inputs and/or the process should be changed to bring actual results into closer alignment with desired results. The ability to determine how inputs and processes should be changed in the event actual results differ from desired results requires that the control unit know the relationship of inputs, processes, and outputs. The control unit must have a model defining the relationships between inputs and processes (the variables that management controls) and the outputs; otherwise changes would be based on random guesses.

There are many systems that operate in this fashion. When the thermostat in a home heating system senses that the temperature has dropped below a desired level, it immediately activates the processing unit (the furnace) and delivers more input (fuel) resulting in a warmer home; when the temperature rises high enough, it shuts off the processing unit. Physicians observe the progress of patients and continuously evaluate the efficacy of the therapy employed. In many cardiac care units, nurses have the authority (standing orders) to administer specific medications to patients exhibiting physiological characteristics requiring immediate action. A chef decides to add further seasoning on the basis of taste. A machinist adjusts a machine tool if parts are beginning to exceed or approach a tolerance limit. Few individuals go through a day without evaluating the results of some activity and deciding that certain changes should be made if actual results are going to approach desired results. Such activities can frequently be described and understood better when they are viewed as a system.

The environment includes everything that is not part of the system. The boundary of a system distinguishes the system from its environment. Sometimes the demarcation between a system and its environment is quite clear. For example, government regulations and customers belong to the environment of most manufacturing organizations. Customers can be considered part of the system itself in self-service establishments. Perhaps nowhere is this more apparent than in public restrooms, where cleanliness and usefulness depend largely on the customers. In some cases the purpose of a study determines system boundaries. For example, in one case it may be desirable to include the inventory costing subsystem as part of the materials management system for an inventory management study and in another case it may not be.

Systems Hierarchy: Suprasystems, Systems, Subsystems

A system frequently has subsystems with objectives that should support the goals of the system. For example, the materials management system objectives should support and be consistent with the goals of the organization. The organization may also be viewed as the suprasystem to which the materials management system belongs. The finished goods storeroom is viewed as a subsystem of the materials management system, and the supplier evaluation system and purchase order release systems are seen as subsystems of the purchasing system. Figure 1–7 illustrates this concept.

The Systems Approach

The systems approach is a group of systems-oriented concepts, methods, and techniques used for problem solving, decision making, analyzing, determining management processes, and evaluating performance. Its essence is viewing each organization or entity as a system, focusing on its role in the suprasystem of which it is a part and on the roles of subsystems that make it up. A system is more than the sum of its parts; the interaction of those parts is significant.

The systems approach encompasses all the systems definitions, concepts, and techniques described in this chapter. The application of the systems approach may be more or less explicit. For example, an organization may

Figure 1–7 Systems Hierarchy

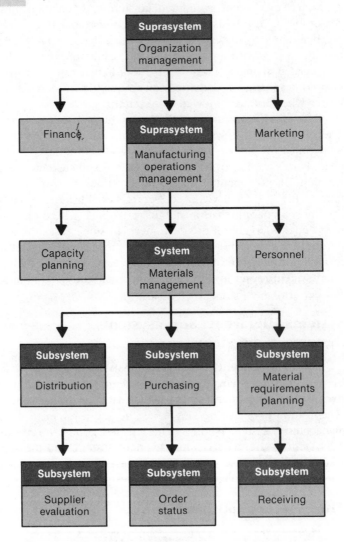

have management and information systems in place without formally or consciously embracing the systems approach. But it is doing so implicitly if it recognizes a hierarchy of objectives and systematically analyzes the impact of each department's activities on the other departments and on the whole organization. Conscious application of the systems approach has proven to be a valuable tool for effective management.

SYSTEMS ANALYSIS. Systems analysis is a somewhat formal methodology for applying the systems approach. It includes the following:

1. Defining the problems of management as decision-making situations with objectives, constraints, resources, alternate courses of action, and criteria by which to measure decision results
2. Analyzing the decision situation to determine the relationship between controlled variables, uncontrolled variables, and the decision results (the outputs) and then developing models that describe those relationships
3. Evaluating the models by inserting different values for the controlled variables, calculating the results, evaluating the alternatives on the basis of these results, and identifying preferred courses of action under various sets of circumstances

A study of the relationships described by the models leads to decision rules and decision guidelines. The following are examples of simple rules and guidelines developed from models: (1) order 1,000 units of Final Assembly J9785 when the quantity on hand drops below 100 units and (2) designate 15 percent of the capacity in work center A, Computer Control Milling, as safety capacity.

MANAGEMENT SYSTEMS. The decision rules and guidelines adopted by an organization to plan, direct, and control its operation are its management systems. A set of decision rules for a given situation implicitly declares that the organization has a model of the situation—that it knows the relationship of the dominant controllable variables to the decision results. For example, a forecast of demand two to four years hence based on the birth rate during the last three years indicates that an organization believes there is a relationship between these variables. Using historical data to run a model will reveal how accurately it would have predicted past events. An organization must also decide if the relationship will hold in the future or if it will be altered by new technology, changing political conditions, or changing social norms.

INFORMATION SYSTEMS. Once the criteria, decision rules, and guidelines for making decisions have been selected, some means of gathering, recording, processing, and communicating the required information to the proper decision makers at the right time must be developed. These methods of gathering, recording, processing, and communicating constitute the information system. The implementation of information systems is the culmination of applying systems concepts to operations management.

PRODUCTIVITY AND OPERATIONS MANAGEMENT

Productivity is the broadest and most versatile measure of operations management performance. Productivity is a measure of how well resources are managed and utilized in achieving a set of desired results. In general it is the ratio of output to input—the ratio of results achieved to resources consumed.

$$\text{Productivity} = \frac{\text{Output}}{\text{Input}} = \frac{\text{Results achieved}}{\text{Resources consumed}}$$

Operations management is a major determinant of an organization's productivity; and the aggregate productivity of organizations in a community plays a dominant part in the standard of living that the community experiences.

In the 1870s the price of barbed wire fell from 18 cents to 3 cents a pound in the United States and, during the same period, the design of the barb was shortened to do less harm when contacted by cattle. The reduced cost was a result of improvements in product design, machinery, processes, and job design, as well as the movement of manufacturing facilities from the eastern United States to Midwest locations that were much closer to the dominant users, the western ranchers (Coleman 1984). The results were dramatic and far reaching. The sale of barbed wire increased from 10,000 pounds in 1874 to 80 million pounds in 1880, total employment in wire manufacturing increased, raising beef cattle became more manageable and efficient, and the diet of an entire nation improved.

These events are a good example of the relationship between operations management, productivity, and the quality of life. Productivity is the ratio of the value of the output produced to the cost of producing that output. In the preceding example, the cost of a pound of barbed wire was reduced approximately 80 percent while at the same time the value (usefulness) of the wire increased due to improved design. These improvements resulted from capable and diligent operations managers and designers who focused on the needs of the customers. There is also more recent evidence of the relationship between operations management, productivity, and the standard of living.

Productivity may be measured for a nation, an industry, an organization, a department, or an individual. It may be measured in terms of all resources consumed (total factor productivity) or of a subset of resources. Labor productivity and capital productivity are examples of partial productivity measures.

Measures of productivity are especially useful when comparing the results achieved during one time period to those achieved in another or when comparing the productivity of two individuals, two organizations, two departments, or two nations. Because productivity can be measured in so many ways, the measurement is often reduced to an index to facilitate comparison. When an index is used, the productivity during a base period is given the value of 100 and subsequent measurements focus on the improvement or decline in productivity. Comparing productivity in successive years or from one period to a base period enables management to measure the increase or decrease in productivity and evaluate management performance and decisions.

Measurement of Productivity

The total factor productivity (TFP) of an organization equals its total output divided by the costs of all the contributing factors. The actual measurement requires defining and measuring the output and inputs. In practice this can be a complex task, but the concept is simple:

$$TFP = \frac{Output}{Labor + Capital + Materials}$$

Similarly, the total factor productivity of a national economy equals the gross national product (GNP) divided by the costs of all the contributing factors.

A partial productivity measure is the ratio of the value of the output to one of the inputs (single factor) or a subset of the inputs (multifactor). For example, two partial single factor productivity measures at the national level are

$$Labor\ productivity = \frac{Output}{Labor\ hours\ (or\ costs)}$$

and

$$Capital\ productivity = \frac{Output}{Capital\ costs}$$

A multifactor measure is

$$Labor\ and\ Capital\ productivity = \frac{Output}{Labor + Capital\ costs}$$

Multifactor productivity measures have the advantage of requiring less data than a total factor productivity model, while still producing a comprehensive indicator. (The Bureau of Labor Statistics multifactor index that combines capital and labor inputs is a good example.)

Relative productivity for any measure of productivity in a given period may be measured by an index such as the following:

$$Productivity\ index = \frac{Productivity,\ a\ specified\ period}{Productivity,\ base\ period} \times 100$$

Table 1–3 contains examples of single factor indices of labor and capital productivity and a multifactor index of labor and capital combined for the United States, using 1977 as a base year.

Table 1–3 Annual Indices of Productivity (1977 = 100)

Item	1960	1970	1977	1980	1983	1986
Private business						
Productivity:						
Output per hour of all persons	67.3	88.4	100.0	99.2	103.1	109.7
Output per unit of capital services	102.1	101.9	100.0	94.2	88.4	92.8
Multifactor productivity	78.1	92.9	100.0	97.4	97.7	103.4
Manufacturing						
Productivity:						
Output per hour of all persons	62.2	80.8	100.0	101.4	112.0	128.6
Output per unit of capital services	102.5	98.6	100.0	91.2	86.9	99.3
Multifactor productivity	71.9	85.2	100.0	98.7	105.1	120.6

Source: U.S. Department of Labor, Bureau of Labor Statistics, *Monthly Labor Review* (Washington, D.C.: U.S. Government Printing Office, January 1988).

National Productivity

Table 1–3 reveals the record of productivity change for the United States in recent years. The total increase in labor productivity in all private businesses was a modest 9.7 percent from 1977 through 1986, while labor productivity increased 28.8 percent in manufacturing. Capital productivity has actually declined 7.2 percent in all businesses during that period, although in manufacturing, capital productivity had recovered to almost the same level in 1986 as in 1977. The decline in capital productivity during much of that period has been attributed primarily to the underutilization of capital. As a general rule, as utilization of capacity increases, productivity tends to increase because fixed costs remain constant while output values increase. The reverse is also true, with decreasing utilization leading to decreasing productivity as fixed costs are spread over fewer units of output.

Many recent examples of the impact of operations management on national productivity and the quality of life also can be cited. The economy and quality of life of any nation depend on its ability to sell its products and services in the world market. This ability in turn depends on its relative productivity. A comparison of postwar Japan and the United States clearly demonstrates these relationships.

The United States had an enviable record of annual improvements in productivity and output during the first half of the twentieth century. However, for the first two decades after World War II, top management of manufacturing companies in the United States, with some notable exceptions, paid relatively little attention to manufacturing management. Hayes and Wheelwright (1984) have pointed out that the following three factors resulted in insufficient interest and time being devoted to operations management: (1) an emphasis on short-term financial results, (2) a dependence on consumer analysis and imitative rather than innovative products, and (3) a concentration on company and equipment acquisitions rather than product innovations and process improvements. On the other hand, Peters and Waterman (1982) have described in detail the management processes of United States companies that avoided these pitfalls.

Prior to World War II, Japanese industry had a reputation for producing shoddy merchandise based on both its design and its manufactured quality. In addition, the war severely damaged their economy. The Japanese decided to change the image of their products by altering reality. This change was imperative if they were to sell in world markets, obtain the foreign income required for imported raw materials, and revive their economy. They reasoned that exports were the best way to obtain the economic means to purchase the natural resources not available in Japan, provide full employment, and revitalize the economy after World War II. The Japanese focused their attention on productivity through operations management and market-driven product development. Their success was not accomplished overnight; it was achieved by a broad strategy encompassing all aspects of customer service, product design, and manufacturing management combined with a painstaking attention to detail. Their approach to improving manufacturing is similar. It encompasses all aspects and attends to detail in a step-by-step approach to productivity improvement. The Japanese studied the theory and practices of the United States, Western Europe, and Eastern Europe and combined the best aspects of each with management practices and techniques particularly suitable to their culture. For example, they paid more attention to Americans W. Edward Deming and Joseph Juran concerning statistical process quality control than most Western companies.

The achievements of the Japanese have been extraordinary; in fact, the Japanese outdid themselves. They have embarrassed the former industrial giants of the world; moreover, they have performed a service for all of humanity. Not only are they providing improved products at lower cost throughout the world, but they have motivated other developed nations to improve their productivity and have provided a role model for many less-developed countries to follow.

The success of their policy and its implementation is well known. The output of the Japanese economy improved dramatically. Figure 1–8 graphs annual indices of manufacturing productivity (output per hour) in Japan and the United States for selected years from 1960 to 1986, with 1977 as the base year. The graph of these indices clearly reveals different rates of productivity improvement between the United States and Japan.

Many organizations in industrialized countries have taken up the gauntlet,

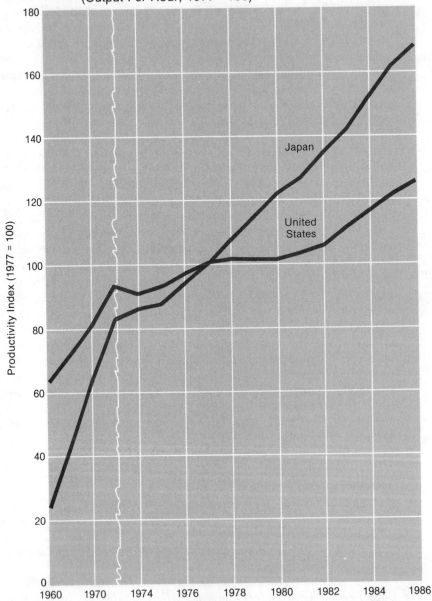

Figure 1–8   Annual Indices of Productivity in the United States and Japan (Output Per Hour, 1977 = 100)

improved manufacturing productivity substantially, and improved their competitive position in a number of world markets. For example, Jaguar Motors of the United Kingdom has tripled its sales primarily by improving its quality; the Swiss have regained a portion of the watch market due to the innovative design, quality, and efficient manufacturing of the Swatch. John Deere, Caterpillar, and the major U. S. automotive companies also have made substantial strides in improving productivity. These and similar improvements throughout the world will improve the quality of life in many areas.

Industry Productivity

The Bureau of Labor Statistics, U.S. Department of Labor, publishes productivity data for a wide range of manufacturing and service industries. Table 1–4 includes industry productivity data from the March 1986 *Monthly Labor Review*. Although these indices are expressed in terms of output per employee hour, many factors in addition to the skills and efforts of the work force determine the level of productivity. Capacity utilization, technological innovation, and managerial skills are three such factors; we discuss these and other factors in greater detail throughout the book. Output per labor hour is a basis for comparison but does not by itself reveal the causes of increases or decreases in productivity. For example, manufacturing of radios and television sets had the greatest productivity increase from 1979 to 1984. Increased capital investment for automated manufacturing, continuing high demand, and high capacity utilization contributed substantially to the productivity increase in this very competitive industry. During the same period, productivity in the farm machinery industry first fell sharply and then struggled to regain lost ground in a depressed farm economy. Increased automation and reduced payrolls have not yet turned around the entire farm machinery industry. Since the degree of automation differs widely among farm equipment manufacturers, one would expect to find major differences in their output per labor hour measures.

In service industries, the undulating productivity of beauty and barber shops from year to year reflects yearly fluctuation in demand, styling changes requiring varying amounts of labor, and pricing changes. The dramatic improvement of productivity in women's ready-to-wear stores is likely due to the increased use of self-service and supermarket-type checkout counters.

Comparing the productivity indices for a given organization to those of its industry as a whole provides management with an assessment of the firm's relative performance. However, the labor productivity of an organization does not tell the whole story. Total factor productivity does. It is determined by the effectiveness of management, availability and utilization of capital, and the price an organization can obtain for its products and services. The price customers are willing to pay is a function of output quality in the fullest sense.

Table 1–4   Annual Indices of Productivity by Industry (1977 = 100)

SIC Code[1]	Industry	1979	1980	1981	1982	1983	1984[2]	Average annual percentage change (1979–84)
111,21	Coal mining	99.4	112.5	122.2	119.2	136.1	149.9	7.7
2011	Meatpacking plants	104.6	108.9	113.9	119.5	124.0	123.4	3.7
2061, 62, 63	Sugar	103.1	100.1	98.8	90.4	98.6	105.2	−0.1
2086	Bottled and canned soft drinks	105.6	109.8	114.3	118.3	127.0	138.0	5.3
251	Household furniture	101.5	99.9	103.0	104.7	109.9	115.2	2.7
2911	Petroleum refining	94.9	94.2	83.7	79.4	81.8	90.7	−2.0
3324, 25	Steel foundries	100.6	99.8	91.6	89.0	90.6	100.9	−0.9
3523	Farm machinery	98.3	91.3	94.1	92.6	92.1	95.4	−0.4
3632	Household refrigerators and freezers	112.3	114.4	117.4	116.1	128.4	135.9	3.8
3651	Radio and television receiving sets	118.5	116.9	133.6	163.9	196.7	[3]	14.5[4]
401	Railroad transportation-revenue traffic	104.7	107.3	111.5	115.8	141.9	152.6	8.2
4511,4521	Air transportation[5]	113.1	106.2	104.9	114.7	126.0	130.1	3.8
5621	Women's ready-to-wear stores[6]	120.7	125.5	139.0	158.2	169.0	184.1	9.4
7011	Hotels, motels, and tourist courts[6]	102.4	98.6	96.2	94.5	95.5	102.9	−0.3
723,724	Beauty and barber shops[6]	107.4	102.9	109.2	108.3	114.1	104.5	0.5

[1] As defined in the Standard Industrial Classification Manual, 1972, published by the Office of Management and Budget
[2] Preliminary data
[3] Not available
[4] Percent change, 1979–1983
[5] Output per employee
[6] Output per hour of all persons

Source: U.S. Department of Labor, Bureau of Labor Statistics, Monthly Labor Review (Washington, D.C.: U.S. Government Printing Office, March 1986).

Organizational Productivity

Productivity is the key to an organization's competitiveness and thus to its profitability, survival, and long-term growth. Peter Drucker (1986) stated it well when he said, "Without productivity objectives a business does not have direction. Without productivity measurements it does not have control." The long-term competitive advantage of an organization is the purpose of productivity objectives. Setting and meeting those objectives is the responsibility of operations management. Establishing productivity objectives and measuring productivity are the first two steps. The third equally important step is determining the factors and the relationships that affect an organization's productivity. Total productivity improvement usually results from many small, mutually supporting changes. Thus, it is important both to measure productivity of specific activities and to verify that actions taken to improve productivity in one area do not decrease it in another.

INDIVIDUAL MEASURES OF PRODUCTIVITY. Figure 1–9 contains examples of productivity measures in different areas of manufacturing, and Figure 1–10 contains examples of measures used in service organizations. Some of these measures are typical productivity ratios of output to input, while others are of different forms. Each has proved useful as a criterion for improvement in its specific application.

On the surface many productivity measures seem to measure one aspect of productivity that is improved at the expense of another measure. For example, quality improvements traditionally are perceived as increasing unit costs; reduced inventory (increased inventory turns) is often viewed as reducing shipments; reduced throughput time is believed to be economically prohibitive due to additional capacity requirements. Although each of these perceptions contains a grain of truth (sometimes magnified by traditional accounting systems), each is misleading. For example, although improved quality may mean increased materials or labor costs, better manufacturing processes and more appropriate materials are frequently less expensive. Furthermore, reduced scrap, fewer customer returns, reduced warranty costs, increased demand, and higher selling prices often outweigh the costs of quality improvements. The point is that an organization needs the proper measures of productivity for the individual decision areas and activities required for producing the final product or service, and each activity must be monitored for its effect on the whole system.

CONCLUSIONS

Operations management is one of the main functional areas of management in most organizations. It involves the management of resources to produce the goods or provide the services offered to the customer, and it includes

Figure 1–9   Productivity Measures in Manufacturing Activities

Labor (direct, indirect, or composite)

$$\text{Labor efficiency} = \frac{\text{Total hours}}{\text{Units Produced}}$$

$$\text{Labor efficiency} = \frac{\text{Total hours in productive activity}}{\text{Standard hours}}$$

Quality

$$\text{Yield} = \frac{\text{Total units} - \text{Rejected units}}{\text{Total units produced}}$$

$$\text{Scrap rate} = \frac{\text{Sales value of scrap} + \text{Cost of rework}}{\text{Total shipments} + \text{Inventory adjustment}}$$

$$\text{Warranty cost factor} = \frac{\text{Cost of warranty repairs}}{\text{Value of shipments during warranty period}}$$

$$\text{Idle cost factor} = \frac{\text{Productive idle time due to poor quality}}{\text{Total productive time}}$$

$$\text{Liability cost rate} = \frac{\text{Liability costs}}{\text{Value of output}}$$

Safety

$$\text{Lost time} = \frac{\text{Productive time lost due to accidents}}{\text{Total productive time}}$$

Materials management ratios

$$\text{Downtime} = \frac{\text{Productive time lost due to materials shortages}}{\text{Total productive time}}$$

$$\text{Shipments} = \frac{\text{Shipments on schedule}}{\text{Total Shipments}}$$

$$\text{Inventory turns} = \frac{\text{Cost of sales}}{\text{Inventory investment}}$$

Manufacturing lead time

$$\text{Manufacturing lead time} = \text{Queue times} + \text{Setup times} + \text{Wait times}$$

$$\text{Manufacturing cycle efficiency} = \frac{\text{Total operation time (setup} + \text{run time)}}{\text{Total manufacturing lead time}}$$

Figure 1–10   Productivity Measures in Service Activities

$$\text{Applications processing} = \frac{\text{Number of applications processed properly}}{\text{Staff hours}}$$

$$\text{Criminal investigations} = \frac{\text{Crimes solved}}{\text{Crimes reported}}$$

$$\text{Ambulance response efficiency} = \frac{\text{Responses within time limit}}{\text{Total number of calls}}$$

$$\text{Hotel occupancy} = \frac{\text{Occupied room-days}}{\text{Total room-days}}$$

$$\text{Circuit court utilization} = \frac{\text{Cases adjudicated}}{\text{Days in session}}$$

$$\text{Theatre occupancy} = \frac{\text{Total number of tickets sold}}{\text{Number of performances}}$$

$$\text{Street cleaning efficiency} = \frac{\text{Cost}}{\text{Miles cleaned}}$$

the management of inventory (materials), quality, capacity, processes, personnel, and information.

Operations managers are required both in organizations that manufacture products and in others that provide services and nonmanufactured goods, such as agriculture and mining. Operations management practices are based on concepts, principles, and techniques, some of which were developed in other disciplines and some of which are inherently operations management concepts.

Productivity is a key contributing factor to the standard of living and the quality of life in a community, whether that community is a region, a nation, or the world. Quality of life is used here in the fullest sense; it encompasses material aspects, such as housing, clothing, and food, as well as health care, the arts, education, and recreation. Operations management influences the productivity of organizations — and their communities — as much or perhaps more than any other functional area of management. This relationship of operations management to productivity and the quality of life is a compelling reason to study operations management.

QUESTIONS

1. Name some positions at your university or college that are responsible for primarily operations management activities.

2. Name and describe at least four different types of service organizations in your community. Describe the inputs and outputs of each.

3. Describe the inputs, transformation processes, and outputs for the following types of organizations:

   a. A lawn and garden service
   b. A hardware store
   c. A small airport
   d. A small manufacturer
   e. A surveying firm
   f. A nursing home

4. The conductor of a major symphony contends that she is an operations manager. Would her activities be consistent with this chapter's definition of operations management? Explain your answer.

5. Describe how and why operations management is important to newspapers such as *The Wall Street Journal* and *USA Today*.

6. How can operations management concepts be important to managing a large municipality such as Chicago or Toronto?

7. The fire chief of a rural volunteer fire department states that operations management is unimportant to the management of the fire department because everyone volunteers their time. Comment.

8. When discussing automation and unemployment, a supporter of automation notes that without automatic switching equipment the United States today would have either fewer phones or approximately half the adult population operating switchboards. Assuming that this is roughly true, what is the lesson?

9. It has been contended that the best known operations managers are Connie Mack, John McGraw, Casey Stengel, Tommy LaSorda, and Whitey Herzog. Describe how baseball and other athletic team managers are operations managers. Describe how their role differs from most operations managers.

10. Jim Birk has just inherited three golf driving ranges, two of which have batting cages, in the suburbs of a Great Lakes metropolitan area. Discuss what some of his concerns might be in the different planning horizons with regard to resources, decision areas, and management functions.

11. What measures of productivity would you use for a public swimming pool?

12. Give a specific example of how the key terms of the definition of operations management are applied to an airline catering service.

13. Draw the organizational chart of your university, a baseball team, a utility company, or a large department store. Use your background knowledge of these activities and other information, such as phone books, to find the function names. If nothing is available, estimate the name of those functional positions. Where do significant operations management decision areas begin for the functions?

14. Identify three problems that might occur if the following organizations did not have an operations manager: a utility company; an airport; a major theme park.

15. Many cab companies and most police and fire units have dispatchers. In what way are these individuals operations managers?

REFERENCES

Coleman, Glen. *The Man Who Fenced the West*. St. Louis: Osthoff-Thalden, 1984.

Drucker, Peter F. "The Changing World Economy." *Foreign Affairs* (Spring 1986): pp. 768–791.

Hayes, Robert H., and Steven C. Wheelwright. *Restoring our Competitive Edge: Competing Through Manufacturing*. New York: John Wiley & Sons, 1984.

Murdick, Robert J., and Joel E. Ross. *Information Systems for Modern Management*, 2nd ed. . Englewood Cliffs, N. J. : Prentice-Hall, 1975.

Peters, Thomas J., and Robert H. Waterman, Jr. *In Search of Excellence*. New York: Harper & Row, 1982.

U.S. Department of Labor. Bureau of Labor Statistics. *Monthly Labor Review*. Washington, D.C.: U.S. Government Printing Office.

CHAPTER 2
MANUFACTURING AND SERVICE ORGANIZATIONS

OBJECTIVES

After completing this chapter, you should be able to

- Describe the main functional areas of operations management

- Describe manufacturing organizations and service organizations, the different types of each, and the differences between manufacturing and service organizations

- Explain the increasing importance of service operations management in the economy

- Discuss the operations management implications of several characteristics in which manufacturing and service operations differ

- Describe the different operations management approaches needed for various types of service organizations

30

OUTLINE

Introduction
Functions of Operations Management
    Capacity
    Process
    Quality
    Materials Management
    Human Resource Management
    Integration of Operations Management Decisions
Types of Organizations
    Manufacturing, Nonmanufacturing, and Service Organizations
        Nonmanufactured Goods
        Manufactured Goods
        Service Organizations
    Process Design
        Line Flow
        Job Shop
        Fixed Site
Service Organizations in the Economy
    Differences Between Service and Manufacturing Organizations
        Multilocations
        Customer Interaction
        Demand Variability
        Perishability
        Intangibility
    Differences Among Service Organizations
        Emergency Service Organizations
        Consumer Service Organizations
        Professional Service Organizations
        Organization Structures of Service Organizations
Operations Management Decisions
    Capacity
    Materials Management
    Quality
    Human Resource Management
    Process
Conclusions
Questions
References

31

INTRODUCTION

Operations management takes place in both service and manufacturing organizations. Much of this book deals with manufacturing primarily because manufacturing applications of operations management are further developed than service applications. However, that is changing due to the increasing economic importance of services. This chapter examines the similarities and differences between service and manufacturing organizations, especially with regard to the main functional areas of operations management. First the functional areas are described, followed by a description of different classifications and types of manufacturing and service organizations. The chapter concludes with a description of the primary differences between manufacturing and service organizations in each of the functional areas of operations management.

FUNCTIONS OF OPERATIONS MANAGEMENT

As noted in Chapter 1, decisions in operations management can be classified on the basis of the major functional area affected. Those areas are capacity, process, quality, materials management, and human resource or work force management. Although operations management decisions sometimes deal primarily with one of these areas, they usually affect two or more areas. Therefore, a description of the nature of each of the major functional areas and their interactions follows.

Capacity

Capacity decisions concern the availability and use of facilities, equipment, and human resources. Long-range capacity decisions include facility size and location decisions; medium-range decisions include the development of planned output and employment levels; and short-range decisions include scheduling of specific jobs and assignment of those jobs to specific work centers. Other chapters in this text detail principles and techniques that relate to the location of manufacturing and service facilities, the development of aggregate plans, and short-range scheduling.

Process

First, it is essential to note that if a cheese producer does not really know how to make good cheese, the best operations management in the world will not save the organization. An organization must know and understand its primary process. Efficiently run hospitals facilitate good patient care, but the appropriate therapy properly applied in a timely manner is a necessity. Injection molding, papermaking, printing, manufacturing printed circuits, producing pharmaceuticals in commercial quantities, freezing seafood or fresh vegetables, freeze-drying coffee, repairing diesel locomotives, treating burn injuries, developing photographic film, designing group insurance plans, and organizing group travel packages are a few examples of the many technologically different service and manufacturing processes. This text does not examine process technologies themselves; it is concerned with the organization of the equipment and personnel in implementing that technology, the management systems used in its operation, major operations strategies and policies, and common problems (decisions) confronting operations managers in service and manufacturing organizations. This text examines the primary classifications of processes (e.g., line flow, job shop, manufacturing cells, and fixed position) and their related strategic and tactical decisions.

Quality

The American Production and Inventory Control Society (APICS) defines quality as "conformance to requirements"; more simply put, it is fitness for use. The degree to which a product or service fulfills the needs and expectations of the customer is its quality. Quality encompasses a wide range of attributes including performance, dependability, availability, reliability, and appearance. The actual quality achieved depends on the product design, the process technology, the quality of materials used, and perhaps most importantly the execution of the transformation process. Rational operations management decisions require an explicit definition of the organizational results desired. For example, a postsecondary educational institution that is training technicians would have different operations policies, procedures, and measures of performance than an institution that is preparing students for a scientific research career. Both would presumably be interested in quality graduates, but their process designs and measurement of results would differ. In a similar manner, an organization designing and manufacturing one-of-a-kind high fashion dresses would have different marketing, design, processing, and materials management strategies and procedures than a firm manufacturing military uniforms. The point is that the operations management decisions should be consistent with the quality requirements of the market being served.

Materials Management

Operations planning and materials management decisions are inextricably interwoven. Thus, they are viewed as a decision area. Policy decisions in this area include the following:

1. Selecting the criteria for measuring the efficiency of operations planning, purchasing, and inventory management
2. Planning the role inventory and operating capacity will have in meeting demand
3. Planning the levels of different inventories, such as raw materials, component parts, subassemblies, and finished goods

4. Determining policies and procedures for selecting suppliers
5. Developing methods of controlling the flow of materials and orders, for example, determining the type of items to be included on the master schedule

It is only after these decisions have been made that rational decisions concerning information system design, computer hardware, and software can be made.

It was not too long ago that a customer had to wait a week or more for eyeglasses after being fitted. Today there are retail optical centers that combine manufacturing and service functions and deliver prescription glasses within one hour. This is a good example of the way competitive factors can lead to reductions in manufacturing and service lead times. Achieving a reduced lead time requires flexible capacity, improved manufacturing processes, and different production planning and inventory management systems. It also requires the physical proximity of the eyeglass fitting and grinding activities.

Human Resource Management

Human resource management recognizes the intrinsic values, needs, and resourcefulness of employees, provides an environment that nurtures and rewards that resourcefulness, and taps it for the benefit of the employee and the productivity of the organization. Human resource management engenders a spirit of cooperation, mutual trust, and common goals; it rejects the adversary model of many traditional labor-management relationships.

The major elements of human resource management are the following:

1. Management policies and attitudes that recognize basic human needs and create an environment supporting those needs
2. A system for determining personnel needs by skill and profession under different marketing and production plans
3. A system that evaluates employee capabilities, skills, potentials, interests, and development opportunities
4. An explicit policy of rewards that recognizes employee interests and objectives and is based on both group and individual performance; this should encourage all employees to act as if they are part of a research group examining data for suggestions of improvements
5. Integration of recruitment and selection policies, personnel levels, capacity requirements, aggregate plans, and processes employed

Ouchi (1981) and Peters and Waterman (1982) have presented many specific examples of this approach to human resource managers in American industry.

Integration of Operations Management Decisions

Explicit statements of values, policies, strategies, and procedures concerning major decision areas of operations management have at least three major benefits. First, they provide a basis for day-to-day tactical decisions often made by managers with limited time and limited access to the organization's officers or staff. Second, they provide the basis for examining decisions made over six months or a year and for evaluating their degree of correspondence with policy and strategy. Third, management is able to verify that the set of policies has internal consistency.

For example, if an organization's strategy is to excel at delivery (taking less time than competitors to fill an order), it should have excess flexible capacity and higher inventory levels than a competitor whose strategy is based on price. The organization should be analyzing its operations to determine how to achieve its primary objective of a fast delivery time with minimum negative effects on price.

TYPES OF ORGANIZATIONS

There are a number of ways of classifying organizations that are useful to the study of operations management. Two of these are by type of product and by type of process.

Manufacturing, Nonmanufacturing, and Service Organizations

An organization does one or both of the following:

1. Produces a physical product or good
2. Produces a service—that is, does something to or for an individual or another organization

Organizations that produce goods are further classified as manufacturing and nonmanufacturing. Many organizations, of course, produce some combination of manufactured and nonmanufactured goods and services, so the classification may be somewhat ambiguous. However, it is a useful method for two reasons: (1) it is a classification used by the government for data collection, which facilitates research along these lines, and (2) many operations management techniques are more applicable within one classification than another, so it is efficient for operations managers and researchers to specialize in one of the areas.

NONMANUFACTURED GOODS. This classification includes those organizations involved in agriculture, fishing, mining, and construction. The first three, namely agriculture, fishing, and mining, are extraction industries. They obtain materials from their natural sources. Many of these industries, particularly mining, require large capital investments long before any output and earned income occurs. Facilities must be located at the source, personnel must work in remote and underdeveloped areas, and materials handling must be considered. The drilling and exploration procedures that must be completed prior to **actual** extraction takes time and capital. Mining also involves another risk; neither the final output nor the demand five to ten years in the future can be predicted with certainty. Forecasting economic, political, and other environmental factors five to ten years hence is a major challenge. Long-range planning is crucial. Process and equipment planning is also very important. Materials handling and movement involves major expenditures. Capacity at the various stages must be balanced (have the same rate of flow), and equipment must be reliable in physical environments that are frequently extreme and hazardous. Recruiting, selecting, and training the personnel who will function well in what sometimes can best be described as an unpleasant environment is a major challenge. Competent and reliable managers and technicians can usually obtain employment in more favorable locations and conditions. The operations managers and engineering staff must select reliable equipment, develop maintenance plans, and maintain an inventory of repair parts in order to keep the equipment operating.

Although construction is classified as a nonmanufactured good, construction exhibits characteristics of both extraction and manufacturing. Construction is performed at the site of the structure being built. As the project progresses, tools, equipment, and workers move to the next structure and site. The continual changing of the job site constitutes a challenge to operations management, even when the structure produced is very similar or even identical to a previous job. Construction is a good example of fixed site production (the product does not move from station to station during its manufacture); and project management approaches (see Chapter 15) are very useful in the management of construction operations.

Many construction firms now manufacture components such as roof trusses and room modules in a plant and then transport them to the site for final assembly. For example, Cardinal Industries manufactures basic room modules at their Columbus, Ohio plant and then transports them to the site where their latest Knights Inn Motel is being built. Thus, they are in both the manufacturing and the construction business. Many organizations have similar overlapping classifications of manufactured and nonmanufactured goods. Furthermore, many nonmanufactured goods producers also perform service functions. However, these activities can be segregated when managing their operation.

MANUFACTURED GOODS. Any organization whose primary purpose is to convert raw materials and/or components into a finished product or assembly through the use of labor and/or machinery falls into this category. The output may be sold to the general public or another commercial organization. The manufacturers of textiles, clothing, shoes, electronic equipment, machine tools, medical equipment, paper products, boxes, cans, soaps, medicine, fertilizers, petroleum products, wine, beer, and other beverages are examples. Some organizations have divisions that produce nonmanufactured goods and others that produce manufactured goods; a company may operate both oil wells and a refinery, for example.

SERVICE ORGANIZATIONS. All organizations whose primary purpose is to do something to or for the customer fall into this category. Restaurants, caterers, financial institutions, educational institutions, hospitals, service stations, consulting firms, software development organizations, accounting firms, engineering design firms, symphony orchestras, insurance companies, repair shops, and government agencies such as license bureaus and social security offices are examples. Many of these organizations also provide products, but that is secondary to the service. For example, a supper club or lounge provides food and beverages, which are essential elements; but, in most cases, table service, entertainment, and ambiance are the primary reasons the customer comes in. Due to the dramatic growth in service organization employment and their contribution to the gross national product, this chapter examines the different types of service organizations, their growth, and the primary differences between service and manufacturing organizations.

Process Design

The process design of an organization is based on the dominant flow pattern of the item being processed. Parts and material are processed in a manufacturing plant; patients are processed in a hospital or clinic; and customer claims are processed in an insurance company. Thus, process flows exist in both manufacturing and service organizations. The three major types of process design are (1) line flow, (2) job shop, and (3) fixed site. Chapter 5 contains a detailed description of each of these process types and their relationships to operations management. The following is only an introduction to these important concepts.

LINE FLOW. The item being processed moves directly from one workstation to the next, which is immediately adjacent to it as illustrated in Figure 2–1. Each workstation, including the required equipment, is designed to perform a limited number of operations on a single item or on relatively few similar items. Line flow is appropriate when high volume demand justifies the relatively high capital investment. The objective is to achieve low unit variable costs with quick delivery and to be competitive in a market for a relatively

Figure 2–1 Line Flow

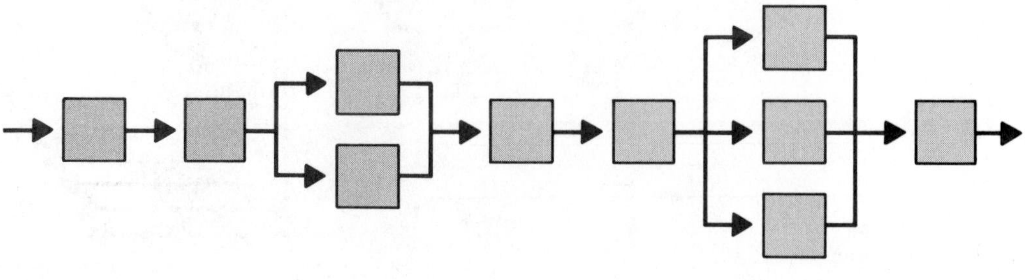

standard product or service. For example, dental clinics specializing in providing false teeth and the related extraction and therapy often use a line flow design. This provides patients with treatment and false teeth at a relatively low cost and delivery the same or the next day. Automobile assembly lines are the classic example of line flows in manufacturing.

JOB SHOP. The spatial and administrative organization of similar equipment by functions, such as welding, painting, forging, assembly, x-ray, dialysis, underwriting, claims processing, check sorting, loan application processing, and accounting is the hallmark of a job shop. Although dominant operations are used to physically arrange the location of departments and minimize the travel of items, a great variety of flow patterns exist, as illustrated in Figure 2–2. Equipment tends to be multipurpose; thus, a greater variety of items may be processed than is possible with a line flow process. Capital investment is also generally lower than with the line flow, and unit variable costs are higher. Compared to line flow, job shop design is more appropriate for make-to-order and lower volume output.

FIXED SITE. In this type of production the materials, tools, and personnel are brought to the location where the process is being performed. Repair services performed at the customer's home, office, or plant are an example. Fixed sites are also used when manufacturing items such as large aircraft and large pressure vessels that are difficult to move from work center to work center. Manufacturing goods or providing services at a fixed site tends to involve custom-designed products or services, highly trained and skillful workers, and unique approaches to the management of inventory, capacity, and production.

Figure 2–2 Job Shop

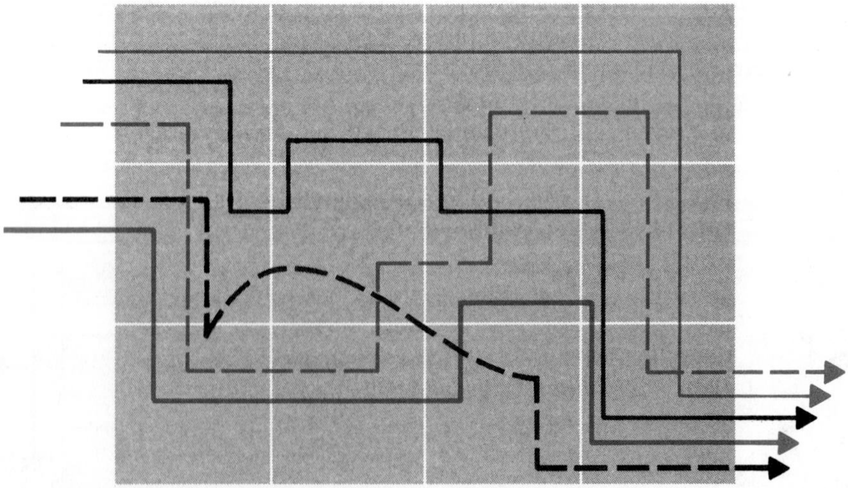

SERVICE ORGANIZATIONS IN THE ECONOMY

Service production makes up the majority of gross national product in the United States, and its share continues to increase (see Figure 2–3). Table 2–1 gives a classification of services based on the type of service. It is very similar to the U.S. Bureau of Labor's classification of service organizations.

As reported by Beeson and Bryan (1986), service organizations accounted for 90 percent of the 42.6 million more people employed between 1950 and 1984 in the United States; they also accounted for 70 percent of the increased output during that same period. The service sector portion of the total output increased from 58 to 66 percent in this period, while the manufactured goods share remained about the same and the nonmanufactured goods share dropped by approximately 8 percent.

While the manufacturing share of output has remained about the same, it has done so with a declining share of employment. The share of employment

Table 2–1 Service Industry Groups

Transportation
   Railroad
   Local transit, intercity buses
   Truck
   Water
   Air
   Transportation services
Communications
   Radio, television broadcasting
   All other (telephone and other)
Public utilities
   Electric, public and private
   Gas, excluding public
Trade
   Wholesale
   Retail, except eating and drinking places
   Eating and drinking places
Finance, insurance, real estate
   Banking
   Credit agencies, financial brokers
   Insurance
   Real estate
Other
   Hotel, lodging
   Health care
   Education
   Nonprofit organizations
   Amusement, recreation
   Miscellaneous business and professional
   Automobile repair
   Government

in the **service** sector, however, has grown even faster than the share of service output, as indicated in Figures 2–3 and 2–4. Productivity has increased in manufacturing much faster than in services. This productivity differential and the relative importance of services has focused increasing attention on operations management in service organizations.

The increase in the service sector of the economy is due primarily to the following three factors: (1) the increase in intermediate services, (2) the income effect, and (3) the relative productivity of the service, manufactured goods, and nonmanufactured goods sectors.

Intermediate services include accounting, insurance, legal, recruiting, engineering, computer software, advertising, and similar services that at one time were produced mainly in-house by manufacturing firms. Today many of these services are purchased from firms that specialize in such activities. Thus, part of the increase in service sector activity is due to a change in where the work is performed rather than in the type of work being performed. Beeson and Bryan (1986) estimate that 20 percent of the growth in the service sector results from the shift toward using external service organizations.

Figure 2–3   Shares of Gross National Product

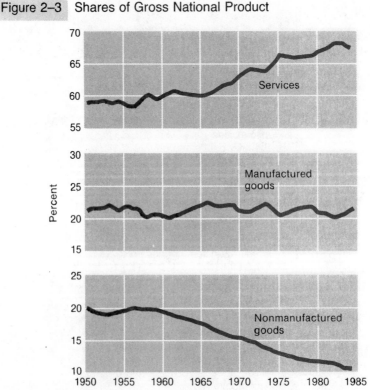

Source: U.S. Department of Commerce, Bureau of Economic Analysis.

Figure 2–4   Total Shares of Employment

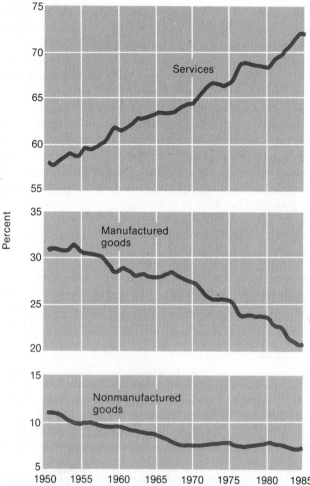

Source: U.S. Department of Labor, Bureau of Labor Statistics.

The income effect is the term given by economists to the shift in the spending pattern as a nation becomes wealthier. The premise is that as a nation becomes wealthier, its need for goods is fulfilled by a smaller proportion of its income. It begins to spend a larger share of its income on services, including education, health care, recreation, and travel.

Beeson and Bryan (1986) also contend that the relatively low productivity of the service sector and the entrance of women and other second-income providers into the labor pool has encouraged the relatively large employment growth of the service sector. But both Collier (1985) and Shelp (1984) have reported on productivity gains in services, the high capital intensity among many services, and the highly skilled personnel required by many service organizations. Shelp noted that the recent rate of growth in business services has been twice that of fast-food franchises and that the growth in service sector employment is as great in professional and paraprofessional fields as it is in the unskilled areas. Thus, many of the new service jobs are well-paid jobs. The cry for productivity improvements in service industries such as health care and education is heard across the nation today. This demand for productivity improvements coupled with increased automation will lead to increased productivity in these and other service areas. The demand for more and better services combined with human ingenuity in developing meaningful and desirable services will allow the growth of the service sector to continue. However, it is more likely that productivity increases in manufacturing will follow the pattern of agriculture; that is, the increases will continue due to competitive pressures and the application of technology. And, similar to agriculture over the last century, substantially fewer employees will be required in manufacturing per unit of output.

Differences Between Service and Manufacturing Organizations

There are noteworthy differences between manufacturing and service organizations that substantially affect the operations management task. Although the degree of difference depends on the natures of both the manufacturing organization and the service organization being compared, major differences include the following:

1. Processing at many small locations is more likely in service organizations.
2. A greater short-term demand variability exists in service organizations.
3. Greater interaction of the customers with the employees, the process, and the facilities exists in a service organization.
4. Flexible capacity is usually more important in a service organization.
5. Output quality and specification are more intangible in a service organization.

These differences are summarized in Table 2–2. The relationships that these differences have to operations management practices are discussed in the sections that follow.

MULTILOCATIONS. Some service organizations have many outlets, with each outlet in a location that is convenient to a local market. Services are produced

Table 2–2   Major Differences Between Service and Manufacturing Organizations

Organization	Locations	Demand variability	Customer interaction	Capacity flexibility	Intangible outputs
Manufacturing	Few	Seasonal	Little	Important	Few
Service	Many	Hourly	Great	Vital	Many

and consumed at each outlet. Banks and other financial institutions have found that, similar to automobile service stations, their volume is dependent on having many locations, preferably in high traffic areas such as shopping centers. Thus, Sears, Roebuck and Co., a nationwide merchandiser with high-volume traffic, has opened stock brokerage offices in their retail stores in cooperation with an established brokerage house; they have had insurance sales offices for some time. The challenge is to obtain consistent and reliable quality throughout the organization. Thus, insurance companies, banks, national real estate firms, and national repair and service firms of all types face the same challenge of offering consistency as McDonald's restaurants. For example, if a customer is having a transmission repaired, that customer should receive the same courtesy and quality of work from garages of the same firm whether they are in Dallas or Toronto. In a similar manner, a hotel in Michigan should offer the same level of service and accommodations as one from the same chain in Athens, Greece.

The implications for operations management in service organizations are clear. Management policies, procedures, and practices must be transportable; that is, the company must be able to install and execute them effectively at each satellite location. To achieve this requires capabilities above and beyond those required to manage one or two sites. These capabilities include corporatewide systems for training regional managers, site managers, and employees concerning all aspects of operating an individual site. This also necessitates documented formal policies and procedures to allow central management to monitor the quality of services provided at each location.

CUSTOMER INTERACTION. In a service organization there is often no buffer between the customer and many of the people doing the work. Furthermore, the customer frequently observes the actual process followed and the equipment used in providing the service. The customer rarely observes the manufacture of the shoes, television, or other products purchased or interacts with the employees actually producing them. The opposite usually occurs when services are purchased. The patient talks to the physician, nurse, and the x-ray technician. The diner frequently observes the chef, interacts with the servers, and may obtain at least a peek at the kitchen. Providers of financial services make it a point to be visible to the potential customer as well as the one being serviced. Repair and maintenance personnel typically operate under the view of the homeowner or with an office staff anxiously awaiting the proper functioning of a computer or copy machine. The business consultant and the accounting auditor do much of their work in full view of the client organization and interact with many members of that organization. The point is that the customer of a service organization observes, knows, and deals with the foot soldier; the service employee is the front line of customer relations.

Again, the implications for operations management are clear. The service employee must recognize the importance of the customer relations role and act accordingly. This means that the organization should recruit and select employees likely to perform well in this role, provide the appropriate training for them, and monitor their performance. Furthermore, decisions regarding the design and selection of the process and equipment must be made after considering its impact on the customer's perception of the service and satisfaction with it. It may be advisable to move some processes, equipment, and personnel to a back room to avoid disenchanting the customer.

DEMAND VARIABILITY. Demand for services typically varies hourly, if not minute by minute, in service organizations. In some cases the variations follow a predictable pattern, and in other cases demand is more random. Restaurants, airline ticket counters, hotel cashiers, and many retail establishments experience demand that is relatively predictable on an hourly as well as a daily basis. On the other hand, organizations providing emergency services experience a more erratic demand. Manufactured goods also experience varying demand, but the products may be made in advance and stored as a finished product for an hour, day, week, or longer. Maintaining a finished goods inventory is one method of coping with varying demand for manufactured goods. Finished service units cannot be stored.

Thus, a service organization must have flexible capacity to cope with surges in demand, must be able to alter demand, or both. (Altering demand will be discussed later.) Furthermore, facility and equipment capacity will be underutilized much of the time. Whereas manufacturing strives to develop formal scheduling procedures for balancing flow, minimizing manufacturing lead time, and maximizing throughput, service operations use queuing theory to evaluate capacity elements such as the number of servers and stages in the process. Both manufacturing and service organizations use simulation to evaluate priority rules for deciding the sequence in which orders or customers should be served.

PERISHABILITY. If a service is not consumed when available, its sale is lost forever. An empty airline seat, motel room, or restaurant table is income lost; unused manufacturing capacity is also lost forever. The difference is that most manufacturers can build finished goods inventory during slack demand periods.

This characteristic also emphasizes the importance of flexible capacity for service organizations and the development of methods that shift demand from high to low demand periods. Such methods include reservations, promotions, and the development of complementary services with different peak demand periods.

INTANGIBILITY. Service customers are usually purchasing some combination of atmosphere, nostalgia, friendliness, security, prestige, reliability, and ambiance in addition to the actual service itself. For example, some retirees gather for breakfast at a fast-food franchise after the morning rush, primarily to socialize; the nutrition they receive is secondary. The friendly and helpful bank teller will obtain the loyalty of some customers in spite of competitors' higher interest rates on savings accounts and more convenient bank-by-mail services. Staying at the Ritz can provide elegance, graciousness, and status to those willing to pay for more than clean sheets and a private bath with hot water. The restaurant that has not changed its decor or good food and service since you ate there with your parents and grandparents can provide a magic time capsule with fond memories. The process, the equipment, and the facility are frequently part of the service. Modifications in any of these or in the behavioral pattern of employees can destroy an essential ingredient of the service package. The point is that the customer is frequently purchasing a complex package in which the ambiance and other aspects that appear to be superficial are as important as the aspects that appear to be primary.

Differences Among Service Organizations

Service organizations may be divided into the following three types:

1. Emergency service organizations (ESOs) that respond quickly to widely varying situations
2. Consumer service organizations (CSOs) that provide relatively standardized services to the public
3. Professional service organizations (PSOs) that provide a high-level professional service to meet a particular need

Before discussing each type it is important to note that, to a degree, most service organizations exhibit characteristics of all three types. Figure 2–5 represents a service organization classification space, a three-dimensional graph that gives a perspective on the relative positions of different organizations. The three axes measure the salient features of each type of service organization: (1) the capacity to respond quickly, (2) standardization of product, and (3) professional expertise. For example, a motel chain and a ski lodge are both CSOs, but the ski lodge has more of the characteristics of a PSO. A hospital trauma center is both a full-fledged ESO and a PSO, while a plumbing firm may provide emergency services to both commercial organizations and private residences and be more of a CSO than a PSO.

EMERGENCY SERVICE ORGANIZATIONS (ESOs). ESOs include medical emergency units, fire departments, police, and a whole host of other organizations and individuals available on short notice to repair plumbing, electrical service, appliances, computers, machinery of all types, marine engines in distant ports, and so on. ESO characteristics include the following:

1. The organization must respond quickly to customer calls frequently at any hour and any day of the week.
2. The organization is frequently faced with unusual problems requiring analysis, diagnosis, and solution.
3. Employees often work without supervision or assistance in far less than the best environment. For example, a marine engine service technician may be

Figure 2–5   Service Organization Classification Space

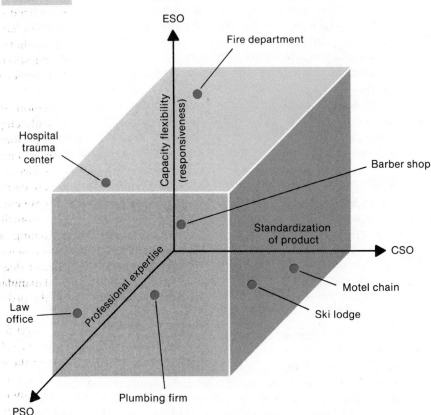

reboring an engine cylinder of a ship docked at Singapore. This is quite different from working on that same engine in a ship repair dry dock.

4. Promptness and performance are more important than price.

Emergency service operators must not only be competent, they must exude competence. They are similar to members of a PSO in that they are the organization as far as the customer is concerned. Although ESOs can use customer feedback and spot field checks to monitor the performance of their operators, they depend on the high motivation and complete trustworthiness of their operators. The satisfaction of solving problems in less than ideal environments, the customer's appreciation of their work (usually expressed directly to them), and the relatively high remuneration for their craft or profession are the primary motivators of ESO employees.

Although the ESO category encompasses a myriad of organizations from oil well fire fighters to the road rescuers of the local auto club, the design and operations of ESO organizations should be substantially different from similar organizations that are not ESOs. Many of these differences are discussed in the Operations Management Decisions section later in this chapter.

CONSUMER SERVICE ORGANIZATIONS (CSOs). Sasser et al. (1978) have defined a CSO as an organization that offers "relatively standardized services to the public." Examples are fast-food restaurants, quick printers, taxis, barbers, retail establishments selling standard products, and repair shops where an item may be brought for repair. Since their products and services are standard, they are similar to high-volume manufacturers. They often can standardize processes.

CSOs offer an explicit service package with minimum variation. Standard operating policies and procedures are common in CSOs, with employees typically required to perform a few relatively simple tasks but perform them well. In most cases, employee education and training is brief, employees operate in the presence of first-line management, and pay scales are relatively low. Thus, the CSO labor pool is large, the cost of training a new employee is relatively small, and employee turnover is usually high. Many CSO employees interact directly with the public and must exhibit desirable personality traits such as courtesy, warmth, reasonable appearance, good grooming, and the ability to listen and communicate. Because of this, employee selection is critical. Marketing and manufacturing are interwoven to a greater degree in a CSO, as well as in an ESO and a PSO, than they are in the typical manufacturing company. For example, the restaurant server performs part of the process and makes the sale.

Motivation of front-line CSO employees comes from the need for some income with flexible hours while they focus on a different primary role, such as student, struggling artist, traveler, or retiree. Others may find it the only job available and see it as an opportunity to gain work experience, some understanding of the marketplace, and job references. In general, consumer service employees are not looking for or expecting mental challenges. However, a small percentage of employees are motivated by the opportunity to become an assistant manager or manager of a CSO.

The first-line CSO manager's task is to see that standard procedures are followed and to handle those relatively few situations when the unplanned or unforeseen occurs. The manager often trains the workers, schedules employees, orders supplies, and nearly always evaluates the workers. Managers also serve as backup for absent employees; this role, as well as their training duties, requires that they be able to perform most if not all of the jobs. The knowledge and experience gained as a manager, the challenge of management, possible advancement in the management ranks, and the income are their primary motivators.

In the case of a small CSO with only one or two locations, managers must possess and use the employee relations skills required of first-line managers and also have the general managerial and financial skills of top management. Corporate management in a large CSO with many branches requires technical, financial, and marketing skills as well as strategic planning capabilities. The transition from a small CSO with one or two branches to even a medium-sized CSO with five to ten branches requires management capabilities, policies, and procedures not necessary in the small CSO. Since the owner's or general manager's on-site presence decreases, standardization of methods and procedures must be increased, training programs developed, and common control points established. CSO changes in size from local to regional, regional to national, or national to international are major challenges. Successful implementation of such changes requires management skills, policies, and practices not guaranteed by previous successes.

PROFESSIONAL SERVICE ORGANIZATIONS (PSOs). Law firms, public accounting firms, computer software developers, management consulting organizations, design engineering organizations, insurance and investment advisers, and research institutes are all examples of PSOs. The distinguishing characteristics of a PSO are the high level of professional and academic training of its staff, the professional certification and licensing of its staff, the relatively high pay, and the fact that customers contract for the service of a PSO on either a task (job) or a time-required basis.

Although there are a few large PSOs in accounting, law, and computer software, they are the exception. Most PSOs consist of relatively few workers, and the performance of each staff member is directly related to the organization's reputation, image, revenue, and profits. Although the style, approach, and methods of each employee may vary, their activities and achievements should be compatible with organizational goals and values. Thus, two lawyers from a firm specializing in labor law and negotiation may have different personalities and styles, but both should project (and possess) integrity, firmness, a concern for just wages and working conditions, and a positive attitude toward new technology. Managing a PSO is sometimes similar to managing an opera company—there are prima donnas, prima dons, and a talented supporting cast of singers and musicians. The major actors, actresses, and conductors may have very individual styles, different native languages, and different national origins; but, when working on the same project, they must be singing the same opera with each vocalist and musician singing the proper note and word at the proper time. Keeping talented and energetic people relatively happy and working toward a common goal is not an easy task for PSO management. Some PSOs are short-lived or continually in turmoil due to their inability either to attract or to hold top professionals.

Some PSOs have managed to grow and prosper by attracting young professionals to perform many of the supporting tasks (sing the chorus) while the stars manage, approve, and present the final report (sing the lead). Young professionals are lured to these PSOs by the experience and status to be gained by working with leaders in the field. The experienced professionals find that their time is frequently spent more efficiently and effectively in such a firm than it would be working alone or with two or three colleagues. As such PSOs increase in size, they reduce their dependence on a few top performers and depend on many very qualified and competent personnel. The transition of a PSO from a handful of leading players to an organization with dozens of leading men and women is a difficult hurdle. In addition, many firms may desire to remain small and rather comfortable with two to five individuals retaining complete control.

ORGANIZATION STRUCTURES OF SERVICE ORGANIZATIONS. Figure 2–6 presents a general picture of the organizational structures of CSOs, PSOs, and ESOs. CSOs have a multilayered structure, with policies and standard operating procedures (SOPs) established centrally to cover most, if not all, branches and situations. Few decisions are left to subordinates, except to decide which SOP applies. Branch managers and assistant managers select, train, motivate, evaluate, and schedule the personnel. CSOs typically have more layers in their organizational structure due to the multiple locations, the standardization of tasks, and the need for corporate staffs for tasks such as site selection, facility and service design, transportation, information system design and operation, and training.

ESOs usually possess some features of a CSO or a PSO. Oil well fire fighting organizations, medical emergency rooms, and organizations involved in clearing train wrecks after an accident are combinations of ESOs and PSOs. Automotive road service organizations (e.g., AAA in the United States and AA in Britain) are a combination ESO and CSO. Nonetheless, the nature of many ESOs requires personnel to act with no supervision. Recruitment and selection of personnel capable of working independently while adhering to the organization's policies is essential. Organizational structures of ESOs tend to have fewer levels and a wider span of control for first-line employees than PSOs.

The organization of a PSO usually has fewer layers than that of a CSO. Employees frequently work as members of a small team on a specific project. Managers and employees in PSOs, such as a software house, management consulting firm, or law firm, have much broader authority and freedom of action within general policies. Middle managers, for example, may play key roles in deciding how a job should be done, whether or not the assignment should be accepted, the cost to be charged, whether or not external resources should be employed, and when the job can be performed and completed. When the project is completed, members may become part of a different team, as different jobs frequently require a different mix of skills.

OPERATIONS MANAGEMENT DECISIONS

Concepts and techniques concerning capacity, materials, quality, and other operations management areas are discussed throughout this text, along with applications in both manufacturing and service organizations. The differences between manufacturing and service organizations and problems central to service operations management are detailed here. Remember that although the following general statements are accurate, there are exceptions.

Figure 2–6   Typical Structures of Service Organizations

Professional service organization

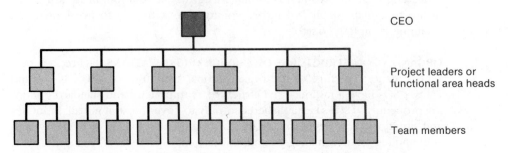

CEO

Project leaders or
functional area heads

Team members

Consumer service organization

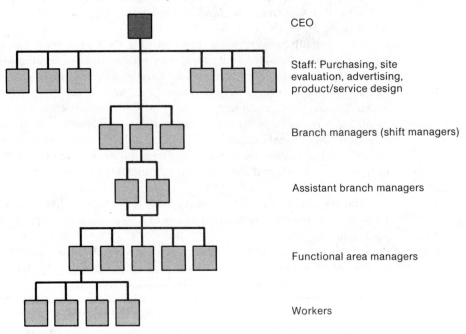

CEO

Staff: Purchasing, site
evaluation, advertising,
product/service design

Branch managers (shift managers)

Assistant branch managers

Functional area managers

Workers

Emergency service organizations

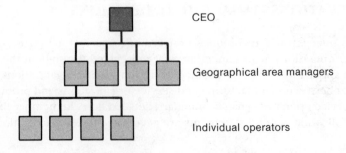

CEO

Geographical area managers

Individual operators

Capacity

Three major factors contribute to the special challenge of managing capacity in a service organization. First, completed service units cannot be stored as finished goods. Although many preparations may be completed in advance, the completed service unit cannot be delivered until the customer calls for it. Second, capacity in service operations is typically constrained by available personnel, whereas manufacturing capacity is typically constrained by equipment and facilities that stand ready twenty-four hours a day, seven days a week. And third, service organizations not only experience the seasonal and daily demand that some manufacturing organizations do, but they also experience hourly and sometimes minute-by-minute variations in demand. Emergency service organizations in particular are subjected to demand at all times of the day, as well as surges in demand due to severe weather and catastrophes. These conditions require that service organizations manage capacity in some ways that are not required, at least not to the same extent, in most manufacturing organizations.

The following are four avenues open to service operations managers to cope with the capacity challenge: (1) obtain excess capacity, (2) provide flexible capacity, (3) control demand, and (4) automate capacity.

Excess capacity is necessary for most service organizations in order to meet peak demand. Motels, restaurants, hospital emergency rooms, airliners, and most service organizations operate at less than full capacity more often than not. This enables them to service most if not all the demand during the rush periods.

Flexible capacity is the key to productivity in many organizations. Organizations with relatively predictable demand patterns may obtain flexible capacity by having part-time employees, by assigning full-time personnel other duties during slow periods, or sharing employees (subcontracting) with other organizations. For example, restaurants and retail establishments often use part-time employees. Waiters and waitresses in a restaurant may spend the slow time setting tables, preparing the salad bar, and cleaning. In a retail establishment, the clerk may attend to stock during low-demand periods and customers during high-demand periods. In addition, some airlines with only one or two flights daily at an airport hire the services of competitors (subcontract) for refueling, baggage handling, and routine service and maintenance.

There are three major methods of controlling demand, namely reservations, promotions, and pricing. Reservation systems reduce both waiting lines and customer frustration by smoothing the arrival of customers for service. Reservation systems may reduce the number of customers in peak periods, but additional motivation is usually required to generate demand in slack periods. Marketing promotions, including price discounts and premiums, frequently increase off-hour demand. For example, theaters offer reduced price performances for matinees, restaurants offer specials during slow periods, and airlines reduce rates during the low-demand traffic periods. On the other hand, many professional service organizations whose capacity is insufficient to meet demand find that raising the price of their service will reduce demand to the level of capacity and will also increase profits.

When possible, converting personnel-constrained capacity to an automated equipment process can increase capacity substantially. The replacement of telephone operators with automatic dialing and switching equipment was perhaps the earliest example of such a conversion. Automatic bank tellers at many remote locations have both disbursed the demand pattern and reduced personnel requirements. Electronic funds transfer systems (EFTS) have reduced the time, paperwork, and personnel required to complete banking transactions.

Materials Management

Many service organizations have been required to develop just-in-time solutions to their materials (production and inventory) management problems (see Chapter 20 for a detailed explanation of this approach). Restaurants, grocery stores, produce markets, and similar establishments have long been required to use short-cycle scheduling of supplies due primarily to their perishable nature and secondarily to space limitations. As a result, many have become adept at managing daily or more frequent deliveries. The major materials management challenge facing CSOs is the development of relationships with reliable providers of quality supplies and materials at a competitive price. As a service organization increases the number and especially the geographic spread of its sites, the selection and management of suppliers becomes more of a challenge. Suppliers in the original areas may not have the capacity to handle quantity increases or to supply competitively at a distance. Successful control of suppliers and supplies is one of the keys to successful management of growth and expansion.

Materials management raises the question of vertical integration in service organizations. For example, should the hospital or large hotel do its own laundry? At what point and under what conditions should a chain of restaurants enter the bakery business? The answers to these questions have major policy and strategic implications (see Chapter 19).

Quality

The intangible and implicit nature of many of the results that constitute a service usually make the quality of services more difficult to measure than the quality of manufactured products. Developing explicit quality measurements should be interwoven with developing the design specification. The service organization must develop methods of measuring employee attributes, such as attitudes toward customers, consistency of performance, and response and timing. Explicit results, such as cleanliness, appearance, taste of food, and complete performance of the service must also be measured.

Measurement of service quality can be obtained from customer feedback, internal inspections and audits, and external audits. Motels, restaurants, hospitals, and automobile service centers are examples of organizations that frequently provide evaluation forms for customers. Some of these organizations also telephone customers after the service to obtain an assessment of quality. Poor quality can be insidious; decaying facilities, slovenly work habits, and a general lack of cleanliness can creep into an organization gradually. Many, including Peters and Waterman (1982), have noted that the best guarantee of quality output is a climate or quality culture that comes from top management. Irons (1983) points out that this means that managers in a service organization must listen to their employees if they expect the employees to treat customers in an attentive and responsible manner. Service employees are the first, and sometimes the only, employees to hear customer complaints and suggestions. They frequently know best the desires of the customer.

Management performance measures and rewards should be based on quality as well as meeting schedule and cost goals. Individuals tend to perform to meet explicit goals. In "How to Create a Culture for Quality in an Existing Organization," Schroeder reports that "Many of the highest quality programs have visible charts and graphs everywhere . . . (recording quality)." Measuring, recording, and rewarding quality performance is essential for its achievement in both service and manufacturing organizations.

Human Resource Management

The very factors that differentiate a service organization from a manufacturing organization require the service organization to have different human resource management policies and practices. These factors include the greater interaction between employees and customers, the personnel-constrained capacity of most services, the varying demand for services, the many locations, and the need to perform many services at the customer's site. These factors affect personnel selection, training, and motivation requirements.

The importance of selecting personnel with personal characteristics that are essential for warm, pleasant, and positive responses to customer inquiries, requests, and comments has been noted. An ESO requires personnel who can work independently, display initiative, and act in a trustworthy manner while working within the policies and guidelines of the organization. An equally important element in achieving the desired employee attitude toward customers is the corporate culture, which is established by the way management interacts with employees. In all service organizations, but especially in PSOs and ESOs, it is essential that all personnel participate in the development of policies and practices. Not only do they have firsthand knowledge of the customers' interests, but they must be able to identify with the policies and perceive themselves as members of the service team.

The varying demand for services requires that many service employees have flexible schedules and flexible assignments and that others be on call. Many workers in CSOs are young, part-time, in their first job, and passing through while they study for future careers in other fields. This, plus the many locations of CSOs, makes the existence of training programs and support on the job essential to quality output and productivity. It should also be noted that CSOs perform an important function for the economy; they educate literally thousands of individuals concerning such things as how customers should be treated, the importance of personal appearance, output quality, and productivity.

Process

The term *process* in this chapter refers to the flow of work and materials, not the specific technique used to perform the service or manufacture the product. Thus, we are concerned with the requirements, advantages, and disadvantages of line flow, job shop, and fixed site processing. The very nature of services involves at least a degree of customization both in the timing and the nature of a service. For example, customers usually order different food at a restaurant, have equipment that requires service at different times, and require computer software that meets their particular needs. Line flow usually requires a relatively high volume of standard products or services to achieve the low unit costs and high productivity associated with it. The nonstandard nature of services has been one of the reasons that productivity increases in service organizations have been lower than those in manufacturing. However, steps can be taken to reduce some of these obstacles. Possible steps include the following:

1. Implement flow lines
2. Adopt the modular service repair approach; replace the entire deficient module or unit and return it to a service center for repair
3. Use modular service components and combine them in a final assembly fashion to meet individual customer requirements
4. Implement automated devices and systems
5. Combine two or more of alternatives 1 through 4

Line flows have been adopted for at least part of the processes used by service industries. Fast-food franchises have developed line flows for preparing different sandwiches on the same line. Using the modular replacement service with a flow line repair process is a natural combination. A major Midwest beverage supplier also leases dispensing equipment at a nominal cost to its customers and replaces the equipment on a scheduled or emergency basis with refurbished or new units. The units pulled from service are returned to a regional refurbishment facility with a flow line process.

The cafeteria-style restaurant is a good example of line flow combined with modular service components; in this case some of the service components are in finished goods inventory. Bands and orchestra leaders have long used the modular service component approach. The number and variety of instruments on any assignment (party, bash, gig) depend on the needs and budget of the customer. Consulting project teams ideally consist of members selected from the organization's retinue so that there is a match of expertise to the task. These last two examples emphasize again the benefits of flexible capacity.

Collier (1983) provides over seventy examples of the use of robots, computers, and totally automated production systems in all sectors of the service economy. Most of us use many of these devices frequently, either directly or indirectly. They include such items as automatic funds transfer systems, automatic car washers, point-of-sale electronic terminals with optical scanners, automatic toll booths, automatic teller machines, electronic mail, and telephone switching systems. Even in this age, it is still rather amazing to pick up a telephone in Budapest or Sydney, dial the proper number, and have one of your children answer the phone in the United States. (The amazing part is that the line is not busy.) Most would agree that developments in automation and their adoption by service organizations will likely continue at a rapid pace with major effects on the service economy.

Two major results of the growth of automation are the increased capital required to compete in many services and the change in personnel capabilities and skills required by service organizations. Initial costs of extensive automation are high; thus, the entry level stakes are higher and entry is more difficult than in the past. Automated equipment, usually computer controlled, and computer data processing requires systems analysts, programmers, computer operators, electronic communications specialists, skilled maintenance personnel, and frequently fewer clerks. Automation increases productivity; it also increases the skill levels required. This gradually increases the average income of service personnel and makes it more difficult for the less skilled to obtain employment.

CONCLUSIONS

Service organizations generate nearly two-thirds of the GNP, earned a $30 billion net trade surplus in 1983, created over 85 percent of the new jobs in the last decade, and employ more individuals than the agriculture, mining, construction, and manufacturing sectors combined. In addition, most of the new jobs in the service sector are not the menial type, as is frequently thought. Shelp (1984) reports that (1) more than half of all U. S. service workers are in white-collar, often highly skilled, occupations and (2) the recent rate of growth in business service employment was nearly double the growth rate for fast-food franchises and eating and drinking establishments. The importance of service organizations in the economy, the importance of service activities to the success of most manufacturers, and the role of operations management in the success of service organizations demand the inclusion of service organizations in an introductory operations management text.

Many applications of concepts, principles, and techniques to service operations management are shown throughout the text, and here we summarize the main points of this chapter. Service organizations fall roughly into three types: (1) ESOs, (2) CSOs, and (3) PSOs. Each type brings with it different challenges for management and usually requires different approaches for managing personnel.

Although service organizations and manufacturing organizations have many similarities, they also differ substantially. The differences between a manufacturing and service organization depend on the two specific organizations being compared; however, in general, the major differences are (1) the greater interaction of the customers with service organization employees, facilities, equipment, and processes, (2) the greater need of service organizations for flexible capacity due to the inability to store service units in finished goods, (3) the less tangible nature of service outputs, (4) the hourly variability of demand for services, and (5) the necessity for most consumer service organizations to have many widely dispersed locations.

Designing a service requires first that the organization have a clear concept of the service they provide and to whom they intend to provide it. This goal is what drives and provides a focus for their activities. Once the overall organizational goal is determined, the desired explicit and implicit attributes of the service must be defined. Consumer surveys have proven valuable in discovering seemingly secondary attributes that the customers consider important. Primary services such as good food, clean accommodations, and on-time repairs are taken for granted; it's going that extra mile that separates the very successful from the mediocre service organizations.

Operations management decisions fall into the same general areas in both manufacturing and service industries—that is, capacity, materials, quality, human resources, and processes. Operations management challenges more commonly found in service organizations include the following:

1. Developing a combination of excess and flexible capacity to handle demand peaks
2. Obtaining qualified suppliers of materials and supporting services for many widely dispersed facilities
3. Measuring service quality
4. Selecting, training, and motivating employees to become both sales and production (service) personnel
5. Improving productivity through more efficient use of human resources, facilities, and equipment without diminishing the very service that the customer is purchasing

Many of the remaining chapters of this text examine operations management decisions in service organizations further. The references at the end of this chapter are also excellent sources of additional information concerning the management of service organizations.

QUESTIONS

For questions 1 through 8, refer to one or more of the following organizations:

Ambulance service	Travel agency	Caterer
Lawn care service	Dance hall	Dance band
Mortuary	Vacation resort	Interior decorator
Stock broker	Car wash	Auctioneer
Real estate agent	Laundromat	Estate planner
Pediatrician	Donut shop	Optical clinic
Fire department	Automotive garage	Instant printing shop

1. Describe the dominant attributes of service.

2. Suggest methods of measuring quality.

3. Indicate where in the service organization classification space you would place them.

4. Develop a proposed organizational chart for any four of the preceding organizations including an ESO, CSO, and PSO.

5. What skills and characteristics might one look for in first-line employees? In the first level of supervision?

6. Describe the capacity problems one might anticipate. What approaches might be taken to cope with these problems?

7. Pick two of the preceding organizations with substantially different training requirements for first-line employees. Describe the similarities and the differences.

8. Pick three of the preceding organizations that likely have substantial inventory and describe the inventory situation including the decisions involved.

9. You recently became the owner and general manager of an automobile dealership in the suburbs of a large city. You believe that the service department is neither as profitable as it should be nor a competitive strength of the organization. Develop a program that will meet the following criteria:

   a. Determine the factors that are essential to the service department being a competitive strength of the organization

b. Include measures of service quality

c. Include methods of achieving service quality

10. The president of a gas and electric company contends that the firm is in all three types of business: service, nonmanufactured goods, and manufactured goods. How might the president justify this statement?

11. Your client has a degree in management information systems and has worked as a programmer and systems analyst for a large retail firm. She also has developed a computerized information system for a radio station in your hometown, a relatively large city. She is considering opening a systems and software firm on a full-time basis. What particular advice would you give her concerning the nature (objectives) of this business?

12. A company that manufactures drilling rigs for obtaining soil samples has increasing sales due to environmental concerns and the need to forecast and evaluate the environmental impact of industrial operations. Although the reliability of their products is quite good, service in the field is still required for some of the hundreds of units they have sold over the years. They now need a new field service representative. What characteristics should this person possess? Where is the first place the company might look for such a person?

13. K-Mart and Wal-Mart both have had great success in what might be called the discount department store market. Wal-Mart entered the field years after K-Mart, Target, Venture, and others established strong footholds and loyal customers in the market. How did Wal-Mart deal with this problem, and what is the general lesson to be learned from that policy?

14. The American Automobile Association (AAA), also known as the Auto Club, was formed primarily to provide assistance to automobile owners whose vehicles break down anywhere in the country. However, as the years went by, they found that individuals who no longer own, rent, or lease a car—that is, they seldom drive—retain their membership. How do you explain this? What is the general lesson to be learned from it?

15. During the last seven years José and Francesca Gonzales have developed a very successful business that specializes in cleanup after water main breaks, sewer backups, floods, and similar catastrophes. They provide both residential and commercial service. They started with just the two of them and have added six individuals, whom they trained one at a time. They are located in San Diego and are considering opening offices in San Bernadino and perhaps Los Angeles. If they asked you for advice, what would you tell them?

16. Jon Von Slydal has inherited a ski lodge from his great uncle. His uncle, a widower, made a comfortable living, but the growth in his business has not compared to his competitors. This lack of growth puzzles Jon because most admit that the slopes are as good or better than any in the region and never are close to being full. What do you suspect?

17. Alex and Alecia Strutwell own a fashionable restaurant. Over the past two years many of their competitors and some less-expensive restaurants have added glass-enclosed awning type frontages that give a sidewalk cafe–type appearance. Their business is slipping while their competitors seem to be doing as well or better than formerly. Alecia believes they should change the front of the restaurant to resemble an awning-type enclosure; the capital cost is not that great. Alex agrees with Alecia that the elegance of the restaurant could be maintained with such a change but says that his visits to those restaurants, discussions with owners, and marketing surveys indicate that only a small percentage of people prefer sitting in those enclosures although the others do not object. How should Alecia respond?

18. Anthony and Vincent own and operate a small restaurant that their father founded. It is located downtown, has a reputation for good food, and has provided reasonably well for the family over the years. The men, now in their late twenties, plan to upgrade the restaurant. They are considering adding a doorman. In fact, they have a distinguished looking retired gentleman who would be perfect and enjoy it. Their uncle, who has given them much good advice, says, "Why spend the money? None of your competitors do it." What would you recommend?

19. Lutheran Hospital is located in an older section of a large city. Over the years the population in the surrounding area has aged and also declined, as the family size has declined. The demand for hospital service has declined, especially the demand for pediatric care. The organization has a new hospital in the suburbs but is interested in maintaining the older hospital primarily because there is still a need. What steps would you recommend to better serve their community (market) and thus increase demand?

20. There is a general feeling among the citizens of a small city that the city is a poor provider of services. The new mayor was, in fact, elected on the promise to change this situation. Now she must take action. What steps might she take? (Suggestion: First she must ascertain the citizens' thoughts about which services should be provided by the city and then those services should be ranked by importance.)

21. You are the supervisor of a plant that manufactures special equipment used by manufacturing companies that operate twenty-four hours a day,

seven days a week. The company has prided itself on services after the sales, which management believes gives it an edge on the competition. There are rumbles from your customers that your company's service is not that outstanding. You have just been promoted and made service manager. The company has approximately 700 customers throughout North America. What would be your plan of action for the immediate future (next week), for the next three to six months, and thereafter?

22. You are the manager of the Chicago office of a software consulting firm that specializes in developing virtually unique engineering and scientific programs for all types of companies. Your current programmer is an extremely creative analyst and programmer who has found solutions to problems that no others on the staff could and perhaps few in the profession could. The problem is that he has alienated customers, some permanently, by his behavior when visiting their facilities. It is imperative that he directly interface with client organizations. Finding a replacement for this programmer would be extremely difficult. What do you do?

REFERENCES

Albrecht, Karl, and Ron Zemke. *Service America!* Homewood, Ill.: Dow Jones-Irwin, 1985.

Beeson, Patricia E., and Michael F. Bryan. "The Emerging Service Economy." *Economic Economy*. The Federal Reserve Bank of Cleveland, June 15, 1986.

Canton, I.D. "Learning to Love the Service Company." *Harvard Business Review* 69 (1984): 89–97.

Collier, David A. "The Service Sector Revolution: The Automation of Services." *Long Range Planning* 16 (1983): 10–20.

Collier, David A. *Service Management*. Englewood Cliffs, N.J.: Reston Publishing Co. Inc., 1985.

Fitzsimmons, James A., and Robert S. Sullivan. *Service Operations Management*. New York: McGraw Hill, 1982.

Irons, Ken. "How to Manage Services." *Management Today* (November 1983): 90–93, 168.

Jones, Norman, et al. "The Hollow Corporation." *Business Week* (March 3, 1986): 52.

Ouchi, William. *Theory Z*. Reading, Mass.: Addison-Wesley, 1981.

Peters, Thomas J., and Robert H. Waterman, Jr. *In Search of Excellence*. New York: Harper & Row, 1982.

Runyon, Herbert. "The Service Industries: Employment, Productivity and Inflation." *Business Economics* 20 (1985): 55–63.

Sasser, W. Earl, et al. *Management of Service Operations*. Boston: Allyn & Bacon, 1978.

Schroeder, Roger G. "How to Create a Culture for Quality in an Existing Organization." Working Paper, School of Management, University of Minnesota, p. 7.

Shelp, Ronald K. "Bum Rap on the Service Economy." *The Wall Street Journal* (April 13, 1984): 26, 32.

Voss, Christopher, et al. *Operations Management in Service Industries and the Public Sector*. Chichester and New York: John Wiley & Sons, 1985.

PART II
LONG-RANGE PLANNING

CHAPTER 3
PRODUCT AND RESOURCE PLANNING

OBJECTIVES

After completing this chapter, you should be able to

- Define planning and identify and describe the four phases of the planning process

- Relate the operations planning process to the corporate planning process, specifically identifying the inputs to the process, the types of transformations that occur, and the outputs

- Identify several key questions that must be answered in the long-, medium-, and short-range operations planning processes

- Understand different management concerns and key management activities during various phases of the life of a productive system

- Relate the operations execution and control phase to the evaluation criteria of the operations manager and view it as an interactive system of inputs, transformations, and outputs

OUTLINE

Introduction
    The Definition of Operations Planning
    The Purpose of Operations Planning
Planning as a System
    Inputs to the Planning Process
    The Corporate Master Plan
Long-Range Operations Planning
    Product Planning
    Capacity Planning
    Location Planning
Medium- and Short-Range Operations Planning
    Human Resources Management
    Facility Layout Planning
    The Production Plan
    Short-Range Materials and Capacity Planning
Operations Execution and Control
Conclusions
Questions
References

65

INTRODUCTION

One of the few truths that operations managers can count on today is uncertainty. New laws, production technologies, competitors, and products, among other factors, have all caused dramatic changes and continuing uncertainty in production and service operations. To adjust operations to these changes and uncertainties in the environment, managers must first define the changes and their effects and then develop response alternatives. Planning assists management in defining and anticipating the future environment and developing appropriate alternatives. Planning activities allow management to operate more effectively by reacting rapidly and accurately to dynamic environments.

Planning is often done at several levels in the firm. For example, the vice-president for corporate planning may be responsible for overall corporate planning and work directly for the chief executive officer. The director of operations for a large production or service firm would probably have an assistant for planning and a small supporting staff dedicated to operations planning. However, at lower levels of the firm or in smaller firms, the planning function is often integrated with line management functions.

The Definition of Operations Planning

Operations planning is defined as follows:

Operations planning, the primary function of the operations manager, is the formalized process of anticipating future conditions by answering basic questions about how the organization may act to achieve its objectives.

Recall from Chapter 1 that there are five basic functions of the operations manager: planning, organizing, staffing, execution, and control. Planning has been called the most important of these five functions because planning must be accomplished before attention is turned to the other functions; however, there are arguments to the contrary.[1] In a well-managed organization, planning generally precedes, but is highly interactive with, other management functions. The initial plan may be imperfect and often will have to be modified, but it is a necessary first step. It would be difficult, time consuming, and very costly to organize, staff, execute, and control an operation without a plan to provide the overall guidance. Because of the importance of planning, Parts

---

[1]The primacy of the planning function is cited by Kreitner, Steiner and Miner, Gerstner, and Hayes and Wheelwright. However, note that there is an argument to the contrary, particularly with regard to daily activities of managers (Mintzberg 1971). Whether planning is the primary operations management function or not may depend upon the specific job; however, in a well-managed operation, planning must be accomplished and is a predecessor to other functions.

II through IV of this book examine the different levels of operations planning (i.e., long-, medium-, and short-range planning).

Planning is a formal, four-phase process that involves a specific series of activities. Although plans may not be written, particularly in very small firms, managers implicitly follow this development process. The planning process includes the phases of inquiry, information input, evaluation, and updating.

> *Phase I—Inquiry.* To initiate the planning process, the operations manager must ask a variety of questions. The exactness of these questions depends upon the time frame (long, medium, or short) of the desired plan.
>
> *Phase II—Information Input.* The answers to the operations manager's questions provide information input to the plan. This input is then formulated as a conceptual plan or an initial draft of a planning document.
>
> *Phase III—Evaluation.* The plan, in its initial format, is reviewed from various perspectives by key line managers and staff. Among the important concerns are whether the parts of the plan fit together well and whether the plan is amenable to management execution and control.
>
> *Phase IV—Updating.* The plan is revised based upon the evaluation accomplished in Phase III. This updating or fine tuning of the plan may have to be performed several times before the plan is acceptable to all parties in the planning process.

Planning, like management, is a process, or a series of activities. But unlike management, it is not necessarily continuous. Often planning will involve several hours or days of very concentrated work by management. Questions must be asked, information must be gathered, options must be considered, and the alternatives updated. Once these processes have been accomplished, managers can turn their attention to other functions, among them control and execution of the plan. The planning process must be regularly, but not necessarily continuously, pursued.

Planning anticipates possible future events (sometimes called contingencies) by developing alternative plans for use should such events occur. A political upheaval disrupting the normal source of a raw material, severe price cutting by a competitor, unexpected inflation, and unusually hot or cold weather are examples of possible events that can affect either supply, costs, or the sales of many organizations. Contingency plans provide for a calm and rational approach to dealing with such events and should eliminate the confusion and panic that could surround such events.

The Purpose of Operations Planning

The purpose of the operations planning process is to permit the operations manager to clarify or focus the operations contribution toward the goals of the firm and then to more explicitly identify the production requirements necessary and the resources available to meet those contributions. The operations plan should be drafted and circulated among top management and functional area managers, as well as the operations staff, for comment. This process gives each manager the opportunity to evaluate the operations plan for its impact on the whole organization and on other activities. Comments developed during the review process may identify critical weaknesses or limitations and permit improvement of the plan prior to final drafting. This drafting and review process is interactive and requires managers to identify the operations contribution to dealing with contingencies. Additionally, the planning interaction focuses the thinking of top management toward organizational goals.

A well-managed planning process (1) is the foundation for other management functions; (2) is regularly, but not continuously, pursued; (3) weighs and anticipates responses to future contingencies; and (4) requires regular top management involvement. Recalling for a moment the definition of management, planning permits management to focus the use of resources so that they are effectively and efficiently integrated toward the goals of the firm.

PLANNING AS A SYSTEM

Operations planning is developed in support of corporate planning. The corporate master plan, as its name implies, is the overall long-range corporate plan. It derives information from a variety of inputs, while simultaneously providing inputs, for plans in various functional areas. The operations planning process must be developed within the well-established framework of the corporate master plan.

Figure 3–1 depicts the corporate planning process as a system. This process includes inputs, transformations, outputs, controls, feedback, and the external environment, all identified in Chapter 1 as elements of a system. Inputs come from various sources, both inside and outside the firm. These inputs are transformed through the long-, medium-, and short-range planning processes into consistent, carefully evaluated assessments of how the firm will act. The outputs are the implementation of the plan and the increased understanding that management and employees have of the firm's objectives and activities. Management controls are exercised at every step, but particularly in the implementation process. Finally, planning must have a review and information feedback process.

Long-range plans deal with questions that can be resolved in a two- to five-year period or longer. Medium-range plans deal with questions that can be resolved in a period of between one to three months and two to five years, and short-range plans deal with questions that can be resolved within the next one to three months. These time frames vary in length because some business environments are very stable, whereas other environments are more dynamic.

Inputs to the Planning Process

Inputs to the corporate planning process represent different perspectives, some of which are consistent and synergistic, while others are conflicting.

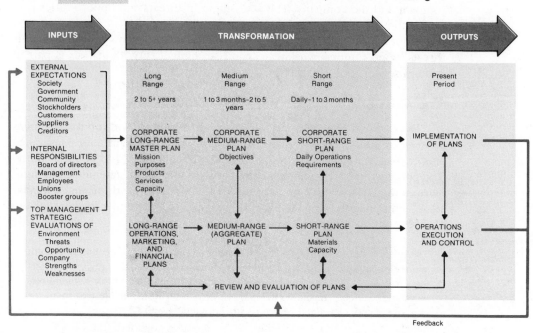

Figure 3–1 An Overview of Corporate and Operations Planning

Among the outside interests, the market expects the firm to provide a useful product or service (or else they will look to competitors), and the local community expects the firm to be a good neighbor by providing jobs and supporting community projects. Of course, the government expects the firm to meet legal requirements, such as paying taxes and operating in a pollution-free and safe manner. Customers expect products or services to be delivered on time, while stockholders, suppliers, and creditors all expect to be paid promptly. Thus, each external stakeholder has expectations about the operations of the firm. These sometimes conflicting expectations usually pertain to the nature and cost of the good or service.

Similarly, inside interests have expectations that are sometimes identified as responsibilities and rewards. Members of the board of directors are responsible for overall direction of the firm and for top management performance. Management and employees are responsible for full-time operations, including many details of product quality, employee welfare, and competitive position. Unions often represent employees, particularly with regard to compensation, security, and welfare issues. Booster groups, such as retiree, family, or social organizations, often provide valuable informal support functions to the organization. Each of these internal interest groups has a position of responsibility toward the firm. The interests of these groups are often conflicting in the short run; however, in the long run they are usually mutually supporting. If the legitimate objectives of any internal interest group are not achieved, the overall objectives of the organization may be imperiled. Likewise, if the organization fails, related internal and external interests fail with it.

Top management is responsible for the strategic evaluation of the environment and the company. The assessment of threats and opportunities present in the environment and the weaknesses and strengths internal to the firm are important parts of the corporate and operations planning processes. This threats, opportunities, weaknesses, and strengths (TOWS) analysis is part of strategy formulation and will be developed in Chapter 19.

The Corporate Master Plan

The external expectations, internal responsibilities, and top management strategy are ultimately aggregated in the corporate or organization long-range master plan, which, in large firms, may be a document of 100 pages or more. The corporate master plan normally contains a mission statement that summarizes the basic service or product, the key external and internal expectations, and the strategy of the firm. An example of a mission statement for the Midwest National Bank follows:

> The mission of the Midwest National Bank is to encourage the economic growth and well-being of the ten-state midwestern business and market region by offering small- and medium-sized businesses competitively priced basic banking services and financial consulting services and by ensuring equitable treatment for employees and a specified return to stockholders.

This corporate mission statement may appear to be very bland. Even so, a careful reading suggests that the Midwest National Bank primarily serves fast-growing entrepreneurial firms by providing low-cost basic banking and financial services. Profitability is sought through standardization, a stable work force, and focusing on low-cost responsive delivery. The Midwest National Bank may not be very flexible or adaptive and may only achieve quality through its well-trained, stable work force. After a specified (depending on current money markets) return to stockholders, the profits are returned to build equity. Of course, the corporate master plan would give more specific details. Figure 3–2 is an outline of the corporate master plan for Midwest National Bank.

Thus, the corporate or organization master plan identifies in broad strokes the mission, purpose, products and services, capacity, and long-range goals of an organization. The process of developing the specific medium- and short-range plans from the more general long-range plan is like exploding the detail of the plan. The long-range plan deals in years and in families of goods or services, while the medium- and short-range plans deal in months, weeks, or days and with individual components or required resource inputs.

The corporate master plan normally requires separate functional plans, appendices, or sections for each major functional activity. Functional plans would be expected from operations, finance and accounting, marketing, human resources, engineering and research, and sometimes from such specialized activities as safety, logistics, legal, labor relations, and others. Each

Figure 3–2   Outline of a Corporate Master Plan

Introduction
The Firm
   Locations and Facilities
   Organization and People
   Levels of Processing Technology
   The Nature of Banking and Consulting Services
   Major Suppliers
   Principal Investors
The Client Base
   Location
   Growth Rates
   Changing Client Needs
The Midwestern Region
   Economic Considerations
   Legal Considerations
   Business Conditions
   Major Competitors
The Business Climate
   Major Variables
   Forecast Projections of Business Growth
   Impacts of Changes in Banking Legislation
   Impacts of the Declining Heavy Industry Base in the Midwest
   Impacts of the Changes in Telecommunications
Growth Opportunities
   Short-Range Growth by Location
   Medium-Range Growth by Business Area
   Long-Range Growth in National Markets
Ownership Obligations
   Stockholder Obligations
   Obligations to Employees
   Long-Range Fixed Obligations
Conclusions

functional plan must be carefully integrated to fit the corporate master plan. This integration process develops a focus by considering the inputs of the five to ten major stakeholders and adjusting functional staff perspectives. This process results in the clearest possible statement of the corporate mission and purpose, objectives, and daily operational requirements, which are, respectively, the core emphases of corporate long-, medium-, and short-range plans. Figure 3–3 shows the channels through which the corporate master plan is focused.

Each of the functional plans and stakeholder perspectives must be tied together. The financial plan must support the marketing plan, the human resource plan must support the operations plan, and so forth. Extensive interaction is necessary among the functional staffs and stakeholders to achieve a good fit. The process is not complete unless these external loops are closed.

Figure 3–3   Channels Used to Focus the Corporate Master Plan

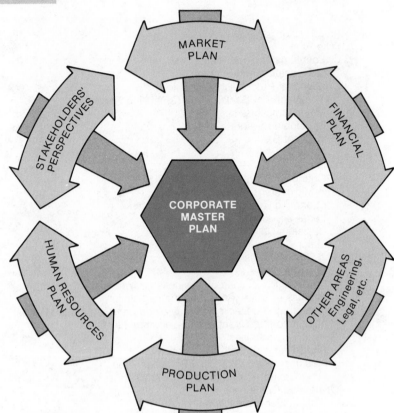

The focusing process forces the integration of the various external stakeholders and the functional staffs. What emerges is one plan that ties together the various functional staff perspectives and the stakeholder positions. Successful planning efforts focus the firm toward goals and missions, objectives, and daily operational requirements.

Numerous different perspectives, or answers, to the basic planning questions are represented by the different functional staffs. Figure 3–4 identifies a number of the areas in which operations may interface with the other staff functions. In more direct terms, these may be sources of conflict between operations and other functional staffs that must be resolved for the good of the organization.

LONG-RANGE OPERATIONS PLANNING

Long-range operations plans normally address questions that impact the firm from between two to five years or more in the future. These topics are

Figure 3–4 Interfaces of Operations with Other Staff Functions

Interfaces with Human Resources Management

a. Staffing Requirements: recruitment, position definition, employee skill levels, overtime
b. Performance Appraisal: performance measurement, employee evaluation, promotion
c. Training Requirements: internal and external programs, conceptual or technical skills
d. Compensation and Benefits: pay administration, program options, incentives
e. Labor Relations: work rules, safety, grievance procedures, quality of work life programs, schedules, time off, shift differentials

Interfaces with Finance and Accounting

a. Production Costing and Job Estimates: job requirements, material and labor costs
b. Inventory/Work in Process Accounting and Accuracy
c. Purchasing or Sales of Production Assets: equipment, facilities, subcontracting
d. Purchasing of Components or Raw Materials: shipping costs, bulk rates
e. Overhead and Labor Costs: time studies, work measurement, overtime, shift pay

Interfaces with Marketing and Sales

a. Product Design: specifications, options, assembly, modules, customization
b. Delivery Requirements: shipping methods and due dates, levels and type of inventory, backorders
c. Packaging Conditions: materials, bulkfill, packing sequence
d. Warranty and Quality Requirements: costs of rejects, costs of returns
e. Product Use, Obsolescence, and Safety: service, maintenance, upgrades
f . Competitor Products: capabilities and limits, price, manufacturing technology

Interfaces with Engineering and Research

a. Product Functioning: design requirements, durability
b. Model Changeover Scheduling: downtime, training requirements
c. Production Technology: process, organization, equipment
d. Equipment Maintenance and Modification: regularity, duration of downtime, alternate routings
e. Product Upgrade or Modification: design of modules
f . Raw Materials or Component Parts Specifications: reliability, performance

introduced here; however, more specific concepts and tools are detailed in the remaining chapters of Part II.

Firms that operate in very dynamic environments, such as computer manufacturers, toy manufacturers, or banks, must be prepared to implement long-range plans in as little as two years; however, the more common time frame for long-range plans of firms in the automobile, steel, drug, and other industries is three to five years or more. Some firms, particularly those that operate in very stable environments, consider a long-range plan as starting at ten years. For example, a manufacturer of small electric motors and portable welding equipment uses a long-range planning time frame of ten to twenty-five years.

Long-range operations planning involves three general areas of consideration: (1) nature of the product(s) or service(s), (2) output capacity, and (3) production facility location(s).

General Motors' decision to build the Saturn Plant at Spring Hill, Tennessee, integrates all three considerations of long-range operations planning. That decision resulted from planning efforts to design and produce a new automobile using computers and robotics technologies. Careful studies were made of the nature of the product and projected automobile sales in the 1990s. Finally, General Motors considered many locations for their new plant (*Business Week*, August 12, 1985 and January 28, 1985). These long-range planning issues are represented in Figure 3–5.

Figure 3–5 Long-Range Operations Planning

The Nature of the Product—What Product?

   a. Number of Products or Services and Range of Product or Service Lines
   b. Product Life Cycle
   c. Market Entry and Exit Timing
   d. Seasonal Nature of Product Demand
   e. Original Manufacturing versus Assembly of Components
   f . Design of Product, Quality, Customized or High Volume

The Facility Output Capacity—How Much?

   a. Economies or Diseconomies of Scale/Scope
   b. Technology and Best Operating Level
   c. Process Specialization
   d. Fixed and Variable Production Costs
   e. Outsource Vendors
   f . Personnel

Facility Location—How Many and Where?

   a. Proximity to Resources or Customers
   b. Few or Many Locations
   c. Level of Product or Service Provided at Each Facility

Product Planning

Initially, the long-range operations plan must consider what product(s) or service(s) will be produced. Product-related information is often developed from the marketing plan or the corporate master plan. The number of products or services and the range of the product or service lines is constrained by the business environment. For example, airlines and trains provide two or three levels of service, sometimes called regular (tourist) fare, business class, and first class. A refrigerator manufacturer might build seven or eight different models of refrigerators and market them regionally, nationally, or internationally.

The number of products or services in a line can vary; similarly, the range of product or service lines can vary. Among the automobile makers, for example, General Motors offers a full range of automobiles in the United States, from the basic transportation Sprint to the luxurious, sporty Cadillac Allante. A similar range of products is offered in Europe. Chrysler markets a narrower range of automobiles, from the Plymouth Horizon to the top-of-the-line New Yorker and LeBaron, with specialty products (Jeep) and a joint operation with Lamborghini in Europe.

Operations management must also be concerned with what stage of the life cycle the product is in. Most products have a life cycle; that is, they are born, they are produced until demand declines, then they are terminated. These phases are important because operations management has different concerns during each phase. Additionally, because of these different concerns, varying management concepts, techniques, and abilities are required. These phases are represented in Figure 3–6.

The research and process design phase involves conceptualization of the product, building an example prototype, and designing and building the production facility. Typically, the operations manager regularly communicates with the engineering and marketing staffs during this phase to define product or service characteristics and determine the best way to produce or provide them. Prototype models are subjected to a variety of in-plant and external customer use tests, as well as market testing. These tests result in numerous design changes and alterations of specifications. The operations objective during the research and design phase is to prove the product and the production process.

Operation of the production system is the second phase in the life of the productive system. After the product or service design has been decided on and the production process built, production is started. System flaws are resolved, and output volume is gradually increased until system capacity is reached. During this phase, production scheduling, product design upgrade, personnel and inventory resource utilization, and reduction of waste are prime concerns of the operations manager. Often, as a result of unexpected changes in the market, such as the entry of a competitor, changes in laws or governmental policies, or the development of new technology, the product design or the production process will be changed. During this

Figure 3–6 Key Concerns in the Life of a Productive System

Phase	Concern
Research and Process Design	1. What product/service will be offered? 2. What is the form and appearance? 3. What is the technology of the production process? 4. How do you determine the demand? 5. What output capacity is needed? 6. Where should the facility be located? 7. What shop layout is best to use? 8. What scheduling controls are required? 9. How do you assure desired quality? 10. What task should each worker perform? 11. How will job performance be evaluated?
Operation of the Production System	1. How do you produce the first product/service? 2. What production process upgrades are required? 3. How long will it take to reach the desired rate of production? 4. How many employees/shifts are needed? 5. What product upgrades can be made to better adjust to the competitive market? 6. How do you control day-to-day production? 7. What maintenance procedures are required? 8. How should quality be evaluated? 9. What scheduling flexibility is required by customers? 10. How can production be adjusted to better fit changing corporate strategy?
Termination of the Production System	1. What termination schedule is best? 2. What repair parts stock should be produced? 3. What is the salvage value of the facility? 4. What other products can be produced in the facility? 5. How do you minimize effects on employees? 6. How do you maintain morale during shutdown? 7. What are the long-range responsibilities for product, process, and production residues?

phase, the operations objective is the efficient operation of the production system.

The third phase of the product life cycle, termination of the production system, involves development of a residual stock of replacement parts and facility shutdown or conversion. The disposition of the facility and the minimization of turbulence and adverse impacts on the employees are the prime concerns of management during this phase. Additionally, recent legal changes encourage management to address long-term liabilities of the firm for the product, possible industrial residues, and negative impacts on the affected employees and communities. The objective of operations during this phase is to achieve a clean and equitable shutdown or product transition.

Product life cycles vary in length depending upon the dynamics of the market environment. The cycle may be as short as three or four months, as in the case of Christmas toys or an advertising campaign, or it may be many years, as in the case of a household appliance or commercial electric motor. Additionally, the relative length of each phase of the life cycle may vary. The research and design phase for a Christmas toy (a month or two) may be relatively short compared with the operations phase (three months). Alternatively, the research and design phase for an entertainment program may be three or four years, while the operations phase may last only half that time.

A third question of long-range product or service planning, one which derives from both the marketing and the operations plan, is the timing of market entry and exit. Depending upon the capabilities and experience of the operations and engineering personnel, the firm may desire to enter the market during early product development, taking advantage of a patent or license, and exit when lower-cost competitors have copied the technology and entered the market. Alternatively, the experience or competitive niche of the firm may lie primarily in low-cost, mass manufacturing or service provision. In that case, the firm should let other companies do the costly research and product development and rely on its own ability to mass produce once designs have been standardized.

A fourth long-range product planning question involves the development of complementary products, required by the seasonal nature of product demand. Customer demand for most products and services is seasonal. Telephone calls during holiday periods, vacation trips away from the cold of northern winters or the heat of southern summers, leisure products such as snow and water skis, motorcycles, and snowmobiles, and the use of electric and gas utilities are all examples of seasonal goods and services. Other goods and services, such as food production, are also highly seasonal, but modern methods of preserving, in the case of food products, provide stable, year-round supplies. Because of this essential seasonal nature of most commodities, firms will often produce countercyclical products or encourage countercyclical service volumes. A manufacturer may produce motorcycles and snowmobiles at different times of the year in the same factory. A hotel chain may schedule conferences in southern cities during the summer or northern cities during the winter to balance tourist business. These techniques of long-range product planning reduce the seasonal impacts on production facilities. (See Chapter 7 for a detailed discussion of operations planning in this situation.)

Another long-range product planning issue is the type of value added, both with regard to inputs and outputs. Service or manufacturing firms may choose to add value at different points of production input or with various amounts of standardization or customization of output. The value added of a manufacturing firm may be to build component parts from raw materials, to assemble finished goods from purchased components, or to produce finished goods from raw materials. In the service environment, some banks specialize in developing customer deposit accounts, while other banks aggregate funds from small accounts to make loans to major corporations. Thus, firms add value at various points of the production or service process.

With regard to output, some firms provide one standardized product, while others customize to desired specifications. Housing contractors, for example, build large developments of standardized condominiums and homes. For a greater cost, they build developments with mixed architecture or individually customized homes. In another product environment, one fast food restaurant offers a standardized hamburger, while a second customizes the hamburger to the customer's specifications, which usually means a higher price and a longer delivery time. Still another restaurant offers a broader menu with yet a longer delivery time. Both manufacturing and service firms select the limits of their value-adding operations and the amount of customization offered.

Long-range operations planning must consider the nature of the product, various market entry timing questions, the nature of demand, the input and output value added, and the product life cycle. These product questions are closely related to the long-range capacity planning questions considered in the next section.

Capacity Planning

The second general area of long-range operations planning involves the capacity of the operation, or how much should be produced? Capacity can be considered in terms of the best operating level and technology, process specialization, and vendor usage.

As the product or service design becomes more standardized and higher-volume production runs are possible, the operation becomes less costly for a variety of reasons. Economies of scale can be attributed to purchasing volume, utilization or scrap rates, and technology, among other factors. Generally, the larger the production lot, the lower the cost per item—up to a point. Unfortunately, at some volume or lot size, inefficiencies of scale may occur and production costs per unit may be more, not less. This phenomenon was initially identified as Parkinson's Law in studies of the British Navy (Parkinson 1957).

Similar findings have been encountered in nongovernmental environments. At the General Motors Vega assembly plant at Lordstown, Ohio, faster assembly lines required workers to reduce task cycle times (the duration of job actions before the cycle was repeated) to thirty seconds. When the assembly line was initially opened, employees were not familiar with these fast cycle times. At first many cars were improperly assembled. The technical economies of scale led to human resource management problems, strikes, and overall diseconomies of scale (Lee 1982). Economies of scale are possible as service volume or production lot size is increased, up to the point called the best operating level. However, after that point diseconomies of scale set in. The economies and diseconomies of scale are suggested by the best operating level (BOL) curve, represented in Figure 3–7.

The BOL curve is based on a specified level of technology. Operations managers must adjust production volumes to achieve the most efficient point of the curve for the specified technology. If the technology is changed, a new curve is created. Improved technology moves the curve downward and to the right, while reduced technology moves the curve upward and to the left. For example, the use of bar code readers at checkout counters of retail stores or public libraries speeds the process. Thus, a grocery checkout clerk or librarian is able to efficiently process more items for more customers per hour. This increases service volume and reduces the number of checkout counters needed. Ultimately, technological improvement reduces the cost per unit and establishes a second, lower BOL curve. Alternatively, the breakdown of a piece of production equipment, for example a robotic welder on an auto assembly line, would require manual welding, temporarily establishing a higher BOL curve. These lower and higher BOL curves are shown in Figure 3–8.

Different BOL curves are defined by the amount of specialized equipment or other fixed costs of production. A check-clearing department of a bank could operate manually, with extensive use of clerks and account books. This method would permit low fixed costs, but high variable costs (wages for the clerks). BOL Curve A in Figure 3–8 represents this option. Note that BOL

Figure 3–7   Operating Efficiencies and the Best Operating Level

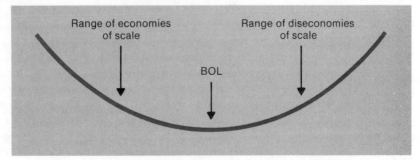

Number of items produced or services rendered
per time period

Figure 3–8 Technology Changes and the Best Operating Level

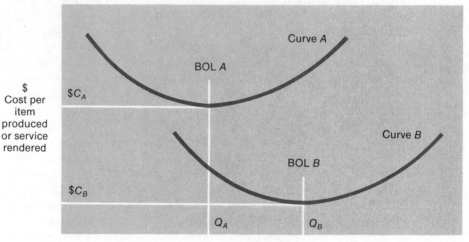

Number of items produced or services rendered
per time period

Curve A results in a lower quantity produced and higher variable cost, but lower fixed cost.

Alternatively, many banks have purchased automatic check processing machines that only require human verification. The equipment is expensive, but it operates faster and has a lower variable (labor) cost per item produced. This second level of technology is represented by Curve B which at the BOL has lower variable costs and higher volume. Manual production and unspecialized production equipment and processes have low fixed costs, but high variable costs. Alternatively, high-technology processing equipment requires a higher fixed cost investment, but has lower variable costs. Selecting the level of technology and adjusting to the BOL of the particular curve is a major capacity issue for the operations manager.

Such increases in the number of items produced, due to technology, are often referred to as efficiencies or economies of scale. That is, the increased volume of production permits the firm to prorate fixed production costs (e.g., the technology) over a greater production volume. Economies of scale often result in very large, high-volume, single (or few) product or service operations. A related concept, economies of scope, is often pursued by firms to broaden the range of their product offering. Recent efficiencies of technology, scheduling, and inventory management techniques, such as just-in-time and flexible manufacturing methods, have permitted firms to prorate fixed production costs over many different products. The resulting economies of scope often result in a generally small, low-volume, highly flexible production process with a wide variety of products.

Another capacity decision permits a firm to keep production rates level every month while making up for seasonal or unexpected demand through the purchase of extra production capacity outside the company. Because much of this extra capacity has been purchased overseas in recent years, the term *outsourcing* (meaning outside of the firm) has developed a negative connotation. This method of adjusting capacity works well for generic products, such as computer chips or long-distance telephone capacity. However, it is more difficult to outsource the capacity of a clearly defined or brand-name identified product or service, such as a drug or an up-scale restaurant.

A very widely used way of integrating resource or capacity planning issues in a manufacturing environment is shown in Figure 3–9. Although this approach was developed for a manufacturing environment, many aspects of this analysis are also applicable to services. The top portions of the figure derive from corporate and operations long-range plans, as noted in Figure 3–1. Long-range resource or capacity requirements planning is used to plan long-term capacity needs out to the time period when it is necessary to make gross capacity adjustments, such as a major facility or equipment purchase. Of necessity, gross estimates, or rough cuts, are often used. These estimates will show any serious production constraints in labor, materials, equipment, or plant capacity and can subsequently be used as the basis for the medium-range master production schedule.

After these resource evaluations have been accomplished, the further medium- and short-range planning activities are pursued, as shown in Figure 3–9. The aggregate plan establishes a production schedule for the medium range, roughly one year. Then materials requirement planning (MRP) and capacity requirements planning (CRP) define the component parts and labor required. Once these planning decisions have been completed and the aggregate plan is workable, short-range purchasing and scheduling are considered. These planning processes and their execution and evaluation are discussed in detail throughout this book.

Location Planning

The third long-range operations planning area is location. Where should facilities be located and what products or services should be produced at each location? Should the same products or services be provided at all locations or should several locations provide different selections? These decisions are interwoven with those concerning production facility size and distribution.

Manufacturing or resource extraction operations normally locate closer to resources in order to reduce transportation or operating costs. Service operations traditionally locate closer to customers or to the competition for convenience and product visibility. Similarly, manufacturing or resource extraction operations normally have one or relatively few production sites, while service facilities operate at many locations. Of course, resource extraction operations must be located near the raw materials. But service operations, such as fast-food restaurants, bank branches or cash stations, retail stores, or gasoline sta-

Figure 3–9   Resource/Capacity Planning

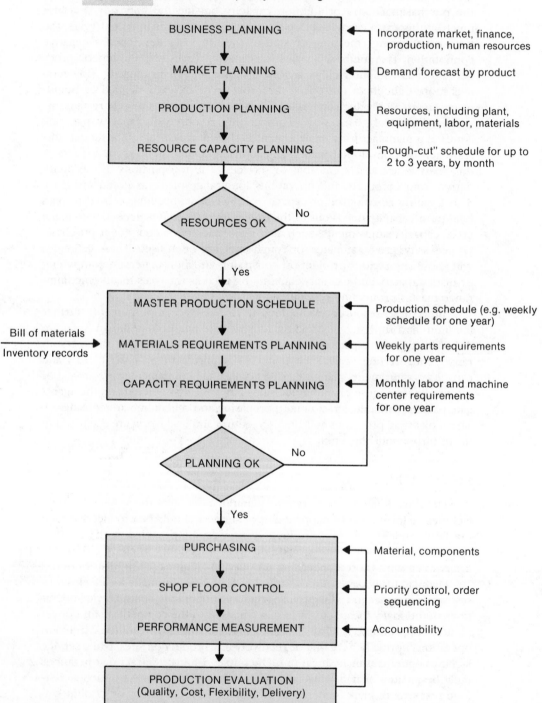

BUSINESS PLANNING ← Incorporate market, finance, production, human resources

MARKET PLANNING ← Demand forecast by product

PRODUCTION PLANNING ← Resources, including plant, equipment, labor, materials

RESOURCE CAPACITY PLANNING ← "Rough-cut" schedule for up to 2 to 3 years, by month

RESOURCES OK — No

Yes

MASTER PRODUCTION SCHEDULE ← Production schedule (e.g. weekly schedule for one year)

Bill of materials
Inventory records →

MATERIALS REQUIREMENTS PLANNING ← Weekly parts requirements for one year

CAPACITY REQUIREMENTS PLANNING ← Monthly labor and machine center requirements for one year

PLANNING OK — No

Yes

PURCHASING ← Material, components

SHOP FLOOR CONTROL ← Priority control, order sequencing

PERFORMANCE MEASUREMENT ← Accountability

PRODUCTION EVALUATION
(Quality, Cost, Flexibility, Delivery)

tions must locate close to the customers to ensure convenience and a steady flow of business. Their location, in itself, provides a service.

The nature of the product or production process may limit the level of goods or services provided at a particular facility. For reasons of security and practicality, the cash station of a bank normally limits the amount of withdrawals and the availability of customer services. However, a candy machine vendor would provide customers with as great a range of product choices as possible. Similarly, some product distribution systems handle all product lines, while others handle only a subset of the product line based on customer or area usage. There would be very little need, for example, for a mail-order distribution point in the southwestern United States to stock arctic parkas.

In manufacturing, the separation of different production processes may or may not be efficient. For example, Toyota mixes the models produced on its assembly line by sequencing first a sedan, then a hardtop, then a sedan, then a wagon, and so forth. This mixing process saves Toyota the cost of a separate facility, or an assembly line changeover process; however, the mixed assembly line requires the increased complexity and probably slower speed of different assembly processes (Wantuck 1983). A similar mixed assembly line production process is used by Cummins Diesel. Other companies have taken a different approach. Texas Instruments concluded that the production technologies of different stages of the digital watch production process should be housed in different plants. Similarly, the Lynchburg Foundry established five plants, each with a different metal-working technology, rather than combine production technologies (Hayes and Wheelwright 1979).

Just as capacity issues are closely related to the nature of the product, so the location issues are directly related to available capacity. The three questions (product, capacity, location) must be simultaneously considered in the long-range planning process. These questions have been briefly introduced here. They will subsequently be developed in detail in Part II, along with appropriate quantitative tools.

MEDIUM- AND SHORT-RANGE OPERATIONS PLANNING

Because most medium-range operations planning activities are directly interrelated with short-range activities, these two time dimensions of planning will be considered together in this section. However, the concepts and appropriate tools will be separated in Parts III and IV of this book for greater clarity of presentation.

Medium- and short-range operations planning deal with issues that are generally of three years or less in duration and three months or less in duration, respectively. The three general areas of concern for medium- and short-range planning are (1) human resources management—medium range, (2) facility layout planning—medium range, and (3) production planning—medium and short range.

Both human resources management and facility layout planning are medium-range considerations. However, human resources management and facilities layout also imply a short-range planning requirement. For example, the selection of specific individuals to work overtime on a particular job, the routing, or a machine setup for a job are short-term activities that are considered in short-range capacity requirements planning. Production planning is also a medium-range activity; however, once the aggregate schedule is established in the medium range, it generates subsequent short-range materials requirements planning and capacity requirements planning activities. These medium- and short-range planning activities are shown in Figure 3–10.

Once the long-range questions of product, capacity, and location have been addressed, planners should consider the medium-range questions of human resources management, facility layout, and production planning or aggregate scheduling. After these medium-range questions have been addressed, planners can consider short-range scheduling of materials, equipment, and labor for each separate job of a job shop or adjustments of materials, equipment, and labor as required for modifications of the assembly line production schedule.

Human Resources Management

Human resources management encompasses the more traditional functions of personnel and work force management, but it is more than that. Human resources management recognizes the intrinsic value, needs, and resourcefulness of employees, provides an environment that nurtures and rewards that resourcefulness, and taps it for the benefit of the employee and the productivity of the organization. Human resources management engenders a spirit of cooperation, mutual trust, and common goals; it rejects the adversary model of many traditional labor-management relationships.

The major elements of human resources management include the following:

1. Management policies and attitudes that recognize basic human needs and create an environment supporting those needs
2. A system for determining personnel needs by skill and profession under different marketing and production plans
3. A system that evaluates employee capabilities, skills, potential, interests, and development opportunities
4. An explicit policy of rewards that recognizes employee interests and objectives and is based on both group and individual performance
5. Integration of recruitment and selection policies, staffing levels, capacity requirements, aggregate plans, and processes

The initial structuring of an organization is a long-range planning function that involves extensive study of organization theory and design. The organizational structure, which can be tailored to fit specific operating environments, is important because it establishes the duties, formal lines of control, num-

Figure 3–10   Medium- and Short-Range Operations Planning

Medium-Range Planning Concerns

Workforce Management—Who?

a. Structuring the Organization: structural alternatives, job descriptions, categories of employees
b. Acquiring Labor: recruiting, hiring
c. Productivity: motivation, training, skills, work measurement
d. Labor Relations: compensation, benefits, and employment security

Facility Layout—How?

a. Purpose of Layout
b. Equipment Positioning and Process Flows
c. Handling Methods: equipment, conveyors
d. Communication Methods and Facilities: bar coding, data capturing

Production Planning (Aggregate Scheduling)—When?

a. Aggregate Planning: Master production scheduling, capacity planning
b. Cost of Operations: raw materials, components, overhead, labor, fixed equipment, quality shrinkage, shipping
c. Integration of Suppliers/Shippers

Short-Range Planning Concerns
(An Explosion of the Aggregate Schedule)

Materials Management—What Materials?

a. Delivery Timing: shipping lead times, frequency of delivery
b. Storage Locations: warehousing versus shop floor
c. Material Specification: quality, shipment volumes, packaging

Capacity Requirements Planning—Which Jobs?

a. Customer Due Dates: costs of late shipment, prioritization, expediting
b. Input-Output Control: order sequencing, order release
c. Routings to Work Stations or Equipment: lot sizes, split batches, job sequencing, queues
d. Work Station/Employee Utilization Rates: productivity, quality, scrap rates, production performance measurement

bers and types of positions by skill and qualifications, and employee classifications of part-time, full-time, and temporary hire. Each position should have a clearly written description of principal functions, responsibilities, and reporting relationships. Normally, the operations manager will only be concerned with medium- and short-range modifications, such as adding a position or combining the functions of two sections. These relatively minor actions can be accomplished with help from the human resources staff. More extensive restructuring of the operation should be planned with the involvement of top management.

When the positions are established and an organizational structure is defined, the positions must be filled. Often human resources will be responsible for recruitment; however, the operations manager must assure that the recruitment process, over which he or she has little control, provides a sufficient range of internal and external candidates. In all cases, operations should have a strong voice in the final hiring decisions.

A major human resources management concern is labor relations issues, including the development of a corporate culture, participative management, and compensation and incentive programs. Carefully planned compensation packages must be worked out with union representatives or employee groups. Such packages involve questions of competitive pay levels and incentives for the work performed; cost-effective benefit programs that satisfy legal requirements and attract qualified employees; and employment security to provide continuing income in the event of employee discharge, job cutbacks, or plant closures. Operations managers must be familiar with the very detailed legal requirements and other constraints of effective labor relations. These topics can be pursued through further study in compensation management and industrial relations.

A final concern of human resources management planning is labor productivity and work measurement. Probably the single most important contributor to productivity is the motivation of the work force. The employee hired for a specific position must have the necessary professional skills and attributes. Additionally, however, an employee must desire to work. Numerous contributors to enhanced motivation and productivity are considered in organizational behavior and labor management courses. Ultimately, the operations manager must consider a program that measures the productivity, performance, and potential of each employee. Work measurement permits standardization of labor and performance data so that management can better estimate the labor costs associated with a product or a specific task.

Facility Layout Planning

In the medium range, operations planning must consider the purpose of the layout, materials handling concerns, and communication methods to be used. There are six general types of operations layouts, each of which is designed to achieve different purposes. These are described in Figure 3–11.

Depending upon the specific purpose, an organization may use different layout types in different parts of the operation. For example, a large Midwest office products distributor uses a storage layout to minimize retrieval time for high-volume items in one section of the warehouse. However, that same distributor uses an administrative layout for order assembly and packaging lines. Similar items are placed at widely separated storage locations, a practice which the company has found to significantly reduce the possibility for errors

Figure 3–11   Layout Alternatives for Operations Managers

Type	Purpose
Product	Sequential flow of a single product or several very similar products occurs through adjacent work stations. The equipment is arranged as required by the sequence of the process. Cost efficiency and standardization of production are emphasized.
Process	Equipment is grouped by function, thus items with different operation sequences follow different paths through the facility. Flexibility of production is emphasized.
Project	Fixed location, production flow is designed to move resources toward production site with minimum job disruption. Minimum duration of operations is emphasized.
Storage	Product location is designed to permit minimum retrieval time or ease of retrieval flow, particularly for the most heavily demanded items. Cost efficiency of storage and retrieval is emphasized.
Marketing	Product location is designed for maximum product visibility and to facilitate customer flow past product locations. Spontaneous sales and product visibility are encouraged.
Administrative	Locations are based on individual comfort, reduction of processing errors, or facilitation of administrative interaction. Administrative efficiency, however defined, is encouraged.

in order assembly. Marketing layouts are used by retail stores that have found that some customer items, such as magazines and candy, sell better if they are located close to the checkout areas. Similarly, many large retailers position counters and displays like a maze, which encourages greater sales visibility.

Traditional manufacturing layouts are designed for either sequential efficiency of assembly, as used in product flow lines, or efficiency of equipment and labor utilization, as used in functional layouts. However, in cases such as the construction of a building, a ship, a bridge, or a fixed mining, agricultural, or timber-harvesting site, it is not practical to move the production site. Materials must be brought to a fixed location. Even so, the layout of materials at a fixed job site is important to minimize disruptions, thus reducing costs and assuring completion deadlines. Storage, marketing, and administrative layouts are more commonly found in service operations, while process, product, and fixed layouts are more widely used in manufacturing and extraction operations.

In addition to the physical layout relationships of processing activities, the operations manager must consider materials and information-handling methods and operations support that might be integrated with the physical site layout. Conveyors are used to move lightweight boxes and wire guidance systems assist forklift trucks in negotiating narrow warehouse aisles. Careful layout planning for these material-handling items is important because this equipment is difficult to install or change after the layout has been established.

Management information and control technology, such as bar code readers located at each work station or at shipping docks, can report the status of each job or identify incoming and outgoing shipments. Direct input of this information to the operations computer will reduce the paperwork and confusion on the plant floor.

Facility layout planning considers capacity requirements and the most efficient flow of the production process, based upon production system goals. Service organizations may desire the efficiencies of storage, marketing, or administrative layouts, while manufacturing operations normally use process, product, or fixed layouts. Material-handling and information-handling methods should be integrated in layout planning.

The Production Plan

The third area of medium-range planning is the production plan or aggregate schedule, as noted in Figure 3–10. The aggregate schedule answers the question of when resources are needed and when products or services will be produced. Aggregate plans normally establish approximate monthly production schedules over one or several years for each major product or product family, based on demand forecasts.

Costs of materials and component parts, skills and numbers of workers, plant capacity, and equipment technology are all considered in rough-cut resource requirements planning. Aggregate planning relates resource planning to estimates of demand by major product or product family. Thus, the aggregate schedule, or aggregate plan, is a rough-cut evaluation of production resources to satisfy demand. This rough-cut estimate is further refined through two, short-range planning processes: materials requirement planning and capacity requirements planning.

A technique that is increasingly being used to improve operations efficiency is the close integration of suppliers and shippers with the production schedule. Delivery of raw materials or component parts close to the point of production and only as needed by the production process reduces inventory and material-handling costs. Additionally, careful scheduling of product or service output with shippers or customers reduces finished goods inventories and the number of customers waiting for service. Careful integration of suppliers and distributors with the aggregate schedule can improve operations efficiency.

Various issues of medium-range human resources management, facility layout planning, and aggregate scheduling, and the associated computational methods, are considered in greater detail in separate chapters in Part III.

Short-Range Materials and Capacity Planning

Materials requirement planning (MRP) uses weekly or daily demands in the master production schedule (MPS), which is based on customer orders or sales forecasts, to compute the quantity of raw materials or components that are required for production. MRP also schedules when those items are needed and when they should be ordered. MRP is a short-range planning tool because, unlike the rough-cut aggregate plan, MRP uses exact production requirements and determines specific order times and need dates for each item. This detailed information permits the finished good to be produced to specified due dates as stated in the MPS. MRP is used in this way to manage materials acquisition.

Capacity requirements planning (CRP) integrates MRP information with process information, available labor hours, equipment utilization rates, out-source vendors, and other production resources to schedule daily production jobs against the facility, equipment, human resources, and material assets of the firm. CRP answers this question: Which jobs with which resources when? Its primary task is to determine whether sufficient capacity is available and if not, it must enable management to determine what should be done.

Medium-range operations plans for the work force and facility layout establish an aggregate schedule or plan, which is a rough-cut computation to determine if there are major shortfalls or overages in production resources. Medium-range plans are then exploded into more specific short-range plans, the MPS, MRP, and CRP, which schedule material and production resources against firm customer orders or which forecast customer demand.

Medium-range plans address three issues: (1) human resources management, (2) physical layout, and (3) aggregate schedule planning. For example, a chemical firm might decide to hire and train a second shift or use an additional processing area of an electrolysis plant, based upon the anticipated receipt of a new contract. Similarly, a tax preparation firm temporarily increases the number of client representatives and office space in the winter and spring of each year. Medium-range planning for these changes in work force, layout, and scheduling concerns specific questions of who, when, and how, in general, rough-cut terms.

Short-range planning is concerned with managing materials, personnel, and other resources to fulfill the requirements (quantity and due date) of specific orders. Thus, it assigns priorities to orders and develops specific schedules. Materials requirements planning determines the need (when and how many) for materials, components, subassemblies, and assemblies. Capacity requirements planning determines the need and availability of capacity resources such as equipment and personnel. Input-output management and order sequencing determine the release of orders and the sequence in which they are processed. For example, a printer receives an order for 1,000 business cards. This order initiates a query to determine if there is enough paper stock in inventory, and, if so, commits that inventory and schedules the job to cutting, embossing, or printing equipment on a specific day. Short-range operations planning activities and quantitative tools are considered in more detail in Part IV.

The long-, medium-, and short-range dimensions of planning raise numerous, very closely interrelated questions. The planning process is used to gradually explode the long-range product, capacity, and location issues into rough-cut aggregate plans in the medium range, and master production schedules in the short range. However, no explicit actions are taken until the implementation phase, which involves the execution and control of the plans. Each level of planning implicitly addresses the four measurement criteria: cost, flexibility, delivery, and quality. However, it is only in the control and execution phase that those criteria of an operation are measured.

OPERATIONS EXECUTION AND CONTROL

The execution and control phase differs in one very critical way from the three planning phases. The planning phases produce only paper and, hopefully, a greater understanding of the operation. The execution phase produces products or services. All the planning in the world does not contribute to the operations goals unless it is executed. On that basis, one might argue that, to minimize costs, a minimum of effort should be committed to planning, and maximum effort should be committed to execution. Unfortunately, the execution of a faulty or improperly prepared plan may be even more costly and less efficient than no production at all.

Five activities are associated with the execution and control phase of operations management: purchasing, production activity control, distribution, quality control, and maintenance. These activities can be viewed as an execution and control system in the sense that there is an input, transformation, and output relationship among them. Figure 3–12 shows that the inputs are acquired through purchasing, the transformation is managed through production activity control, and the outputs are handled through the distribution system. Maintenance activities and quality control feedbacks assure that the transformation process is operating properly.

Four criteria are used to evaluate the effectiveness of operations execution and control. These criteria were introduced in Chapter 1, are defined here, and will be discussed in detail and applied in Chapter 19.

1. *Cost*—Maintaining production costs at acceptable levels
2. *Quality*—Product fitness for use and performance to specification
3. *Flexibility*—Responsiveness to product design modifications or changes in output volume
4. *Delivery*—Production and shipment of orders in a prescribed manner

Purchasing of raw materials and components emphasizes careful market evaluation for cost. However, vendor flexibility to changes in delivery require-

Figure 3–12   The Execution and Control System

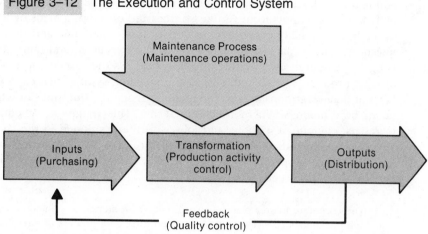

ments and meeting of required delivery dates with high-quality goods and services may also be very important criteria in purchasing decisions.

Production activity control (PAC) manages the execution of scheduled production, including the maintenance of equipment and quality evaluation. The criteria of cost, flexibility, and quality are all important considerations in the evaluation of the transformation process. Are production costs competitive? How flexibly can the process be changed to meet revised customer needs? Are quality levels acceptable? These questions are central to transformation process management.

Of the four criteria, delivery is probably the most important to consider in production output or distribution activities. However, this final step also requires the delivery of the right goods or services to the specified customer location on time and in good condition with minimum delivery costs. Implicitly, cost, flexibility, and quality are also considered. Thus, the four criteria of evaluating operations—cost, flexibility, quality, and delivery—are each potentially applicable to each aspect of the execution system, depending upon the specific production environment.

More importantly, the execution system depends, to a large degree, upon the effectiveness of the planning that preceded it. It is difficult and costly to double capacity, change production location, hire a second shift, or change layouts in the middle of a production run. The operations planning process of identifying and answering the long-range, medium-range, and short-range questions must be directed toward the four criteria by which operations effectiveness is measured.

CONCLUSIONS

The product and resource planning process is the primary function of management and has been defined as a formalized process to anticipate future contingencies by answering a number of questions. The planning process initially integrates inputs from various sources and develops a focus by logically developing internally consistent answers to long-, medium-, and short-range questions. These plans are acted upon in the execution and control phase. Long-range operations planning questions address the essence of how much of what product is produced where. The planning system then explodes the level of detail and considers in the medium range the questions of who produces how much when in rough-cut terms. This rough-cut scheduling of materials, equipment, people, and jobs is further exploded in the short run to meet the demands of specific orders or forecasts. These questions and the answers drive the planning process. Several characteristics of the planning process should be reemphasized:

1. The corporate master plan receives inputs from numerous conflicting inside and outside sources. These are integrated through a process of interchanges among the major external stakeholders and internal staff directors of the firm.
2. The corporate master plan is exploded in detail to develop the corporate medium- and short-range plans. These corporate plans are the basis for implementation.
3. The corporate master plan provides major guidelines for the long-range operations plan, which, in turn, drives the medium-range (aggregate) plan and short-range (master production schedule) plan. Simultaneously, the corporate medium- and short-range plans must be integrated with the medium- and short-range operations plans.
4. Execution and control may be viewed as a system, with elements of purchasing, distribution, production activity control, quality feedback, and process maintenance.
5. The implementation is measured by one or several of four criteria: delivery, flexibility, cost, and quality. These criteria must be carefully considered at each phase of planning.
6. The process is cyclical and ongoing, although it may not be continuous. A review and evaluation of plans is conducted regularly to revise and update inputs to the planning process.

QUESTIONS

1. Define planning. Consider and describe the elements of the definition.

2. Why is planning considered to be the primary operations management function? Do you agree? Note an argument against planning as the primary operations management function.

3. What are the four phases of the planning process? Why are they necessary?

4. Consider a specific manufacturer or service production company that you are familiar with. Identify several of the external and internal stakeholders

and note existing conflicts between them. (If you are not familiar with any specific organization, consider your university, a service provider, or consult a recent issue of *Business Week* or another practitioner periodical.)

5. Does your selected firm have a long-range, a medium-range, a short-range plan? How long is the duration of each planning time frame? Is that what you would have expected?

6. What is the corporate mission of your selected firm?

7. For your selected firm, give the titles of each of the principal staff members.

8. For your selected firm, identify several conflicts between the operations function and other staff members.

9. List three questions that are considered by each of the following: long-range plans, medium-range plans, and short-range plans.

10. Select a durable goods manufacturer and a service firm that you are familiar with. Give examples of long-range planning questions that each firm should consider.

11. Would you expect that the product life cycle of a manufactured good would generally be longer than for a service? Why or why not?

12. Describe BOL curve movement in the following four situations:
    a. Increasing the number of employees on a work team
    b. Decreasing the number of word processing work stations for a secretarial pool (no other equipment is available as a replacement)
    c. Raising the weight limitations for tractor-trailers carrying goods in interstate commerce
    d. Using microwave ovens in restaurants to reduce food preparation times

13. The range of products or services produced at a particular facility may vary. Give examples of both products and services with their different ranges of production at different facilities.

14. Select a durable goods manufacturer and a service firm that you are familiar with. Give examples of medium- and short-range planning questions that each firm should consider.

15. Why might medium- and short-range planning processes consider the same questions, but differ in substance?

16. Why is the execution and control phase considered to be a system?

17. You are the owner of a local theater. Identify in outline form several issues that you would address in the long-range plan, the medium-range plan, and the short-range plan.

18. You are the owner of lake or seashore rental property, a fast-food restaurant franchise, a small printing business, a travel agency, a medium-sized plastic products molder, a blank audio cassette assembler, or a service organization. Identify the issues presented in Question 17.

REFERENCES

Daft, Richard L., and Richard M. Steers. *Organizations: A Micro/Macro Approach*. Glenview, Ill.: Scott, Foresman and Company, 1986.

Fogarty, Donald W., and Thomas R. Hoffmann. *Production and Inventory Management*. Cincinnati: South-Western Publishing Co., 1983.

Gerstner, Louis V., Jr. "Can Strategic Planning Pay Off?" *Business Horizons* (December 1972): 5–16.

Hayes, Robert H., and Roger W. Schmenner. "How Should You Organize Manufacturing?" *Harvard Business Review* (January–February 1978).

Hayes, Robert H., and Steven C. Wheelwright. "Link Manufacturing Process and Product Life Cycles." *Harvard Business Review* (January–February 1979).

———. *Restoring Our Competitive Edge*. New York: John Wiley & Sons, 1984.

"How GM's Saturn Could Run Rings Around Old-Style Carmakers." *Business Week* (January 28, 1985): 126.

Kreitner, Robert. *Management*. Boston: Houghton Mifflin Co., 1983.

Lee, Hak-Chong. "Lordstown Plant of General Motors" from Gordon K. C. Chen and Robert E. McGarrah, *Productivity Management: Text and Cases*. Hinsdale, Ill.: Dryden Press, 1982.

Mintzberg, Henry. "Managerial Work: Analysis from Observation." *Management Science* (October 1971).

Parkinson, C. Northcote. *Parkinson's Law*. Boston: Houghton Mifflin Co., 1957.

Shapiro, Benson P. "Can Marketing and Manufacturing Coexist?" *Harvard Business Review* (September–October 1977).

Skinner, Wickham. "The Focused Factory." *Harvard Business Review* (May–June 1974).

Steiner, George A., and John B. Miner. *Management Policy and Strategy*. New York: Macmillan Publishing Co., 1977.

Wantuck, Kenneth A. "The Japanese Approach to Productivity." Proceedings of the American Production Inventory Control Society Annual Conference, 1983.

Wells, Louis T., Jr. ed. *The Product Life Cycle and International Trade.* Cambridge, Mass.: Harvard University Press, 1972.

Wheelwright, Steven C. "Strategic Planning in the Small Business." *Business Horizons* (August 1971): 51–58.

"Why A Little Detroit Could Rise in Tennessee." *Business Week* (August 12, 1985): 21.

Wight, Oliver. *MRP II: Unlocking America's Productivity Potential.* Boston: CBI Publishing Co., 1981.

CHAPTER 4
FACILITY
LOCATION

OBJECTIVES

After completing this chapter, you should be able to

- Describe reasons for the importance of location decisions

- State the four-step, sequential, site selection process and some factors that affect the decision at each step of the process

- List the different factors that affect site location decisions for the following:

    1. nonmanufacturing organizations
    2. manufacturing organizations
    3. warehousing and transportation organizations
    4. service organizations

- Select and compute varying location decision models using qualitative and quantitative data inputs

- Identify the differences between and approaches to site location decisions for single and interrelated multiple facilities

OUTLINE

Introduction
Long-Range Capacity and Location Planning
    Dealing with Capacity Change
    Capacity Evaluation
    Capacity and Location Planning
    The Location Decision Process
Decision Factors and Organization Types
    Nonmanufacturing Production Facilities
    Manufacturing Facilities
    Warehouses and Distribution Facilities
    Service Facilities
Location Decision Models
    Models to Evaluate Qualitative Factors
    Models to Evaluate Combined Qualitative and Quantitative Factors
    Models to Evaluate Quantitative (Distance) Factors
    Models to Evaluate Quantitative (Cost) Factors
Integration of New Facilities
    The Northwest Corner Method
    Vogel's Approximation Method
    The Modified VAM
    Optimality Testing and Stepping Stone Adjustment
    Multiple Facility Integration
Service Facilities
Conclusions
Questions
Problems
References

INTRODUCTION

Location is crucial. It affects the efficiency and effectiveness of nonmanufacturing production facilities, manufacturing plants, warehouses, and service organizations. For example, location affects shipping costs to customers, the transportation costs of materials, and the availability and cost of personnel. Location decisions usually are long range; once made, they take considerable time and money to change. Thus, they usually affect operating costs for a long time and are an integral part of the long-range strategic planning process.

Location decisions occur more frequently than the casual observer might believe. New organizations, expanding and contracting organizations, organizations coping with changing economic factors, and organizations implementing policy changes resulting from revised strategies all face the location decision challenge. Expansion includes both the addition of new products and entrance into new geographic markets. Changing production factors include the availability of required personnel, supplies, or supporting services. The demographic features of communities change; populations in one area may decrease while populations in another area increase. Such changes affect the demand of retail establishments and the availability of personnel to staff those businesses. Such shifts also dramatically affect the demand for health care services and generate site location decisions for hospitals and health care clinics. Examples of changes in strategy and policy that generate relocations are (1) the decision to change from one centralized warehouse to several regional warehouses or (2) the decision to manufacture goods at a number of small single-purpose focused factories instead of one large multipurpose facility. In many respects, the location decision process involves a continuous, long-range review of capacity needs, given the changing environmental conditions.

LONG-RANGE CAPACITY AND LOCATION PLANNING

Most location decisions are originally necessitated by changing capacity requirements. The requirements for production, specified in terms of volume, product or service design, and timing and location of delivery, can be expected to vary significantly over time. These aggregate capacity requirements are based upon known demands, firm customer orders or backlog, or a forecast estimate of probable sales. Aggregate capacity needs can normally be projected with relatively high accuracy. However, as Figure 4–1 suggests, it is

Figure 4–1 Aggregate Capacity Planning Subsets

When to Produce	→ Required Delivery Date (RDD)
Where to Produce	→ Location or Distribution Plan
How Much to Produce	→ Volume, Product Mix

also necessary to accurately estimate subsets of aggregate capacity. For example, the location breakout by specific region, the monthly required delivery dates (RDD), or the product breakout by type or model (product mix) are three subsets of aggregate capacity that are central to location planning.

Dealing with Capacity Change

Some change of capacity, even in relatively stable aggregate capacity, is inevitable. Shifts in the external environment, including population demographics, production technology, and communication linkages, impose these capacity changes upon the competitive production environment. John Naisbitt has identified four "critical restructurings" of society that impact on capacity and location planning (Naisbitt 1982). Population growth in the southern and western United States has been dramatically increasing as people move to the Sunbelt. These shifts primarily involve the cities, which in the South are experiencing very rapid growth, while cities in the North are generally declining or remaining stable. A second demographic shift is the decentralization away from these cities through the proliferation of suburban and beltway communities. Increasingly, major corporations, businesses, and jobs are moving away from the central city to suburban areas.

Enhanced specialization and communications have permitted the internationalization of production processes. A simple product like a baseball glove is made from Texas cowhides, tanned in Brazil, stitched in the Far East, and then sold in the United States. Additionally, major portions of growth, both in manufacturing and service sectors, have not been found in major institutions, but rather in the smaller and more entrepreneurial firms. This downsizing of American business clearly affects location decisions. These four critical restructurings—North to Southwest, decentralization, national to world, and institutional to entrepreneurial—have shifted both the location of markets and the location of available labor.

The changing technologies of manufacturing have also caused some notable shifts in the methods of production. Traditional manufacturing methods worked toward large capacities and were generally not concerned with the inventory, labor, and overhead inefficiencies that large capacities caused. For example, high amounts of automation, long setup times, and complex, highly differentiated production processes all lead to high capacity outputs, but incur the expense of very specialized and inflexible labor and equipment, high inventories, and increased overhead. Recent research suggests that smaller facilities, production cells, and selective automation can substantially reduce costs (Hill 1984). Similar efficiencies have been achieved in service organizations through miniaturization; examples are point-of-sale photo-processing laboratories and one-stop eye care centers. These developments are discussed in greater detail in Chapter 9 and Chapter 20.

The third external environmental impact results from improved communication linkages, particularly in the service area. Communication enhancements permit a variety of customer interface efficiencies, such as cash stations, toll-free catalog ordering, various travel and entertainment reservation services, and customer product inquiry and maintenance services. For example, admissions offices of many universities now provide toll-free telephone inquiry services. Telephone communications and customer identification (through credit card numbers, for example) permit convenient, direct-ordering processes. Additionally, facsimile and graphics transmission and other data transfer services provide information that is the life blood for services and increasingly for manufacturing firms. The efficiency of these linkages has notably changed the capacity requirements by (1) shortening the competitive lead time, that is, the time from order acceptance to the required delivery date (RDD) (the "when" subset of aggregate capacity planning) and (2) permitting service response from otherwise impossible locations.

Thus, changes in the social structure, process technology, and communication all impose capacity requirements changes. These changing capacity needs necessitate facilities adjustment either through redistribution of production to existing facilities, expansion or contraction of specific facilities, the purchase of new facilities, or the sale of present facilities. However they are handled, changes of capacity are complex and require the full application of the four-step planning process described in Chapter 3.

Capacity Evaluation

Capacity is considered in terms of the rate of output of a facility or process. It is the maximum possible output of a transformation facility or process, given several known constraints, such as number and length of shifts per day, average nonproductive time, and average waste rates. Capacity is formally defined as follows:

> The highest reasonable output from a transformation facility or process over a stated time period, given product design specifications, model mix, work force, plant, and equipment limitations.

Examples of capacity are the seating space of a sports stadium or an auditorium. Such facilities will hold a specified number of customers at one time. A more complex application of capacity might be passenger air miles per month or tons of metal production per week. In these latter applications, the time period is longer and includes periods of maintenance and repair, employee rest, material transit, and other necessary requirements for the continuation of the process. In each case, the notion of maximum possible capacity is constrained by some limitations that are either known or predicted. Additional production inefficiencies, however, limit capacity in ways that cannot be anticipated. Examples are strikes, quality failure, inventory shortage, and machine breakdown. To differentiate between anticipated and unanticipated capacity constraints, a more specific definition is required. The following terms are widely used to clarify different approaches to capacity:

1. *Design capacity*—the maximum output that can possibly be attained per time period under ideal conditions.
2. *Effective capacity*—the output that can realistically be achieved, given product mix, quality, maintenance, labor, and other defined and known specifications. Due to these constraints, effective capacity is normally less than design capacity. Actual output is normally less than effective capacity because of unanticipated or unscheduled production inefficiencies.

This classification permits the development of two measures of the capacity-related effectiveness of a production system: efficiency and utilization. Recall that efficiency was generally defined in Chapter 1 as "minimizing waste through the optimal use of resources." The following definition of efficiency is much more specific and is related to utilization. These measures are defined as follows:

$$\text{Efficiency} = \frac{\text{Effective capacity}}{\text{Design capacity}}$$

$$\text{Utilization} = \frac{\text{Actual output}}{\text{Effective capacity}}$$

Actual output will equal design capacity only if the production system is completely efficient and fully utilized. Efficiency is primarily a short- and medium-range measure of how well a system is being used; utilization measures how much it is being used. Utilization also can be expressed in terms such as the ratio of hours actually used to hours available. If a facility sits idle, it is not being fully utilized.

If a facility is inefficient, various motivational, work rule, equipment setup, process design, and policy variables can be adjusted for improvements. There are also numerous short-run methods to increase or decrease capacity utilization. These include adjusting the work force with part-time or temporary workers, hiring, firing, and using shifts, overtime, and outsourcing. These methods of increasing output usually require higher costs and are effective only in the short run. However, once these variables have been fine-tuned and the process is reasonably efficient, then the operations manager will have to address longer-range concepts of facility utilization and design capacity. Organizations that expect to have too high or too low rates of utilization over the long range would expand or contract their design capacity through adjustment of existing facilities, building and relocation programs, or both.

Capacity can be specified by date, by area, and by product (the when, where, and how much). For example, an automobile manufacturer may need more capacity in light trucks and less capacity in compact models. The efficiency and utilization of each plant, each model, and each geographical sales area and estimates of growth or decline must be computed. Capacity must be defined in terms of changes in total output, as well as adjustments to the product mix, required delivery dates, and delivery locations among several subsets of the product line.

Capacity and Location Planning

Once the need for more or less total capacity, or a specified subset of capacity, has been identified, then capacity planning, and if necessary, location planning, must be undertaken. Capacity and location planning is generally defined in Chapter 3 as a "formalized process of anticipating future conditions by answering basic questions about how the organization may act." Capacity variables such as economies of scale, technology, specialization, fixed and variable production costs, and outsource vendors, must all be carefully considered as ways for the organization to better fit the desired capacity goals. If present facilities cannot meet those goals (either because facilities are too small and cannot be expanded or because they are too large and cannot be economically contracted), the facility location question must be addressed. Alternatives include expansion (or contraction) of present facilities, the purchase of an existing facility, or building a new facility from the ground up. The costs, time requirements, and advantages of each of these options must be carefully evaluated, through a formal location plan process.

More specifically, the planning process should gather information on all inputs (machines, labor, materials), the functional interrelationships of these inputs (material flows, routes and speeds, material-handling capabilities), and the process of the proposed facility (overhead, labor costs, value added). Thus, the initial facility planning considerations should be as specific as possible. The process should be formalized; it should clearly define and assign costs to the alternatives; and it should answer the basic who, what, when, where, and how questions about those alternatives. The two single most important contributors to the success of a location decision, according to recent research, are clear objectives and good input data (Muther and Phillips 1983).

The Location Decision Process

Making a location decision is a sequential process. It begins with the selection of the general area and then continues to narrow the choice down to the specific site in four sequential steps: (1) the general region (e.g., Western Europe), (2) the subregion (e.g., the state, province, or county), (3) the community or metropolitan area, and (4) the specific site. Many organizations are committed to operating within a given country, city, or neighborhood. Thus, the site selection process often involves only the last one or two steps. On the other hand, a decision by an international firm concerning whether to build its next manufacturing facility in Malaysia, Mexico, Brazil, or the United

States, for example, will involve each of the four steps in the site selection process.

DECISION FACTORS AND ORGANIZATION TYPES

The location decision process can be affected by the nature of the business (nonmanufacturing, manufacturing, distribution, or service) and by the number of facilities that must be relocated or integrated. Figure 4–2 lists the major criteria for each type of business and also indicates the likelihood that decisions will involve single or multiple sites. The location decision will first be examined with regard to each of the organization types listed in Figure 4–2. Then differences between the development of independent sites and integration with existing facilities, both as single and multiple facility decisions, will be considered.

Nonmanufacturing Production Facilities

Possible locations of oil wells, coal mines, stone quarries, and most nonmanufacturing facilities were determined long ago. The location of the essential natural resources limits the available sites and is the dominant consideration. Similarly, construction operations usually take place at the sites where the finished structures are to be located. (Such site locations are the result of separate location decisions.) The nonmanufacturing production site selection is also based on physical and political accessibility, as well as on economic factors such as the cost of bringing the product to market and the value of the output in the marketplace. Agricultural, forestry, and fishery products are similarly, but less absolutely, dependent upon proper soil, water, and other environmental conditions. Within limits, however, technology has permitted the development of the product cultivation industries in areas where resources are not naturally available. Dams for irrigation and fish-

Figure 4–2 Location Decisions by Type of Organization

	General Location Decision Criteria	Number of Facilities Single ⟷ Multiple
Nonmanufacturing production	Resource availability Accessibility	—
Manufacturing	Market, resources, services Capacity	—
Warehouse or distribution	Customer service Cost	—
Service	Customer location	—

ery management, improved fertilizers, and plant hybridizing have all expanded the possible sites for the production of cultivated products.

Manufacturing Facilities

Figure 4–3 lists some of the factors that influence the decision at each step in the process of deciding where to locate a manufacturing facility. These factors are not the same for all types of facilities or for all products. For example, automobiles are raw material–intensive products and require good transportation networks; alternatively, computer chips are relatively more knowledge intensive. Differences in factor importance occur even among products that are functionally similar (e.g., the differences in labor and material necessary to produce a basic automobile versus a luxury automobile).

Figure 4–3   Manufacturing Facilities Location Decision Factors

Factors	Region	Sub-region	Community	Site
Market availability	■	■		
Raw material availability	■	■		
Transportation infrastructure				
Highways	■	■	■	■
Railroads	■	■	■	■
Waterways	■	■	■	■
Airfields	■	■	■	■
Human resources availability and support				
Wage scale	■	■	■	
Climate	■	■		
Tax structure, incentives		■	■	
Education	■			
Churches, housing, and recreation			■	
Supporting services				
Technical			■	
Financial			■	
Supplies			■	
Police, fire, etc.			■	
Facilities construction and overhead				
Energy (power) supply	■	■	■	
Waste disposal			■	
Construction costs		■	■	■
Environmental impact			■	■
Zoning			■	■
Soil and terrain				■

Warehouses and Distribution Facilities

Warehouse location should enable an organization to achieve a desired level of customer service at minimum cost. Customer service has a number of components: (1) the time from the receipt of an order until its delivery to the customer; (2) the availability of the items ordered; and (3) the response of the firm to customers' questions, complaints, and requests for information, assistance, or repair. The first two components (delivery time and availability) are an integral part of distribution and inventory management goals. The customer response issues are usually considered part of customer field service, which often (but not necessarily) reports to the marketing department. In many cases these service activities are performed in a location that is separate and distinct from the strictly warehousing and distribution activities. Transportation costs are the major component of the operating costs of most warehouses.

Service Facilities

In the service location decision there is an important distinction between services that go to the customer (delivered services) and those for which the customer must travel to obtain the service (fixed services). In the delivered services location decision, travel distances and time are crucial. With fixed services, accessibility, visibility, and ease of entry are important. These two types of services are often combined; for example, a blood bank operation is a fixed service with regard to visibility, donor proximity, and convenience, yet it is a delivered service with regard to mobile blood bank operations and blood product deliveries (Price and Turcotte 1986).

Locations for delivered services are based on their market (service) area and the time required to respond. Delivery response time is often the decisive factor for customer services such as office equipment repairs, and is the critical measure for emergency or health-related services, such as hospitals and emergency ambulance services. Additionally, modern communication systems are widely used by service organizations to permit vehicle operators to directly respond to customer needs without returning to their home base.

In the case of many fixed services there is often little brand loyalty; accessibility is the critical factor in the customer's purchasing decision. For example, most interstate travelers will stop at the automobile service station, restaurant, or motel adjacent to the highway exit rather than drive another mile or two to an otherwise equally attractive competing establishment. In addition, shopping centers in high customer density areas will have more customers than centers in a location with less traffic. As a result, access, visibility, and population density are crucial, and prime locations are priced accordingly.

Location decisions must consider and apportion weights to numerous factors, which is not an easy process. It is especially difficult when the decision will locate two or more interdependent facilities. A further difficulty is that relevant data are often not available, and the appropriate models are very "data hungry" (Price and Turcotte 1986). However, the application of models can sometimes reduce and focus the problem, even though it may not give one best solution. Models aid the analyst in conceptualizing the decision, organizing the relevant information, and assessing the importance of different factors, even if they do not completely differentiate proposed locations. This is particularly important in service location decisions for which the decision factors are less tangible. The next section examines various models of location decisions.

LOCATION DECISION MODELS

Location decisions are usually based on a combination of factors, some that are relatively difficult to measure (qualitative factors) and others that are more tangible (quantitative factors). Quantitative factors include both the initial fixed costs for the land and building and the variable operating costs for items such as labor, utilities, and transportation. Location analysis at the regional and subregional levels generally involves more qualitative factors, while analysis at the community and site level often involves more quantifiable factors.

All location decisions should consider both the qualitative and quantitative factors. Often separate models are used to evaluate the qualitative and quantitative factors, and the results of both are then considered in the decision process. Most organizations evaluate the qualitative (intangible) factors first and eliminate from further consideration those locations that do not meet the minimum requirements. This frequently leaves a few candidate sites roughly equal with respect to the qualitative factors, and then cost considerations are more important in the final selection process. In other situations, however, qualitative factors may dominate a selection decision. For example, a community may be selected for a research laboratory on the basis of climate, cultural attractions, educational facilities, and recreational facilities—all of which attract competent personnel. In such cases, the attraction of the best possible personnel is viewed as more important than differences in the initial costs or operating costs.

In other cases, initial costs and operating costs may be roughly equivalent; the decision in such a case is based on a distinct difference in a critical qualitative factor. For example, the initial and operating costs of two prospective manufacturing plant sites may be about the same, but one might be in an area with a substantially better labor climate. Finally, situations exist in which there are substantial differences among both the qualitative and quantitative factors for the final candidates. In these cases, the quantitative (often cost) advantage of one site may be counterbalanced by a qualitative disadvantage of that site, and a model that combines qualitative and quantitative factors is required. Management must be able to integrate numerous qualitative and quantitative factors to make a decision that will significantly affect company costs over the long run. Thus, this section includes a model for evaluating qualitative factors, a second approach that permits the combination of qualitative and quantitative factors, and a third model that is best for evaluating quantitative factors.

Models to Evaluate Qualitative Factors

The supply of labor, availability of suppliers, labor relations, government regulations, and environmental factors such as the climate, medical facilities, schools, and recreational opportunities are all examples of qualitative factors that are often important in selecting a location for a manufacturing facility. Although these factors are intangible, they can be evaluated and structured in a composite measure. There are three steps to this approach:

1. Identify the critical factors for a desirable location. (A critical factor is one for which an evaluation of "unacceptable" eliminates a site from further consideration.)
2. Assign a weight to each factor commensurate with its importance. The weights are values between 0 and 1, the total of which should equal 1.
3. Evaluate each factor for each possible location on an arbitrarily chosen scale of 1 to 5, for example, where 5 represents excellent and 1 represents unfavorable. A minus infinity ($-M$) represents a rating of "unacceptable" for a critical factor.

Thus, the model is

$$LV_j = \sum_{i=1}^{m} W_i E_{ij}$$

where

$$LV_j = \text{Location value for location } j$$

$$W_i = \text{Weight for factor } i$$

$$E_{ij} = \text{Evaluation of factor } i \text{ for location } j$$

$$i = 1 \text{ to } m \text{ different factors}$$

$$j = 1 \text{ to } n \text{ different locations}$$

Example: Qualitative Factor Evaluation of the Location of a Manufacturing Plant. The following example illustrates a basic model for evaluating locations using qualitative factors. It involves the selection of one of three metropolitan areas in the Mid-Atlantic region of the United States for a plant to manufacture a family of products for distribution, primarily within a one-day transportation distance. The transportation and manufacturing costs are estimated as roughly equal for each of the three sites. Table 4–1 lists the critical qualitative factors, the weight assigned to each, and the evaluation of each factor for each city by the company's site selection committee.

The summation of the products of the weight times the evaluation score for each location gives the highest score (4.0) to Area B, even though the sum of the unweighted scores gave Area B the lowest rating. In this case, because of possibly contradictory results, the site selection committee might need to reassess the weights used or consider other factors before making a location decision. Once the ratings are confirmed, selection of a specific site within the selected area is the next step. Remember that, in this example, the initial costs and operating costs for the different plants are estimated as roughly equal.

Models to Evaluate Combined Qualitative and Quantitative Factors

Combining qualitative factors and quantitative factors into a single evaluation model requires that the importance of cost and other quantifiable factors be weighted along with the qualitative factors. For example, if the previous decision could be supplemented with cost data, management might decide that the weight of the cost factor is .40. Since weights of the qualitative factors must then sum to .60, multiply the factor weights by .6 to derive new qualitative factor weights. The costs of the three sites have been evaluated as A = 4, B = 3, and C = 5. This gives the evaluation shown in Table 4–2.

In this case, Area C receives the highest scores, both unweighted and weighted, and is the logical choice. This method of combining qualitative and

Table 4–1 Qualitative Factor Evaluation of Three Areas

Factor	Weight	Evaluation Score for Three Areas			Product of Weight Multiplied by the Evaluation Score for Three Areas		
		A	B	C	A	B	C
Labor supply	.3	5	5	4	1.5	1.5	1.2
Labor relations	.3	2	5	3	.6	1.5	.9
Supporting services	.1	3	1	3	.3	.1	.3
Schools	.2	3	4	4	.6	.8	.8
Recreation	.1	4	1	4	.4	.1	.4
Total	1.0	17	16	18	3.4	4.0	3.6

Evaluation scores are as follows: 5 = excellent; 4 = very good; 3 = good; 2 = fair; 1 = unfavorable; and −M = unacceptable.

Table 4–2   Combined Factor Evaluation of Three Areas

Factor	Weight	Evaluation Score for Three Areas			Product of Weight Multiplied by the Evaluation Score for Three Areas		
		A	B	C	A	B	C
Labor supply	.18	5	5	4	.90	.90	.72
Labor relations	.18	2	5	3	.36	.90	.54
Supporting services	.06	3	1	3	.18	.06	.18
Schools	.12	3	4	4	.36	.48	.48
Recreation	.06	4	1	4	.24	.06	.24
Cost	.40	4	3	5	1.60	1.20	2.00
Total	1.00	21	19	23	3.64	3.60	4.16

Evaluation scores are as follows: 5 = excellent; 4 = very good; 3 = good; 2 = fair; 1 = unfavorable; and −M = unacceptable.

quantitative data has one possibly serious shortcoming because it converts interval measures (costs) to an ordinal scale. For example, although the costs of Area C are obviously the lowest and Area B costs are the highest, the cost difference between Area C and Area A may not equal the cost difference between Area A and Area B. However, the difference between their cost evaluation scores is the same. This method of assigning scores on a common scale implies not only rank order but also an interval scale, where a score of 4 is twice as good as a score of 2. Although this assumption may be tenuous, it is necessary in order to combine these factors in an aggregate measure. See Siegel (1956) or Conover (1980) for a further discussion of the measurement scale.

Models to Evaluate Quantitative (Distance) Factors

Location decisions must consider initial costs and operating costs. Initial costs include the cost of the land, building, transfer and recruitment of personnel, and all the start-up costs associated with beginning operation in a new plant, warehouse, office, retail store, or other service facility. These costs vary in importance for different types of facilities. For example, land costs per square foot are usually much higher for retail stores than for the typical warehouse. The initial costs of competing sites may vary widely due to many factors, including inducements offered by competing communities. For example, a large religious denomination selected Louisville, Kentucky from four final candidates for its national headquarters due in large measure to the donation of a building in that city. The many other attractive features of Louisville cemented the decision. Many communities provide tax incentives, free land, and other benefits to attract new industries.

Operating costs include the costs of transportation, personnel, supporting services, energy, supplies, and other variable costs of producing a product or service. Many of these factors involve consideration of distances for either transportation of goods and services or travel of personnel. Because of their significance, transportation costs are often separated from other operating costs. In other cases, transportation costs may be minimal and not worthy of consideration. In still other cases, production costs might be essentially the same for all sites and thus excluded from the location analysis. Decisions concerning the location of warehouses frequently include transportation costs only.

In addition to the distance itself, the cost per unit of distance and the frequency a given route is traveled must be considered. Of course, once the distance has been measured, it is a relatively simple matter to incorporate the number of trips per period and the cost per unit of distance to get a total cost. The four common methods of measuring distances are (1) the empirical approach, (2) the rectilinear distance method, (3) the euclidean distance method, and (4) the euclidean distance squared method.

The empirical approach uses the actual travel distances, times, or costs, and includes fuel consumption, tolls, and the variance in time due to varying weather, highway, or traffic conditions. Good travel data exists among many cities; however, data between specific locations within a community are often not available and must be found by trial runs. The costs of water routes, rail routes, and many truck routes are best measured by the empirical approach.

The rectilinear distance method finds the distance between two points based upon the sum of the two legs of a triangle. For example, in Figure 4–4, the rectilinear distance (D_R) from A to B is the sum of the distance from Y_1 to Y_2 and the distance from X_1 to X_2, or $D_R = (X_2 - X_1) + (Y_2 - Y_1)$. This distance is 15. This is a good measure of distances over city streets that are laid out in square blocks.

The euclidean distance (the straight line between two points) is calculated using the Pythagorean theorem for finding the hypotenuse of a triangle given the two sides. That is, the euclidean distance (D_E) equals the square root of the sum of the squares of the X and Y distances. In Figure 4–4, the euclidean distance is 10.8. This method is especially useful for measuring air travel distances, although these distances and related costs are often available from shippers.

A fourth measure of distance, the euclidean distance squared (D_{ES}), is like the euclidean distance, except that it does not take the square root of the function (see Figure 4–4). Thus, it significantly penalizes increases in distance and travel time; the larger the increase, the greater the penalty. Of course, the euclidean distance squared method will give a greater value than either the rectilinear distance or the euclidean distance methods. However, the euclidean distance squared method is preferable in some cases; delivery of emergency services or perishables are two examples. As the adoption of just-in-time manufacturing and distribution increases, distance computation models that penalize larger delivery times become more appropriate.

Figure 4–4   Measures of Distance Between Two Sites

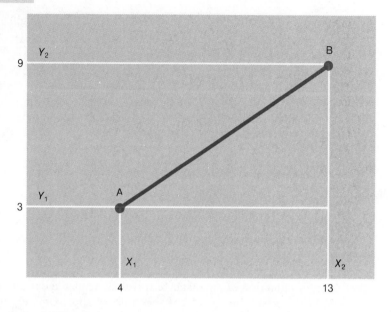

1. Rectilinear distance

$$D_R = (X_2 - X_1) + (Y_2 - Y_1)$$
$$D_R = (13 - 4) + (9 - 3) = 15$$

2. Euclidean distance

$$D_E = \sqrt{(X_2 - X_1)^2 + (Y_2 - Y_1)^2}$$

$$D_E = \sqrt{(13 - 4)^2 + (9 - 3)^2} = 10.8$$

3. Euclidean distance squared

$$D_{ES} = (X_2 - X_1)^2 + (Y_2 - Y_1)^2$$
$$D_{ES} = (13 - 4)^2 + (9 - 3)^2 = 117$$

Models to Evaluate Quantitative (Cost) Factors

Some location decisions, such as warehouse decisions, involve factors that are often reducible to a common scale, such as cost, for comparison. The prerequisite is that all minimum requirements be met by the evaluated sites.

For example, the location of a single warehouse to supply a known number of fixed-location customers, such as company-owned retail outlets, is a relatively simple decision. The objective is to select the one site that will result in the minimum transportation costs. The analyst must determine the transportation cost of each possible location and identify the one with the lowest total cost as the solution. Locations with unusually high initial or operating costs are eliminated from further consideration in the first stages of the decision process.

Example: Quantitative (Cost) Model Evaluation of the Location of a Single Warehouse. A department store chain must select a warehouse location to serve its five retail stores in a metropolitan area. After examining

Table 4–3   Travel Data for Warehouse Location Decision

Retail Stores	Trips per Week	Roundtrip Miles to Possible Warehouse Sites			
		1	2	3	4
A	6	5	23	25	19
B	9	12	19	10	8
C	8	22	8	24	8
D	10	31	17	2	28
E	5	40	9	18	21
Total	38	110	76	79	84

available sites, four are judged to possess adequate railway and highway access for incoming and outgoing shipments, appropriate zoning, and initial and operating costs that are roughly equivalent and within budget. The task is to find the site with the lowest estimated transportation costs, which are, in this case, a function of the distance traveled. Available data are shown in Table 4–3. In this case, the travel cost per mile is approximately the same for all the potential sites due to ready access to freeways, the absence of tolls, and the ability to use the same equipment on all routes. Multiplying the distance by the average number of trips gives the matrix of average miles per week listed in Table 4–4.

Location 3 is the minimum cost site, assuming that other factors, including cost per mile, are equal. In this example, the minimum cost site has been selected. However, in other cases different criteria, such as minimizing the maximum time or distance to any customer, are more appropriate. For example, a local blood bank may seek a location that is no more than 25 minutes from any of its participating hospitals or clinics.

Table 4–4   Average Miles Per Week Per Warehouse Location

Retail Stores	Possible Warehouse Sites			
	1	2	3	4
A	30	138	150	114
B	108	171	90	72
C	176	64	192	64
D	310	170	20	280
E	200	45	90	105
Total	824	588	542	635

INTEGRATION OF NEW FACILITIES

Frequently, an organization must decide where to locate a new warehouse or plant with the intention of integrating it into a network of existing facilities. The location of the new facility must be evaluated both for inherent costs as well as impacts on existing transportation patterns. Several approaches may be used to solve what is sometimes called the transportation problem. The problem is to allocate stated amounts of available supplies from several sources to meet stated demands at several destinations, given transportation costs for each supply-demand pair. The following inputs are required: (1) amount available at each supply source, (2) amount required by each demand point, and (3) the transportation cost from each supply point to each demand point.

The transportation problem can also be specifically defined in numerous variations, the most common of which are the following:

1. The number and type of supply or demand points can vary from the present sites only to one or several additional supply or demand sites under consideration.
2. The problem may be defined in aggregate planning terms, where "supply points" are months when goods are produced and "demand points" are months when goods are required. Costs are defined as backorder or inventory costs when an item is produced before or after the month required.
3. The costs can be defined in a variety of ways, including distance in miles, distance in travel time, or travel costs in dollars.
4. A variety of measures of distance can be used, including rectilinear distance, euclidean distance, and euclidean distance squared.
5. Costs can be defined as any combination of fixed facility overhead and per-unit production and transportation values.

The total supply available must equal the total demand required; if not, a dummy must be created. If total supply is greater than total demand, a dummy demand is created to receive allocations. However, those allocations are not shipped and remain as unused inventory at the particular supply point. If total demand is greater than total supply, a dummy supply is created to represent the required backorder to fulfill the known demands.

Several methods are used in the solution of the transportation problem, including the northwest corner method, Vogel's approximation method (VAM), modified VAM, optimality testing, stepping stone adjustment, and linear programming. These methods represent a range from very simple approaches, which do not usually give a very good solution, to rather complex algorithms, which are optimal for the given data. The northwest corner method is rather easy to solve, but rarely gives an optimal solution, particularly with larger data sets. VAM usually gives very close to an optimal solution, but is much more complex. The optimality testing and stepping stone adjustment can be used to optimize the initial solution found by the northwest corner method or VAM. Linear programming is the most complex method, but it will give an optimal solution. Linear programming is covered in Chapter 22, Mathematical Programming.

The following general steps are used to solve the transportation problem:

1. Remove from consideration all sites that do not meet the critical requirements
2. Define the problem in terms of specific sources and amounts of supply available, specific demands and amounts of demand required, and costs of movement from each source to each demand
3. If total supply is not equal to total demand, create a dummy supply or dummy demand, as appropriate
4. Find an initial feasible solution using VAM or the northwest corner method
5. Test the solution for optimality—if optimal, the solution has been found; if not optimal, proceed to Step 6
6. Improve the solution using the stepping stone adjustment; go to Step 5
7. If there is more than one possible site, compute the optimal cost of each separately; then compare and select the site with the lowest optimal cost

In the example that follows, the list of possible locations of a new warehouse has been narrowed to Omaha, Nebraska and Des Moines, Iowa. Initially, various methods are used to find a solution to the Omaha part of the problem. Subsequently, the Des Moines problem will be solved, and that total cost will be compared with the total cost for Omaha.

The Nuweave Textile Manufacturing Company has plants (sources) in St. Louis, El Paso, and Raleigh, North Carolina; it has distribution warehouses (demands) in Los Angeles, New York, and Columbus, Ohio. Another warehouse is planned for either Omaha, Nebraska or Des Moines, Iowa to handle increasing demand in the north central states. The supplies available, demands required, and costs of shipment from all sources to all demands, including the two planned warehouses, are shown in Figure 4–5 in the standard trans-

Figure 4–5 Transportation Cost Tableau

PLANTS	WAREHOUSES						Total Supply (Units)
	Los Angeles	New York	Columbus	Omaha	Des Moines	Dummy	
St. Louis	43	31	20	21	15		130
El Paso	28	48	40	32	36		130
Raleigh	51	22	23	35	21		110
Total Demand	100	100	80	80	80	10	370

portation tableau format. Because the available supply is 10 greater than the available demand, a dummy demand was created for 10 units. No costs are associated with the dummy, because units will not really be moved to it.

Figure 4–5 gives a per unit shipping cost matrix from each source to each demand. For example, the cost of shipping one unit from St. Louis to New York is $31. The tableau also gives total supplies available at each source and total demands required at each destination. For example, 130 units are available in El Paso and 80 units are required in both Columbus and Omaha. Units in this example are standard shipping containers. The decision to be made is: How many units should be shipped from each plant (source) to each warehouse (destination) to minimize transportation costs?

The Northwest Corner Method

The northwest corner method is computationally quite easy and will give an initial feasible solution, but it is rarely optimal and normally not very efficient. The approach starts at the northwest corner (upper-left cell) and allocates a quantity equal to the smaller of the supply available and the demand required for that northwest cell. If there is excess supply, allocate it to the cell immediately to the right of the northwest cell; if there is excess demand, allocate it from the cell immediately below the northwest cell. In this manner, sequentially allocate from the northwest corner to the southeast corner. Incidentally, the method could just as easily start with the northeast corner and proceed southwest, or it could start with any other corner and proceed to the opposite corner. The following specific rules are used to solve the transportation problem with the northwest corner method:

1. Allocate all items possible to the northwest-most cell of the matrix
2. Adjust the column (demand) and row (supply) totals. Cross out the column if demand is met; cross out the row if supply is used up
3. If supply remains, allocate remaining supply to cells east; if demand remains, allocate from cells south
4. Sequentially move south and east until all demand is fulfilled

Figure 4–6 shows the northwest corner solution to the Omaha part of the Nuweave problem. Allocations are shown moving progressively from the northwest to the southeast corner. Because the total demand did not equal the total supply, 10 units from the Raleigh plant were allocated to a dummy demand (i.e., in this solution, Raleigh would ship 10 units fewer than its capacity).

The total cost of this solution is found by multiplying the cell costs times the amounts allocated, as shown in Table 4–5.

This solution is relatively costly. Note that it allocates to several of the higher-cost cells, specifically to St. Louis–Los Angeles ($43), El Paso–New York ($48), and El Paso–Columbus ($40). However, the solution is feasible and the method is easy to compute. Because rather sizeable fixed costs are

Figure 4–6   Northwest Corner Solution for Omaha

PLANTS	WAREHOUSES					Total Supply (Units)
	Los Angeles	New York	Columbus	Omaha	Dummy	
St. Louis	43 100	31 30	20	21		130
El Paso	28	48 70	40 60	32		130
Raleigh	51	22	23 20	35 80	10	110
Total Demand	100	100	80	80	10	370

often committed based on location decisions, the northwest corner method is usually only used to produce an initial estimate. For any serious investment, an analyst would want to compute the allocations using other methods.

Vogel's Approximation Method

Vogel's approximation method (VAM) will almost always give a better solution than the northwest corner method; however, it is more complex. The advantage of VAM is that it will be close enough to the optimal solution that only one optimization test and one stepping stone modification are usually required. The northwest corner method may require many such searches for optimization. VAM uses an opportunity cost principle. At each sequential

Table 4–5   Allocations and Costs of the Northwest Corner Method

Route	Units	Unit Cost	Total Cost
St. Louis–Los Angeles	100	$43	$4,300
St. Louis–New York	30	31	930
El Paso–New York	70	48	3,360
El Paso–Columbus	60	40	2,400
Raleigh–Columbus	20	23	460
Raleigh–Omaha	80	35	2,800
Raleigh–Dummy	10	0	0
Total			$14,250

trial, the difference between the lowest and second lowest cost is computed for each row and column. This difference represents the opportunity cost of not making the low-cost assignment. Thus, at each sequential trial, the analyst selects the allocation that would save the most over the second best alternative. VAM rules are as follows:

1. For each row and for each column, calculate the difference between the two least-cost cells—this is the VAM row and column number
2. Find the largest VAM number and allocate as much as possible to the least-cost cell in that row or column; in case of ties, allocate to the lowest costs
3. If unallocated supply or demand remains, go to Step 1; the number of allocations will usually be ($m + n - 1$), where m = the number of rows and n = the number of columns

Figures 4–7 through 4–12 show the sequential tableaus for each VAM trial allocation. The results of the first VAM trial are shown in Figure 4–7. In the column and row called VAM Trial 1, the VAM numbers are indicated, as calculated in Step 1. The largest VAM number, 15 ($43 − $28), is indicated by an asterisk. Therefore, the maximum allocation of 100 units is made to the least-cost cell in that column, the $28 of El Paso–Los Angeles. El Paso has 130 total units of supply available, but Los Angeles only requires 100, so 100 are allocated, leaving 30 available at El Paso and the Los Angeles demand satisfied.

Figure 4–7   Vogel's Approximation Method—Tableau 1

PLANTS	WAREHOUSES					Total Supply (Units)	Unallocated Supply	VAM Trial 1
	Los Angeles	New York	Columbus	Omaha	Dummy			
St. Louis	43	31	20	21		130	130	1
El Paso	28 / 100	48	40	32		130	30	4
Raleigh	51	22	23	35		110	110	1
Total Demand	100	100	80	80	10	370	270	
Unmet Demand	0	100	80	80	10	270		
VAM Trial 1	15*	9	3	11				

In VAM Trial 2, shown in Figure 4–8, the recomputed VAM numbers are indicated. The Los Angeles column is disregarded because there is no further demand there. The largest VAM number, 11 ($32 − $21), is highlighted by an asterisk, and an allocation is made to the least-cost cell in that column, the St. Louis–Omaha cell. Since 130 units are available but only 80 are required, 80 are allocated, leaving 50 available at St. Louis and no further demand at Omaha.

VAM Trial 3, shown in Figure 4–9, recomputes the VAM numbers. The Los Angeles and Omaha columns are disregarded because there is no further demand there. The largest VAM number, 11 ($31 − $20), is highlighted by an asterisk, and an allocation is made to the least-cost cell in that row, the St. Louis–Columbus cell. Since 50 units are available (see Figure 4–8) and 80 are required, 50 are allocated, leaving no units available at St. Louis and 30 still in demand at Columbus.

VAM Trial 4, shown in Figure 4–10, recomputes the VAM numbers. The Los Angeles and Omaha columns and the St. Louis row are now all disregarded because there is no further supply or demand at those locations. The largest VAM number, 26 ($48 − $22), is highlighted by an asterisk, and an allocation is made to the least-cost cell in that column—the Raleigh–New York cell. Since 110 units are available and 100 are required, 100 are allocated, leaving 10 available at Raleigh and no further demand at New York.

VAM Trial 5, in Figure 4–11, shows the only VAM number that can be computed, 17 ($40 − $23), indicated by an asterisk. An allocation of 10 units

Figure 4–8   Vogel's Approximation Method—Tableau 2

PLANTS	WAREHOUSES					Total Supply (Units)	Unallocated Supply	VAM Trial 2
	Los Angeles	New York	Columbus	Omaha	Dummy			
St. Louis	43	31	20	21 80		130	50	1
El Paso	28 100	48	40	32		130	30	8
Raleigh	51	22	23	35		110	110	1
Total Demand	100	100	80	80	10	370	190	
Unmet Demand	0	100	80	0	10	190		
VAM Trial 2		9	3	11*				

Figure 4–9   Vogel's Approximation Method—Tableau 3

PLANTS	WAREHOUSES					Total Supply (Units)	Unallocated Supply	VAM Trial 3
	Los Angeles	New York	Columbus	Omaha	Dummy			
St. Louis	43	31	20 _50_	21 _80_		130	0	11*
El Paso	28 _100_	48	40	32		130	30	8
Raleigh	51	22	23	35		110	110	1
Total Demand	100	100	80	80	10	370	140	
Unmet Demand	0	100	30	0	10	140		
VAM Trial 3		9	3					

Figure 4–10   Vogel's Approximation Method—Tableau 4

PLANTS	WAREHOUSES					Total Supply (Units)	Unallocated Supply	VAM Trial 4
	Los Angeles	New York	Columbus	Omaha	Dummy			
St. Louis	43	31	20 _50_	21 _80_		130	0	
El Paso	28 _100_	48	40	32		130	30	8
Raleigh	51	22 _100_	23	35		110	10	1
Total Demand	100	100	80	80	10	370	40	
Unmet Demand	0	0	30	0	10	40		
VAM Trial 4		26*	17					

Figure 4–11 Vogel's Approximation Method—Tableau 5

PLANTS	WAREHOUSES					Total Supply (Units)	Unallo-cated Supply	VAM Trial 5
	Los Angeles	New York	Columbus	Omaha	Dummy			
St. Louis	43	31	20 50	21 80		130	0	
El Paso	28 100	48	40	32		130	30	
Raleigh	51	22 100	23 10	35		110	0	
Total Demand	100	100	80	80	10	370	30	
Unmet Demand	0	0	20	0	10	30		
VAM Trial 5			17*					

is made to the least-cost cell in that column—the Raleigh–Columbus cell—and total supply and demand are adjusted accordingly. The remaining supply at El Paso of 30 units meets the demand of 20 at Columbus, with the remaining 10 allocated to the dummy. Those final allocations, the sixth and seventh, are shown in Figure 4–12. Note that 7, including the one to the dummy, is the correct number of allocations, because there must be $(m + n - 1)$ allocations $(5 + 3 - 1 = 7)$.

The total cost for the VAM solution is found in the same manner as in the northwest corner method—by multiplying the cell costs times the units allocated. The VAM allocation cost of $8,710, as calculated in Table 4–6, is a notable improvement over the $14,250 allocated by the northwest corner method.

The Modified VAM

The VAM procedure is rather clumsy to fully iterate, but it will frequently give an optimal or nearly optimal solution, thus eliminating many iterations of optimality tests necessary with the northwest corner method. However, particularly for smaller matrices, a modification of VAM is useful. That modification uses only the first set of VAM trial numbers. Consider the original VAM trial from Figure 4–7. Using the first VAM trial numbers, the modified version finds the largest VAM number and labels it with a 1. The next largest VAM number is labeled 2, and so forth, until all VAM numbers are labeled. Figure 4–13 shows the modified VAM tableau. In this case, two VAM

Figure 4–12   Vogel's Approximation Method—Final Tableau

PLANTS	WAREHOUSES					Total Supply (Units)
	Los Angeles	New York	Columbus	Omaha	Dummy	
St. Louis	43	31	20 50	21 80		130
El Paso	28 100	48	40 20	32	10	130
Raleigh	51	22 100	23 10	35		110
Total Demand	100	100	80	80	10	370

numbers (the two 1s) are labeled with 6 because they are a tie. The dummy does not get a VAM number, and thus allocations are not made to it until all other demand is satisfied. Allocations are then made in the same manner, to the least-cost cell in the row or column associated with the largest VAM number. The first allocation is 100 units to the El Paso–Los Angeles cell, based on the VAM number of 15. The second allocation is to the St. Louis–Omaha cell, based on the VAM number of 11, and so forth. In this case, the modified VAM procedure gives the same solution as the full VAM procedure. But, with other matrices, the modified VAM could be expected to give a less accurate approximation of the optimal than the full VAM, and sometimes it will be only a minor improvement over the northwest corner method.

Table 4–6   Allocations and Costs of VAM

Route	Units	Unit Cost	Total Cost
El Paso–Los Angeles	100	$28	$2,800
Raleigh–New York	100	22	2,200
St. Louis–Columbus	50	20	1,000
El Paso–Columbus	20	40	800
Raleigh–Columbus	10	23	230
St. Louis–Omaha	80	21	1,680
El Paso–Dummy	10	0	0
Total	370		$8,710

Figure 4–13 Modified Vogel's Approximation Method

PLANTS	WAREHOUSES					Total Supply (Units)	VAM # (Rank)
	Los Angeles	New York	Columbus	Omaha	Dummy		
St. Louis	43	31	20 50	21 80		130	1 (6)
El Paso	28 100	48	40 20	32	10	130	4 (4)
Raleigh	51	22 100	23 10	35		110	1 (6)
Total Demand	100	100	80	80	10	370	
VAM # (Rank)	15 (1)	9 (3)	3 (5)	11 (2)			

Optimality Testing and Stepping Stone Adjustment

The total transportation cost of the VAM solution is $8,710. The next step is to evaluate the solution using an optimality test called the MODI (modified distribution) technique, using the following steps:

1. Assign a value U_i to each row and V_j to each column. Begin by selecting any row or column and assigning a value of 0 to it.
2. Assign U_i and V_j values to all remaining sources and destinations such that for each cell with an allocation, $U_i + V_j$ equals the cell cost.
3. The solution is optimal if, for each cell with no allocation, the sum of $U_i + V_j$ is less than or equal to the cost of the cell, or $U_i + V_j \leq C_{ij}$. If $U_i + V_j = C_{ij}$ for one or more cells without an allocation, alternate optimal solutions can be found by shifting allocations to those cells. If $U_i + V_j > C_{ij}$ for any cell, the current allocation is not optimal and allocations must be shifted toward that cell.

Figure 4–14 shows the MODI technique for the Nuweave data.

In Figure 4–14, column 1 or V_1 was arbitrarily designated as 0. According to Step 2, for each cell with an allocation, $U_i + V_j$ must equal the cell cost. Thus, for cell El Paso–Los Angeles, $28 = 0 + U_2$ or $U_2 = 28$. Following the same logic, V_3 must equal 12 because $40 = 28 + V_3$. In this manner, the other U and V values can be found. The remaining cells (those without allocations) are assigned values equal to the sum of $U_i + V_j$. For example, cell El Paso–Omaha equals U_2 plus V_4, or $C_{2,4} = 28 + 13 = 41$. In Figure 4–14, the $U_i + V_j$ values have been computed for each cell and are shown in the upper-left corner of each cell.

Figure 4–14   Optimality Testing—MODI Technique Tableau 1

PLANTS		WAREHOUSES							
		Los Angeles		New York		Columbus		Omaha	
		$V_1 = 0$		$V_2 = 11$		$V_3 = 12$		$V_4 = 13$	
St. Louis	$u_1 = 8$	8	43	19	31	20	20	21	21
							50		80
El Paso	$u_2 = 28$	28	28	39	48	40	40	41	32
		100				20			
Raleigh	$u_3 = 11$	11	51	22	22	23	23	24	35
				100		10			

Subtracting each of the $(U_i + V_j)$ values in the upper-left corner of each cell from the transportation cost in the upper-right corner of each cell gives the shadow cost listed in the matrix in Figure 4–15. By the way they were calculated, this shadow price equals 0 for each allocated cell. For unallocated cells, the shadow price may be positive or negative. For example, the value of the St. Louis–Los Angeles cell is $43 - 8 = 35$. A positive shadow price indicates the additional cost of allocating to that cell if the analyst desires to select a nonoptimal solution. A negative shadow price indicates that the current solution is not optimal.

Figure 4–15   Shadow Price Matrix

PLANTS	WAREHOUSES			
	Los Angeles	New York	Columbus	Omaha
St. Louis	35	12	0	0
El Paso	0	9	0	-9
Raleigh	40	0	0	11

Since one of the values is negative, the solution is not optimal; improvement is possible. The location of the negative value (the El Paso–Omaha cell) indicates that shipping from El Paso to Omaha will improve the solution (reduce the total cost) by $9 for every unit changed to that route from the best alternative cell. An examination of the original cost matrix reveals that shipping 20 units from El Paso to Omaha instead of Columbus reduces the shipping cost by $8 per unit. The 20 units for Columbus must be replaced by 20 units from another source. As it happens, these units can be shipped from St. Louis to Columbus for $1 per unit less than from St. Louis to Omaha.

This process is called the stepping stone adjustment, the rules for which are as follows:

1. Identify the cell(s) to which the allocation must be increased (i.e., negative shadow price values).
2. Select a loop containing that cell (or if there are several, the cell with the largest negative shadow price) and at least three allocated cells where each sequential cell is in either the same row or column.
3. Allocate one unit to the selected cell and then move around the loop, reallocating one unit at each step so the row or column total is restored. Check the effect on the solution by sequentially adding or subtracting cell costs around the loop. A negative sum means you can improve the solution. Find a loop that improves the solution.
4. Reallocate as many units as possible around the loop.
5. Check for optimality again. Repeat the process if necessary.

This stepping stone solution considers demands at Columbus and Omaha and supplies at St. Louis and El Paso. This loop meets the conditions of Rules 1 and 2, and is shown in Figure 4–16.

Start at the El Paso–Omaha cell (the empty cell) and move around the loop in either direction, adding and subtracting cell costs ($+32 - 21 + 20 - 40 = -9$). Twenty items (the maximum allocation) can be reallocated with a cost improvement of $9 per item. The result of this modification and the total cost of the reallocation are shown in Figure 4–17 and Table 4–7.

Since the cost of the VAM solution was $8,710, a savings of $180 is achieved by this optimization of the VAM solution for a net cost of $8,530. Another iteration of the MODI technique reveals that this solution is optimal; no cells have negative shadow prices.

Multiple Facility Integration

Recall that Figure 4–5 and the original problem statement suggested two possible sites, Omaha and Des Moines. Now the optimal shipping pattern and related costs must be determined for Des Moines. A comparison of the two optimal solutions will reveal the low-cost site. The transportation cost tableau

Figure 4–16   Stepping Stone Reallocation

PLANTS	WAREHOUSES					Total Supply (Units)
	Los Angeles	New York	Columbus	Omaha	Dummy	
St. Louis	43	31	20	21		130
			50 ⬅	80		
El Paso	28	48	40	32	10	130
	100		20 ➡			
Raleigh	51	22	23	35		110
		100	10			
Total Demand	100	100	80	80	10	370

and the optimal solution found by applying the VAM transportation algorithm to the data for Des Moines are shown in Figure 4–18. The costs of the optimal solution are shown in Table 4–8.

Since the Des Moines cost of $8,230 is less than the Omaha cost of $8,530, Des Moines is the preferable site. If shipments are to be made each week, the savings would be $15,600 (52 × $300) annually. Although the cost savings is not overwhelming, the apparel manufacturing business is very competitive and every possible savings should be seized. However, because

Figure 4–17   Optimal VAM Solution—Omaha

PLANTS	WAREHOUSES					Total Supply (Units)
	Los Angeles	New York	Columbus	Omaha	Dummy	
St. Louis	43	31	20	21		130
			70	60		
El Paso	28	48	40	32	10	130
	100			20		
Raleigh	51	22	23	35		110
		100	10			
Total Demand	100	100	80	80	10	370

Table 4–7   Allocations and Total Cost of the Optimal
VAM Solution—Omaha

Route	Units	Unit Cost	Total Cost
El Paso–Los Angeles	100	$28	$2,800
Raleigh–New York	100	22	2,200
St. Louis–Columbus	70	20	1,400
Raleigh–Columbus	10	23	230
St. Louis–Omaha	60	21	1,260
El Paso–Omaha	20	32	640
El Paso–Dummy	10	0	0
Total			$8,530

Figure 4–18   Transportation Cost Tableau and Optimal
Solution—Des Moines

PLANTS	WAREHOUSES					Total Supply (Units)
	Los Angeles	New York	Columbus	Des Moines	Dummy	
St. Louis	43	31	20 / 50	15 / 80		130
El Paso	28 / 100	48	40 / 20	36	10	130
Raleigh	51	22 / 100	23 / 10	21		110
Total Demand	100	100	80	80	10	370

Table 4–8   Allocations and Total Cost of the Optimal
Solution—Des Moines

Route	Units	Unit Cost	Total Cost
El Paso–Los Angeles	100	$28	$2,800
Raleigh–New York	100	22	2,200
St. Louis–Columbus	50	20	1,000
Raleigh–Columbus	10	23	230
St. Louis–Des Moines	80	15	1,200
El Paso–Columbus	20	40	800
El Paso–Dummy	10	0	0
Total			$8,230

the cost difference is quite small, all cost and other data about the two sites should be verified.

SERVICE FACILITIES

The wide diversity in service organizations produces literally dozens of criteria for locating a service facility; the importance of these criteria depends on the type of service and the objectives of the organization. Similarly, the number of different methods that can be used to address service location problems is extensive. Certainly the techniques already discussed and adaptations of those techniques are appropriate. However, service organizations face a greater influence from social and political concerns (particularly governmental services), the need for collocation with competitors for visibility, and often the challenge of a large number of relatively small facilities. Therefore, service location planning and decision making is generally more complex and nebulous than such decisions in other environments. Service decisions normally require more input data and subjective assessments, but may involve less fixed capital outlay and financial commitment. Figure 4–19 lists some major characteristics of service organizations that affect the location decision.

Even within these classifications, there are differences that affect the location decision dramatically. For example, organizations grouped under the classification of consumer, fixed, and having a community market include all types of restaurants, retail stores, and automotive service stations. Although some commonality in location criteria would exist, there would also be substantial differences. For example, a restaurant interested in the evening dinner trade might seek a site in or convenient to the theater district, while a retail store would seek a high pedestrian traffic site.

The location of a delivered emergency service depends on the geographic area to be served, the density of the customer population, the nature of the service, the response time objectives, and the access mode. For example, response time for emergency medical care is more important than for emergency equipment repair. As a result, medical helicopter emergency service

Figure 4–19   Service Classification Factors

Type	Mobility	Market	Location
Professional	Fixed	National	Multiple
Consumer	Delivered	Regional	Single
Emergency		Community	
		Traveler	

is now relatively common for rural areas and traffic clogged metropolitan areas. Rapid access overcomes the need for multiple sites. Thus, in many cases the location decision criteria vary even within classifications depending upon the nature of the service provided. Although the criteria for service location decisions are notably different than those for manufacturing decisions, once the criteria are defined, the decision process itself follows roughly the same steps and uses the same general methods of evaluation as the manufacturing location decision process.

CONCLUSIONS

Although it can be argued that each location decision is unique, most have characteristics that are shared by a group of similar organizations. As a result, the somewhat generic models employed to address qualitative and quantitative (distance and cost) factors must be adapted to analyze specific location decision situations. Perhaps the greatest variety of location decision criteria exists among service organizations. This is due to the broad diversity in the objectives and operations of service organizations. A very wide range of methods to address the location and transportation problems have been demonstrated in this chapter, along with the limits of applicability of those methods. These methods assist in formalizing the long-range, yet generally continual, location planning process.

QUESTIONS

1. Explain why location decision processes for banks and other service organizations are more widely used today than twenty years ago.

2. Given banking by mail and electronic funds transfers, why are location decisions important to banks?

3. The administrator of a local hospital with an established reputation for excellence comments that "the hospital's location is killing it financially." How might you explain her statement?

4. What are the three capacity questions that must be answered in location planning? Give an example of each.

5. Nick Kanoza has been a stylist at a local salon with carriage trade for over ten years. He has many customers who demand his services rather than any other operator's. Nick has decided to open his own salon and is

talking to real estate representatives about finding a low-rent facility in a nearby semi-industrial area. His objective is to keep overhead low. What do you think of this objective?

6. What measures would you recommend to evaluate a potential department store site for intangible (qualitative) criteria?

7. What is the difference between design capacity, effective capacity, and actual capacity? How does this difference affect the concepts of efficiency and utilization?

8. Under what circumstances would the rectilinear distance, euclidean distance, and the euclidean distance squared methods be used to compute travel distance?

9. Give an example, possibly suggested by a recent magazine or newspaper article, of a company that has gone through the four-step location decision process.

10. Differentiate the decision factors pertaining to location for delivered services and fixed services.

11. What is the effect of using the euclidean distance squared technique when computing travel costs? Give examples of situations that should employ this technique.

12. What one aspect of a nonmanufacturing production facility location decision differentiates it from all other production facility location decisions?

13. The regional marketing director of a major oil company sounds like a real estate agent when she says that there are three primary factors determining the company's sales, namely "location, location, and location." What do you think might be the basis for that statement?

14. What site selection criteria might be used by a university to select a suburban branch campus site if most students are night students who are employed full-time?

15. How might the criteria for selecting a site for a new Ritz Hotel differ from the criteria for locating a new Super 8 Motel?

16. How does the decision concerning the location of a plant to produce a new product differ from the decision concerning the location of a plant to increase the production capacity of a product currently being produced in two plants?

17. What are some of the special problems of locations in other nations?

18. What are some of the problems of quantifying intangible factors?

PROBLEMS

1. The transportation and processing costs for the three final candidate locations for a manufacturing plant are roughly equal. The critical qualitative factors have received the following weights and evaluation scores on a 5-point scale (5 = excellent) from the site selection committee. Select the best site on the basis of the weighted scores.

Factor	Weight	Location		
		A	B	C
Labor supply	0.20	5	4	4
Labor relations	0.30	3	4	5
Supporting services	0.25	5	3	3
Waste disposal	0.15	4	4	4
Community attitude	0.10	5	4	3

2. Shortly after completing the analysis in Problem 1 the selection committee receives new information that the operation costs of location B are substantially less than those of locations A and C, which are still the same. If operating costs are weighted as 0.50 and all the others combined as 0.50 with the previous relative weights, select the best site on the basis of the new weighted score. Operating costs of the three sites are evaluated as: A = 4, B = 5, and C = 4.

3. The site committee in Problems 1 and 2 recommends site B to the company president. The president examines the data and selects site C. What conclusions can be drawn? Consider what weight the president assigned to the factors.

4. The site selection committee has narrowed the alternatives to three sites, A, B, and C. They have identified four criteria—labor supply, climate, availability of raw materials, and market availability. Based on a scale of 1 to 5 (5 is best), three executives are asked to evaluate each site on the four criteria. The results are as follows.

	Location		
Factors	A	B	C
Labor supply	3.3	4.0	3.7
Climate	3.7	3.3	3.3
Raw materials	3.0	3.7	3.3
Market availability	4.7	3.3	3.0

    a. Which site would you select, assuming equal weights?

    b. The executives have decided to weight the factors. The weights selected are (1) labor supply $= 0.4$; (2) climate $= 0.3$; (3) raw materials $= 0.2$; and (4) market availability $= 0.1$. Under these conditions which would be the best site selection?

  5. Following is a table of evaluation scores received by eight possible plant sites for each of the critical decision factors. The evaluations (5, 4, 3, 2, 1, and $-M$) have the same meaning as was given in Table 4–1.

	Weight	A	B	C	D	E	F	G	H
Labor									
Supply	0.20	$-M$	2	4	3	5	$-M$	4	5
Relations	0.20	5	1	5	4	4	5	4	$-M$
Productivity	0.20	4	2	3	2	4	5	4	2
Services									
Financial	0.05	3	5	2	5	3	4	4	3
Accounting	0.05	2	4	1	4	3	2	3	2
Engineering	0.05	1	3	1	5	3	3	4	4
Suppliers	0.10	5	2	1	5	4	4	3	4
Data processing	0.05	3	4	1	4	4	3	4	3
Waste disposal	0.05	4	2	2	2	3	2	3	3
Community attitude	0.05	5	4	4	4	4	3	4	2

    a. Which location(s) should be eliminated from further consideration?

    b. Of the remaining locations, which would you select?

    c. If the weights were (1) labor supply $= 0.15$; (2) labor relations $= 0.15$; (3) data processing services $= 0.10$; and (4) community attitude $= 0.10$, what would be your recommendation?

  6. An organization has four large stores, A, B, C, and D, located as shown on the grid. They are serviced by a centralized warehouse located at the origin (0,0). Calculate the distance from the warehouse to each store using the

   a. rectilinear distance
   b. euclidean distance
   c. euclidean distance squared

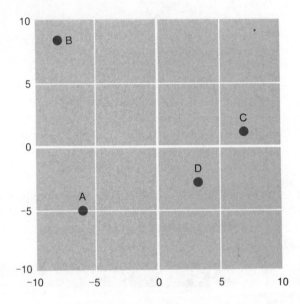

7. Using the data shown in the preceding problem, which method would you recommend for measuring the following distances:

   a. If the stores are in different cities, linked by air routes?
   b. If the delivered goods are primarily perishable items?
   c. If the stores are in the downtown area of a large metropolitan business district?

8. The following table shows the average number of trips per week. Using this table and the data in the two preceding problems, answer the following questions.

Store	Trips/Week
A	15
B	9
C	8
D	12

   a. The executive committee has decided to relocate the warehouse to adjoin one of the store locations. Using the rectilinear distance method, calculate which store location would provide the least distance to travel for the other stores.

b. Use the euclidean distance method to calculate which store location would provide the least distance to travel for the other stores.

c. What are the advantages and disadvantages of locating the warehouse at one of the stores?

9. Hayes Department Stores is opening four of their discount stores in a metropolitan area in which none presently exist. They also are building a new warehouse in that area to supply the four stores. Four possible sites have been found for the warehouse; each of these sites meets all requirements. Select the best site on the basis of the following transportation data (trips per week and miles between stores and possible warehouse sites).

Retail Stores	Trips per Week	Warehouse Sites			
		1	2	3	4
A	10	7	23	18	5
B	8	20	8	14	12
C	5	7	22	12	15
D	7	18	6	8	17

10. In the south central region, the Spud Beer Company has three full-service production plants and three separate distribution points. The following tableau gives total volume, demand and supply data, and transportation costs per unit for each route.

Plant	Distribution Point			Supply
	1	2	3	
A	3	5	6	20
B	2	6	3	40
C	4	2	5	30
Demand	15	30	45	90

a. Use the northwest corner method to find a feasible solution for this transportation problem. Calculate the total costs for this method.

b. Use Vogel's approximation method to find a solution for the transportation problem above. Calculate the costs using this technique.

11. The Spud Beer Company of problem 10 decides to increase its volume and needs one more distribution point. It is the company's option to select between points 4 and 5. The revised data follow. Calculate the optimal solution for each of the configurations.

Plant	Distribution Point					Supply
	1	2	3	4	5	
A	3	5	6	3	6	40
B	2	6	3	4	2	40
C	4	2	5	7	4	40
Demand	15	30	45	30	30	

12. A company has three plants, each manufacturing the same family of products, that supply four regional warehouses. The weekly demand for each warehouse, the weekly capacity for each plant, and the cost of shipping from each plant to each warehouse is given in the tableau on page 135.

a. Solve the problem using the northwest corner method.

b. Solve the problem using VAM.

c. Evaluate the optimality of the solution in part b, and, if appropriate, use the stepping stone adjustment technique to optimize the solution.

Plant	Warehouse				Supply
	A	B	C	D	
1	12	10	8	6	120
2	10	13	10	7	120
3	6	7	11	8	120
Demand	80	80	110	90	360

13. The Wholesale Grocery Chain has five retail sectors serviced by three large warehouse complexes. The matrix below represents the demand and supply data and the cost rates.

Warehouse	Retail Sector					Supply
	1	2	3	4	5	
A	10	15	10	12	20	400
B	17	20	22	15	10	350
C	14	12	18	10	17	450
Demand	300	200	250	150	300	1,200

  a. Use the northwest corner method to solve for a feasible solution to this transportation problem. Calculate the cost for this technique.
  b. Use the modified VAM technique to find a feasible solution for this transportation problem. Calculate the cost for this technique.
  c. Use the full VAM to find a feasible solution for this transportation problem. Calculate the cost for this technique.

14. The Johnson Aluminum Company presently has two distribution points in the Midwest to handle the requirements for four customers. The company plans to open a new warehouse to better serve these customers. The monthly data on existing and proposed sites is provided in the following tableau. If construction of site 3 costs $600,000 and of site 4 costs $500,000, and a three-year payback (in terms of reduced transportation costs) is required, make a recommendation to the site planning committee.

Distribution Point	Customers				Supply
	A	B	C	D	
Present 1	45	51	50	51	180
Present 2	48	54	50	52	110
Proposed 3	44	50	48	49	100
Proposed 4	45	50	48	51	100
Demand	90	90	75	100	

15. The Lakeland Furniture Company has three warehouses and eight retail stores. Each warehouse carries all furniture items. The demand and supply data and the cost matrix follow.

Warehouse	Stores								Supply
	1	2	3	4	5	6	7	8	
	4	3	7	2	8	4	9	2	150
	7	9	3	6	4	9	7	3	220
	2	8	9	7	3	9	3	9	230
	65	70	80	65	90	75	90	65	600

Find a feasible solution using the northwest corner method. Calculate the cost for this method.

16. Use Vogel's approximation method to find a feasible solution of the data in Problem 15. Calculate the cost using this method.

17. For Problem 16, check for optimality by using a computer and the appropriate software, if available.

REFERENCES

Ardalan, Alireza. "An Efficient Heuristic for Service Facility Location." Proceedings of the Northeast American Institute for Decision Sciences (1984), pp. 181–182.

Carroll, T. M., and R. D. Dean. "A Bayesian Approach to Plant Location Decisions." *Decision Sciences* (January 1980): 87.

Conover, W. J. *Practical Nonparametric Statistics*. New York: John Wiley & Sons, 1980.

Hill, I. D. "Modern Manufacturing Techniques Require Flexible Approach to Facilities Planning." *Industrial Engineering* (May 1984): 86–93.

Muther, R., and E. J. Phillips. "Facility Planners Cite Clear Objectives and Proper Input as Main Success Factors." *Industrial Engineering* (March 1983): 44–48.

Naisbitt, John. *Megatrends: Ten New Directions Transforming Our Lives*. New York: Warner Communications, 1982.

Price, W. L., and Michel Turcotte. "Locating a Blood Bank." *Interfaces* (September 1986): 17–26.

Schilling, David A. "Dynamic Location Modeling for Public Sector Facilities: A Multi-Criteria Approach." *Decision Sciences* (October 1980): 714–724.

Schmenner, Roger W. *Making Business Location Decisions*. Englewood Cliffs, N. J.: Prentice-Hall, 1982.

Siegel, S. *Nonparametric Statistics for the Behavioral Sciences*. New York: McGraw-Hill, 1956.

Tompkins, J. A., and J. A. White. *Facilities Planning*. New York: John Wiley & Sons, 1984.

CHAPTER 5
PROCESS DESIGN

OBJECTIVES

After completing this chapter, you should be able to

- Define and differentiate the characteristics of line flow, job shop, and fixed site processes

- Define and differentiate continuous, repetitive, and batch flows

- Appreciate the strategic implications of process design

- Understand constraints that bind process selection alternatives on a process design continuum

- Identify and characterize several emerging dimensions of process design

- Appreciate the potential contribution of computer integration in manufacturing and service environments

OUTLINE

Introduction
    Definition
    Competitive Process Design
Production Process Designs
    Line Flow
        Continuous Flow
        Repetitive Flow
        Characteristics of Continuous and Repetitive Flow Processes
        Batch Flow
        Classification of Line Flows
            Process and Item
            Models
            Objectives
    Job Shop
    Fixed Site (Project)
The Process Continuum
Emerging Process Design Dimensions
    Manufacturing Cells
    Flexible Manufacturing Systems (FMS)
    Computer Integrated Manufacturing (CIM)
        The Elements of CIM
        CIM and Management
        Technological Change on the Shop Floor
            Numerically Controlled Machines
            Group Technology
            Automated Materials Handling
            Robotics
        The Implications of CIM
    The Emerging Service Process Environment
Conclusions
Questions
References

INTRODUCTION

Process design is the third consideration in long-range planning. It is closely integrated with product and resource planning and facility location, the two areas covered in Chapters 3 and 4. Product and resource planning answer the questions of how much and when to produce, which are basically capacity issues. Facility location planning addresses the question of where to produce, which is normally a location and cost issue. Process design answers the third long-range planning question of how to produce and primarily involves scheduling and efficiency issues. Process design can be viewed as a way of interrelating these different aspects of long-range planning, because it focuses the considerations of how much product to produce where and when toward the question of how to build the product or provide the service.

The impact of these long-range planning decisions can be felt in a variety of medium-range and short-range planning activities, including the technology and equipment of the process, the layout of the process, and the specific schedules of production. Thus, process design integrates the long-range, medium-range, and short-range plans and, ultimately, the execution of the plan. Coverage of process design in this chapter will be limited to long-range planning issues. The medium- and short-range planning activities will be mentioned only briefly and will be covered more completely in later chapters.

Process design is a vital link between product, capacity, and location planning and the subsequent layout, scheduling, and control decisions. As with product, capacity, and location planning, the time focus of process design must vary from long-range planning to execution.

Definition

Process design is a specialized planning process for manufacturing or service operations to integrate product or service location and capacity decisions with subsequent layout, scheduling, and execution actions by defining the production steps and their necessary sequence.

This definition highlights several key elements of process design. First, process design is a planning process; it is formalized, it anticipates future conditions, and it answers basic questions about how an organization will act. However, it is a specialized type of planning process in that it deals with only one area; how the product or service will be produced. Second, it applies equally to the production of manufactured goods or to the delivery of a service. Third, it demonstrates the integration between long-, medium-, and short-range planning activities and their execution. Fourth, process design is concerned with the definition and sequencing of production steps.

Competitive Process Design

Process design decisions coincide with and depend on capacity and location decisions, as well as manufacturing and marketing (product positioning) strategy. Product positioning strategy is concerned with (1) whether to produce a few standardized products in large volume, several product families in lower volumes, or custom-designed items and (2) whether to sell the products through distributors, manufacturers' representatives, or direct sales. Product-positioning decisions, and thus process flow, scheduling, and layout decisions, are influenced by competitive factors in the industry, the product demand rate, the strengths of the organization, and the market niche the company desires to fill. Product-positioning decisions also influence whether an item is made to stock or made to order.

Made to stock means that a product, or sometimes a service, is completely produced and placed in inventory awaiting a purchaser. *Made to order* means that production is not started until a customer order is received. In some cases, these two production strategies are combined. For example, a company might build component parts or subassemblies to stock and then assemble these modules of component parts to individual customer orders.

One organization may decide to produce relatively standard items at low cost, planning to have high-volume sales. Such a decision usually results in continuous or repetitive flow production with a line layout (these terms are described in detail later). Ready-to-wear clothing purchased off the rack is such an example. Another organization producing a similar product may decide to produce to customer orders. This strategy is designed to fulfill the exact needs of each customer. It is usually consistent with low-volume, higher-unit-cost job shop production with a functional layout (also described later). Tailor-made shirts are a good example of this strategy.

In the service area, restaurants provide good examples of these two strategies. Fast-food restaurants emphasize standardized products (often made to stock several minutes before the sale), high volume, and low cost. Process line flow layouts exist in many such establishments. Other restaurants offer a wide selection of made-to-order entrees with specialized preparation (for example, rare, medium, or well done) and have higher unit costs, relatively low volume, and a functional layout in the kitchen. Both types of restaurants must provide quality, although the quality requirement differs based on customer expectations. The exact process design selected is thus clearly related to the competitive strategy of the firm.

PRODUCTION PROCESS DESIGNS

There are three traditional process design strategies that are useful for classifying operations environments—flow, job shop, and fixed site design. Figure 5–1 depicts a classification of processes and their typical layouts and product-positioning strategies.

Line Flow

The line flow is sometimes called a product flow because the product always follows the same sequential steps of production. There are three

Figure 5–1   Traditional Classification of Process Designs

Process Design	Typical Layout	Typical Product Positioning

Line flow (product)
  Continuous flow
  Repetitive flow
  Batch flow
	Line
	Product emphasis
		Make to stock (MTS)
		High volume
		Low unit cost

Job shop	Functional Process emphasis	Make to order (MTO) Low volume Higher unit cost
Fixed site	Fixed position project emphasis	Custom order (CO) Specialized products High unit cost

types of line flow: (1) continuous flow, (2) repetitive flow, and (3) batch flow.

CONTINUOUS FLOW. This term usually refers to the production or processing of fluids, wastes, powders, basic metals, and other bulk items. A hydroelectric dam is an example of a continuous flow; both water and electricity are flowing continuously through the process. Similarly, an oil refinery that gradually refines crude oil into various petroleum products or a pipe line for water, oil, or natural gas are examples of continuous flow processes. In the service area, telephone, radio, and television communication systems are examples of continuous flow services.

REPETITIVE FLOW. Discrete parts, such as shafts and connecting rods, and discrete assemblies, such as toasters and amplifiers, may be produced by a repetitive flow process. Examples of repetitive flow processes in the service sector include a barber shop or an all-night gas station. In each case, consistent service is provided on a repetitive basis in response to customer demand.

CHARACTERISTICS OF CONTINUOUS AND REPETITIVE FLOW PROCESSES. A line flow process may be an automated line with equipment and tooling designed and built specifically for processing and handling a given product (hard automation), or it may be nonautomated, with the combination of workers and machines designed specifically for the manufacture of a given product. Figure 5–2 depicts a typical flow line, although many flow lines have fifty or more stations.

The following are the general characteristics of continuous and repetitive flow processes:

Figure 5–2   Typical Flow Line

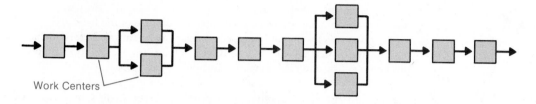

Work Centers

1. Work moves through the process at a fixed rate.
2. The processing and materials-handling equipment is individually designed and built (or modified) for the production of a product type.
3. The process is generally arranged in a direct line to minimize materials handling, queues, and work in process.
4. Minor changes may be made in the line to incorporate product or process improvements. Most major changes are expensive.
5. The line tends to be run (or remain idle) for a relatively long time.
6. Inventory planning and control is driven by the rate of flow. The continuous availability of materials and parts is critical.
7. The capacity of the different work stations is balanced along the line.
8. The rate of flow cannot be significantly changed without substantial modifications to the equipment or the number of personnel.
9. Fixed costs are high and variable costs are relatively low.

BATCH FLOW. The batch flow production or service delivery process is functionally the same as continuous and repetitive flows, but it is interrupted for updating control or due to limited production volume. An example might be a newspaper printing operation. In the service area, batch flows occur in airline flight check-in and cafeteria food service; firms that specialize in coupon handling and rebate administration also use batch flows.

The batch flow process overlaps the line flow and job shop classifications. Batch flow is used when the cost of a line process is justified, even though the item is not produced continuously. Relatively low demand parts, assemblies, and nondiscrete items (e.g., pharmaceuticals) are often produced using interrupted or batch flow production. Quality control requirements, such as those present in the production of pharmaceuticals, frequently demand batch processing.

The following are characteristics of an interrupted or a batch flow production process:

1. Equipment tends to be more general purpose, thus less efficient, than in continuous or repetitive production.
2. Equipment and personnel must be continuously scheduled.
3. In some cases, tooling and small equipment is moved into temporary storage when a batch is complete. It is replaced by tooling and equipment for the next item.

4. In batch processing lines with larger equipment, the equipment is not moved, but it is cleaned and adjusted for the required temperature, pressure, and time prior to running a different item.
5. Material requirements are often predicated on the size of the batch.
6. Production batch lot size and order release depend on various factors, including demand, production capacity, lead time, setup costs, availability of supply, product mix, and the commonality of production processes.

In some organizations a substantial portion of the orders may have the same flow pattern, while others have a different flow in terms of departments or sequence. Thus, the organization might simultaneously have several flow processes or a flow process and a job shop process. When an area within a plant is dedicated to manufacturing one product or product family, it is sometimes called a plant within a plant.

CLASSIFICATION OF LINE FLOWS. Classifying flow lines on the basis of the attributes listed in Figure 5–3 aids in describing, analyzing, designing, and managing them. A given line may be described by a combination of these attributes, with one being selected from each of the categories of process, item, models, and objectives.

Process and Item. Some lines are fully automated (closed loop and self-adjusting machine controlled); others, including many assembly lines, are manual; and some are a combination of machine controlled and manual operations. This distinction is important for purposes of line balancing, which is discussed in Chapter 9. For example, most automobile assembly lines, even the modern robotics lines, use both manual and automated processes. A flow line may be used for assembly fabrication, for part manufacturing, or for a combination of part and assembly production. In the latter case, it is usually described as an assembly line. For example, an assembly line may be used to make and package sandwiches that are then sold through coin-operated (automatic) machines.

Models. A single-model line is a line dedicated to manufacturing one item (part or assembly). Such a line is necessary when either the demand (and consequently the capacity requirements) for the item justifies the exclusive use of a line or the manufacturing requirements are sufficiently different from any other item. In the latter case, excess capacity may exist and either the

Figure 5–3   Flow Line Attributes

Process	Item	Models	Objectives
Automated	Assembly	Single	Balance
Combination	Combination	Batch (multi)	Other
Manual	Parts fabrication	Mixed	

production flow (output) rate is adjusted to match the demand rate or the line is periodically idle.

In some cases, a given work space may be used for two or more single-model lines when each is not run continually. These are batch lines consecutively occupying the same space, but they are not multimodel lines. For example, in the assembly of certain carburetors that have a relatively low demand, a line may be operated until the required quantity (production lot) for a specific model is completed. The tools and assembly fixtures for that model are then placed in adjacent storage, and different tools and equipment required for the next scheduled model are then used to set up the new line. Such lines are being replaced with mixed-model lines as just-in-time and zero inventory concepts are adopted by many organizations.

A batch or multimodel line manufactures two or more items requiring similar processes. The items are manufactured in batches due to the setup time required to change the line from one item to another. The diesel engine line at the John Deere plant in Waterloo, Iowa is used to manufacture batches of several different engines (Spencer 1980).

Mixed-model lines are also used to manufacture two or more models; however, the changeover time between models is minimal (frequently zero), and the different models are intermixed on the same line. Hall describes such a mixed-model line with the following flow sequence, where A, B, C, and D represent different models: A-B-C-A-B-C-A-B-A-D. Thus, for every D produced, there would be four A's, three B's, and two C's manufactured (Hall 1983).

Objectives. Traditionally, discussions of line flow design have emphasized capacity, precedence requirements, and line-balancing objectives. Other possible objectives of a flow design are as follows:

1. Combine activities requiring one or more of the following: the same special skill, the same tooling or equipment, or the same materials or parts
2. Meet operation relationship requirements, such as segregating dust-producing activities from activities requiring a clean environment
3. Limit the number of physically demanding tasks at each workstation in a manual line
4. Provide flexibility to meet changes in output rates. Workstations can be reorganized by changing assignments of activities with minimum difficulty and cost
5. Minimize the space requirements
6. Limit the initial cost of making the layout revisions required to implement the line; this objective is important whenever available capital is limited, the projected life of the product is relatively short, or a major change in the manufacturing process is anticipated
7. Achieve a minimum level of job satisfaction at each workstation

Numerous heuristic approaches have been developed to address flow design objectives; several of these are described in Chapter 9. The authors have observed multiple flow design objectives in their extensive work with manufacturing and service organizations. To develop a flow line for an environment that has several objectives, the relative priority of each objective, essential objectives, and the rank order of all objectives must be determined. An effective way to address multiple flow design objectives using a goal-programming formulation is presented by Gunther, Johnson, and Peterson (1983).

Job Shop

The spatial and administrative organization of similar equipment by function (e.g., milling, drilling, turning, forging, and assembly) is characteristic of a job shop process. As jobs flow from work center to work center, or department to department, a different type of operation is performed in each center or department. Orders may follow similar or different paths through the plant, suggesting one or several dominant flows. The layout is intended to support a manufacturing environment in which there can be a great diversity of flow among products. Figure 5–4 depicts a job shop process design.

The following are salient characteristics of job shop processes:

1. Multipurpose production and materials-handling equipment can be adjusted and modified to handle many different products.
2. Many different products are run in lots or batches through the plant, and many lots are usually being processed at a given time. Low demand per product usually does not justify flow production.
3. The processing of orders requires detailed planning and control, due to the variety of flow patterns and the separation of work centers.

Figure 5–4   Job Shop

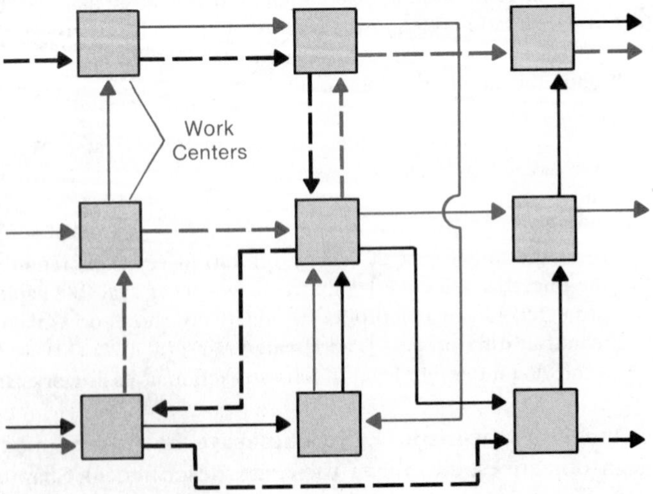

4. Control requires detailed job and shop information, including processing sequence, order priority, time requirements of each job, status of jobs in process, work center capacity, and capacity requirements of each work center by time period.
5. Work center loads differ greatly; that is, they have different percent capacity utilizations. Critical capacity centers (bottlenecks) caused by relative scarcity of labor or machinery must be determined. Change in product mix may cause the bottlenecks to shift (roam) from work center to work center.
6. Resource availability, including materials, personnel, and tooling, must be coordinated with order planning.
7. Each work center is decoupled or allowed to work independently of the others through buffer inventories (work-in-process queues). This amount of work-in-process material tends to be high relative to that in a flow process due to the queues and long in-process times.
8. The total time, from the beginning of the first operation to the end of the last, is relatively long compared to total operation time. An order often spends 75 percent or more of its time in the plant waiting to be moved to the next work center or waiting at a work center for processing.
9. Direct labor personnel are usually more highly trained and skilled than those in a flow process operation.

Job shop operations, like interrupted flow operations, are characterized by batches. However, unlike the interrupted flow where batches and batch size are specified by quality constraints or by demand volumes, the batch size of job shop processes is often dictated by the size of a specific order. Thus, large and small batches of very similar, or in some cases identical products, are processed concurrently by the job shop.

Job shop operations typically produce anywhere from one unit to several hundred units per setup, and consequently they rely upon highly flexible labor and low-cost, flexible, general-purpose equipment. A small commercial printer is typical of a small job shop. Jobs are often quoted in terms of setup costs and then additional costs per unit, per hundred, or per thousand of production.

Fixed Site (Project)

The key identifying characteristic of this type of process is that the materials, tools, and personnel are brought to the location where the product is being fabricated or the service is being provided. This type of process is found in shipbuilding, construction, road building, and the final assembly of large, special-purpose trucks, turbines, aircraft, pressure vessels, and any other items that are difficult to move from work center to work center. In the service area there are many instances where the service process must move to a fixed site. Examples include a tow truck that goes to the location of a disabled car, repair or installation services that must be taken to the location of the job, and many delivery services, such as food, flowers, and shut-in care.

This type of process is sometimes used in conjunction with other processes. After the product reaches a certain size, it is often more practical to keep it stationary and move the necessary components to its location.

Characteristics of fixed position production include the following:

1. Tooling, personnel, materials, and other resources should be available at the proper time to avoid nonproductive capacity.
2. Order quantities are small, and orders frequently have custom design features.
3. Direct labor personnel frequently are highly trained, very skillful, and independent. They work from blueprints and general instructions rather than detailed process sheets.
4. An order control system is usually used.
5. Scheduling of design engineering, manufacturing engineering, and tool fabrication is frequently an essential part of manufacturing (order) planning and control.
6. Network scheduling models—for example, PERT and CPM (discussed in Chapter 15)—are useful in determining the sequential requirements of tools and materials.

THE PROCESS CONTINUUM

These generalized process designs (flow, job shop, and fixed) are rarely found in a totally pure form. Most production and service operations are a combination of two, or sometimes all three, of these designs. For example, the construction of a building is usually regarded as a fixed project; however, the construction of suburban housing units is often done with techniques that are associated with job shop and flow designs. Earthmovers dig cellars, create lakes, and build noise-dissipation berms for all houses in the particular subdivision. Then paved roads, utility lines, concrete forms for basements, and curbs are sequentially added for each of the twenty or more homes. Because the houses are sequentially produced with the same type of flow as an automobile assembly line, such housing construction can be likened to a flow process. One difference is that the car is moving on the assembly line, but the house assembly tools and processes are sequentially moving to different fixed sites in the housing development. Thus, housing production combines some elements of a fixed site operation with some elements of a line flow.

Further, consider that some houses are built without cellars and thus require different concrete forms. This and other design customizing would quickly suggest characteristics of a job shop flow process. Thus, as labor moves from house to house, building the skeleton, finishing the outside, placing the individual accoutrements, and performing interior finishing work, the sequencing and pace of a line process is approximated. Simultaneously, each house must be adjusted for various semicustom modifications, as in a job shop. To minimize the amount of investment in fixed inventory (in this case, a finished but unsold house), this integrated production process must be closely coordinated with the progress of house sales.

These three processes, when considered in terms of applications, are better represented as a continuum. Examples of a continuous flow might be an oil pipeline, a sugar refinery, or a radio transmission. At the other extreme, a plumbing repair or bridge construction project are reasonably fixed processes. Between these two relatively pure extremes there are numerous possible adjustments of process design.

One of the important reasons for identifying the design of the production process in the long-term plan is that each process requires different types of job flow, implying specific layout and scheduling techniques and different management concerns and tasks in executing the plan. In turn, these decisions suggest different competitive strategies. The interrelationships of product, process, strategy, and execution have been ably developed by Hayes and Wheelwright (1979) as shown in Figure 5–5.

Figure 5–5 identifies a matrix of the product and process relationships over the life cycle of the product. The process continuum is shown at the top with several further descriptors, including volume, standardization, and number of products. The dominant competitive criteria continuum is at the bottom, ranging from flexibility/quality to delivery/cost. The flow continuum is shown at the left side, and a range of key management tasks is included at the right side of the figure.

Companies can define their exact position within the framework of the matrix, although they are constrained somewhat by the type of product and the stage of product development. For example, auto assembly is generally considered to be a repetitive process, but many luxury and sports automobiles are built in job shops; sometimes even in a semifixed position. Examples are Rolls Royce, some Volvo models, and the Avanti. Additionally, the type of process selected depends, to some degree, upon the stage of the product life cycle. The first prototype of a product is often built as a fixed project, but as the volume increases, the efficiencies of job shop and then flow processes are sought and developed. Within some limits, then, the operations manager can select the exact product/process relationship position of the operation and use that position as a competitive advantage.

EMERGING PROCESS DESIGN DIMENSIONS

Manufacturers are constantly looking for the right balance or combination of process characteristics that will give them a competitive edge. With the dynamics of changing process developments, product technology, information management, and product distribution methods, numerous and highly changing process designs might be expected to emerge. However, among the many different possibilities, three general and related approaches appear to have developed; namely, manufacturing cells, flexible manufacturing systems, and computer integrated manufacturing.

Figure 5-5   Product/Process Matrix

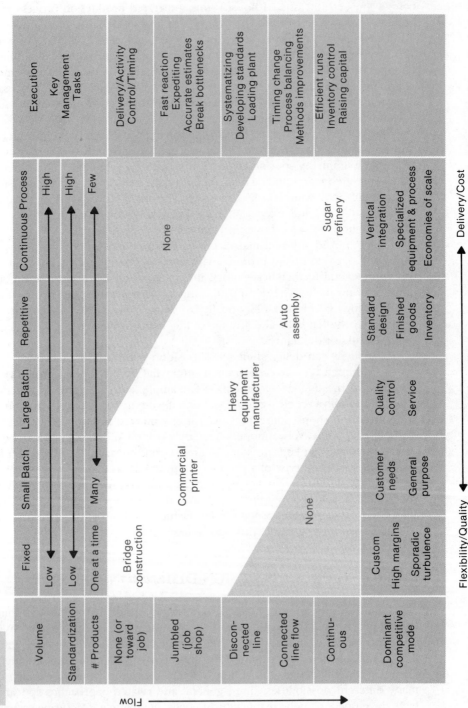

Source: Adapted from Robert H. Hayes and Steven C. Wheelwright, "Line Manufacturing Process and Product Life Cycles," *Harvard Business Review*, Jan–Feb 1979.

Manufacturing Cells

Cellular manufacturing is a loosely defined term that involves the organization of a small group of workers and/or machines in a repetitive production flow layout, frequently a U-shaped configuration, to produce a group of similar items. The cell will often be organized to accomplish all manufacturing or service operations, from order receipt to shipping, for one product or product group, or for one or several customers. Figure 5–6 shows several examples of manufacturing cells.

The manufacturing cell achieves economies due to the modified equipment dedicated to the group, special tooling, reduced setup and run time, reduced materials handling, shorter throughput time, and reduced work-in-process. New (1977), for example, reported a 70 percent average reduction in throughput time for a group of U.K. firms using cellular manufacturing. The use of manufacturing cells reduced the inventory of diesel engines required for final assembly at John Deere's Waterloo, Iowa engine plant (Spencer 1980).

Manufacturing cells are generally differentiated into two types: (1) those

Figure 5–6   Manufacturing Cells

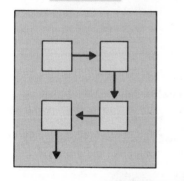 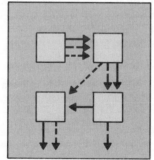 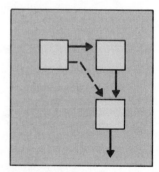

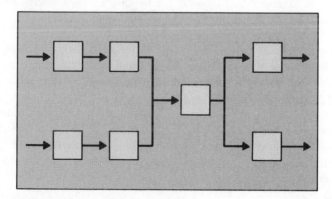

with manual steps and setups and (2) those with automated steps and setups. This latter type of automated manufacturing cell is usually called a flexible manufacturing system (FMS).

Flexible Manufacturing Systems (FMS)

The ability to avoid a new setup each time a different item is processed is the differentiating characteristic of an FMS. The absence of setup requirements allows manufacturing to switch from one item to another without an economic penalty for the setup. Thus, the system is more flexible.

The typical FMS is an automated cell (integrated materials handling and processing equipment) used to produce a group of parts or assemblies. Although all items require similar manufacturing processes, the sequence of operations is not necessarily the same in each case. However, a nonautomated production line that can switch from one product to another without any setup time can also be called an FMS. For example, a salad bar in a restaurant or cafeteria kitchen that can switch production between a combination salad, spinach salad, quarter head of lettuce salad, or Caesar salad without any setup time is technically an FMS. In an automated FMS, either computers or operators or both might perform the following required functions.

1. Computers control the
   a. Machine tools
   b. Material-handling equipment
   c. Integration of the activities of the machine tools and material-handling equipment
2. Operators
   a. Perform emergency and preventive maintenance
   b. Enter data, such as part numbers
   c. Enter new or revised programs
3. Either the operators or the computer-controlled, automated equipment can
   a. Load materials (rough castings, for example) into the material-handling system
   b. Unload completed parts from the material-handling system
   c. Remove or add tools to the tool magazines of different machines

An FMS is dedicated to manufacturing a family of items. In an ideal situation, each item in the family is designed with a standard set of mounting bosses (lugs, holes, or ears, for example) or is mounted on a standard plate or frame. Thus, all items in a group are secured to the table, bed, or faceplate of a machine tool in the same manner. As a result, it is not necessary to change fixtures or holding devices when switching from one item to another. Because there is no setup time, a lot size of one is economically feasible. In some situations different mounting fixtures may be required, but automatic sensing devices can recognize these variations and, through the computer, instruct the equipment to make the necessary adjustments.

In addition to product mounting, setup time may also include adjustments to control the length and depth of a cut. This is not necessary in an FMS, as each machine tool performs the programmed operation with an accuracy matching or surpassing that of the best operator. The computer controlling the machine's operation accesses the program for machining the particular item and follows that program. The machine also may have the capability to read a coded identification on an item and verify its identity.

The use of computers and software in the FMS provides an economy of scope. Economies of scope are defined broadly as those reduced costs and increased revenues that result from the ability to shift inexpensively from the production of one product or service to another due to improved production technologies and management. This ability enables an organization to efficiently produce small quantity lots (small production runs) and thus respond quickly to customer requests for product variability, short lead times, and reasonable costs. This is sometimes called *soft automation*. In contrast, *hard automation* can produce only one item in a large volume very efficiently, and thus is associated with economies of scale.

Setup costs still exist, however, as does the need for human skill and ingenuity. The cost of programming the process instructions for each item is a fixed setup cost. In an FMS it is spread across many production lots (frequently one unit each) and is not incurred each time a lot is produced. Further, just as the efficiency of a traditional job shop depends on the art and craft of the setup operator, the efficiency of an FMS depends on the skill of the programmer. System design and programming of the direction, monitoring, and control of the integrated materials-handling and machining processes also are key factors in the efficiency of the FMS. Thus, the setup (software) costs must be considered when deciding to establish an FMS. Other factors affecting the decision are quality, lead time reductions, and reduced inventory.

Computer Integrated Manufacturing (CIM)

Computer integrated manufacturing (CIM) is a natural extension of FMS. It is an application of computer technology to take full advantage of both hardware and software developments in conjunction with manufacturing technology and management practice. It combines these to provide truly flexible automation. CIM ties together both information technology and systems concepts to achieve greater efficiency and effectiveness. The precise definition of CIM is evolving; and it sometimes means different things to different people. Basically, however, it integrates the six concepts shown in Figure 5–7 to achieve greater productivity.

THE ELEMENTS OF CIM. These six elements of CIM are also difficult, in some cases, to precisely define because of the dynamic development in the field and the numerous different applications. However, several elements have become increasingly standardized, particularly as a result of efforts by the American

Figure 5–7 Elements of a Computer Integrated Manufacturing System

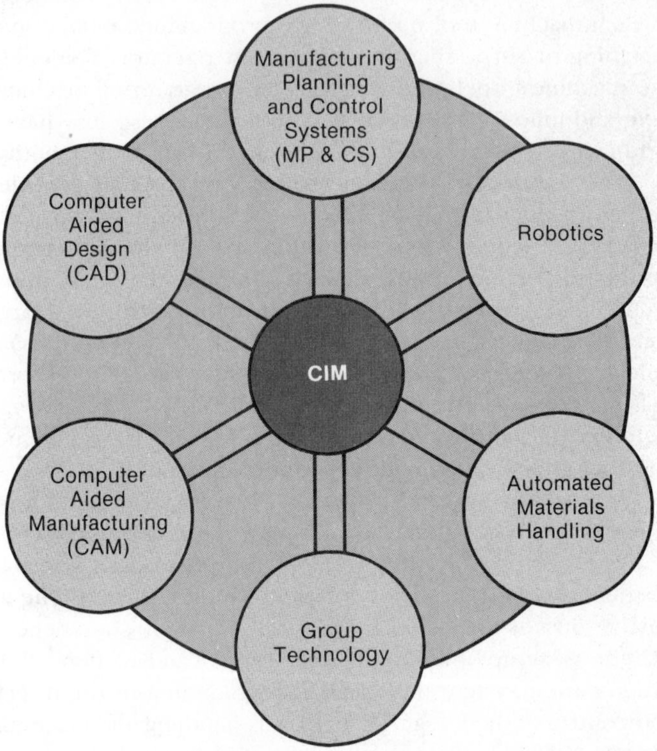

Production and Inventory Control Society (APICS). The following definitions are generally accepted:

1. *Group technology* is an engineering and manufacturing philosophy that identifies the sameness of parts, equipment, or processes. It provides for rapid retrieval of existing designs and anticipates a cellular-type production equipment layout. Manufacturing cells, discussed earlier, are often considered to be an integral part of group technology.
2. *Computer aided design (CAD)* is the use of computers in interactive engineering drawing and storage of designs. Programs complete the layout, geometric transformations, projections, rotations, magnifications, and interval (cross-section) views of a part and its relationship with other parts.
3. *Computer aided manufacturing (CAM)* is the use of computers to program, direct, and control production equipment in the fabrication of manufactured items.
4. *Robotics* is the use of programmable machines designed to handle materials or tools in the performance of a variety of tasks.
5. *Manufacturing planning and control systems* interface with the master production schedule and execute that plan, subject to imposed capacity and resource constraints.

6. *Automated materials handling* equipment permits automated storage, retrieval, and movement of materials and component parts from storage to various work stations, finished goods inventory storage locations, and shipping docks.

CIM then integrates these elements to manufacture a product. For example, computer chip makers use CAD to visualize, test, and develop circuitry of new computer chips. Once a design has been selected, the design information is passed to the manufacturing planning and control system (MPCS) and to the CAM system. The MPCS schedules the production, given demand information, current usage of the production process equipment, and resource constraints. Then the direction to build one unit or one lot is passed on to the CAM system. The CAM system directs the robotics and automated materials handling systems and adjusts the production of an existing group technology (GT) cell to manufacture the specified chip or lot. This development process for one new product may take three to four weeks or more, depending upon complexity.

CIM represents the final stage in the automation of the manufacturing process. It builds on the traditional manufacturing processes and incorporates engineering design techniques and information-handling technologies. The result of this integration is a dramatic reduction of information handling and transmission times in the product development, process design, and execution cycle. Figure 5–8 shows the stages of growth toward CIM.

The process development continuum in Figure 5–8 shows how CIM relates to various other concepts in the manufacturing area. While produc-

Figure 5–8 Process Development Continuum

Stage	Manufacturing Process	Engineering and Information Handling	
Stage 1	Traditional manufacturing	Batch/Lot processing Buffer inventories	
Stage 2	Group technology manufacturing cells	Focused factory, CAPP Reduced inventory	
Stage 3	Islands of automation	CAD/CAM/CAE Robotics FMS	
Stage 4	Computer integrated manufacturing	Information network Complete system integration	

Process Development

Time ⟶

Source: Adapted from James H. Greene, *Production and Inventory Control Handbook,* 2nd ed. (New York: McGraw-Hill, 1987).

tion was progressing through the first three stages (traditional manufacturing, GT/Manufacturing cells, and islands of automation), engineering was also progressing. Engineering advanced from manual, disjointed activities through computer aided process planning (CAPP), part of the MPCS, to CAD, CAM, and computer aided engineering (CAE). At the same time, information technology was moving from batch processing to fourth generation languages, data base systems, communications and networking, artificial intelligence, and decision support systems. CIM is the union of all three: manufacturing, engineering, and information technology. It ties together these diverse aspects of manufacturing processes to create an enhanced, total system.

CIM has been evolving for the past twenty years, and the Bureau of Labor Statistics estimates that the market for CIM is growing by 25 percent a year. Manufacturing automation alone is a $20 billion a year business. The Sikorsky Aircraft Division of United Technologies Corporation currently has seventy machine tools tied together with CIM and will increase that number to one hundred very soon (*Industry Week* 1987).

CIM AND MANAGEMENT. Besides the technology considerations, CIM also incorporates recent developments in manufacturing management. These are not unique to CIM but are the building blocks for a well-designed and well-managed production system.

1. Inventory is viewed as a liability.
2. Quality must be designed and built into the product and the process; it cannot be inspected in.
3. Manufacturing can be viewed as a flow rather than a set of discrete activities.
4. The focus of control switches from a materials flow to a materials and information flow.
5. Design and manufacturing activities must be closely coordinated so that product requirements can drive the process configurations.
6. Simple is better. Arthur Anderson advises its clients to "simplify, automate, integrate."

These fundamental management considerations are more apparent when the characteristics of a typical, traditional, manufacturing facility are compared with those of a CIM facility. This distinction is shown in Figure 5–9.

While manufacturing management concepts have been evolving over the past twenty years, computer and information systems concepts have also been changing. Historically, the application program has dominated data processing management; however, today it is recognized that the data base is what endures and that programs must change and evolve to meet new demands. Thus, data integration must precede CIM, and there must be an information architecture or structure of data relationships to support various systems.

TECHNOLOGICAL CHANGE ON THE SHOP FLOOR. Technological change, particularly the extreme reduction in the cost of computer memory accompanied

Figure 5–9   Traditional Production Processes Compared with CIM

Traditional processes can be described by:	In contrast, the CIM factory is described by:
Economy of scale	Economy of scope
Learning curve	Truncated product life cycle
Task specialization	Multimission facilities
Work as a social activity	Unmanned systems
Separable variable costs	Joint costs
Standardization	Variety
Expensive flexibility and variety	Profitable flexibility and variety

Leading to factories that exhibit characteristics of:	Leading to factories that exhibit characteristics of:
Centralization	Decentralization
Large plants	Disaggregated capacity
Balanced lines	Flexibility
Smooth flows	Inexpensive surge and turnaround ability
Standard product design	Many custom products
Low rate of change and high stability	Innovation and responsiveness
Inventory used as a buffer	Production tied to demand
"Focused factory" as an organizing concept	Functional range for repeated reorganization
Job enrichment and enlargement	Responsibility tied to reward
Batch systems	Flow systems

Source: Reprinted by permission of Joel D. Goldhar and Mariann Jelinek, "Computer Integrated Flexible Manufacturing: Organizational, Economic, and Strategic Implications," *Interfaces*, Vol. 15, No. 3, May–June, 1985, Copyright 1985, The Institute of Management Sciences.

by the escalation in computer power, has been pulling us toward CIM. Other forces have also been pushing the need for CIM: increased competition in world markets, a need for higher productivity, the goal of higher quality at lower cost, and the importance of a quick response to market forces. CIM has been made possible because of a number of technological developments on the shop floor, several of which are discussed in this section. While this is not an exhaustive listing, it represents the range of ideas that have come together under the general concept of CIM.

Numerically Controlled Machines. Manufacturing technology began to change significantly with the advent of numerically controlled (NC) machines. The first NC machines were controlled by electronic signals from devices that read punched paper tape that had been prepared off-line by a computer. Eventually, the machines were directly attached to the computer and the process was called direct numeric control (DNC). Then, the computer was incorporated into the machines and it was called computer numeric control (CNC). Both of these terms are common today.

Control of machines occurs at three levels: unit, area, and supervisory. Unit control refers to direct control of tool movements for individual machines. This includes CNC-type installations and may be performed by a simple programmable controller. Area control involves coordination of a number of machines from a central device that downloads instructions to the unit level and uploads information from each unit as it completes its assigned tasks. This level of integration is often described as a manufacturing cell and may be accomplished with a microcomputer. The supervisory level coordinates all of these by linking design, manufacturing, and planning activities. This is done by maintaining a centralized library of parts and product design programs, routing and scheduling information, and inventory status. Mainframe and super-minicomputers are usually required for these tasks.

John Deere's tractor works in Waterloo, Iowa is a good example of this type of system in action. An IBM mainframe directs nine Digital Equipment Corporation minicomputers, which control operations in four separate buildings. Each night the mainframe sends instructions to the minis regarding what parts to withdraw from the automated storage system for the next day's work. Other minis are instructed on what items to process and in what order to process them. The result is a highly efficient factory.

Group Technology. Group technology (GT) is used in two different yet related contexts. First, GT is useful in engineering design; it recognizes the similarity in shape and other characteristics among diverse parts in order to reduce the proliferation of engineering drawings and different part numbers for identical items. Second, GT identifies parts with common tooling or machining requirements, or similarity based on manufacturing process, so as to facilitate manufacturing as described in the section on manufacturing cells. The importance of the GT concept is that significant time savings in design and cost savings in manufacturing are possible. The key to its implementation is a good coding scheme to facilitate a data base search that can be used in designing products and processes. A number of software packages exist to support this function.

Automated Materials Handling. Automated materials handling (AMH) and automated storage/retrieval systems (AS/RS) are an integral part of a CIM system. AMH integrates by physically linking islands of automation into a single, plantwide entity. The AS/RS serves as the front end and back end to the manufacturing process and controls the receipt and storage of inventory, the shipping of finished goods, and the timing of operations. Through automatic identification equipment, the AS/RS is linked to the manufacturing information system and provides on-line control of the process.

Automatic identification can make use of optical character recognition, magnetic strip readers, voice recognition, and bar coding. The importance of the accuracy of data entering the system cannot be overstated; bar coding, according to Department of Defense tests, proved 300 times more effective than optical character recognition and 10,000 times more effective than manual entry of the information into a computer, due to improved accuracy and speed. General Electric estimated annual savings of $280,000 at its manufacturing plant in Portmouth, Virginia as a result of implementing a bar coding system (*Modern Industry* 1984).

Robotics. The Robot Institute of America defines a robot as a "reprogrammable, multifunctional manipulator." Common usage labels any automatic device that performs functions ordinarily done by humans, but without human direction, as a robot. While some feel that robots are introduced to replace unionized workers, the most common placement is for dull, dirty, or dangerous jobs (the three D's) or hot, heavy, and hazardous jobs (the three H's). As a result of robotics, worker compensation claims have decreased significantly. Workers often fear loss of jobs because of the introduction of robots, but if the introduction of robots is well planned, normal attrition and a shift of job opportunities to avoid the three D's or three H's should avoid layoffs.

A common fallacy is to assume that problems with people can be avoided by automation. In fact, to realize the full benefits of automation and robotics, people and robots must be integrated. Careful job analysis is a first step toward planning that integration. Prudent managers should make long-term forecasts of job requirements before introducing robotics.

THE IMPLICATIONS OF CIM. The managerial implications of CIM are numerous. As was pointed out previously, CIM encompasses the entire range of activities of a manufacturing organization. It goes well beyond simple mechanization or automation of production tools and includes the information and planning systems as well. The strategy of CIM is to integrate design and production, and the approach is sometimes referred to as design for assembly. One goal of this strategy is to reduce the number of parts in a product so as to facilitate its production. According to Morgan Whitney, director of Ford Motor Company's robotics and automation laboratory, "When you reduce complexity, you improve quality and the cost benefits flow back through the system, cutting overhead" (*Minneapolis Star Tribune* 1987).

Decision-making authority tends to move to lower levels in a CIM environment as more powerful equipment and systems become available on the shop floor. The results are faster decisions and an improvement in job satisfaction. Other changes in corporate culture include having marketing, engineering, and production work together on product and process development—often in a unified direction. Even vendors and customers may be involved in these decisions at a very early stage. Vendors in particular may be in a position to supply needed technical information.

While robot suppliers exist (Unimation Inc. and Cincinnati Milacron are the two oldest and largest in the United States), there really are no CIM vendors. What does exist are systems integrators; firms that link together equipment, systems, and communication devices from various suppliers to create a CIM-like environment. Implementation of CIM is not an overnight proposition; it may take several years or more to incorporate.

Traditional equipment replacement and investment analyses applied to decisions about CIM have been a major barrier to adoption of this new concept. Often these historical techniques fail to recognize adequately the strategic, integrative nature of CIM. CIM's greatest benefits come not from doing old things cheaper, but from doing things not previously possible. Flexibility and reduced lead time for new product development are strategic benefits that do not fit into traditional return-on-investment calculations. According to J. Tracy O'Rourke, President of Allen-Bradley Co. (a subsidiary of Rockwell International Corporation), "Traditional financial justification procedures based on internal rates of return or short payback periods are perhaps the greatest single barrier to adoption of new manufacturing technologies" (*Industry Week* 1987).

The Emerging Service Process Environment

Much of the previous discussion has implied a manufacturing environment, which is where the various techniques of CIM have been developed. Even the name, computer integrated manufacturing, suggests that it applies only to manufacturing, not to services. That is absolutely not the case, and as the applications in the service environment become more visible, perhaps the acronym CIP, for computer integrated production, may be more appropriate. Consider the following situations:

1. An ambulance paramedic uses a radio-linked data input device to measure and monitor the vital signs of an accident victim. The data are transmitted to a central computer, and a medical status evaluation program suggests further diagnostic checks and defines emergency treatment and doses.
2. A doctor uses various sensing devices to guide an instrument to the site of an internal operation through the arteries or various body openings. The doctor is able to complete major surgery with little or no external cutting.
3. An energy conservation specialist records information about a house during a short inspection on a hand-held data input device, and then, through a telephone, interacts with a central computer to get a complete analysis of the expected costs and probable savings of various weatherproofing strategies.
4. The check-out process of most retail stores adjusts inventories and identifies items that need to be reordered, and in some cases, actually posts the order.
5. A police artist uses computer graphics to establish a composite sketch of a criminal, uses the image to confirm the accuracy of the sketch, and then transmits the data of the sketch, but not the sketch itself, for a national identity check.
6. At a restaurant, a sensor monitors and adjusts the temperature and viscosity of cooking fat to assure that french fries are golden brown.
7. A computer monitors market data and computes various financial ratios, which are the bases for recommendations to sell or buy specific securities.

Many such programs, assisting many thousands of investors, may have been responsible for part of the stock market decline of October 1987.

8. Turn-lane sensors at busy traffic intersections count the number of cars that enter the left-turn lane, then adjust the length of the left-turn arrow accordingly.

9. Credit-card readers check the status of the purchaser's account before the transaction is completed.

These are just a few ways in which an adjustment of the service is accomplished based on an evaluation of factors in the service environment. In each case, information about the service condition was detected and relayed to a computer or similar device. That device was preprogrammed to use decision rules and to relay the outcome of the decision back to the service location for implementation.

Although service delivery differs from the production of manufactured goods in various ways, the design of the service process, the evaluation of the service needs, the movement of resources, and the execution of the service delivery are all highly amenable to computer integration. There seems to be little difference whether the service is a high-contact or a low-contact operation (Chase 1978) or whether the service is generally customized or quite standardized. Even as simple and standardized a service process as shining shoes can be blueprinted and carefully analyzed for both the process design and the service delivery (Shostack 1984).

CONCLUSIONS

This chapter has described the varying ways that manufacturing and service delivery processes may be designed. The three traditional approaches, line flow, job shop, and fixed position production were described and differentiated through the identification of process characteristics. The very distinctive approaches of these pure processes are not normally encountered in application; rather, some combination of processes is usually found. The specific process design is constrained, to some degree, by the nature of the product or service, but operations managers do have some strategic choice in the positioning of their product/process relationship. This choice in placement along the process continuum is a very important part of strategic, long-range operations planning.

Increasingly, technological developments have reduced the differences between line flow, job shop, and fixed position processes. These emerging process technologies integrate manufacturing or service operations with engineering design methods and computer information technology to provide economic unit lot sizes and fully individualized service in a rapid and flexible manner. Full integration is highly complex and very difficult to develop; however, once achieved it offers many efficiencies and a new way of viewing the product manufacturing or service delivery process.

The implications of these changes for management are far reaching. Most notably, they mean turbulence in the work force, although not necessarily work force reduction. The nature of the contribution of labor, however, will change dramatically. The quality of work life will improve as work becomes safer and less onerous and as responsibility shifts to a level that is closer to the dynamic, computer integrated production environment. While labor skills, requirements, and decision-making authority increase, management's function becomes that of a facilitator; a remover of barriers and a provider of the tools necessary to do the job with efficiency and effectiveness. In such an environment, operations management is required to look toward the long-run competitive edge and growth of the product/process relationship.

QUESTIONS

1. A list of operation characteristics follows. For each characteristic, select the type(s) of process with which it is most likely to be found.

Process Type
a. Continuous flow
b. Repetitive flow
c. Batch
d. Manufacturing cell

e. Flexible manufacturing system
f. Job shop
g. Fixed position

Operation Characteristics

(1) Similar equipment is grouped together; many different flow patterns exist; and detailed order planning and control is required.
(2) Materials, tools, equipment, and personnel are brought to the location where the work is performed.
(3) Inventory planning is driven by the rate of flow.
(4) Work-in-process is high relative to other flow patterns.
(5) Direct labor personnel are highly trained, very skillful, and work from blueprints and general instructions rather than from detailed process sheets.
(6) Equipment is specialized
(7) The total time from the beginning of the first operation to the end of the last operation in manufacturing a product is relatively short.
(8) There are no machine setup savings per unit when manufacturing more than one unit.
(9) Computers control the machine tools and materials-handling equipment.
(10) Machines and personnel dedicated to manufacturing a group (family) of items are arranged in a flow pattern in one location.
(11) Items with similar setups are run in sequence.

(12) Lead time tends to be long due to the time orders spend waiting to be processed or to be moved. (This can be reduced by good management.)

(13) Equipment tends to be general purpose.

2. Define process design.

3. What area does process design address? What does it involve?

4. What does made to stock mean? Give two examples of companies that produce goods or services by following a made-to-stock strategy.

5. What does made to order mean? Give two examples of companies that produce goods or services by following a made-to-order strategy.

6. When and how might an organization integrate the two strategies, made-to-stock and made-to-order? Give two examples of such a situation.

7. Name and differentiate the three traditional process design strategies. Give several examples of each.

8. Flow design can be differentiated into three categories: continuous flow, repetitive flow, and batch flow. What are the distinguishing differences among them?

9. What is a plant within a plant?

10. Describe a single-model line. When is such a line justified?

11. What is the difference between a multimodel line and a mixed-model line?

12. Name six possible operations objectives that could affect the configuration of a process design. Give an example of how consideration of these objectives might dictate the configuration of a process design.

13. What are the salient characteristics of job shop processes?

14. Generally, what dictates the batch size of a job shop process?

15. What is the key identifying characteristic of the fixed site (project) process?

16. What are the general characteristics of fixed site production?

17. Refer to Figure 5–5. Would it be advantageous for an organization considered to be a job shop to produce under a repetitive or continuous process mode of manufacturing? Why? Why not?

18. How does batch flow production differ from job shop production?

19. How might a job shop achieve a large batch or repetitive manufacturing method?

20. What is a manufacturing cell? What are some of the factors that contribute to the manufacturing cell's increased efficiency and reduced overall costs?

21. What is the distinguishing characteristic of a flexible manufacturing system (FMS)?

22. Contrast soft automation with hard automation.

23. What skills are key to the efficiency of an FMS?

24. Besides the setup (software) costs, what other factors may affect the decision to form an FMS?

25. Based on your observations either through employment or tours of manufacturing and service organizations, give an example of each of the following process types:

    a. Continuous flow   e. Manufacturing cell
    b. Repetitive flow   f. Flexible manufacturing system
    c. Batch flow   g. Fixed position
    d. Job shop

26. What is the essential difference between an FMS and a manufacturing cell that is not an FMS?

27. Name and define the six elements of computer integrated manufacturing (CIM). Give an example of how each of these elements are currently integrated within a production system or how you perceive they might be integrated.

28. Describe the difference between economy of scale and economy of scope.

29. What are the basic concepts of good management that serve as building blocks for a well-designed and well-managed CIM system?

30. What driving forces have been pulling and pushing organizations toward CIM?

31. In the CIM environment, the location of decision-making authority tends to change as more powerful equipment and systems become available on the shop floor. Where does it move to and why? What are the results of this move?

32. What changes in the corporate culture result from the CIM environment?

33. What is perhaps the greatest single barrier to the adoption of new manufacturing technologies?

34. Select two of the following service organizations and describe the items (materials, customers, employees, etc.) whose movement should have a major influence on the process.

a. Hospital
b. Restaurant
c. Coronary care unit
d. Insurance claims processing office
e. Airline ticket office
f. University registration

35. A planner has a new item that can be machined either in the traditional shop or on an NC machine. In this case, both the traditional shop and the NC machining center produce acceptable quality, but the machining of each unit will cost $20 more in the traditional shop. Only two items are required, and further orders are unlikely. Capacity is available in both the NC department and the traditional job shop. Where should the order be run? Why? What cost factor is not mentioned?

REFERENCES

Chase, Richard B. "Where Does the Customer Fit in a Service Operation?" *Harvard Business Review* (November–December, 1978).

Dar-El, E. M. "Solving Large Single Model Assemble Line Balancing Problems—A Comparative Study." *AIIE Transactions* 7, no. 3 (1975): 302–310.

Fogarty, Donald W., and Thomas R. Hoffmann. *Production and Inventory Management.* Cincinnati: South-Western Publishing Co., 1983.

Greene, James H. *Production & Inventory Control Handbook* 2nd ed. New York: McGraw Hill, 1987.

Groover, Mikell P. *Automation, Production Systems, and Computer-Aided Manufacturing.* Englewood Cliffs, N.J.: Prentice-Hall, 1987, pp. 119–128.

Gunther, Richard E., Gordon D. Johnson, and Roger S. Peterson. "Currently Practiced Formulations for the Assembly Line Balancing Problem." *Journal of Operations Management* 3, no. 4 (August 1983): 209–221.

Hall, Robert W. *Zero Inventories.* Homewood, Ill.: Dow-Jones Irwin, 1983, p. 61.

Hayes, Robert H., and Steven Wheelwright. "Link Manufacturing Process and Product Life Cycles." *Harvard Business Review* (January–February 1979).

Helgeson, W. B., and D. P. Bernie. "Assembly Line Balancing Using Ranked Positional Weight Techniques." *Journal of Industrial Engineering* 12, no. 6 (1961): 394–398.

Industry Week (March 9, 1987), p. 34.

Minneapolis Star Tribune, September 22, 1987 p.7B

Modern Industry (August 1984), p.77.

Muther, Richard. *Systematic Layout Planning.* Boston: Industrial Education Institute, 1961.

New, C. Colin. "MRP and GT: A new Strategy for Component Production." *Production and Inventory Management* 18, no. 3 (1977): 50–62.

Shostack, G. Lynn. "Designing Services that Deliver." *Harvard Business Review* (January–February 1984).

Spencer, Michael S. "Scheduling Components for Group Technology Lines." *Production and Inventory Management* (Fourth Quarter, 1980): 43–49.

Talbot, F. B., et al. "A Comparative Evaluation of Heuristic Line Balancing Techniques." Working Paper No. 215, University of Michigan, Ann Arbor, Michigan, 1980.

PART III
MEDIUM-RANGE PLANNING

CHAPTER 6
Forecasting

CHAPTER 7
Aggregate, Production, and Resource Capacity Planning

CHAPTER 8
Master Scheduling and Capacity Planning

CHAPTER 9
Facility Layout

CHAPTER 10
Work Design and Measurement

CHAPTER 6
FORECASTING

OBJECTIVES

After completing this chapter, you should be able to

- Understand the reasons for forecasting and the types of data that may be used in forecasts

- Understand various characteristics of a data series and how those characteristics contribute to the quality and accuracy of forecasting

- Distinguish between qualitative and quantitative forecasting techniques and appreciate when each method is appropriate

- Use various quantitative techniques to analyze data series

- Measure forecast accuracy by various techniques and identify methods of improving forecast accuracy and effectiveness

OUTLINE

Introduction
Characteristics of a Data Series
    Sources of Data
    Time Frame and Data Dimensions
    Data Quality and Accuracy
Basic Forecasting Techniques
    Qualitative Techniques
    Quantitative Techniques
        Simple and Moving Averages
        Exponential Smoothing
        Seasonal Indexing or Smoothing
        Extrinsic Forecasting Methods
        Box-Jenkins Method
        Econometric Modeling
Summary of Forecasting Techniques
Forecast Error Measurement and Accuracy
    Bias and Deviation
    Tracking Signals
Conclusions
Questions
Problems
References

INTRODUCTION

Forecasting may be the most widely used, but least understood, activity of the operations manager. The fundamental purpose of forecasting is to reduce, or at least clarify, the uncertainty of a future event or group of events. Forecasting is often misunderstood, however, because everyone, even expert forecasters, has different perceptions of future events and the risks associated with those events. To accomplish the forecast, we may rely on the results of experience or we may make an evaluation of present factors. Ultimately, we must make a decision to accept or modify the forecast and then use it, based on the risks involved.

For example, in most parts of the country it is necessary to check the weather before taking a short trip. The uncertainty is whether or not the weather will change, and the risk is getting caught in the rain or cold. For a short trip, a quick look at the sky, a thermometer, or a barometer would be sufficient, since the risks, or consequences of error, are not too great. However, if the risks were greater, for example, if the trip were longer or involved many people (as a large picnic would), consideration might be given to the weather report, particularly if the weather forecaster had a reputation for accuracy.

This very simplistic example expresses numerous aspects of the sometimes very complex forecasting environment. First, there are many different forecasting techniques available, both qualitative and quantitative. Second, except for the most trivial situations, the forecast is almost always wrong. That is, it does not exactly predict an outcome. Third, the error of the forecast will vary, depending upon the type of situation and the forecasting method used. Fourth, the risks associated with errors of forecasting may also vary. In some cases, forecasts must be very accurate because the risks or costs of errors are high. In other cases, increased accuracy is not worth the trouble.

Most production forecasting systems are built upon extrapolating time series data—that is, an historical record of past activity (sales or use of a product or component) is made and used to project future demand or need. A fundamental assumption of this approach is that the future is related to the past in some (possibly complex) way. Since even in today's rapidly changing environment fundamental relationships still hold, this is a reasonable assumption as long as the look backward is not too far back and the look forward is not too far distant. It does not necessitate that tomorrow be just like today (although in weather forecasting one can observe a very high correlation of just this sort); it only requires a stability of relationships. Some typical time series are shown in Table 6–1. Some of the characteristics to note are the time intervals (weeks, months, years, etc.), the dimensions (units, dollars, kilograms, etc.), and the variability or lack thereof.

The foundation for any production activity is either an actual order or the forecast of an order. However, even in the make-to-order (actual order) case, forecasts are used to maintain inventories of raw materials or component parts and to plan and schedule production. Thus, forecasting is used (1)

Table 6–1 Typical Time Series Data

Weekly Demand for Item 05880—Red Desk Lamp						
Week Number	122	123	124	125	126	127	128
Demand	9	7	8	13	18	22	27

Monthly Shipments of Part 5149—Detergent 127					
Month	March	April	May	June	July	August
Kilograms	10	15	10	25	10	30

Net Sales of XYZ Corporation						
Year	1973	1974	1975	1976	1977	1978	1979
Dollars (in thousands)	437,626	475,998	480,700	641,283	711,193	765,818	802,295

Japanese Imports of Manufactured Goods					
Year	1972	1973	1974	1975	1976	1977
Dollars (in thousands)	6,000	9,200	11,300	9,400	10,900	12,000

Number of Jobs Run per Hour on Computer A					
Time	1000	1100	1200	1300	1400	1500
Quantity	78	85	40	75	105	120

to evaluate future sales volume and operations requirements, (2) to plan for inventories of supplies, raw materials, or component parts, and (3) to estimate facility, equipment, and human resource requirements. Forecasting is thus a key activity of the operations manager in the long and medium range. Because forecasting is most accurate and more focused in the medium range, it is treated here as a medium-range topic, although some applications of forecasting certainly are appropriate in the long range as well. Even so, forecasting is still an art, not an exact science. It can reduce the uncertainty of the future, but it will never eliminate the uncertainty or the risk.

Generally discussions of forecasting focus almost exclusively on techniques, primarily on quantitative techniques. But before discussing those means of manipulating data to yield informative forecasts, let's examine the characteristics of data, including the sources of data, the data's dimensions and time characteristics, and the inherent quality and accuracy of data. Following that, forecasting techniques and forecasting accuracy will be discussed.

CHARACTERISTICS OF A DATA SERIES

Forecasts are used to evaluate a data series. The forecasting process gives a prediction for one or several periods in the future and permits an estimation of the amount of error that can be expected in the forecast. A data series can be defined as three or more observations that are derived in the same manner. Many of the problems associated with forecasting result from difficulties in developing the data. These differences may be found in the source of the data, the time frame of reference or the dimensions of the data, or the accuracy of measurement techniques used.

Sources of Data

Foremost among external data sources are various types of market intelligence, such as survey information, test panel data, and salesforce feedback. Frequently this type of data is considered of questionable value to the operations manager; the fault, however, is often not in the quality or accuracy of the data, but rather in their interpretation and timeliness. Market survey data are primarily obtained to aid in sales, promotion, and service or product introduction decisions. The specific procedures for selecting proper samples, designing questionnaires, and conducting interviews will not be covered in this text. Rather, we wish to point out that since the data obtained by these methods are intended primarily for marketing purposes, they must be viewed carefully, instead of being ignored, in making production decisions. Specific recognition of the time dimensions of the data should be noted; for example, a survey that establishes an intent to increase purchases may be more useful in planning capacity than in establishing schedules. The operations manager should know the characteristics of the sample, not just the number of items the people in the sample say they will purchase. This may shed some light on the mix (size, color, configuration) of the demand—these attributes being more important in determining manufacturing units than in establishing aggregate sales dollar estimates.

Another source of data is salesforce feedback. As salespeople contact customers or potential buyers, they accumulate information about what customers say they want and what competitors are offering, plan to offer, or plan to withdraw from the market. There are several difficulties in using these data for production decisions. Since these types of data are not obtainable in an orderly and regular manner, their comparability to other information is difficult to establish. Does the reported fact that customer X intends to buy 15 percent more next month represent demand over that already scheduled, or does it just compensate for the unreported decline by customers Y and Z? Since it is quite common to use previously forecast sales to set salesforce goals and hence compensation, the incentive exists to manipulate and withhold data to influence personal pay. The nature and extent of these modifications are difficult to determine and control. Thus, the data from this source are often questionable, but not altogether unusable.

One difficulty that sometimes arises between marketing and production is caused by sales promotions or new advertising campaigns. While it is obvious that production should be aware of any such activities, it nevertheless happens sometimes that such activities are not communicated adequately. Perhaps of greater concern is that the effects of such campaigns or promotions cannot be estimated accurately. It is necessary that marketing and operations agree in advance on both a forecast and a schedule in order to share responsibility for those decisions. Of course, once the market forecast is agreed upon, then various operations forecasts (e.g., raw materials, components, capacity and equipment usage, and human resource) are easily developed. Needless to say, changes in the market forecast (e.g., revisions of delivery dates, production volumes, or product specifications) can have serious operational and cost impacts. A mutually agreed upon master production schedule will reduce this kind of problem.

Most market research is intended to yield information about new products, new packages, or new promotion strategies. It is not directed toward ongoing demand for existing products. However, some market research is directed toward detecting fundamental changes in demand patterns. This is often called econometric forecasting and usually addresses itself to aggregate demand for product lines or groups. The techniques often employ very elegant statistical and mathematical methods, but since the underlying relationships are poorly understood, such forecasts are often inaccurate. Also, the time frame and level of detail of such forecasts make them useful in production and warehouse capacity planning, but they are not well suited for scheduling decisions.

Time Frame and Data Dimensions

One source of confusion that is sometimes related to marketing data is that demand is expressed in dollars for certain purposes, while for other purposes, units, kilograms, or meters are required. Care must be exercised in converting data between these dimensions. Cost dollars are not sales dollars; twenty one-liter bottles do not cost or sell for the same amount as forty half-liter bottles, but they do contain the same amount of liquid. Problems arise here because conversion ratios and detailed product mix data may not be available. More importantly, the dollar data may be subject to price changes that have no effect on units demanded.

The other dimensional aspect is time. Total demand is not sufficient for scheduling, since the timing and rate of demand must be accounted for. Often the duration or length of the forecast period will be significant. While it is well recognized that the accuracy of detailed forecasts diminishes when they are projected further ahead in time, it is also true that the exact timing of orders may be difficult to predict even in the short range. Thus, it is probably most easy to predict aggregate demand in the medium range. The significance of this is that explicit recognition of these timing issues should be considered and operations policies established that recognize these timing problems.

For the forecasting systems based on historical data, as most are, the amount of past data available and/or needed is of great significance. For some forecast methods, adaptive exponential smoothing, for example, substantial, data histories may be necessary to get started; but very little information is required to keep the model functioning in the future. When little historical data are available, data on similar or related products may be used.

Another dimensional aspect of data is the level of detail represented. As has already been pointed out with the one-liter versus the half-liter example, aggregate (20 liters) demand data may be satisfactory for some uses but insufficient for others. This conflict is aggravated by the fact that aggregate data are usually easier to forecast than detailed data; hence, forecasts are more often obtained by decomposing aggregate data than by aggregating detailed data. In addition, a number of top-level decisions (work force, plant, cash needs, etc.) can best be made by predicting aggregate dollar sales without detailed unit demand. Table 6–2 shows an example of a relationship between aggregate and composite data. The four model types, A, B, C, and D, have dollar values of $10, $9, $8, and $7, respectively. Demand for each of the models varies considerably from period to period, but the aggregate units of demand per period have a relatively small variation. A careful examination of the dollar values shows that they are growing at a fairly uniform 1 percent per period. Depending on the decisions being made and the technological differences between the models, these data may present a difficult or an easy forecasting problem.

Data Quality and Accuracy

The byword in data processing is GIGO, Garbage In–Garbage Out. This is equally true in forecasting. Not only must we concern ourselves with the validity and appropriateness of the data sources and the physical and time dimensions of the data, but we must control the data for errors and make modifications for changes in price or product.

A most obvious source of errors is in recording data. These errors may regard numeric quantity (recording 71 instead of 11), identification (part

Table 6–2 Aggregate and Composite Data Relationships

Period	Units of Model Type				Aggregate Units of Demand	Aggregate Dollar Value of Demand
	A	B	C	D		
1	28	79	46	91	244	$1,996
2	79	70	49	29	227	2,015
3	82	26	56	76	240	2,034
4	77	77	44	35	233	2,060
5	28	98	79	41	246	2,081
6	87	38	84	31	240	2,101
7	95	56	44	45	240	2,121
8	86	79	35	41	241	2,138
9	68	47	50	94	259	2,161
10	48	63	70	82	263	2,181

SA5Z instead of SA52), or dimensionality (seven dozen in place of seven gross). The data processing system, whether manual or computerized, should be developed to find such errors and correct them or at least point them out for further investigation.

Various techniques, such as check sums, cross tabs, and dual entries (possibly in dollars and quantity), can be built into the data entry system. Verifying that a part number actually exists before accepting an order should be standard procedure. Reasonableness checks should also be used. For example, if order quantities are normally (95 percent of the time) for 50 units or less, then any order in excess of 50 should be questioned. (This type of check would have caught the 71 in place of the 11.) The imposition of such a demand filter to check for reasonable input data will highlight any outliers—that is, values outside normal expectations. Whether these are correct values or errors must be determined through specific examination of each instance. Thus, the operations manager must identify appropriate limits and ranges in various policies and procedures to identify the tradeoffs between (1) spending time looking for nonexistent errors and (2) permitting erroneous data to enter the system.

Many forecasting errors and hence many scheduling errors have been made through failure to recognize the difference between orders and shipments. For example, they differ in timing. Orders precede shipments by the manufacturing lead time or at least by the order filling time. Quantities shipped may be less than quantities ordered, as partial shipments are made over a period of time to fill one order. Shipments may exceed orders because spare parts or allowances for defects are included. Whatever the reason, the distinction between orders and shipments must be taken into account when using historical data for forecasting.

Another factor to consider is that price changes may cause an increase in dollar sales but not an increase in unit sales. Historical variations in unit prices are frequently overlooked, and errors arise because a single conversion factor is used in translating past dollar sales into past unit sales. For example, a price increase from $2.50 to $2.75 last July means that the second six months' sales of $32,000 actually represent a decline from the first six months' sales of $30,000 in unit sales. Similarly, past product changes may have resulted in aggregate shipments that do not reflect constant ratios of component parts and subassemblies. Thus, a package that currently contains five subassemblies of type Z20 may have had three Z20 subassemblies and two Y17 subassemblies six months ago. Care must be exercised in making conversions or erroneous forecasts will result.

To summarize, before forecasting techniques and the accuracy of forecasts can be evaluated, the source and accuracy of the data on which forecasts are built must be examined. No amount of ordinary photographic developing techniques can transform a fuzzy negative into a clear, sharp picture. Similarly, elegant (or simplistic) forecasting techniques applied to poor data cannot yield good forecasts. The first place to look for forecasting inaccuracies is in the quality and accuracy of the source data and the subsequent transformations (e.g., dollars to units) applied to that data. Explicit recognition of the purpose for collecting the data and the inclusion of techniques to point out possible errors will enhance the likelihood of producing good forecasts.

BASIC FORECASTING TECHNIQUES

Forecasting techniques can be divided into two categories: qualitative and quantitative. The former methodology, although it may involve numbers, is basically not mathematical. Qualitative techniques rely on judgment, intuition, and subjective evaluation. Quantitative techniques can be divided into intrinsic and extrinsic. The intrinsic techniques are often referred to as time series analysis techniques. They involve mathematical manipulation of the history of demand for an item; that is, they make use of the historical, period-by-period (time-phased) series of numeric values of the demand for an item. The other group of quantitative techniques, extrinsic, attempts to relate demand for an item to data about another item, group of items, or outside factors (e.g., general economic conditions) to create a forecast for the item of interest.

Qualitative Techniques

Qualitative forecasting has been maligned as a seat-of-the-pants approach. In fact, qualitative forecasting techniques can be very helpful in situations in which other techniques, notably the quantitative methods, are not effective. More specifically, qualitative techniques are normally used to consider long-range, aggregate, and strategic issues. These evaluations are usually concerned with one-time or irregular decisions that integrate diverse, external, nebulous patterns and interrelationships. Decisions pertaining to capital investments, new products, or new markets would normally require an operations manager to use a more qualitative-oriented forecasting approach. Market research, the Delphi method, forecasting techniques for new markets or new products, and management estimation will be considered.

We have previously mentioned some aspects of market research in discussing data sources. The important factor to keep in mind is that, while market research techniques are based on good theory and can yield valuable information for marketing decisions, they are not intended to directly support operations management decisions. An intent-to-buy survey, or a market research project to determine preferred packaging or product characteristics, is intended to support product development and promotion strategies. Data gathered by these methods can and should be considered in some aggregate inventory or capacity-planning decisions, but should not be considered as a market forecast and should not be the sole input for production planning.

The Delphi, or panel consensus, method may be useful in technological forecasting—that is, forecasting, based on expert opinion, the general state of the market, economy, or technology for five years or more into the future. (The name for this method comes from the ancient Greek oracle of Delphi who forecast future events.) The following example demonstrates the process of creating a Delphi forecast.

A panel of futurists is asked the following question: In the next ten years, which consumer products do you envision containing microcomputers as an integral part? Each specialist independently submits a list of items to the panel coordinator. The combined lists are then sent back to each panel member for evaluation and rating of likelihood of occurrence. Panel members may see something that they had not thought of and rate it highly. Members may also have second thoughts about items they themselves previously submitted. This evaluated list is then condensed by removing items not rated highly, and the shortened list is recycled. After a sufficient number of cycles, generally two or three, the result is a list with high consensus and usefulness for new product ideas, long-range corporate strategy, and the like. It is not a suitable technique for short-range forecasting and certainly not for individual stockkeeping units.

When attempting to forecast demand for a new item, there may be a shortage of historical data. One approach to this problem is to look at the historical demand for an analogous product. If the related product is very similar, quantitative techniques may be used; however, if the relationship is tenuous, it may be more appropriate to relate the products qualitatively in order to get an impression of demand patterns or aggregate demand. For example, the seasonal demand pattern for an established product such as ski gloves may be used to estimate the expected demand for ski goggles. The actual levels and trends for the latter cannot be determined in this manner with any precision, but the demand pattern may be similar.

Finally, we must not overlook management estimation (intuition) as a forecasting method. It is widely practiced, often successfully by talented people, with regard to new products or unexpected changes in demand for established product lines. Not everyone has such talent, however. Some studies have shown that a mathematical technique consistently followed will lead to better results than the expert modification of those forecasts. Nonetheless, many mathematical techniques need significant quantities of historical data that may not be available. When substantial data are lacking, subjective management judgment may be better than objective manipulation, poor quality data, or trying to establish tenuous relationships with existing product families.

Quantitative Techniques

Intrinsic techniques use the time-sequenced history for a particular item to forecast future activity for that item. Such a history is called a time series. Some typical time series patterns are shown in Figure 6–1. The characteristics of such series can be graphed, and the algebraic representations can be accomplished as suggested.

Generally a time series can be thought of as consisting of any or all of the following five components: (1) level, (2) trend, (3) seasonal, (4) cyclical,

Figure 6–1 Typical Time Series Patterns

Where D = demand in period x

a = the level or y-intercept

R = the random effect

b = the slope of trended data

S_i = the seasonal effect

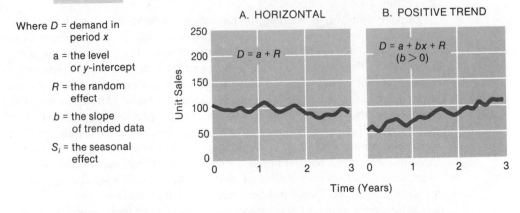

A. HORIZONTAL
$D = a + R$

B. POSITIVE TREND
$D = a + bx + R$
($b > 0$)

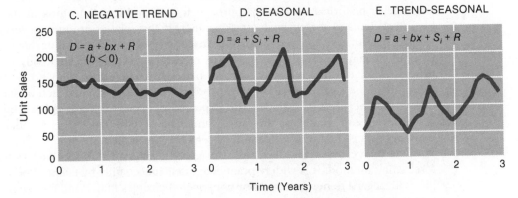

C. NEGATIVE TREND
$D = a + bx + R$
($b < 0$)

D. SEASONAL
$D = a + S_i + R$

E. TREND-SEASONAL
$D = a + bx + S_i + R$

Time (Years)

and (5) random (or irregular). These components are sometimes represented as $L, T, S, C,$ and R, respectively. In other words, the components that give rise to a particular pattern of demand consist of an average demand or level that may be modified by a trend, which may be further modified by a seasonal or cyclical phenomenon, all of which are somewhat muddied by a random, irregular, or otherwise unpredictable variation.

While a series is actually only a set of point values, it is common to connect those points and thus imply continuous variables. For example, quantities are really 6, 8, and 104; not 5.917, 8.003, and 104.172. Time is expressed in whole days or weeks, not in fractions thereof. This is of significance in trying to determine aggregate demand, in converting forecasts to orders, and in interpolating for values between two points in time.

While it may seem straightforward to use the approach of determining each component of the series (sometimes referred to as decomposition) that is not always possible or practical. It is a lot easier to create the series given the components than it is to deduce the components given the series, as can be seen by examining Table 6–3. This section will use several methods to separately decompose the level, trend, and periodicity (or cycle) of the data.

Table 6–3   Table of Typical Time Series For One Year

Week	1	2	3	4	5	6	7	8	9	10	11	12	13
Quantity	42	63	115	250	59	83	143	279	69	75	117	184	357
Week	14	15	16	17	18	19	20	21	22	23	24	25	26
Quantity	61	93	158	307	46	75	150	279	54	65	108	137	298
Week	27	28	29	30	31	32	33	34	35	36	37	38	39
Quantity	49	70	115	238	40	51	86	200	37	37	70	81	180
Week	40	41	42	43	44	45	46	47	48	49	50	51	52
Quantity	29	49	72	143	46	67	107	203	51	75	112	149	237

SIMPLE AND MOVING AVERAGES.   Perhaps the simplest of all time series forecasting techniques is a simple average. To use this method, we calculate the average of, say, three periods of actual demand and use that to forecast the next period's demand. For example,

$$F_4 = \frac{D_1 + D_2 + D_3}{3}$$

This average forecasts the demand for period 4. To forecast period 5, each average is moved ahead one period each time, and this adjustment is referred to as a moving average. The number of periods to use in computing the average may be two to twelve or more, with three or four periods being common. If the time series is a level series, like that in Figure 6–1A, then this is a satisfactory technique from an accuracy standpoint. However, if there is any trend or seasonal effect, a moving average will not work very well because it lags behind any changes. This is illustrated in Figure 6–2. Note also that the moving average requires a start-up period where no forecasts are available.

On the assumption that the most recent actual data are more indicative of the future than older data, a weighted moving average can be computed. A typical equation for this might be

$$F_4 = \frac{2D_1 + 3D_2 + 5D_3}{2 + 3 + 5}$$

or simply

$$F_4 = .2D_1 + .3D_2 + .5D_3$$

Weighting factors can be any values, and the denominator is the sum of the weights. The average is moved just as in a simple moving average method. As a comparison, examine Table 6–4 and Figure 6–3. Note that the error for each forecast has been computed as demand minus forecast $(D - F)$, and the sum of the errors has been computed to give a comparison between the simple moving average and the two weighted average examples. In this case,

Figure 6–2   Moving Average Lags Behind Actual Data

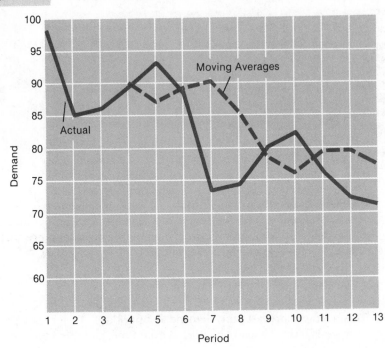

the second weighted average gives the least total errors, although that may not always be the case. On this basis, the forecast of 76 might be selected.

A major difficulty in using moving averages to forecast thousands of different items is that $N - 1$ periods (N being the number of demand periods used in the average; three in our example) of data must be retained, and N multiplications, $N - 1$ additions, and 1 division must be performed for each forecast. This amounts to a great deal of data and many calculations. Additionally, moving averages are easy to compute and good for the level data series; but they are usually less accurate because they forecast behind the movement of trend or seasonal data.

EXPONENTIAL SMOOTHING. Probably the most popular method for forecasting is exponential smoothing. Simple or first-order exponential smoothing can be viewed several ways. One approach is to build a forecasting technique based on the forecasting errors. If the forecast, F, for period n is F_n and the actual demand for period n is D_n, then one can forecast the next period as being F_n plus some fraction, α, of the current error ($D_n - F_n$), or

$$F_{n+1} = F_n + \alpha(D_n - F_n)$$

Table 6–4   Comparison of Moving Averages

Period	Actual Demand	3-Period Moving Average		3-Period Weighted Average Weights—2,3,4		3-Period Weighted Average Weights—1,5,9	
		Forecast	Error	Forecast	Error	Forecast	Error
1	98						
2	85						
3	86						
4	89	90	− 1	88	1	86	3
5	93	87	6	87	6	88	5
6	88	89	− 1	90	− 2	91	− 3
7	73	90	−17	90	−17	90	−17
8	74	85	−11	82	− 8	79	− 5
9	80	78	2	77	3	75	5
10	82	76	6	76	6	78	4
11	76	79	− 3	80	− 4	81	− 5
12	72	79	− 7	79	− 7	78	− 6
13	71	77	− 6	76	− 5	74	− 3
14		78		78		76	
Sum of Errors			−32		−27		−22

A much more widely used statement of this same formula is

$$F_{n+1} = \alpha D_n + (1 - \alpha)F_n$$

Since α must be between 0 and 1, simple exponential smoothing amounts to a weighted moving average with the following weights: α, $\alpha(1 - \alpha)$, $\alpha(1 - \alpha)^2$, $\alpha(1 - \alpha)^3$ and so forth. As shown in Table 6–5, the weights decrease rapidly for α values close to 1 and slowly for α values close to 0. In practice, the relationship between α and an equivalent moving average of N periods may be approximated by

$$\alpha = \frac{2}{N + 1}$$

As can be noted, high alpha values, say .6 and above, cause a great deal of weight to be placed on the current period. To provide stability, forecasters usually choose alpha values between .1 and .3. The value of .3 is usually used for relatively turbulent data, and alpha values closer to .1 are favored for more stable data. As suggested by the preceding formula, a formula using an alpha value of .3 is roughly equivalent to a simple moving average with five

Figure 6–3 Relation of Actual to Moving Averages

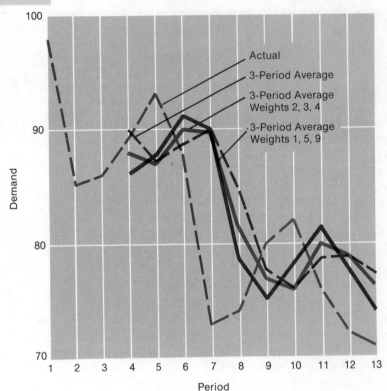

periods, and an alpha value of .1 closely relates to the moving average with about twenty periods.

The problem with simple exponential smoothing is that, as with any simple averaging technique, it lags behind changes in the series. To compensate for this, several methods have been devised to permit adjustment for trend. Simple differencing merely forecasts based on the difference between the current actual observation and the prior observation. Simple differencing works

Table 6–5 Decreasing Weights for Older Time Periods

Period	1	2	3	4	5
Weights	α	$\alpha(1-\alpha)$	$\alpha(1-\alpha)^2$	$\alpha(1-\alpha)^3$	$\alpha(1-\alpha)^4$
$\alpha = .9$	.9	.09	.009	.0009	.00009
$\alpha = .6$	.6	.24	.096	.0384	.01536
$\alpha = .3$	.3	.21	.147	.1029	.07203
$\alpha = .1$	.1	.09	.081	.0729	.06561

well if there is a stable trend in either direction. The formula for simple differencing is

$$F_{t+1} = D_t + (D_t - D_{t-a})$$

where a is some number to identify the lag.

If the trend shifts sharply, the forecast is often very bad for several periods. To protect the forecast against such rapid shifting of data, the difference can be smoothed in the same way as exponential smoothing. The forecasting results of the single exponential smoothing and the simple differencing with $a = 1$ are noted in Table 6–6.

SEASONAL INDEXING OR SMOOTHING. The third component of a data series is the seasonal movement, that is an annual pattern, whether stated in observations (or periods) of 365 or 360 days, 52 weeks, 12 months, or 4 quarters per year. The index method of evaluating seasonality uses the following four steps to develop a seasonally smoothed or revised series, which can then be used with other forecasting methods:

1. Identify the cycle of the data
2. Identify the difference between the observations and a centered moving average (or similar method)
3. Find the common index for each period
4. Smooth the data by factoring out, or deseasonalizing, the seasonal effect

Table 6–6 Exponential Smoothing and Differencing

Period	Actual	$\alpha = .1$ Forecast	$\alpha = .1$ Error	$\alpha = .3$ Forecast	$\alpha = .3$ Error	Differencing, $a = 1$ Difference	Differencing, $a = 1$ Forecast	Differencing, $a = 1$ Error
1	98.00							
2	85.00	98.00	− 13.00	98.00	−13.00	−13		
3	86.00	96.70	− 10.70	94.10	− 8.10	+ 1	72	+ 14
4	89.00	95.63	− 6.63	91.67	− 2.67	+ 3	87	+ 2
5	93.00	94.97	− 1.97	90.87	2.13	+ 4	92	+ 1
6	88.00	94.77	− 6.77	91.51	− 3.51	− 5	97	− 9
7	73.00	94.09	− 21.09	90.46	−17.46	−15	83	−10
8	74.00	91.98	− 17.98	85.22	−11.22	+ 1	58	+16
9	80.00	90.19	− 10.19	81.85	− 1.85	+ 6	75	+ 5
10	82.00	89.17	− 7.17	81.30	0.70	+ 2	86	− 4
11	76.00	88.45	− 12.45	81.51	− 5.51	− 6	84	− 8
12	72.00	87.21	− 15.21	79.86	− 7.86	− 4	70	+ 2
13	71.00	85.68	− 14.68	77.50	− 6.50	− 1	68	+ 3
14		84.22		75.55			70	
Sum of Errors			−137.84		−74.55			+12

These steps are shown in Table 6–7. Columns 1 and 2 identify the data and the periodicity of the data, as in Step 1. Columns 3 through 5 provide a centered moving average, and Column 6 finds a proportional difference for each observation from that centered moving average in Step 2. Steps 3 and 4 are accomplished in Columns 7 and 8, respectively.

The series of thirteen observations shown in Table 6–7 represents quarterly data. Columns 3 through 5 develop a centered moving average using the normal four-period moving average technique (appropriate because this is quarterly data). The actual center of a four-quarter average falls between two of the quarters; for example, the average for quarters 1, 2, 3, and 4 actually falls at 2.5. To center each average on a quarter, Column 3 is shifted back by 1/2 period and Column 4 is shifted forward by 1/2 period. Column 5 averages Columns 3 and 4. This process gives a moving average of the data that is exactly centered on the time period of that data. As with any moving average, data are lost at the beginning and end of the series, so values can only be calculated for quarters 3 through 11. Column 6 computes the seasonal index value for each quarter by taking the ratio of the original data to the centered moving average, or Column 2 divided by Column 5. Column 7 finds the average of the seasonal index values in Column 6 for each quarter. The values for quarters 3, 7, and 11, for example, represent the third quarters of three consecutive years. The seasonal index for the third quarter is $(.968 + .908 + .995)/3 = .957$. Similarly, the first, second, and fourth quarter values are averaged. Column 8 gives the smoothed, or deseasonalized, value of the data, found by dividing the actual data by the seasonal index. Forecasting this seasonally smoothed data using a three-period moving average and simple exponential smoothing ($\alpha = .3$) gives the results shown in Table 6–8.

Deseasonalization improves the accuracy of the exponential smoothing forecast and has no effect on the three-period simple moving average forecast (compare the sum of errors from Tables 6–4, 6–6, and 6–8). Note that the forecast values for Period 14 should be factored by the appropriate seasonal index when using this method. In actuality, at least two years of data are required to develop accurate seasonal component factors from intrinsic data. However, several years of data are desirable in order to sort out random variations (e.g., weather pattern fluctuations from year to year) within these factors. Furthermore, the pattern would have to be stable over that period. If the trend itself were increasing, a single value would not suffice. Obtaining sufficient data to do this may not be possible if the average life of a product is less than three years. The result is that seasonal factors are often determined for a family of items by assuming groupings based on judgments. In addition, the accuracy of the data and the large random components for individual items, which work to cancel each other out when aggregated over a family of items, tend to make these decomposition techniques appropriate for high-level forecasts and aggregate planning only.

This example suggests that forecasting methods can simultaneously

Table 6–7   Seasonal Indexing

1 Period (Quarter)	2 Actual Series	3 4-Quarter Moving Average Shifted Back 1/2 Quarter	4 4-Quarter Moving Average Shifted Forward 1/2 Quarter	5 Centered 4-Quarter Moving Average Column 5 = (Column 3 + Column 4)/2	6 Ratio of Original Data to Centered Moving Average Column 6 = Column 2 ÷ Column 5	7 Seasonal Index Column 7 = Column 6 Average for each Quarter	8 Deseasonalized Value Column 8 = Column 2/Column 7
1	98					1.047	93.60
2	85					1.052	80.80
3	86	89.50	89.50	88.875	.968	.957	89.86
4	89	88.25	88.25	88.625	1.004	.976	91.19
5	93	89.00	89.00	87.375	1.064	1.047	88.83
6	88	85.75	85.75	83.375	1.049	1.052	83.65
7	73	82.00	82.00	80.375	.908	.957	76.28
8	74	78.75	78.75	78.000	.949	.976	75.82
9	80	77.25	77.25	77.625	1.031	1.047	76.41
10	82	78.00	78.00	77.750	1.055	1.052	77.95
11	76	77.50	77.50	76.375	.995	.957	79.41
12	72	75.25	75.25			.976	73.77
13	71					1.047	67.81

Table 6–8 Forecasting with Seasonally Adjusted Data

Period	Actual	Simple Moving Average 3-Period Forecast	Error	Simple Exponential Smoothing ($\alpha = .3$) Forecast	Error
1	93.60				
2	80.80			93.60	−12.80
3	89.86			89.76	0.10
4	91.19	88.09	3.10	89.79	1.40
5	88.83	87.28	1.55	90.21	− 1.38
6	83.65	89.95	− 6.30	89.79	− 6.14
7	76.28	87.88	−11.60	87.95	−11.67
8	75.82	82.92	− 7.10	84.45	− 8.63
9	76.41	78.58	− 2.17	81.86	− 5.45
10	77.95	76.17	1.78	80.22	− 2.27
11	79.41	76.72	2.69	79.54	− 0.13
12	73.77	77.92	− 4.15	79.50	− 5.73
13	67.81	77.04	− 9.23	77.78	− 9.97
14		73.66		74.79	
Sum of Errors			−31.57		−62.67

Note: To compute the first forecast of the three-period moving average, add 93.60, 80.80, and 89.86 and divide by 3 (264.26/3 = 88.09). This is the forecast for the fourth period. For the simple exponential smoothing with $\alpha = .3$, the actual data for period 1 are used to forecast period 2. Then the forecast for period 3 is 93.60 (.7) + 80.80 (.3) = 89.76

address several components of the data. To further illustrate this, let us construct a set of underlying factors and then observe the resulting time series. First, let us pick an initial level of 100 units per week; then we will presume that this is increasing at a rate of one unit per week, its trend. A possible seasonal pattern is shown in Table 6–9, where the numbers represent the fraction of total annual demand that occurs each month. Remember that if there were no seasonal or trend effect 8.33 percent (1/12) would be demanded each month. Thus, the seasonal index values are computed in this method as the ratio of the monthly percentage to 8.33 percent and are shown in the third column of the table.

Within each month demand is not uniformly distributed so that the cyclical factors are as shown in Table 6–10. (The cyclical index is the function of monthly demand divided by 25 percent.)

The irregular component causes about a plus or minus ten-unit fluctuation each week. Using these factors, we can construct a time series by the following process. Considering only level and trend, the first week's demand will be 100, the second 101, the third 102, and the fourth 103, for a cumulative total of 406. Since January represents 10 percent of the total (from the seasonal factor table), January base demand will be multiplied by a factor of 1.20 to

Table 6–9   Seasonal Demand Factors

Month	Fraction of Total Annual Demand	Seasonal Index
January	.10	1.20
February	.11	1.32
March	.12	1.44
April	.11	1.32
May	.10	1.20
June	.09	1.08
July	.08	.96
August	.06	.72
September	.05	.60
October	.04	.48
November	.06	.72
December	.08	.96

adjust for seasonality. Similarly, taking into account the cyclical factors, by week the demand will be as shown in Table 6–11.

With the additional modification for random fluctuations, actual demand may be as follows:

Week	Quantity
1	42
2	63
3	115
4	250

You may recognize this as the series that was initially presented in Table 6–3. Mathematically, this process is based on a combination multiplicative and additive model of the following sort:

$$D = (L + T) \times S \times C + R$$

Table 6–10   Cyclical Demand Factors

Week	Fraction of Monthly Demand	Cyclical Index
1	.10	.40
2	.15	.60
3	.25	1.00
4	.50	2.00

Table 6–11   Computation of Demand

Period	Trended Demand	×	Seasonal Factor for January	=	Seasonal Demand	×	Weekly Cyclic Factor	=	Trend/Seasonal and Cyclic Adjusted Demand
1	100		1.2		120		.4		48
2	101		1.2		121.2		.6		73
3	102		1.2		122.4		1.0		122
4	103		1.2		123.6		2.0		247

where D is demand and L, T, S, C, and R represent level, trend, seasonal, cyclical, and random components respectively.

Winters has developed another exponential smoothing type model that applies the smoothing concept more broadly (Winters 1960). It incorporates in one equation the separately defined average, trend, and seasonal factors. The smoothed, deseasonalized value, A_t, is

$$A_t = \frac{\alpha D_t}{S_{t-L}} + (1 - \alpha)(A_{t-1} + T_{t-1})$$

where L is the length of the season (number of periods per year). Trend is updated by

$$T_t = \beta(A_t - A_{t-1}) + (1 - \beta)T_{t-1}$$

and seasonality by

$$S_t = \frac{\gamma D_t}{A_t} + (1 - \gamma)S_{t-L}$$

The forecast for period m is then

$$F_{t+m} = (A_t + mT_t)S_{t-L+m}$$

Note that different smoothing coefficients (α, β, and γ) may be used in these relationships. While the computations for this seem much more complex than for simple smoothing, the technique has proved feasible in practice and appears to work well, particularly if computers are used for computational support.

EXTRINSIC FORECASTING METHODS. The previously discussed methods were designed to quantitatively evaluate historical patterns intrinsic to the data (the components) and then use those to develop the forecast. Alternatively, extrinsic forecasting methods use a second series of data, which is chosen because it moves in a pattern similar to the first series, to forecast the data. The simplest method is often referred to as *trend line analysis*. In its most elemental form, trend line analysis involves two series; the dependent series or variable (that to be predicted) and the independent series or variable (the predictor). Each observation consists of two values, a dependent variable y and an independent variable x. The trend line involves plotting each pair of data, then visually estimating a straight line that shows the general upward or downward trend in the data. For example, if the average weekly demand for food items at a local convenience store was based on the number of people living within one mile, the observations in Table 6–12 could be plotted as shown in Figure 6–4.

A more sophisticated approach is to compute the slope and y-intercept of the line that most closely represents the data by using linear regression. This technique calculates a best (in a statistical sense) line by selecting a line in such a manner as to minimize the differences between the observed values and the corresponding values on that line.

If we compute the average x value and the average y value, we can then plot a line that passes through that point. Regardless of the slope of that line, we will find some observed values above it and others below it. If we add those differences, they will sum to 0 no matter what the slope of the line is. To get the best line, we must minimize the sum of the squares of the differences. When this is done, we can then use the familiar statistical measures of standard deviation and variance to make statements about the accuracy of our forecasts. This is true as long as certain statistical assumptions hold true (e.g., the series is stable and the random component is normally distributed.)

The specific model we use has $\hat{y}$ as the estimate of y, and its equation is

$$\hat{y} = a + bx + r$$

Table 6–12   Trend Line Analysis

Demand (Y variable)	Population (X variable)
34	3
43	4
51	5
54	6
62	7
70	8
73	9
80	10
90	11
97	12

Figure 6–4 Scatter Diagram and Trend Line

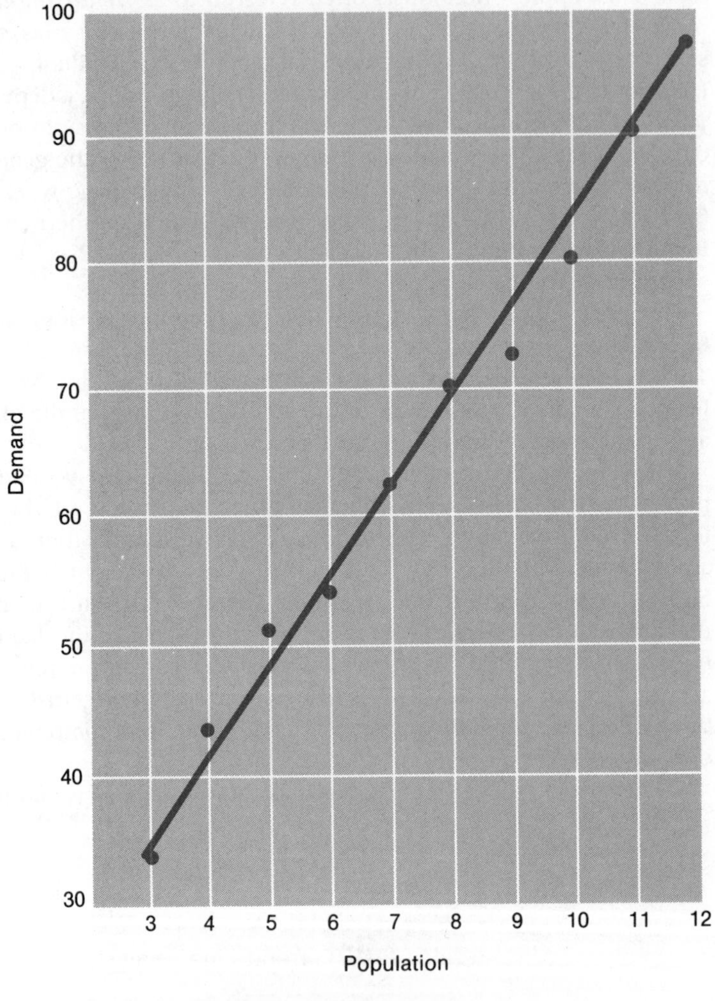

where r is a random component. We estimate a and b by

$$b = \frac{(n \sum xy) - (\sum x \sum y)}{(n \sum x^2) - (\sum x)^2}$$

and

$$a = \bar{y} - b\bar{x}$$

where the $x's$ and the $y's$ are the observed values, $\bar{x}$ and $\bar{y}$ are their respective means, and n is the number of observations. The computations for these equations are given in Table 6–13. Substituting in the equations for a and b, the following occurs:

$$b = \frac{10 \times 5,458 - 75 \times 654}{10 \times 645 - 75 \times 75} = \frac{54,580 - 49,050}{6450 - 5625}$$

$$b = \frac{5,530}{825} = 6.703$$

and, therefore,

$$a = \frac{654}{10} - 6.703 \times \frac{75}{10} = 65.40 - 50.27$$

$$a = 15.13$$

Thus, our equation is

$$\hat{y} = 15.13 + 6.703x$$

This line passes through the mean of the x and y values.

From Table 6–13, the mean of x ($\bar{x}$) is 75/10 or 7.5 and the mean of y ($\bar{y}$) is 65.4. Substituting $\bar{x}$ in the preceding equation

$$\hat{y} = 15.13 + 6.703 \times 7.5 = 65.4 = \bar{y}$$

It is also true that the sum of the differences between the y's and the corresponding $\hat{y}$'s is 0 or without bias. (The sum of differences in Table

Table 6–13 Computation of Regression Line Coefficients

	x	x^2	y	y^2	xy	$\hat{y}$	$y - \hat{y}$
	3	9	34	1,156	102	35.239	−1.239
	4	16	43	1,849	172	41.942	1.058
	5	25	51	2,601	255	48.645	2.355
	6	36	54	2,916	324	55.348	−1.348
	7	49	62	3,844	434	62.051	−0.051
	8	64	70	4,900	560	68.754	1.246
	9	81	73	5,329	657	75.457	−2.457
	10	100	80	6,400	800	82.160	−2.160
	11	121	90	8,100	990	88.863	1.137
	12	144	97	9,409	1,164	95.566	1.434
Totals	75	645	654	46,504	5,458		−0.025

6–13 is −0.025 because of rounding effects.) Compared to any other line that might be drawn through the data, this is the one for which the sum of the squares of the differences is least. Thus, linear regression is called the *best linear unbiased estimator.*

Closely related to regression analysis is statistical correlation. If two phenomena are observed to move in the same or opposite directions consistently, whether that direction be up or down or back and forth, they are said to be correlated. This does not mean that one causes the movement of the other, but only that they are related. An example might be that whenever the gross national product (GNP) of the United States moves up 1 percent, the Jones Company sales increase by $40,000. Conversely, whenever there is a similar drop in GNP, sales decrease by approximately a corresponding amount.

It is often helpful to have a measure of the amount of variance explained by the regression line. The coefficient of determination (r^2) measures the percent of variance of the dependent variable, which is explained by the variance of the independent variable. A coefficient of determination of .8 or .9 indicates that 80 or 90 percent of the variance is explained and that there is a strong linear relationship between the x and y variables. If a coefficient of determination is .3 or less, it would suggest that much of the relationship between x and y is unexplained. In that case, the regression line would not have strong predictive power and perhaps another predictor should be used. The formulation and computation of r^2 using the data in Tables 6–12 and 6–13 is as follows:

$$r^2 = \frac{(n \sum xy - \sum x \sum y)^2}{(n \sum x^2 - (\sum x)^2)(n \sum y^2 - (\sum y)^2)}$$

$$r^2 = \frac{(10 \times 5,458 - 75 \times 654)^2}{(10 \times 645 - (75)^2)(10 \times 46,504 - (654)^2)} = .967$$

Regression analysis thus finds the best linear relationship between two variables and then identifies the strength of that relationship by measuring the error around that line. But we need not limit this relational concept to just one variable (say, spare parts) tied to one other variable (machines sold). We can extend this to include many factors. For example, spare parts demand could be a function of machines sold, dollar cost of the machines, fraction of that cost represented by the part's cost, and expected useful life of the machine. In this case, spare parts demand is the dependent variable and all of the others are the independent variables. A whole body of knowledge is devoted to this concept of multiple regression and correlation. Further, there are numerous methods of defining the regression relationship as nonlinear using various exponential or logarithmic curves. Such techniques can be very useful if (1) the indicators, or independent variables, lead the dependent variables by enough time so that one can take action, (2) correlation is strong, and (3) data are available. Primarily these techniques are useful at aggregate planning levels.

BOX-JENKINS METHOD. In studying time series data, evidence often shows that when sales are up one month they are up the next month also. Such a situation—the relationship of one period's increase (or decrease) to a subsequent period's increase (or decrease)—is called *autocorrelation*. The periods need not be successive, that is, January and March may move together. The direction of movement need not be the same; for example, an increase in July may mean a decrease in August. Because this relationship is generally true in examining the time series for a particular item, it taints the purity of the mathematical assumptions underlying regression analysis. However, it also provides a powerful tool for forecasting time series—for example, the Box-Jenkins method.

In regression analysis, or in exponential smoothing for that matter, it is necessary to postulate an underlying model such as

$$y = a + bx$$

or

$$y = a + bx + cx^2$$

In the Box-Jenkins approach the autocorrelation between observed values for various time lags—that is, the relationship between adjacent values, those separated by two periods, those separated by three periods, and so on—is examined. The mathematical procedure for doing this is quite complex and can only be done effectively with a computer, but the accuracy can be very good. Regardless of whether there are trend, seasonal, or cyclical factors present, if sufficient data are available (more than one cycle), the coefficients relating the time-spaced values can be determined. Generalized statistical software, such as Minitab, and other special programs are becoming increasingly available to facilitate use of this powerful technique (Ryan, Joiner, and Ryan 1976).

ECONOMETRIC MODELING. One other method that deserves mention is econometric modeling. Econometric modeling, as its name implies, is most often used in forecasting aggregate economic measures such as the GNP. The basic concept is to develop a set of regression equations relating various factors in the economy and then to solve these equations simultaneously, either by analytical methods or simulation, in order to forecast economic developments. Although the number of equations may be large, numbering in the hundreds, the accuracy of the forecasts is not particularly good because the true causal, as opposed to correlation, relationships are not known. However, these models are useful in examining the direction of change that may occur at macroeconomic levels.

SUMMARY OF FORECASTING TECHNIQUES

Forecasting then is used to reduce risk by using one or several qualitative or quantitative techniques to project intuition or historical data toward future events. Table 6–14 provides a summary of forecasting methods, their description, and a time frame of usage. Note that the quantitative techniques are generally of use in the short range, while the qualitative methods may be longer range in nature. It is also worth noting that the appropriate techniques can be expected to vary over the life cycle of a product, as shown in Figure 6–5. The use of qualitative techniques dominates the beginning and end of the product development cycle, while quantitative techniques prove most useful during the production phase.

FORECAST ERROR MEASUREMENT AND ACCURACY

As the various forecasting methods were presented, the sum of error as a measure of forecast accuracy was computed. However, that measure is only a very tenuous evaluation because it does not consider the effects of data errors, modeling errors, or negative and positive errors canceling each other. Additionally, it does not consider the number of error observations or whether the errors are generally high or generally low. Each of these factors can be measured and can affect the validity and usefulness of the forecast.

Error is generally measured in two ways, (1) as bias and (2) as deviation. *Bias* is defined as a tendency of the forecast to be either consistently higher than or consistently lower than the actual observation. For example, recall that the moving average methods always forecast behind the trend—that is, below an increasing trend and above a decreasing trend. Thus, the moving average is inherently biased below the actual data in the case of the increasing trend and above the actual data in the case of the decreasing trend. Alternatively, *deviation* measures address the amount that the forecast is in error, whether in a positive or negative direction. Deviation was noted as the difference between the forecast and the actual in the preceding discussion. Thus, bias is the direction of the error and deviation is the amount of that error. As you might expect, there are several different ways to measure bias and deviation.

It is common to label all differences between actual and forecast values as errors. But this is like saying that all poor performances, be they in games, the classroom, or life, are mistakes. Sometimes poor forecasts (those with serious errors), like poor grades, are because of lack of knowledge; other times errors are due to inherent difficulties in the task. Once in a while they are caused by real mistakes, such as adding 2 and 2 to get 5.

We should recognize real errors. These have been discussed previously in

Table 6–14 Summary of Forecasting Methods

Method	Description	Time Horizon
Qualitative		
Market Surveys	Questionnaires and panels used to anticipate customer behavior	Medium to Long Range
Delphi	Experts answer series of questions (anonymously), receive feedback, and reach a consensus	Long Range
Historical Analogy	Forecast from comparison with similar product whose history is known	Short to Long Range
Sales Force Estimates	Composite of field salespeople's estimates	Medium Range
Management Intuition	Knowledgeable managers prepare forecast	Short to Long range
Quantitative		
Decomposition	Time series is divided into level, trend, seasonal, cyclical, and random components	Short Range
Moving Average	Forecast is a simple average of *n* most recent periods; may be weighted average	Short Range
Exponential Smoothing (including various multiple smoothing methods)	Forecast uses exponentially weighted factors to consider level, trend, seasonal, and random series	Short Range
Regression and Correlation	Forecast via a least-squares equation (regression) or via close association (correlation) with an explanatory variable; may use multiple factors	Short to Medium Range
Box-Jenkins Method	Autocorrelation effects are used	Short Range
Econometric Modeling	Uses simultaneous multiple-regression equations that relate broad range of economic activity	Medium range

Figure 6–5   Forecasting Methods and Product Life Cycle

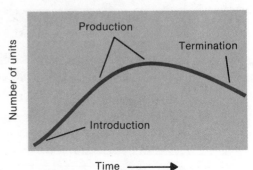

Introduction
Data: No time series history;
             rely on qualitative methods
Time: Need medium and long horizon
Methods: Judgment, Delphi, and
             historical analogy are useful;
             market surveys important

Production
Data: Data increasingly available
Time: Still need long horizon; trends important, but trends change only gradually
Methods: Market surveys and historical analogy useful
             Tracking product history important

             Quantitative methods useful.
             Regression with leading indicators possible.
             Exponential smoothing very useful.

Termination
Data: Abundant data (but not necessarily pertinent to decline)
Time: Shorter horizon
Methods: Judgment, historical analogies, and market surveys may signal changes

talking about data quality on the input side of forecasting. The same comments can be extended to cover recording the dimension errors and the use of wrong values in preparing a forecast. These are real errors that must be eliminated.

Errors also occur when the wrong model is selected to match the series it is to forecast. For example, if the true series is actually a level demand affected only by random fluctuations, then use of a higher-order model that incorporates a trend and a change in the trend, for example, will cause the forecasting model to amplify each random fluctuation, since it is looking for a trend and a change in trend that does not really exist. Any mismatch between the model and the series can thus be viewed as a true error that should be eliminated. However, this is often difficult because we do not really know the nature of the real-world phenomena we are trying to forecast.

Another type of error is caused by the random component of the process that is generating the time series. Thus, the observed error reflects the true variability of the underlying process, something that cannot be forecast and for which we must accommodate. The statistical distribution of these errors may contain valuable information about the process and may be used to establish contingency plans to deal with an uncertain future.

The problem in labeling all these differences as errors, whatever their cause, is that the forecasting system is too often the scapegoat for inadequate actions in other areas. For example, controlling the variability of suppliers in meeting delivery dates and specified quantities may be overlooked as a way of reducing forecast errors. Similarly, improving quality control on a production process may not be seen as a way to improve forecasts of shipping quantities.

On the other hand, it should be pointed out that many forecasting systems fail to explicitly use forecast errors to improve future forecasts. In contrast to moving average systems, exponential smoothing averages can feed back into the forecast the forecast error, as noted in the $(D_n - F_n)$ formulation.

The use of forecast errors lies in two directions. One is to permit the improvement of the forecast itself, including selection of the correct model, use of proper coefficients in that model, and elimination of real errors. The other direction is as a measure of the uncertainty in the future caused by inherent fluctuations in the process that generated the time series. The use of this latter measure in developing plans and procedures for dealing with forecast errors will be covered in later chapters concerning such topics as setting safety stocks, revising schedules, and planning capacity changes.

Bias and Deviation

The sum of errors computation is useful in computing the bias, which is often defined as mean error, or

$$\text{Bias} = \frac{\sum (D - F)}{n_e}$$

This is the sum of errors divided by the number of error observations. This definition of bias is probably the most widely used, although bias can also be defined as mean percent error. The bias will show the amount that a particular forecast method will overforecast (forecast is high) or underforecast (forecast is low). The bias is very important in some cases. Consider, for example, the situation of a public administrator forecasting the number of swimmers at a public beach in order to schedule lifeguards or the number of police or fire calls for which to schedule available protection. The risk of forecasting too high, and thus scheduling too many employees (slightly higher overall operating costs), is small compared with the negative results of not having enough lifeguard, police, or fire protection to handle the uncertain future events. Thus, the administrator would probably desire a forecast method that usually overforecasts rather than one that usually underforecasts.

Alternatively, consider a real estate sales organization predicting the number of new condominiums that will be sold in a certain community. The sales organization would want to underforecast because of the relatively high costs of financing an unsold house compared with the relatively low costs of delaying a closing date for a customer. These risks and costs make every forecasting situation unique, and thus forecasting is an art, not a precise science.

The deviation is normally measured by the mean absolute deviation, or MAD. Other measures of deviation are the mean absolute percent error (MAPE) and mean square error (MSE). The mean absolute deviation is defined as

$$\text{MAD} = \frac{\sum |D - F|}{n_e}$$

Often, however, an exponentially smoothed MAD is used, of the form

$$\text{MAD}_t = \alpha|e_t| + (1 - \alpha)\ \text{MAD}_{t-1}$$

where $|e_t|$ means the absolute value of the error. All errors, regardless of sign, contribute to the total. Thus, the MAD reflects variability of the forecast from the actual demand. Table 6–15 shows the bias and MAD values for some of the models explained in this chapter.

Not including the regression computation, which uses a different series, the seasonally smoothed simple moving average gives the lowest MAD and the differencing method gives the lowest bias. Note also that the MAD and the bias are equal in absolute value in the two cases where the error is entirely negative (exponential smoothing, $\alpha = .1$; seasonally smoothed exponential smoothing). At this point the forecaster must decide whether bias or deviation is more important in terms of the risk of the decision. Then the forecaster must decide if the present results are worth the time and effort or if the method should be improved. In these decisions, the forecasting process becomes more an art than a science.

Tracking Signals

Tracking signals are designed to provide an evaluation of the forecast over the range of the forecast. Of course, a comparison of the forecast and the actual value, or the error of a particular observation, could be made, but then the signal might be readily tripped by an error in the information collection system. Tracking signals provide an evaluation of the forecast error that has been smoothed over several observations. As with many forecasting techniques, several different computational approaches have been developed, but they usually use either the smoothed error or the running sum of the current error (RSCE) as the numerator and some computation of the absolute error as the denominator. A widely used formulation (Wheelwright and Makridakis 1985) is the smoothed error tracking signal, which consists of two smoothing equations and a tracking signal as follows:

$$E_t = \alpha e_t + (1 - \alpha)E_{t-1}$$

$$M_t = \alpha|e_t| + (1 - \alpha)M_{t-1}$$

$$T_t = \frac{|E_t|}{|M_t|}$$

Table 6–15 Forecasting Bias and Deviation

Table	Method	Sum of Errors	Number of Error Observations	Bias	Absolute Error Sum	MAD
6–4	3-period moving average	− 32	10	− 3.2	60	6.0
6–4	3-period weighted moving average (2,3,4)	− 27	10	− 2.7	59	5.9
6–4	3-period weighted moving average (1,5,9)	− 22	10	− 2.2	56	5.6
6–6	Exponential smoothing ($\alpha = .1$)	− 137.84	12	− 11.4	137.84	11.4
6–6	Exponential smoothing ($\alpha = .3$)	− 74.85	12	− 6.23	80.5	5.7
6–6	Differencing	− 12	11	− 1.09	74	6.7
6–8	Seasonally smoothed simple moving average	− 31.57	10	− 3.16	50.99	5.1
6–8	Seasonally smoothed exponential smoothing	− 62.67	12	− 5.19	65.68	5.4
6–13	Regression	− .025		− .0025		1.44

Table 6–16 Measures of Forecast Errors

Actual	Forecast	Current Error e_t	Absolute Error $|e_t|$	Smoothed Error E_t $\alpha = .3$	Smoothed Absolute Error M_t $\alpha = .3$	$T_t = \dfrac{E_t}{M_t}$
150.00	153.00	−3.00	3.00	− .9	6.33	.14
146.00	155.00	−9.00	9.00	−3.33	7.13	.46
156.00	147.00	9.00	9.00	+ .37	7.69	.05
152.00	145.00	7.00	7.00	+2.36	7.48	.31
145.00	155.00	−10.00	10.00	−1.35	8.24	.16
146.00	154.00	− 8.00	8.00	−3.35	8.17	.41
153.00	148.00	5.00	5.00	− .85	7.22	.12
157.00	146.00	11.00	11.00	+2.71	8.35	.32

Mean absolute error (MAE) = 7.75; M_0 = MAE; E_0 = 0

Examples of the tracking signal computations shown in Table 6–16 follow:

$$E_1 = .3(-3.0) + .7(0) = -.9$$

$$M_1 = .3(3.0) + .7(7.75) = 6.33$$

$$T_1 = .9/6.33 = .14$$

Note that the value of M_0—the mean absolute error (MAE)—is usually calculated after five or more periods.

Table 6–16 shows the computation of the current error and the absolute error. The smoothed error and the smoothed absolute error are computed next. The tracking signal is the smoothed error divided by the smoothed absolute error. A common application of the tracking signal uses an upper or lower limit of confidence. If the tracking signal exceeds some specified value, this suggests that a fundamental change has taken place in the series. The forecaster should then either search for the cause by reevaluating the nature of the error and the fit of the forecast technique or by treating the errant tracking signal as a temporary aberration that will quickly be corrected. For $\alpha = .3$, a 95 percent confidence interval is defined by a tracking signal less than or equal to .69. For other tracking signal values, see Wheelwright and Makridakis (1985).

CONCLUSIONS

This chapter has considered several very important aspects of improving forecasting accuracy. Initially, the source, dimensions, and quality of the series were considered. Then, the components of a series were introduced, and various qualitative and quantitative methods were described. Finally, measures of accuracy or fit of the forecast to the series were suggested.

Certainly, these concepts are fundamental for a good forecast. Failure or omission in any one of these areas can result in a forecast that seriously misrepresents the future. However, there is a further requirement for a good forecast. Currently, available computer software offers numerous programs that can reduce the tedium of the forecasting process to merely data input and printout interpretation of the results. Unfortunately, these mechanical enhancements of speed and accuracy tend to bypass one of the most important aspects of forecasting—that is, the human involvement and intimacy of the forecaster with the series. A forecaster must develop a feel for the data; a subtle, integrated, and proactive appreciation of the factors that will influence the series. No amount of quantification can provide this intuition; it must be gained through careful observation and study. It is this developed perception of the series that is truly an art, and this is why forecasting is so widely misunderstood.

QUESTIONS

1. What are the categories of forecasting techniques? Generally, how do they differ from each other?

2. What is the purpose of forecasting?

3. Why is forecasting important in a made-to-order environment?

4. Forecasting is more accurate and more focused in which range of planning?

5. Define the term *data series*. Give an example of a data series with which you are familiar.

6. What are the common problem areas in developing the data for forecasting? Give an example of each.

7. Why is it inherently important for the marketing and production functions to work closely in planning? Give three examples of how operational costs can be affected by changes in the marketing plan.

8. What is econometric forecasting? How might econometric forecasting be used in the production functon?

9. What is a demand filter?

10. Why is it important for the operations manager to identify the appropriate limits and ranges for data inspection?

11. Explain why it is important that a distinction be made between orders and shipments when using historical data for forecasting?

12. How might variations in the selling price of a product or service affect a forecast? Give an example.

13. What types of criteria for evaluation can be employed in the qualitative method of forecasting?

14. Compare and contrast the intrinsic and extrinsic techniques of quantitative forecasting.

15. Qualitative methods of forecasting are more appropriately used for what type of issues? Why?

16. What is the Delphi method? How might this technique be applied at your workplace or school? What might the results be?

17. When might the intuitive management estimation or expert modification method of forecasting be better than a quantitative method of forecasting?

18. What is a coefficient of determination? In what way does the value of the coefficient of determination suggest the predictive power of a regression line?

19. Why is it useful to calculate the error of a forecast?

PROBLEMS

1. Monthly sales (in thousands of units) of the new talking teddy bear are as follows:

Month	Units
1	12
2	14
3	15
4	15
5	17
6	21

    a. Plot these observations.
    b. Estimate the best technique for determining an accurate forecast for month 7.

2. Monthly demand (in thousands) for component parts is as follows:

First Year		Second Year	
Month	*Demand*	*Month*	*Demand*
1	10	1	12
2	8	2	11
3	7	3	11
4	4	4	8
5	5	5	10
6	9	6	17
7	12	7	22
8	19	8	27
9	25	9	32
10	29	10	33
11	19	11	21
12	15	12	19

    a. Plot these observations.
    b. Estimate the best method of forecasting future demand.

3. Recordland, a local audio store, has had monthly sales (in thousands) as follows:

Month	Sales
April	$23
May	25
June	25
July	24
August	28
September	30

    a. Using a simple average of the six values, forecast October's sales.
    b. Calculate a two-period moving average forecast for the months June through October.
    c. Calculate a three-period moving average forecast for the months July through October.
    d. In your estimation, which is better and why?
    e. Forecast July through October sales employing a weighted moving average using weights of .2, .3, and .5 respectively for the earliest through the latest period.

    f. Compute the mean absolute deviation and bias for part c.

    g. Compute the mean absolute deviation and bias for part e.

    h. Which is the best forecast; the three-period moving average or the three-period weighted moving average? Why?

4. The score and the number of points by which the Bears have won or lost (− indicates a loss) their last six games are as follows:

Bears	Opponents	Difference
30	22	+ 8
24	28	− 4
41	21	+20
7	32	−25
21	14	+ 7
14	3	+11

    a. Forecast the average number of points the Bears score against their opponents.

    b. Forecast the average number of points the opponents score against the Bears.

    c. Using a two-period simple moving average, forecast the score and the points difference for the Bears' next game.

    d. Forecast the score and the points difference for the Bears' next game using a three-period simple moving average.

    e. Using a three-period weighted moving average, forecast the score and the points difference for the Bears' next game (weights of .2, .3, and .5).

    f. Using a three-period weighted moving average, forecast the score and the points difference for the Bears' next game (weights of .05, .25, and .7).

5. The City College copier usage for the first six months of the year is as follows:

Month	Number of Copies (in thousands)
January	78
February	77
March	79
April	77
May	82
June	83

    a. Forecast the usage for April through July using a three-period weighted moving average. Use weights of .1, .3, and .6.

    b. Forecast the usage for April through July using a weighted moving average. Use weights of 3, 6, and 9, by adjusting the weights to sum to 1.

    c. Calculate the bias and mean absolute deviation for parts a and b.

    d. Which forecast is more accurate? Why?

6. The monthly demand (in hundreds of gallons) at Robinson's Ice Cream Parlor is as follows:

Month	Demand
1	37
2	39
3	40
4	43
5	45
6	49

    a. Calculate the forecast and error for months 4 through 7 using a three-period moving average.

    b. Use the exponential smoothing technique to calculate the forecast and error for months 4 through 7 ($\alpha = 0.1$).

    c. Follow the directions from part b ($\alpha = 0.3$).

    d. Follow the directions from part b ($\alpha = 0.5$).

    e. Which of the forecasting methods is best? Why?

7. Your local pharmacist is attempting to forecast the demand for a very expensive heart medication. She places a large order at the beginning of each month, for which she receives an added discount for quantity purchases. The pharmacist is attempting to maintain an adequate supply of the medication while not overstocking, because she can better invest the inventory dollars in other necessary medications. Demand for the current year is given at the top of page 206.

    a. Calculate a three-period moving average forecast and error for April of the current year through January of the following year.

    b. Calculate a three-period weighted moving average for the same periods as in part a using as weights .2, .3, and .5, respectively.

    c. Calculate a three-period weighted moving average for the same periods as in part a using as weights 1, 3, and 6, respectively.

    d. Which method gives the least sum of errors?

    e. Calculate the bias and mean absolute deviation for all three methods of forecasting.

    f. Based on the calculation of the bias and mean absolute deviation, which forecasting technique is best for this situation? Why?

Month	Bottles of 100 Sold
January	80
February	95
March	87
April	82
May	97
June	94
July	89
August	82
September	87
October	72
November	94
December	89

8. The data below represent the weekly ridership (in thousands) for the Jackson Street bus route. The Transit Authority wants to forecast ridership for week 13 to facilitate the scheduling of drivers and maintenance.

Week	Actual
1	36
2	39
3	35
4	39
5	40
6	43
7	40
8	43
9	44
10	43
11	46
12	47

a. Prepare a forecast and calculate the error for periods 2 through 13 using simple exponential smoothing with $\alpha = 0.1$.
b. Follow the directions from part a, but use $\alpha = 0.3$.
c. Follow the directions from part a, but use $\alpha = 0.5$.
d. Compare the forecasts from parts a, b, and c. Which forecast is the best? Why?
e. Prepare a forecast and calculate the error for periods 2 through 13 using the differencing technique.

9. The Johnson Company's sales record has exhibited seasonal tendencies. Last year's sales are listed by quarter as follows:

Quarter	Sales
1	$15,000
2	40,000
3	35,000
4	10,000

Calculate the seasonal index for each quarter.

10. Next year's sales for the Johnson Company are forecast to be $120,000. Using the seasonal index calculated in Problem 9 above, forecast the demand by quarter for next year's sales.

11. During the past three years, the quarterly guest registration at the Club Caribbe was as follows:

Year	Quarter	Registered Guests (in thousands)
1	1	29
	2	25
	3	16
	4	18
2	1	33
	2	27
	3	17
	4	21
3	1	31
	2	28
	3	18
	4	19

a. Compute the seasonal index for the first year.
b. Compute the seasonal index for the second year.
c. Compute the seasonal index for the third year.
d. Compute the twelve-period seasonal index for all three years.
e. Use a three-period average of first quarter data only to forecast the number of guests registered during the first quarter of the fourth year.
f. Use a three-period average of second quarter data only to forecast the number of guests registered during the second quarter of the fourth year.
g. Use a three-period average of third quarter data only to forecast the number of guests registered during the third quarter of the fourth year.

h. Use a three-period average of fourth quarter data only to forecast the number of guests registered during the fourth quarter of the fourth year.

12. The Department of Agriculture publishes the feed grain price index quarterly. The index is adjusted annually for inflation and is based on the average price of feed grain from 1957 to 1959. The index is used as a basis for government purchases and price supports.

Year	Quarter	Index Price ('57–'59 = 100)
1982	1	95
	2	99
	3	102
	4	93
1983	1	95
	2	98
	3	96
	4	92
1984	1	102
	2	103
	3	98
	4	96
1985	1	93
	2	97
	3	103
	4	105
1986	1	102
	2	99
	3	97
	4	99

Deseasonalize the quarterly data for 1982 through 1986. Use the four-period moving average technique, centering the calculations.

13. The municipality's Bureau of Human Services tracks and forecasts rent rates for apartments within the city limits. The data on page 209 list the average rental rate for apartments during the year. (Hint: Define 1970 as the base year of 0, therefore, 1971 = 1, 1972 = 2, and so forth.) Calculate the rent rate and the standard error of estimate for 1986.

Rent	Year
$140	1970
165	1971
185	1972
215	1973
240	1974
245	1975
250	1976
290	1977
350	1978
450	1979
560	1980
590	1981
610	1982
640	1983
650	1984
660	1985

14. Using the data from Problem 13, calculate the coefficient of determination. Does this coefficient of determination suggest that a high or low percentage of the variance in rent rates is explained by the variance in years?

15. Demand for ski equipment at Eric's Ski Chalet is related to the amount of snowfall in the area. Data pertaining to the real dollar demand for equipment and the measurement of snowfall are as follows:

Year	Demand in Real Dollars (thousands)	Snowfall (feet)
1979	$ 70	11
1980	140	10
1981	135	7
1982	80	5
1983	70	9
1984	125	12
1985	150	6
1986	70	10
1987	140	12
1988	130	6

a. Use linear regression to identify the a, b, and r^2 values.

b. Consider that demand is related not to the present year's snowfall, but to the prior year's snowfall. Use linear regression to identify the a, b, and r^2 values of the relationship between the snowfall each year (from 1979 to 1987) and the dollar expenditures for ski equipment the next year.

16. Data on yearly demand for luxury automobiles (in hundreds of thousands) and a stock market average for those years are as follows:

Year	Luxury Automobile Demand	Stock Market Average
1976	8	925
1977	5	870
1978	7	911
1979	9	979
1980	7	1,017
1981	10	1,058
1982	11	1,275
1983	13	1,215
1984	12	1,370
1985	13	1,416

Use linear regression to compute the a, b, and r^2 values in order to ascertain the relationship between demand for luxury automobiles and a stock market indicator.

17. Monthly demand for automobile headlights (in thousands) as spare parts from the factory is as follows:

	Demand			
	1979	*1980*	*1981*	*1982*
January	232	226	228	219
February	247	239	251	239
March	219	256	268	259
April	211	247	278	277
May	199	231	256	287
June	183	199	217	255
July	167	182	203	242
August	174	185	189	231
September	170	174	181	215
October	169	162	184	202
November	187	177	169	188
December	213	198	188	217

a. Plot the data and evaluate it.

b. Identify a forecasting method that would be effective with this type of data.

c. Using the method chosen, calculate the seasonal index and forecast demand for January, February, and March of 1983.

REFERENCES

Box, George E., and G. M. Jenkins. *Time Series Analysis: Forecasting and Control.* San Francisco: Holden-Day, Inc., 1970.

Brown, Robert G. *Smoothing, Forecasting, and Prediction of Discrete Time Series.* Englewood Cliffs, N.J.: Prentice-Hall, Inc., 1963.

Fogarty, Donald W. and Thomas R. Hoffmann. *Production and Inventory Management.* Cincinnati: South-Western Publishing Co., 1983.

Ryan, Thomas A. Jr., Brian L. Joiner, and Barbara F. Ryan. *MINITAB Student Handbook.* North Scituate, Mass.: Duxbury Press, 1976.

Trigg, D. W., and A. G. Leach. "Exponential Smoothing With an Adaptive Response Rate," *Operational Research Quarterly* (March 1976).

Wheelwright, Steven C., and Spyros Makridakis. *Forecasting Methods for Management.* 4th ed. New York: John Wiley & Sons, 1985.

Winters, P. R. "Forecasting Sales by Exponentially Weighted Moving Averages," *Management Science* (April 1960).

CHAPTER 7
AGGREGATE, PRODUCTION, AND RESOURCE CAPACITY PLANNING

OBJECTIVES

After completing this chapter, you should be able to

- Describe aggregate planning and illustrate the relationship of the business plan, the market plan, and the production plan

- Define and describe production planning

- Define and describe the aggregate planning problem

- Identify the costs relevant to the aggregate planning decision and the effect of different approaches to the problem

- Describe commonly used methods to the solution and control of aggregate planning

- Discuss the relevance of aggregate planning to service organizations

OUTLINE

Introduction
Aggregate Plans
The Business Plan
Resource Requirements Planning
    Resource Profile
    Resource Requirements
    Financial Resources
    Integration of Plans
    Resource Planning in Service Organizations
Aggregate Capacity Planning
    Managing Demand
    Managing Supply
Costs Relevant to the Aggregate Planning Decision
    Inventory Costs
    Production Rate Change Costs
        Facility and Equipment Costs
        Hiring and Releasing Employees
        Overtime and Undertime
        Part-Time and Temporary Personnel
        Subcontracting
        Cooperative Agreements
Aggregate Capacity Planning Models and Decision Techniques
    Trial and Error
    Mathematical Aggregate Planning Models
        Linear Programming
        The Linear Decision Rule
        Goal Programming
        Simulation
Sensitivity Analysis
Controlling the Aggregate Plan
Aggregate Planning in Nonmanufacturing and Service Organizations
Conclusions
Questions
Problems
References

INTRODUCTION

In Chapter 3 we developed the general framework for operations planning within the context of the corporate master plan and the long-, medium-, and short-range planning horizons. Chapter 3 also pointed out that long-range plans concern changes in the services offered, the product line, the marketing plan, and aggregate output levels, as well as major changes in the production process and the acquisition of new facilities and equipment. Long range planning may take place anywhere from one to ten years prior to execution, depending on the nature of the organization. Medium-range planning concerns aggregate employment, inventory, and production levels within long-range planning constraints. Process and layout planning take place in the long, medium, and short range. The more substantial the change or development in the process or layout, the longer the planning horizon. Quality is usually an explicit part of the product, service, layout, and process planning. This chapter examines aggregate planning in the long and medium range, with an emphasis on aggregate production planning. Although long- and medium-range planning activities often overlap, each has distinct characteristics.

AGGREGATE PLANS

The term aggregate planning denotes planning for a group in order to obtain a view of the planned total results. An aggregate plan may encompass a product line; the output of a plant, division, or entire organization; or planned sales in a geographic area. Aggregate financial plans are expressed in dollars and are based on the corresponding sales, production, employment, and inventory plans. All of the latter are expressed in both the appropriate units and dollars. In a large organization the grand aggregate is the total of the aggregate plans for all divisions, incorporating the sales of many different products in many different markets. The example developed in this chapter is relatively simple; there are only three product lines (Groups A, B, and C) and only one market. Aggregate plans are developed in the long range and used through the medium and short range as an overall control and guide for more detailed plans, such as the master production schedule (MPS). On occasion they may be modified in the medium or short range to cope with unforeseen developments such as a plant fire or flood, an energy crisis, or an abrupt shift in demand due to a strike at a competitor or a sharp price decrease by a competitor.

Figure 7–1 illustrates the relationships among marketing and financial planning, production planning, and resource capacity planning, all of which are aggregate plans. It is a more detailed development of Figure 3–1.

THE BUSINESS PLAN

The planned aggregate sales income, the planned cost of sales, and all other planned operating expenses for all products and services per period

Figure 7–1 Output and Capacity Planning and Control

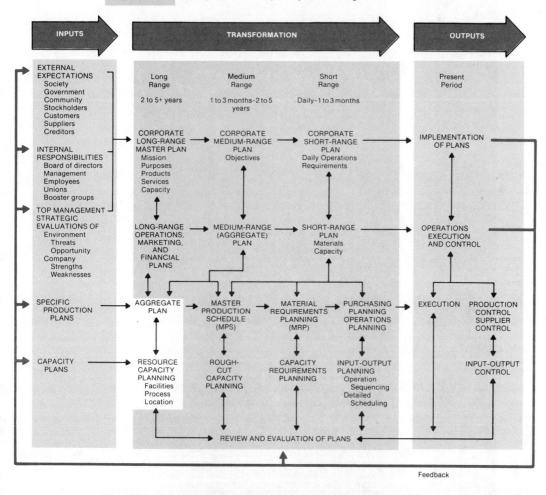

provide a basis for calculating the planned net income of an organization. This enables the organization to calculate the planned return on investment (ROI) or return on assets (ROA) and to estimate what funds will be available for either distribution to stockholders or reinvestment in the organization.

The business plan, the market plan, and the production plan must be consistent and mutually supportive. Table 7–1 uses October data developed from the data in Tables 7–2 through 7–6 to illustrate the relationships among the production plan, the market plan, and the business plan. For example, the planned income is based on planned shipments, the sales prices of the products shipped, the projected cost of sales, and other allocated costs. The market plan projects sales (shipments) of 700 units of Product Group A in October at $45 each, thus generating $31,500 revenue. The total variable and fixed costs allocated to these units is $28,000. Subtracting the total costs from revenue renders a net income of $3,500 for Product Group A in October.

Table 7-1 Relationship Among Market, Production, and Financial Plans

Product Group	Production (Units) Sept.	Production (Units) Oct.	Financial (Dollars)		
A			Cost	$ 40	
			Price	45	
	180	720	Production costs	28,800	
		700	Revenue	31,500	
Production		200	Ending inventory	8,000	
Shipments			Cost of sales	$28,000	Income $3,500
Ending inventory			Change in inventory	800	
B			Cost	$ 33	
			Price	38	
	250	240	Production costs	7,920	
		250	Revenue	9,500	
Production		240	Ending inventory	7,920	
Shipments			Cost of sales	$8,250	Income $1,250
Ending inventory			Change in inventory	−330	
C			Cost	$ 35	
			Price	40	
	50	160	Production costs	5,600	
		110	Revenue	4,400	
Production		100	Ending inventory	3,500	
Shipments			Cost of sales	$3,850	Income $ 550
Ending inventory			Change in inventory	1,750	
				Total income	$5,300

Aggregate Financial Plan

Revenue	$45,400
Cost of Sales	40,100
Income	$ 5,300
Ending inventory	$19,420

216

During that period the planned profit from the sales of Product Groups A, B, and C is $5,300. The natural question is, From where do the income and cost values come? The income of each product group is based on the projected weighted average sales price for the anticipated (forecast) product sales of the items that constitute the group (the product mix); and the total revenue is the the sum of the revenue from all groups. The variable costs of each group are calculated and then added to the other costs allocated to the group to obtain the group's total costs. Summing the costs of all product groups renders the aggregate costs. The net total income then equals the difference between the total revenue and the total costs. (The costs are a natural derivative of the resource requirements planning system, as described in the following sections, and the projected revenue is a natural derivative of the market plan.)

RESOURCE REQUIREMENTS PLANNING

The resources required by the production plan in any period include labor, materials, facilities and equipment (usually identified by work center), and the funds required to pay the employees, purchase the materials, and pay other expenses. (This analysis omits resources required for capital improvements, such as building new facilities, purchasing new equipment, or substantially modifying existing facilities and equipment.)

The resource requirements are determined in the following manner:

1. Obtain the planned production for each product group by period.
2. Determine the resource profile for each product group.
3. Determine the materials profile for each product group.
4. Using the planned production, resource profile, and materials profile, calculate the resource and material requirements.

Resource Profile

The product group *resource profile* states the resources required to produce one unit of a product group. It is based on the anticipated product mix of the group and includes the processing time required for all components and subassemblies, and for the final assembly. Table 7–2 illustrates how

Table 7–2   Assembly Labor For Average Unit
Product Group A

Item	Typical Percentage (1)	Standard Assembly Hours per Unit (2)	Average Assembly Time (1) × (2)
1	.50	.342	.171
2	.30	.294	.088
3	.20	.210	.042
	1.00		.301

assembly labor is determined for Product Group A, which consists of three different items: 1, 2, and 3. The anticipated percentage of each item in the group is multiplied by the standard assembly time for the item; these results are then summed to obtain the standard assembly time for the average item in Product Group A. For example, for Item 1 sales are forecast to be 50 percent of Product Group A total sales and to have a standard assembly time of .342 hours. Multiplying .50 by .342 gives .171 hours. Adding .171 hours to the values obtained in a similar computation for Items 2 and 3 gives an average assembly time of .301 hours for Product Group A as shown in Table 7–2.

Thus, using the information in Table 7–2 concerning the labor (time) required for assembling a typical unit of Product Group A, and similar information for all of the product groups and resource centers, the resource profiles for Product Groups A, B, and C are developed as shown in Table 7–3.

Since all of the processes required to produce a complex assembly and its components must be included and since many of the components must be manufactured a week or so in advance of the assembly activities, the timing of the requirements for various resources must be recognized. This is accomplished using lead time offset information as shown in Figure 7–2. This lead time offset information reveals that the mechanical subassembly is usually completed one week prior to the final assembly and the processing of components in the CNC machining department takes place two weeks prior to the final assembly. This information is especially important when planning on a weekly basis, but it will not affect less-refined plans made on a monthly basis. As an organization achieves just-in-time production (See Chapter 20), most resources will be required in the same week.

Resource Requirements

The standard labor hours required for each product group in a resource center during a period are obtained by multiplying a product group's standard

Table 7–3   Resource Profiles for Product Groups A, B, and C
Average Standard Hours Per Unit

	Standard Hours			
Resource Center	A	B	C	Week
Assembly	0.301	0.285	0.256	1
Electrical subassembly	0.274	0.222	0.241	1
Mechanical subassembly	0.250	0.185	0.241	2
CNC machining	0.112	0.098	0.108	3
Other	0.205	0.182	0.198	
Total	1.142	0.972	1.044	

Figure 7–2   Lead Time Offsets Product 1

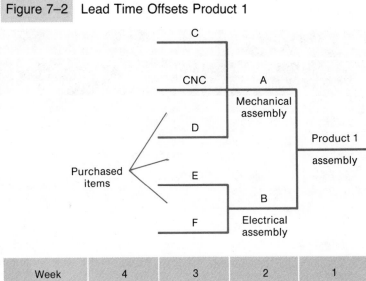

| Week | 4 | 3 | 2 | 1 |

time per unit in the resource center by the quantity of the group to be produced during the period. For example, multiplying the .301 hours required for assembling one unit of Product Group A by the 720 units planned in October renders a requirement of 216.72 standard hours for Product Group A during October in the assembly department. Performing similar calculations for Product Groups B and C and summing the requirements for all groups gives 326.08 standard hours required in the Assembly Department for Product Groups A, B, and C during October. To arrive at the actual hours required, the efficiency of the resource centers must be considered. Efficiency can be measured as follows:

$$\text{Efficiency} = \frac{\text{standard hours}}{\text{actual hours}}$$

which may be transformed to

$$\text{Actual hours} = \frac{\text{standard hours}}{\text{efficiency}}$$

In our example, the efficiency of the Assembly Department is .95; thus the actual total hours required for Product Groups A, B, and C in the assembly department during October is 343.24 hours. The resource requirements for

Table 7–4   Resource Requirements (Standard and Actual Hours in October)

Product Group	Resource Center				
	Assembly	Electrical Subassembly	Mechanical Subassembly	CNC Machining	Other
A	216.72	197.28	180.00	80.64	147.60
B	68.40	53.28	44.40	23.52	43.68
C	40.96	38.56	38.56	17.28	31.68
Total standard hours	326.08	289.12	262.96	121.44	222.96
Efficiency	.95	.95	.95	.95	.95
Actual hours	343.24	304.34	276.80	127.83	234.69

all periods and all departments are calculated in the same manner. These values are shown in Table 7–4.

Although a group of chapters is devoted to the issue of control later in the text, it is important to note that control begins in the planning process as the planned resource requirements are compared to the available capacity as shown in Table 7–5. The available capacity in standard hours is based on the actual output that each department (resource center) has achieved in standard hours of output in the recent past. Table 7–5 reveals that sufficient capacity exists in all departments except assembly. This means that management must take some action to eliminate this imbalance. Possibilities include overtime, adding personnel, or changing the process, such as moving some of the assembly department operations to the electric subassembly department. In this example, management discovers this capacity deficiency shortly before the execution of the plan; however, in most cases this deficiency would have been discovered long ago and remedial action taken.

Table 7–5   Comparison of Required and Available Capacity by Resource Center

Resource Center	Capacity Requirements (Standard Hours)				Available (Demonstrated) Capacity	Deficiencies
	A	B	C	Total		
Assembly	216.72	68.40	40.96	326.08	300	−26.08
Electrical subassembly	197.28	53.28	38.56	289.12	320	
Mechanical subassembly	180.00	44.40	38.56	262.96	280	
CNC machining	80.64	23.52	17.28	121.44	200	

Table 7–6	Total Cost Per Unit

Product Group	Total Standard Hours	Total Actual Hours	Cost of Labor	Cost of Materials	Other* Costs	Total Cost
A	1.142	1.202	$24.04	$7.96	$8.00	$40.00
B	.972	1.023	20.46	5.54	7.00	33.00
C	1.044	1.099	21.98	6.02	7.00	35.00

*Sales and administrative costs.

Financial Resources

The financial resources required are the sum of materials, direct labor, and all other costs. The direct labor costs per unit are equal to the cost of labor per hour times the estimated actual labor hours required. The total cost of labor is $20 per hour, which includes wages and fringe benefits such as insurance, holidays, and vacation. Since 1.142 standard hours are required for the typical unit of Product A (see Table 7–3), the projected actual hours required equal 1.202 (1.142/.95), and the labor cost per unit is $24.04 (1.202 × $20). This information is recorded in Table 7–6 along with the labor requirements and costs for Product Groups A, B and C.

Materials costs are available from the bill of material, which lists all purchased materials and components, as well as their costs (see Chapter 8). The composite cost per unit of a product group is obtained in the same manner as the average labor cost per unit. That is, the typical materials costs of Product Group A equal the weighted average of the materials costs of the three products in the group.

Integration of Plans

Tables 7–7 and 7–8 depict an example of an integrated marketing, production, and financial plan for the next twenty-four months. Table 7–7 gives the shipments (sales), production, and inventory investment in units. Table 7–8 lists the same information, as well as the change in inventory and net income in dollars. Both plans are stated in monthly periods for the next six months and in quarterly periods for the last eighteen months of the two-year plan. It is a common practice to present plans for the more proximate periods in smaller time increments. For example, in the chapters that follow, master planning and rough-cut capacity planning will develop weekly plans for the first few months.

Resource Planning in Service Organizations

Resource planning in service organizations is similar to that in manufacturing and the details differ as much between types of service organizations

Table 7–7 Two-Year Production Plan Product Groups A, B, and C

Period	Month						
	Sept.	Oct.	Nov.	Dec.	Jan.	Feb.	March
Weeks/Period[1]	5	4	4	5	4	4	5
Production Days/Period		20	18	22	19	19	25
Group A Production rate: units/day[2]		36	36	36	36	36	36
Production		720	648	792	684	684	900
Shipments		700	760	850	500	500	875
Ending inventory	180	200	88	30	214	398	423
Group B Production rate: units/day[3]		12	12	12	12	4	4
Production		240	216	264	228	76	100
Shipments		250	300	350	250	60	180
Ending inventory	250	240	156	70	48	64	104
Group C Production rate: units/day[4]		8	8	8	8	20	20
Production		160	144	176	152	380	500
Shipments		110	115	120	180	400	460
Ending inventory	50	100	129	185	157	137	177

[1] The weeks per month in each quarter are assigned arbitrarily as 4, 4.5. For example, April and May have 4 weeks, June has 5. The plant does not close for vacation.

[2] 36 units per day for first three quarters, 40 units per day thereafter; level production throughout the year; rate change due to long-term positive demand trend

[3] 12 units per day September through January, and 4 units per day February through August due to seasonal sales.

[4] 8 units per day September through January, and 20 units per day February through August. These rates increase to 9 and 22 units per day, respectively, due to long-term positive demand trend.

as they do between service and manufacturing organizations. In Chapter 2 we noted that there are three types of service organizations: (1) professional service organizations that provide a high-level professional service to meet a particular need, (2) consumer service organizations that provide a relatively standardized service to the public, and (3) emergency service organizations that respond promptly to an immediate need in widely varying situations. The emergency service organization also possesses characteristics of a professional or consumer service organization to some degree.

Planning personnel resource requirements is important in most service organizations, but it is usually crucial in professional service organizations. This is due primarily to two factors. Level of available personnel is the dominant factor determining the capacity available, and additional personnel usu-

Period	Quarter					
	2	3	4	1	2	3
Weeks/Period	*13*	*13*	*13*	*13*	*13*	*13*
Production Days/Period	*64*	*63*	*60*	*63*	*64*	*63*
Group A Production rate:						
units/day	36	40	40	40	40	40
Production	2304	2520	2400	2520	2560	2520
Shipments	2500	2500	2300	2600	2700	2700
Ending inventory	227	247	347	267	127	−53
Group B Production rate:						
units/day	4	4/12	12	12/4	4	4/12
Production	256	444	720	404	256	444
Shipments	180	370	900	370	180	370
Ending inventory	180	254	74	108	184	258
Group C Production rate:						
units/day	20	22/9	9	9/22	22	22/9
Production	1280	1034	540	1060	1408	1034
Shipments	1340	1060	500	1100	1450	1000
Ending inventory	117	91	131	91	49	83

ally can not be added on short notice. For example, both of these conditions are true in the case of law firms, public accounting firms, and computer software development organizations. This is not to deny the fact that some professional service organizations, such as hospitals, must plan equipment and facility capacity with the same attention given to personnel requirements.

Emergency service organizations have special needs in planning capacity requirements. In particular, they must estimate the maximum number of expected calls during peak demand periods. In addition they must include the maximum time a customer can wait for service, a time that will differ, for example, between emergency medical care and the repair of one of a customer's many copying machines. Other factors are described in the following example.

A service firm involved in field repair and the installation of new units must have information that enables that organization to convert the projected number of service calls and new installations into the equipment (vehicles, testing devices, and other special equipment) and personnel required. Personnel required will depend on estimates of travel time, repair time, installation time, and the organization's objectives concerning how long a customer

Table 7–8 Two-Year Production Plan (Units and Dollars)

Period	Sept.	Oct.	Nov.	Dec.	Jan.	Feb.	March
Group A							
Production		720	648	792	684	684	900
Shipments		700	760	850	500	500	875
Inventory (End)	180	200	88	30	214	398	423
Cost of Sales		$28,000	$30,400	$34,000	$20,000	$20,000	$35,000
Revenue		$31,500	$34,200	$38,250	$22,500	$22,500	$39,375
Profit		$ 3,500	$ 3,800	$ 4,250	$ 2,500	$ 2,500	$ 4,375
Inventory value	$7,200	$ 8,000	$ 3,520	$ 1,200	$ 8,560	$15,920	$16,920
Group B							
Production		240	216	264	228	76	100
Shipments		250	300	350	250	60	60
Inventory (End)	250	240	156	70	48	64	104
Cost of Sales		$ 8,250	$ 9,900	$11,550	$ 8,250	$ 1,980	$ 1,980
Revenue		$ 9,500	$11,400	$13,300	$ 9,500	$ 2,280	$ 2,280
Profit		$ 1,250	$ 1,500	$ 1,750	$ 1,250	$ 300	$ 300
Inventory value	$8,250	$ 7,920	$ 5,148	$ 2,310	$ 1,584	$ 2,112	$ 3,432
Group C							
Production		160	144	176	152	380	500
Shipments		110	115	120	180	400	460
Inventory (End)	50	100	129	185	157	137	177
Cost of Sales		$ 3,850	$ 4,025	$ 4,200	$ 6,300	$14,000	$16,100
Revenue		$ 4,400	$ 4,600	$ 4,800	$ 7,200	$16,000	$18,400
Profit		$ 550	$ 575	$ 600	$ 900	$ 2,000	$ 2,300
Inventory value	$1,750	$ 3,500	$ 4,515	$ 6,475	$ 5,495	$ 4,795	$ 6,195

Table 7–8   Two-Year Production Plan (Units and Dollars) (cont'd.)

Period	Quarter					
	2	3	4	1	2	3
Group A						
Production	2,304	2,520	2,400	2,520	2,560	2,520
Shipments	2,500	2,500	2,300	2,600	2,700	2,700
Inventory (End)	227	247	347	267	127	−53
Cost of Sales	$100,000	$100,000	$92,000	$104,000	$108,000	$108,000
Revenue	$112,500	$112,500	$103,500	$117,000	$121,500	$121,500
Profit	$12,500	$12,500	$13,000	$13,000	$13,500	$13,500
Inventory value	$9,080	$9,880	$13,880	$10,680	$5,080	($2,120)
Group B						
Production	256	444	720	404	256	444
Shipments	180	370	900	370	180	370
Inventory (End)	180	254	74	108	184	258
Cost of Sales	$5,940	$12,210	$29,700	$12,210	$5,940	$12,210
Revenue	$6,840	$14,060	$34,200	$14,060	$6,840	$14,060
Profit	$900	$1,850	$4,500	$1,850	$900	$1,850
Inventory value	$5,940	$8,382	$2,442	$3,564	$6,072	$8,514
Group C						
Production	1,280	1,034	540	1,060	1,408	1,034
Shipments	1,340	1,060	500	1,100	1,450	1,000
Inventory (End)	117	91	131	91	49	83
Cost of Sales	$46,900	$37,100	$17,500	$38,500	$50,750	$35,000
Revenue	$53,600	$42,400	$20,000	$44,000	$58,000	$40,000
Profit	$6,700	$5,300	$2,500	$5,500	$7,250	$5,000
Inventory value	$4,095	$3,185	$4,585	$3,185	$1,715	$2,905

must wait. For example, if an organization that is engaged primarily in the repair of Apple computers changed its market plan and decided to repair IBM and IBM-compatible microcomputers as well, it would be necessary to project the number of additional personnel required, how many of the present staff should be trained to repair the IBM equipment, the additional service parts inventory requirement, and the new vehicles and equipment required. These estimates would be based on the number of IBM-type units the organization plans to service each week.

Consumer service organizations have resource requirement planning situations that are similar to manufacturing in that they have standardized services and relatively high volume. As a result, they can use bill-of-labor and resource profile data as illustrated by the following example.

The market plan of a fast-food restaurant that predominantly serves hamburgers includes the addition of a drive-through service to its existing counter service. This requires facility planning for the addition of a window, a communication system, driving space, and parking space for those waiting for delayed orders. The addition also requires an estimate of the increase in sales volume. If additional sales are projected, additional requirements for preparation, cooking, storage, and refrigeration capacity must be calculated to determine if the facility must be enlarged or modified and if any additional equipment must be purchased. Additional employees will be required to serve at the window, and others may be required for food preparation. Calculating equipment and personnel requirements necessitates evaluating the information available in a bill-of-labor and resource profile. These documents convert output rates (hamburgers and fries per hour) into the number of personnel and machines required to achieve that output rate.

Although aggregate planning is a generic term covering many different plans, references to "the aggregate planning problem" are concerned with the specific decision situation described next.

AGGREGATE CAPACITY PLANNING

The aggregate planning problem concerns the allocation of resources such as personnel, facilities, equipment, and inventory so that the planned products and services (the output) are available when needed. The aggregate plan usually covers a twelve to twenty-four month period; and as time passes, may be updated monthly or quarterly. Prior long-range facility decisions limit the capacity available and may limit aggregate planning options. Thus, long-range facility planning must consider the aggregate planning strategy.

Let's examine the cause of the aggregate capacity planning problem and some approaches for meeting the challenge. Not only do snow-blowers and lawn mowers have seasonal demand, but furniture, appliances, automobiles, clothing, small tools, and many other items have demand with substantial seasonal variation, year after year. Variation in the demand for consumer goods generates seasonal demand for the raw materials, components, and supplies used in their manufacture. Figure 7–3 shows three typical situations: (1) relatively stable demand—bread and milk, for example, (2) single cycle demand, or one high and one low demand cycle annually—retail sales of many items at Christmas, for example, and (3) dual high and low cycles annually—shaving lotion peaks at Christmas and Father's Day for example. Other seasonal variations in demand are possible, but examination of these three patterns will provide a basis for studying the concepts and techniques useful for aggregate planning under all situations.

With relatively steady demand, there is no aggregate planning problem. Facilities, capacity, the work force, and materials are planned for production at that steady rate. However, seasonal demand patterns present management with the following options:

1. Modify or manage demand.
2. Manage supply (output) in the following ways:
   a. Produce at a level rate and store some of the output to meet peak demand (the level production strategy).
   b. Provide ample capacity and flexibility to have the output match demand (the chase strategy).
3. Some combination of 1 and 2.

Figure 7–3 Typical Monthly Aggregate Demand Patterns

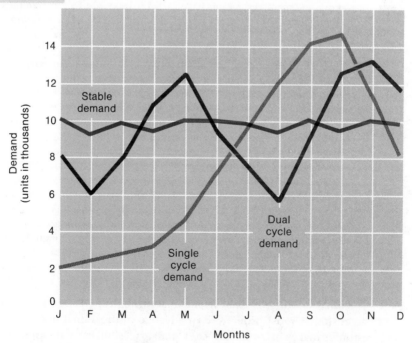

Managing Demand

Changing the demand pattern can reduce the aggregate planning problem and in some cases uncover other sources of income and profit. Possible methods of modifying demand include the following:

1. **Complementary products**. Developing and marketing new products whose primary demand is in the present off-season can reduce the demand-capacity imbalance. For example, some lawn equipment companies have been successful in manufacturing and marketing snow removal equipment, while swimsuit manufacturers have entered the ski-apparel business. Many service organizations have developed complementary services. Examples include heating and air conditioning repair organizations; adding weekend courses and evening continuing education programs at educational institutions traditionally offering only weekday programs; and McDonald's adding a breakfast menu during the morning.

2. **Promotion, advertising, and price incentives.** The right combination of a desired service or product, value for the price, and promotion can increase customer demand in normally slack periods. Major league baseball in the United States has been very successful in using attractions such as glove night and jacket night to increase attendance at games that normally have small- to medium-sized crowds.

   Reduced pricing can shift demand to periods that normally have low demand. Local transit companies offer shoppers reduced bus fares in non-rush hours. Theaters often have reduced prices for matinee and dinner-hour shows, and many restaurants have early bird specials. Other examples include reduced rates for off–season travel and time period differentials in long distance telephone rates. Special financing arrangements may also be used to manage demand. For example, department stores offer November purchasers the option of a late January payment without interest. Similarly, some manufacturers of recreational boats offer retailers the option of later payment without interest for purchases in the preseason months. Thus, the manufacturing company reduces its storage space needs and obtains the sale, while the retailer avoids the financial cost of the inventory and has a better opportunity for early sales to the final customer.

3. **Reservations and backlogs**. Service organizations frequently ask or require that customers reserve capacity by means of an appointment. This could include a reservation for dinner where a specific time is reserved, or a specific space reservation, such as a hotel room or airline seat. This practice enables both the customer and the service provider to plan with greater certainty. In other instances, customers are willing to enter a waiting line for a service. For example, customers often must wait until a restaurant table, service technician, or emergency room physician is available. The service provider agrees to serve the customer as soon as the capacity is available.

Similar conditions exist in manufacturing, especially in a seller's market. The customer must order well in advance of the actual need date. Thus, the customer makes an order for later delivery (similar to an appointment), and the manufacturer produces to a backlog of orders. For example, the Custom Shirt Shop of New Jersey has retail outlets throughout the United States that accept the customer's order with payment; then the factory mails the tailor-made shirts to the customer six to eight weeks later. Using a backlog as a planning approach is feasible only when the customer perceives the quality of the product worthy of the wait—and the cost.

Although modifying demand often makes an important contribution to solving the aggregate planning problem, it rarely solves it completely. Other actions are required to manage the supply so that it meets surges in demand. The primary methods of doing this are described next.

Managing Supply

Two basic strategies represent opposite ends of the spectrum of supply management approaches used in solving the aggregate planning problem. One, the *chase strategy*, is designed to allow for sufficient capacity and flexibility to enable production output to match the demand. Using this approach, the production rate may vary widely, as illustrated in Figure 7–4. The rationale of the chase strategy is to avoid high inventory carrying cost when demand varies substantially by varying employment levels, using overtime, subcontracting,

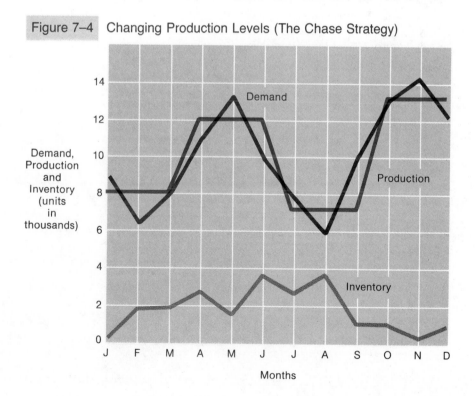

Figure 7–4 Changing Production Levels (The Chase Strategy)

and/or assigning production employees to maintenance or training activities during low demand periods. In some cases, such as agriculture, this is a necessity; harvesting must take place when the crop is ready. It also is a necessity for some service organizations, for example, the hospital emergency room must be able to handle trauma cases as they arrive. However, the chase strategy is not necessary or economically practical in many situations. Examples include situations in which employees have a guaranteed annual wage and those in which equipment capacity is well below the maximum demand rate.

The other end of the spectrum, the *level production strategy*, is designed to allow for the same production rate throughout the year and to have inventory or backorders absorb variations in demand, as illustrated in Figure 7–5. This makes sense when demand is relatively stable; but following this approach in some situations, such as the manufacture of artificial Christmas trees, will result in excessive inventory carrying costs.

Traditionally the aggregate planning problem has been viewed as an analysis of the tradeoff between production rate change costs and inventory carrying costs. (These and other costs will be examined in the next section of this chapter.) However, more flexible manufacturing and service systems that have the ability to change output rates quickly and inexpensively are being developed in many organizations.

Figure 7–5 Level Production Strategy

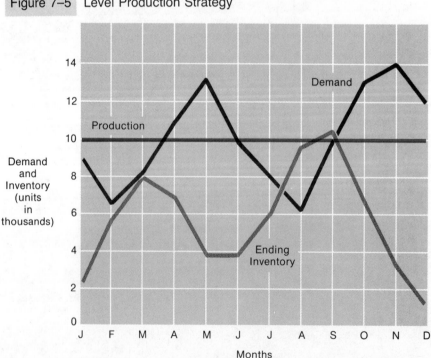

COSTS RELEVANT TO THE AGGREGATE PLANNING DECISION

The costs resulting from the aggregate planning decision fall into two major categories: (1) Inventory costs and (2) production rate change costs.

Inventory Costs

Inventory costs include the following: (1) the costs of carrying inventory and (2) the capital costs of added storage facilities beyond those required for level production. Manufacturing items in one period for sale in later periods during which forecast demand exceeds planned production results in inventory carrying costs. These carrying costs include the costs of storage, capital invested, insurance, taxes for the items held in storage, as well as breakage, deterioration, and obsolescence. In addition, increasing inventory beyond certain levels requires additional storage capacity, which requires additional storage facilities, equipment, and possibly personnel. Furthermore, when working capital requires additional debt, interest rates may be increased due to the altered capital structure of the organization. This, in turn, may increase the carrying cost rate.

Management often views inventory as occupying free space—that is, space not useful for any other purpose. This is misleading. Marion Laboratories, Inc. of Kansas City has reduced its inventory space requirements by over 75,000 square feet through improved inventory management; Miller Fluid Power of Bensenville, Illinois has achieved similar savings. Both companies achieved these savings through increased production flexibility and improved production planning, purchasing, and aggregate planning. Both have also converted this space to income-producing activities. Figure 7–6 depicts the general nature of the inventory costs that affect the aggregate planning decision. Note that carrying costs increase at a constant rate from that point at which inventory exists. Discontinuities occur when additional capacity is required (Point B). As inventory shortages (negative inventory investments) increase, backorder and stockout costs rise exponentially.

Production Rate Change Costs

Production rate change costs include the following items:

1. Facilities and equipment (greater capacity)
2. Hiring and releasing employees
3. Overtime and undertime
4. Part-time and temporary personnel
5. Subcontracting
6. Cooperative agreements

FACILITY AND EQUIPMENT COSTS.   The processing capacity required to match peaks in demand (a chase strategy) is greater than that required

Figure 7–6   Aggregate Inventory Costs

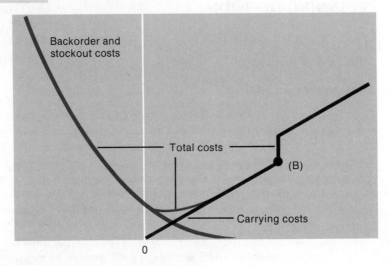

Backorder and
stockout costs

———— Total costs ————

(B)

———— Carrying costs

0

Inventory investment

to maintain a level production rate. This often means that a larger facility and more equipment are required when initiating or changing to a chase strategy than when following a level production strategy. These decisions and costs are usually part of long-range facility planning; thus, they provide de facto policy constraints within which aggregate capacity planning decisions must be made. For example, restaurants have a given number of tables, man-ufacturing plants have equipment with specific processing capabilities and speeds, and elementary schools have a limited number of classrooms and seats. Increasing the facility capacity usually takes longer than one year. The exception is when an existing facility can be purchased and readied for use in a few months. For example, beverage bottling companies occasionally are able to purchase and modify a competitor's plant in a relatively short time. Automobile dealers can often purchase and use the facility of a competitor. Operations managers should be involved in these long-range plans, but in the medium range the option of switching to a chase strategy may not be available.

HIRING AND RELEASING EMPLOYEES.   In some cases, increased capacity requires hiring and training new employees—an expensive activity. There are learning curve effects (see Chapter 10) and new employees usually require more instruction than experienced employees. In general new employees are more susceptible to accidents, more likely to generate scrap, and generally less productive. In a tight market, new employees tend to be marginal and the situation is worsened. Even in a labor market with an abundance of skilled labor, the recruiting, selection, and training costs can be substantial.

Releasing employees increases unemployment insurance and often lowers morale and productivity. Organizations with a policy of seasonal layoffs often have difficulty obtaining the more competent employees. In addition, some labor agreements require the employer to pay furloughed employees a substantial portion of their base pay for periods up to one year.

OVERTIME AND UNDERTIME.   Increasing labor capacity by scheduling overtime avoids the costs of hiring and training and does not increase the total fringe benefit costs for holidays, vacations, and insurance. However, direct costs usually increase due to both premium wages and decreasing productivity rates. This decrease in productivity is especially true when weekly overtime becomes excessive or lasts for more than a month or so. Undertime exists when there are more personnel on the payroll than required to produce the planned output. The costs of undertime can be reduced by having a flexible work force, flexible work rules governing personnel utilization, and appropriate planning. For example, Sunnen Products Company, a St. Louis manufacturer of honing equipment and hones, has avoided layoffs during slack periods for approximately a half century by (1) using production personnel for plant and equipment maintenance and factory layout changes, (2) running smaller production quantities (more setup time), and (3) providing training programs. Sunnen has operated profitably with a no-layoff policy, good wages and benefits, no strikes, and a productive work force.

Flexible employees and flexible scheduling have long been the practice in service industries. For example, although nurses may have a primary assignment, such as the cardiac care unit or the thoracic surgery recovery unit, many are available to switch from their primary assignment to another for which they are qualified, should the need arise. Similarly, many operations management, finance, and other business school faculty members have taught the basic business statistics course when the need arose.

PART-TIME AND TEMPORARY PERSONNEL.   Part-time employment is often beneficial for both the employer and the employee. Many individuals in the work force desire less than full-time employment and fill the organization's need for personnel to work only during peak demand periods. Relatively permanent part-time employees can be effective and efficient members of an organization. Some temporary personnel also return on a regular basis, every Christmas or summer for example, and possess much of the experience and knowledge of permanent full-time employees. Since the wages and fringe benefits of part-time employees are frequently less than that of full-time employees, there is a savings in both hours worked and rate of pay. On the other hand, since temporary and part-time employees have a minimal relationship with an organization, it is difficult to imbue them with a full understanding and appreciation of organizational goals and policies concerning critical areas such as quality and customer service. Inconsistent quality and service from excessive use of poorly trained part-time or temporary personnel can more than counterbalance the cost savings.

SUBCONTRACTING.   Using other firms on a regular basis to perform manufacturing and professional services such as engineering, marketing research, and software development can be an effective method of balancing supply and demand. Subcontractors can be especially valuable when treated as an important link in the production chain. They should be provided with an adequate description of the product requirements, (specifications, quantity, and due date) and production process, as well as assistance with tooling. As trust and confidence develop, subcontractors often suggest improvements in the product design, manufacturing process, or marketing approach.

Subcontracting is a two-way street. Manufacturing companies producing a product for either an industrial market or the general public often subcontract their excess capacity. For example, the Kidder-Stacy Company of Springfield, Massachusetts machines parts for other firms when their machine shop capacity is not utilized fully.

COOPERATIVE AGREEMENTS.   Working agreements based on the sharing of personnel and equipment to meet surges in demand or the need for expertise or equipment possessed by only one or two members of a group of organizations is common. For example, neighboring fire protection districts, hospitals, and police departments often share in providing paramedic services; and electric utilities often have cooperative agreements through power sharing. In addition, many universities offer off-campus courses and programs at community colleges; and some share faculty.

AGGREGATE CAPACITY PLANNING MODELS AND DECISION TECHNIQUES

Many different approaches are available for solving the aggregate capacity planning problem. The more prominent methods include the following:

1. Trial and error or heuristic methods
2. Linear programming cost minimization (LP)
3. Linear decision rules (LDR)
4. Search decision rules (SDR)
5. Goal programming (GP)
6. Simulation

Trial and error is by far the most commonly used method. However, methods 2 through 6 are slowly gaining greater acceptance and they are usually used in conjunction with proven established practices.

Trial and Error

Nearly all organizations have developed a set of aggregate planning rules based on their experience. These rules of thumb vary from firm to firm but often include information and guidelines such as the following:

1. Identify bottleneck work centers and their capacity.
2. Know the point at which overtime produces diminishing results. For example, working the fifth, six-day week in succession is usually followed by at least 25 percent of the work force being absent at least one day in the following week.
3. Avoid reducing the work force below 75 percent of the normal or there will be a permanent loss of skilled and efficient workers.
4. Avoid changing the work force level more than four times a year or the administrative capability of the organization will be overloaded; the industrial relations department has insufficient time for handling grievances, negotiating the labor contract, and promoting labor productivity through cost reduction and profit-sharing plans.

The archetypal trial and error method consists of the following steps:

1. Prepare an initial production plan on the basis of forecast demand and established guidelines.
2. Determine if the plan is within capacity constraints. If not, revise it until it is.
3. Cost the plan.
4. Alter the plan to lower costs, perform steps 2 and 3 on it, and compare the costs of the two plans.
5. Continue this process until a satisfactory plan is developed.
6. Perform sensitivity analysis to evaluate the effect of changes in such parameters as the carrying cost rate, the cost of hiring, and demand.
7. Track the plan (compare actual results to the planned results).

This approach leads to a feasible and satisfactory solution, but not necessarily the optimum one. Frequently the two extreme plans, a level production rate and a production rate that approximates demand, are developed first. Compromises within these extremes are then developed and evaluated.

Trial and Error Example.   First, the cost of the two production plans illustrated in Figure 7–4, the chase plan, and Figure 7–5, the level plan, are determined. Then the costs of the two plans are compared. A later section examines the sensitivity of the results to changes in the values of certain parameters.

The following information is available from the product's resource profile and operating policies. Production is planned in increments of 1,000 units.

1. Stockouts are not permitted.
2. The minimum planned level of inventory is 1,100 units.
3. Unit costs equal $50 (labor = $8, materials = $30, and overhead = $12).
4. Overtime unit costs equal $53.50 (labor = $12, materials = $30, and overhead = $11. 50).
5. Carrying cost rate equals .30 per year per dollar of inventory.
6. Hiring cost equals $600 per worker. (This is a weighted average of hiring and rehiring costs.)
7. Layoff costs equal $200 per worker.

8. Labor cost per hour equals $10.
9. Capacity per worker per month equals 160 hours.

There is a direct ratio of 1:200 between direct laborers and output when production is in the range of 5,000 to 12,000 units per month. That is, one additional worker is required for each additional 200 units produced per month. Overtime must be used to produce more than 12,000 units per month. Since management policy limits overtime to 40 hours per worker per month, the maximum monthly capacity is 15,000 units (12,000 units in regular time + (60 direct laborers × 1.25 units per hour × 40 overtime hours per worker)).

Table 7–9 gives the total cost, $84,125, of the level production plan. The values in the table are calculated as follows:

$$EI_i = BI_i + P_i - D_i$$

and

$$BI_{i+1} = EI_i$$

where:

$$EI_i = \text{ending inventory of period i}$$

$$BI_i = \text{beginning inventory of period i}$$

$$D_i = \text{demand in period i}$$

For example

$$EI_1 = 1,100 + 10,000 - 9,000$$

$$= 2,100$$

Inventory carrying costs are calculated as follows:

$$IC_i = EI_i \times C \times \frac{k}{12}$$

where:

$$IC_i = \text{the inventory carrying cost of period i}$$

$$EI_i = \text{the ending inventory of period i}$$

$$C = \text{the unit cost}$$

$$\frac{k}{12} = \text{the monthly carrying cost rate}$$

Table 7-9   Cost of Aggregate Production Plan I—Level Production

Month	Beginning Inventory (thousands)	Production (thousands)	Demand (thousands)	Ending Inventory (thousands)	Overtime Cost	Production Rate Change Cost	Inventory Carrying Cost
January	1.1	10	9.0	2.1	—	—	$ 2,625
February	2.1	10	6.2	5.9	—	—	7,375
March	5.9	10	8.0	7.9	—	—	9,875
April	7.9	10	11.0	6.9	—	—	8,625
May	6.9	10	13.2	3.7	—	—	4,625
June	3.7	10	10.0	3.7	—	—	4,625
July	3.7	10	8.0	5.7	—	—	7,125
August	5.7	10	6.0	9.7	—	—	12,125
September	9.7	10	9.5	10.2	—	—	12,750
October	10.2	10	13.0	7.2	—	—	9,000
November	7.2	10	14.0	3.2	—	—	4,000
December	3.2	10	12.1	1.1	—	—	1,375
Total	—	120	120.0	67.3	—	—	$84,125

Total cost of level production $84,125

Previous December (Period −1) production level was 10,000 units.

For example

$$IC_1 = 2,100 \times \$50 \times \frac{.30}{12}$$

$$= \$2,625$$

The total cost of the level production plan is \$84,125; consisting entirely of inventory carrying costs. The total cost of the chase plan, in which the planned monthly production equals the forecast demand, is \$76,750 as shown in Table 7–10. The models for calculating these costs and some examples follow.

$$If \ WF_i > WF_{i-1} \ then \ CL_i = 0 \ and \ CH_i = \$600(WF_i - WF_{i-1})$$

$$If \ WF_i < WF_{i-1} \ then \ CH_i = 0 \ and \ CL_i = \$200(WF_{i-1} - WF_i)$$

$$WF_i = P_i/200$$

The maximum value of WF for any period is 60; production from 12,001 to 15,000 units is on overtime.

$$If \ P_i < 12,000, \ then \ COT_i = 0$$

$$If \ P_i > 12,000, \ then \ COT_i = \$3.50(P_i - 12,000)$$

where:

$$P_i = the \ production \ quantity \ in \ period \ i$$

$$WF_i = the \ number \ of \ workers \ in \ period \ i$$

$$CL_i = the \ cost \ of \ layoffs \ in \ period \ i$$

$$CH_i = the \ cost \ of \ hiring \ in \ period \ i$$

$$COT_i = the \ cost \ of \ overtime \ in \ period \ i$$

For example,

$$WF_1 = \frac{9,000}{200} = 45$$

$$WF_2 = \frac{6,200}{200} = 31$$

Table 7-10 Cost of Aggregate Production Plan II—Chase Strategy

Month	Beginning Inventory (thousands)	Demand and Production (thousands)	Change in Work Force	Overtime Cost $3.50 Each	Hiring Cost $600 Each	Layoff Cost $200 Each	Inventory Carrying Cost
January	1.1	9.0	−5			$1,000	$ 1,375
February	1.1	6.2	−14			2,800	1,375
March	1.1	8.0	+9		$ 5,400		1,375
April	1.1	11.0	+15		9,000		1,375
May	1.1	13.2	+5+OT	$4,200	3,000		1,375
June	1.1	10.0	−10			2,000	1,375
July	1.1	8.0	−10			2,000	1,375
August	1.1	6.0	−10			2,000	1,375
September	1.1	9.5	+18− UT		10,800		1,375
October	1.1	13.0	+12+OT	3,500	7,200		1,375
November	1.1	14.0	0+OT	7,000			1,375
December	1.1	12.1	0+OT	350			1,375
Total	—	120	—	$15,050	$35,400	$9,800	$16,500
Total cost of chase strategy							$76,750

Previous December (Period −1) production level was 10,000 units. OT = overtime and UT = undertime.

$$CF_2 = \$200(45 - 31) = \$2,800$$

$$CH_2 = 0$$

$$CF_3 = 0$$

$$CH_3 = \$600(40 - 31) = \$5,400$$

$$COT_{11} = \$3.50(14,000 - 12,000) = \$7,000$$

The other values in Tables 7–9 and 7–10 are calculated in the same manner—with one purposeful exception. The planned increase in production from August to September for the chase plan in Table 7–10 is 3,500 units, which requires the addition of 17.5 workers. Since workers are added as full-time employees, 18 are added. This means that one worker will not be fully employed in October (undertime exists). Therefore, in the following period when an additional 12.5 workers are required, we need add only 12. In addition, the ending inventory is never less than 1,100 units in either the chase or level plan. This is because management is planning a reserve (safety) aggregate stock of 1,100 units to cover the contingency of actual demand exceeding forecast demand. The annual cost, \$16,500, of carrying these units results from that decision and is not affected by the selection of a chase plan, level plan, or some combination of the two. It is a result of the decision concerning the aggregate level of safety stock in the capacity plan.

Since the estimated cost of the chase plan is \$7,375 less than that of the level plan, the next step is to attempt to modify the chase plan and reduce the total cost. Consecutive periods with oscillations in employment levels (April through September, for example) are a logical place in a chase plan to look for a possible cost reduction. One approach for reducing these oscillations is to have only three or four employment levels throughout the year. Table 7–11 gives the cost of a compromise solution that includes only three production levels and less inventory than the level plan. Its total cost is \$66,125; \$10,625 less than the cost of the chase plan.

Plan III, the compromise plan, is the most economical. However, before adopting it some additional questions should be addressed. For instance, could the five workers scheduled for layoff in January and rehiring in March be assigned temporarily to other duties? Also, what is the expected effect of labor force attrition on the costs of the various plans? The level production plan costs \$18,000 more than the compromise plan. If new workers are not hired to replace retirees, those who voluntarily resign, and any who take extended sick or injury leave, what is the expected cost difference? This requires estimates of the probability of these events. (Note that up to this point the cost of replacing workers lost to attrition was treated as the same for all plans).

Table 7–11 Cost of Aggregate Production Plan III—Compromise Solution

Month	Beginning Inventory (thousands)	Production (thousands)	Demand (thousands)	Ending Inventory (thousands)	Overtime Cost	Production Rate Change Cost	Inventory Carrying Cost
January	1.1	9	9.0	1.1	—	$1,000 (−5 workers)	$ 1,375
February	1.1	9	6.2	3.9	—	—	4,875
March	3.9	10	8.0	5.9	—	$3,000 (+5 workers)	7,375
April	4.9	10	11.0	4.9	—	—	6,125
May	3.9	10	13.2	1.7	—	—	2,125
June	.7	10	10.0	1.7	—	—	2,125
July	.7	10	8.0	3.7	—	—	4,625
August	2.7	10	6.0	7.7	—	—	9,625
September	6.7	10	9.5	8.2	—	—	10,250
October	7.2	10	13.0	5.2	—	—	6,500
November	5.2	11	14.0	2.2	—	$3,000 (+5 workers)	2,750
December	2.2	11	12.1	1.1	—	—	1,375
Total	—	120	120.0	47.3	—	$8,000	$59,125
Total cost of compromise plan							$67,125

Previous December (Period −1) production was 10,000 units.

241

Mathematical Aggregate Planning Models

The following sections present an overview of various mathematical aggregate planning models. These models are used by relatively few operations managers on a regular basis. The most common reasons include:

1. Aggregate planning decisions may be dominated by a policy decision, such as a no-layoff policy.
2. A single factor such as a labor contract, available capital, capacity limitations, or product shelf life may dominate the decision.
3. Trial and error methods based on years of experience have developed acceptable decision rules.
4. Much of the literature on mathematical aggregate planning models is written for management scientists and not operations managers.

Although these mathematical models have shortcomings, they can provide management with improved insight concerning a situation and possible opportunities to improve productivity substantially. Thus, the adoption of these modeling techniques is expected to increase gradually as operations managers gain experience with them and as microcomputer software becomes more available.

LINEAR PROGRAMMING. Linear programming (LP) formulations that range from simple to very complex exist for solving the aggregate planning problem. The LP formulation of the problem generally establishes an objective function and identifies constraints on the decision. In aggregate planning, the objective function usually is to minimize the total costs of carrying inventory, changing production rates, subcontracting, and overtime. Typical constraints include the maximum production capacity, the maximum investment in inventory due to either storage or capital limitations, limits on overtime, and restrictions concerning the furloughing or reassignment of the work force. (An example of a relatively simple formulation is contained in Chapter 22.) Shortcomings of the LP approach to aggregate planning include the assumptions that cost functions are both linear and continuous. Both assumptions often are false. For example, the overtime cost per hour may increase as overtime increases due to a decrease in production efficiency. Larger production quantities may result in a lower unit cost at certain points due to quantity discounts or changes in the manufacturing process—justified by the larger quantity. Nonetheless, Greene et al. (1959) have reported that LP models can provide a reasonable estimate of costs in some situations and also provide valuable insights and guidance to management.

THE LINEAR DECISION RULE. Holt, Modigliani, Muth, and Simon raised the level of interest in the aggregate planning problem with their description of the linear decision rule (Holt, Modigliani, and Simon 1955; Holt et al. 1960.) The linear decision rule (LDR) represents the costs associated with production rate changes, inventory, and overtime as quadratic functions of the production and work force level. Linear decision rules for determining the optimum work force levels and production rates are derived by differentiating the aggregate quadratic cost function.

Although this approach was a valuable step in the continued development of aggregate planning models, it has not had widespread industrial acceptance due to certain inherent limitations. First, it requires that cost functions be quadratic for differentiating, and this is often not a valid assumption. Second, it places no constraints on the decision variables, which are in practice frequently constrained.

GOAL PROGRAMMING.   There are usually multiple goals when developing the aggregate capacity plan or master production schedule for the medium range. A typical set of such goals might include the following:

1. The schedule must be within productive capacity.
2. Production should be sufficient to meet demand requirements.
3. Production and inventory costs should be minimized.
4. Inventory investment should not exceed a specified limit.
5. Overtime costs should be within a specified limit.
6. Any decrease in employment levels will be handled by attrition.

Since most mathematical programming methods require that all goals be expressed in a single dimension, these goals either are formulated in terms of dollars or converted into constraints. This approach has two shortcomings: (1) the actual constraints may not be as rigid as indicated in an LP formulation and (2) not all goals have the same priority. For example, there may be no objection to exceeding either the overtime cost or inventory investment limits on occasion if substantial improvements in delivery performance are achieved.

Goal programming overcomes these objections. It allows the different goals to be expressed in their natural form and provides a solution that achieves the goals in priority order. Since some of the goals are in opposition to each other, it may not be possible to achieve all of them. For example, a goal of stable employment may be inconsistent with minimized production costs. Goal programming enables the manager to analyze the deviations from a given goal, which are required to achieve another and to decide how much the organization may deviate from one goal to achieve another.

Lee and Moore (1974) have described the application of goal programming to the development of a schedule for a manufacturer of large electric transformers. The goals and their priorities in that situation were as follows:

1. Operate within the limits of productive capacity.
2. Meet the contracted delivery schedule.
3. Operate at a minimum level of 80 percent of regular-time capacity.

4. Keep inventory to a maximum of three units.
5. Minimize total production and inventory costs.
6. Hold overtime production to a minimum.

The first four goals were achieved. However, overtime production and costs for production and inventory were not kept to a minimum in one month in order to meet the delivery schedule, which is a higher priority goal. Goal programming provides for a straightforward analysis of such tradeoffs.

SIMULATION.   The inherent difficulty of developing a realistic analytical model that is easily solved invites the application of simulation techniques to the aggregate planning decision (see Chapter 23). Analytical aggregate planning models rigidly assume specified relationships between decision variables. For example, some require that costs are linear in relation to the production quantity; others require that the cost-quantity relationship is quadratic; and none allow these relationships to change over the planning horizon. In an actual situation, some costs may vary linearly while others vary in a quadratic relationship to production quantities. In addition, labor and material costs may change over a twelve- to eighteen-month period due to the labor contract and changes in the prices of purchased materials. The arrival of new equipment may be scheduled during the planning horizon, which results in increased setup costs and capacity and decreased unit processing costs. Analytical approaches cannot handle these changes without a prohibitive increase in model complexity.

Simulation enables the planner to formulate a model with different types of cost relationships (linear, quadratic, exponential, etc.) and with costs that change at specific points in time or abruptly at specific production quantities. Thus, simulation models can approximate reality more closely than their analytical counterparts in most situations. Analytical models such as linear programming, however, guarantee an optimum solution—albeit to an oversimplification of reality—while running a simulation model does not guarantee an optimum solution.

SENSITIVITY ANALYSIS

The aggregate production plan is based on a set of forecast demands and costs. They are treated as certain, but that is rarely the case. Important questions to answer include: If the actual demand is higher or lower than the forecast, what penalty will the organization pay in each case? Will the plan selected still be the most economical if the actual production rate change costs and inventory carrying costs turn out to be substantially different from the estimates?

In the latter case, the production planner can use the existing forecast demand and revised estimates, both higher and lower, of inventory carrying

Table 7–12 Sensitivity Analysis for Carrying Cost Rate Change

| Plan | $.30 Carrying Cost Rate | | | $.40 Carrying Cost Rate | | |
	Level	*Chase*	*Compromise*	*Level*	*Chase*	*Compromise*
Inventory	$84,125	$16,500	$59,125	$112,167	$22,000	$78,833
Hire/Fire	—	45,200	8,000	—	45,200	8,000
Overtime	—	15.050	—	—	15.050	—
Total	$84,125	$76,750	$66,125	$112,167	$82,250	$86,833

costs and production rate change costs to determine how sensitive the decision is to changes in these parameters. For example, if the cost of money changes rather quickly and the actual carrying cost per dollar of inventory per year is $.40 instead of the forecasted $.30, then the cost of the three plans described previously in Tables 7–9, 7–10, and 7–11 change as shown in Table 7–12.

The information in Table 7–12 reveals that the compromise plan now costs nearly $5,000 more than the chase plan, whereas it had cost a little more than $9,000 less. Clearly, the economics of the decision are sensitive to a one-third increase in the carrying cost rate. The effect of changes of different degrees and direction, a decrease to 25 cents per dollar of inventory for example, and of changes in other costs can be examined in a similar manner.

CONTROLLING THE AGGREGATE PLAN

Once the plan is implemented and execution occurs, management must exercise control. Rarely are actual production and demand quantities equal to the planned quantities. Comparing actual cumulative demand and production with forecast demand and production enables us to determine if the situation is under control. Either unexpectedly high demand or actual production that is substantially below the planned level will result in insufficient inventories to fill all orders during subsequent peak demand periods. Unusually low demand or production exceeding the plan can result in excessive inventory. Tabulating and plotting actual and planned results enables the planner to determine if the spread between planned and actual requires remedial action.

Case A in Table 7–13 and Figure 7–7 illustrates a situation in which demand for the initial periods is below the forecast, production is as planned, and inventories are becoming excessive. Management must decide if the lower demand levels will continue or if purchases have been postponed and will increase in the future. Case B depicts a situation in which demand has exceeded the forecast for the first few periods, production is as planned,

Table 7–13   Inventory Under Planned, Low, and High Demand

Production Period		The Plan		Case A Decreased Demand		Case B Increased Demand	
Period	Production	Cumulative Demand	Ending Inventory	Cumulative Demand	Ending Inventory	Cumulative Demand	Ending Inventory
1	8	9.0	1.1	8.5	1.6	9.1	1.0
2	8	15.2	2.9	14.0	4.1	16.6	1.5
3	8	23.2	2.9	21.5	4.6	24.8	1.3
4	12	34.2	3.9	31.7	6.4	36.8	1.3

Beginning inventory is 2.1.

Figure 7–7   Effect of Demand Variation On Inventory

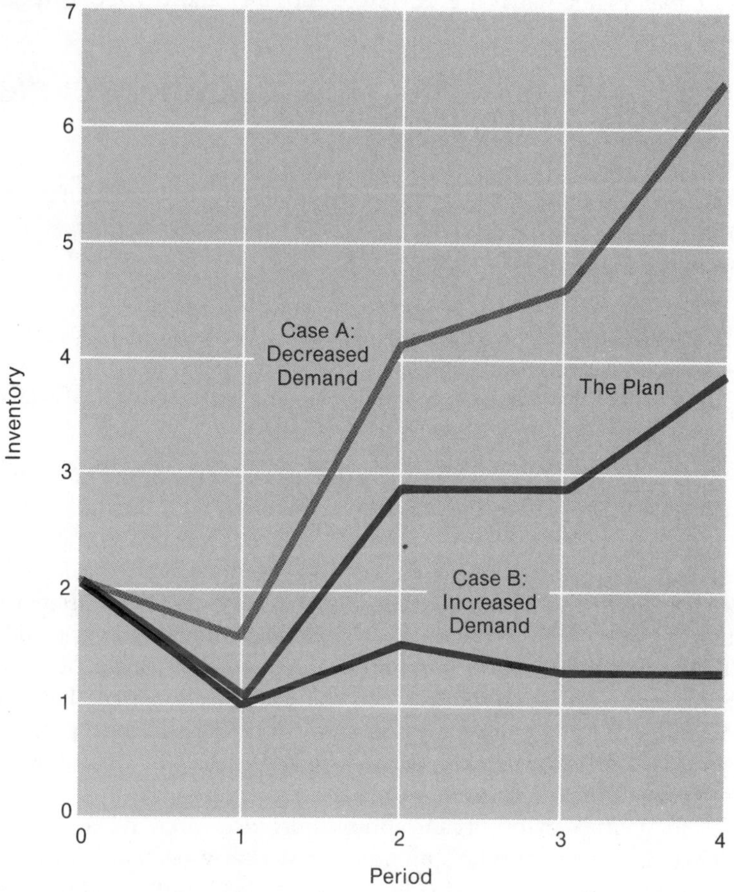

and inventories are precariously low. They are insufficient to meet the fore-cast peak demand in the immediate future. Management must decide if this increased demand will continue or if purchases were made early and demand in the immediate future will be less than forecast.

The point is that the graphs and tables can often alert operations planners and the master scheduler that a significant difference exists between planned and actual demand, production, or inventories. However, the numbers do not in themselves reveal the causes of the difference between actual and planned demand. For example, if increased demand is due primarily to early purchases, no action is required; demand will be less than planned in the near future. If, on the other hand, increased demand is due to a strike at a competitor or the unforeseen development of a new market, the aggregate plan should be increased. This will affect the entire production schedule as noted in Chap-ter 8.

Aggregate planning is a dynamic planning and control device. The aggregate plan is not static; it is reviewed monthly and revised as required.

AGGREGATE PLANNING IN NONMANUFACTURING AND SERVICE ORGANIZATIONS

Medium-range capacity planning problems in nonmanufacturing and service industries differ from those in most manufacturing organizations in one or more of the following ways:

1. Completed products or services usually cannot be stored in inventory.
2. Demand may occur only once a year and in some cases for a relatively short period, or may exist only in a particular season.
3. Demand may vary widely within a month, week, day, or hour with customers expecting a quick response to their needs.

Harvesting of crops and the preparation of income tax returns are once-a-year activities, with the season for income tax preparation perhaps being longer. Harvesting of crops traditionally has been accomplished either by subcontractors (the wheat harvest, for example) moving from area to area as the harvest dates change by climatic conditions. Additional capacity for the harvest often is obtained from longer hours of work and marshaling all the members of a community, most of whom have other occupations. Students and migrant workers also have been part of the harvest task force. Accounting firms work long hours in the tax season, hire part-time workers, and occasionally employ retirees. The key is that the organization must have the capability to increase its capacity in a given period.

In many service organizations there are often three to four cycles of demand: hourly, weekly, monthly, and yearly. Demand in a restaurant, at the front desk of a motel (check-in and check-out), at a bank, at an airline baggage claim, and in a retail establishment varies widely from hour to hour and sometimes from day to day. However, much of this variation follows a predictable pattern. Coping with these variations requires flexible capacity— flexible in that it can be varied throughout the day, week, or month and in that resources can switch from one type process to another without major cost penalties. Most restaurants, catering organizations, nursing divisions, and public works departments have developed rules of thumb for achieving work force and equipment flexibility. Some techniques are common throughout an industry. For example, garbage trucks and other heavy trucks often serve as snowplows in emergencies. Caterers often have a battalion of part-time workers available to serve with a full-time cadre of supervisors during the busy holiday and wedding seasons. Organizations such as amusement parks, the National Park System, and the local swim club all make good use of students who are available in the summer.

Service organizations also can take steps to manage demand—that is, to reduce the hourly capacity requirement variations. There was a time when long lines at bank drive-up tellers would extend into the street and tie up traffic every payday. Banking by mail and direct deposits of paychecks to an employee-designated bank have reduced these lines. Direct deposit of government checks, such as those from Social Security, has also helped. Tennis and racquetball clubs, resorts, and hotels have smoothed demand by offering lower rates and special packages during off hours and days. For example, the lowest airfares frequently require a Saturday flight.

Reservation systems and off-loading techniques also are used to control demand and reduce the level of customer disappointment. The airlines have been successful in reducing ticket and check-in lines immediately preceding a flight through a combination of preticketing and seat assignments, provision of boarding passes by either the airline or a travel agency, and curbside baggage check-in by porters for preticketed passengers.

Another approach is to make the waiting for an available service an enjoyable or at least less disagreeable experience. Restaurants provide lounges (some of which have been known to contribute to the profit margin); and other organizations provide televisions and reading material for the customers' entertainment. At first glance these problems may seem entirely different from that of the manufacturer planning for a three-month peak in sales. While it is true that the time frame of the problem is different, the basic problem of balancing capacity and demand is the same.

CONCLUSIONS

Facility planning, resource planning, aggregate capacity planning, master production planning, and capacity requirements planning are all elements of capacity planning, each encompassing the degree of detail appropriate to its planning horizon and the organization's environment and objectives. Just as resource planning must be connected to the planning of production in gross measures for periods of twelve months or longer, capacity requirements planning is driven by one material requirements plan to calculate requirements in much greater detail.

Capacity planning at all levels in the capacity planning hierarchy is connected to measures of product and service outputs. These measures usually are stated in both physical and monetary units. In fact, both the required new capacity resources (facilities, equipment, labor, and information) and required material inputs must be converted to financial terms for the financial planning management system.

Capacity planning at all levels should focus on critical resources (bottlenecks) which may be processing centers, engineering, nursing, left-handed pitchers, or systems programmers.

Aggregate planning decisions are inherent to facility planning, resource planning, and master production planning. Although most organizations do not use mathematical aggregate planning models, they do recognize the aggregate planning problem and make decisions concerning it.

When the aggregate planning problem is viewed as planning for varying demand over time, some service operations can be perceived as facing aggregate planning periods within the month, week, or day as well as over long-range planning horizons. The aggregate capacity planning challenge can be met by attempting to alter demand, by managing supply through control of production output and inventories, or a combination of the two.

The chase and level production strategies are at the opposite ends of the spectrum of aggregate capacity planning strategies. The costs of carrying inventory to meet future demand peaks and the cost of changing output rates are the two major costs affecting the management of supply in the aggregate planning decision.

Sensitivity analysis should be performed on the aggregate capacity plan to evaluate the effects of changes in costs or demand. This analysis can be used to develop contingency plans to deal with the situation when actual parameters differ substantially from projected parameters.

As time unfolds and the plan is implemented, control must take place. This requires that actual inventory, shipments, and costs be compared to the plan and that corrective action be taken as required. The following are some of the principles found in this chapter:

1. The production plan should be consistent with and support the market plan, the financial plan, and the business plan.
2. Aggregate plans, including the aggregate production plan, are not static. They should be reviewed at least quarterly to determine that marketing, finance, and production are operating as a team with the same game plan.
3. The more accurate and reliable the resource and production planning, the fewer the difficulties that will occur in master scheduling.
4. Both service and manufacturing organizations should perform aggregate planning of production and resource capacity.
5. Available capacity should be based on the actual (demonstrated) output of the key work centers.
6. Control begins in the planning process by comparing the planned resource requirements to the estimated available requirements.

QUESTIONS

1. Relate aggregate planning to resource planning.

2. Answer the following questions with regard to the aggregate planning decision process:
   a. What does it decide?
   b. How long a period does it usually cover, and how often is it done?
   c. What cost factors affect the decision?

d. What other factors (some perhaps indirectly related to costs) may affect the decision?

3. What are the three factors necessary for the calculation of ending inventory?

4. Compare resource planning as it is used in manufacturing versus service operations.

5. Define aggregate capacity planning. What are several of the key terms? What do they mean?

6. Describe the two basic strategies that represent opposite ends of the aggregate planning spectrum.

7. Differentiate between three methods that can be used to manage seasonal demand.

8. Identify several products or services that fit each of the demand patterns in Figure 7–3.

9. Describe the relationship between facility planning and the aggregate plan.

10. Describe aggregate planning in the following service organizations:
    a. A college such as a school of business or engineering
    b. An auto body repair shop
    c. A heating and air conditioning repair service

11. When is the level production strategy most appropriate in managing supply?

12. When is the chase production strategy most appropriate in managing supply?

13. Describe the relationship the aggregate plan has with marketing, finance, and engineering.

14. Describe some humanistic or social considerations that should enter into aggregate planning decisions. How will including these considerations in the decision process benefit an organization?

15. Describe methods that might be used by each of the following to alter the demand pattern (manage demand). Each may use a different method.

      a. An indoor Racquetball Facility
      b. A resort hotel
      c. An airline
      d. The local utility company

16. Review the major costs considered in the aggregate planning problem and rank them on a certainty-to-uncertainty dimension—that is, rank first the estimated cost you believe would usually be closest to the actual.

17. From Question 16 explain your selections of the following:

      a. The cost possessing the greatest uncertainty
      b. The cost possessing the greatest certainty

18. Organizations A and B are in the same industry and have very similar manufacturing processes. The undertime cost estimate used by Organization A is twice the undertime cost estimate used by Organization B. Describe a set of conditions under which both estimates could be relatively accurate.

19. A restaurant owner is heard to state that his organization faces daily, weekly, and seasonal aggregate capacity planning problems. Explain his meaning.

20. The owner and general manager of a small manufacturer of circuit boards and other electronic items comments that, "We only plan our work force levels for the next two months; we can always get good workers in this community. " (There has been an abundant supply of labor in this region for the last four or five years.) Comment. What advice or suggestions might you give?

21. What is the major benefit of the aggregate production plan?

22. You visit the dean of the college to talk about taking an operations management course in summer. You tell her that you are interested in studying aggregate planning. She responds by saying that she never understood aggregate planning and it is not a real-world problem. She also responds by saying that very few courses are offered in the summer session. Comment. Do you have any creative ideas about managing demand?

PROBLEMS

  1. The Allswell Manufacturing company estimates that it will have an inventory of 1,000 units at the beginning of January, which is the company's minimum requirement for ending inventory. It is mid-December, and the current production is 8,000 units per month. Projected monthly demand (in thousands) for the coming year is as follows:

Month	Jan.	Feb.	Mar.	April	May	June	July	Aug.	Sept.	Oct.	Nov.	Dec.
Demand	7	8	9	12	13	15	10	10	12	13	12	11

  a. Plot this data and analyze it.
  b. If management decides to follow a level production strategy, what level of production should be planned?
  c. If each item in inventory at the end of the month costs $1.00, what is the total cost of changing inventory at the end of the year?

2. Use the information in Tables 7–9, 7–10, and 7–11, to calculate the cost of each plan for each of the following conditions. Determine which, if any, of these conditions results in a different, more economical plan.

  a. The carrying cost rate is .25 per dollar of inventory rather than .30.
  b. The cost of hiring an employee is $200 instead of $600, and the cost of a layoff is $300 per worker instead of $200.
  c. The cost of manufacturing on overtime is $54.00 rather than $53.50.
  d. All of the preceding conditions exist.

3. Concerning Tables 7–9 through 7–11, added information that confirms that the company loses an average of two workers each month due to normal attrition. Take this information into consideration and develop a revised plan.

4. Use the data applicable to Tables 7–9 through 7–11 , except that the regular labor cost of an item is $10 and overtime cost is $11, to determine what the most economical plan would be.

5. Use the data applicable to Tables 7–9 through 7–11, except that back-orders are now permissible at a cost of $10 per unit, and determine what plan to recommend.

6. Referring to the data in Table 7–10, an unexpected slowdown in the economy has occurred. Actual demand in August is 5,000 units; the forecast for September and October has been revised downward by 500 units for each month. The forecasts for November through December have been decreased by 1,000 units each. What change in the plan do you recommend?

7. Given the following forecast demand and production data
   a. What is the cost of the chase strategy?
   b. What is the cost of the level production strategy?
   c. If you were the production manager which cost factor would you pay the most attention to? What suggestions do you have that might reduce that burden?

Month	Jan.	Feb.	Mar.	April	May	June	July	Aug.	Sept.	Oct.	Nov.	Dec.
Demand	40	40	40	32	32	32	48	48	48	60	60	60

Required safety stock	5
Holding cost per unit per month	$300
Hiring cost per worker	$50
Layoff cost per worker	$100
Labor cost per month	$480
Overtime cost per hour	$18
Units of production per worker per period	8
Workdays per month	21
Current work force	5

8. Demand for price-marking machines for the next eight quarters is as follows:

Quarter	1	2	3	4	5	6	7	8
Demand	35,000	40,000	39,000	32,000	39,000	46,000	44,000	45,000

Hiring cost per worker	$400
Layoff cost per worker	$600
Straight-time wages	$3,000
Inventory carrying cost per unit per period	$1
Overtime factor	1.5
Units of production per worker per period	1,000
Current work force	40
Initial inventory	10,000
Minimum safety stock level	10,000

   a. What would be the total cost of production for the chase strategy, not including raw material costs or overhead charges?
   b. What would be the total cost of production for the level production strategy, not including raw material costs or overhead charges?

REFERENCES

Bowman, E. H., "Production Scheduling by the Transportation Method of Linear Programming." *Operations Research* (February 1956): 100–103.

Britan, Gabriel R., and Arnoldo C. Hax. "On the Design of Hierarchical Planning Systems." *Decision Sciences* no. 8 (January, 1977).

Galbraith, Jay R., "Solving Production-Smoothing Problems." *Management Science* 15, no. 12 (August 1969): 665–673.

Graziano, Vincent J., "Production Capacity Planning—Long Term." *Production and Inventory Management* 15, no. 2, second quarter (1974).

Greene, J. H. et al.,"Linear Programming in the Packing Industry," *Journal of Industrial Engineering* 10, no. 5 (September/October 1959): 364–372.

Hax, Arnoldo C. and H. C. Meal. "Hierarchical Integration of Production Planning and Scheduling." *Studies in Management Sciences, Logistics*, vol. 1. Edited by M. A. Geisler. New York: North Holland Publishing Co., 1973.

Holt, Charles C., Franco Modigliani, and Herbert Simon, "A Linear Decision Rule for Production and Employment Scheduling," *Management Science*, 2, no. 1 (October 1955): 1–30.

Holt, Charles C., et al. *Planning Production, Inventories, and Work Force.* Englewood Cliffs, N. J.: Prentice-Hall, 1960).

Lee, Sang M., and L. J. Moore. "A Practical Approach to Production Scheduling." *Production and Inventory Management*, 15, no. 1, first quarter (1974): 79–92.

Lee, W. B., and B. M. Khumawala. "Simulation Testing of Aggregate Production Planning Models in an Implementation Methodology." *Management Science* 20, no. 6 (February 1974): 903–911.

Lee, W. B. and C. P. McLaughlin. "Corporate Simulation Model for Aggregate Materials Management," *Production and Inventory Management* 15, no. 1 (first quarter 1974).

Schwarz, Leroy B. and Robert E. Johnson. "An Appraisal of the Empirical Performance of the Linear Decision Rule for Aggregate Planning." *Management Science* 24, no. 8 (April 1978), 844–849.

Silver, Edward A., "A Tutorial on Production Smoothing and Work Force Balancing." *Operations Research* (November–December 1967): 985–1011.

CHAPTER 8
MASTER SCHEDULING AND CAPACITY PLANNING

OBJECTIVES

After completing this chapter, you should be able to

- Describe the purpose and the process of master scheduling and rough-cut capacity planning

- Describe the relationship of master scheduling to production planning, capacity planning, and order promising

- Describe how different production environments affect master scheduling and capacity planning

- Describe the importance of the bill of material, routing data (including standard times), and load profiles in master scheduling and capacity planning

OUTLINE

INTRODUCTION

Chapter 7 described production planning and resource capacity planning, which are aggregate plans of production and capacity generally made one to ten years prior to execution. These plans aggregate similar products into product groups, combine weeks into months, and often group personnel requirements across departments. However, the time comes when specified quantities of specific products and services must be scheduled and produced in specific work centers to meet actual or forecast demand. This is accomplished by master scheduling which produces a plan to manufacture specific items or provide specific services within a given time period. Rough-cut capacity planning (RCCP) is the process of determining if the plan is feasible; it determines whether the organization has sufficient capacity to carry out the plan. Although RCCP is more refined than resource requirements planning (RRP), it is called rough-cut because it is less refined than capacity requirements planning (CRP). In particular, the RCCP does not consider any existing inventory of components that will be used in producing the master production schedule (MPS) assemblies, nor does it consider the specific sequencing of component production orders. Both of these factors can affect the capacity required in some work centers.

Figure 8–1 illustrates how master scheduling and rough-cut capacity planning relate to corporate and operations planning as described in Chapter 3. In this chapter, a general picture of master scheduling, the master production schedule, and a rough-cut capacity plan are presented. Since these terms and processes are used primarily in manufacturing operations, they are described in that context. However, their counterparts do exist in many service organizations, and these are also noted. A description of the development of the master production schedule and the rough-cut capacity plan follows.

Master Scheduling and the MPS

The American Production and Inventory Control Society defines the master production schedule as the primary output of the master scheduling process. The MPS specifies the end items that the organization anticipates manufacturing each period. End items are either final products or component parts from which final products are made. Thus, the MPS is the plan for producing the supply to meet demand. The master schedule is a presentation by planning period of the demand, including the forecast and backlog (customer orders received), the supply plan, the ending inventory, and the available to promise (ATP) quantity. An example of a master schedule that includes the MPS is shown in Table 8–1. The ATP quantity is calculated using the cumulative method with lookahead, which will be described later in the chapter. The example in Table 8–1 is developed further in the discussion of rough-cut capacity planning.

Figure 8-1   Corporate Operations Planning and the MPS and RCCP

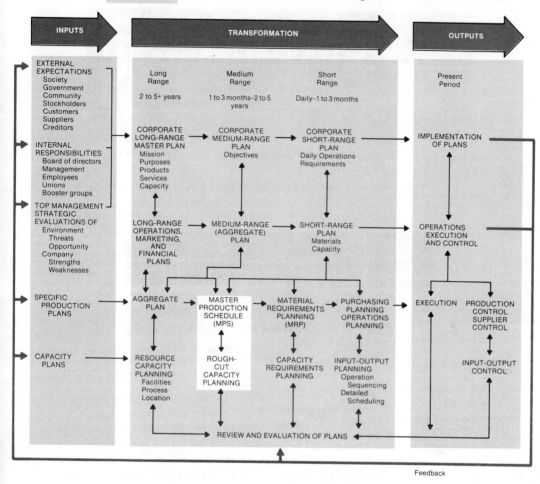

The Rough-Cut Capacity Plan

The rough-cut capacity plan (RCCP) calculates the capacity, often in standard hours, required to achieve the MPS. Table 8–2 is an example of an RCCP. Its development is described toward the end of this chapter. It is based on the MPS in Table 8–1.

INTERFACES

The MPS is a key link in the manufacturing planning and control chain. The MPS interfaces with marketing, distribution planning, production plan-

Table 8–1   Master Schedule

Product 1, Group A	Week				
	31	*32*	*33*	*34*	*35*
Forecast	—	90	90	90	90
MPS*	—	169	169	22	0
Orders (booked)	—	100	85	50	20
Projected on hand*	90	159	238	170	80
Available to promise**	90	159	195	195	195

*End of period; **Cumulative ATP with lookahead

Table 8–2   Rough-Cut Capacity Plan for Group A Assembly Work Center in Standard Hours

Product	Standard Hours			
	32	*33*	*34*	*35*
1	57.80	57.80	7.52	—
2	—	—	47.04	16.46
3	—	—	—	37.15
Total	57.80	57.80	54.56	53.61

ning, and capacity planning. It drives the material requirements planning (MRP) system as shown in Figure 8–1.

Master scheduling is the activity that produces the MPS. The MPS enables marketing to make legitimate delivery commitments to field warehouses and customers, enables production to evaluate capacity requirements in a more detailed manner, and provides the information necessary for production and marketing to agree on a course of action when customer requests cannot be met by normal capacity. It also provides all levels of management with the opportunity to ascertain whether the business plan and its strategic objectives will be achieved. Before describing the activities involved in developing and maintaining the MPS, the following section examines the different organizational environments in which master scheduling takes place. These environments are determined in large measure by an organization's response to the interests of customers and to the actions of competitors.

THE ENVIRONMENT

The competitive strategy of a manufacturing organization may be any of the following:

1. Make finished items to stock (sell from finished goods inventory)
2. Assemble final products to order and make components, subassemblies, and options to stock
3. Custom design and make to order

While service organizations typically face a different competitive environment, they may adopt strategies analogous to these. The competitive nature of the market and the strategy of the organization determine which of the MPS alternatives it should use. It is not unusual for an organization to have different strategies for different product lines and thus use different MPS alternatives.

Make to Stock

The competitive strategy of make to stock emphasizes immediate delivery of reasonably priced, off-the-shelf standard items. In this environment, the MPS is the anticipated build schedule of those items required to maintain the finished goods inventories at the desired level. Quantities on the schedule are based on manufacturing economics and the forecast demand, as well as desired safety stock levels. An end item bill of materials (BOM)—described later in this chapter—is used in this environment. Items may be produced either on a continuous or repetitive line or in batch production. Note that the MPS is the same as the final assembly schedule (FAS). Case I in Figure 8–2 represents this situation.

Figure 8–2 Manufacturing Environments

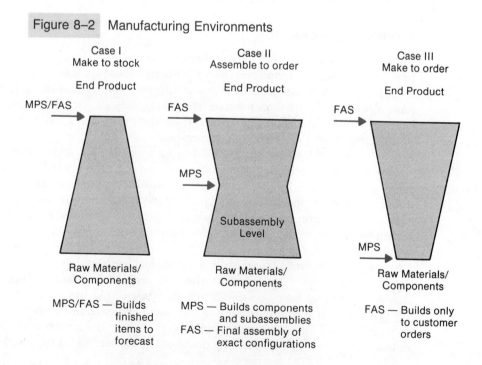

Assemble, Finish, or Package to Order

In this environment, options, subassemblies, and components are either produced or purchased to stock. The competitive strategy is to be able to supply a large variety of final product configurations from standard components and subassemblies within a relatively short lead time. For example, a Ford Taurus may be ordered with or without air conditioning, and Burger King will deliver your hamburger with or without lettuce. This requires a forecast of options as well as total demand. Thus, there is an MPS for the options, accessories, and common components as well as an FAS. This is Case II in Figure 8–2.

Custom Design and Make to Order

In many situations the final design of the item is part of what is purchased. The final product is usually a combination of standard items and custom designed items to meet the special needs of the customer. An example of custom designed products includes special trucks for off-the-road work on utility lines and facilities. Thus, there is an MPS for the standard items that are fabricated or built to stock and an FAS for the custom engineering, fabrication, and final assembly. Case III in Figure 8–2 represents this situation. As we proceed with the discussion of the policies and procedures of master scheduling and rough-cut capacity planning, we will examine further the relationship of these environments to the MPS task.

Service Organizations

As noted in Chapter 2, service organizations fall into three categories: professional, consumer, and emergency. Although there are some exceptions, most service organizations do not use master schedules; instead most perform rough-cut capacity planning, or something very similar, to provide the capacity to meet the anticipated demand for their provide-to-order services. Professional service organizations such as law firms, public accounting firms, and software development organizations obtain the number and type of personnel required to provide the anticipated demand for their services. In consumer service organizations, materials are usually ordered on the basis of the organization's capacity and anticipated demand. Capacity planning begins with the production plan and the resulting plan of resources, for example, restaurant seating capacity and facilities, hospital beds and facilities, and university classrooms, laboratories, and staffing plans. Thus, there may be an MPS for a hotel, which lists forecast occupancy, special banquets, and conferences. This document drives the orders for the daily arrival of foodstuffs, with variations in quantities based on the day of the week or the special events. The key in most cases is the scheduling of adequate personnel. In the short range, staffing plans and the planning of supply orders are the counterpart to the MRP and capacity requirements planning discussed in Chapter 13. Thus, additional ushers, vendors, beverages, and hot dogs may be planned for a sporting event with a forecast large attendance.

Emergency service organizations fulfill the medium- to short- range planning function by planning capacity in terms of both equipment and personnel and by planning the inventory of essential service (replacement) parts through time-phased order point systems and adequate safety stocks. As noted in Chapter 2, they also develop cooperative agreements with other organizations and individuals for providing additional capacity in very high demand situations.

It is worth pointing out that universities do use master scheduling. For example, business schools usually publish two or three terms in advance a schedule of courses to be offered that includes the time and location by term. This enables students to plan their programs and department chairs to plan capacity (faculty) requirements and utilization well in advance. In a similar manner, many travel agencies that provide packaged tours also have a master schedule of tours a year in advance. An example is INTRAV, Inc. of St. Louis, which provides luxury international tours. This master schedule enables them to prepare the promotional material, determine tour director requirements, reserve capacity in hotels from Shanghai to Stockholm, determine the need for and reserve the services of local guides in places such as Stockholm, Leningrad, and Budapest, as well as reserve capacity on Russian ships sailing up the Danube from Izmail to Vienna. Master scheduling and capacity planning in this type of service organization is as challenging as that encountered in most manufacturing organizations.

THE BILL OF MATERIALS (BOM)

An inclusive definition of a final product includes a list of the items, ingredients, and/or materials needed to assemble, mix, or produce that end product. This list is called a bill of materials (BOM). The BOM can take several forms and can be used in many ways. It is created as part of the design process and is then used by manufacturing engineers to determine which items should be purchased and which items should be manufactured. Production control and inventory planning use it in conjunction with the master production schedule to determine the items for which purchase requisitions and production orders must be released. Accounting uses it to cost the product. The BOM is a basic required input for many operations planning and control activities and its accuracy is crucial. In computerized systems, the BOM data are contained in *BOM files*, a data base organized by the *BOM processor*, which produces the BOM in the various formats required by the organization.

Single-Level Bill of Materials

The way in which the data in the BOM files are organized and presented is called the structure of the bill of materials. The simplest format is a single-

Table 8–3   Single-Level Bill of Materials for Assembled Lamp

ABC Lamp Company Bill of Material Part LA01-Lamp			
Part Number	Description	Quantity for Each Assembly	Unit of Measure
B100	Base assembly	1	Each
S100	14" Black shade	1	Each
A100	Socket assembly	1	Each

level BOM, as depicted in Table 8–3. It consists of a list of all components needed to make the end item, including for each component (1) a unique part number, (2) a short verbal description, (3) the quantity needed for each single end item, and (4) the part's unit of measure.

Multilevel Tree Structure and BOM Levels

While the single-level BOM is sufficient when a product is assembled at one time from a set of purchased parts and raw materials, it does not adequately describe a product that has subassemblies. If we decided to make the base and socket assemblies, each of these would have subitems that are purchased or manufactured. To illustrate the product structure, we can draw a tree having several levels as shown in Figure 8–3. Note that by convention the final product is at Level Zero and the level numbers increase as one looks down the tree.

Corresponding to this tree structure is the multilevel BOM shown in Table 8–4. Each part or assembly is still given a unique number, but to aid in understanding the structure the numbers for the components of each subassembly are indented under the respective subassembly numbers. When

Figure 8–3   Multilevel Tree Structure and BOM Levels

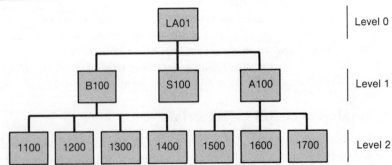

Table 8–4 Indented Bill of Materials

ABC Lamp Company Bill of Materials Part LA01			
Part Number	**Description**	**Quantity for Each Assembly**	**Unit of Measure**
B100	Base assembly	1	Each
1100	Finished shaft	1	Each
1200	7"-Diameter steel plate	1	Each
1300	Hub	1	Each
1400	1/4-20 Screws	4	Each
S100	14" Black shade	1	Each
A100	Socket assembly	1	Each
1500	Steel holder	1	Each
1600	One-way socket	1	Each
1700	Wiring Assembly	1	Each

a component is used in more than one subassembly, a common parts bill may be produced for use by purchasing in which there is only one occurrence of the item, along with its total quantity per final assembly.

If the wiring assembly were itself a subassembly, then its components would be listed and on the indented BOM the component part numbers would be further indented as shown in Table 8–5. As you see, the multilevel product structure is really made up of building blocks of single-level product trees; that is, a BOM can be drawn up for each subassembly and only these single-level bills need be retained. This is important when producing many different end items that have common subassemblies. We do not need to change every end item BOM when an engineering change takes place in a single common subassembly.

To illustrate this and several other real-life complexities, assume that we now manufacture lamps with three different shades, two alternate base plates, and two types of sockets. Working with the different components we now can have twelve different final products. To clarify this we can create a common parts BOM in a matrix format, for this family of twelve different models as shown in Table 8–6. An examination of the matrix shows that some parts are common to all models. To ease the planning task we could group together the wiring assembly and the finished shaft with a new part number, say 4000. These components are produced independently of one another and thus can be grouped as common parts. Part number 4000 is never stocked and so it is called a phantom part. Its only purpose is to reduce the number of items on the BOM. We can go further with the concept of restructuring our BOM and, for some products, create new numbers to represent new subassemblies in order to shorten lead times; for example, subassemblies of plate, hub, and screws.

Table 8–5 A Three-Level Bill of Materials

ABC Lamp Company Bill of Materials Part LA01			
Part Number	Description	Quantity for Each Assembly	Unit of Measure
B100	Base assembly	1	Each
1100	Finished shaft	1	Each
2100	3/8" Steel tubing	26	Inches
1200	7"-Diameter steel plate	1	Each
1300	Hub	1	Each
1400	1/4-20 Screws	4	Each
S100	14" Black shade	1	Each
A100	Socket assembly	1	Each
1500	Steel holder	1	Each
1600	One-way socket	1	Each
1700	Wiring Assembly	1	Each
2200	16-gauge lamp cord	12	Feet
2300	Standard plug terminal	1	Each

Another type of BOM is often useful in planning and handling engineering changes. It is referred to as a planning bill, a pseudo bill, a phantom bill, a super bill, or a family bill. From the matrix form of the summary bill, a simplified product structure diagram (see Figure 8–4) could be created for the family of lamps that consisted of pseudo subassemblies—namely base assemblies, shades, and socket assemblies. For each of these, in place of the quantity for each unit assembled, the percentage split for each type of component is stated. In planning for a total of 10,000 lamps for each month, this planning bill can be used to derive the number of each type of component to build.

Figure 8–4 A Planning or Family Bill

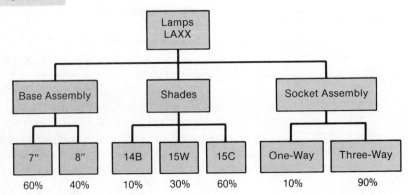

Table 8–6   Planning Bill of Materials in Matrix Format Part LA01 (Quantity for Each Assembly)

Part Number	Description	Unit of Measure	Model 01	02	03	04	05	06	07	08	09	10	11	12
1100	Finished shaft	Each	1	1	1	1	1	1	1	1	1	1	1	1
2100	⅜" Steel tube	Inches	26	26	26	26	26	26	26	26	26	26	26	26
1200	7"-Diameter steel plate	Each	1	1	1	1	1	1	1	1	1	1		
1200	8"-Diameter steel plate	Each											1	1
1300	Hub	Each								1	1	1	1	1
1400	¼-20 Screws	Each	4	4	4	4	4	4	4	4	4	4	4	4
S100	14" Black shade	Each	1			1			1					
S101	15" White shade	Each		1		1			1		1		1	
S102	15" Cream shade	Each			1	1			1		1	1		1
1500	Steel holder	Each	1	1	1	1	1	1	1	1	1	1	1	1
1600	One-way socket	Each	1	1	1	1	1	1	1	1	1	1	1	1
1601	Three-way socket	Each					1	1	1	1	1	1	1	1
1700	Wiring assembly	Each	1	1	1	1	1	1	1	1	1	1	1	1
2200	16-Gauge lamp cord	Feet	1	1	1	1	1	1	1	1	1	1	1	1
2300	Standard plug terminal	Each	1	1	1	1	1	1	1	1	1	1	1	1
B100	Base assembly—7"	Each												
B101	Base assembly—8"	Each												
A100	Socket assembly—one-way	Each	1	1	1	1					1	1	1	1
A101	Socket Assembly one-way	Each					1	1	1	1				

THE PLANNING HORIZON

A principle of planning is that a plan must cover a period at least equal to the time required to accomplish it. This means that the MPS planning horizon (the time period that it covers) must be at least as long as the lead time required to fabricate the MPS items. This includes production and procurement time, as well as engineering time in a custom-design environment. The customer order response times in the different production environments are illustrated in Figure 8–5.

Many organizations divide the planning horizon into periods with different controls on schedule changes. The closer a period is to the present, the tighter are the controls on schedule changes. For example, time fences (the boundary between different periods) may be established at the fourth and eighth weeks with the limitations on changes in the MPS as shown in Table 8–7.

The location of the time fences and the nature of the approval required is dependent on the product and the process. Varying lead times, market conditions, and processing flexibility make for different time fences, sometimes at different plants within the same firm. Time fences should be tailored to specific product groups because lead times may vary widely between groups.

Figure 8–5   Manufacturing Environment and Customer Order Response Time

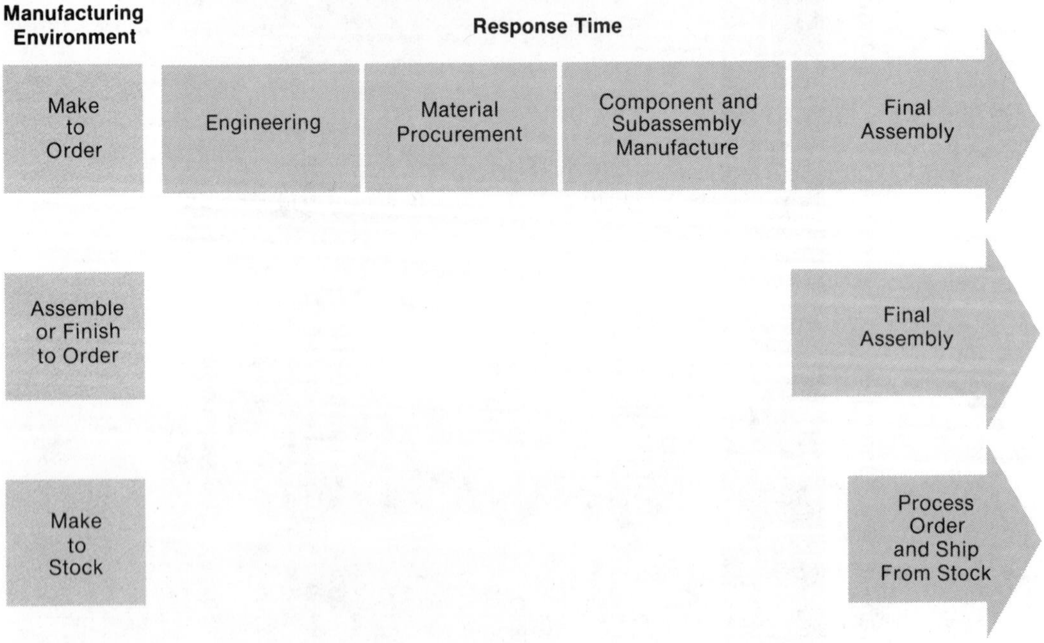

Table 8–7 MPS Planning Horizons

Period	Time Horizon	Conditions	Approval Required
A	0 to 4 weeks	Emergency	Top management
B	4 to 8 weeks	Dramatic shift in requirements	Marketing-manufacturing negotiation
C	Beyond 8 weeks	Normal	Master scheduler

In all cases, the MPS is the vehicle for coordinating the achievement of marketing and manufacturing goals.

In Period C (beyond 8 weeks in Table 8–7) the MPS is consistent with the production plan. A good production plan will make preparation of the MPS straightforward in this time frame. Product families are extended into MPS items, as illustrated in Figure 8–6.

In Period B (4 to 8 weeks in Table 8–7) things become a bit sticky when operating at full capacity. A zero sum game exists—that is, any additions to the schedule must be counterbalanced by comparable deletions. Changes in demand patterns, unusual orders, or equipment failures may warrant changes in the MPS. These changes are usually negotiated between marketing and manufacturing, with the master scheduler determining their feasibility before the final decision. The product mix may change, but the production rate will not. In Period A only an act of God or top management can change the MPS.

As the time for order execution and manufacturing approaches, labor and materials are committed. Changes in the schedule can be disruptive

Figure 8–6 Relationships of Items and Planning Activities

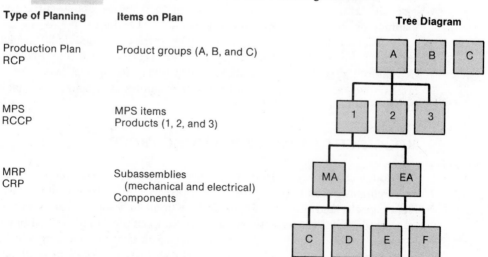

Type of Planning	Items on Plan	Tree Diagram
Production Plan RCP	Product groups (A, B, and C)	
MPS RCCP	MPS items Products (1, 2, and 3)	
MRP CRP	Subassemblies (mechanical and electrical) Components	

and costly. These costs must be compared with the benefits of the change. Following time-fence-control guidelines, which reflect realistic lead time constraints and competitive factors, will result in an MPS that promotes manufacturing stability and productivity while providing reasonable flexibility in meeting marketing demands. The competitive environment may force decisions to restructure the BOM, to develop a modular BOM, to produce to stock at a higher level in the BOM, or to move time fences.

Service Organizations

The type of service organization affects the necessary planning horizon and the policies followed in changing the MPS. As noted earlier, the MPS in emergency service organizations consists of scheduling the available capacity. Since many of these organizations must cope with dramatic increases in demand on very short notice, they often have established procedures for rapidly expanding capacity on short notice, such as using overtime, shifting personnel assignments, and using part-time personnel. For example, in the event of a heavy snowstorm the street departments of large cities commonly use overtime, assign drivers and trucks with snowplows from other departments to snow removal, and occasionally hire independent firms to aid in the task.

Professional service organizations such as accounting, engineering, management, and software development firms fulfill contracts; they operate in a make-to-order environment. Their MPS typically lists the orders under contract and the time required to complete them, as well as the capacity available for future orders within the MPS planning horizon. Many others, such as educational institutions, airlines, and railways have a schedule of the services (courses, flights, etc.) to be offered in the next year or six months. In each case, the feasibility of the MPS must be verified by the rough-cut capacity planning process applied to critical personnel and facilities.

Consumer service organizations typically have a schedule of available capacity planned for the next quarter to one year. This capacity may differ by time of day and day of the week, and will vary for special occasions e.g., holidays. Restaurants, hotels, and banks are examples of organizations that use this type of schedule.

ROUGH-CUT CAPACITY PLANNING (RCCP)

Rough-cut capacity planning calculates the critical work center capacity requirements for all items on the MPS. It provides an early warning of insufficient capacity and the need for capacity actions. In some situations, capacity in a certain work center—the paint shop, for example—may be well beyond that ever required; while capacity in other work centers—welding and heat treating, for example—may be relatively low, creating a frequent bottleneck.

Capacity actions is the term used to describe correcting situations in which the available capacity is less than the required capacity.

Table 8–8 and Figure 8–6 show the relationship of resource capacity planning (RCP), rough-cut capacity planning (RCCP), and capacity requirements planning (CRP). RCP was described in Chapter 7, and CRP is described in Chapter 13. Table 8–8 highlights the salient characteristics of these different stages of capacity planning.

The primary differences between RCP and RCCP are that the RCCP plans in smaller time increments, and considers the production lead time of the various components and subassemblies required to produce the products on the MPS. Since all of the processes required to produce a complex assembly and its components must be included and since many of the components must be manufactured a week or so in advance of the assembly activities, the timing of the capacity requirements varies. This requires a product load profile with lead time offsets for each item on the MPS. A load profile is a list of the critical resources required to produce a specific quantity—often one unit—of a given product, as shown in Figure 8–7. This profile reveals that the mechanical subassembly is usually completed one week prior to the final assembly and the processing of components in the CNC machining department takes place two weeks prior to the final assembly. Notice in Figure 8–7 that the lead time weeks are counted backwards; that is, the week of final assembly is Week 1, the week preceding that is Week 2, and so on. The rough-cut capacity requirements are calculated by multiplying the resource profile by the quantity required.

In Chapter 7 we calculated the resource requirements of Product Group A for the month of October. Now we will calculate the resource requirements for each of the weeks of October using the data for Products 1, 2, and 3 of Product Group A. Figure 8–8 presents an overview of the information flow in

Table 8–8 Capacity Planning Stages

Stages	Input	Outputs
Resource capacity planning (RCP)	Production plan (product groups) Resource profile (bill of labor, capacity bill) Resource capacity available	Resource requirements by month
Rough-cut capacity planning (RCCP)	MPS Product load profile with lead time offset	Rough-cut capacity requirements by week
Capacity requirements planning (CRP)	Material requirements plan Capacity available Inventory status	Capacity requirement plans by week or day

Figure 8–7 Lead Time Offsets—Product 1

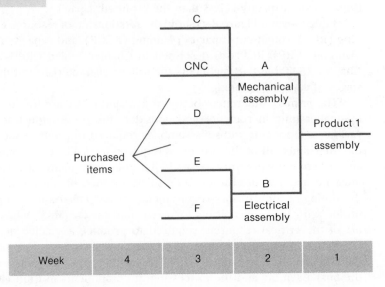

the RCCP process. Using BOM and routing data that include lead time offsets and standard time data, a load profile is developed for each item on the MPS. For example, the lead time offsets of Group A are shown in Figure 8–7 and Table 8–9, the standard time data for all Group A products are given in Table 8–10, and the October MPS for the products in Group A is given in Table 8–11.

The information in these tables can be used to calculate capacity requirements. For each product on the MPS, multiply the quantity required

Figure 8–8 Data Flow, MPS, and RCCP

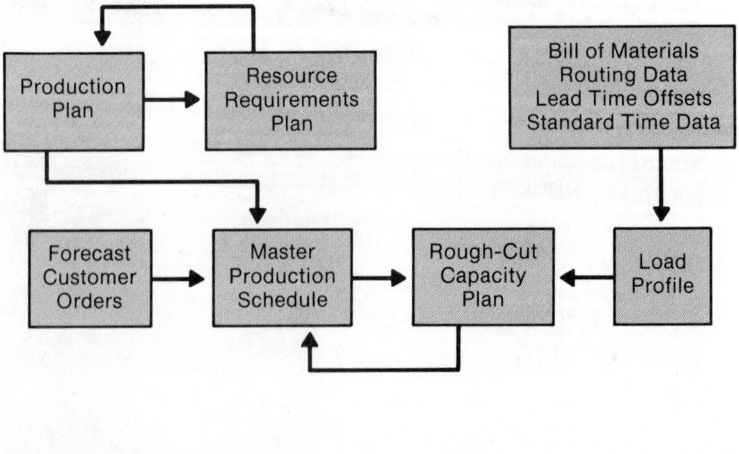

Table 8–9 Product Group A Load Profile— Product 1

Item	Work Center	Standard Hours	Week
1	Assembly	.301	1
A	Mechanical assembly	.250	2
B	Electrical assembly	.274	2
C	CNC	.112	3

by the load profile standard time and add to the resource requirements of the appropriate department in the period as determined by the lead time offset. Using the delivery requirements for Product 2 in Week 35 as an example, its assembly work center capacity requirements are 36 times .294 or 10.58 standard hours in Week 35; its mechanical assembly work center requirements are 36 times .255 or 9.18 standard hours in Week 34 (due to lead

Table 8–10 Standard Time Data—Product Group A

Work Center	Product			Weighted Average
	1	*2*	*3*	
Assembly	.342	.294	.258	.301
Mechanical assembly	.244	.255	.267	.250
Electrical assembly	.280	.268	.268	.274
CNC	.112	.112	.112	.112

Table 8–11 MPS for Product Group A—October

Product	Week				Total	Percent
	32	*33*	*34*	*35*		
1	180	180			360	50
2			180	36	216	30
3				144	144	20
Total	180	180	180	180	720	100

Table 8–12　Rough-Cut Capacity Requirements
Week 35—Products 2 and 3

Work Center	Item	Standard Hours Per Week		
		33	34	35
Assembly	2			10.58
	3			37.15
				47.73
Mechanical	MA2		9.18	
assembly	MA3		38.45	
			47.63	
Electrical	EA2		9.65	
assembly	EA3		38.59	
			48.24	
CNC		4.03		
		16.13		
		20.16		

time). These values are recorded in Table 8–12 along with the other capacity requirements resulting from the 36 units of Product 2 and the 144 units of Product 3 scheduled for delivery in Week 35. The capacity requirements resulting from scheduled shipments in other weeks are calculated in the same manner. Table 8–13 shows the total capacity requirements for Group A in the assembly department and compares it to the available capacity. (Groups B and C are assembled in a different work center.) The available capacity of 58 standard hours is based on the actual output of the Group A assembly work center with the present personnel and equipment, often called the demonstrated capacity. This information is required to determine if any changes in the MPS or available capacity are required.

This section reveals once again that control takes place in the planning process. The comparison of capacity requirements to available capacity reveals whether or not the present MPS is feasible. Table 8–13 shows a shortfall of 3.56 hours of capacity in both Weeks 32 and 33 and surplus

Table 8–13　Capacity Report—Assembly Work Center

Type of Capacity	Capacity in Hours Per Week			
	32	33	34	35
Required	61.56	61.56	52.96	47.73
Demonstrated	58.00	58.00	58.00	58.00
Shortfall	3.56	3.56	−5.04	−10.27

Table 8–14   Revised MPS and Capacity
Requirements

MPS

Product	Week			
	32	33	34	35
1	169	169	22	
2			160	56
3				144

Capacity Requirements

Product	Week			
	32	33	34	35
1	57.80	57.80	7.52	
2			47.04	16.46
3				37.15
Total	57.80	57.80	54.56	53.61

capacity in Weeks 34 and 35. This presents the master scheduler with the following options:

1. Increase capacity in Weeks 32 and 33
2. Reduce production quantities in Weeks 32 and 33 and increase production quantities in Weeks 34 and 35.
3. Some combination of options 1 and 2

In this case, the choice is Option 2 as shown in Table 8–14, a revision of the MPS in Table 8–11. Table 8–14 also reveals that sufficient capacity is available with the revised MPS. This decision is possible only if the 22 units of Product 1 are not required prior to Week 34.

Many organizations have computerized the calculation of rough-cut capacity requirements, while others have standard forms and procedures that facilitate manual computations. In any event, the rough-cut capacity required to implement the MPS must be compared to available capacity to determine if any capacity actions are required.

ORDER-PROMISING INFORMATION

The ability to make legitimate delivery promises to a customer is very important to an organization. It is an attribute of customer service that is part of the overall quality of an organization's output. Two pieces of infor-mation are required for making reliable delivery promises: (1) the available-to-promise (ATP) quantity and (2) the projected-on-hand (POH) quantity of inventory. The POH is the number of units that will be physically in stock. Methods for calculating both quantities are described next.

Calculating the ATP

Two different methods are commonly used for calculating the ATP—the period-by-period discrete method and the cumulative method. A description of these methods in a make-to-order environment with one week lead time for final assembly follows. Components are made to stock.

PERIOD-BY-PERIOD METHOD. Table 8–15 is an example of period-by-period calculation of the ATP in a make-to-order environment. In each period with scheduled production, the backlog is subtracted from the scheduled produc-tion to give the ATP. Thus the ATP in any period is independent of the ATP values in other periods.

In Week 5, for example, the ATP = 30 − 20 or 10 units. Weeks in which production is not scheduled are left blank. Thus, some of the 20-unit backlog in Week 5 might be on the shipping schedule of Weeks 6 and 7. This approach often is called consuming the schedule.

In addition, the planner may look ahead and decide to use the 10 units available in Week 5 to cover the 10-unit short in Week 8. In that case the planner must add a note indicating that the 10 units (the ATP) in Week 5 are not available. (Software programs often provide text space for such notes.)

CUMULATIVE METHOD. The cumulative method can be used with or without this lookahead feature. Table 8–16 is an example of cumulative calculation of the ATP without lookahead in a make-to-order environment using the same backlog and MPS data in Table 8–15.

Using this approach, the ATP in a period equals the ATP of the preceding period plus the MPS minus the backlog. Thus, the ATP in Week 5 is 5 + (30 − 20), which equals 15. The difference between this method and the discrete method is that the ATP in any period using the cumulative method without

Table 8–15 ATP, Make to Order, Period-by-Period Method (Discrete)

Production Data	Week												
	1	2	3	4	5	6	7	8	9	10	11	12	13
Backlog	0	25			20			40			5		
MPS		30			30			30			30		
ATP	0	5			10			−10			25		

Table 8–16   ATP, Make to Order, Cumulative Without Lookahead

Production Data	Week												
	1	2	3	4	5	6	7	8	9	10	11	12	13
Backlog (BL)	0	25			20			40			5		
MPS		30			30			30			30		
ATP	0	5	5	5	15	15	15	5	5	5	30	30	30

$$ATP_i = ATP_{i-1} + MPS_i - BL_i$$

lookahead is likely to include units also included in the ATP of other periods. For example, the 15-unit ATP of Week 5 includes the 5 units also in the ATP of Week 2. Furthermore, when there is no lookahead procedure, the ATP for a period may include units committed to fill requirements for a later period. For example, 10 of the units in the ATP of Weeks 5, 6, and 7 are committed to customer orders promised for delivery in Week 8. Although some planners may function well with such a system because they understand the data and are available to extract accurate information from it, the data available are not being used efficiently. The lookahead approach combined with the addition of projected-on-hand information regarding inventory resolves this problem.

Table 8–17 is an example of the cumulative method with lookahead calculation of the ATP in a make-to-order environment.

With this method, units produced in one period and committed for use in a future period are omitted from the ATP in all periods preceding that in which they are promised. Thus, the 10 units of the 40 promised for delivery in Week 8 but produced earlier, in Week 5, are not included in the ATP of Week 5. The ATP values in Table 8–17 illustrate this clearly: there are 5 units that can be promised for any of the Weeks 2 through 10, and a total of 30 units, which includes the previously mentioned 5, that can be promised for delivery in Weeks 11 through 13. In addition, the ATP information displayed in Table 8–17 does not confuse ATP quantities with the number of units that will be in the physical inventory.

Table 8–17   ATP, Make to Order, Cumulative with Lookahead

Production Data	Week												
	1	2	3	4	5	6	7	8	9	10	11	12	13
Backlog	0	25			20			40			5		
MPS		30			30			30			30		
ATP	0	5	5	5	5	5	5	5	5	5	30	30	30

$$ATP_i = ATP_{i-1} + MPS_i - \Sigma(BL_j - MPS_j) \text{ for all future periods } j \text{ until MPS > BL.}$$

Projected-On-Hand (POH)

The estimated number of units on hand each period gives management the information they need to evaluate the MPS fully. Table 8–18 illustrates the calculation of POH information and provides questions for the master production scheduler to resolve with manufacturing and marketing. Since delivery lead time is one week, no new orders will be accepted for Week 1. Thus, we are concerned with Weeks 2 through 13. In Table 8–18 we have omitted the forecast and ATP and POH values in weeks without schedule production. The forecast is actually 10 units per week, which is accumulated in the preceding MPS periods. For example, the forecasts for Weeks 3 and 4 have been added to that of Week 2 giving a total of 30.

The projected ending inventory physically in stock equals the POH value of the preceding period plus the MPS quantity minus the larger of the forecast or the backlog. The rationale of using the greater of the forecast or booked orders is that if the latter is greater, the forecast was obviously too low; if the forecast is greater, not all of the orders have been received yet. Thus, the POH of Week 5 equals $0 + 30 - 30$ or 0; and the POH of Week 8 equals $0 + 30 - 40$ or -10. This information raises the following questions:

1. How many more orders for delivery in Weeks 2 through 7 are likely? Is the forecast too low or have delivery requests expected for those weeks been delayed to Week 8?
2. Are sufficient capacity and materials available to manufacture additional units in Week 2 or in Week 5 if necessary?
3. If the MPS quantity in Week 2 is not increased, what is the latest time that the MPS quantity in Week 5 or in Week 8 can be increased?

These questions illustrate some of the management decisions prompted by the information in Table 8–18. A knowledge of the market and an analysis of the orders is required to answer these questions.

Table 8–18   ATP, Cumulative With Lookahead, and POH

Production Data	Week												
	1	2	3	4	5	6	7	8	9	10	11	12	13
Forecast (F)		30			30			30			30		
Backlog (BL)		25			20			40			5		
MPS	0	30			30			30			30		
ATP	0	5			5			5			30		
POH	0	0			0			−10			−10		

$POH_i = POH_{i-1} + MPS_i - F_i$, when $F_i > BL_i$

$POH_i = POH_{i-1} + MPS_i - BL_i$, when $BL_i > F_i$

Table 8–19 Consuming the Forecast, ATP with Lookahead, and POH

Production Data	Week												
	1	*2*	*3*	*4*	*5*	*6*	*7*	*8*	*9*	*10*	*11*	*12*	*13*
Forecast		5			15			0			25		
Backlog		25			20			40			5		
MPS	0	30			30			30			30		
ATP	0	5			5			5			30		
POH	0	0			−5			−15			−15		

$$POH_i = POH_{i-1} + MPS_i - F_i - BL_i$$

Consuming the Forecast

Using the consuming-the-forecast concept enables the planner to have the master schedule (i.e., the output on the computer screen) present the revised forecast and the resulting revised POH data for two different situations. In the first instance, the original forecast still is viewed as accurate. Thus, the revised forecast equals the original forecast minus the backlog, and the forecast is consumed by the orders received. This situation is illustrated in Weeks 2 and 11 of Table 8–19. The second situation differs in that the original forecast no longer is viewed as accurate. For example, unexpected orders may have been received from a new customer and there is no reason to believe that the regular customers will not order as forecast. This situation is illustrated in Weeks 5 and 8 of Table 8–19. The backlog of 20 units in Week 5, for example, includes 5 units from an unexpected source, thus the forecast has been reduced by only 15 units. No further sales are expected for delivery in Week 5; but sales already exceed the forecast. (The total forecast for the period is now 35 units of which 20 have been consumed.)

The POH now equals the preceding POH plus the MPS minus the sum of the backlog and the revised forecast. For example, the POH in Week 8 is $-5 + 30 - (40 + 0) = -15$. The calculation of the ATP is not affected. The ATP is positive while the POH is negative because the cumulative booked orders are less than the cumulative forecast.

The primary difference between a make-to-order and make-to-stock environment is that the latter will normally have some safety stock to cover variations in demand. The POH would not be allowed to approach 0. Calculation of the ATP and the POH completes the development of the master schedule.

THE FINAL ASSEMBLY SCHEDULE

The final assembly schedule (FAS) is a statement of those final products that are to be assembled from MPS items in specific time periods. In some organizations, such as Black and Decker, MPS items and final products are identical and one document serves as both the MPS and the FAS. In many other situations the two are separate and distinct.

In some cases final products differ only by the labeling or packaging of the same MPS item, in others painting or finishing may constitute the difference, while in still others a vast difference may exist in the transformation of MPS items into a variety of final products. In each of these cases an FAS that is distinct from but consistent with the MPS must be prepared.

In the manufacture of automatic washers, for example, the motor, transmissions, control units, consoles, tubs, sets of assembly hardware, and various optional accessories would be MPS items, and the different models available to the customer would be final assemblies. Thus, the manufacture of motors can be authorized long before each motor is committed to the assembly of a particular model. The FAS is constrained by the availability of those items scheduled on the MPS plus those in inventory, the lead time required for assembly, and the assembly capacity.

In an assemble-to-order environment the FAS frequently is stated in terms of individual customer orders and must be consistent with the shipping schedule. In a make-to-stock environment it is a commitment to produce specific quantities of catalog final products. The shipping schedule depends on available inventory and available capacity. Capacity is required for assembly and for any items that may be controlled by the FAS and not the MPS. Examples are painting, packaging, crating, and preparing shipping documents.

In any event, authorization of the final assembly schedule (the release for execution) should be held to the last possible moment. This provides the greatest flexibility in meeting actual demand and improves customer service. Since assembly lead time and MPS item availability constrain the FAS, any planning and design that reduces this lead time and increases flexibility aids in achieving customer service objectives.

Preparation, measurement of actual output, and control of the FAS should rest with the master scheduler. This enables one person to control all demands on resources and coordinate MPS items with the FAS, order entry items, and order-promising activities.

DEVELOPING THE MPS

The following steps are required in the development and preparation of the MPS.

1. Select the items and the levels in the BOM structure to be represented by the items scheduled (both components and final assemblies may be included).
2. Make the revisions necessary in the BOM to obtain consistency between the BOM and the listing of items on the MPS.
3. Organize the MPS by product groups.
4. Determine the planning horizon, the time fences, and the related operational guidelines. The planning horizon is the span of time covered by the MPS; it must be equal to or longer than the time required to carry out the plan.

Time fences are boundaries between planning horizon subperiods in which different guidelines govern schedule modifications.
5. Obtain the necessary informational inputs.
6. Prepare the initial draft of the MPS.
7. Calculate the rough-cut capacity plan.
8. Revise the initial draft of the MPS to obtain a feasible schedule.

The first four steps are clearly system design activities, while the remainder are steps in the ongoing master scheduling process.

The Master Scheduler

Most organizations should have a master scheduler. This individual is the link between marketing, distribution, engineering, manufacturing and planning. The tasks of the master scheduler include the following:

1. Providing delivery promise dates for incoming orders and matching actual requirements with the master schedule as they materialize
2. Evaluating the impact of top-down inputs, such as a request for the introduction of a new product in much less than the normal delivery time
3. Evaluating the impact of bottom-up inputs, such as anticipated delay reports from the shop or purchasing indicating that particular components will not be available as scheduled or planned production rates are not being attained
4. Revising the master schedule when necessary due to lack of material or capacity
5. Calling basic conflicts between demand and capacity to the attention of other members of management who need to resolve the problems in advance

Whether or not a firm has someone formally designated as the master scheduler, the tasks are essential. Combining them under the jurisdiction of one individual improves the likelihood that they will be coordinated and managed properly. Most importantly, it provides a focal point for the required coordination of marketing, manufacturing, distribution, and planning as well as a place to look when things are not going well.

MPS Information Systems and Analysis

The complexity of most manufacturing and service organizations requires a computerized operations planning and control system with human interfaces at appropriate decision points. As noted previously, the master scheduler requires such an interface. The requirement for computer-assisted planning is due to (1) a combination of the number of items on the MPS, (2) the large number of subassemblies and components, and (3) the magnitude of recording and processing inventory transactions, materials requirements, and capacity requirements. Today there are literally hundreds of commercial software systems available; they can be used with mainframe computers, minicomputers, and personal computers.

The installation and availability of such a computer system often allows the organization to perform what-if analyses to answer questions such as (1) What will be the effect of a shift in product mix on capacity requirements? (2) What will be the effect of a 10 percent increase in demand on capacity requirements? Answers to these questions, available from a computerized simulation run, will enable management to prepare plans for such contingencies.

CONCLUSIONS

Although the preparation and maintenance of all the elements of the master schedule may be complex in some situations, the following principles and concepts are not.

1. The MPS is a vital link in the operations planning and control system due to its interfaces with many other activities and systems in manufacturing, marketing, and engineering (product and process design).
2. The items on the MPS, in particular their level in the BOM, should be consistent with the organization's competitive strategy.
3. The efficacy of the master scheduling process and the MPS requires an accurate and reliable capacity planning system.
4. The master scheduler plays a key role in the master scheduling function and keeps marketing and manufacturing working on the same plan.
5. Available-to-promise information is very useful for responding to customer requests for delivery.

QUESTIONS

1. In what way(s) does the master production schedule (MPS) relate to the production plan?

2. The production plan affects what factors of production?

3. When is the final assembly schedule (FAS) the same as the master production schedule?

4. Differentiate between an MPS in a make-to-order environment and an MPS in a make-to-stock environment.

5. In the context of the MPS, define the term ending inventory.

6. What is a time fence?

7. What are some of the factors that cause time fences to vary?

8. What is the terminology used when any additions to the schedule must be counterbalanced by comparable deletions?

9. At what level is the bill of materials (BOM) normally aggregated? Why are cases I to III in Figure 8–2 significant? Give an example of each.

10. Why might it be necessary to restructure the BOM? What would be the outcome of that restructuring?

11. Sequentially, what steps should be accomplished in the preparation of an MPS? What is accomplished at each step?

12. What are the two principles of available-to-promise (ATP) computations?

13. Why is there a tendency for an MPS to be overstated? What are the impacts?

14. What measures should be used to evaluate scheduling performance?

15. How are the resource capacity plan of a service organization and the MPS of a manufacturing firm related?

PROBLEMS

1. The indented BOMs (without item descriptions) for four final assemblies (B100, B200, B300, and B400) are shown in the following table. Prepare a multilevel tree structure BOM for each of the four assemblies. Identify the levels.

Item	Quantity	Item	Quantity	Item	Quantity	Item	Quantity
B100	1	B200	1	B300	1	B400	1
B101	1	B201	1	B201	2	B201	2
X	2	X	3	X	3	X	3
Y	1	Y	1	Y	1	Y	1
Z	1	Z	1	Z	1	Z	1
B102	1	T	2	T	2	T	2
R	3	B103	1	B104	1	B101	1
Y	1	R	1	R	1	X	2
Z	1	S	3	S	2	Y	1
B103	1	Z	3	Z	3	Z	1
R	1			Q	1		
S	3			T	1		
Z	3						

2. Prepare a matrix summary BOM combining the four asemblies.

3. The typical ratio of demand among the four asemblies is B100:B200:B300:B400 = 4:3:2:1. The forecast demand for this product group is 10,000 units for each of the next three months. What is the forecast demand for each assembly during each of these months?

4. Items R, T, X, and Z are purchased parts. How many of each must be purchased each month?

5. The lead time for all items except the following is one week:

Item	Lead Time
B102	2 weeks
T	3 weeks

a. If all items are purchased or produced to order, what is the minimum planning horizon of each assembly?
b. If no items are available, which assembly would be the first scheduled in the final assembly department (for which assembly would the sub-assemblies be ready first)?

6. B100, B200, B300, and B400 are fabricated in the final assembly department; all other nonpurchased items are fabricated in the subassembly department. The following are the capacity requirements for each item:

Item	Capacity Required per 100 Units	Item	Capacity Required per 100 Units
B100	40 work hours	B103	15 work hours
B200	20	B104	25
B300	30	B201	25
B400	20	Q	5
B101	15	S	5
B102	15	Y	5

a. How many workers are required in the assembly department? How many in the subassembly department (use 160 work hours per person per month)?
b. If the forecast is stated with a plus or minus 10 percent on the total and on the mix ratio, what are the minimum capacity requirements in the subassembly and final assembly departments?

7. Use the MPS, forecast, and orders booked (backlog) information in Table 8–1 to calculate the POH and the ATP, cumulative with lookahead.

8. Given the following data, calculate how many units are available to promise (ATP) and the projected inventory (POH) for each period. Use the discrete method. Beginning inventory is 20.

	Week					
	1	2	3	4	5	6
Forecast	15	15	15	15	15	15
Backlog	19	0	10	10	0	0
MPS	30	0	30	0	30	0

9. Given the following data, calculate how many units are available to promise (ATP) and the projected inventory (POH) for each period. Use the cumulative method with lookahead. Beginning inventory is 10.

	Week					
	1	2	3	4	5	6
Forecast	15	15	15	15	15	15
Backlog	19	10	15	18	20	0
MPS	30	0	30	0	30	0

10. Use the load profiles in Table 8–10 to calculate the monthly capacity required in each of the four departments to manufacture the following:

Product	Quantity
1	60
2	60
3	60

11. Using the data in Problem 10, calculate the capacity required each week in each department if final assembly of the four products is spread over four weeks, namely Weeks 11 through 14. Decide the weekly schedule of the assemblies.

REFERENCES

Aherns, Roger. "Basics of Capacity Planning and Control." *APICS 24th Annual International Conference Proceedings*, 1981, pp. 232–235.

Berry, William L., Thomas E. Vollmann, and D. Clay Whybark. *Master Production Scheduling: Principles and Practice*. Washington, D.C.: American Production and Inventory Control Society, 1979.

Campbell, Kenneth L. "Rough-Cut Capacity Planning—What It Is and How to Use It." *APICS 25th Annual International Conference Proceedings*, 1982, pp. 406–409.

Capacity Planning Reprints. Falls Church, Va.: American Production and Inventory Control Society, 1986.

Lankford, Ray. "Short Term Planning of Manufacturing Capacity." *APICS 21st Annual Conference Proceedings*, 1978, pp. 37–68.

Malko, Richard. "Master Scheduling; A Key to Results." *APICS 23rd Annual International Conference Proceedings*, 1980, pp. 408–412.

Proud, John J. "Consuming the Master Schedule with Customer Orders." *APICS 26th Annual International Conference Proceedings*, 1983, pp. 21–25.

Sodahl, Lars O. "How Do You Master Schedule Half a Million Product Variants?" *APICS 24th Annual International Conference Proceedings*, 1981, pp. 70–72.

Wemmerlov, Urban. *Capacity Management Techniques for Manufacturing Companies with MRP Systems*. Falls Church, Va.: American Production and Inventory Control Society, 1984.

CHAPTER 9
FACILITY LAYOUT

OBJECTIVES

After completing this chapter, you should be able to

- Define layout and relate that definition to both process design and the criteria by which an operations manager is evaluated

- Use qualitative and quantitative methods to analyze functional layout situations

- Identify various measures of performance for the line layout and relate those measures to different assembly line–balancing methods

- Solve assembly line–balancing problems for both maximum cycle time and fixed number of workstation criteria

- Appreciate some of the considerations in project, or fixed position, layout analysis

OUTLINE

INTRODUCTION

The layout of a facility deals with the physical organization and interrelationship of equipment and people in a production or service process. As noted in Chapter 7, facility layout is dependent upon such process design considerations as resource availability, demand, and capacity. In this sense, facility layout decisions become the implementation of the process design. Once the production process is defined as a line flow, a job shop, or a fixed project, further decisions can be made with regard to the physical layout of the production or service process.

Similarly, the layout of a facility, and the decision to change a layout design, are closely related to the criteria by which an operation is evaluated, as noted in Chapter 1. In fact, the layout contributes to productivity, which is measured in terms of cost, quality, flexibility, and delivery. Thus, facility layout is the implementation of process decisions; it directly affects the productivity of the manufacturing or service process, however measured.

Layouts can be designed to achieve productivity in many different ways. A layout supports productivity by minimizing or eliminating material travel, or by using gravity or other mechanical efficiencies to move heavy products. For example, in the assembly of components, lighter-weight components are often assembled on the upper floors of a multilevel facility, and the product is moved downward as it gains weight. This method reduces the need to raise heavy or bulky objects and permits the use of gravity.

In other situations, the reduction of employee or customer movement may be the key to a good layout design. Many large airports, for example, are designed around somewhat circular hubs. By using the inside circumference of the hubs and radial spokes for traveler movement and by placing taxiways and runways near the outer circumference of the hubs, traveler walking distances are reduced. Similarly, in a manufacturing environment, manufacturing cells often involve U-shaped lines that permit workers to move more rapidly from one process to another.

A third facet of facility layout design involves the sequencing or interrelatedness of specific activities. Manufacturing processes often rely upon the sequencing and timing of tasks (e.g., the application and drying time of glue or paint). Similarly, with a computer or software installation or a complex consulting job, this sequencing and interrelatedness of activities and human resources are closely managed.

This chapter will introduce the basic concepts of facility layout and then address the measures of effective functional (process) layout, product line layout, and fixed position or project layout. Throughout the discussion, measured production performance is a central consideration, yet one that is difficult to operationalize and almost impossible to optimize. This is because numerous assumptions, constraints, and methodological conveniences are often required to permit the evaluation of facility layouts.

Layout Defined

The issues of facility layout vary depending upon resource and capacity decisions, facility location decisions, the production process selected, and the criteria by which productivity is measured. The planning and decision process for layout evaluation must take all of these factors into consideration. Facility layout is thus defined as follows:

> A planning process that considers alternatives of resource utilization, facility location, and process design, often through the use of mathematical algorithms, for the purpose of greater productivity, defined in terms of quality, cost, flexibility, or delivery.

The key points of the definition are briefly highlighted in the following discussion.

Planning process. Facilities layout evaluation and implementation is a planning process. As noted in Chapter 3, the planning process has four steps: inquiry, information input, evaluation, and updating. These steps are all considered in facilities layout evaluations, although the emphasis of these steps, when applied to layout planning, may be more specific.

Alternatives. After the general resource utilization, facility location, and process design approaches have been selected, specific site design alternatives are evaluated, including resource movement patterns, types of equipment, labor skill levels, and contingencies for emergency action, safety, and maintenance.

Mathematical algorithms. Such tools are often used to evaluate a particular layout pattern prior to implementation. The algorithm permits the operations manager to model or simulate each alternative without incurring extensive setup costs to test the process. In this manner, one or several of the more efficient designs may be selected for additional testing. The use of algorithms permits low-cost focusing of the solution process toward several of the more cost-effective alternatives.

Purpose. Layout analysis is used to increase process productivity through better integration of facilities and other resources.

Recent Developments in Facilities Layout Techniques

The three traditional production processes were identified in Chapter 3 as the line (product), job shop (process), and fixed position (project) approaches. Subsequently, in that chapter, a variety of recent developments, such as manufacturing cells and flexible manufacturing systems, were suggested as ways of integrating or mixing these processes and using the best characteristics of each. These developments have been made possible through computers and information control, which permit memory of complex actions and implementation of those actions without long setups; these developments have encouraged some of the more specific recent trends in facilities layout, including the following:

1. *Robotics*—Computer-controlled mechanical devices perform repetitive production operations.
2. *Automated Material Handling (AMH)*—Conveyors, fixed equipment movement paths, programmable delivery carts and other such devices reduce and simplify handling.
3. *Product/Process/Resource Identification*—Bar coding or other symbols are used for control, automation, and identification.
4. *Miniaturization*—Automation permits the use of smaller, more flexible equipment, thus saving space and cost.
5. *Process Flexibility*—The ability to rapidly change from one production process to another is an important trend.

Despite these developments, most traditional facility layout evaluation techniques still apply. This makes sense, of course, because the recent automation of production processes merely permits the integration of the best characteristics of the traditional processes. Thus, in the remainder of this chapter facility layout evaluation methods will be related primarily to traditional production techniques. The job shop layout, sometimes called a functional layout, is examined first.

FUNCTIONAL LAYOUT

The design objectives of the functional layout, which supports a job shop design, fall into two basic categories:

1. *Activity Relationships*—The objective is to obtain the desired distance (near or far) between two activities or departments due to reasons other than movement volume.
2. *Movement Distance*—The objective is to minimize the distance traveled by materials, customers, or employees.

Activity Relationships

In both service and manufacturing operations there are often conditions that make it desirable for two activities to be relatively close or relatively distant. The requirements of these conditions may supersede material, employee, or customer movement considerations and are as many and varied as are the diverse service and manufacturing operations. Some conditions are environmental, for example, the avoidance of noise, dust, fumes, or other toxic substances. Other requirements are for safety, such as protection from high voltages or radiation. Security, privacy, supervision, and quality of work life objectives are other factors that suggest either closeness or distance of specific work activities. Muther (1961) has described a relationship chart that is very useful for analyzing qualitative aspects of layout design.

THE ACTIVITY RELATIONSHIP CHART.   All of the activities of a particular process must be identified; then the relationships, in terms of closeness or distance, and the underlying reasons for the relationships must be developed. These relationships are often expressed in codes such as those shown in Table 9–1.

There are many variations of this coding structure, including some that have an associated numeric value. After the coding structure has been decided upon and the relationship requirements for each pair of activities has been identified, the information is often depicted in a chart similar to Figure 9–1.

To solve this type of layout problem, start with a floor diagram, that includes the walls, doors, corridors, and any other construction that has a bearing on location requirements. For example, a hospital emergency room would require a driveway and outside door for ambulance access. Typically, the layout analyst begins with the A (absolutely essential) relationships and places them on the diagram, often toward the center, so that as many of the A relationship cells can be joined as possible. Once the A relationships have been satisfied, the X (not desirable) relationships are considered. If X relationships are identified among activities that have already been placed on the layout chart and those X activities are adjoining, then one or both activities are moved, consistent with the A relationship requirements. Subsequently, the remaining X activities are placed near opposite edges of the chart. When all X relationships have been satisfied, the analyst considers the E, I, O and U relationships, fitting the activities together in the best way possible, consistent with the closeness constraints. This general description can be stated as the following set of rules:

1. Allocate all activities with an A relationship in adjacent positions on the layout chart, usually near the center.
2. Check to assure that this allocation to the layout chart does not include any X relationships.
3. Place one activity of each X relationship toward an edge of the layout chart and the other activity of the pair near an opposite edge of the chart, in such

Table 9–1   Activity Relationship Chart Codes

Code	Value	Closeness	Code	Reason
A	4	Absolutely essential		
E	3	Extremely important	1	Material flow
I	2	Important	2	Dust and dirt
O	1	Ordinary importance	3	Safety
U	0	Unimportant	4	Temperature
X	−10	Not desirable	5	Odor

Figure 9–1   Activity Relationship Chart

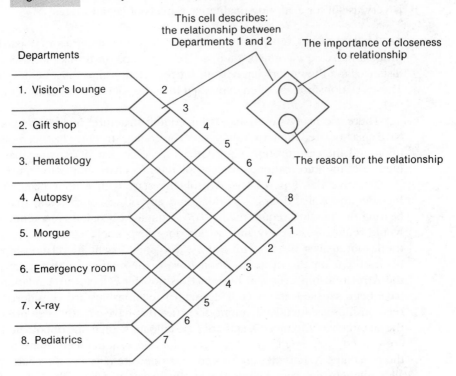

a manner than no X activities are adjacent. Continue until all X interrelated activities have been allocated.

4. Sequentially place E, I, O, and U activities in available positions.

This method of allocating positions based on activity relationships is not very precise, nor can it be. For this reason, it is sometimes called the qualitative method of facility layout evaluation. It may be necessary, for example, to place two X related activities together because of constraints imposed by A relationships. Thus, the layout analyst must weigh the value of having A activities together against the problems created by adjacent X activities. Additionally, there is no way to assess how good this particular solution is relative to other solutions, except as a subjective evaluation. For this reason, a numeric value is sometimes applied to the closeness codes. A commonly used set of values is shown in Table 9–1, although any sequenced set of values can be defined.

After all activities have been allocated a position, the analyst computes the value of each adjacent location. There are several methods, but one popular method sums the value of each horizontally and vertically adjacent activity pair. Sometimes diagonally adjacent pairs are also included. Thus, when evaluating several alternatives, the layout with the highest value sum

Figure 9–2 Example Activity Relationship Chart

Departments (Partial List)

1. Visitor's lounge
2. Gift shop
3. Hematology
4. Autopsy
5. Morgue
6. Emergency room
7. X-ray
8. Pediatrics

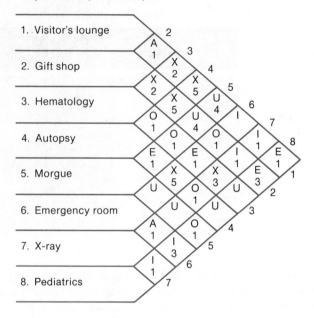

is the best. Of course, negative totals are possible if negatively valued X relationships are in close proximity.

An Example Activity Relationship Problem. Consider that the available floor space is a two room by four room rectangle with one internal corridor and internal and external doors for each room. Department pairs are evaluated using the codes shown in Table 9–1, which results in the activity relationship chart depicted at Figure 9–2.

To solve this problem, first identify that there are two A relationships, those of activities 1–2 and 6–7. Place these activities near the center of the floor space diagram, as shown at Figure 9–3. Then identify the six X pairs, 1–3,

Figure 9–3 Available Floor Space Diagram

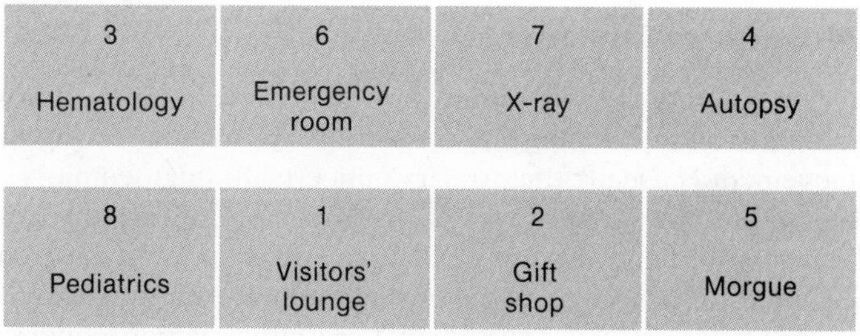

3
Hematology
6
Emergency room
7
X-ray
4
Autopsy
8
Pediatrics
1
Visitors' lounge
2
Gift shop
5
Morgue

Table 9–2   Value Computations for the
Example Activity Relationship
Problem (Adjacent
Departments Only)

Activity	Relationship Closeness Code	Value
3–6	E	3
3–8	U	0
8–1	E	3
6–7	A	4
6–1	I	2
1–2	A	4
7–2	I	2
7–4	O	1
2–5	U	0
4–5	E	3
Total		22

1–4, 2–3, 2–4, 3–7, and 4–6. Note that the four presently allocated activities do not have any X relationships among them. Place the unallocated activities that have an X relationship, that is, activities 3 and 4, in such a manner that none of the six X relationships are violated. Because activity 3 can not be directly (horizontally or vertically) adjacent to activities 1, 2, or 7, place activity 3 adjacent to activity 6 in the upper-left corner. Because activity 4 cannot be directly adjacent to activities 1, 2, or 6, place activity 4 adjacent to activity 7 in the upper-right corner. The remaining two activities, 5 and 8, have no binding constraints, although it would be nice to satisfy the E relationships of activities 5–4, 8–1 and 8–2. These can be partially satisfied by placing activity 5 adjacent to activity 4 and activity 8 adjacent to activity 1. The numeric structure introduced in Table 9–1 can be used to compute the value of this layout. This particular allocation has a total score of 22, based on computations of horizontal and vertical adjacencies (see Table 9–2). This score could be compared with other layout allocations using the same value system and method of computation.

Movement Distance

A common layout design objective is to minimize movement distance within activity relationship constraints. In manufacturing facilities, material movement is usually the primary concern although employee movement may be important in some cases. In many service operations, employee and customer movement distances are more important than material movement. For example, in a speech pathology or communications disorder clinic where many of the patients (customers) are either young children or the elderly, sequential workstations for diagnosis and therapy should be reasonably close; they should not be on different floors or in different buildings.

A number of different methods, some computerized, are available to analyze movement distance. Most of these methods are minor variants of the travel charting method, which is discussed here. Because movement distance methods use numeric values to directly express activity relationships, they are sometimes called quantitative layout analysis methods.

TRAVEL CHARTING.   Travel charting is a common-sense approach for calculating the total travel distance of a layout; it uses tables similar to mileage charts on roadmaps in the following five-step procedure.

Step 1. Collect the prerequisite information. Typical data requirements include the following:
   a. Ground rules, such as restrictions or assumptions on sizes and shapes of activity areas, and penalties, such as for backtracking
   b. The operational sequence (process) for the production of each item
   c. The production volume of each item during a typical production period
   d. The load factor, relative difficulty or cost of moving an item on this particular route
   e. A proposed layout

Step 2. Construct the distance table for the layout. If the same route is used traveling in both directions between departments, it will be a symmetrical matrix. In a distance table
   a. Each department should be located in the same row and column.
   b. The physical proximity of departments should be reflected by the proximity of the rows and columns selected for the departments.

Step 3. Construct the volume (move) table showing the total number of moves between all departments for all products. If appropriate, incorporate product loading or construct the cost-per-unit distance table to reflect that some movements are more costly than others. Requirements a and b in Step 2 are also necessary for a volume table.

Step 4. Construct the travel chart by multiplying each entry in the volume table by the corresponding entry (cell) in the distance table (and in the cost table if used) and entering that number into the corresponding cell in the travel chart.

Step 5. Examine the travel chart to determine functions (departments) whose relocation would likely lower the total travel. Compute costs and continue to adjust.

Travel costs can be incorporated in two ways. If there are several widely used predetermined routes, such as the product or service delivery flows for a small number of products or services, a common practice is to compute the product/process loads. Alternatively, if costs or loads vary notably for each activity pair, as they do with personnel or mail movement between offices, it is more appropriate to use a cost-per-unit distance matrix that incorporates different costs for each cell. For example, in an administrative environment, the cost of executive time spent in interoffice movement would differ from that of staff or clerical travel time. Thus, routes around an office that are heavily used by executives are more costly than other routes. An overview of the total cost of a particular allocation is presented by the formula:

$$TC = \sum_{i=1}^{n} \sum_{j=1}^{n} C_{ij} V_{ij} D_{ij}$$

where

i = The first activity in a pair

j = The second activity in a pair

n = The number of activity pairs

C = Cost/Volume/Unit Distance

V = Volume of flow, which may incorporate load factors if appropriate

D = Distance between activities

The travel distance approach is often preferred over qualitative methods if reasonable data are available. At a minimum, accurate volume and distance data are required. If appropriate, loading factor or cost data are useful; otherwise, loading factors or costs are assumed to be equal among all activity pairs.

Numerous factors, such as multiple routes, several floors of a building, placement of external exits, controlled areas (for example, security restricted areas for drugs or maintenance operations) and different movement patterns for employees or customers can all complicate layout analysis problems. Thus, analysts must make some basic assumptions, such as movement within an activity (or room) is not measured; distance is measured from the nearest door; and the most direct route to the destination is used. For this reason even the highly quantitative movement distance approach should be regarded as an approximation, not an exact representation, of the total loaded or cost-adjusted travel distance of a particular layout.

An Example Travel Charting Problem.   The following example of the travel charting or movement distance method incorporates many, though for simplicity, not all, of the previous considerations. The data required for Step 1 include the following ground rules:

1. The dimensions of the building are fixed at 20 feet × 80 feet; there are no internal walls.
2. All departments are 10 feet × 20 feet and can be moved anywhere within the building.

Table 9–3 Example Travel Charting Problem Data

Item	Process Sequence (by department)	Parts per Month	Parts per Load	Loads per Month	Load Factor	Movement Units per Month
1	RI – A – E – D – F – PD	1,000	40	25	5	125
2	RI – B – D – C – E – PD	4,000	80	50	2	100
3	RI – C – A – D – F – PD	8,000	100	80	3	240
4	RI – A – D – B – E – PD	3,000	60	50	1	50

Note: RI = resource input; A–F = departments; and PD = product delivery.

3. Aisles are north-south and east-west. Distances are right-angle measures from department centers.
4. There is no penalty for backtracking. The operation sequence, production volume, parts per load, load factor, movement of units per month are provided in Table 9–3. A proposed layout is shown in Figure 9–4.

Note that parts per load depends on the containers, pallets, skids, and other material-handling devices or, in a service environment, facility constraints such as customer group size. The load factor represents the relative difficulty or cost of moving each item or group along the specified route. Multiplying the load factor by the loads per month incorporates the variable cost of movement. Because there are only four items in this problem, the loading factor approach is used.

This completes all parts of Step 1. That is, restrictions and assumptions have been stated, the operational sequence, production volume, and load factors for each item have been defined; and a proposed layout has been established. From this information, the distance table (Step 2) and the volume table (Step 3) can be constructed. If products flow in one direction only, a one-sided computation of the distance table is used. In the case of human resource (employee or customer) movement where the flow involves round trips, if the number of trips and costs in the to-and-from directions are the

Figure 9–4 Example Travel Charting Problem Proposed Layout

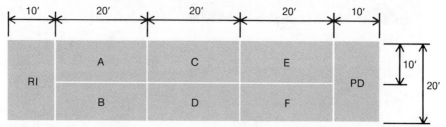

Note: RI = resource input; A–F = departments; and PD = product delivery

Table 9-4 Example Travel Charting Problem Distance Table

To \ From	RI	A	B	C	D	E	F
RI	—						
A	15	—					
B	15	10	—				
C	35	20	30	—			
D	35	30	20	10	—		
E	55	40	50	20	30	—	
F	55	50	40	30	20	10	—
PD	70	55	55	35	35	15	15

same, the one-sided computation results can be multiplied by 2 to get the total round-trip value. Otherwise, a nonsymmetrical flow matrix must be used. The distance table is shown in Table 9-4.

Note that the position of the activities in columns and rows suggests the proximity of those activities. Since this flow is forward and there is no penalty for backtracking, it is only necessary to use one side of the table. This has been done in Table 9-5, which shows the volume (move) table.

Using the example data, from Resource Input (RI) to Department A there are 125 trips for Item 1 and 50 trips for Item 4, for a total of 175 trips. This value is placed in Row A, Column 1 of the Volume Table. The values in the other cells are determined in the same manner. A blank column indicates there is no material moved from the column department to the row department. In this case, there is no need for a cost matrix; the use of the load factor results in all loads being cost equivalent. Steps 2 and 3 have now been completed. The fourth step, constructing the travel chart, is shown in Table 9-6.

Note that the product of the distance table and the volume table cells is divided by 100 and rounded off to simplify the travel chart. For example, for the RI to A Cell, multiply 175 by 15 and enter 26, which is 2,625/100.

Table 9-5 Example Travel Charting Problem Volume Table

To \ From	RI	A	B	C	D	E	F	PD
RI	—							
A	175	—						
B	100		—					
C	240	240		—				
D		290	150	100	—			
E		125	50	100	125	—		
F					365		—	
PD						150	365	—

Table 9–6   Travel Chart for Proposed Layout
(Unit Load in Feet Per Month)

To \ From	RI	A	B	C	D	E	F	PD	Total
RI	—								
A	26	—							26
B	15		—						15
C	84	48		—					132
D		87	30	10	—				127
E		50	25	20	38	—			133
F					73		—		73
PD						23	55	—	78
Total	125	185	55	30	111	23	55		584

The total unit load in feet traveled per month with the proposed layout is approximately 58,400. This completes Step 4 of the analysis.

In this travel chart, the diagonal represents travel from one location to the same location, or the internal travel, which is not considered here. Cells just off the diagonal represent travel to a directly adjacent location. Cells that are distant from the diagonal represent nonadjacent travel. To reduce total loaded distance, the analyst desires that heavy loads be in cells that are close to the diagonal and lighter loads be in cells away from the diagonal. This permits the following definitions of the Type A and Type B cells.

Type A cells possess large values and are a relatively long way from the diagonal. An examination of the travel chart reveals that the RI–C cell and the A–D cell have relatively large values, 84 and 87 respectively, and are some distance from the diagonal.

Type B cells possess relatively small values and are relatively close to the diagonal. Cells A–B, B–C, and E–F meet this description.

Step 5 examines the travel chart to determine which relocations would be likely to lower the costs. The following process is effective in analyzing the travel chart:

1. Interchange the positions of Type A and Type B cells
2. Check the activity relationship chart for possible violations
3. Calculate the aggregate movement cost of the revised layout

The objective is to revise the layout so as to move Type A cells closer to the diagonal and Type B cells further from the diagonal. The conclusions are that, if possible the following changes should be made:

1. Cell RI–C should be closer to the diagonal.
2. Cell A–D should be closer to the diagonal.
3. Cells E–F, A–B, and B–C need not be adjacent and should be moved further from the diagonal.

Figure 9–5   Example Travel Charting Problem
Revised Layout

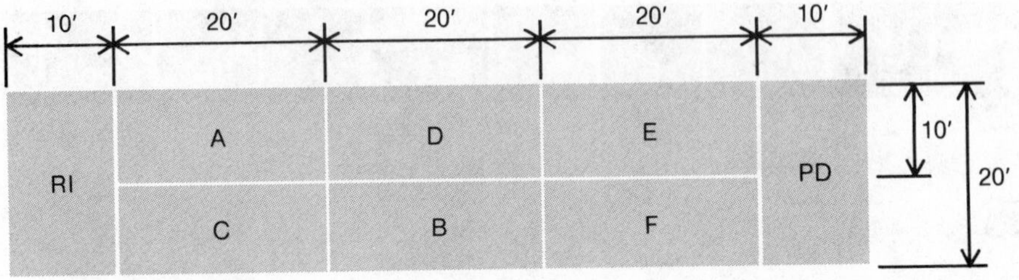

An examination of both the volume table (Table 9–5) and the travel chart (Table 9–6) reveals that Department B has less travel between itself and Department RI than either Department A or C do. Thus, this analysis reveals that the following changes should be made:

1. Move Department C to Department B's initial position
2. Move Department D to Department C's initial position
3. Move Department B to Department D's initial position

These changes are reflected in the revised layout shown in Figure 9–5.

At this point it is necessary to check the relationship chart to see if any prohibitions are being violated. The previous moves result in the combined distance-volume table shown in Table 9–7 and the travel chart shown in Table 9–8.

The total improvement equals 58,400 minus 55,200 or 3,200 unit load-feet per month, a 5.5 percent improvement. A further examination of the travel chart suggests that interchanging Departments E and F should be considered. This would improve the layout by about 2,600 unit load-feet per month in total movement, for a revised total of approximately 52,600.

This example reveals that travel charting can be laborious, but it can be useful in analyzing relatively small layouts, of ten or fewer departments.

THE NEARNESS PRIORITY RANKING METHOD.   For the analysis of a larger layout problem, the nearness priority ranking (NPR) method may be more helpful. This method ranks the cells of the loaded (or costed) volume table and identifies the costliest cells, in terms of flow, which have the highest priority for placement close together in the layout. Using the data from the volume table in Table 9–5, a ranking is created, as shown in Table 9–9.

The NPR method focuses the analyst's attention sequentially on the most important location relationships to satisfy. The analyst should initially place the RI and PD (product delivery) activities at the left and right sides of the chart respectively, because they are the first and last activities in a left-to-right job flow. The highest priority for nearness placement is the F–PD activity. To satisfy that priority, place Department F in the upper-right corner, as close as possible to PD. Then satisfy the other first-ranked priority

Table 9–7   Combined Distance-Volume Table for Revised Layout

To \ From	RI	A	C	D	B	E	F	PD
RI								
A	15 175							
C	15 240	10 240						
D	35	20 290	30 100					
B	35 100	30	20	10 150				
E	55	40 125	50 100	20 125	30 50			
F	55	50	40	30 365	20	10		
PD	75	55	55	35	35	15 150	15 365	

Note: Distance is the upper value in cell; volume is the lower value in cell.

Table 9–8   Travel Chart for Revised Layout

To \ From	RI	A	C	D	B	E	F	PD	Total
RI									
A	26								26
C	36	24							60
D		58	30						88
B	35			15					50
E		50	50	25	15				140
F				110					110
PD						23	55		78
Total	97	132	80	150	15	23	55		552

Table 9–9   Nearness Priority Ranking of Volume Chart Data

Rank	Activities	Loaded Volume
1	F–PD	365
1	D–F	365
3	A–D	290
4	RI–C	240
4	A–C	240
6	RI–A	175
7	E–PD	150
7	B–D	150
9	A–E	125
10	C–E	100
10	RI–B	100
10	C–D	100
14	B–E	50

(D–F) by placing Department D directly across from F in the lower-right location. This decision permits the analyst to minimize the distance of the movement load between these two departments. The third priority is then considered by placing Department A in the lower-center location, directly adjacent to Department D. Both of the fourth-ranked priorities can be satisfied by placing Department C in the lower-left location, between Departments A and RI. The E–PD and B–D priorities cannot be satisfied by direct proximity. However, if Department E is placed as close as possible to PD, the ninth priority (the proximity of activities A and E) can be satisfied. This leaves Department B in the upper-left corner. This possible NPR layout allocation is depicted in Figure 9–6.

The NPR method ranks the volume loads for each pair of a large number of activities; then the analyst satisfies the high-priority ranks with proximate locations. This process is much like the diagonal method; it will give a good solution to the layout problem, but not necessarily an optimal solution. It may not be optimal because it is difficult for the analyst to see the benefits that

Figure 9–6   NPR Layout Allocation

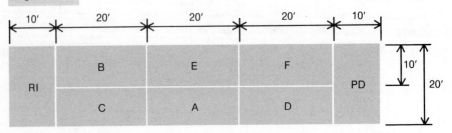

Table 9–10   Nearness Priority Ranking of Volume Chart Data
with Distance and Totals

Rank	Activities	Loaded Volume	Distance	Load × Distance
1	F–P	365	15	5,475
1	D–F	365	10	3,650
3	A–D	290	20	5,800
4	RI–C	240	15	3,600
4	A–C	240	20	4,800
6	RI–A	175	35	6,125
7	E–PD	150	35	5,250
7	B–D	150	50	7,500
9	A–E	125	10	1,250
10	C–E	100	30	3,000
10	RI–B	100	15	1,500
10	C–D	100	40	4,000
14	B–E	50	20	1,000
Total				52,950

are possible by disregarding a higher-ranked pair in favor of the improvement of several lesser-ranked pairs. The NPR chart is shown again in Table 9–10, with the distance and total calculations added.

Note that the total cost of movement is 52,950, an improvement over the initial layout, but not as good as the layout that was finally achieved by the diagonal method. Recall that the second layout allocation made, the placing of Department D directly opposite Department F, saved 10 feet of movement times the loaded volume of 365. However, had Department D been placed beside Department F, at an additional cost of $3,650, several subsequent costs would have been reduced. This would have led to the final solution of the travel charting method, including the final adjustment of swapping the locations of Departments E and F. This example shows the advantages (ease of use and rapidity of computation) and the disadvantages (difficulty in improving the solution toward optimization) of the NPR method. The NPR method is particularly effective for a large number of departments; it identifies a good, but not necessarily optimal, solution.

COMPUTERIZED LAYOUT EVALUATION.   For larger layouts, the use of computerized layout evaluation techniques is almost mandatory. The analyst just cannot visualize all of the possible tradeoffs. The most widely used computerized program is the Computerized Relative Allocation of Facilities Technique (CRAFT). This program uses the volume or cost-loaded matrix and the distance matrix as inputs. With these inputs the CRAFT program finds an initial layout, such as might be developed by the NPR method, and then tries to improve on that initial layout by making pairwise location exchanges and recomputing the total cost. If the total cost is improved, the exchange is made and the process is continued until several iterations yield no improvement.

Computer models are particularly useful because they can quickly identify low-cost solutions to layout decision and compare the costs of several feasible solutions. However, computer models have traditionally been regarded only as aids to decision-making. Certainly, some subjective or judgmental decision-making processes also must be incorporated. The best use of quantitative layout methods is to focus the decision on several low-cost alternatives and permit more qualitative considerations.

LINE (PRODUCT) LAYOUT

Line layouts are typically used to produce relatively large quantities of a single item or a closely related family of items. Ideally the work in process consists of one unit being processed at each workstation. The workstations are located so as to minimize the travel distance between them. Thus, a line layout approaches some objectives of just-in-time (JIT) production: space requirements and work-in-process requirements are relatively small.

Until recently the manufacturing line was usually designed to produce a large volume of one item with some minor variations. This is no longer the case; manufacturing cells enable a flow line to be used for much shorter runs of different items. The widespread implementation of manufacturing cells and flexible manufacturing systems in traditional job shop (manufacturing and service) environments has led to the need for increased specialization and co-ordination in the development and implementation of manufacturing and service cells, flexible manufacturing systems, and mixed model assembly lines.

Measures of Performance

In analyzing, developing, and evaluating a flow line, the three major considerations are as follows:

1. Process efficiency
2. Line capacity and utilization
3. Line-balancing efficiency

These all contribute to line process efficiency in an interrelated manner and are defined as follows:

Process (line) efficiency is the proportion of time a line is producing good parts while running. The line can fail to perform for various reasons, including bad parts, jammed or failed equipment, or maintenance or adjustment downtime.

Line capacity is the output rate performance, often stated in terms of the number of good units produced per time period. Utilization measures the proportion of available capacity used in production.

Line balancing efficiency measures the proportion of time the workstations in a line are not idle and waiting because one workstation has a longer operating time than the others. Line balancing seeks to ensure that all workstations in a particular line sequence require exactly the same amount of time to perform the required tasks. This ensures minimum queues and facilitates a smooth flow of product along the line.

These issues are treated more completely in the following sections.

PROCESS EFFICIENCY. The technology of some manufacturing processes has developed to the point that relatively little line downtime is caused by machine or part jamming, tool breakage, or equipment failure. In addition, relatively few bad parts are produced. Some metal machining and bottling lines fall in this category. Other operations have not developed these levels of process efficiency. For example, printing and page collating lines frequently jam and destroy some of the work-in-process. In either case, production planners must consider the process efficiency when determining capacity requirements, material requirements, and production schedules. The variables defined in Table 9–11 are used here in analyzing the production cycle times, efficiency, and process yields.

Production capacity requirements must be based on C, the production cycle time, incorporating machine downtime due to jamming and other minor malfunctions. Note that these breakdowns do not include major failures, such as the burnout of a bearing, motor failure, or control system failure. Major failures are usually repaired by the maintenance department and result in a relatively lengthy downtime. Such events are classified as emergency repairs rather than equipment or work piece adjustments made by the operator. Time for major emergency repairs is downtime; the production process cycle time concerns running time.

Table 9–11   Terms Related to the Analysis of
Line Layout Performance

Term	Definition
c	Ideal cycle time; no downtime adjustments
C	Cycle time of the process, taking adjustments for minor malfunctions into consideration
E_p	Process efficiency
N	Number of workstations
$P(A)$	Probability of adjustment (jamming) in a cycle
Q_s	Average number of units scrapped per jam
$\overline{RM}$	Average raw material units required
R	Requirements per time period
T	Time length of shift
T_A	Average time a line is down for an adjustment
T_P	Time required to produce a given quantity
U	Utilization expressed as a percentage

Cycle Time. Production cycle time (C) equals the total cycle time (c) plus the probability of an adjustment, multiplied by the average time of that adjustment. This is expressed mathematically as:

$$C = c + (P(A) \times T_A)$$

For example, a line can produce one unit every 2.0 minutes, but it jams an average of once every fifty cycles, and one unit is scrapped each time the line jams. Adjustment of the line and work in process takes 3.5 minutes on the average. In this example, the cycle time is as follows:

$$CA = 2.0 + (.02 \times 3.5) = 2.07 \text{ minutes}$$

where

$$c = 2.0 \text{ minutes}$$

$$P(A) = 0.02$$

$$T_A = 3.5 \text{ minutes}$$

$$Q_s = 1 \text{ unit}$$

Efficiency. The process efficiency (E_p) equals the ideal cycle time divided by the production cycle time. This is expressed mathematically as

$$E_p = \frac{c}{C} = \frac{c}{c + (P(A) \times T_A)}$$

In the example given, the process efficiency is

$$E_p = \frac{2.0 \text{ minutes}}{2.0 \text{ minutes} + (0.02 \times 3.5 \text{ minutes})} = \frac{2.0 \text{ minutes}}{2.07 \text{ minutes}} = 0.966$$

When there are two or more workstations in a line, line-balancing efficiency must also be considered. The line-balancing efficiency (E_L), expressed as a percentage, equals the sum of the operation times of all workstations divided by the total workstation time or the number of stations (N) times the longest workstation cycle time. Thus,

$$E_L = \frac{\sum\limits_{i=1}^{N} c_i}{NC} \times 100\%$$

Figure 9–7   Multiple Workstation Example

Layout Diagram

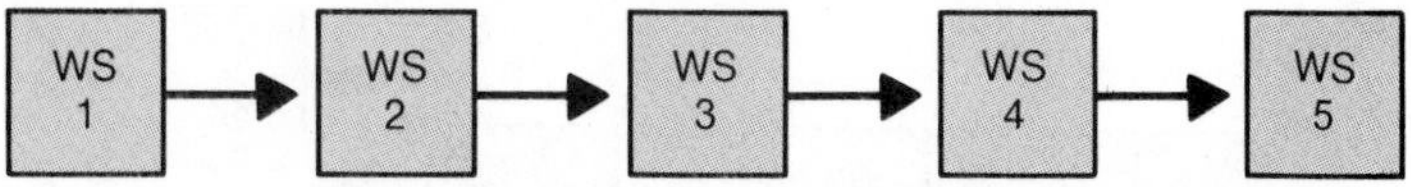

Workstation	Machine	Activity Time c_i (minutes)	Delay Time $C - c_i = d_i$ (minutes)
1	1	1.3	2.5
2	2	1.6	2.2
3	3	2.0	1.8
4	4	3.8	0
5	5	1.6	2.2
		10.3	8.7

For example, consider the number of workstations, activity times and delay times shown in Figure 9–7. The line-balancing efficiency for this multiple workstation example is

$$E_L = \frac{10.3 \text{ minutes}}{5 \times 3.8 \text{ minutes}} \times 100\% = 54.2\%$$

This means that, when the line is operating, the average workstation is in use 54.2 percent of the time.

Continuing with this example, consider a cycle time of 2.0 minutes. This can be achieved by adding another machine to Workstation 4. This layout and data are shown in Figure 9–8. The new line-balancing efficiency is:

$$E_L = \frac{10.3 \text{ minutes}}{(6 \text{ workstations})(2.0 \text{ minutes})} = 85.8\%$$

Thus, the line-balancing efficiency increases dramatically with the addition of one machine. However, adding a machine is expensive and may not be justified if the output rate requirement is low and the line utilization (U) decreases precipitously as a result. For a low-output line that is manually operated, the cost of added equipment and personnel may be justified by the increased labor efficiency due to improved line balancing and the use of personnel for other tasks during nonutilization of the equipment.

Yield.   For a given output requirement (R), the average raw materials requirements (inputs) are calculated as follows:

Figure 9-8   Modified Multiple Workstation Example

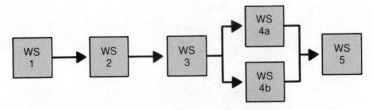

Layout Diagram

Workstation	Machine	Activity Time c_i (minutes)	Delay Time $C - c_i = d_i$ (minutes)
1	1	1.3	0.7
2	2	1.6	0.4
3	3	2.0	0
4	4a	1.9	0.1
	4b	1.9	0.1
5	5	1.6	0.4
		10.3	1.7

$$\overline{RM} = \frac{R}{1 - (P(A) \times Q_s)}$$

If the production required in the example is 48,000 units, $\overline{RM}$ is calculated as follows:

$$\overline{RM} = \frac{48,000 \text{ units}}{1 - (.02 \times 1 \text{ unit})} = 48,980 \text{ units}$$

LINE CAPACITY AND UTILIZATION.   Utilization is usually measured by the percentage of time a line must be run to achieve the required output quantity. Consequently,

$$U = \frac{T_p}{T} \times 100$$

$$T_p = R \times C$$

For example, a plant operates one shift, forty hours a week, fifty weeks a year. The line is dedicated to manufacturing one product; it is a single-model line. Preventative maintenance is performed on another shift. The line produces an acceptable unit every 2.07 minutes on average, as calculated previously. The production plan calls for 48,000 units annually at a steady rate throughout the year. Therefore

$$R = 48,000 \text{ units}$$

$$C = 2.07 \text{ minutes}$$

$$T = 40 \text{ hours} \times 50 \text{ weeks} = 2,000 \text{ hours per year}$$

$$T_p = 48,000 \text{ units} \times 2.07 \text{ minutes} = 99,360 \text{ minutes}$$

$$= 1,656 \text{ hours per year}$$

and

$$U = \frac{1,656 \text{ hours per year}}{2,000 \text{ hours per year}} \times 100 = 82.8\%$$

The line has 344 hours (2,000 − 1,656) of excess capacity per year; consequently, it has the capacity to meet a surge in demand. On the other hand, increasing the cycle time leads to balanced demand and output rates and increased line utilization, which is more efficient from a manufacturing perspective. The maximum cycle time (the upper limit given the output requirements) equals the production time divided by the required quantity. This is expressed mathematically as

$$C_{\max} = \frac{T}{R}$$

$$C_{\max} = \frac{2,000 \text{ hours}}{48,000 \text{ units}} = .0417 \text{ hours or 2.5 minutes}$$

VARYING REQUIREMENTS.   In the preceding example, the output requirements were projected as a constant 960 units per week; that is, 48,000 units in 50 weeks. However, production plans frequently call for the manufacture of varying amounts in different weeks or months. In such cases the capacity requirements for different output rates should be analyzed. If, for example, all of the preceding information is the same except that the production requirements vary from a minimum of 600 units per week to a maximum of 1,200 units per week, analysis would usually begin with the maximum weekly output rate ($R_{\max}$) required. The analysis of this example is as follows:

$$R_{max} = 1,200 \text{ units per week}$$

$$T_p = 1,200 \text{ units} \times 2.07 \text{ minutes} = 2,484 \text{ minutes}$$

$$= 41.4 \text{ hours}$$

Consequently, either overtime must be employed or the cycle time decreased. If the planned weekly production rates over the next four quarters are 600, 800, 1,000, and 1,200 units respectively, production capacity and utilization are summarized in Table 9–12.

Assembly Line Balancing

Capacity utilization and process efficiency studies treat the process line as a single unit when, in fact, lines have many workstations. Each workstation may have different jamming and scrap rates. Such conditions and the effect of adding work-in-process banks between workstations, sometimes called internal storage, are discussed in detail by Groover (1987). In addition, a production line may be used 100 percent of the time (U equals 100 percent), but individual workstations can be idle a proportion of the operating time. (In actuality, Parkinson's law often takes effect; workers sometimes reduce their pace and appear to be busy throughout their work cycle.) This occurs when the operations performed at one workstation take longer than the time required to complete the operations at other stations. Thus, a major objective of line balancing is to have the total operation time at each workstation be approximately the same.

The terms and symbols that are used throughout the discussion of assembly line balancing are shown in Table 9–13.

More than one operation may be performed at most workstations. Figure 9–9 schematically represents an example solution in which Operations 1, 2, and 3 are assigned to Workstation A; Operations 4 and 5 are assigned to Workstation B; and Operation 6 is assigned to Workstation C. Planning the assembly line involves assigning each operation to a specific workstation. Note

Table 9–12 Summary of Capacity Requirements

Weekly Production Requirements in Units	Production Hours Available	Production Hours Required	Percent Utilization	Percent Overtime Required
600	40	20.7	51.8	0
800	40	27.6	69.0	0
1,000	40	34.5	86.25	0
1,200	40	41.4	100.0	3.5

Table 9–13   Terms Related to Assembly Line Balancing

Symbol	Term	Definition
i	Operation	Element of a task performed at a workstation
j	Workstation	Physical location with operators and/or machines where one or more operations (activities) are performed
A_i	Activity time	Time required to complete Operation i
C	Cycle time	Length of time between the completion of two successive units on a line; determined by the workstation with the longest cycle time
c_j	Cycle time in Workstation j	Time required to complete the activities assigned to Workstation j and to move the item to the next station
R	Required production	Quantity of units required in time T
T	Production period	Number of operating hours in the period
d_j	Delay time	Idle (delay) time per cycle at Workstation j while the line is operating
D	Total delay	Total of idle (delay) time per cycle at all workstations while the line is operating (inefficiency due to imperfect line balance)
N	Number of workstations	Number of workstations in the line
t	Throughput time	The average time to complete all activities, sometimes called the makespan
E_L	Line efficiency	Line-balancing efficiency expressed as a percentage
N_m	Number of machines	Number of machines in an automated line
n	Number of activities	Number of activities (operations)

that in this case, the operations have been assigned so that the cumulative times at each workstation (C_i) are less than or equal to 6.3 minutes.

Many analytic and heuristic approaches exist for solving assembly line–balancing problems (Dar-El 1975). Balancing an assembly line involves combining and assigning tasks to workstations. There are basically two different situations in which assembly line balancing takes place.

Type I. The maximum cycle time is established by production requirements (C_{max} equals time available divided by the units required); and the objective is to minimize the number of workstations.

Type II. The number of workstations is fixed, and the objective is to minimize the cycle time and load the stations equally.

Figure 9–9   Assignment of Operations to Workstations

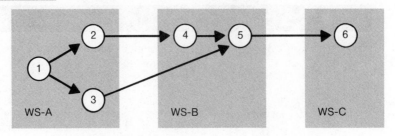

Workstation	Operation	Time (A_i) (minutes)	C_i
A	1	1.5	
	2	3.4	
	3	1.3	6.2
B	4	4.1	
	5	1.8	5.9
C	6	6.3	6.3

SITUATION TYPE I—MAXIMUM CYCLE TIME.   This situation is more common than the Type II problem in both manufacturing and service organizations, and there are literally scores of methods available to solve it.

Empirical approaches include using more than one of a given workstation, task sharing among workers in two or more stations, reorganizing tasks by using off-line subassembly, scheduling overtime for certain tasks, and using work-in-process banks. Some approaches, such as off-line subassembly, can be useful in the short run and are occasionally justified as permanent solutions.

As mentioned previously, there are many techniques, both exact and heuristic, that have been developed to solve this problem (Baybars 1986, Hoffmann 1963, Johnson 1988, Mastor 1970). While the Hoffmann heuristic has been shown to be superior in computation (Talbot, Patterson, and Gehrlein 1986), the longest candidate rule and the ranked positional weights method are more easily described for manual calculation and will be used to provide insight into the line-balancing problem. Their use will also show that multiple, equally efficient solutions frequently exist for this problem.

Longest Candidate Rule (LCR).   Since activities with the longest times are the most difficult to schedule within cycle time constraints, it makes sense that their assignments would have priority. That is the rationale of the longest candidate rule. The procedure is as follows:

Table 9–14   Job Activities, Times, and
Precedence Relationships

Activity i	Activity Time A_i (minutes)	Immediate Predecessors
1	.8	—
2	3.1	—
3	.6	1
4	1.2	1, 2
5	2.0	2
6	2.4	4
7	4.2	2, 4
8	.8	5
9	1.6	6
10	2.2	3, 7, 9
11	1.0	8, 10

Step 1. Prepare the precedence network.

Step 2. List the activities in descending order of A_i.

Step 3. Start with the longest A_i and assign the first feasible activity to Workstation 1. A feasible activity meets the precedence requirements and does not cause the total workstation time to exceed the cycle time (C). Add the next longest feasible activity to the workstation and continue until no more activities can be added.

Step 4. Repeat Step 3 for Workstation 2, and all additional workstations until all activities have been assigned and workstations formed.

Using the data provided in Table 9–14, a C_{max} of 6 minutes, and the LCR procedure as outlined here, a network can be determined and assignments to workstations made.

Step 1. The precedence network begins with Activities 1 and 2, which have no predecessors. Activities 3, 4, and 5 are added next since their predecessors are Activities 1 and 2. This allows Activities 6, 7, and 8 to be added, then 9, and finally 10 and 11. The network shown in Figure 9–10 is the result.

Step 2. Table 9–15 lists the activities in descending order of A_i.

Step 3. Working down the list, the first feasible activity is Activity 2, the next is Activity 5 (its predecessor, Activity 2, has been completed), and then Activity 1. Since the total time of these three activities is 5.9 minutes, all three are assigned to Workstation 1. Since no other activities can be added to Workstation 1 without exceeding the 6-minute cycle time, go to Step 4.

Step 4. The status is as follows: Activities 2, 5, and 1 have been assigned; prerequisites for Activities 4, 8, and 3 have been completed. Starting at the top of the list, Activity 4 is the first for which precedence requirements have been met, so assign it to Workstation 2. Since this fulfills the prerequisites for Activity 7, we can add it to Workstation 2. Activity 3 is the only

Figure 9–10   Network Depicting Precedence Relationships

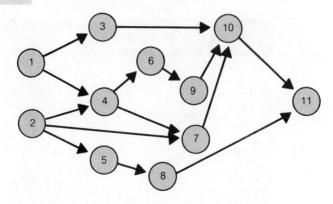

remaining feasible addition. Thus, Workstation 2 consists of Activities 4, 7, and 3. Continuing in the same manner, Workstation 3 consists of Activities 6, 9, and 8, with a total time of 4.8 minutes, and Workstation 4 includes Activities 10 and 11 with a total time of 3.2 minutes. This results in the assignment of activities to workstations as shown in Table 9–16.

The theoretical minimum number of workstations is determined by dividing the sum of the activity times by the maximum cycle time as follows:

$$N_{min}(\text{integer}) \geq \frac{\sum_{i=1}^{n} A_i}{C_{max}}$$

Table 9–15   Job Activities in Descending Order of Activity Times

Activity i	Activity Time A_i (minutes)	Immediate Predecessors
7	4.2	2, 4
2	3.1	—
6	2.4	4
10	2.2	3, 7, 9
5	2.0	2
9	1.6	6
4	1.2	1, 2
11	1.0	8, 10
1	.8	—
8	.8	5
3	.6	1
	19.9	

Table 9–16	Assignment of Activities to Workstations Using the LCR Method—Type I Problem		

Workstation	Activity i	Activity Time A_i (minutes)	Workstation Time
1	2	3.1	
	5	2.0	
	1	.8	5.9
2	4	1.2	
	7	4.2	
	3	.6	6.0
3	6	2.4	
	9	1.6	
	8	.8	4.8
4	10	2.2	
	11	1.0	3.2
		$\Sigma A_i = 19.9$	

Therefore, for this example

$$N_{\min} \geq \frac{19.9 \text{ minutes}}{6 \text{ minutes}} \geq 3.1 = 4 \text{ workstations}$$

Thus, the above solution is the minimum number of workstations possible. However, it is not the only possible solution, as an application of the ranked positional weights method will demonstrate.

Ranked Positional Weights (RPW) Rule. The ranked positional weights rule assigns activities to workstations on the basis of the total time required for an activity and all following activities in its precedence chain. It was described by Helgeson and Bernie in 1961. The procedure is as follows:

Step 1. Develop the precedence network.
Step 2. Calculate the ranked positional weight for each activity by adding its own activity time to the times of all activities that follow it on the precedence chain. This is expressed mathematically as

$$RPW_i = \sum_{i=p}^{f} A_i$$

where p to f includes all the activities on activity i's precedence chain.

Step 3. List all activities in descending order of their RPW_i.
Step 4. Assign activities to workstations by working down the list meeting station cycle time and precedence constraints.

Table 9–17 Ranked Positional Weights of Activities

Activity i	Activity Time A_i (minutes)	Precedence Chain Activities	RPW_i
1	.8	1, 3, 4, 6, 7, 9, 10, 11	14.0
2	3.1	2, 4, 5, 6, 7, 8, 9, 10, 11	18.5
3	.6	3, 10, 11	3.8
4	1.2	4, 6, 7, 9, 10, 11	12.6
5	2.0	5, 8, 11	3.8
6	2.4	6, 9, 10, 11	7.2
7	4.2	7, 10, 11	7.4
8	.8	8, 11	1.8
9	1.6	9, 10, 11	4.8
10	2.2	10, 11	3.2
11	1.0	11	1.0

The RPW method is applied to the example data in Table 9–14 in the following manner.

Step 1. The precedence network developed in the LCR approach (Figure 9–10) remains unchanged.

Step 2. All activities except Activities 2, 5, and 8 are in the precedence chain of Activity 1; and all activities except Activities 5 and 8 are in the precedence chain of Activity 2. Therefore, their RPW_i's are 14.0 and 18.5, respectively. For example, to compute the RPW_i of Activity 1, sum the activity times of each activity in the precedence chain—that is, .8 + .6 + 1.2 + 2.4 + 4.2 + 1.6 + 2.2 + 1.0 = 14.0. Table 9–17 shows the RPW of each activity.

Step 3. Table 9–18 lists the activities in descending rank order.

Table 9–18 Activities in RPW Order

Activity i	RPW_i	Activity Time A_i (minutes)	Immediate Predecessors
2	18.5	3.1	—
1	14.0	.8	—
4	12.6	1.2	1, 2
7	7.4	4.2	2, 4
6	7.2	2.4	4
9	4.8	1.6	6
3	3.8	.6	1
5	3.8	2.0	2
10	3.2	2.2	3, 9, 7
8	1.8	.8	5
11	1.0	1.0	8, 10

Table 9–19   Assignment of Activities to Workstations Using
the RPW Rule

Workstation	Activity i	Activity Time A_i (minutes)	Workstation Time
1	2	3.1	
	1	.8	
	4	1.2	
	3	.6	5.7
2	7	4.2	4.2
3	6	2.4	
	9	1.6	
	5	2.0	6.0
4	10	2.2	
	8	.8	
	11	1.0	4.0
		$\Sigma A_i = 19.9$	

Step 4. Assigning activities to workstations by working down the table and
meeting cycle time and precedence constraints gives the organization
of workstations shown in Table 9–19.

Each method obtains a different solution, but both use the minimum
feasible number of workstations. Other solutions are also possible. Examining
the other objectives for the assembly line, described previously, and their
relative importance will assist in making the final decisions concerning the
assignment of activities to workstations.

SITUATION TYPE II—FIXED NUMBER OF WORKSTATIONS.   First, the cycle
time (C) must be less than C_{max} if output requirements are to be met. This
also means that the longest time for any operation must be less than C_{max}.
Since the number of workstations is fixed in a Type II assembly line–balancing
problem, the objective is usually to assign the activities to the workstations so
that the maximum time required at any one workstation (i.e., the cycle time)
is minimized. One or more of the empirical objectives also may influence the
assignment of activities to workstations.

The Type II Problem.   Let the manufacturing environment be such that
management has decided to use six workstations for producing an assembly,
and it is not feasible to assemble any other product in this area. In a Type
II problem, one objective is to obtain the minimum cycle time (C_{min}) given
a fixed number of workstations (N). In a system with perfect balance, C_{min}

equals the sum of the activity times divided by the number of workstations; that is,

$$C_{\min} = \frac{\sum\limits_{i=1}^{N} A_i}{N}$$

or in this example

$$C_{\min} = \frac{19.9 \text{ minutes}}{6 \text{ workstations}} = 3.32 \text{ minutes with perfect balance}$$

Longest Candidate Rule—Type II Problem. The solution of the example problem using the data in Table 9–14, the LCR method, and a fixed number of workstations follows. These data reveal that $C_{\min}$ equals 4.2 minutes, the duration of Activity 7, unless Activity 7 could be divided between two workstations. Since the perfect balance cycle time is 3.32 minutes, 3.7 minutes (approximately 110 percent of 3.32) will arbitrarily be set as the limit on workstation times except for the workstation that includes Activity 7. (This approach is just one of many that could be applied here.) The procedure for solving a Type II LCR assembly line–balancing problem is as follows:

Step 1. Prepare the precedence network. This network is exactly the same as the network shown in Figure 9–10 for a Type I problem.

Step 2. List the activities in descending order of A_i. This step is exactly the same as the Type I example. Table 9–15 shows the accurate list.

Step 3. Start with the longest A_i and assign the feasible activities to a workstation until no more activities can be added. Repeat for all additional workstations. Working down the list, Activity 2 is the first feasible assignment to Workstation 1, and the next is Activity 5. However, their times total 5.1 minutes, thus violating the 3.7-minute upper limit. Since there is no activity that when added to Workstation 1 does not bring the total workstation time over the 3.7-minute limit or violate precedence relationships, Activity 2 alone is assigned to Workstation 1. Proceeding to Workstation 2, Activities 5, 1, and 8 are assigned to it; thus, Workstation 2's total time is 3.6 minutes. Assignment of the remaining activities yields the results shown in Table 9–20.

The efficiency for this solution is as follows:

$$E_L = \frac{\Sigma A_i}{NC} = \frac{19.9 \text{ minutes}}{(6 \text{ workstations})(4.2 \text{ minutes})} = 78.9\%$$

The foregoing is only one of many possible solutions. It does a reasonable job in minimizing the variance of the workstation times, however, improvements may be possible. An approach worthy of investigation is to combine

Table 9–20 Assignment of Activities to Workstations Using the LCR Method—Type II Problem

Workstation	Activity i	Activity Time A_i (minutes)	Workstation Time
1	2	3.1	3.1
2	5 1 8	2.0 .8 .8	3.6
3	6 4	2.4 1.2	3.6
4	7	4.2	4.2
5	9 3	1.6 .6	2.2
6	10 11	2.2 1.0	3.2
		$\Sigma A_i = 19.9$	

Activities 7, 9, and 3 of Workstations 3 and 4 and have two such combinations. If this were feasible, each combined workstation would have a cycle time of 6.4 minutes. Since there are two such combinations, the effective cycle time of the two stations will be 3.2 minutes. Recomputing the efficiency using a cycle time of 3.6 minutes yields an improvement in efficiency from 78.9 percent to 92.1 percent.

$$E_L = \frac{\Sigma A_i}{NC} = \frac{19.9 \text{ minutes}}{(6 \text{ workstations})(3.6 \text{ minutes})} = 92.1\%$$

Many software packages are available for line balancing. Most are based on the solution logic described previously. Three of the most popular are COMSOAL (Computer Method of Sequencing Operations for Assembly Lines), CALB (Computer Assembly Line Balancing), and ALPACA (Assembly Line Planning and Control Activity). The primary advantage of computerized programs is that they can evaluate many of the possible solutions in a very short time.

Most approaches to line-balancing problems assume constant activity times. This is reasonable when balancing some automatic lines; the times are constant and the machines seldom fail. In other cases, for example, manual operations, times may vary widely. This may be handled by using work-in-process banks of inventory to absorb the variance in activity times, by providing off-line workstations for catchup, or by using the average time plus some number of standard deviations to increase the probability of adequate time at each workstation. Each of these approaches has disadvantages; the best approach is to develop work methods with consistent times and minimum rework and scrap.

Balancing the Plant

Just-in-time (JIT) and zero inventory (ZI) principles point out that parts fabrication and subassembly lines should have the same cycle time as the assembly line they are feeding. Stockless production (JIT and ZI) calls for a cycle time based on demand rate. Balancing individual lines only to have inventory stand idle between departments is a shifting of the point of waste rather than an elimination of waste. The finished goods consumption rate, however, is rarely perfectly smooth. Thus, safety stock is usually held in finished goods or by the customer. Consumption rates can also vary daily, weekly, or seasonally. Thus, parts fabrication and assembly lines must have the flexibility to change output rates without excessive costs or it will be necessary to build anticipation inventories.

PROJECT (FIXED POSITION) LAYOUT

Determining a layout for a group of activities that takes place in a single area is very similar to designing the individual workstation. Factors that must be considered include the following:

1. Space required for equipment and its operation
2. Storage space for tools, fixtures, and supplies
3. Operator space
4. Materials space, protection, and handling
5. Material-handling equipment, storage, and movement
6. Access for maintenance, service, and adjustments
7. Testing and inspection requirements
8. Environmental requirements such as temperatures, humidity, and contamination prevention
9. Relationships of various processes and materials.

A kitchen and an operating room are both examples of fixed position workstations in which different services may be performed at different times. Environmental considerations and personnel movement are important in both, as is access to equipment for maintenance, service, and adjustments. Often, projects will be laid out with the product, such as a building under construction, in the center, with materials flowing toward the center. Consider, for example, the sequenced movement of cement, glass, steel, and facing materials for each floor of a highrise building. Many fine project management models are available (see discussion in Chapter 15). However, activity relationship charts and travel charts can also be applied to the design of facilities for these processes, as well as those for aircraft assembly, shipbuilding, and large pressure vessel or turbine assembly facilities.

CONCLUSIONS

This chapter has only begun to scratch the surface of the layout analysis problem. There are many more algorithms that are designed to address specific subsets of the job shop, line, and fixed site processes. Methodologically these algorithms vary; however, no one method has been shown to be consistently better than another. These methods are generally not optimal, except in extremely simple situations, and only rarely consider the variances of activity times due to human or other uncontrollable situations. The best approach to use in solving the layout problem is to run several algorithms and develop the costs or efficiencies of each. Then select the better alternatives and evaluate them for quality of work life and other considerations.

Computer programs are often used to solve these types of problems, particularly with more complex situations. But those programs, although computationally efficient, have the same definitional and activity timing difficulties as the manual methods described here. Additionally, the layout decision process is dependent upon a careful definition of job activities and the measurement of those activities in terms of effort committed (and thus rest breaks required) and time required per activity. Without accurate work measurement data, layout studies are hypothetical estimates. Unfortunately, like layout analysis studies, work measurement studies are also subject to measurement vagaries. Work design and measurement is the subject of Chapter 10.

QUESTIONS

1. Briefly identify the three traditional production processes and give an example of each.

2. Briefly but specifically, apply the four key points of the definition of facility layout to the layout of a fast-food restaurant, an automobile production plant, an airport, or a grocery store.

3. Differentiate Type A cells and Type B cells. When should the position of these cells be switched in travel charting?

4. When would a layout analyst select the nearness priority ranking method over the diagonal method of solving a layout problem?

5. Give four examples of characteristics that will increase the load factor of an item when analyzing material flow.

6. Why is knowledge of flow manufacturing more important for the manufacturing planner today than it was ten to fifteen years ago?

7. Traditionally, the design of assembly lines has emphasized capacity, precedence requirements, and line-balancing objectives. Describe at least four other objectives that may be important in designing an assembly line.

8. Name and describe three major measures of performance for a flow line. Give an example in which each is applied.

9. Two lines, A and B, are available to manufacture an item. Line A has a speed 10 percent greater than Line B. What characteristics might Line B possess that would make it a better line?

10. How can a production line that produces no scrap and is operated 100 percent of the time have an efficiency less than 100 percent?

11. Describe the difference between Type I and Type II assembly line–balancing problems.

12. In a repetitive manufacturing plant, three subassembly lines feed the final assembly line. Using this situation, explain the concept of balancing the plant.

13. Is a processing line in a service organization more similar to an assembly line or machining line? Why?

14. If two organizations have the same annual demand but one has a level production rate while the other has a seasonally varying production rate, which has the greater capacity requirement? Why?

15. When using the term "cycle time" in a line-balancing context, does it affect the output rate or the throughput time of manufacturing?

PROBLEMS

1. A small service organization has four departments arranged as shown on page 325 on the left, with interdepartment distances based on the center of the department. The number of trips between departments during a typical week is given on the right. The department sizes are appropriate, and the cost of a trip is primarily a function of distance. What do you think of the present layout? Would you suggest any changes?

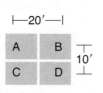

	A	B	C	D
A	—	25	15	20
B		—	20	10
C			—	5
D				—

2. The North Star Construction Supply Company manufactures cement block products in the volumes given below. The company plans to use a process layout.

Product	Process Sequence	Volume per Month	Area Available for Manufacturing
1	A, D, & E	1,032	25,000 square feet
2	A, B, & D	10,600	
3	C & E	250	
4	B & D	900	
5	A, C, & F	160	
6	C, E, & F	340	

   a. Calculate the number of units processed per month in each department.

   b. Develop a volume (move) table.

   c. Using the data calculated in B, classify the proximity of each pair of cells (A–B, A–C, B–C, and so on) on the basis of volume movement as:

    1. Very important

    2. Important

    3. Less important

   State the rationale for your classification system.

   d. Since work-in-process storage is critical, the space allocated to each department should be roughly proportional to the volume processed by the department. Calculate the space allocated to each department. Note that 25,000 square feet are available for manufacturing.

   e. The land available and building construction technology permit the sides of the building to vary from a minimum of 100 feet to a maximum of 200 feet in increments of 25 feet. Determine length and width of the building, size of departments, and layout of the building given the preceding constraints and layout objectives.

3. A printing plant has a line that collates and folds eight stacks of double pages (for example, the first stack has a sheet with pages 1 and 32 on one side and 2 and 31 on the other side, while a second stack has a sheet

with pages 3 and 30 on one side and 4 and 29 on the other). It produces 200 completed brochures every minute.

   a. If the line never jams or fails, calculate the cycle time (the ideal cycle time) and the capacity in an eight-hour shift.

   b. If the probability of a jam (adjustment) in a cycle is 0.0002 (0.02%) and the average time for an adjustment is five minutes, calculate the cycle time (C) and the capacity of an eight-hour shift.

   c. Given the information in Problems 3a and 3b, calculate the process efficiency.

4. Each time the line described in Problem 3 jams, it runs for fifteen seconds before the operator can shut it off. All of the input material during that period is mutilated and therefore scrapped.

   a. Calculate the units of final product scrapped each time the line jams.

   b. If 20,000 good units are required, calculate the quantity of raw material (the number of eight sheets) that will be required on average.

5. Refer to the information in Problems 3 and 4. Preventive maintenance is performed on another shift; the line is scheduled to run only that one product in a given week; and cycle time (C) = 0.006 minutes.

   a. Calculate the expected (average) time required to produce 300,000 good units.

   b. Calculate the line utilization for that week.

   c. Calculate the maximum cycle time the line could experience that week while still producing the required output of good products (300,000).

6. A part is routed through five operations in a batch production shop (process flow layout). The averge setup and operation times are given below. If the batch size is 200 parts and the interoperation (nonoperation = queue plus transit time) time is eight hours for each operation, what is the total throughput time (manufacturing lead time)?

Operation	Setup Time (hours)	Operation Time (minutes)
1	3.0	2.2
2	2.5	2.5
3	4.0	3.0
4	6.0	2.7
5	1.5	2.1

7. Using the data in Problem 6, assume the setup is complete and all operations are connected by a materials-handling operation requiring 1.0 minute between each workstation. Thus, a production line now exists. The same minimum operation times exist.

   a. What is the production rate of the line?
   b. What is the throughput time of 200 parts?

8. In the operation of a certain fifteen-station transfer line, the ideal cycle time is 0.58 minutes. Breakdowns on the entire line occur at a rate of once every 10 cycles, and the downtime per breakdown ranges between two minutes and nine minutes, with an average of 4.2 minutes. The plant is operated eight hours per day, five days per week.

   a. How many parts will the line be capable of producing during an average week?
   b. If the line has a scrap rate of 1 percent, how many hours must it operate to produce 1,000 parts?

9. Draw a precedence network representing the following relationships:

Activity	Immediate Predecessors
1	—
2	1
3	1
4	2, 3
5	4
6	5
7	4
8	6, 7

10. Given the data that follows for eleven activities that are performed in sequence, with a maximum cycle time of eleven minutes:

Activity	1	2	3	4	5	6	7	8	9	10	11
Time (in minutes)	0.8	3.1	0.6	1.2	2.0	2.4	4.2	0.8	1.6	2.2	1.0

   a. Calculate the minimum number of workstations.
   b. Calculate the capacity of an eight-hour shift.

11. The following information is for three different models of an assembly.

Weekly Requirements		Operation Times in Minutes Per Assembly			
Model	Quantity	Operation	A	B	C
A	200	1	2	2	1
B	300	2	1	1	3
C	400	3	–	3	3
		4	.5	1	1
		5	.5	2	–
		6	–	–	1
		7	2	4	2

Precedence Requirements

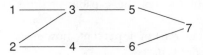

a. Determine the weekly capacity required in minutes for each operation.
b. Determine the theoretical minimum number of workstations.
c. Assume this assembly line is a flexible manufacturing system producing a three-item group that requires a minimum of four workstations. Determine the daily requirements, the segment patterns, the maximum cycle time, and assign operations to workstations so as to meet the weekly output and operation precedence requirements.

12. The following data are applicable for Problems 12, 13, and 14. The maximum cycle time is 6.0 minutes.

Activity	Immediate Predecessors	Average Time (in minutes)
1	—	1.8
2	—	3.2
3	1	0.6
4	2	3.4
5	2	2.0
6	4	1.4
7	4, 5	3.1
8	5	1.6
9	6	1.2
10	3, 7, 9	2.6
11	8, 10	1.8

a. Construct the precedence network.
b. What is the minimum number of workstations?

13. Use the longest candidate rule to allocate activities to workstations and balance the line (see data from Problem 12).

14. Use the rank positional weights to construct a precedence network and allocate activities to workstations (see data from Problem 12).

15. The tasks, times required, and precedence relationships for the tasks in assembling a portable backyard barbecue stand are given below.

Task	Immediate Predecessors	Average Time (in minutes)
A	—	0.6
B	A	0.4
C	A	0.8
D	A	1.0
E	B	1.2
F	B	0.6
G	B	0.4
H	C	0.2
I	D	0.3
J	E	0.6
K	F, G	0.2
L	H, I	0.3
M	J, K	0.6
N	K	0.2
O	L	0.9
P	M, N, O	0.2
		8.5 minutes

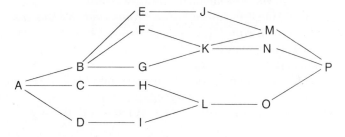

Thirty six hours of capacity are available each week. Planned production is 1,620 barbecue stands each week.

a. Calculate the maximum cycle time.
b. Calculate the theoretical minimum number of workstations.

c. Define the activities of workstations using the longest candidate rule.
d. Calculate the rank positional weights for the following tasks: A, G, J, and L.

16. Define the activities of workstations for the data in Problem 15 using the rank positional weights method.

17. Compare the longest candidate rule solution of Problem 15 and the rank positional weights solution of Problem 16. Which, if either, do you recommend? Why?

18. The planned output for the line described in Problem 15 is only 500 units per week in November and December. How would you alter the workstation design?

a. Calculate the maximum cycle time.
b. Calculate the minimum number of workstations required.
c. Define the activities of workstations using the longest candidate rule.
d. Define the activities of workstations using the rank positional weights method.

REFERENCES

Baybars, Ilker. "A Survey of Exact Algorithms for the Simple Assembly Line Balancing Problem." *Management Science* 32, no. 8 (August 1986): 909–932.

Dar-El, E. M. (Mansoor). "Solving Large Single Model Assembly Line Balancing Problems—A Comparative Study." *AIIE Transactions* 7, no. 3 (1975): 302–310.

Fogarty, Donald W., and Thomas R. Hoffmann. *Production and Inventory Management.* Cincinnati: South-Western, 1983, Chapter 8.

Groover, Mikell P. *Automation, Production Systems, and Computer-Aided Manufacturing.* 2nd ed. Englewood Cliffs, N.J.: Prentice-Hall, 1987, pp. 119–128.

Gunther, Richard E., Gordon D. Johnson, and Roger S. Peterson. "Currently Practiced Formulations for the Assembly Line Balancing Problem." *Journal of Operations Management* 3, no. 4 (August 1983): pp. 209–221.

Hall, Robert W. *Zero Inventories.* Homewood, Ill: Dow Jones-Irwin, 1983, p. 61.

Helgeson, W. B. and D. P. Bernie. "Assembly Line Balancing Using Ranked Positional Weight Techniques." *Journal of Industrial Engineering* 12, no. 6 (1961): 394–398.

Hoffmann, Thomas R. "Assembly Line Balancing with a Precedence Matrix." *Management Science* 9, no. 4 (July 1963): 551–562.

Johnson, Roger V. "Optimally Balancing Large Assembly Lines with 'FABLE'." *Management Science* 34, no. 2 (February 1988): 240–253.

Mastor, Anthony A. "An Experimental Investigation and Comparative Evaluation of Production Line Balancing Techniques." *Management Science* 16, no. 22 (July 1970): 728–745.

Muther, Richard. *Systematic Layout Planning.* Boston: Industrial Education Institute, 1961.

New, C. Colin. "MRP and GT: A New Strategy for Component Production." *Production and Inventory Management* 18, no. 3 (1977): 50–62.

Spencer, Michael S. "Scheduling Components for Group Technology Lines." *Production and Inventory Management* (1980): 43–49.

Talbot, F. Brian, and James H. Patterson. "An Integer Programming Algorithm with Network Cuts Solving the Assembly Line Balancing Problem." *Management Science* 30, no. 1 (January 1984): 85–89.

Talbot, F. Brian, James H. Patterson, and William V. Gehrlein. "A Comparative Evaluation of Heuristic Line Balancing Techniques." *Management Science* 32, no. 4 (April 1986): 430–454.

CHAPTER 10
WORK DESIGN AND MEASUREMENT

OBJECTIVES

After completing this chapter, you should be able to

- Understand the impacts of work evaluation techniques and the reasons why work evaluation is necessary

- Identify the general and specific factors in the work environment and their impact on the design of work

- Understand the effects of work specialization and various techniques to make work more compatible with human needs

- Differentiate and apply motion study and time study techniques

- Understand and compute learning curve effects with various types of data, using both unit and cumulative concepts

OUTLINE

333

INTRODUCTION

Work evaluation, consisting of work design and work measurement, makes an essential contribution to the integration of human resources and production technology. Any mismatch of the human-machine interface will likely have serious quality and productivity impacts.

Human Resource Impacts of Work Evaluation

Before the nineteenth century, the human contribution to production was to provide power by carrying, lifting, shaping, or performing other easily measurable manual tasks. However, as the Industrial Revolution spread, people were increasingly used to manage the resources of water, steam, or electric power. At first, the processes were crude and wasteful, but enormous improvements in work design have been made. Today's technology permits the accurate control of production power and on-line feedback about production outcomes. Automation has progressed to the point that some products are being manufactured in fully or largely automated factories (Barnes 1980). Because technology removes labor from easily measurable direct production, the design of the human-machine interface becomes increasingly important and complex and, simultaneously, more difficult to measure and cost. This is significant because the contribution of different resources to the productive process must be accurately identified and rewarded.

Work evaluation, consisting of work design and work measurement, is the process of designing tasks to accommodate human needs, while simultaneously achieving necessary levels of productivity and quality. Work design specifies human actions and integrates technology to define this balance of human and organizational requirements, while work measurement formally evaluates productivity against measured standards. The following statements formally define work design and work measurement:

Work design specifies the content, functions, processes, and relationships for an individual or small group to achieve defined tasks while simultaneously satisfying personal needs. Work design addresses the human-machine interface.

Work measurement develops time standards for various specific work activities and measures actual performance against those standards.

The Reasons for Work Evaluation

While work design and work measurement are very important, they are also controversial and often misunderstood. For that reason, the operations manager must clearly communicate the need for work design and the appropriateness of work measurement methods. Work evaluation techniques are necessary for the following closely interrelated activities:

1. Facilitation of operations planning
   a. *Capacity definition.* Given specific equipment, materials, processes, labor, job design and performance estimates, the operations manager plans the sustainable output level and adjusts resource inputs for an optimal human-machine interface.
   b. *Production process costing.* Cost evaluation permits budgeting, competitive pricing, and an assessment to be made of the cost or productivity changes resulting from improved work methods or process technologies. Comparison of process alternatives is facilitated.
   c. *Job scheduling.* The production activity control (PAC) function requires the accurate measurement of task times to efficiently schedule jobs across the available capacity.
2. Assessment of labor productivity
   a. *Job descriptions.* Work study data are often a major input to the job description, which is used for recruiting, hiring, training, and other personnel and operations decisions.
   b. *Performance measurement.* Individual and group employee performance can be directly measured against the time standard, which is formalized in the job description and used extensively for promotion, discipline, training, and other personnel actions.
   c. *Incentive compensation programs.* Programs to reward high performance and motivate labor productivity require accurate measurement of both task data and performance to be fair and effective.

Capacity definition is a long-range activity and must precede process costing and job scheduling. Job description is a long- or medium-range function, preceding performance measurement and incentive programs. Of course, a well-managed company must have accurate work data for capacity, cost, and schedule planning. Additionally, work data are used for job descriptions and professional skill classifications. However, further use of work data for performance measurement and incentive programs has been resisted in some cases. A study by Rice (1977) surveyed 1,500 firms to identify the reasons for work evaluation and found that 89 percent of respondents used work design to estimate and cost work and 55 percent of respondents used work design to schedule production.

Similarly, work design studies were used for wage incentive and performance measurement purposes by 59 and 41 percent, respectively, of the respondents; however, there was less use of long-range job descriptions. Interestingly, long-range applications of work design are not as widely used, but short-range applications are more accepted. Nevertheless, the study supports widespread use of work evaluation methods.

WORK DESIGN

Work design initially defines the overall professional environment and reinforces management expectations for a particular job. Work design can be conducted at two levels, the general work environment and the immediate task situation. Although work design is guided by numerous laws and common-sense necessities, there are no consistently clear guidelines.

The General Work Environment

The general physical environment of the workplace consists of such variables as temperature and humidity, light and color intensity, noise and vibration, and ventilation. A range of human tolerance and efficient human performance can be established for each of these variables. Additionally, these variables are interrelated with the specific task situation variables.

TEMPERATURE AND HUMIDITY. Temperature and humidity are closely interrelated because the normal human body temperature of 98.6 degrees must be maintained during work. Increased humidity, more protective clothing, or greater physical movement generally permits workers to be comfortable at slightly lower temperatures. For most indoor work, however, an upper limit of roughly 90 degrees and a lower limit of roughly 65 degrees is best for prolonged exposure (McCormick 1970).

LIGHT AND COLOR. Light and color intensity have a notable effect on the work environment. Natural light is generally preferred to artificial light, quite possibly because contact with the external environment may reduce claustrophobia. Additionally, rough surfaces should be used to reduce glare where possible. Table 10–1 shows the illumination required for different levels of activities.

Color is used in the work environment for two purposes: (1) to achieve psychological effects and (2) to visually discriminate. Bright colors are used to suggest high creativity or danger. The more natural colors (brown, green,

Table 10–1 Levels of Illumination for Comfortable Work

Level of Activity	Function of Light	Illumination (in foot-candles)
Limited activities Theaters, corridors	Safety of movement	.1 to 10
General activities Warehouses, filing, rough machining	Gross viewing	10 to 50
Detailed activities Reading, assembly, art, benchwork	Fine viewing	50 to 100
Intense activities Surgery, detailed inspections	Critical viewing	100 to 500 +

Table 10–2   Effects of Color in the Workplace

Color	Discriminating Impact	Psychological Impact
Red	Danger, emergency, warning	Heat and action High visibility
Orange	Start buttons, safety equipment, dangerous equipment	Warmth and stimulation Highest visibility
Yellow	Caution, heavy equipment	Cheerful and fresh
Green	Safety, first aid, go lights	Calm and restful
Blue	Inoperative equipment	Cool and thoughtful Depression
Purple	Radiation hazards	—
Brown	—	Natural and peaceful

and blue) are used where thoughtful, calm behaviors are desired. Table 10–2 identifies the discriminating and psychological impacts of colors.

NOISE AND VIBRATION. Excessive noise or vibration can cause irritability, pain, or injury; but surprisingly, total silence can also cause some uneasiness. Noise is measured in decibels (db), with each increase of ten decibels indicating a ten-fold increase in intensity. The permissible noise levels in the work environment are related to the duration of exposure. The Occupational Safety and Health Act (OSHA) of 1971 permits employees to be exposed to noise levels of 90 db for eight hours, but exposure to noise levels of 115 db (which is 500 times the 90-db level) is permitted for only fifteen minutes. The noise intensity of several common work activities is shown in Table 10–3.

AIR QUALITY. Attention is increasingly being directed at the proper ventilation of work areas, primarily because of long-range health concerns. The build up of toxic fumes and handling of harmful chemicals in work areas has long been addressed through various monitoring techniques. Strict administrative and legal constraints apply. For example, an Illinois court found several

Table 10–3   The Noise Level of Work Activities

db	Activity
10 to 30	Whisper, soft speaking, clock ticking
40 to 60	Average home, large store, noisy office, fan, ventilation systems, air conditioning
70 to 100	Traffic, vacuum cleaner, typical factory, train, circular saw, subway
130 to 160	Aircraft, large unmuffled engines

executives guilty of manslaughter in the cyanide poisoning of an employee because they did not follow required OSHA procedures in a chemical recovery process. Similarly, smoking restrictions and the requirement that employees be nonsmokers are gaining acceptance, from both a job-safety and long-range health perspective. (*Business Week* July 27, 1987).

The factors of temperature and humidity, light and color, noise and vibration, and ventilation establish the general conditions of the work environment. More importantly, they affect performance in the immediate task situation.

The Immediate Task Situation

The immediate task situation involves the labor-technology interface, workplace organization, energy expenditure, and rest and safety needs. Most tasks require an interaction between the human and the technology, as embodied in a tool or a machine. Thus, the work environment technology can be placed within a continuum from purely manual tasks to purely information-based, or technological, tasks, as shown in Figure 10–1.

THE LABOR-TECHNOLOGY INTERFACE. Manual tasks are defined as those that require effort of the major muscle groups. Mechanical tasks require response of the central nervous system and actions of smaller muscle groups, such as fingers moving control knobs or neck muscles turning for viewing. Information tasks require mental evaluation, which is often based on visual perceptions or displays, such as an instrument control panel; imagination or conceptualization of a new method; a programming logic; or a layout alternative. Each of these tasks results in a different type of fatigue and requires a different rest or recovery process.

Manual tasks necessitate the opportunity for major muscle groups to recover through rest and the replacement of body liquids. Mechanical tasks involve less general fatigue and more nervous system fatigue. Finally, mental tasks involve almost no physical fatigue and extensive mental fatigue. For this reason, manual workers often require rest breaks, but information workers often like mild stimulants, such as coffee or tea, as a substitute for the lack of physical exertion on the job.

Figure 10–1 The Labor-Technology Interface

Manual	Mechanical	Information
Physical	<------------------->	Mental
Simple Work	<------------------->	Complex Work
Direct Work	<------------------->	Indirect Work
Easily Measured	<------------------->	Difficult to Measure
Early Basic Processes	<------------------->	Recent, High-Tech Processes
Human Paced	<------------------->	Machine Paced

To improve the labor-technology interface, the operations manager must be aware of the contributing factors. Many years ago, Frederick Taylor designed shovels specifically for different materials and the varying size of workers (Taylor 1911). Small shovels were designed for heavier materials, such as coal or iron ore, and large shovels for lighter materials, such as ashes. The shaft of the shovel was cut to the worker's height, the blade of the coal shovel was rounded to prevent loads from tipping, and the toe was rounded for digging into a hard coal pile. In today's mechanized environment, the operation of a mechanical steam shovel to move materials requires very different skills than manual shoveling. The operator, sitting in a cab, must see from a distance the material to be moved and the location where it is to be placed. The various mechanical shifts, levers, and knobs are placed so that they can be reached easily and cannot be confused based on touch and location. Additionally, the environment of the work area is often controlled, as with an operator's cab, which eliminates dust and may be air conditioned.

Materials may also be moved by conveyor systems. A control room has instrument panels to show the speed of movement, temperature, weight of material, and other important variables. Depending on the specific job, the operator has a variety of information displayed and a series of control buttons and emergency cut-off switches. In critical or sensitive operations, such as a nuclear reactor or an airplane cockpit, monitors evaluate information displays and record operator actions. In some cases, a computer may recommend or even override a decision. Careful configuration of displays permits easy viewing and minimizes operator errors.

WORKPLACE ORGANIZATION. Ergonomics, or human factor engineering, is the science of workplace design. The objective of ergonomics is to improve productivity by increasing the speed, accuracy, and safety of the task performance. Typically, ergonomics will start with the measurement of the employee; and then design the work location for comfort and efficiency of operation. Initial ergonomic studies were conducted to design fighter aircraft so that pilots could better monitor their flight conditions. Subsequently, data entry equipment, automobile design, operations control consoles, and many other workstations have been subjected to ergonomic analysis.

Information display rules include the following:

1. Use the same scale (Celsius or Fahrenheit) for like information
2. Use consistent colors (red, yellow, or green) for like information
3. Place like information (status of gates 1, 2 and 3) in parallel positions
4. Align the displays consistently (0 or straight up is the normal range)
5. Place important data and switches directly in front of the operator

Physical anthropology is the evaluation of the human profile. Measures of reach or height, range of movement, rapidity of movement, and lifting capacity are used. These measurements are normally profiled by percentile, often including the 1st, 5th, 50th, 95th, and 99th percentiles. A child-proof medicine bottle cap might be designed to be opened by less than 1 percent of children under ten years old but 99 percent of persons older than sixteen years. Similarly, doors and beds should be designed for all but the tallest persons, and fire extinguishers should be operable by 99 percent or more of adults. But chairs, automobiles and work benches should be designed for the average person.

WORK AND HUMAN ENERGY. The design of the workplace to ergonomic specifications permits increased safety and accuracy of work but, more importantly, it reduces fatigue. Physiologists use various measures of fatigue, including heart pulse rate and oxygen consumption. Pulse rates are easy to measure but are less accurate than oxygen consumption, which can be converted to calories consumed per unit of time. Thus, more thorough studies normally measure oxygen consumption. Approximate energy expenditures for various work activities are shown in Table 10–4.

Unfortunately, there are no standardized data on calorie expenditure other than for very simple tasks. This is because the conditions of the task, including regularity of cycle, temperature, humidity, reach required, as well as the individual, vary enormously. Thus, measurement of the specific task

Table 10–4   Energy Expenditures for Various Tasks

Task/Activity	Energy Expenditure in Calories per Minute
Sitting—idle	1.2
Clerical work—sitting	1.65
Light bench work	1.8
Tailor—machine sewing	2.6
Tailor—hand sewing	2.0
Sheet metal work	3.0
Punch press operator	3.8
Tailor—pressing suit	4.3
Pushing wheelbarrow 2.8 m.p.h. with 125-lb. load on smooth surface	5.0
Shoveling 18 lbs. of sand a distance of 3 ft. with 1.5-ft lift at 12 throws per min.	5.4
Pushing wheelbarrow 2.8 m.p.h. with 330-lb. load on smooth surface	7.0
Shoveling 18 lbs. of sand a distance of 3 ft. with 3-ft. lift at 12 throws per min.	7.5
Digging a ditch in clay soil	8.5
Tending furnace in a steel mill	10.2

Source: Passmore, R., and G.V.G.A. Durnin. "Human Energy Expenditure." *Psychological Reviews*, vol. 35, no. 4 (October 1955): 816–834.

situation is required for accuracy. However, Table 10–4 provides a starting point; more comprehensive data are available (Barnes 1980, p. 453).

Caloric expenditure can be used to estimate the approximate amount of rest needed for various types of physical labor, as shown by the following formula adapted from Murrell (1965). The formula is valid for physical work with calorie expenditure above a minimum standard.

$$R = \frac{60(C - S)}{C - 1.5}$$

where

R = Rest required in minutes per hour for sustained work

C = Calories expended in average calories per minute

S = Standard for minimum energy expenditure
(normally about 4.0 calories per minute)

For example, an individual handling heavy boxes would use roughly 6.5 calories per minute. Rest for this activity would be computed as follows:

$$R = \frac{60(6.5 - 4.0)}{6.5 - 1.5} = 30 \text{ minutes per hour}$$

This formulation establishes a standard for energy expenditure, in this case 4.0 calories per minute, and increases the rest period for heavier effort. It does not accommodate the worker's need for mental relaxation or recreation, such as vacations or time off. Long-term burn out is prevented by scheduling a work week of roughly forty hours with appropriate holidays and vacations.

Thus, the work environment for even the simplest of jobs requires careful planning and extensive operations management controls. The general work environment involves controlling temperature and humidity, light and color intensity, noise and vibration, and ventilation. The design of the immediate task situation involves an evaluation of ergonomic considerations ranging from work physiology to psychometry to the need for rest. Of course, the ultimate goal of work design is to assure employee productivity and safety.

ON-THE-JOB SAFETY. Until this century, human injuries in the workplace have accounted for most major injuries. Injuries due to recreational activities and in-the-home accidents have only recently become the major categories of human injury. There are many reasons for this shift, such as the increasing amount of time and energy available for recreation, new types of recreation, and the like.

One important but often ignored reason for the decline in injuries is the attention given to working conditions. Labor laws and business policies in the twentieth century have limited the hours an employee can work, reduced fatigue-based health and safety problems, and controlled the age of workers. Additionally, unions have traditionally placed a high priority on employee safety. However, in 1971, the U.S. government became directly involved with worker safety through the Occupational Safety and Health Act. This act provides for the National Institute of Occupational Safety and Health, an overview agency with broad powers of policy making, regulating, and inspecting, in addition to legal responsibilities and prerogatives. Unfortunately, OSHA initially established some unrealistic goals and was given a bad name. However, those matters are largely resolved, and OSHA now performs primarily a consultative and facilitative role.

Labor Specialization

The degree of labor specialization is a key issue of work design. Specialization of labor has permitted the development of greater productivity and contributes to a high standard of living. However, extreme specialization has an adverse effect on labor. The degree of specialization can be viewed as a continuum of generalized to specialized. Highly generalized jobs (e.g., the individual carpenter who both makes and sells the product) are probably not competitive in most work environments. However, at the other end of the continuum, high specialization creates monotony, boredom, and lack of involvement with the work. The dimensions of the generalization-specialization continuum that suggest in a very general fashion the benefits to management and labor are illustrated in Table 10–5.

One interpretation of Table 10–5 is that the advantages of specialization, including costs, productivity, and quality, accrue primarily to management, particularly in the short run. Similarly, the advantages of generalization accrue to labor. However, this typecasting of labor and management is much too stereotypical; a more effective approach is to define specialization in terms of work environment or technology level. Recent developments in just-in-time production encourage cross-training of labor (more generalization), which increases labor flexibility and is advantageous to both labor and management. Costs associated with the level of specialization are shown in Figure 10–2.

Curve 1 shows that increased specialization leads to lower costs, other factors being constant. These cost efficiencies are limited, however, because the curve decreases at a decreasing rate, and ultimately inefficiencies of specialization become operative. The abruptly increasing costs of greater specialization are suggested by strikes or labor dysfunctions. However, a change in production technology, represented by Curve 2, would permit lower average costs and greater specialization. Operations managers should seek the optimal specialization level and the employees, who by talent and inclination, are appropriate for a given technology. The relationships between specialization and cost, including the designation of a best specialization level, are very similar to the best operating level concepts explained in Chapter 3.

Table 10–5   The Generalization Specialization Continuum

Generalization	Factor	Specialization
Benefits to Management		
Lower	Productivity	Higher
Lower	Management control	Higher
Lower	Overhead	Higher
Lower	Hidden costs (absenteeism, grievances, turnover, disruption, tardiness)	Higher
Neutral Benefit (roughly equal benefits to management and labor)		
Mental	Fatigue	Physical
Higher	Wages	Lower
Higher	Worker innovation	Lower
Benefits to Labor		
Higher	Training (self-development)	Lower
Higher	Employee involvement	Lower
Higher	Worker social interaction	Lower

Figure 10–2   The Relationship Between Specialization and Cost

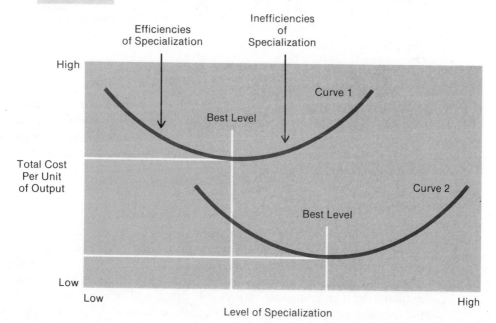

Table 10–6   Work Specialization Adjustments

Dimension	Method	Effect
Task variety	Job enlargement	Increase number of tasks
	Job rotation/shifts	Rotate among different but similar tasks
	Work modules	Rapid rotation through 10-to-20-minute modules
	Integrated work teams	Teams of 3 to 20 workers vary tasks among them
Time scheduling	Variable work week	Typically four-day work weeks
	Flex time	Variable, but controlled, daily schedule
	Job sharing	Two part-time workers in one job
	Part-time, temporary hire	Nontraditional classes of employees
Work redesign	Job enrichment	Motivational factors such as growth, achievement, recognition, advancement, and the work itself[1]
	Autonomous (self-supervised) work teams	Team responsibility for all aspects of production
	Quality circles	Training, interface, involvement
	Motivation potential evaluation	Factors such as significance, autonomy, feedback, identity, and variety[2]

[1]Herzberg, et al. 1959.
[2]Hackman and Oldham 1976.

Efforts to accommodate the desire for generalization, yet simultaneously achieve competitive levels of specialization, have taken a variety of forms. Some have been purely cosmetic and have generally resulted in problems. However, the majority, and particularly the more successful, have been clear efforts to balance the priorities and needs of management and labor. Table 10–6 shows several dimensions of the level of specialization.

Job Descriptions

Formalization of work design often results in a job description. This document provides various details to identify the job and the job qualifications and a written overview of the knowledge, skills, and abilities (the KSAs) of the task, normally in measurable terms. The job description should be prepared by the immediate supervisor, often with direct assistance from the human resource staff, process designers, or methods engineers. It is used for a variety of purposes, such as recruitment, placement, training, pay grading, and industrial relations contract negotiations. Additionally, job descriptions identify performance standards that are the basis for performance evaluation.

In summary, work design considers general factors of the work environment and immediate task situations. These general and specific conditions must be carefully considered because they can have extensive effects on the productivity, satisfaction, health, and safety of the labor force. Management and labor often have distinctly different interests in work design, particularly with regard to the degree of specialization. The work design process finds the optimal level of specialization and then considers various methods, such as variety, scheduling, or redesign, to make the job more palatable. These general approaches to work design are often formalized in the job description.

There are numerous examples of such work redesign projects, including several in the automotive industry (*Business Week* January 28, 1985), the steel industry, and more generally in the post-industrial corporation (*Business Week* March 3, 1986). At Nucor steel, CEO Ken Iverson's success is based on backward integration toward raw materials, lean management, employee involvement, and constant upgrading of technology (*Scanorama* September 1987). In each of these areas, as changes are implemented there are extensive impacts on the design of individual jobs. The next section, work measurement, considers the various techniques of describing and measuring work.

WORK MEASUREMENT

The first part of this chapter discussed work design, which is concerned with properly specifying work tasks for the greatest productive efficiency and worker satisfaction. The remainder of the chapter examines ways that worker performance standards can be set and individual worker performance can be evaluated once job tasks have been precisely defined.

Motion Study

The detailed evaluation of employee work actions is called a motion study and is conducted by a methods analyst. The objectives of a motion study are to improve work methods in order to make the task easier or safer and to increase quality and productivity. Motion studies evaluate work methods, workstation layout, and employee motions. Modern motion studies can be traced to Frederick Taylor (1911) and Frank and Lillian Gilbreth (1917). They observed the differences between methods employed by neophyte apprentices and those used by experienced journeymen. It was obvious that the journeymen were faster; but, with further study it also became apparent that the journeyman's speed resulted from improved motion patterns, not just

Figure 10–3   Principles of Motion Economy

1. The two hands should begin and complete their motions at the same time.
2. The two hands should not be idle at the same time except during rest periods.
3. Arm motions should be made in opposite and symmetrical directions and should be simultaneous.
4. Materials and tools should be located to permit the best sequence of motions.
5. Hand and lower arm movements are preferred to upper arm and shoulder movements for light work.
6. Rhythm is essential to smooth, automatic performance.
7. Tools, materials, and controls should be located close to and directly in front of the operator.
8. Gravity feed bins and containers should be used to deliver materials close to the point of use.
9. Drop deliveries should be used wherever possible.
10. The hand should be relieved of all work that can be done more advantageously by a jig, fixture, or a foot-operated device.
11. Smooth, continuous motions are preferable to straight-line or zigzag motions involving sudden and sharp changes in direction.

a speeding up of the apprentice's motions. Taylor and the Gilbreths examined many activities to increase efficiency through improved work methods. Such motion studies attempted to eliminate movements, to shorten necessary movements, and to make necessary movements less tiring. Evaluation of the motion economy is normally the first step of a motion study.

MOTION ECONOMY. Over the years many principles of motion economy have been developed. The most widely used are shown in Figure 10–3. Through these principles, the motion analyst ensures that the movements are efficient and necessary.

PROCESS CHARTS. Process charts are schematic models used to evaluate motion economy; they formalize the existing work method and assist in planning improved procedures. Among the principal types of process charts are the assembly flow chart, flow process charts, right- and left-hand charts, man-machine charts, and simultaneous motion (SIMO) charts. The assembly flow chart, sometimes called the "gozinto" chart (see Figure 10–4), identifies the operations, their sequencing, and their relationships. The flow process chart shows the timing and distance of a method. Right- and left-hand charts, man-machine charts, and simultaneous motion charts all concern the operator, rather than a product, and show, respectively, the interaction of the hands, the human-machine interface, and a micromotion analysis. These charts and diagrams highlight potential areas of methods improvement through the use

Figure 10–4   Assembly Flow Chart

Subject Charted: Stud and Casting Mount	Chart No.: L8
Drawing No.: B-161-2	Part No.: 810-23-79X
Chart of Method: Current	Charted By: S Stone
Chart Begins: Raw Stock	Date: 8-23-86
Chart Ends: Assembly Dept. Stock	Sheet: 121

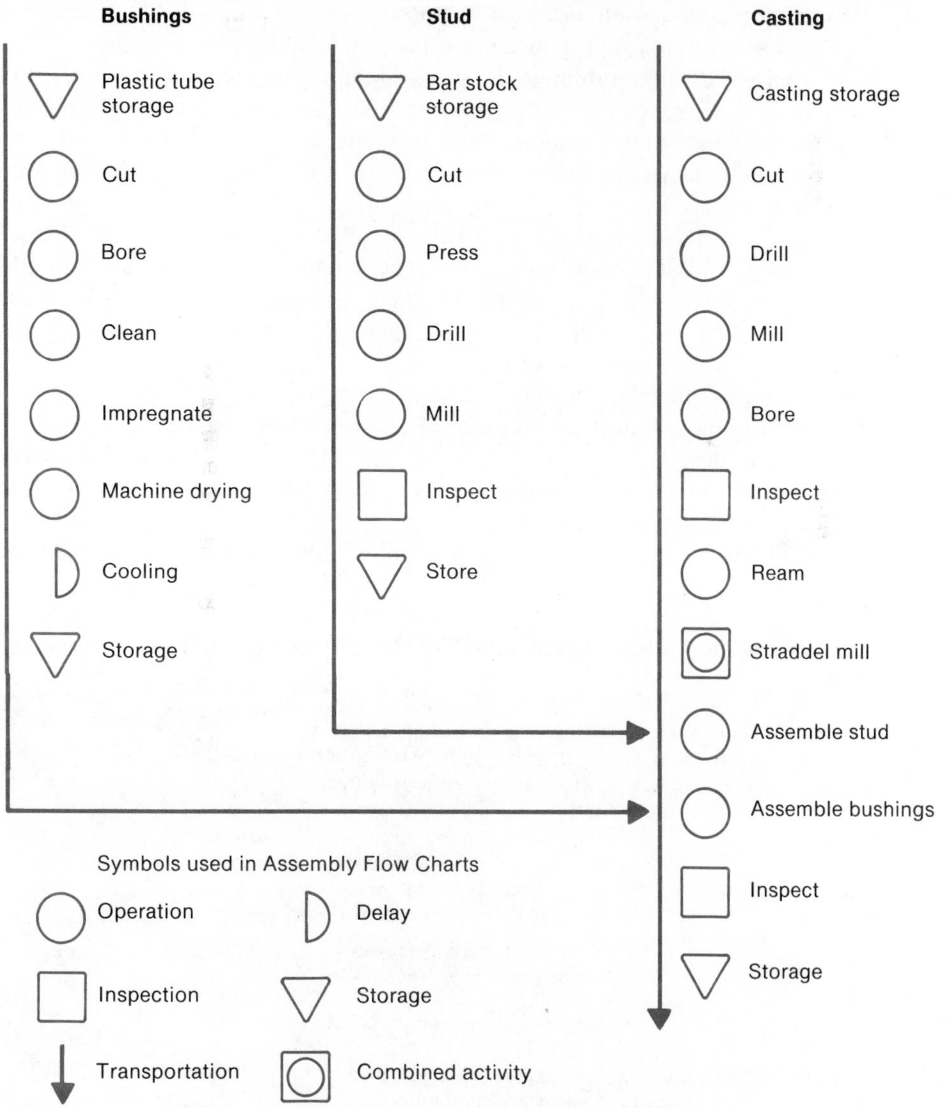

Bushings

▽ Plastic tube storage
◯ Cut
◯ Bore
◯ Clean
◯ Impregnate
◯ Machine drying
◗ Cooling
▽ Storage

Stud

▽ Bar stock storage
◯ Cut
◯ Press
◯ Drill
◯ Mill
▢ Inspect
▽ Store

Casting

▽ Casting storage
◯ Cut
◯ Drill
◯ Mill
◯ Bore
▢ Inspect
◯ Ream
◉ Straddel mill
◯ Assemble stud
◯ Assemble bushings
▢ Inspect
▽ Storage

Symbols used in Assembly Flow Charts

◯ Operation   ◗ Delay

▢ Inspection   ▽ Storage

↓ Transportation   ◉ Combined activity

of the standard symbols shown in Figure 10–4. Process charts show detail and identify and sequence the operations to help the analyst combine and eliminate operations according to motion economy principles, thereby permitting improved micromotions.

MICROMOTION STUDIES. In micromotion studies, moving pictures taken of the motion patterns are examined frame by frame. Several different techniques can be used. In time-lapse photography, pictures are taken at either ten frames per second or 1,000 frames per minute, which permits, in addition to motion analysis, detailed timing of the work. Memomotion studies are similar to time-lapse photography, but they conserve film because pictures are taken at 60 to 100 frames per minute. Slow motion effects may be obtained for more detailed analysis by taking high-speed pictures and showing them at a normal rate.

Another method is used in the detailed study of motion. Taylor initially thought to subdivide tasks into small common elements, such as pick up piece, place in rack, etc. Frank and Lillian Gilbreth (1917) carried this concept further by subdividing tasks into standard elements, such that all motions could be described as combinations of therbligs. (Therblig spelled backward is, approximately, Gilbreth.) The seventeen therbligs listed in Figure 10–5, are the basic building blocks for all micromotion patterns.

By describing a job in terms of these elementary motions, an analyst can identify which operations are unnecessary, fatiguing, or nonproductive. For example, the Hold therblig involves using the hand as a vice and probably violates the tenth principle of motion economy (see Figure 10–3). Similarly,

Figure 10–5   Therbligs—The Basic Building Blocks of Motion

  1. Search—locate an object visually or by groping for it
  2. Select—choose one part from among several
  3. Grasp—close the fingers around a part
  4. Reach—motion of the empty hand
  5. Move—motion of the hand while carrying something
  6. Hold—manual support or control of an object
  7. Release—relinquish manual control
  8. Position—locate an object in specific position
  9. Preposition—orient object correctly
 10. Inspect—compare object with standard
 11. Assemble—bring together mating parts
 12. Disassemble—disunite mating parts
 13. Use—manually implement production procedure
 14. Unavoidable delay—interruption beyond operator's control
 15. Avoidable delay—idle time for which operator is responsible
 16. Plan—mentally determine next action
 17. Rest to overcome fatigue—a periodic delay due to operator fatigue

Search and Select can be eliminated by proper workplace design, and Reach can be shortened by proper tool and part locations.

Motion study eliminates unnecessary movements, standardizes the task, and shortens the work cycle, with the result that jobs are done more rapidly. For this reason, the effects of increased standardization must be considered by the motion analyst.

Time Studies

Time studies are often conducted following motion studies because there is no sense in establishing a time standard for a poor method. Four sources of time data are available to time study analysts: stopwatch data, work sampling data, published time data, and nonscientific data.

STOPWATCH STUDIES. The objective of a stopwatch study is to establish an average cycle time for a normal operator performing at a normal level of effort. This gives a time that most workers, operating at a normal pace, will be capable of exceeding by some given percentage, say 25 percent. The basic method for establishing time standards is through the use of a stopwatch. Although other methods have been developed to overcome the weaknesses of stopwatch studies, they are more easily understood after examining the way in which a stopwatch study is carried out. The following are the seven steps of a stopwatch study:

1. *Determine the proper work method.* The workplace and method must be checked to ensure that the proper method is being followed. This is why the motion study should precede a time study.
2. *Select a representative operator.* This may be difficult; if the job is new, an operator must be trained and the learning effect, described later, may bias the standard. If the standard is used to develop an incentive system, some operators may attempt to create a loose standard (one that they can exceed easily). Other operators may perform in an unusually skillful way.
3. *Define the work elements.* Break down the method used into logical elements and record them in the sequence performed. Elements should be chosen with clear-cut beginnings and endings, possibly identifiable by listening to the pattern of job noises. This eases the time study analyst's job since the timer can detect breaks between elements and still view the stopwatch. Work elements paced by machines should be separated from those controlled by the operator. The duration of machine-paced elements does not vary and is determined by establishing the method, not by timing them during the study.
4. *Conduct observation and timing.* Now comes the actual observation and stopwatch timing. Watches marked off in hundredths of a minute, rather than seconds, are normally used. Observe and record the elapsed time of a sufficient number of cycles to assure that the sample represents the population. The number of cycles to time can be computed through statistical analysis. The continuous method of observation records the total elapsed time; subsequently, the time per element is obtained by a series of subtractions. Other

observers prefer the snapback method. This technique eliminates the need to perform the successive subtractions, but it may lose time in reading and restoring the watch back to the zero position. The three-watch method combines the advantages of having a watch running continuously while allowing direct reading of the element times. Three watches, mounted on a clipboard, are controlled by depressing one bar. Since it takes three strokes to complete a stopwatch cycle (start, stop, and reset), each watch is initially set in a different state. As the study progresses the observer can stop one watch, start another, and reset the third in preparation for the next observation.

5. *Calculate the average time.* Care must be exercised in deciding which observations to exclude from the calculation as unrepresentative of the population. Extraneous elements, such as dropped tools, poor materials, or operator mistakes must be included if they are inherent to the method, even if infrequent (for example, if operator fatigue causes the mistakes).

6. *Rate operator performance and compute the normal time.* Since an operator may be better or worse than normal, adjust the average elemental times. This is the most difficult, sensitive, and controversial aspect of stopwatch time studies. What constitutes normal performance, and how does an observer recognize small deviations? One approach is that normal performance may be related to some physical act, such as walking three miles per hour. A better approach provides both a standard and a training device, such as a set of films that depict numerous work activities rated by experts. The Society for the Advancement of Management (SAM) has published such film sets showing a succession of different performance levels for each activity. The ratings are based on the pooled judgments of 1,200 experienced time study people. Other groups have produced multiple-image films in which the same tasks, performed at different rates, can be viewed simultaneously (Barnes 1980). By having time study people regularly view and rate these films, advocates claim that observers learn what constitutes normal performance. Nevertheless, this highly subjective job of performance rating is a weakness in establishing a stopwatch time standard. Ideally, each work element should be rated separately; however, this is quite difficult, and so most studies rate only the overall performance.

7. *Adjust for allowances.* Allowances must be added to normal times for personal needs, unavoidable delays, and fatigue—all factors not encountered to any significant extent during the short observation period. These allowance values are determined separately and are often established by department or plant, frequently as part of the labor contract. After performing this step, a standard time for the task has been determined.

The time study relationships can be simply stated as

$$NT = AT \times PR$$

$$ST = NT \times PA$$

where

NT = Normal time

ST = Standard time

AT = Average time

PR = Performance rate

PA = 1 + percent allowances (where allowance is a percent of normal time)

The computation of the number of cycles to count involves two formulae.

$$S_x = \sqrt{\frac{\sum (X_i - \bar{X})^2}{N - 1}}$$

$$n = \frac{Z^2 S_x^2}{e^2}$$

where

X_i = Each observation

N = Number of cycles observed in sample

S_x = The sample standard deviation

e = The acceptable error

Z = The standard score of the confidence interval, normally 2 for 95 percent and 3 for 99 percent confidence

$\bar{X}$ = The average of observations

n = Number of cycles to count

This approach assumes that the sample standard deviation is an accurate estimate of the population standard deviation. Careful sample selection to ensure random sampling and independence can help assure this.

For example, for six work times of 70, 72, 76, 80, 79, and 73 seconds, the average is 75, and in calculating S_x the numerator $(\Sigma X_i - \bar{X})^2$ equals 25 + 9 + 1 + 25 + 16 + 4, or 80. Dividing by $N - 1$ and taking the square root gives $\sqrt{80/5} = 4$. If the analyst desired that the mean time be accurate to within plus or minus 3 seconds with a 95 percent confidence level, the number of cycles would be

$$n = \frac{2^2 4^2}{3^2}$$

$$= \frac{4 \times 16}{9}$$

$$= 7.11 \text{ or } 8$$

Therefore, 2 more cycles should be observed.

The full time study computation with an example series is shown in Figure 10–6. The data in Figure 10–6 give a continuous time sample in decimal fractions of a minute, followed by computed unit times, for ten cycles of five work elements. Average times are computed for each work element; then adjustments are made for the performance rating and allowances. Standard times sum to .9454 minutes per unit produced, or about 63 units per hour. Standard deviations of each cycle are computed, and the number of cycles necessary to observe are shown, given the element standard deviation and a confidence level of 99 percent that the sample average would be plus or minus .003 from the population mean if twenty-one (or the largest necessary cycles for any work element) cycles were observed. Considering that the shortest work element takes roughly six seconds and the longest takes fifteen seconds, an error of .003 minute, or approximately one-fifth of a second, is reasonable. This means more cycles should be observed or the high confidence level or relatively tight error range should be relaxed.

WORK SAMPLING. Stopwatch time studies are not appropriate for all situations. For example, it would be necessary to observe a worker for many hours to establish how much time is spent waiting for materials (the unavoidable delay allowance), to establish maintenance standards, or to get good fatigue and personal allowance times. Such continuous overviewing of a worker is expensive and could cause problems of extraneous elements or lack of cooperativeness. The technique of work sampling overcomes these problems.

Work sampling is based upon statistical sampling principles that allow generalizations about the time required for activities with irregular patterns on the basis of a sample of that period. Figure 10–7 shows an example of how a machine operator actually spent time over a five-day period, based on continuous observation.

Rather than continuously observing this operator, it is possible to use a random sample of observations and arrive at a reasonably accurate estimate of waiting time. Using the last column of the random number table (Appendix

Figure 10–6 Time Study Computations

Department Name: _____ Date: _____
Operator: _____ Methods Analyst: _____
Task: _____ Type of Data: Continuous
Number of Work Elements: 5 Number of Observed Cycles: 10
Percent Allowances: Personal   Unavoidable Delay   Fatigue   Total
            5.00%   7.00%   6.00%   18.00%
Amount of Error = .003 Confidence Level = 99%

Cycle #	Work Element Continuous Times (in minutes)				
	1	2	3	4	5
1	.252	.408	.591	.690	.808
2	1.049	1.214	1.386	1.488	1.601
3	1.834	2.016	2.191	2.246	2.415
4	2.655	2.813	2.990	3.090	3.204
5	3.449	3.610	3.788	3.889	4.006
6	4.253	4.412	4.594	4.694	4.809
7	5.060	5.217	5.394	5.498	5.614
8	5.860	6.018	6.197	6.299	6.416
9	6.660	6.819	7.000	7.103	7.216
10	7.466	7.626	7.806	7.906	8.021

Cycle #	Work Element Unit Times (in minutes)				
	1	2	3	4	5
1	.252	.156	.183	.099	.118
2	.241	.165	.172	.102	.113
3	.253	.162	.175	.105	.119
4	.240	.158	.177	.100	.114
5	.245	.161	.178	.101	.117
6	.247	.159	.182	.100	.115
7	.251	.157	.177	.104	.116
8	.246	.158	.179	.102	.117
9	.244	.159	.181	.103	.113
10	.250	.160	.180	.100	.115

Work Element	Average Time	Perform Rating	Normal Time	Standard Time	Standard Deviation	Desired Cycles
1	.2469	.95	.2345	.2767	.0045	20.2 ≅ 21
2	.1595	1.10	.1754	.2070	.0026	6.7 ≅ 7
3	.1784	1.00	.1784	.2105	.0022	4.8 ≅ 5
4	.1016	.90	.0914	.1079	.0019	3.6 ≅ 4
5	.1157	1.05	.1215	.1433	.0020	4.0 = 4
				.9454		

Additional Observations for Desired Accuracy and Confidence Level: 11
Standard Units of Output per hour: 63.4

Figure 10–7   One-Week Study of Time Allocation
               for Machinery Operation

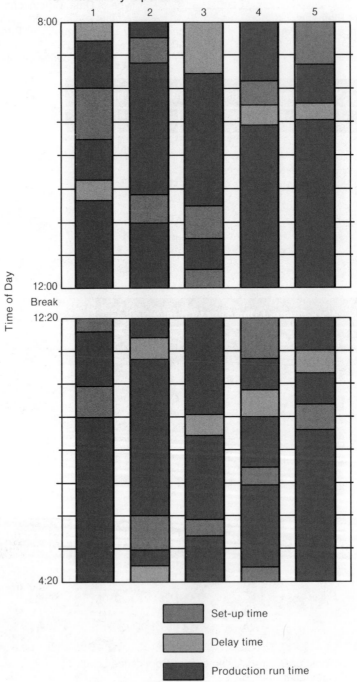

Set-up time

Delay time

Production run time

B) and considering the numbers to be decimal fractions of a day, random observations are made at the following times on a sample day:

Random Number	Hours After Start of Day	Actual Time
.9856	7.88	4:13 PM
.2010	1.61	9:37 AM
.9540	7.63	3:58 PM
.2865	2.29	10:17 AM
.7145	5.72	2:03 PM
.7801	6.24	2:34 PM
.8669	6.94	3:16 PM
.0816	0.65	8:39 AM
.0113	0.09	8:05 AM
.5912	4.73	1:04 PM

To convert the random numbers to observation times, multiply the random number by the length of day (8 hours) and add that to the starting time (8:00). Provision must also be made for the 20-minute lunch break and the decimal fraction of an hour must be converted to minutes. For example, in the preceding table the first random number is .9856; this is multiplied by 8 to give 7.8848 hours. Since this time is after lunch (greater than 4), 20 minutes (.3333 hours) are added. That sum is then added to 8 a.m. to yield l6.2181, from which 12 hours are subtracted to give 4.2181 p.m. To convert .2181 to minutes, it is multiplied by 60, which yields approximately 13. Thus, the first time is 4:13 p.m. The calculations for the second random number, .2010, are as follows:

$$8 + (.2010 \times 8) = 9.608 \text{ a.m.}$$

$$.608 \times 60 = 36.48 \text{ minutes or } 9:36 \text{ a.m.}$$

Such a simulation would be developed to identify various random times to observe a worker. If the observations are made on the fifth day, the operator would be involved in seven production runs, two setups, and one delay. This one day sample of worker activities may not adequately represent all possible days (the population), and a larger sample may be necessary. The technique is useful, however, in determining the allocations of time over a long period without extensive direct monitoring.

The use of a camera is also much less obtrusive than the stopwatch. Certain situations such as banks, hospitals, or retail stores, require a camera for security. The analysis of randomly snapped photographs provides a very good representation of the overall time spent by employees at various activities. Examples are the time spent by clerks with customers, the time duty nurses spend answering the telephone, or the utilization rates of pieces of equipment. Work sampling methods also have extensive applications in the setting of maintenance and quality control standards. Estimates of the number of hours (sometimes as a fraction) of process maintenance required for each unit or hour of production can be easily developed using work measurement methods. Additionally, work sampling can be used to determine the proportion of time spent on quality conformance checks as the product is made. For example, a piece may be milled to a designed tolerance and then the exact measure checked by placing it in a quality control jig or high-tech measuring instrument.

PUBLISHED SOURCES OF TIME DATA. In order to do a time study or work sampling, you must observe an operator performing the work. Because this is often difficult or inconvenient, the establishment of time standards without taking observations has long been a goal of time study departments. Two somewhat different methods for accomplishing this end have been developed. The first, called standard data, uses work element times from past studies. The second, called predetermined time studies, regards all jobs as a collection of very short movements like therbligs. Once a catalog of these times is established, it is easy to describe the method and find the times in the catalog.

The standard data approach assumes that although many different products are produced at a workstation, the work elements that the worker performs are relatively few. Therefore, once the elemental times have been set, operational standards can be built by prescribing the method and referring to an elemental times table. This technique is particularly useful in planning the production of new products.

Predetermined time systems eliminate (1) performance ratings, (2) variations of individual operator ability, and (3) inadequate job methods. Several predetermined time systems have been developed, the most common of which are the work factor method and methods time measurement (MTM). Because times are stated as normal times, performance rating is not necessary. However, since the task is subdivided into very small elements, these techniques are rarely used to build time standards for a complete job. Nevertheless, they are useful in determining times for small segments of work, which are used with standard data measurement techniques.

The work factor method uses original times developed from the study of thousands of operations in shops and laboratories. Studies were conducted during regular working hours with experienced operators of normally varied skills, effort, and ability who were earning wages on jobs under production rates. Each operation was rated by two experienced engineers according to individual motions and total operation cycle. Time values were established for basic motions, including arm, forearm swivel, finger, hand, foot, leg, trunk, walking, body turns, focus, inspection, reaction, step up, and step down. Basic motions occur without any resistance, weight, or change in direction; they involve only distance. Five work factors add time to the basic motion: weight or resistance, directional control or steer, care or precaution, change of direction, and definite stop. Applying the work factors results in a select time, which is the time required for an average experienced operator with good skill and effort to do a task. Allowances must be added to the select time to complete an operational time.

MTM, developed by Maynard, Stegemerten, and Schwab (1948), is based on micromotion film analysis. The motions defined are reach, move, turn, grasp, position, disengage, release, apply pressure (foot, leg, and body), walk, eye travel, and eye focus. Each motion is assigned a constant time value and, sometimes, a formula. Time values are stated in multiples of 0.00001 hour, called a time measurement unit (TMU). The time value for any motion is the time required for an average operator working with average effort under average conditions to perform that motion.

In addition to the basic motion and the MTM, industry standards and work rates have been developed for almost every major industry group. Automotive mechanical tasks, most job shop machine operations, and construction activities such as bricklaying and painting are among the numerous activities with published time study data. The use of published time data creates an attitude of motion-mindedness. The standards technician must review the motion patterns of each operation, identifying the nonproductive motions often overlooked in stopwatch studies.

NONSCIENTIFIC STUDIES. Other methods used in establishing time standards may be classified as nonscientific; among these are estimation and historical records. These methods may be required if scientific data are not initially available. The best estimate from an expert in the field or related historical data is better than no estimate at all. Accounting records of elapsed time incurred in the production of similar products may be used for gross estimating purposes. Unfortunately, these data usually contain hidden delays, moves, and other variations that may have been peculiar to the past performance.

THE USES OF TIME STUDIES. In summary, four methods (stopwatch studies, work sampling, published sources of time data, and nonscientific studies) are used to accomplish the time study phase of work measurement. Which of these methods is selected depends upon numerous considerations, among them the available time and data, the importance of accuracy, the sensitivity of the labor situation, and the ease of getting accurate measures of tasks.

If no information is available, a first step would be to use nonscientific evaluations, including data from related but slightly different tasks. Estimates by experienced and knowledgeable supervisors or workers are certainly appropriate. In some situations, labor relations constraints may require the use of published industry standard data. If the task involves relatively simple, easily describable actions, standard data and predetermined time study techniques can be used. However, these techniques are not effective in situations where extensive knowledge or judgment are required to complete the task. Stopwatch studies are used when other less costly methods are not available or when other such methods would be expected to give less accurate results than required. Stopwatch studies are best when used with tasks that have clearly definable start and finish actions and a fairly rapid cycle time (usually less than five minutes). Work sampling becomes appropriate as the cycle time increases or as the duration of the observation increases. Certainly, however, these general considerations should not be taken as hard and fast rules. Careful evaluation of the task and experience with the capabilities and limits of each technique are necessary to select the best method for a particular time study.

The Learning Curve

The time standard set in the previous ways assumes that the workers are experienced and the process is relatively stable. However, in many instances the workers are just becoming familiar with the tasks or the process is undergoing evolutionary improvement. When such learning is occurring, the time required for production of successive units is declining, productivity and quality are improving, and unit costs are going down. In general, such gains are easy to make at first; but, as more units are produced, improvements become more difficult. Several long-range studies have found that improvement due to learning is quite predictable. The learning or improvement phenomenon can be illustrated by any of the curves in Figure 10–8.

However, a learning rate may be interrupted as product design, production technology, or market conditions change (Hirschmann 1964 and Abernathy and Wayne 1974). Although the operations emphasis should be on the volume or cost reduction achieved through the learning curve, opportuni-

Figure 10–8 Possible Learning Curve Patterns

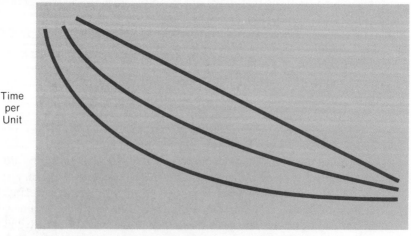

Time
per
Unit

Number of Individual Units Produced

ties for product, process, or technology innovations should not be ignored. Overemphasis of the learning curve may reduce the opportunities for innovation; particularly when the learning curve flattens as products and processes reach maturity.

THE LEARNING OF WORK BEHAVIORS. Mathematically, the learning curve may be represented in two ways. In the first way, it solves for the actual hours to produce the Nth unit or the cumulative hours to produce N units. In the second way, it solves for the average hours to produce N units. Because the actual data method permits easy compilation of both unit and cumulative production times as well as averages, it is used here.

The learning curve is described by the following equation:

$$T_N = TN^R$$

where

T_N = Time required to produce the Nth unit

T = Time required to produce the first unit

N = The number of units

R = The improvement rate = $\dfrac{\text{Natural log L}}{\text{Natural log 2}}$

L = The learning percentage

Note that R, the improvement rate, is a factor of the logarithm of the learning percentage divided by the logarithm of 2. The learning curve is stated in the following terms: every time production quantity doubles, the direct labor time per unit reduces to 75 percent of its former level. The exponent denominator of the natural log 2 is used because the improvement is computed based on a doubling of production; the natural log of 3 or 4 could be used for tripling or quadrupling of production. In other words, if the first unit required 100 direct labor hours, the second unit would require 75 hours, the fourth unit would require 56.25 hours (75 × .75), and so on. The cumulative time that would be required for the first four units would be 100 + 75 + 63 + 56.25 or 294.25 hours (the 63 hours for the third unit is a computed value).

Similarly, if the improvement rate was 80 percent and the first unit required 100 direct hours of labor, the fourth unit would require 64 hours (100 × .8 × .8), and the cumulative time of the first four units is 100 + 80 + 70 + 64 or 314 hours (again, the third unit value of 70 was computed).

Needless to say, these computations would be difficult for complex problems. Thus, the formula is an important assist. For example, given a 100-

hour first unit time and a 90 percent improvement rate, compute the 2,050th time.

$$T_{2,050} = 100(2,050)^{\ln 0.9/\ln 2}$$

$$T_{2,050} = 100(2,050)^{-.1054/.6419}$$

$$T_{2,050} = 100(2,050)^{-.1520}$$

$$T_{2,050} = \frac{100}{2,050^{.1520}}$$

$$T_{2,050} \cong 31.38$$

These computations can get tedious and require the use of logarithms. While spreadsheet programs are an increasingly popular method of computing learning curves, learning curve tables are still widely used for unit and cumulative values, and of course, are the basis for spreadsheet computations (see the learning curve tables in Appendices C and D).

These learning curve tables have numerous applications. Initially, the time to do the fourth unit and the first four units (cumulative), with a first-unit time of 100 and 75 percent and 80 percent improvement rates (as computed above) could be confirmed. Read down either the 75 percent or the 80 percent column to the fourth unit row in either table to find the correct unit or cumulative value, then multiply that value times 100, the time for the first unit. Most learning curve tables, including this one, are based on unitary values for the first unit, stated in any consistent time unit such as months, weeks, days, hours, or minutes. These computations are

Fourth unit, unit values

$$80\% = .64 \times 100 = 64 \text{ hours}$$

$$75\% = .5625 \times 100 = 56.25 \text{ hours}$$

Fourth unit, cumulative values

$$80\% = 3.14 \times 100 = 314 \text{ hours}$$

$$75\% = 2.95 \times 100 = 295 \text{ hours}$$

An average unit time in a range can also be found. For example, with a 100-hour first-unit time and a 75 percent learning rate, the average time of the 11th to the 20th unit is computed from the cumulative table by subtracting the 10th unit factor from the 20th unit factor, multiplying by the first-unit time, then dividing by the number of observations. Computationally, this is

$$\frac{100(8.83 - 5.59)}{10} = 32.4 \text{ hours average time for the 11th to 20th units}$$

WORK EVALUATIONS WITH LEARNING CURVES. There are numerous situations when the learning percentage rate may not be known and time study methods are required. The typical approach is to measure the first performance of an operation and then measure the second or a subsequent performance. For example, if a time study resulted in the data for the first two performances being 21 minutes and 18 minutes, the learning percentage would be found by dividing the time of the second performance by the time of the first: 18/21 = .857 (roughly 85 percent).

Similarly, if the learning rate is known and one unit time is known, any other unit time can be computed by dividing the known unit time by the appropriate Unit Table value. This would give the time for the first unit, which could be used to compute the time for any other unit. Additionally, if the first and any other time were known, the learning rate can be computed by dividing and reading the table. For first and third operation times of 21 and 16.25 minutes, the third operation divided by the first operation = 16.25/21 = .7738. To convert this value to a learning improvement, read across the appropriate row (here, row 3) and interpolate. In this case, .7738 is roughly the table value .7729, which is the three-units row and the 85 percent column.

Learning percentage rates may vary over time. That is, an initially fast-learning worker measured for the first ten units at a 75 percent learning rate may slow down to 80 percent or 85 percent for units 11 through 20. This learning rate change, if it continues, will impact the accuracy of the learning curve, particularly as the learning curve is applied further into the future. Thus, it is a good idea to recompute the learning curve at regular intervals. However, some of this individual variance is reduced by the common practice of averaging learning rates across several workers. Labor time data are often initially computed in hours per job; however, they are later converted to dollars per job so that it can be added to raw materials and overhead cost, to get a total cost. A typical example problem is presented in the following paragraphs:

An auto manufacturer has been told to recall and modify the brakes of a certain model. To evaluate the ability of local dealerships to do the work, the manufacturer developed the following labor time data, overhead cost, and raw material cost.

1. Find the missing learning curve data for each dealership.
2. Which dealership has the lowest per-unit time for the 400th unit? 500th unit?
3. Which dealership has the lowest cost based on 1,000, 1,400, and 2,000 estimated modifications and labor cost? Based on an average of 1,000 to 2,000 units?
4. Given the per-unit overheads, find the total cost for 1,400 modifications.

5. If the original learning curve estimated labor costs are expected to vary within a range of ± 5 percent for modification of 1,400 automobiles, does it make any difference who does the work?

Dealership	Work Test (in hours)				Learning Rate	Labor Rate per Hour	Overhead Costs
	1	2	3	4			
Seneca Motors	10	8.5	7.7		?	$8.00	$4.00
Bob's Auto	17		11.9		?	7.85	4.10
Heavy's Chevy	?		8.5		.85	8.25	3.90
Crosby Brothers	?		5.1	4.9	?	8.30	4.05

To answer Question 1, for Seneca Motors, divide the second job time by the first job time (because the increase from one to two jobs involves a doubling of the work) to get 8.5/10 or 85 percent. Similarly, the rate for Bob's Auto is solved by dividing the third job time by the first job time, or 11.9/17 = .7; next look across the three-units row of the unit learning curve table for the closest value, or .7021 = 80 percent rate. A similar process is used for Crosby Brothers. To find the improvement, divide the fourth job time by the third job time, or 4.9/5.1 = .9607, then look across rows 3 and 4 (which were the units in this problem) for a similar ratio. In this case, .8100/.8462 = .9572; this is in the 90 percent column. The first work test can be calculated at six hours. To find the first unit time for Heavy's Chevy, divide the time of the third unit by the 85 percent table value for that third unit, or 8.5/.7729 = 10.997 $\cong$ 11 hours.

To answer Question 2, which dealership has the lowest per-unit time for the 400th unit or the 500th unit, use the learning rates and first work test times found in Question 1. Multiply the time for the first unit by the table value for the appropriate improvement ratio of the 400th or 500th item. For example, Seneca Motors has a first-unit test time of ten hours and an 85 percent learning rate, thus .2454 $\times$ 10 = 2.4540 hours for the 400th unit. The other times are shown.

Dealership	Learning Rate	First Work Test Time	Time of 400th Unit	Time of 500th Unit
Seneca Motors	85%	10 hours	2.4540	2.3290
Bob's Auto	80%	17 hours	2.4701	2.2984*
Heavy's Chevy	85%	11 hours	2.6994	2.5619
Crosby Brothers	90%	6 hours	2.4132*	2.3328

To answer Question 3, the dealership with the lowest cost based on 1,000, 1,400, and 2,000 estimated modifications and labor cost, use the cumulative learning curve table, and multiply that figure by the labor cost per hour. Seneca Motors, with the ten hour first-unit time and an 85 percent improvement ratio, would take 10 $\times$ 257.9, or 2,579 hours to complete 1,000 units. At $8.00 per hour, the total labor cost would be $20,632. Other times and costs are shown. To compute the average hours per unit between 1,000 and 2,000 units for Seneca

Motors, subtract the cumulative time for 1,000 units from that for 2,000 units and divide by the number of units, or 4,389 − 2,579 = 1,810. That value, divided by 1,000 = 1.81. If you multiply by the labor cost, the result is 1.81 × $8.00 = $14.48.

Dealership	Total Hours			Hours × Labor Costs			Average 1,000 to 2,000	
	1,000	1,400	2,000	1,000	1,400	2,000	Hours	Cost
Seneca Motors	2,579	3,339	4,389	$20,632	$26,712	$35,112	1.81	$14.48
Bob's Auto	2,697	3,393	4,324*	21,178	26,636*	33,949*	1.62	12.77*
Heavy's Chevy	2,836	3,672	4,827	23,404	30,301	39,830	1.99	16.41
Crosby Brothers	2,473*	3,290*	4,453	20,527*	27,310	36,966	1.98	16.43

To answer Question 4, the total cost, including per-unit overhead for 1,400 modifications, is computed by multiplying the per-unit overhead by 1,400, and adding the labor costs, which were computed in Question 3 for 1,400 units. Those computations are shown as follows:

Dealership	Overhead per Unit	× 1,400	+ Labor Costs	= Total
Seneca Motors	$4.00	$5,600	$26,712	$32,212*
Bob's Auto	4.10	5,740	26,636	32,376
Heavy's Chevy	3.90	5,460	30,301	35,761
Crosby Brothers	4.05	5,670	27,310	32,980

To answer Question 5, compute the labor costs for each dealer at 5 percent less and 5 percent more than the present estimated learning curve rate. Evaluate the difference of cost between the +5 percent rate and the −5 percent rate against the differences between dealerships. For example, for Seneca Motors, 1,400 units at the 80 percent rate takes 1,996 hours times $8.00 = $15,968. At the 90 percent rate, takes 5,484 hours times $8.00 = $43,872. The difference is $27,904. Other dealers are similarly computed. Thus, it does not matter who does the work because the difference between the −5 percent and +5 percent rate costs (of between $27,405 and $31,654) is so much greater than the difference of costs for 1,400 modifications of $3,449 ($35,761 − $32,312) between the dealerships.

Dealership	Rate	Rate & Cost (−5 percent)		Rate & Cost (+5 percent)		Difference Between +5% and −5%
Seneca Motors	85	80	$15,968	90	$43,872	$27,904
Bob's Auto	80	75	15,639	85	44,558	28,921
Heavy's Chevy	85	80	18,113	90	49,767	31,654
Crosby Brothers	90	85	16,628	95	44,033	27,405

This example problem explores various computations and relationships that can be used to evaluate task learning rates of change. The learning curve permits the use of time study data, particularly in situations where the work times have not stabilized. This permits estimates of future unit, average, and cumulative production times. These times can be converted to dollar values of labor and integrated with raw materials or overhead to permit a more realistic overall cost computation per unit. Of course, periodic evaluation of the learning rate is appropriate, because as the computation is carried further into the future, inaccuracies of the initial estimate can cause very significant deviations in the future data.

CONCLUSIONS

This discussion has identified numerous work environment and task situation variables as central to work design; however, joint labor-management cooperation to determine the level of specialization and to negotiate job descriptions and allowances is critical to successful work evaluation. Although it is not possible to identify the best level of specialization or to specify a performance rate for tasks, once the task is given management and labor can negotiate appropriate work rules.

Certainly employee health and safety, competitive production rates and costs, and employee welfare are relevant. Sometimes they are conflicting factors in the short run, but often they are mutually supportive of long-run productivity. Union involvement in work evaluation has been extensive and, with some minor exceptions, union studies correspond closely with the findings of management studies. In this area, a strong union can be a significant asset to management. The specification of reasonable work rules that protect and encourage labor, yet are conducive to organizational growth and productivity, combined with formalized job descriptions, are of benefit to both management and labor.

Of course, the accuracy of a time study or a learning curve computation is only as good as the input data. Operations managers should never forget the possible limitations of their data when applying studies and planning jobs. Although results of studies or problems are often stated in decimal fractions, it is wise to use this computation only as a rough estimator of the expected outcome. There are many other variables that these computations do not consider.

QUESTIONS

1. List several reasons for work design and work measurement. Which are most likely to be used?

2. List several possible outcomes if work evaluation were not used or were used improperly.

3. Identify general environment variables that affect a day care center, a bank teller operation, a computer board drilling operation, a highway toll booth, a product gluing operation, and a suburban construction site office. What would you do to improve the work environment of these jobs.

4. If improvement of the working conditions were not possible, what would you expect to happen? How would you manage that?

5. Describe several major effects of improving the technology of work.

6. What is ergonomics? What is physical anthropology?

7. Describe several variables that are important contributors to the specific task environment.

8. Identify the key benefits to management and labor by increased specialization.

9. Identify four methods of conducting time studies. Which would be most appropriate for a furniture gluing operator, a toll booth money changer, a receptionist, a printing press operator, an industrial robot programmer developing new computer programs, a retail clerk, a telephone operator, and a counter clerk at a fast-food restaurant.

10. Name three ways that process charts assist the time study analyst.

11. In what ways are micromotion and memomotion studies different? When would they be used?

12. Why should a motion study be done before the time study of the same task?

13. Why is the method of defining the normal time so important? Describe three methods of developing normal time data.

14. Why is it necessary to compute the number of cycles of a task to observe?

15. What limitation of time studies do learning curves help the time study analyst consider?

16. What circumstances may cause learning curves to be inaccurate?

17. Why are learning curves less accurate when computing expected outcomes further into the future?

18. List several long-run outcomes of an effective work evaluation system.

19. Identify several general limitations of the time evaluation and learning curve methods. How would the time analyst overcome these?

PROBLEMS

1. If the following tasks were measured for caloric expenditure, how much rest would be required?

Activity	Calories per minute
Typing	2.5
Standing at a grinding machine	5.5
Directing automobile traffic	6.5
Lifting wooden pallets	8.0
Carrying furniture	10.0
Using a pneumatic drill	12.0

2. A manufacturer of portable radios has mechanized most functions, but one series of tasks must be done manually. Task cycle times vary from five to twenty seconds. Recommend how this work environment should be designed.

3. Using the principles of motion economy, describe how you would place the disks on a checkerboard, set a restaurant table for ten guests, and plant 100 annuals in a garden.

4. Develop an assembly flow chart to build a tricycle from the following parts:

Part No.	Part Name
1	Seat post and seat
2	Handlebars
3	Handlebar grips
4	Gooseneck (between the fork and handlebars)
5	Fork
6	Fork bearing and bolt assembly
7	Front wheel and tire
8	Front pedals, axle and bearing assembly
9	Rear step and axle assembly
10	Rear wheel and bearing assembly
11	Frame assembly

5. Given the data in Figure 10–6,

   a. Compute the task standard times if the total allowances were 12 percent and if they were 25 percent

   b. Compute the total standard time if the performance ratings were: Task 1 = 1.10; Task 2 = 1.05; Task 3 = 1.20; Task 4 = 1.15; Task 5 = 1.25.

   c. Compute the total standard time if the performance ratings were: Task 1 = 0.95; Task 2 = 0.90; Task 3 = 0.75; Task 4 = 0.80; and Task 5 = 0.85.

   d. If the amount of error permitted and the confidence levels were changed, compute the necessary cycles of observations.

Error	Confidence
0.0005	95%
0.005	99%
0.001	95%

6. Given the following ten continuous time observations (time in hundredths of minutes) for five work elements:

Cycle #	Element # 1	2	3	4	5
1	23	36	52	62	74
2	94	108	129	139	150
3	171	187	205	214	224
4	243	258	275	285	298
5	320	335	353	362	374
6	393	406	425	437	448
7	469	485	502	511	524
8	547	564	582	593	605
9	625	641	660	670	681
10	704	721	741	750	763

   a. Compute the average time.
   b. Compute the normal time.
   c. Compute the standard time.
   d. Compute the number of cycles to observe given a 95 percent confidence level and an acceptable error.

7. Given the following random numbers determine the distribution of activities (Figure 10–7) for the third day.

.8621	.3145	.5218	.7916	.6832
.9461	.1025	.0169	.4210	.0103

8. Refer to the learning curve example on page 358 to answer the following:

   a. Compute the revised curve if:

Dealership	1	2	3	4	Learning Rate
Seneca Motors	10	9.0			?
Bob's Auto	15			9.6	?
Heavy's Chevy	?	14.0			90%
Crosby Brothers	17		13	11.5	?

   b. Find the cost-per-unit time for the original data for the 300th, 450th, and 600th job.
   c. Find the cumulative time for the original data of the 1,200th, 1,500th, and 1,800th completed job.
   d. Find the average time for the original data of the 1,200th to the 1,600th jobs.
   e. Within a range of plus or minus 5 percent error for 200 modifications, does it make any difference who does the work?

9. The Metro Rail Company has received a contract to produce 200 passenger cars for a mass transit system. Given previous experience in building train passenger cars, an 80 percent learning curve is planned. The first car takes 1,400 direct labor hours.

   a. How many direct labor hours will it take to build the 200th car?
   b. How many direct labor hours will it take to build 140 cars?
   c. What is the average number of labor hours for the 101st to the 140th car?
   d. If labor is $12.50 per hour and overhead is prorated at $200 per unit, what is the total cost of the contract?
   e. Should Metro use the 80 percent learning assumption if labor hours for the first eight units were: 1,400, 1,206, 1,172, 1,145, 1,101, 1,083, 1,033, and 1,005?
   f. Should Metro use the 80 percent learning assumption of labor times for the first eight units were: 1,400, 1,089, 887, 801, 728, 684, 600, and 586?

REFERENCES

Abernathy, William J., and Kenneth Wayne. "Limits of the Learning Curve." *Harvard Business Review* (September–October 1974).

"And Now the Post-Industrial Corporation." *Business Week* (March 3, 1986): 64.

Barnes, Ralph M. *Motion and Time Study*. 7th ed New York: John Wiley & Sons, 1980.

Floyd, W. F., and A. T. Welford. *Symposium on Human Factors in Equipment Design*. London: H. K. Lewis & Co., 1954.

Floyd, W. F., and A. T. Welford. *Symposium on Fatigue*. London: H. K. Lewis & Co., 1954.

Gilbreth, Frank and Lillian. *Applied Motion Study*. New York: Sturgis & Walton, 1917.

Hackman, J. Richard, and Greg R. Oldham. "Motivation Through the Design of Work: A Test of Theory." *Organizational Behavior and Human Performance* 16 (1976): 256.

Henderson, Richard I. *Compensation Management: Rewarding Performance*. Reston, Va.: Reston Publishing Co., 1985, pp. 202, 203.

Herzberg, F. B., et al. *The Motivation to Work*. New York: John Wiley & Sons, 1959.

Hirschmann, Winfred B. "Profit from the Learning Curve." *Harvard Business Review* (January–February, 1964).

"How GM's Saturn Could Run Rings Around Old-Style Carmakers." *Business Week* (January 28, 1985): 126.

Maynard, H. B., G. J. Stegemerten, and J. L. Schwab. *Methods-Time Measurement*. New York: McGraw-Hill, 1948.

McCormick, Ernest J. *Human Factors Engineering*. New York: McGraw-Hill, 1970.

Murrell, K. F. H. *Human Performance in Industry*. New York: Reinhold Publishing Co., 1965.

Mundel, Marvin E. *Motion and Time Study*. Englewood Cliffs, N. J.: Prentice-Hall, 1978.

"'No Smoking' Sweeps America." *Business Week* (July 27, 1987): 40–52.

Rice, Robert S. "Survey of Work Measurement and Wage Incentives". *Industrial Engineering* 9, no. 7 (July 1977): 20.

Schrieber, Albert N. , et al. *Cases in Manufacturing Management*. New York: McGraw-Hill, 1965.

"Stealing an Edge." *Scanorama* (September 1987): 93.

Taylor, Frederick W. *The Principles of Scientific Management*. New York: Norton, 1911.

Van Cotte, Harold, and Robert Kinkade. *Human Engineering Guide to Equipment Design*. U. S. Government Printing Office, 1972.

Werther, W. B. "Going in Circles with Quality Circles." *Journal of Management Development* 2, no. 1 (1983).

Wilson, Frank W., and Philip D. Harvey. *Manufacturing Planning and Estimating Handbook*. New York: McGraw-Hill, 1963.

PART IV
SHORT-RANGE PLANNING

CHAPTER 11

Independent-Demand Inventory Management

CHAPTER 12

Material Requirements Planning

CHAPTER 13

Capacity Requirements Planning

INDEPENDENT-DEMAND INVENTORY MANAGEMENT

OBJECTIVES

After completing this chapter, you should be able to

- Distinguish between independent and dependent inventory demand and describe situations in which each type of demand exists

- Describe the general type of information that is contained in an inventory record file and know how that information is used

- Describe inventory-ordering rules that establish a quantity to order and those that establish the timing of the order and understand the situation in which each is appropriate

- Understand how to incorporate safety stock into inventory-ordering rules

- Appreciate various practical applications of inventory-ordering rules that facilitate inventory management

OUTLINE

INTRODUCTION

Individual items include assemblies, subassemblies, fabricated components, purchased components, and purchased materials. They are found in finished goods, spare parts, work in process, and raw materials. Prior to analyzing individual items, decisions have been made at the aggregate and intermediate levels concerning such things as constraints on inventory, grouping of items, customer service objectives, and the development and implementation of inventory management information systems.

Individual item management activities begin with selecting the appropriate inventory management system (i.e., decision rules for how much to order and when to release the order) for the different individual items. Table 11–1 lists some of the basic methods for managing individual items.

Many different combinations of lot size and order point rules are possible and are appropriate under different conditions. In this chapter we will examine the data required for inventory management decisions, the situational characteristics that determine the appropriateness of different management systems, and the nature of basic inventory management decision rules and the systems that they constitute.

DATA REQUIREMENTS

Certain data concerning each item are required for inventory management decisions. In less complex situations (low-volume transactions) these data may be processed manually and stored on cards. However, the complexity of most situations and the availability of relatively inexpensive computer hardware and software have led to increased computerization of inventory management support systems. The data usually are organized in the following manner:

1. The inventory record file, also called the part master file or the item master file
2. The bill of materials file (discussed in Chapter 8)
3. The master production schedule (discussed in Chapter 8)

Table 11–1 Names of Basic Ordering and Lot Size Rules (Grouped by Type of Rule)

When-to-Order Rules	Quantity-to-Order Rules
Order point	Economic order quantity
Periodic review	Variable order quantity
Time-phased order point	Discrete order quantities

The inventory record file contains a record, identified by part number, for each item. Each record usually contains inventory status and cost data required for cost estimating and production activity control in addition to the following data required for inventory management:

1. *Part number*—the unique part number assigned to the item
2. *Part description*—the name of the item
3. *On-hand quantity*—the number of units of this item in stock
4. *Allocated quantity*—the number of units of this item that has been assigned to previously planned future orders
5. *Available quantity*—the difference between the on-hand quantity and the allocated quantity
6. *Lot size quantity*—the normal number of units of this item produced at one time (the order quantity), the quantity of which will vary in many situations
7. *Lead time*—the normal time required to manufacture (or purchase) this item in a typical lot quantity range
8. *Item cost*—the standard cost of the item
9. *Preparation costs*—the sum of administrative, clerical, and shop costs incurred in issuing and monitoring the order (machine setup time is included in these costs for manufactured orders)
10. *Carrying cost*—the annual cost of carrying one unit of this item in inventory
11. *Group code*—An indication as to whether this item is to be purchased or produced as one of a group of items in a joint lot size decision process
12. *Where used (next assembly)*—the identification of the assembly or assemblies in which this item is used
13. *Safety stock*—a number of units usually held in inventory to protect against fluctuations in demand and/or supply
14. *Average demand*—the average quantity required per period

FACTORS IN INVENTORY DECISIONS

The nature of a situation determines the appropriateness of an inventory management system. Although it is not possible to examine all combinations of factors, each of which can define a unique situation and set of considerations, it is possible to describe those that are most important in selecting an inventory management system and why they are important. Those factors are (1) demand pattern, (2) source, that is, common suppliers or production process, and (3) customer requirements.

The Demand Pattern

The nature of the demand pattern has an effect greater than any other possible factor on the appropriateness of the when-to-order decision rules—and thus on the design of the inventory management system. The relation of a demand pattern to the quantity on hand (in stock) is the key factor in

Figure 11–1 Relation of Demand and Inventory Dissipation Patterns Over Time (Independent Demand)

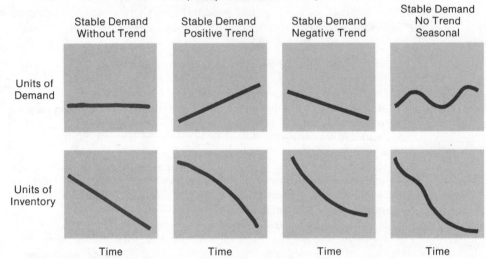

classifying demand patterns. A pattern that results in a relatively gradual and steady decrease in inventory is representative of independent demand (see Figure 11–1). On the other hand, a pattern that causes abrupt and dramatic changes in stock is representative of dependent demand (see Figure 11–2).

INDEPENDENT DEMAND. Distribution inventories (i.e., items held as finished goods for sale) and service parts purchased by many different customers in small quantities per time period relative to total annual demand usually experience a relatively stable demand, as illustrated in Figure 11–1. This demand, which may be affected by trends and seasonal patterns, does not depend on demand for other items; it is independent demand.

Figure 11–2 Relation of Demand and Inventory Dissipation Patterns Over Time (Dependent Demand)

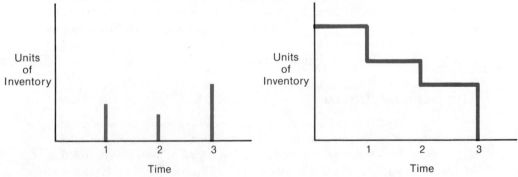

DEPENDENT DEMAND. Subassemblies, component parts, and raw materials have a demand that is primarily dependent on the demand for the final products in which they are used. If the final products are fabricated intermittently in lots (batches), which occurs in all situations except continuous and repetitive production, the demand for these items is relatively abrupt and dramatic as illustrated in Figure 11–2. Except for service part requirements (usually a small portion of an item's demand), the demand for these items results from the demand for other items; they are dependent demand items. Materials requirements planning should be used for these items.

Of course, there are exceptions. Finished goods purchased in relatively large quantities only a few times a year by one or two customers will likely exhibit an abrupt and irregular demand pattern similar to dependent demand. On the other hand, raw materials, common hardware items, and components used in many different final products may experience a relatively stable demand similar to that usually associated with independent demand items. The demand pattern for each item must be evaluated on its own merits.

Source—Common Supplier or Production Process

Inventories also can be grouped on the basis of the supplier, the process, and the departments through which the items are processed. For example, parts that are to be purchased from a single supplier frequently are grouped together to facilitate joint purchase orders, joint product quantity discounts, transportation, and communications with suppliers. Items produced in the same department or on a similar group of machines also should be grouped for analyzing the relationship of the aggregate order quantity capacity requirements to the capacity availability and the possibility of common setups. Methods available for analyzing such situations are discussed in Fogarty and Hoffmann (1983). Items purchased from a common supplier or produced on common facilities are candidates for periodic review inventory management when the combination of orders or joint orders generates savings greater than the possible increase in inventory investment costs.

Customer Requirements

When a group of items has been ordered or usually is ordered by a single customer, the production or purchase of these items may be grouped to enable concurrent delivery, unless the purchase order specifies different delivery dates for different items. This practice not only enables joint shipping and invoicing, but in many cases none of the items are of value to the customer unless all are delivered, and, in practice, some purchase orders predicate payment upon receipt of all items. This situation may exist when all the items are required in an assembly produced by the customer.

Other Factors

Demand and design stability, shelf life, and lead time also affect inventory decisions. Items susceptible to the whims of fashion or engineering changes may be ordered in quantities smaller than otherwise would be the case. Limited shelf life also imposes limits on the quantity ordered. Dependent demand parts and materials with long lead times relative to final assembly delivery requirements may require an order point system to achieve customer service objectives.

INVENTORY MANAGEMENT MODELS AND DECISION RULES

A company may manufacture or purchase an item in three different ways: (1) after receiving an order for the item (production to order), (2) in anticipation of customer orders (production to stock), or (3) as modular components that are produced to stock and are assembled after receiving an order.

In the first instance, production to order, the firm may produce the quantity ordered by customers, or it may produce that quantity plus additional units in anticipation of further orders.

The principles and techniques of material requirements planning (MRP), discussed in Chapter 12, are used in determining the order release dates and lot sizes of items produced only to order. In the case of production to stock or production of modular components, the decision rules governing lot size and order release timing are a function primarily of an item's demand characteristics. A fixed order quantity—order point system or a periodic review system—is usually appropriate for managing independent demand items. Dependent demand items usually are managed best by an MRP type system.

Production of customer order requirements plus anticipated requirements upon receipt of an order frequently involves a combination of MRP and order point management systems. In fact, most real-world systems are hybrid; they combine features of the different systems to cope with real-world complexities. This introduction to lot size and order release decision rules views inventory management situations as relatively simple and neat. The principles and techniques developed under these conditions will aid in handling more complex situations.

The two objectives of an inventory management system are to provide a level of customer service and to minimize the costs of providing that service. The order release mechanism is used by the operations manager as the major determinant of the level of customer service, while order quantity size is the primary determinant of inventory costs. This is important because the operations manager selects the inventory management model that best achieves the system objectives.

First, we will examine the fixed order quantity model because it clearly illustrates the cost structure of lot size decisions. Presentation of the statistical order point model follows as the concepts involved are relevant to any demand situation. Treatment of periodic review systems, visual review systems, and the time-phased order point system follow. Material requirements planning is described in Chapter 12.

Economic Order Quantity

The fixed order quantity lot size decision rule specifies a number of units that are ordered each time an order is placed for a particular item. This quantity may be arbitrary, such as a two-week supply or 100 units, but it is frequently the economic order quantity (EOQ). The EOQ is the most economical quantity available under a given set of conditions. The fixed order quantity lot size determination method can be combined with each of the different methods for determining the order release. These methods and the conditions appropriate for their combination will be examined later in the chapter.

The conditions under which the basic economic order quantity model is valid are

1. Demand is relatively constant and known; there are no stockouts.
2. Preparation costs, total carrying costs, and lead time are constant and known.
3. Replenishment is instantaneous; items arrive at an infinite rate at a given time.

Situations in which all the relevant factors—demand, lead time, and costs—are known with complete certainty are rare. But assuming deterministic conditions, certainty is a legitimate expectation when analyzing some inventory situations. There are three reasons for this. First, situations do exist in which the facts are known with near certainty (e.g., the newsprint necessary to publish a Sunday paper or the requirement for staple food items such as milk or bread). Second, the effect of the decision frequently is relatively insensitive to small changes in decision factors. Third, understanding the fixed order quantity model can aid in the modeling of more complex situations.

Two graphs are essential in analyzing inventory management situations. One displays the relationship of the quantity on hand to time, and the other illustrates the relationship of lot size to cost (see Figure 11–5). In the case of the fixed order quantity, the quantity versus time relationship takes the sawtooth shape in Figure 11–3.

The straight vertical line in Figure 11–3 represents the arrival of items in inventory just as the stock level reaches zero. The number of units in stock then increases instantaneously by Q, the amount ordered and received. This graphic representation of the arrival of an order instantaneously is a very accurate depiction of the arrival of a lot of purchased parts. It is also an accurate representation of the arrival of parts produced within the organization when the time between the manufacture of the first item and the last is relatively brief.

Figure 11–3 Units in Inventory Versus Time (Fixed Order Quantity Model with Demand and Lead Time Certain)

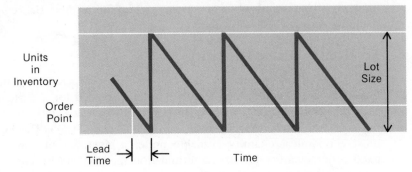

Withdrawals of items from inventory under constant demand conditions actually take place in an incremental step fashion that is approximated by the straight line slope shown in Figure 11–4.

Costs incurred in a lot size decision include carrying costs, preparation costs, stockout costs, and the cost of the item itself. The cost of the item, the purchase price or the cost of material, and labor and overhead in the case of an item produced internally can change in situations in which purchase or production of larger quantities will achieve economies of scale. For the purpose of this analysis, the cost of an item is treated as a constant, and stockouts do not occur. Therefore, the total costs incurred during a period as a result of the lot size decision when using the basic fixed order quantity decision rule are formulated as follows:

Total costs equal preparation costs plus carrying costs.
Preparation costs equal cost per preparation times the number of preparations in the period.
Carrying costs equal the average quantity in inventory times the cost of carrying one unit for the period or equivalently, the average quantity in inventory times unit cost times the cost rate of carrying one dollar of inventory for the period.

Figure 11–4 Constant Withdrawals from Inventory over Time

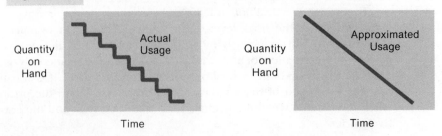

Therefore,

$$TC = \frac{SR}{Q} + \frac{QK}{2} \text{ or } \frac{SR}{Q} + \frac{QCk}{2}$$

Where

TC = total costs per period, usually a year

S = cost per preparation in dollars

R = period requirements in units

Q = lot size in units

$K = Ck$ or cost of holding one unit in inventory for the period

C = cost of one unit

k = cost rate per dollar of carrying inventory for the period

From Figure 11–3 it can be determined that average inventory equals one half the lot size. Inventory decreases at a constant rate from a maximum lot size to a minimum of 0. Thus, the average inventory equals $(Q + 0)/2$ or $Q/2$.

The period used for these calculations is usually one year. However, it may be appropriate to use a different length period; for example, the planning period of some items may be only six months. You should note that the requirements, demand, and the carrying cost per unit will be proportionately less for the shorter period. Either a calculus or a graphic approach can be used to find the lot size that results in minimum costs.

THE GRAPHIC SOLUTION. Graphing carrying costs, preparation costs, and total inventory costs in relation to lot size reveals a critical relationship between carrying costs and preparation costs at that point, lot size, where total costs are at a minimum. Let's look at an example.

A ball bearing distributor has an item that has an annual demand of 60,000 units at a relatively constant rate throughout the year. Preparation costs are $45 each time an order is placed; the carrying cost rate is .3 or 30 cents per dollar of inventory per year; and the units cost $2 each. To graph the relationship of lot size and total costs, it is necessary to calculate the total costs for different lot sizes, as shown in Table 11–2 and graphed in Figure 11–5.

Note that the preparation cost (SR/Q) decreases at a geometrically decreasing rate and that the carrying cost $(QCk/2)$ increases at an arithmetically increasing rate. Additionally, the total cost values and the graph reveal

Table 11–2   Tabulation of Inventory Costs for Different Lot Sizes

S = $45	R = 60,000	k = .30	C = $2
Lot Size (Q)	Preparation Costs (SR/Q)	Carrying Costs (QCk/2)	Total Cost
10	$270,000	$ 3	$270,003
100	27,000	30	27,030
500	5,400	150	5,550
1,000	2,700	300	3,000
1,500	1,800	450	2,250
2,000	1,350	600	1,950
2,500	1,080	750	1,830
3,000	900	900	1,800
3,500	771	1,050	1,821
4,000	675	1,200	1,875
6,000	450	1,800	2,250
10,000	270	3,000	3,270
15,000	180	4,500	4,680
30,000	90	9,000	9,090
60,000	45	18,000	18,045

Figure 11–5   Fixed Order Quantity (Costs Versus Lot Size)

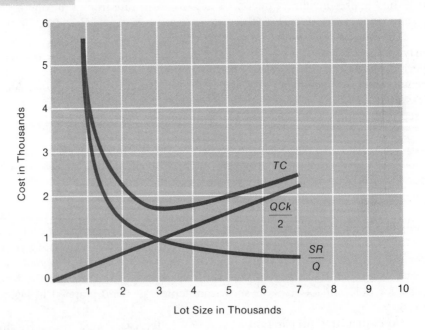

two interesting facts: (1) total costs are lowest at that point at which preparation costs equal carrying costs (lot size equals 3,000) and (2) the total costs are approximately the same for a wide range of lot sizes centered on the minimum cost lot size. In fact, preparation costs are approximately equal to carrying costs for the minimum total cost lot size in most continuous demand situations. You may want to tabulate and graph other examples to verify this. The width of the span of lot sizes in which there is little change in total costs is called the inelastic portion of the total cost curve and depends on the values of the parameters (e.g., carrying costs, preparation costs, and annual demand). We will return to this topic later when discussing the sensitivity of the model. The first observation enables us to establish the general procedure for setting preparation costs equal to carrying costs and for solving for the EOQ.

Since the EOQ is that quantity where preparation costs equal carrying costs,

$$\frac{QkC}{2} = \frac{SR}{Q}$$

Thus, solving for Q gives

$$Q^2 = \frac{2SR}{kC}$$

and, therefore,

$$Q^* \text{ (optimum value)} = \left(\frac{2SR}{kC}\right)^{1/2}$$

The EOQ can be determined using this model. Graphing the cost functions versus lot size will also provide valuable insight concerning the increase in total cost as the lot size is increased or decreased in a particular case.

THE CALCULUS OPTIMIZATION APPROACH. The calculus approach is presented to illustrate a technique useful for deriving a decision rule in many inventory situations. One need not possess a knowledge of calculus to use the resulting decision rule.

Using the basic calculus optimization technique, the first derivative of the total cost expression with respect to Q is set equal to 0. The value of Q that satisfies the equation is an optimum. Taking the first derivative of TC (TC') with respect to Q,

$$TC = \frac{RS}{Q} + \frac{KQ}{2}$$

$$TC' = \frac{-RS}{Q^2} + \frac{K}{2} = 0$$

and, so,

$$\frac{K}{2} = \frac{RS}{Q^2}$$

Multiplying both sides of the equation by Q^2 and $2/K$ gives

$$Q^2 = \frac{2RS}{K}$$

$$Q^* = \left(\frac{2RS}{K}\right)^{1/2}$$

This is the same decision rule we obtained using the graphic approach, except that kC has been replaced by K.

To determine if this point is a maximum or minimum we must next take the first derivative of TC (TC'') and determine if it is positive or negative at Q^*. This is formulated as follows:

$$TC'' = \frac{2RS}{Q^3}$$

Since R, S, and Q are always positive, the test of a minimum solution is met; TC'' will be positive for Q. Therefore, the solution obtained by solving the first derivative is a minimum—that is, it gives the value of Q that will result in the minimum total period costs.

TOTAL PERIOD COSTS AND SENSITIVITY. Both approaches result in the same lot size, 3,000 units. The total annual costs resulting from using a lot size of 3,000 are determined in the following manner:

$$TC(Q^*) = \frac{SR}{Q^*} + \frac{CkQ^*}{2}$$

$$TC(3,000) = \left(\$45 \times \frac{60,000}{3,000}\right) + \left(\$2 \times 0.3 \times \frac{3,000}{2}\right)$$

$$= \$900 + \$900$$

$$= \$1,800$$

Increasing the lot size (Q) by 10 percent results in a little less than a one-half percent increase in total costs given the parameters of this situation.

$$TC(3,300) = \left(\$45 \times \frac{60,000}{3,300}\right) + \left(\$2 \times 0.3 \times \frac{3,300}{2}\right)$$

$$= \$818.18 + \$990$$

$$= \$1,808.18$$

Decreasing the lot size (Q) by 10 percent results in slightly more than a one-half percent increase in the total annual inventory costs.

$$TC(2,700) = \left(\$45 \times \frac{60,000}{2,700}\right) + \left(\$2 \times 0.3 \times \frac{2,700}{2}\right)$$

$$= \$1,000 + \$810$$

$$= \$1,810$$

Total costs resulting from the lot size decision do not seem to be overly sensitive to changes in the lot size if the foregoing examples are any indication. Let's examine the general case.

The relationship of the total cost, TC, of a nonoptimum lot size to the total cost, TC^*, of the optimum lot size can be determined as follows:

$$TC^* = \frac{SR}{Q^*} + \frac{Q^*K}{2}$$

and

$$TC = \frac{SR}{Q} + \frac{QK}{2}$$

therefore

$$\frac{TC}{TC^*} = \left(\frac{SR}{Q} + \frac{QK}{2}\right) \div \left(\frac{SR}{Q^*} + \frac{Q^*K}{2}\right)$$

Substituting $Q^* = \sqrt{\frac{2SR}{K}}$ and then manipulating algebraically to remove S, R, and K gives:

$$\frac{TC}{TC^*} = \frac{1}{2}\left(\frac{Q^*}{Q} + \frac{Q}{Q^*}\right)$$

Thus, the effects of a specific percentage change in Q can be calculated. For example,

$$\text{let } Q = 1.10Q^* \text{ (a 10 percent increase)}$$

Then,

$$\frac{TC}{TC^*} = \left(\frac{Q^*}{1.10Q^*} + \frac{1.10Q^*}{Q^*} \right) \div 2$$

$$= (.909 + 1.10) \div 2$$

$$= 1.0045$$

These results correspond to those obtained when analyzing the sensitivity of total costs to changes in the lot size of the previous examples. Thus, in general, the percentage difference in inventory costs is relatively small in comparison to the difference in lot sizes around the EOQ. This inelasticity of the total cost curve in the vicinity of the EOQ gives the operations manager some flexibility.

VARIATIONS OF THE EOQ MODEL. There are literally dozens of ways the basic EOQ model can be modified to fit different situations. Because of their broad applicability, two commonly used and widely applicable techniques are the dollar lot size model and the noninstantaneous receipt model. Other variations are described in Fogarty and Hoffmann (1983).

The total cost (inventory) model may be formulated to provide the optimum lot size value in monetary units rather than physical units. This approach is especially useful when developing and applying a model to determine the minimum cost lot size of a group or family of related items. If

$$Q_\$ = \text{lot size in dollars}$$

$$A = \text{period requirements in dollars}$$

$$TC = \frac{kQ_\$}{2} + \frac{SA}{Q_\$}$$

Following the calculus approach to determine the value of $Q_\$$ that results in the minimum total period costs, TC^* yields the following:

$$Q_\$^* = \left(\frac{2AS}{k} \right)^{1/2}$$

And, using data from the previous example:

$$C = \$2$$

$$R = 60,000$$

$$k = .3$$

$$S = \$45$$

$$A = CR = \$2.00 \times 60,000 = \$120,000$$

$$Q_\$^* = \left(\frac{2 \times 120,000 \times 45}{.3}\right)^{1/2}$$

$$= \$6,000$$

$$Q^* = \frac{Q_\$^*}{C} = \$6,000/\$2 = 3,000$$

Note that this is the same answer obtained earlier.

NONINSTANTANEOUS RECEIPT. Frequently when items are produced internally, they enter inventory gradually on a day-to-day basis during a substantial portion of the consumption period rather than at once as when a purchased lot arrives. Thus, the investment of dollars in inventory takes place day by day during the production run, as illustrated in Figure 11–6, and units continue to be withdrawn from stock as the newly produced items arrive. Thus, in this case of noninstantaneous receipt, known lead time, and no safety stock, the inventory level is never as large as the lot size.

Inventory is both produced and consumed during the period of production (T_p). The rate (P) at which an item is produced is equal to the production

Figure 11–6 Inventory Versus Time, Fixed Order Quantity (Noninstantaneous Receipt)

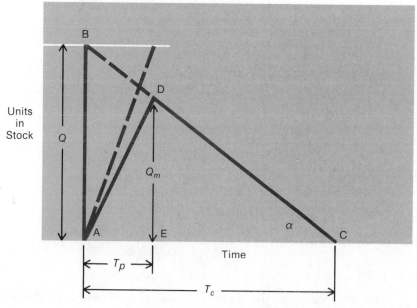

lot size (Q) divided by T_p; and the demand rate (D) is equal to Q divided by the consumption period (T_c). These are, then, formulated as follows:

$$P = \frac{Q}{T_p} \text{ and } D = \frac{Q}{T_c}$$

Therefore,

$$T_p = \frac{Q}{P} \text{ and } T_c = \frac{Q}{D}$$

Both P and D are expressed in units per time period. In this case, as in the instantaneous receipt case, the TC resulting from the lot size decision is equal to the preparation cost plus the carrying cost. Preparation costs again equal the cost per preparation times the number of preparations in the period, as described previously. Carrying costs equal average inventory quantity (or value) times the cost (or cost rate) of carrying one unit for the period. The difficulty is that average inventory is not one-half the lot size, $Q/2$, in this case. An examination of Figure 11–6 reveals that average inventory is equal to $Q_m/2$, but the value of Q_m isn't immediately apparent. A little basic geometry will allow us to determine it from the known parameters. Two similar triangles, each having a common angle alpha (α), can be seen in Figure 11–6. Triangle ABC has sides of Q and T_c while triangle EDC has corresponding sides of Q_m and $T_c - T_p$. From the rules of geometry:

$$\frac{Q}{T_c} = \frac{Q_m}{T_c - T_p}$$

since both ratios describe the angle alpha, α. Thus

$$Q_m = \frac{Q(T_c - T_p)}{T_c}$$

Previously described relationships between Q, T_c, T_p, P, and D, showed that:

$$T_p = \frac{Q}{P} \text{ and } T_c = \frac{Q}{D}$$

Substituting Q/P for T_p and Q/D for T_c,

$$Q_m = \frac{Q\left(\frac{Q}{D} - \frac{Q}{P}\right)}{\frac{Q}{D}}$$

Dividing the numerator on the right side of the equation by the denominator, Q/D, gives:

$$Q_m = Q\left(\frac{D}{D} - \frac{D}{P}\right) = Q\left(1 - \frac{D}{P}\right)$$

And thus the average inventory is equal to $Q_m/2$, which equals

$$\frac{Q\left(1 - \frac{D}{P}\right)}{2}$$

The average inventory, therefore, in the noninstantaneous receipt case is equal to one-half the lot size multiplied by one minus the ratio of the consumption rate to the production rate. Intuitively, this makes sense; one would expect the average inventory to decrease in proportion to the ratio of the consumption and production rates due to the fact that units are being withdrawn from stock as they are produced and enter stock.

This example illustrates a useful approach for determining average inventory under many different circumstances that do not correspond exactly to the basic model. Thus, substituting

$$\frac{Q\left(1 - \frac{D}{P}\right)}{2}$$

for Q/2 in the basic decision rules gives the following:

$$TC = \frac{SR}{Q} + kCQ\frac{\left(1 - \frac{D}{P}\right)}{2}$$

$$Q^* = \left[\frac{2RS}{kC\left(1 - \frac{D}{P}\right)}\right]^{1/2}$$

Noninstantaneous Receipt Example. Let's return to the previous example of the ball bearings with the same facts except that the situation has changed to one of a manufacturer producing these items for finished goods with a production capacity of 960 units per eight-hour shift. Thus, we have the following:

$$R = 60,000 \text{ units per year}$$

$$S = \$45 \text{ per order}$$

$$k = .30 \text{ per dollar of inventory per year}$$

$$C = \$2 \text{ each}$$

$$P = 960 \text{ units per eight-hour shift}$$

$$D = 60,000 \text{ units per year}$$

If we casually insert the given demand and production rates directly into the formula we have developed for this situation, we will have a mixture of apples and oranges—or fruit salad. Consequently, we must first convert either P or D to the same base. They should not be stated in units for different time periods. In this case, let's convert P to the same base as D, an annual one.

Since the plant works one shift a day, five days a week, and fifty weeks a year, the annual production capacity is calculated next as:

$$P = 960 \times 5 \times 50 = 240,000 \text{ units/year}$$

and the minimum cost order quantity is:

$$Q^* = \left[\frac{2RS}{kC\left(1 - \frac{D}{P}\right)} \right]^{1/2}$$

$$= \left[\frac{2 \times 60,000 \times 45}{2 \times .3\left(1.0 - \frac{60,000}{240,000}\right)} \right]^{1/2}$$

$$= 12,000,000^{1/2}$$

$$= 3,464.1$$

The exactness of this answer raises practical considerations. First, a fractional ball bearing is not a meaningful quantity; second, it probably makes sense to round off the lot size to 3,500 or 3,400 units. The increased unit costs should be relatively small and the record keeping much easier. Using a lot size of 3,464 or 3,465 is attributing greater precision to the estimated parameter values than is justified in most cases.

In summary, the fixed order quantity model is useful for determining the lot size under relatively stable, independent demand. Total costs are relatively insensitive to the actual lot size differing slightly from the optimum lot size. Minor modifications to the basic model are required to provide decision rules for more complex situations.

QUANTITY DISCOUNTS. The cost of purchased items frequently is a function of the number of units purchased reflecting order entry, shipping, or manufacturing economies in the supplier's operation. For a three-tier cost structure, illustrated graphically in Figure 11–7, this situation can be described as:

$$\text{Unit cost} = C_1 \text{ when } Q > 0, \text{ but } < X_1$$

$$\text{Unit cost} = C_2 \text{ when } Q \geq X_1, \text{ but } < X_2$$

$$\text{Unit cost} = C_3 \text{ when } Q \geq X_2$$

Where

$$C_3 < C_2 < C_1$$

X_1 and X_2 are price break quantities, and

Q is the order quantity (purchased lot size)

The objective is to purchase the quantity that results in minimum total costs and violates no constraints. (One typical constraint is to never purchase more than a year's supply, due to the probability of deterioration, product changes, etc.)

The following procedure gives the minimum total cost lot size:

1. Calculate the EOQ for each unit cost. If an EOQ is feasible, calculate its total lot size decision-related costs. (A feasible EOQ is one that is greater than the quantity required to obtain the unit cost used in the EOQ calculation.)
2. Calculate the total lot size decision-related costs of each of the minimum quantities that must be purchased to obtain the cost breaks.
3. The minimum cost order quantity is that quantity found in either Step 1 or 2 that has the lowest total costs and does not violate any constraints.

Figure 11–7   Total Costs Versus Lot Size Breaks in Unit Cost

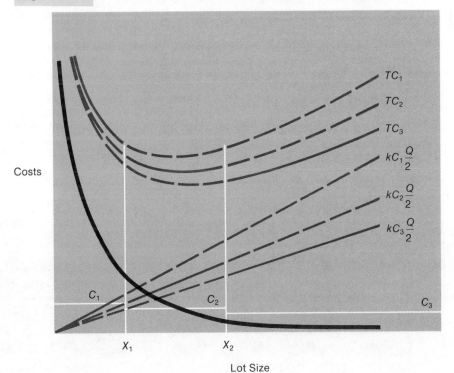

Table 11–3 EOQs for Different Unit Costs

Unit Cost	Minimum Order Quantity	EOQ	EOQ Feasible?
$80.00	—	163	Yes
70.00	200	174	No
65.00	500	181	No

Let's look at an example. A company experiences a rather steady independent demand of 8,000 units annually for an item that it purchases. The item costs $80 when purchased in order quantities less than 200, $70 when purchased in order quantities of at least 200 and less than 500, and $65 when purchased in order quantities of 500 or more. Ordering costs are $40 per order, and the carrying cost rate is .30.

Table 11–3 lists the EOQ calculated for each of the three costs. The EOQs for $70 and $65 are not feasible since they are less than the quantity required to obtain the cost break. Table 11–4 lists the total lot size decision-related costs of the feasible EOQ (163), and the two cost break quantities (200 and 500). In this case the minimum cost lot size is 500 units; it results in the lowest total costs. If the only constraint is that the order quantity must not exceed a year's supply, the order quantity would be 500 units. The quantity discount dominates the decision. Today most organizations would attempt to negotiate weekly or more frequent deliveries with a blanket order to obtain the benefits of both the quantity discount and just-in-time inventory management policies. See Chapters 16 and 20.

Statistical Order Point

As mentioned previously, deciding when to release an order for purchase or production and deciding the quantity to order are the two objectives of

Table 11–4 Total Lot Size Decision-Related Costs of Feasible EOQs and Cost Break Quantities

Column 1	Column 2	Column 3	Column 4	Column 5	Column 6
Lot Size (Q)	Unit Cost (C)	Annual Item Costs (CR)	Annual Ordering Costs (SR/Q)	Annual Carrying Costs (Ck Q/2)	Total Costs (Columns 3 + 4 + 5)
163	$80.00	$640,000	$1,963	$1,956	$643,919
200	70.00	560,000	1,600	2,100	563,700
500	65.00	520,000	640	4,875	525,515

individual item management. There are three basic methods of deciding when to order independent-demand inventory items: (1) statistical order point, (2) periodic review, and (3) time-phased order point.

When to order an item depends on when an item is needed. The first two methods consider need implicitly, while the third recognizes it explicitly.

Traditionally the EOQ, fixed order quantity, lot-sizing approach has been combined most frequently with the statistical order point method of deciding when to order. Thus, we will examine the statistical order point first. The periodic review method of ordering and the variable order quantity are interwoven inextricably; an examination of this method and its most common variations follows. The use of the time-phased order point in conjunction with the EOQ in independent demand situations, a relatively recent development, also is presented.

The statistical order point system places an order for a lot whenever the quantity on hand is reduced to a predetermined level, known as the order point (*OP*), as illustrated in Figure 11–8. This system can be used effectively for independent demand items with relatively stable demand.

If the demand rate and the replenishment lead time (*L*) are constant, it is not difficult to determine exactly how low the stock level of an item can drop before an order must be placed to avoid a stockout. For example, if an automobile parts distribution warehouse experiences a constant demand for 250 ball joint sets every two weeks— month in and month out—and it always takes exactly two weeks to obtain a replenishment order from the factory, the order point should be set at 250 sets, exactly two weeks of stock. However, this is not the common case, More typically the demand would vary, for example, from approximately 200 to 300 sets during lead time, which itself might vary from between 1 1/2 to 2 1/2 weeks. An order point without safety stock will result in stockouts in 50 percent of the ordering periods if demand and lead time vary randomly. In this more realistic case, the order point is

Figure 11–8   Typical Quantity in Stock Versus Time (Order Point System)

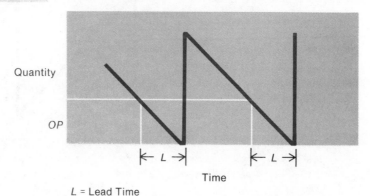

Quantity

OP

|← L →| |← L →|

Time

L = Lead Time

established to cover average usage during average lead time plus some of the expected high side variations in demand or in lead time. Stock held to cover these variations is called safety stock, buffer, or reserve stock (Q_s). The amount of variation covered depends on the level of customer service desired. The relationships among order point, lead time, and safety stock are shown in Figure 11–9.

The purpose of carrying a safety stock is to allow routine handling of the normal fluctuations that can be expected in any real situation. Safety stock is not intended to prevent all stockouts or to eliminate completely the need for expediting (i.e., emergency follow-up on delayed orders or requests for quick delivery in unusual situations). Safety stock is present to allow management by exception, where the exceptions are truly unusual delays or surges in demand. For most statistical distributions the maximum demand rate can be infinite, but analysis of actual data should suggest a usage rate that is exceeded only rarely. If it is exceeded, management considers it an exception to deal with as a special case.

Safety stock can be determined using techniques based on statistical measures of forecast error that may be due to random variations in demand or on the ratio of maximum covered demand to normal demand during lead time. We will examine each.

Bias in the estimate of demand is discussed in Chapter 6. Assuming that the forecasting method is adaptive and bias has been eliminated, this section determines the safety stock required to cover a proportion of forecast errors due to variations in demand. Thus, the order point is equal to normal usage during normal lead time plus the safety stock ($OP = DL + Q_s$).

The required safety stock is a function of the random variation in demand per forecast period, the desired customer service level, and the ratio of

Figure 11–9 Relationship Among Inventory Level, Order Point, Safety Stock, and Lead Time

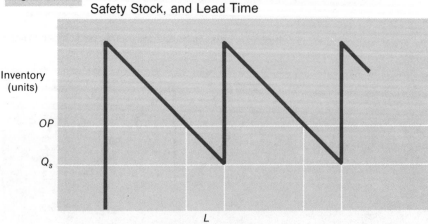

the lead time (L) to the forecast period (FP). Variation in demand may be measured by two different techniques: standard deviation (S) or mean absolute deviation (MAD). The standard deviation of demand per forecast period equals the square root of the sum of the squared differences per period, between the forecast (F_i) and the demand (D_i) divided by the number of periods (n) (or ($n - 1$) if the observations are a sample). Formulated, we have the following:

$$S = \sqrt{\frac{\sum (F_i - D_i)^2}{n}}$$

The MAD measure of variation is calculated by summing the absolute values of the recorded forecast demand deviations (forecast errors) and dividing that sum by the number of periods. Thus,

$$\text{MAD} = \frac{\sum |F_i - D_i|}{n}$$

As discussed in Chapter 6, a smoothed value of MAD may be preferred in order to place greater emphasis on recent variations as in the following equation (wherein b, the smoothing factor, is between 0 and 1):

$$\text{MAD}_i = b|F_i - D_i| + (1.0 - b)\text{MAD}_{i-1}$$

The primary advantage of using the mean absolute deviation rather than the standard deviation is that it requires fewer calculations. This factor may be important when computer capacity is limited and the number of items is extremely large. If computers are not being used, this factor is equally important as it reduces the risk of human error.

The service level is defined as the percentage of order cycles in which inventory is sufficient to cover demand, or $1 - r$, where r is the stockout probability. A safety factor may be defined for any desired customer service level; it is used with the measure of variation to compute safety stock. Assuming that forecast errors are normally distributed as shown in Figure 11–10, the safety factor to be used with the standard deviation is the Z value from the table of areas under the normal curve in Appendix A. Since 50 percent of the time (the left hand side of the curve) demand is less than the forecast and is covered without any safety stock, adding enough safety stock to cover 42 percent of the times when demand is above forecast during lead time (the right side of the curve) gives a 92 percent service level. The safety factor corresponding to a 92 percent customer service level is 1.40. The Z value of 1.40 corresponds to an area of .4192, or approximately .42 of the right half of the curve. Safety factors required to provide other levels of customer service can be determined in the same fashion.

Figure 11–10   Typical Distribution of Demand During Lead Time

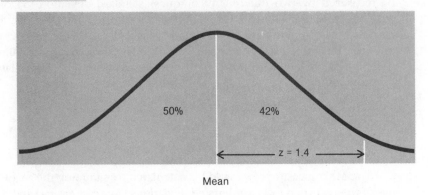

50%   42%

z = 1.4

Mean

If the distribution of deviations $(F_i - D_i)$ is normal, the value of MAD calculated for a distribution approximates .8 times the standard deviation of this distribution. Thus, MAD safety factors (SF) can be derived from a list of Z values by merely multiplying the corresponding Z value by 1.25.

Safety stock can be calculated as follows:

$$Q_s = MAD \times SF \times \sqrt{\frac{L}{FP}}$$

or

$$Q_s = S \times Z \times \sqrt{\frac{L}{FP}}$$

and the statistical order point (OP) can be calculated as the normal demand during lead time (DL) plus safety stock (Q_s).

$$OP = DL + Q_s$$

We can see how this would work with an example. A demand of 250 ball joint sets was forecast for each of ten two-week periods during the preceding twenty weeks. (For ease of calculation this problem uses data from only ten periods. In a real-world example analysis of more data is desirable.) Lead time equals the forecast period, two weeks. Table 11–5 lists the demand that then occurred in each period.

Inspection of these data reveals that the sum of the absolute deviations for the ten periods is 150 units. Dividing 150 by 10 (the number of forecasting periods covered in the data) yields a MAD of 15. If management desires a customer service level of 95 percent, the safety factor is 2.06 (see Table 11–6). The safety stock, and the order point are calculated as:

Table 11–5 Determination of Deviation in Demand
(MAD and Standard Variation)

Period	Demand (D)	Deviation (Forecast Error) (F − D)	(F − D)²
1	262	−12	144
2	276	−26	676
3	240	10	100
4	252	−2	4
5	236	14	196
6	282	−32	1024
7	240	10	100
8	237	13	169
9	222	28	784
10	253	−3	9

Forecast = 250 units/period.

$$Q_s = 15 \times 2.06 \sqrt{\frac{2}{2}} = 30.9$$

$$OP = 250 + 30.9 = 280.9$$

or 281 for practical purposes.

For purposes of comparison, let's determine what OP would result from using the standard deviation as a measure of variation. From the ten periods observed as a sample, the estimated standard deviation is 18. 87 and the value of Z for a service level of 95 percent (corresponding to 45 percent of the area under the right half of the normal curve) is 1.65. Therefore,

Table 11–6 Common Safety Factors (Multiples of MAD
and the Normalized Standard Deviation
Corresponding to Given Customer Service
Levels and Stock-Out Probabilities)

MAD SF Values	Z Values	Service Level	Stock-out Probability
1.60	1.28	.90	.10
2.06	1.65	.95	.05
2.56	2.05	.98	.02
2.91	2.33	.99	.01
3.75	3.0	.9986	.0014
5.0	4.0	.9999	.0001

$$OP = 250 + 18.87 \times 1.65 \times \sqrt{\frac{2}{2}}$$

$$= 250 + 31.14 = 281.14 \text{ or } 282$$

The results of these two methods differ only because the sample distribution is not a perfect normal distribution. The observed measure of variation is based on sample data and is always, therefore, an estimator of the true standard deviation.

MAXIMUM/NORMAL DEMAND RATIO APPROACH. For most statistical distributions the maximum demand rate can be infinite. However, analysis of actual past data should suggest some usage rate that is exceeded only rarely so that if it is exceeded management treats it as an exception.

In many situations both demand rate and lead time vary. Protection against stockout to a maximum tolerable rate of combined demand rate and lead time variations can be obtained using a relatively simple analysis. Figure 11–11 illustrates what happens when demand rises from a normal rate (D_n) to a maximum rate (D_m) just after an order has been placed and lead time increases from a normal length (L_n) to a maximum length (L_m). In that case:

$$Q_s = L_m D_m - L_n D_n, \text{ and}$$

$$OP = L_n D_n + Q_s, \text{ thus}$$

$$OP = L_m D_m$$

Figure 11–11   Safety Stock Required to Meet Maximum Demand During Maximum Lead Time

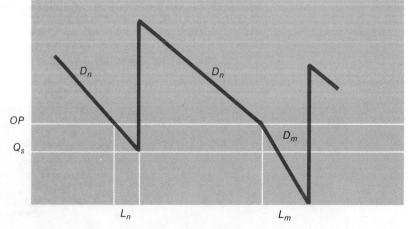

For example, if normal lead time is five days with an average demand of twenty units per the five days, while the maximum lead time has been nine days with the maximum demand over any nine-day period being fifty units, an order point of fifty units would likely provide coverage for virtually all situations.

These discussions of safety stock apply to a fixed order quantity system. Safety stock in a periodic review system must be provided not only for demand during the lead time but also for demand over the time between reviews as well. This will be examined in the section covering the periodic review system later in this chapter.

OTHER CONSIDERATIONS. A number of additional questions arise. What measure of customer service is being used in these calculations? What if the forecast period and lead time are not equal? In fact, do not the demand rate and the length of the lead time both vary simultaneously? What if the distribution of demand is not normal? In the following sections, we will examine these issues.

When using the standard deviation or MAD in calculating safety stock, customer service is defined as the percentage of replenishment periods during which the stock available will be equal to or greater than the demand. Little work has been done in defining order points using other measures of customer service.

UNEQUAL LEAD TIME AND FORECAST PERIOD. If the lead time is greater than the forecast period, then we must modify our calculations accordingly. Let lead time be four weeks (two periods) in the previous example, with all other factors remaining the same. Then,

$$OP = (250 \times 2) + (18.87 \times 1.65) \times \sqrt{\frac{4}{2}}$$

$$= 500 + 43.91 = 543.91 \text{ or } 544$$

In this case, do not overlook the fact that the calculation of normal usage during lead time must reflect the fact that lead time includes multiple forecast periods, in this case two periods. Whenever practical, the forecast period is set equal to the lead time. This is done by recording demand during lead time and developing a forecast for that length of time.

SIMULTANEOUS VARIATIONS IN LEAD TIME AND DEMAND. Safety stock is held to cover both the variations in the demand rate and variations in lead time, as illustrated in Figure 11–12. Operationally there are a number of ways of handling these concurrent variations. Perhaps the simplest is merely to record the actual joint variations and treat the result as a single distribution.

Figure 11–12   Lead Time and Demand Distributions

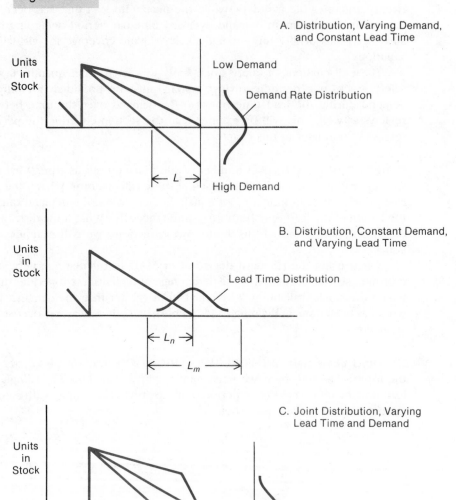

A. Distribution, Varying Demand,
   and Constant Lead Time

Units in Stock

Low Demand

Demand Rate Distribution

L

High Demand

B. Distribution, Constant Demand,
   and Varying Lead Time

Units in Stock

Lead Time Distribution

L_n

L_m

C. Joint Distribution, Varying
   Lead Time and Demand

Units in Stock

Time

For example, if Table 11–5 contains data for ten periods during which both lead time and demand vary, we have an average demand of 250 units per lead time and a standard deviation of 18.87.

Greene (1974) presents an excellent discussion of the factors that influence the demand, withdrawal, distribution lead time, replenishment, and distribution. He also points out—and we should remember—that basing order point calculations on withdrawal and replenishment distributions of historical data assumes that the future will correspond to the past. Changing economic conditions, the actions of competitors, new products, and unusual events such as strikes, wars, and threats of war may make that assumption tenuous. Additionally, Chapter 6 reminds us that demand forecasts must consider seasonal factors, trends, and special promotions. Order point calculations also should recognize these factors.

IMPLEMENTATION OF AN ORDER POINT SYSTEM. A statistical order point system requires a mechanism that alerts management when the order point has been reached. There are two basic methods of accomplishing this: (1) a perpetual inventory system and (2) a two-bin inventory system.

Perpetual Inventory System. A record is kept of each transaction, receipt or withdrawal from inventory, and the new on-hand balance recorded. Computerized systems of this type usually are programmed to output an exception message when the stock balance is at or below the order point. Manual systems require the inventory planner to compare the stock balance to the order point after each transaction.

Two-Bin System. The inventory is physically separated into the order point quantity and the remaining units. The latter are consumed first, and an order is placed upon their consumption. Material may be placed in different bins or physically separated within the same bin. The order point quantity may be placed in a special container or designated by a line on the storage bin or drum. When the container is opened or stock reaches the designated line, an order is placed. This system depends on stockroom personnel recognizing that an order point has been reached. The two-bin system is best suited for independent demand and for low value items with short lead times. Office supplies and common hardware items are likely candidates.

Periodic Review

The characteristics of many items in inventory do not make them amenable to the continuous review inherent in a statistical order point system. Some items, especially dependent demand items, are managed best by a material requirements planning system, while some others are managed more appropriately by a periodic review system.

The adoption of a periodic review system, or one of its derivatives, is suggested when one or more of the following conditions is met:

1. Independent demand is the usual situation.
2. It is difficult to record withdrawals from stock, and continuous review is expensive. Although optical scanning and modern computer systems have reduced this problem—even in some grocery stores—it still exists in many situations.

Figure 11–13   Units in Stock Versus Time (Periodic Review System)

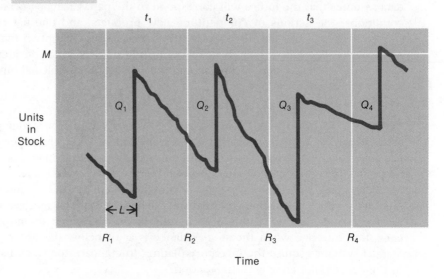

3. Groups of items are purchased from a common supplier, and the total preparation costs per item are greatly reduced by combining the items into one order. Small tools, manufacturing supplies, common commercial parts (e.g., nuts, bolts, washers), and office supplies are examples.
4. Items have a limited shelf life (perishables). Dairy items and fruits and vegetables are the classic examples. Many chemicals, pharmaceuticals, and solvents used directly or indirectly in the manufacturing process also may be managed most effectively by a periodic review system.
5. There is an economic advantage in generating full carload shipments or fully utilizing available production capacity.

THE SYSTEM. A periodic review system in its basic form involves determining the amount of an item in stock at a specified, fixed, time interval and placing an order for a quantity that, when added to the quantity on hand, will equal the sum of the estimated demand during lead time plus the estimated demand during the review period plus the safety stock (see Figure 11–13). Since the time period between reviews of the quantity on hand is fixed, this approach sometimes is called the fixed review period system.

The sum of the anticipated demand during lead time and the replenishment period plus the safety stock is called the target level inventory or the maximum level. We will use the term maximum inventory level (M). The inventory on hand never will reach this level unless demand (withdrawals from stock) ceases during the lead time.

This system is described by the following model:

$$M = D(R + L) + Q_s$$

Where

$$M = \text{Maximum inventory level}$$

$$L = \text{Lead time duration}$$

$$D = \text{Demand per unit of time}$$

$$R = \text{Review period duration}$$

$$Q_s = \text{Safety stock}$$

And with

$$I = \text{Inventory}$$

$$Q = \text{Order quantity}$$

$$O = \text{Quantity on order}$$

The order quantity is equal to the maximum level minus the sum of the quantity on hand (inventory) and the quantity on order:

$$Q = M - (I + O), \text{ or } Q = D(R + L) + Q_s - (I + O)$$

In those cases where the lead time is greater than the review period $(L > R)$, there will be some items on order unless Q equaled 0 in a previous period.

Figure 11–13 illustrates the relationship of the inventory versus time (t) for a periodic review system. It clearly reveals that $t_1 = t_2 = t_3$ and that Q_1, Q_2, Q_3, and Q_4 are not necessarily equal. Thus, the review period is fixed, and the order quantity may vary; whereas in the traditional fixed order quantity order point system, the order quantity is fixed and the period between orders may vary. Let's examine a periodic review example.

A company uses a zinc-based primer that is obtained along with other paints and solvents from a local supplier. Normal usage is three gallons per day; the review period is every two weeks (ten working days); lead time is three days; safety stock is four gallons. Inventory is reviewed at the appropriate time, and there are fifteen gallons in stock. Thus, the maximum inventory level and the order quantity can be calculated as follows:

$$M = D(L + R) + Q_s$$

$$= 3(3 + 10) + 4$$

$$= 43$$

$$Q = M - I$$

$$= 43 - 15$$

$$= 28$$

An order should be placed for 28 gallons every 10 working days.

What if the inventory on hand had been six gallons instead of fifteen? This is insufficient to cover normal usage during the three-day lead time. In all likelihood, the company will be able to obtain some on short notice by special order. However, if this is not possible, the question of the permissibility of backorders must be addressed. In this example, a stockout in primer paint can result in a schedule delay and in some items being painted late (after the paint arrives). The order quantity then will be calculated in the normal fashion as follows:

$$Q = M - I$$

$$= 43 - 6$$

$$= 37 \text{ gallons}$$

Let's look at a slightly different situation. When a stockout occurs, the company uses a substitute primer. In this case the minimum inventory on hand will be nine gallons since the requirements during the lead time are covered by a substitute; Q, then, $= 43 - 9$ or 34 gallons.

A similar situation frequently exists when the periodic reordering system is used in managing finished goods. If the customer usually goes to a second source when an item is not available, the minimum value of I in the calculation is the demand during lead time, D_L. Hardware stores, grocery stores, drug stores, and manufacturing supply houses frequently operate under such conditions.

SAFETY STOCK CONSIDERATIONS. The purpose of safety stock is to cover high side variations in demand from the placement of an order to the arrival of a subsequent order. In an order point system, unusually heavy demand will trigger another order as soon as the order point is reached. This may occur immediately after the receipt of the first order. In a strictly periodic system (one without an order point mechanism) another order will not be placed until the review period has passed. Therefore, in an order point system, safety stock must cover variations in demand during lead time only. However, in a strictly periodic system the safety stock must cover variations in demand during the combined review and lead time period. As illustrated in Figure 11–14, the quantity ordered at R_1 must recognize possible variations in demand from R_1 to D_2 (date of delivery of order No. 2). Thus, safety stock is

Figure 11-14   Safety Stock (Periodic Review System)

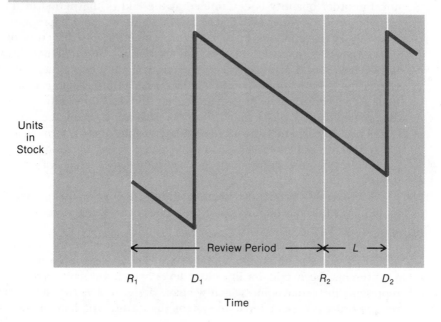

Order size determined at R_1 and R_2.
Deliveries occur at D_1 and D_2.

calculated by multiplying the safety factor times the standard deviation of demand during lead time plus the review period. The value of the safety factor depends, of course, on the customer service level desired. For example, the safety factor for a customer service level of 95 percent is 1.65 (see Table 11–6), when using the standard deviation as the measure of variation. Service level is defined here as the percentage of periods during which all customer orders are filled (a stockout does not occur). Without any safety stock, the service level will be 50 percent since demand is less than or equal to the average demand 50 percent of the time.

Returning to our earlier example of the zinc-based primer, let the standard deviation of demand during the combined lead time and review period be 2.43 units and the desired service level be 95 percent. Then, safety stock will be equal to 2.43 times 1.645—that is, 3.997 or 4 units.

Hybrid Systems

There are many different ways of combining the features of the periodic ordering system and the order point system. The two most common will be described.

The first (the order point–periodic review combination system) combines the order point feature with the periodic review. In brief, if the inventory level drops below a specified level prior to the review date, an order is placed; if not, the order quantity is determined at the end of the period in the basic periodic review manner (see Figure 11–15). This system is appropriate when relatively large variations in demand are common and the costs of safety stocks required to cover these variations during the combined lead time and review period are excessive (greater than the costs of a combination system). A combination periodic review–order point system requires safety stock to cover variations in demand during the lead time only. To function, this system must have a mechanism for indicating when the order point is reached. If perpetual records are not available, then a form of the two-bin system, described earlier, must be installed. A combination order point–periodic review system frequently is used to manage families of independent items.

If an item is frequently reaching the reorder point before the review period has expired, examination of the values of D, demand per unit of time, and M, the maximum inventory level, is in order.

The second hybrid inventory management system is the optional (s,S) replenishment system. This method is also known as the s,S model where S represents the maximum inventory level, which we have called M, and s represents the order point, which we have designated as OP. In this periodic review–order point combination system, the quantity on hand is reviewed at regular intervals and an order is placed only if the quantity on hand is below a specific level (see Figure 11–16). This method enables an organization

Figure 11–15   Units in Stock Versus Time (Periodic Review–Order Point Combination)

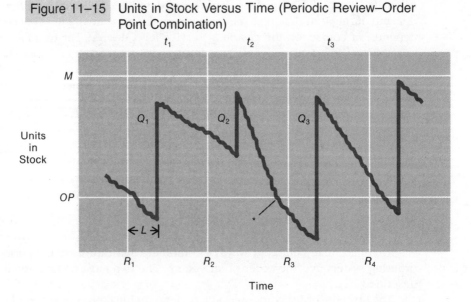

*Order is placed before scheduled review as stock drops below order point.

Figure 11–16   Units in Stock Versus Time (Optional
Replenishment System)

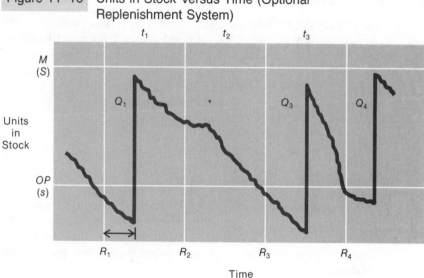

*Order is not placed. Stock level is above the order point.

to avoid placing orders for relatively small quantities, and it is useful when periods of dormant demand are possible, shelf life is important, and aging is undesirable. Although staleness, dust, rust, oxidation, and other attributes of age may not prevent an item from being sold if it is needed, they do not enhance customer satisfaction. The optional replenishment system diminishes the probability of these deficiencies, but it does increase the probability of a stockout.

Establishing the order point in this system is extremely complex if one desires to have the mathematical assurance that the order point guarantees that the sum of holding costs, ordering costs, and expected stockout costs are being minimized. This assurance is always tempered by a few assumptions including one concerning the demand distribution.

The main point is that this system is used successfully by numerous organizations. We have observed on many occasions a storeroom or supply clerk who reviews commercial items on a periodic basis (e.g., on the fifth and twentieth of every month) and orders only if an item has reached the order point. In some such cases, the order point may be relatively high since the carrying costs are relatively low compared with the cost of ordering, which includes the costs of writing the order, receiving, moving to stores, and processing the payment. In other cases, such as fresh food markets, bookstores, restaurants, and pharmacies, the order point may be set relatively low since the cost of a stockout is balanced against the cost of obsolete, unusable, inventory.

Visual Review Systems

Both periodic review and order point systems can be implemented using a physical review of the stock on hand rather than a perpetual inventory record system. For example, in many retail outlets the customer is the stock picker and real-time records of the quantity on hand do not exist. Thus, a periodic physical count of the stock is used to determine the order quantity.

The two-bin system of inventory storage is a common method of operating a visual review order point system. It is appropriate for the management of independent demand, low-value items with short lead times, such as office supplies and common hardware items.

Time-Phased Order Point System

The time-phased order point system applies the logic of material requirements planning to independent demand items. The information prerequisites for this system include a forecast of requirements, the lead time of the item, and the order quantity. The procedures to compute a time-phased order point are as follows:

1. Requirements, scheduled receipts, and the on-hand quantity are projected by week for the short-range planning period, usually two to six months.
2. The week is determined in which the on-hand quantity, excluding safety stock, falls below zero. This is the outage period.
3. An order release is planned for the outage period minus the lead time. For example, if the lead time is two weeks and the projected outage occurs in Week 8, an order release should be planned for Week 6.

Let us see how this works with an example. The following is known about a service part that is not used in currently produced assemblies:

Lead time is 3 weeks.
Weekly demand forecast is 20 units.
Safety stock is 30 units.
Order quantity is 100 units.
An order of 100 units is scheduled for receipt in Week 2.
On hand quantity is 40 units.

The projected gross requirements, scheduled receipts, and on-hand quantity by week are given in Table 11–7.

The on-hand quantity will fall below the safety stock level of 30 in Week 6. An order release must be planned for Week 3 to have a scheduled receipt in Week 6. The release of an order in Week 3 and its scheduled receipt in Week 6 is incorporated in the planning document in Table 11–8. We also have determined that an order receipt will be required in Week 11 and have included its planned release and scheduled receipt.

Table 11–7 Material Requirements Forecast

Production Data	Week									
	1	2	3	4	5	6	7	8	9	10
Gross requirements	20	20	20	20	20	20	20	20	20	20
Scheduled receipts		100								
On hand	20	100	80	60	40	20	0	(20)	(40)	(60)
(40 on hand prior to week 1)										
Planned order releases										

<------------------------>
Lead Time Offset

The time-phased order point system reveals when orders for an item likely will be placed during the entire planning horizon. Thus, it provides the information necessary for projecting capacity requirements and for planning the gross inventory requirements of parts and materials used in the fabrication of the item. Other basic systems do not have this capability.

Other Considerations

Even the most complex inventory management models only approximate reality; and the cost, demand, and lead time values used in calculating lot sizes and order release timing are estimates. The inventory planner should not use the results of lot size and order release calculations without considering practical factors such as rounding off, material usage, tool life, package or container size, and yield.

Table 11–8 Material Requirements with Time-Phased Order Points

Production Data	Week										
	1	2	3	4	5	6	7	8	9	10	11
Gross requirements	20	20	20	20	20	20	20	20	20	20	20
Scheduled receipts		100									
On hand	20	100	80	60	40	120	100	80	60	40	120
(40 on hand prior to weeks)											
Planned order releases			100					100			
Planned order receipts						100					100

<-------------------->   <-------------------->
Lead Time Offset   Lead Time Offset

ROUNDING OFF. Lot size and safety stock calculations frequently result in fractional values that are obviously infeasible in the case of discrete parts. For example, one cannot sell 97.2 transmissions. Rounding such a number to 98.0 or up to 100 makes sense in most cases. Total carrying and setup costs would change little, and numbers ending in one or more zeros facilitate human memory and recognition.

MATERIAL USAGE. Frequently it makes sense to increase a lot size to use all of the material available in coil, rod, sheet, or container rather than returning a small leftover amount to stores. The added material and processing costs may be less than the costs of handling and storing small amounts.

TOOL LIFE. The required periodic replacement or maintenance of a tool or process such as a dye, cutting blade, filter, or treatment solution may consume as much production capacity (machine downtime) as the machine setup. Increasing production lot sizes so that the end of the production run and the maintenance requirement occur concurrently will decrease downtime. Since such tools, solutions, and filters must be replaced or cleaned when a different item is run, coordinating required maintenance and setup activities may be equivalent to eliminating a setup.

   Care should be taken not to reduce the lot sizes of dependent demand items required for an assembly. The savings in machine downtime and maintenance costs will be small compared to the costs that result from the missing parts.

PACKAGE OR CONTAINER SIZE. Items often are purchased or stored in standard size containers or packages. Increasing lot sizes to fill containers may be justified by reduced transportation, storage, and handling costs per unit.

YIELD. The scrap or yield rate of a process should be considered when calculating lot sizes. In a material requirements system using lot-for-lot order quantities, scrap and yield factors require that the actual order quantity be greater than the net requirements. This quantity can be calculated in the following manner for lot sizes in a given range.

$$Q = \frac{\text{net requirements } (NR)}{1.0 - \text{maximum likely scrap percentage } (MLS)}$$

Or

$$Q = \frac{\text{net requirements}}{\text{yield rate } (y)}$$

Where

$$y = 1 - MLS$$

For example, if the net requirements were 500 and the maximum likely scrap percentage were 10 percent, then

$$Q = \frac{500}{1 - .10}$$

$$= 556$$

MINIMUMS AND MAXIMUMS. Floors and ceilings may be established by policy to eliminate overloading of production and order handling capacity by a large number of small orders and to prevent production of quantities greater than required in a reasonable planning horizon. These limits may be stated in absolute terms, such as no fewer than ten units and no more than 100 units, or in demand-related terms, such as no less than two weeks supply and no more than six months supply. Rarely does it make sense to produce more than a year's supply.

IMPLEMENTATION OF MULTIPLE FACTORS. It is common for more than one practical consideration to affect the order quantity decision. When ordering dependent demand items, the top priority is to order at least the net requirements. Maximum and minimum limits usually rank next, followed by yield calculations, tool life, and material usage. However, the planner should evaluate each situation on its own merits, as the costs related to the various factors can differ widely from case to case.

CONCLUSIONS

In summary, individual item management concerns when to order (the order point) and how many to order (the lot size). The dependent demand–independent demand dichotomy is the major determinant of the appropriateness of the different models for a given item. The lot-sizing decision rules are based on models that minimize the sum of carrying and preparation costs. Order point decision rules are predicated on a customer service level objective. A timely and accurate information processing system is required to implement these decision rules. Figure 11–17 is a schematic representation of data flow in a typical system.

Figure 11–17 Schematic Inventory Management Information System

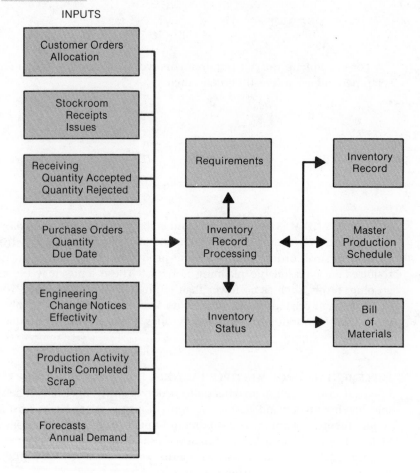

QUESTIONS

1. What is the first step of individual item management?

2. In general, how are inventory data organized?

3. Demonstrate two general patterns of demand. Give an example where each applies.

4. Differentiate independent and dependent demand. Give an example of each.

5. What are two objectives of an inventory management system? Why must these objectives be clearly defined?

6. Even if exact demand, lead time, and cost information is not available, inventory management approaches often assume certainty of information. Give three arguments why this is reasonable.

7. Why is it that total inventory costs change by small amounts in the vicinity of the EOQ?

8. Suppose the annual demand rate is relatively small compared to the annual production rate. Why would the noninstantaneous receipt model give roughly the same solution as the EOQ model in these circumstances?

9. What two basic issues must be determined in deciding ordering policies?

10. What are three basic methods of deciding when to order independent inventory items?

11. What conditions must exist to ensure the effectiveness of the statistical order point system?

12. Give several examples of situations that explain why demand rates and lead times cannot be assumed to be constant.

13. What justification is there for maintaining safety stocks of a good when those stocks cost money to carry?

14. Define service level. How is service level related to stockout probability?

15. How should lead time calculations be varied if lead time is greater than the forecast period? In practice, how can this be resolved?

16. How should simultaneous variations of lead time and demand be managed?

17. The two-bin system can function very effectively with only one bin. Describe how an order point and a periodic review could work with a single bin.

18. What advantages and disadvantages do hybrid systems have over basic inventory systems?

19. Suggest several practical considerations that are used to adjust inventory computations.

20. Given the following items, determine the type of demand that is predominant for the product and suggest an appropriate inventory management procedure.

Boxes of copier paper
Grill ornaments for new automobiles
Tons of steel for stock used to make automobile replacement fenders
Feet of wire to repair small electric motors
Plastic tubing for disposable medical items

PROBLEMS

1. A building materials supplier has an annual demand for 4,000,000 linear feet of wood siding, which costs $1.61 per linear foot. Assume the ordering cost is $120.00 and the annual carrying cost is 24 percent.

    a. Compute the EOQ.
    b. How many orders are placed each year?
    c. What is the total annual cost of maintaining inventory?
    d. Evaluate the effect on total cost of a 10 percent increase and decrease in lot size.

2. A finished good has an annual demand of 15,250 units. Unit cost is $7, annual holding cost is estimated to be 35 percent, and the ordering cost is $50 per order.

    a. What is the EOQ?
    b. How often should an order be placed?
    c. What is the total annual inventory cost?

3. The Far East Communications Co. sells 19,000 receivers each year. They pay a supplier $125 for each receiver, carrying costs are 30 percent, and ordering costs are $40 per order. What is the economic purchase lot size? What is the total annual cost for the system?

4. A vacuum cleaner distributor wants to show that the EOQ computed in physical units is the same as in monetary units. Answer the questions that follow given this data: (1) item cost is $250; (2) cost of an order $20; (3) annual demand is 1,500 units; (4) carrying costs are estimated to be 32 percent; (5) period requirements in dollars is equal to $375,000.

    a. What is the EOQ in physical units?
    b. What is the minimum cost lot size?
    c. How many orders are made annually?
    d. What is the annual inventory cost?

5. A manufacturer of lanterns forecasts a steady demand of 12,000 units next year for its most popular model. The company can produce 100 units per day, and there are 250 working days available. It costs $900 to set up the production line, and the unit production cost is estimated at $17. The holding cost per unit per year is $5.

    a. What is the economic production quantity?
    b. How many runs should be made during the year?

6. A pencil company experiences a rather stable annual demand of 240,000 boxes of 12 #2 pencils. They are capable of producing 2 million boxes of 12 #2 pencils in a 250-day year. Set-up costs are $500, and the annual carrying cost per box is $0.25.

    a. What is the economic lot size?
    b. How many lots should be run annually?
    c. What is the total cost?

7. Refer to Problem 3. If the Far East Communications Co. were to manufacture the receivers with a production capacity of 38,000 receivers each year, a cost of $100 for each receiver, a production set-up cost of $2,000, and 260 days per year available for production, with all other information the same:

    a. What is the best production lot size?
    b. What is the total cost?

8. Retail merchants can purchase glass picture frames for $5 each if the quantity ordered is less than 100 frames, $4 each if the order is between 100 and 300 frames, and $3 each in quantities over 300 frames. If annual demand is 2,000 frames, the cost of ordering is $25, and the carrying cost is 30 percent, what is the best ordering policy?

9. A large pharmacy chain has annual demand for adhesive tape of 500,000 units. The manufacturer offers price discounts at the following quantity points:

0 to 50,000	$1.25
50,001 to 100,000	1.20
100,001 to 250,000	1.15
250,001 to 500,000	1.10
500,001 to 1,000,000	1.05

If ordering costs are $30 and carrying costs are 25 percent determine which ordering plan is best.

10. A construction supply company had forecast a monthly demand for electric drills of 150 units for the past 10 months. To receive the maximum discount, only one order is placed each month for the next month's demand; therefore, lead time is equal to the forecast period—one month. Determine the amount of safety stock and order point for this data based on a desired service level of 90 percent.

Period	Demand
1	137
2	142
3	159
4	166
5	174
6	157
7	155
8	144
9	149
10	139

11. A spirits distributor had forecast demand for the local brewery's brand as 4,000 cases per month for the months of September through May. Determine the safety stock quantity and order point using the MAD safety factors with a desired service level of .99. Data for actual demand follows:

Period	Demand
September	4,250
October	4,175
November	3,950
December	4,125
January	4,050
February	3,775
March	3,900
April	3,950
May	4,150
June	4,300

12. An independent pharmacy in northern Minnesota is scheduled for delivery from a St. Paul drug wholesaler every two weeks. During the morning of the day the order is placed, the owner systematically assesses the inventory on hand for the over-the-counter drug items. Normal daily demand for a popular cough medicine is six bottles; the store is open six days per week; safety stock is twelve bottles; lead time between order delivery and order receipt is three days; and the current on-hand inventory is twenty bottles. Calculate the maximum inventory level and order quantity.

13. The local hardware store orders from a cooperative wholesaler once a week. Lead time between the day of the order and receipt of shipment is 3 days. Daily demand for eight-foot fluorescent bulbs is 24 bulbs; safety stock is 36 bulbs; the store is open 6 days per week; on the day of the order there are 56 bulbs on hand. Because the bulbs are shipped in

protective boxes, orders are calculated to the next dozen quantity (e.g., if 65 bulbs are needed, 72 bulbs are ordered). Determine the maximum inventory level and the order quantity in this situation.

14. Weekly requirements for an independent demand replacement automobile starter motor are below:

Requirements	Week									
	1	2	3	4	5	6	7	8	9	10
Gross requirements	40	40	40	40	40	40	40	40	40	40
Scheduled receipts	75									
On hand 15	50	10	(30)	(70)	(110)	(150)	(190)	(230)	(270)	(310)
POR										

Use a time-phased order point to determine when planned order receipts (PORs) should occur, given a lot size of 75.

REFERENCES

Arrow, K. J., S. Karlin, and H. Scarf. *Studies in the Mathematical Theory of Inventory and Production.* Stanford, Calif.: Stanford University Press, 1958.

Buchan, Joseph, and Ernest Koenigsberg. *Scientific Inventory Management.* Englewood Cliffs, N.J.: Prentice-Hall, 1963.

Fogarty, Donald W., and Thomas R. Hoffmann. *Production and Inventory Management.* Cincinnati: South-Western Publishing Co., 1983, pp. 241–266.

Greene, James H. *Production and Inventory Control.* Homewood, Ill.: Richard D. Irwin, Inc., 1974, pp. 300–301.

Orlicky, Joseph. *Material Requirements Planning.* New York: McGraw-Hill Book Company, 1974, pp. 22–25.

CHAPTER 12
MATERIAL REQUIREMENTS PLANNING

OBJECTIVES

After completing this chapter, you should be able to

- Describe MRP I, Closed Loop MRP, MRP II, and their relationships

- Describe the advantages of an MRP system

- Interrelate material requirements planning with scheduling and inventory management processes

- Accomplish the gross to netting computations of a bill of materials and appreciate the inventory savings that result from gross-to-net adjustments of requirements

- Offset a bill of materials for purchasing or manufacturing lead times

- Define material requirements using a material requirements planning chart and gross-to-netting and lead time offset techniques

- Establish discrete production lot sizes using various methods and describe various lot-sizing methods

- Appreciate the effects of firm planned orders and pegging methods on material requirements planning

- Explain the necessity for accurate data in managing a material requirements planning information system

OUTLINE

INTRODUCTION

The acronym for material requirements planning, MRP, is used in three different but related contexts. They are

1. MRP I—material requirements planning
2. Closed loop MRP
3. MRP II—manufacturing resource planning

Each of these contexts marks a stage in the development of MRP concepts. MRP I calculates the exact quantity, need date, and order release date for each of the subassemblies, components, and materials required to manufacture the products listed on the master production schedule (MPS). Prior to MRP I, the vast majority of manufacturing organizations controlled subassemblies and components using traditional order point methods. This chapter describes MRP I in detail and its advantages over the traditional order point approach for managing dependent demand items.

Closed loop MRP is a natural step in the development of a more formal and explicit manufacturing control system. On the input end it links the master production schedule to the production planning process. It uses the output of MRP I, the material requirements plan, to develop a capacity requirements plan and compares the planned capacity utilization resulting from the MPS and the MRP to the available capacity to determine if the plan is attainable. Once an attainable plan is developed, shop floor control and purchasing control close the planning and control system—that is, actual orders are released, and production and supplier performances are measured and compared to the plan. This feedback enables management to determine if corrective action is required; and if it is, it helps to determine the most appropriate action.

Manufacturing resource planning (MRP II), which is sometimes called business resource planning (BRP), is an explicit and formal manufacturing information system that integrates marketing, finance, and operations. It converts resource requirements (e.g., facilities, equipment, personnel, and material) into financial requirements and converts production outputs into monetary terms. These conversions aid in evaluating the organization's ability to execute the plan financially and in determining the financial merit of the plan in terms of such measures as profit, return on investment (ROI), and return on assets (ROA). Figure 12–1 is an overview of MRP I, closed loop MRP, and MRP II. MRP I is part of closed loop MRP, which is part of MRP II.

MRP I provides the logical tie between the MPS and the detailed inventories and/or purchase or shop orders needed to satisfy the MPS. It is designed to do this on an ongoing basis and to create either new or revised shop or purchase orders as requirements change. The objectives of MRP are (1) to determine what to order, how much to order, when to order, and when to schedule delivery and (2) to keep priorities current for inventory planning, capacity requirements planning (CRP), and shop floor control.

Figure 12–1 Overview of MRP II, Including Closed Loop MRP and MRP I

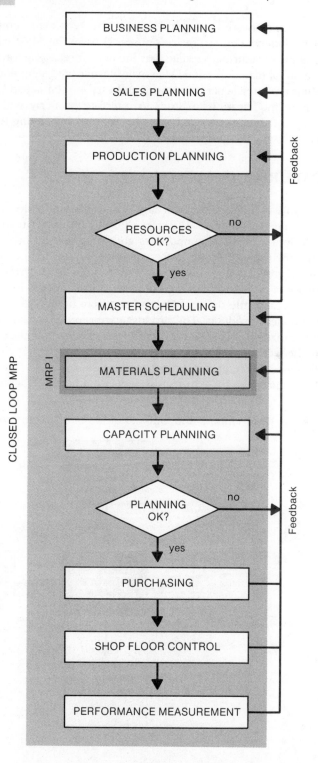

MRP software has been developed by most major computer vendors and many independent software houses. Usually the MRP program is part of a total manufacturing package that includes forecasting, order entry, inventory and bill of materials (BOM) file maintenance, and shop floor control. The programs are often separately priced and vary in their capabilities. They generally require modification in order to interface properly with other information systems in a company and may also require fine tuning to operate efficiently with a firm's unique product characteristics.

DATA REQUIREMENTS

MRP is accomplished through a time-phased explosion of the production schedule. To do this, MRP uses demand information from the MPS with a description of what components go into a finished product (the BOM), the order or production times for components, and the current inventory status (see Figure 12–2). This information is used to determine the quantity and timing of orders to be placed or issued. This process is called product explosion because the demand for one end item breaks up into demand for many component products. The product explosion process also illustrates vertical and horizontal dependent demand. Vertical dependent demand is exemplified by the fact that the requirement for wiring assemblies for lamps depends on the schedule (requirement) for socket assemblies (see Figure 12–3). Similarly, the requirement for terminals is dependent on the schedule for wiring assem-

Figure 12–2 Inputs and Outputs of Material Requirements Planning

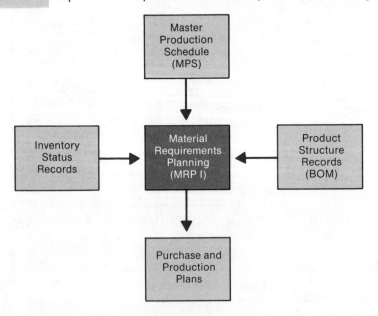

Figure 12–3   Simplified Product Structure for a Lamp

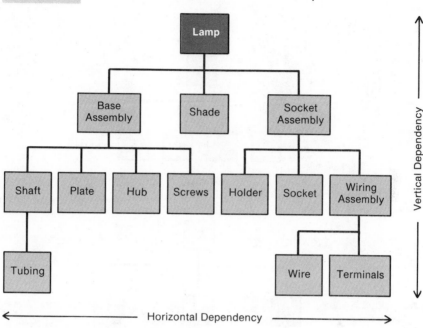

blies because terminals are a component of wiring assemblies. This type of dependency may involve one or more subcomponents and occurs between different levels of the BOM. The holder, socket, and wiring assembly are horizontally dependent—that is, they are at the same level in the BOM and all are required in the socket assembly. Having two of the three is of little value; all three are required. In contrast, the demand for the lamp itself is independent as is the demand for the wiring assembly as a service (repair) part. Thus, the MPS might contain forecast demand for wiring assembly service parts in addition to requirements to build new lamps.

MRP MECHANICS

Individual products may have only a few components, or they may have thousands. Each component itself may be composed of a single item or many sets of items. The relationships can be shown in list or graphic forms. Figure 12–4 illustrates product structure diagrams and product structure levels. The end product or end item is set at Level 0, and its immediate components and/or subassemblies are at Level 1. Each level is similarly divided into successively lower (but by convention, numerically higher) levels down to fundamental components—that is, purchased parts and/or raw materials. The multilevel structure shown has both horizontal and vertical demand dependency relationships.

Figure 12–4   Simple and Multilevel Product Strategies

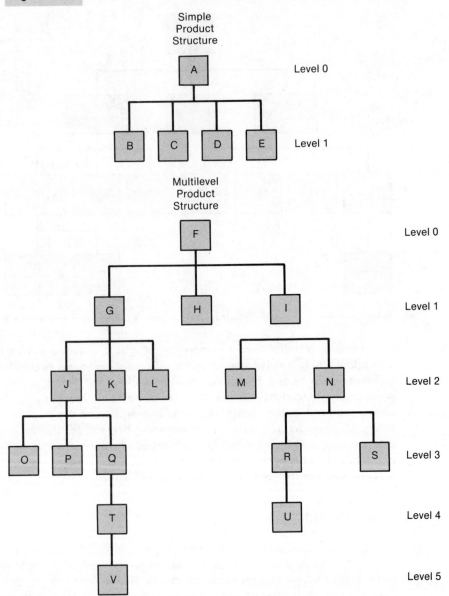

Gross to Net (Netting)

In order to understand the basic problem that MRP I addresses and how its logic works, consider again Figure 12–3. To simplify the example, consider only the left branch of this diagram—lamp, base assembly, shaft, and tubing.

Assume we receive an order for 25 lamps. We have the following items on hand:

Lamps	3
Base assemblies	7
Shafts	4
Tubing	16 feet

(In this instance each shaft requires two feet of tubing.) How many of each of these items should we order? A simple response would be 22 lamps (25 − 3), 18 base assemblies (25 − 7), 21 shafts (25 − 4), and 34 feet of tubing (25 × 2 − 16). This is incorrect, because each unit in a level contains all of the components that are below it. Each lamp already contains one base assembly; each base assembly already contains one shaft; and each shaft already contains two feet of tubing. Thus, the gross requirement for 25 lamps must be analyzed sequentially at each level to get the net requirement. The gross-to-net logic is as follows:

Lamp
Gross requirement	25
Quantity on hand	3
Net requirement	22

Base Assemblies
Gross requirement	22
Quantity on hand	7
Net requirement	15

Shaft
Gross requirement	15
Quantity on hand	4
Net requirement	11

Tubing
Gross requirement (feet)	22
Quantity on hand	16
Net requirement	6

Note that in each case, the gross requirement of a subassembly is equal to the net requirement of the next higher item. These net requirements are considerably less than the previous, simplistically computed ones and represent the true needs to meet the demand for 25 lamps. This process, referred to as netting or gross-to-net calculation, must now be combined with a knowledge of how long it takes to either manufacture or purchase the components in order to schedule a start date for each assembly. These time intervals are referred to as the lead times, and in this case are as follows:

Lamps	2 weeks
Base assemblies	1 week
Shafts	2 weeks
Tubing	3 weeks

Figure 12–5   Lead Time Offsets

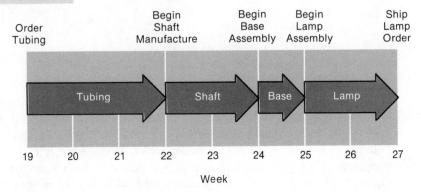

These lead times are used to compute lead time offsets for each component. If the order is to be shipped in Week 27, then the offsets are as shown in the schematic representation in Figure 12–5. Notice how the beginning date for one level is the completion or arrival date for the next. Thus, an order for 6 feet of tubing must be placed in Week 19 in order for the lamps to be shipped in Week 27.

The essence of the MRP logic can be expressed in three relationships: (1) horizontal and vertical dependencies (2) gross to net and (3) lead time offset. Specifically, horizontal and vertical dependencies establish gross number relationships; gross-to-net relationships consider current inventories; and the lead time offset backs off production or order lead time. The logic for a simple product like this is quite straightforward. However, when dealing with thousands of items and varying product structures, the situation in practice is much more complicated.

The MRP Chart

A table or chart similar to Table 12–1 is often used to illustrate the management of a dependent demand item. The gross requirements come

Table 12–1   MRP Chart

Production Data	Period					
	1	*2*	*3*	*4*	*5*	*6*
Gross requirements	10	15	15	10	15	10
Scheduled receipts			25			
Projected ending inventory	20	5	15	5	15	5
Net requirements					10	
Planned order releases		25				
Planned order receipts					25	

Lead time: 3; lot size: 25; BOM level: 0; quantity on hand: 30

from the MPS; the beginning inventory in Period 1 comes from the inventory records; and the projected ending inventory in each period is calculated.

Note that scheduled receipts, by definition, come from orders already released either to manufacturing (production, manufacturing or shop orders) or to suppliers (purchase orders). When an order is released it becomes an open order and has scheduled receipts. Lower-level requirements due to scheduled receipts of production orders (released earlier) were added earlier to the gross requirements of lower-level items. Purchase orders have no lower-level requirements for the purchaser. However, production order releases result in planned order receipts and cause requirements at lower levels. Planned order receipts differ from scheduled receipts in that they have not been released. Since net requirements exist in Period 5 and the lead time is three periods, a planned order release is required in Period 2. This is a plan, however, and if gross requirements in Period 3 should fall to five, then the plan would change to that shown in Table 12–2.

It is important to note that planned order releases are easier to change than released order (open orders). Changes or cancellation of open purchase orders can result in cancellation charges. Open production orders frequently are in process with lower-level purchase and production orders also having been issued; and change is disruptive and costly. Changes in released orders also reduce manufacturing's confidence in the systems and their adherence to it.

TIME PERIODS (BUCKETS).   Time periods also are called time buckets in MRP jargon. The time buckets in the previous example are weeks. The immediate (current) period in the planning horizon, Period 1 in the example, is the action period (the action time bucket); planned order releases usually are not released until this period. This practice provides the planner with maximum flexibility and diminishes disruptions in the plant and at suppliers' facilities.

Bucketless MRP systems use a time period of one day. (Thus, they are not truly bucketless.) Scheduled receipts, planned order releases, and planned

Table 12–2   MRP Chart with Gross Requirements Adjustment

Production Data	Period					
	1	2	3	4	5	6
Gross requirements	10	15	5	10	15	10
Scheduled receipts			25			
Projected ending inventory	20	5	25	15	0	15
Net requirements						10
Planned order releases			25			
Planned order receipts						25

Lead time: 3; lot size: 25; BOM level: 0; quantity on hand: 30

order receipts are specified by a specific date. The smaller the time bucket, the more time buckets there are in the planning horizon, and the greater precision possible in planning and controlling lead times. The costs of smaller time buckets include larger computer storage requirements and increased computer processing and outputs. Many companies have successfully implemented bucketless systems.

If lead time precision permits it, a bucketless system can specify requirements, releases, and receipts in terms of a specific shift, four-hour period, or an hour. As the execution of manufacturing planning and control continues to improve, this will be achieved in some firms. It is consistent with the objectives of just-in-time and zero inventory (see Chapter 20).

TIME CONVENTIONS. Interpreting production and inventory management records requires an understanding of the timing conventions used. Inventory quantities, for example, frequently are listed explicitly as either beginning inventory or ending inventory. When a production quantity is stated for a given period, the understanding usually is that the quantity will be produced by the end of the period. MRP charts also require the use of such conventions for consistent use. The charts in this chapter use the following conventions:

Gross requirements	Needed by end of period
On hand	Ending inventory
Net requirements	Needed by end of period
Scheduled receipts	Needed by end of period
Planned order receipts	Needed by end of period
Planned order releases	Needed by end of period

Thus, if the lamp has net requirements in Week 27 and lead time is two weeks, a planned order release for lamps must exist in Week 25. Note that if the order is released at the beginning of Week 25, manufacturing has a one-week safety lead time.

LOW-LEVEL CODING. Some items are required at more than one level in the BOM. Item B in Figure 12–6 is an example. Net requirements for such an item are obtained by summing gross requirements for that item through the lowest level at which the code is found in the BOM structure. BOM software assigns a level code to each item corresponding to the lowest level at which it is required. This is known as low-level coding.

In a very complex bill of materials, the low-level code would limit the search for all requirements for a common part. The computer would search down to the coded low level, then it would compute the total gross requirements and net those requirements against available inventory.

Lot Sizing

In the preceding example we assumed a lot size of 25, but one of the key questions in implementing MRP is what is the proper lot size. Consider

Figure 12–6   Low-Level Coding

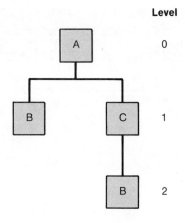

the situation shown in Table 12–3. It might be proper given capacity and other factors. The seeming lack of correlation between quantities needed and quantities ordered raises questions concerning the appropriateness of this schedule. There are several methods of selecting lot size that may improve this situation.

If this particular lot-sizing algorithm were costed over the nine-period planning horizon, it would require five setups and the holding of inventory as indicated in the on-hand row. If setup costs were \$5.75 each and inventory holding costs were \$.05 per period, total setup costs would be 5 x \$5.75 or \$28.75; total holding costs would be 13 + 23 + 14 + 22 + 14 + 4 + 13 + 6 + 20 or 129 part periods at \$.05, or \$6.45. (One part period is equivalent to one item held in inventory for one period.) The total costs over the nine-period horizon would be \$28.75 + \$6.45, or \$35.20.

Table 12–3   Revised MRP Chart with Lead Time Adjustment

Production Data	Period								
	1	2	3	4	5	6	7	8	9
Gross requirements	12	15	9	17	8	10	16	7	11
Scheduled receipts	25	25							
On hand (ending inventory prior to Period 1 was 0)	13	23	14	22	14	4	13	6	20
Planned order releases		25			25		25		
Planned order receipts				25			25		25

Lead time: 2; lot size: 25

Table 12–4   MRP Chart with L4L Lot Size

Production Data	Period								
	1	2	3	4	5	6	7	8	9
Gross requirements	12	15	9	17	8	10	16	7	11
Scheduled receipts	12	15							
On hand (ending inventory prior to Period 1 was 0)	0	0	0	0	0	0	0	0	0
Planned order releases	9	17	8	10	16	7	11		
Planned order receipts			9	17	8	10	16	7	11

LOT FOR LOT (L4L).   Assuming that orders can be for any quantity, then ordering the exact quantity that is actually needed (referred to as the lot-for-lot, or L4L, ordering rule) results in no on-hand inventory. In practice, this doesn't always occur for several reasons: orders arrive late or early, orders are canceled, quantities made or delivered are under or over those ordered, or the economics or technology dictate constant lot sizes or multiples thereof.

If we use our previous example and plan lot-for-lot order releases, the situation would be described by Table 12–4.

To cost the lot-for-lot method, there are nine setups at $5.75 each, and no inventory is held. The total cost by this method is $51.75. In this particular example, the total costs are notably higher for the lot-for-lot method; however, there are situations in which a production planner would have no choice but to select the lot-for-lot method—for example, perishable food items or items for which the market fluctuated widely.

LEAST UNIT COST (LUC).   A second method of defining the lot size is the least unit cost. This method produces the demands of the present period, and then, on a trial basis, evaluates future periods. The algorithm chooses the least unit cost (setup cost + inventory carrying cost per period) over successive periods by adding the total carrying costs to the setup costs and finding the period for which the per unit cost is the smallest. The LUC lot sizing of our example data is shown in Table 12–5 and the computations are as shown in Table 12–6. The data in this table include the cost of the scheduled receipts quantity, which was based on this method.

For Period 1, the number ordered is 12, the setup cost is $5.75, and carrying costs are 0; thus, the total cost of $5.75 is divided by the number of units to get the cost per unit of $.479. The per-unit cost for Periods 1 and 2 is then evaluated as follows: Demands are 27 (i.e., 12 + 15) and setup costs are $5.75. Carrying costs are $.05 for each of the 15 items demanded in Period 2, or $.75. Thus, the total cost is $6.50, and the cost per unit is $.240. Further similar computations would indicate that the cost per unit decreases when the demands through Period 4 are ordered in one lot; but these per-

Table 12–5   MRP Chart with LUC Lot Size

Production Data	Period								
	1	*2*	*3*	*4*	*5*	*6*	*7*	*8*	*9*
Gross requirements	12	15	9	17	8	10	16	7	11
Scheduled receipts	53								
On hand	41	26	17	0	44	34	18	11	0
(ending inventory prior to Period 1 was 0)									
Planned order releases			52						
Planned order receipts					52				

unit costs increase when the demand for the fifth period is ordered. Thus, the model would order the 53 items through Period 4 and plan a subsequent order to cover Periods 5 through 9. Similar computations would result in a planned order release of 52 in Period 3, with an expected receipt at Period 5.

The total cost of the LUC method to manage demand for the nine-week horizon would be two setups at $5.75, or $11.50 for setup costs, and a total of 191 part periods ($41 + 26 + 17 + 0 + 44 + 34 + 18 + 11 + 0$) at $.05, or $9.55 total carrying cost. The total cost of the LUC method would be $9.55 + $11.50, or $21.05.

LEAST TOTAL COST (LTC). This approach selects lot sizes (order quantities) and the timing of their release so as to obtain the least total cost (the minimum sum of ordering and carrying costs) over the planning horizon. It does this by combining requirements until carrying costs approximate ordering costs.

Table 12–6   Lot-Sizing Computations of the LUC Method

Period	Number Ordered	Setup Cost	Carrying Cost per Period	Total Cost	Cost per Unit
1	12	$5.75	0	$ 5.75	$.479
1 and 2	27	5.75	$15 \times .05 = \$ .75$	6.50	.240
1 through 3	36	5.75	$15 \times .05$ $+ 9 \times .10 = \$1.65$	7.40	.206
1 through 4	53	5.75	$15 \times .05$ $+ 9 \times .10$ $+17 \times .15 = \$4.20$	9.95	.188
1 through 5	61	5.75	$15 \times .05$ $+ 9 \times .10$ $+17 \times .15$ $+ 8 \times .20 = \$5.80$	11.55	.189

Based on the logic—similar to the EOQ—that the total cost curve is discrete for dependent demand decisions, the minimum total cost still usually occurs at the point closest to a balance of carrying and ordering costs. This approach is executed as follows:

1. Begin with the first period in which an order is required.
2. Add the requirements of future periods, one at a time; order up to and including that period at which the cumulative carrying costs come closest to the ordering cost. (Another method of exercising the LTC logic is to add requirements in all future periods until the period in which cumulative carrying costs exceed the order cost.)
3. Begin the next order with the first period excluded and continue in the same manner.

Using the same data as the L4L and LUC examples, the ordering cost is $5.75, the carrying costs are $.05 per period per unit, and the requirements and scheduled receipts are given in Table 12–7. (The scheduled receipts order quantity was determined using the LTC method as described shortly.) Table 12–8 shows the calculations for this example.

The first order is for at least the 12 units required in Period 1. The first decision is whether or not to add the 15 units required in Period 2 to the order arriving in Period 1. If the carrying cost of adding these units is less than the cost of ordering again, they are added. Since total carrying costs are $15 \times \$.05 \times 1$, or $.75, the 8 units for Period 2 are included in the order arriving in Period 1. Considering Period 3 requirements next gives a total carrying cost of $1.65, therefore, these units also are added to the first order. The results of continuing these calculations are given in Table 12–8. The 10 units required in Period 6 are not included in the first order because their addition generates a carrying cost much greater than the ordering cost. The planned order receipt for forty-four units in Period 6 is calculated in the same manner. The total costs using the LTC method in this situation equal the setup costs of $11.50 plus the carrying costs of $8.95, or $20.45.

Table 12–7 MRP Chart with LTC Lot Size

Production Data	Period								
	1	2	3	4	5	6	7	8	9
Gross requirements	12	15	9	17	8	10	16	7	11
Scheduled receipts	61								
On hand (ending inventory prior to Period 1 was 0)	49	34	25	8	0	34	18	11	0
Planned order releases				44					
Planned order receipts						44			

Table 12–8   Lot-Sizing Computations of the LTC Method

Period	Units	Periods Carried	Period Carrying Costs	Cumulative Carrying Costs
2	15	1	15 × .05 × 1 = $ .75	$ .75
3	9	2	9 × .05 × 2 = .90	1.65
4	17	3	17 × .05 × 3 = 2.55	4.20
5	8	4	8 × .05 × 4 = 1.60	5.80

PART-PERIOD BALANCING.   Part-period balancing is a variation of the LTC approach. It converts the ordering cost to its equivalent in part periods, the economic part period (EPP), by dividing the ordering cost by the cost of carrying one unit for one period. The EPP is calculated as follows:

$$EPP = \frac{S}{K}$$

Where

   EPP = the economic part period

   S = the cost of ordering

   K = the cost of carrying one unit for one period

Using the data from the previous LTC example, the EPP equals $5.75 divided by $.05, or 115 part periods. Using part-period balancing, requirements are added period by period until the generated part periods approximate the EPP. This approach is shown in Table 12–9.

Since 116 is the closest value to 115, the requirements for Periods 2 through 5 should be included in the order due in Period 1. The advantage of this approach is that it is usually easier to compute part periods than carrying

Table 12–9   Application of Part-Period Balancing

Period	Requirement	Periods Carried	Part Periods	Cumulative Part Periods
2	15	1	15	15
3	9	2	18	33
4	17	3	51	84
5	8	4	32	116
6	10	5	50	166

costs. It always gives the same answer as the LTC approach using carrying costs.

Another technique, which in theory produces optimal orders, is the Wagner-Whitin dynamic programming algorithm (Wagner and Whitin, 1958). Given a finite time horizon and known demands, it optimally balances costs. In the example problem, the Wagner-Whitin method selects the same sizing as the LTC method. A major problem is its complexity and its sensitivity to change. While our planning horizon must be long enough to cover the total lead times for all our items, the dynamics of the real world cause the specific quantities and times to change; hence, the optimal solution changes. Small changes at high levels of the BOM can cause "nervous" changes and instability in dependent demand plans. This is quite undesirable and is one factor that argues for fixed lot sizes. For example, if the demand changes slightly in our first example and the lot size were 30, there would be no change in planned orders.

The difficulty with fixed lot-sizing techniques is that they only look at one level in a multilevel system. The setting of lot sizes for Level 1 of the product structure has an impact all the way down through the explosion of that structure. Trying to take into account the carrying and setup costs for all levels simultaneously to establish optimal lot sizes is an area still being investigated.

THE PERIOD ORDER QUANTITY (POQ). This method uses the standard EOQ to calculate a fixed number of period requirements to include in each order. Thus, the POQ avoids remnants—that is, quantities carried in inventory until the next requirement—whereas using the EOQ for discrete demand frequently results in remnants. In cases with low demand per period and relatively high setup costs it results in lower total inventory costs than the L4L method by combining the requirements for more than one period in a single order. The procedure follows:

1. Calculate the EOQ in the standard manner.
2. Use the EOQ to calculate N, the number of orders per year by dividing the annual requirements (R) by the EOQ.
3. Calculate the POQ by dividing the number of requirements planning time periods per year by N. Round off the result to obtain the POQ.
4. Begin with the first period that has requirements and place an order to cover them plus those in the periods that follow until the number of periods specified by the POQ are covered.

This can be illustrated with an example. If $R = 1,440$ units annually, S = $60 per order, $k = .3$ per year, C = $90 per unit, and there are 50 planning weeks per year, then follow this procedure:

1.
$$EOQ = \sqrt{\frac{2RS}{kC}} = \sqrt{\frac{2 \times 1,440 \times \$60}{.3 \times \$90}}$$

$$= 80$$

2.
$$N = \frac{R}{EOQ} = \frac{1,440}{80}$$

$$= 18$$

3.
$$POQ = \frac{\text{Planning periods per year}}{18}$$

$$= \frac{50}{18} = 2.8 \text{ or } 3$$

4. Applying this result to a given set of requirements when the lead time is two weeks results in the planned order releases shown in Table 12–10.

This approach does not minimize ordering and carrying costs, but it frequently is less costly than ordering each period or arbitrarily selecting a fixed order period.

Safety Stock and Safety Time

As long as parts procurement and manufacturing lead time are constant and the MPS is frozen (fixed) for a sufficient period of time to allow for parts procurement or production, no safety stock is required. Competitive pressures frequently prevent the MPS from being fixed for a period as long as the total lead time. Figure 12–7 illustrates a situation in which the MPS must be frozen for at least sixteen weeks if there is to be no variability in any requirements. However, if customers expect delivery in six weeks, then subassemblies are planned to a forecast. Parts and materials requirements are

Table 12–10 MRP Chart with POQ Lot Size

Production Data	Period											
	1	*2*	*3*	*4*	*5*	*6*	*7*	*8*	*9*	*10*	*11*	*12*
Net requirements	*	*	20	34	8	50	0	51	0	9	38	13
Planned receipts			62			101				60		
Planned order releases	62			101				60				

*The beginning on hand quantity equals the requirements in Periods 1 and 2.

Figure 12–7   Master Production Schedule of Lead Time

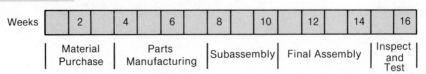

based on the schedule of subassemblies; safety stocks are required at the subassembly level to assure that all demands for final assembled products will be filled within the six-week lead time.

Given a fixed schedule for an assembly (either a final assembly or a subassembly as described previously), both the delivery of purchased material and the manufacturing of parts involve uncertainties. Parts are scrapped late in the manufacturing process, and a new lot cannot be produced within normal lead time. Vendors often do not ship the quantity promised. Vendors also have manufacturing and procurement problems; late delivery and short quantities result. If an item experiences either vendor delivery or manufacturing problems in a regular fashion, safety stock is appropriate. Safety stock requirements are determined as described in Chapter 11.

To illustrate how safety or buffer stocks impact system behavior, consider our previous example with a fixed lot size of 15. With a safety stock of 10 units, the plan is illustrated in Table 12–11. Planned order releases are calculated as before, except that the trigger point is when the inventory falls below 10 rather than below zero. The direct impact of such safety stock is to raise the average inventory level. This negative aspect is offset by the system's ability to handle unexpected demand increases or time advancements. For example, if an additional demand for 10 units were suddenly to occur in Period 3, it could be accommodated; if the demand of Period 5 were to move up to Period 4, it could be met. And, if a future demand increase occurred— that is, if the demand in Period 4 were to suddenly become 25—no change in the order release for Period 2 would be required with the safety stock. A

Table 12–11   MRP Chart with Provisions for Safety Stock

Production Data	Period								
	1	2	3	4	5	6	7	8	9
Gross requirements	12	15	9	17	8	10	16	7	11
Scheduled receipts	15	15							
On hand (ending inventory prior to Period 1 was 10)	13	13	19	17	24	14	13	21	10
Planned order releases	15	15	15		15	15			
Planned order receipts		15	15	15			15	15	

Lead time: 2; lot size: 15; safety stock: 10

shortage would have occurred if no buffer stock were present. An alternative to safety stocks is safety lead times. By overstating the lead time in the plan, the actual deliveries may arrive early and can then be used to satisfy changed demand. A simulation study by Whybark and Williams (1976) showed that if the uncertainties are in the demand quantities then safety stock quantity is desirable; however, if the uncertainty is in the timing of demand, safety lead times are preferred. Since demand for component items is certain, in the sense that it is dependent demand, in theory there should be no need for safety stock except for independent demand items and end products in the MPS. In practice, however, uncertainty in supply, whether it is caused by purchasing or manufacturing problems, may warrant some type of safety or uncertainty preparedness.

It is important that the MRP system output (e.g., report, charts, etc.) clearly distinguish between safety stock requirements and upper-level requirements. Safety stock requirements should be visible. In the previous example, if the on-hand quantity falls to five units in Period 1 (the action period), an order with insufficient lead time would be triggered. Expediting, broken setups, overtime, and considerable expense could result if the source (safety stock) of the requirement was not recognized. Replenishing safety stock usually is not a legitimate cause for special orders. The planner can override the MRP system's call for a safety stock only order by using the firm planned order.

Firm Planned Orders

One of the difficulties in establishing lot sizes is that the traditional EOQ formula looks only at the costs associated with one level in the product structure; but, in the manufacture of multilevel products, as most are, a lot size decision results in requirements for items at all lower levels. For example, the act of producing a gear box assembly necessitates the production of all components at levels below it—that is, gears, castings, shafts, bolts, etc. Research concerning the impact of end item lot sizes on these components is progressing but widespread acceptance of specific practices based on proven results has not occured.

Examine the MRP chart in Table 12–12, in which the rotor is a component of the motor assembly. The need for motor assemblies in Period 4 triggers a planned receipt for a lot size of 35. This in turn generates a planned order release in Period 2 and hence a gross requirement for the rotor in the same period. MRP logic causes a past due condition for the planned order release for the rotor. In actuality, the 25 on hand could cover the true need caused by the gross requirements for motor assemblies (5 + 10 + 10), but the lot sizing forces a past due situation. Manual intervention by a production scheduler may be required to either expedite the past due order, change the lot size for the motor assemblies, or introduce a firm planned order (FPO). An FPO is an order entered by the planner that supersedes the computer's MRP logic—

Table 12-12   MRP Chart—Motor Assembly and Rotor

Production Data for the Motor Assembly	Past Due	Period						
		1	2	3	4	5	6	7
Gross requirements					5	10	10	10
Scheduled receipts								
On hand		0	0	0	30	20	10	0
Planned order release			35					
Planned order receipts					35			

Lead time: 2; lot size: 35

Production Data for the Rotor	Past Due	Period						
		1	2	3	4	5	6	7
Gross requirements			35					
Scheduled receipts								
On hand		25	25	0				
Planned order release	10							
Planned order receipts			10					

Lead time: 2; lot size: 10

that is, the planner does not allow the normal MRP gross to net and lead time offset logic to take place, but rather the planner freezes a particular order. In this example, an FPO for 25 could be entered for the motor assembly and then all lower-level gross requirements would be determined by its value. The FPO technique can also be used if the planner believes the lead time can be compressed. In this case, the planner might decide that the motor assembly can be done in one week instead of two. Therefore, he or she enters as an FPO a planned order receipt of 35 in Week 5 instead of Week 4. This allows the MRP logic to proceed normally in scheduling the rotor. The computer program will probably issue a warning message (action notice) because it notes the discrepancy between the time the FPO will arrive and when it is logically needed, but the planner just uses this message to prompt expediting.

In practice, it may be possible to have complicated lot-sizing rules, although fixed sizes (as illustrated) or minimum lot sizes (for example, order at least 20) are the most common alternatives to L4L ordering. Even the fixed size rule should be subject to reevaluation and periodic recomputation as costs, normal demand levels, or technology change. In addition, production planners should review schedules and use firm planned orders when appropriate.

Figure 12–8   Product Structures

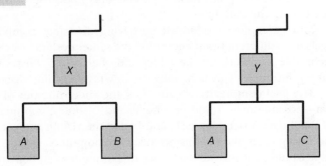

Pegging

Frequently, engineering designs families of end products that have a common component. MRP must pool the demands for these items. Consider, for example, the two product structures and their time-phased demands shown in Figures 12–8 and 12–9, respectively.

This introduces some interesting complexities. If for some reason the production lot of 25 units of A in period 4 is reduced to 20 units (damage and scrap, low-level delays, etc.), what impact should this have on X and Y? The first question is: Have you kept track of which items gave rise to A's gross requirement of 25 in Period 4? In order to have such a record, valuable computer space must be used to note these parent demands. Furthermore, if this is a multilevel product structure, and it usually is, will you also keep track of succeeding generations (parents, grandparents, etc.) or derive such information from a knowledge of each parent and/or offspring? These are important data processing considerations. This process of keeping track of parents and offspring is termed pegging; most systems do at most single-

Figure 12–9   Time-Phased Demands

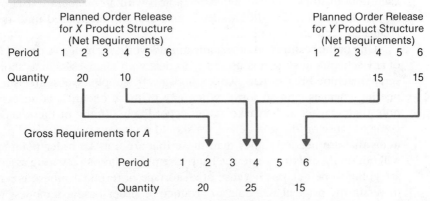

level pegging (keeping track of parents only) because of the complexities of maintaining the data base.

More complexity is added by having the same component at different levels or in different branches within the same product; for example, matching decorative hardware on the tables and chairs that constitute a dining room suite of furniture. This is handled by low-level coding, discussed earlier.

The final complexity is caused by the sheer number of parts in a typical firm—possibly over 1,000 end items and 20,000 components. The result is no small data processing task, and hence the rise in the use of MRP parallels decreasing costs and increasing speed of computers. In fact, without computers it would probably be necessary to assume that all demand is independent demand and hence MRP cannot be used. Also, in some instances, although the product structure relationship of the demand for a given item may be dependent, the effect of the many different requirements can be an aggregate demand of a relatively steady rate—in short, an independent demand profile—and a time-phased order point may be used.

DATA ACCURACY AND DEPENDENCIES

At the base of all MRP computations are correct BOM and inventory status records. If they are inaccurate, the MRP system will plan the wrong items and the wrong quantities—garbage in, garbage out. This is because an MRP system calculates requirements using inventory balance data and an explosion of the BOM. Thus, if an engineering change has been communicated to the shop floor but not to the BOM file, the MRP system will order the wrong item; the item withdrawn from inventory—if it is available—will not be the same as the system records as withdrawn. The salient resulting problems are the lack of required items, disrupted production, and late deliveries. While it may seem that any company, regardless of whether it uses MRP, order point techniques, or just estimates, should have an accurate data base, many do not. Order point systems combined with frequent periodic physical reviews of the quantity of each item in stock will usually enable a firm with an inaccurate data base to survive longer than an MRP system. Thus, they are often used until the firm attains an accurate data base.

One of the realities of the manufacturing world is change. A critical aspect of any scheduling system is its ability to deal with changes such as shortages, scrap, machine breakdowns, work stoppages by suppliers, absenteeism, engineering changes, and so forth. When any of these occur, it is necessary to note their impact and to take action accordingly. If any of these actions is going to cause production delays, we should revise our priorities and produce items that are needed rather than those that are not. An order point system will not do this. Returning to the lamp assembly example, if wiring assemblies are going to be delayed because of a shortage of terminals, there is no need to retain the original schedule to produce or order base assemblies. Wiring assemblies and base assemblies are horizontally dependent. We may as well work on another order, or we will have an inventory of base assemblies gathering dust while waiting for the socket assemblies. From this example, it can be seen that a key feature of MRP is its ability to de-expedite work when necessary and hence to maintain correct priorities so that production can be accomplished on what is really needed.

As information regarding changes becomes available, we can immediately revise our schedule; however, this is often both unnecessary and undesirable. First, notice that MRP I provides plans; it does not just issue orders. Frequently only the priorities need to be changed, not the orders already issued to the shop floor. Second, the time frame of MRP is usually weeks, although bucketless systems are becoming more common. Changes that cause delays of less than a week aren't recognized by the system. Third, it is desirable to have stability in the system since excessive changes will diminish production efficiency. This is a stage at which MRP interfaces with the MPS (discussed in Chapter 8). The planner must decide which changes are feasible and desirable on the basis of customer requirements, material, capacity, and tooling availability, and the status of work in the shop.

System Processing

Somewhat associated with change (but equally the result of time passing and hence production being accomplished and new orders being received) is the necessity to revise the MRP. This can be done in two ways. One is to start with the current plan and change it incrementally based upon new information(e.g., delays, cancelled and new orders, scrap, etc.). This is termed the net change approach.

Second, while the net change approach may seem simple, in practice it has often been found to be easier to start over using the same basic information—the MPS, BOM, and inventory status data—and to regenerate the entire schedule. This is often called "regen" or regeneration.

A number of factors influence the choice of a net change or a regenerative system. One of these is computer processing time. To effectively perform a net change, the program must have pegging capabilities. For example, in a given computer environment, about ten parts per minute might be handled; thus, 2,400 parts could be done in four hours. For a pegged, regenerative system perhaps two or three times as many parts could be handled per unit time, but many more parts must be handled each time the program is run. For example, it may take eleven hours to do a complete replanning run on 20,000 parts. If a regenerative system does not contain pegging capabilities, processing time is speeded up by a possible factor of three or four. Because product structures, software implementations, and the dynamics of change vary so greatly from company to company, it is impossible to state categorically whether net change or regenerative MRP will require less computer time. Inherently a net change system, particularly if it is an on-line system in which changes can be input as soon as they occur rather than grouping them for periodic processing, is very responsive to changes. This makes the plan very current, but also causes it to be "nervous," or extremely volatile in response to changes. The use of time fences to limit the planning horizon within which changes can be made is a very effective way to reduce nervousness. Regenerative systems are less responsive but more stable; hence fewer variations from the plan are noticed. Thus, closer control may be possible with a net change system, but computer costs and stability may argue for a regenerative system. A possible compromise is to net change weekly and to regenerate monthly.

Closed Loop Manufacturing Control

The MRP system in Figure 12–2 is an open loop system; there is no feedback. The manufacturing control system illustrated in Figure 12–10 is a closed loop system; the capacity requirements planning (CRP), supplier performance control (SPC), and production activity control (PAC) systems provide feedback. The CRP system determines if critical work centers have sufficient capacity during each period in the planning horizon. The PAC and SPC systems provide information concerning the status of orders in the plant and the performance of suppliers. This information enables planners to decide what, if any, action is required to bring production outputs in line with production plans. These systems are described in detail in Chapters 14 and 16.

This action may include: (1) changes in the MPS and everything dependent on it, (2) overtime and/or additional suppliers, (3) expediting, (4) firm planned orders, and (5) some combination of the foregoing.

CONCLUSIONS

A closed loop MRP system has four major advantages over the traditional order point system in the management of dependent demand items. These advantages are the correspondence of MRP orders to actual demand requirements; the recognition by MRP of vertical and horizontal dependencies among items, the proactive planning and forward visibility of MRP; and the ability of closed loop MRP to integrate materials and capacity planning and control consistency while maintaining the progress of orders and capacity in the production facility.

Figure 12–11 illustrates a typical relationship of inventory to independent demand for Assembly A, an item on the MPS, and of inventory to dependent demand for Component B when managed by an MRP system, as well as when managed by an order point system. The shaded area represents the additional time the same inventory is carried when using an order point system. In the order point system the example uses a component lot size that is the same as the assembly requirements. In order point systems this is often not the case.

Figure 12–10 Closed Loop Manufacturing Control

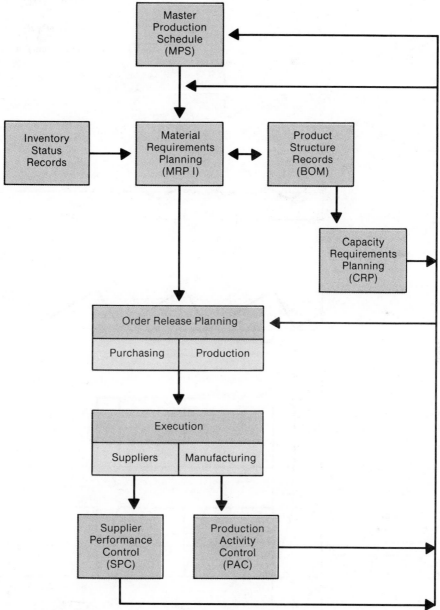

As a result, an additional ordering or setup may be required, or additional units beyond the safety stock may be carried until the next order.

Order point systems do not consider vertical or horizontal dependencies. For example, if Component C also is required for Assembly A but will arrive

Figure 12–11   MRP Versus Order Point

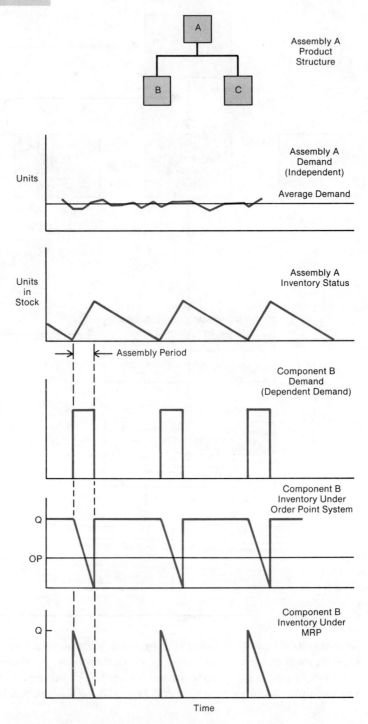

three weeks late from a supplier, an order point system does not consider this factor in deciding when to order Component B. However, the MRP system does.

An MRP system looks into the future and calculates when items are needed; it is proactive. An order point system calls for action when inventory reaches the order point; it is reactive. MRP facilitates formal and explicit planning. Order point systems for dependent demand items make life more exciting by increasing the number of surprises and decreasing the time operations management has to cope with capacity management challenges.

However, order point systems do have certain advantages. Whereas MRP systems can collapse if bills of material are incomplete or inaccurate, and also if inventory records are inaccurate, physical review order point systems will call for orders when inventory reaches the order point even if the records are inaccurate. The point is that an MRP system requires accurate bills of material and accurate and timely recording of inventory transactions to be effective. Thus, some firms that have not attained these prerequisites, continue to use an order point system.

QUESTIONS

1. What is the relationship between MRP and other planning actions and status files?

2. How does the gross-to-net concept assure that requirements for components are correctly computed?

3. Lead time offsets are part of the computation of an MRP chart. Why are lead times necessary? Why must they be added together for a multilayer bill?

4. How does the fact that MRP systems refer to planned order releases and planned order receipts relate to the responsiveness of an MRP system?

5. Describe the benefits and negative aspects of using a small time bucket in an MRP system.

6. What is a low-level code? How does such a code reduce computations in an MRP system?

7. How do lot-sizing techniques affect MRP decisions?

8. Why does lot sizing, at the final assembly level, cause problems in a multilevel system?

9. In what ways do safety stock and safety lead times affect finished good inventories?

10. Describe the term firm planned order. When should the concept be employed?

11. Differentiate the concepts of safety stock and safety time. Give an example of the appropriate use of safety stock and the appropriate use of safety time.

12. What is pegging? When is pegging advantageous? Identify and explain the primary obstacle(s) to using this system effectively.

13. Upon what types of information is the MRP system dependent?

14. What is the difference between a net change system and a regeneration system?

15. How does closed loop manufacturing control supplement the basic MRP system?

16. Define MRP II and describe the relationship between MRP II, Closed Loop MRP, and MRP I.

PROBLEMS

1. Refer to the multilevel structure in Figure 12–4. If the gross requirement for Product F is 75 units, what are the net requirements for Parts F, G, J, O, P, Q, T, and V given the following on-hand quantities?

Part/Assembly	On Hand
F	6
G	5
J	2
O	4
P	7
Q	9
T	6
V	9

2. Referring to Problem 1, what are the net quantities to be ordered for Parts F, G, J, O, P, Q, T, and V if the lot sizes are 15 for all parts/assemblies?

3. Refer to Figure 12–4. If 75 units of Product F are to be shipped in Week 25, when must Part V be ordered, given the following lead times?

Part/Assembly	Lead Time (Weeks)
F	3
G	4
J	2
O	4
P	3
Q	2
T	1
V	2

4. For the following situation, determine the planned order releases.

Production Data	Period 1	2	3	4	5	6	7	8	9
Gross requirements	15	10	20	5	15	25	10	15	20
Scheduled receipts	25								
On hand (ending inventory prior to Period 1 is 25)									
Planned order release									
Planned order receipt									

Lead time: 3; lot size: 25

5. If in Problem 4 the lot-for-lot (L4L) order size rule is employed, what are the planned order releases?

6. If in Problem 4 the lot size is 15, what are the planned order releases?

7. If the ordering cost is $10.00 per order and the carrying cost is $1.00 per unit per period, calculate the total cost for Problems 4, 5, and 6.

8. For the following situation determine the planned order releases using the least total cost (LTC) procedure. Ordering cost is $10.00. Holding cost is $.15 per unit per period.

Production Data	Period 1	2	3	4	5	6	7	8	9	10	11	12
Gross requirement	8	6	5	11	9	12	7	7	10	8	6	8
Scheduled receipts												
On hand (ending inventory prior to Period 1 is 20)	12	6	1									
Planned order releases												
Planned order receipt												

Lead time: 2

9. Using the requirements in Problem 8, calculate the order quantities and releases by the LUC method. Compare the costs of that method to those of the LTC solution found in Problem 8.

10. Given the information in Problem 8, what would the total cost for ordering and holding inventory be if the lot size is fixed at 40 units, and the holding cost is $.15 per unit per period.

11. Refer to the information in Problem 8, determine the planned order releases using the least total cost (LTC) procedure. Ordering cost remains at $10.00 per order; however, the holding cost is $.25 per unit per period.

12. Using the period requirements, ordering costs, and carrying cost in Problem 8 and estimated annual requirements of 400 units and 50 ordering periods per year, apply the Period Order Quantity method to determine the order quantities for the net requirements in Periods 4 through 12. Periods are weeks.

REFERENCES

DeMatheis, J.J., "An Economic Lot-Sizing Technique: The Part Period Algorithms," *IBM Systems Journal* 7, no. 1 (1968): 50–51.

Fogarty, Donald W., and Thomas R. Hoffmann, *Production and Inventory Management*, Cincinnati: South-Western Publishing Co., 1983.

Orlicky, Joseph. *Material Requirements Planning*. New York: McGraw-Hill, 1974.

Schultz, Terry. *BRP: The Journey to Excellence*. Milwaukee, Wis.: The Forum, 1982.

Wagner, Harvey M., and Thomson M. Whitin. "Dynamic Version of the Economic Lot Size Model," *Management Science*, (October 1958): 89–96.

Whybark, Clay D., and J. G. Williams. "Material Requirements Planning under Uncertainty," *Decision Sciences* 7, no. 1 (October 1976): 595–606.

Wight, Oliver. *MRP II: Unlocking American Productivity Potential*. Boston, Mass.: CBI Publishing, 1982.

CHAPTER 13
CAPACITY REQUIREMENTS PLANNING

OBJECTIVES

After completing this chapter, you should be able to

- Explain the relationship of short-range capacity planning to medium-range planning

- Identify the contributors to short-range capacity planning

- Identify the five-step capacity planning process and be able to compute the capacity requirements for a specific order or group of orders

- Understand the effects of controlling inputs and outputs

- Compute changes in lead time and work in process.

- Differentiate the principle methods of capacity requirements planning in service operations

- Plan and control the capacity of a service operation

OUTLINE

INTRODUCTION

Short-range capacity requirements planning (CRP) develops from long-range resource capacity planning (RCP) and medium-range rough-cut capacity planning (RCCP). Both the RCP and the RCCP are estimates, albeit often quite accurate estimates, of resource needs; however, they are not exact, either in volume or in timing. CRP includes actual lead times and other information from the materials requirement plan (MRP) and the purchasing plans. Thus, CRP serves as a bridge to link the long- and medium-range capacity planning estimates and operations activity control in the execution phase.

Short-range CRP takes place in virtually all organizations. For example, parents who are planning a holiday dinner party for three generations of their family not only must determine material requirements (beverages, ice, vegetables, salads, entree, etc.) but also the number of dinner places, tables, chairs, table settings, silverware, cooking utensils, and ovens required to prepare the dinner according to an acceptable delivery schedule and quality standard. Upon determining the total capacity requirements, the parents may decide to ask one of their children to bring a large card table, four chairs, and a toddler's high chair. Additionally, they may subcontract the baking of pies to another child to reduce conflicting requirements on the oven, and another child might be asked to bring some games to entertain the toddlers while dinner is being prepared. This basic example demonstrates how short-range requirements planning integrates capacity and materials—a process inherent in all operations.

Short-range capacity planning should occur in every type of organization. An effective short-range capacity plan should consider the timing and volume of both resource availability and capacity scheduling. Methods of measuring capacity vary widely by activity and the type of organization. Thus, this chapter will consider capacity planning in both manufacturing and service organizations.

In any organization, short-range capacity planning examines operations (activities) planned in the near future to determine the capacity required to carry out these activities in the time periods planned. It then compares required capacity to available capacity. If sufficient capacity is not available, it determines the additional capacity necessary and the possibility and cost of obtaining it. This cost then is compared to the cost of changing the schedule. Once a final schedule is defined, control plans are established to manage the execution.

RELATIONSHIP OF SHORT-RANGE CRP TO MEDIUM-RANGE PLANNING

The master production schedule (MPS) is one of the primary inputs to the short range planning process (see Figure 13–1). However, the case also

Figure 13–1   Output and Capacity Planning and Control

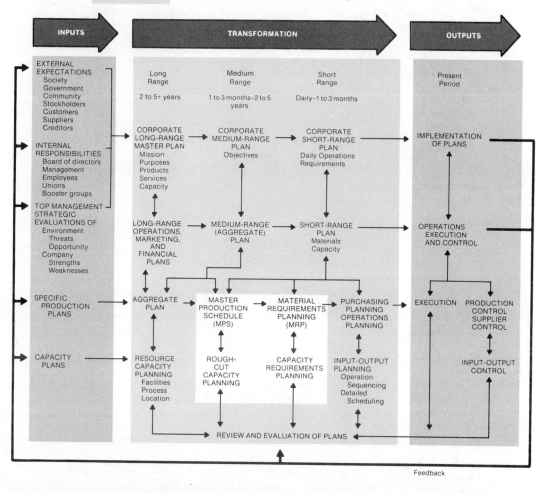

could be made that commitment to a master schedule is the first step of short-range planning. Thus, the master production schedule may be viewed either as a medium- or short-range plan; it assures the continuity, consistency, and integrity of the planning process.

In the case of a make-to-order or an assemble-to-order operation, the final assembly schedule (FAS) often requires components and processing capacity not called for by the MPS. Thus, in some organizations both the MPS and the FAS are inputs to short-range planning. The item requirements stated in the MPS and FAS are inputs to MRP, material requirements planning, which determines the time-phased requirements for individual components and materials. Thus, MRP is a prerequisite to short-range CRP. Figure 13–2 is a detailed illustration of the flow of that process and its iterative nature.

The MPS and the resulting MRP accomplish the priority planning objec-

Figure 13–2   Short-Range Planning Diagram

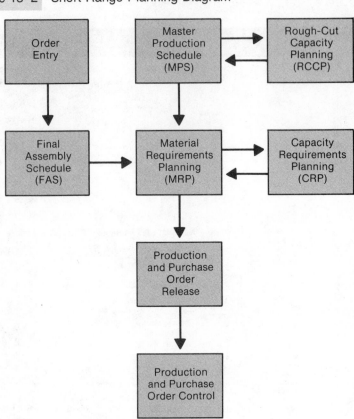

tives of production inventory management. They determine what items are needed and when they are needed. The RCCP may be used during medium-range planning to identify that there is not enough capacity; this information may serve as a basis for choosing external purchasing, subcontracting, or some other option. The output of the MRP is the input to the CRP system.

CAPACITY REQUIREMENTS PLANNING

RCP and RCCP fulfill the capacity planning function in the long- and medium-range planning horizons, respectively. Ideally, they should result in an MPS for which sufficient capacity is available; however, this often is not the case. Additionally, even when the capacity required by the MPS is within capacity limits, a mismatch between available and required capacity can occur either in the timing of the entire production process or in one or more work centers. This mismatch could be a result of unplanned events. Equipment failure or a strike at a key supplier could significantly alter available capacity.

Similarly, an unusually high level of scrap or an unexpected emergency order for service parts can increase the capacity required beyond that planned earlier.

Inherent differences in the RCCP and CRP can also cause a mismatch between available and required capacity. The difference between the RCCP and the CRP can occur because the RCCP processes often plan by month or week, whereas the MRP and the corresponding (linked) CRP may plan by week, day, or even hour. Also, the RCCP does not consider inventory on hand or work in process, whereas the CRP does. Thus, the more detailed MRP and CRP can lead to requirements in a given time period in excess of those defined by the more general RCCP. The RCCP may be feasible but the additional information available to the CRP may necessitate further adjustments. In fact, the CRP results in a schedule that is known to be executable.

The capacity requirements planning process provides the answers to the following questions:

1. Is sufficient capacity available to fulfill the capacity requirements plan as derived from the MRP and the MPS?
2. If sufficient capacity is not available, what work centers and suppliers have inadequate capacity and how much additional capacity is required by each and when is it required?
3. What are the costs to correct capacity shortages? Is it worth the additional costs, often subcontracting or overtime, to meet the MPS?

CRP determines the capacity required in each work center by time period to produce a given output. Although presently used primarily in manufacturing, the principles and examples of CRP included in this chapter are applicable to planning in many service settings including those of an educational institution, editorial office, hospital, or architectural firm. The output, the process, the lead times, and the nature of capacity resources will differ but the concepts remain the same. Most of the techniques are applicable with only minor adjustments.

The CRP Procedure

CRP consists of the following steps:

1. Obtain the requisite data.
2. Backward schedule each item on the basis of the MRP.
3. Compute the required capacity.
4. Load all capacity centers in accordance with the schedule without considering resource capacity constraints (infinite loading).
5. Compare capacity requirements to available capacity. If available capacity is sufficient, the planned release of orders conforms to the schedule developed in Step 4. If available capacity is insufficient, either available capacity must

be increased or the schedule must be revised (finite loading) until available capacity is sufficient.

These five steps are discussed in detail in the following sections.

DATA REQUIREMENTS. Step 1 of the CRP process is to obtain the data necessary for capacity requirements planning to take place. For the present purposes, these data can be divided into three types: (1) the data concerning each required item—from the final assembly to the seemingly least significant purchased part or raw material—(2) the data concerning each work center, and (3) the data describing supplier capabilities. Although these data can be organized in many different ways, typically three separate files are used: the routing file, the work center file, and the purchase file.

A routing file exists for each manufactured part. The record for each part includes a list of the required processing operations identified normally by number in ascending order. This list would normally include:

1. A brief description of the operation
2. The setup time
3. The run time per unit (operation time)
4. The typical scrap rate or yield

Table 13–1 is an example of routing file data required for capacity requirements planning for a gear. The process involves turning the gear blank from bar stock (Operation 10), cutting the gear teeth on a gear cutter (Operation 20), and inspecting and packing the gear (Operation 30).

The work center file contains a separate record for each work center; each record usually contains the following data:

1. *Number of shifts*—The number of shifts worked per planning period.
2. *Machine hours per shift*—the number of machines available per shift.
3. *Labor hours per shift*—The availability of labor may determine the number of machines that can be used.
4. *Efficiency*—The ratio of standard performance to actual performance in terms of labor or machine hours per unit produced.

Table 13–1 Routing File Data

Operation	No.	Setup Time*	Operation Time*	Scrap Rate
Turn	10	15	3.0	.04
Cut gear	20	60	5.0	.05
Inspect and pack	30	6	0.2	.01

*Times are in minutes.

5. *Utilization*—The ratio of hours of effective capacity usage to scheduled work hours. Noneffective usage includes downtime due to machine failure, lack of materials, and employee absenteeism. Coffee breaks, clean up, and fatigue allowances are reflected in standard times and efficiency calculations. For example, five operators are assigned to the first shift and three to the second in a work center with five machines, each requiring an operator. Assuming a 40 hour week, 320 clock hours of capacity are available each week. If an average of 40 hours is lost each week due to machine failure, lack of material, or employee absenteeism, the utilization rate is .876 (280/320).

6. *Effective or actual capacity (EC)*—The number of standard hours of output per time period that can be expected from a department. The best measure of capacity is the output of the department, fully loaded, in the recent past. Rated capacity equals the product of the number of shifts, the number of hours per shift, the number of machines or workers (whichever is the limiting factor), the work center efficiency, and the utilization. If utilization and efficiency factors are accurate, rated capacity will equal actual capacity.

7. *Planned queue*—The planned average time a lot waits before processing.

8. *Planned wait*—The planned average time a lot (or part of a lot) waits before being moved to the next workstation in its sequence of operations.

9. *The work waiting to be processed*—Measured in capacity terms of standard hours.

10. *The work scheduled to arrive*—Includes released orders (work in process) and planned orders.

The purchase parts file usually contains the following data:

1. Alternate sources of supply
2. The lead time of each source
3. The normal yield associated with lots received from each source
4. The capacity of each source

Short-range planning of purchased items is discussed in Chapter 16.

MANUFACTURING LEAD TIME. Step 2 of the CRP process is to backward schedule based on the MRP. The MRP reveals when an item is required by the master schedule and when an order for that item must be released to produce or procure it on schedule, given normal lead times. It does not necessarily reveal when capacity is required to produce the item. Some items, such as a small rod, are produced on one machine, a turret lathe or automatic screw machine for example. Production of a lot of such items may be expected to occur in a week or less. However, many other items require processing in numerous work centers; production of these items requires five or more weeks. This is especially true when lot sizes are large, processing time per unit is relatively long, and a particular process is subcontracted. Thus, the nature of the process and lot size influence when specific types of capacity are required and when an order must be released to be produced on schedule.

Figure 13–3   Components of Manufacturing
Lead Time

1. Operation time	a. Setup (and tear down)
	b. Run time
2. Interoperation time	a. Wait time
	b. Movement time
	c. Queue time

The components of manufacturing lead time can be divided into operation time and interoperation time as described in Figure 13–3.

The flow of a job through a production facility can be represented as in Figure 13–4 and Table 13–2. Each part's lead time profile is necessary to determine the time periods when specific elements of capacity are required. This profile is available from the data described earlier; its use will be demonstrated later in the discussion of scheduling.

AVAILABLE RESOURCE CAPACITY. Step 3 of the CRP process is to compute the capacity of available resources. Differences exist between capacity requirements planning in flow line (repetitive or continuous) manufacturing environments, functional layout (job shop) environments, and project environments. The mechanics of the calculation differ, but the major differences are in the objectives and constraints of the environment. The flow line and the functional layout are examined here; projects are examined in Chapter 15.

Flow Lines.   The required capacity is designated as T_p (the production time required to produce the quantity for all orders); for a single model line, it is calculated as follows:

$$T_p = R \times C$$

Figure 13–4   Manufacturing Lead Time Profile

Day	11	12	13	14	15	16	17	18	19	20	21	22	23	24	25	26
Hour	120	112	104	96	88	80	72	64	56	48	40	32	24	16	8	0

Move and queue   Turn   Wait, move, and queue   Cut gear   Wait, move, and queue   Inspect and pack   Wait and move

Table 13–2 Backward Schedule of Gear Manufacture

Order Number: 5
Completion due date: 26 days
Capacity: 8 hours per day
Quantity Required: 500 units
Normal wait, move, and queue time: 8.0 hours

Operation	Set-up Time*	Operation Time*	Units	Scrap Qty	Scrap Rate	Total Time	Backward Cumulative Time
Move and queue						8.0	107.09
# 10, Turn	.25	.05	555	23	.04	28.0	99.09
Wait, move, and queue						8.0	71.09
# 20, Cut gear	1.00	.0833	532	26	.05	45.32	63.09
Wait, move, and queue						8.0	17.77
# 30, Inspect and pack	.1	.0033	506	5	.01	1.77	9.77
Wait and move						8.0	8.0
						107.09	

*Data corresponds to Table 13–1, but times are in hours.

where

$$R = \text{the number of units required}$$

$$C = \text{the average cycle time per good unit}$$

For example, if 532 units are required and the average cycle time is 5 minutes, or .0833 hours, then

$$T_p = 532 \times 5 = 2,660 \text{ minutes}$$

$$= 532 \times .0833 = 44.32 \text{ hours}$$

Because the example problem in Table 13–2 and Figure 13–4 is not a flow line, the one-hour set-up time is added there, but not here. Since, by definition, single model lines produce only one item, no setup is required. Preventive maintenance would be scheduled separately or might be factored in the setup time or operations time.

Determining capacity requirements for a group of items produced in lots (a batch multimodel line) rather than a mixed model line requires that capacity requirements be calculated for each item and summed as follows:

$$T_p = \sum_{i=1}^{n} S_i + \sum_{i=1}^{n} R_i C_i$$

where

$$S_i = \text{Set-up time for item } i \text{ (the time required to change} \\ \text{the line from running one item to running another)}$$

$$R_i = \text{Requirements (quantity) of item } i \text{ to be processed}$$

$$C_i = \text{Cycle time of item } i$$

$$n = \text{Number of items}$$

Consider the case of four hydraulic cylinders—with minor differences in attachments—being assembled on the same line. The following data describe the set-up times, requirements, and cycle times.

Item (i)	S_i*	R_i*	C_i*
A	5	100	1.5
B	3	200	2.0
C	2	300	1.1
D	4	50	1.2

*Times are in minutes.

The capacity requirement is

$$T_p = (5 + 3 + 2 + 4) + (100 \times 1.5) + (200 \times 2)$$

$$+ (300 \times 1.1) + (50 \times 1.2)$$

$$= 14 + 150 + 400 + 330 + 60$$

$$= 954 \text{ minutes} = 15.9 \text{ hours}$$

For further study of calculating capacity for many different types of flow lines see Groover (1987).

Intermittent (Job Shop) Production. Capacity planning is generally more complex in a job shop manufacturing environment than in a flow shop. In its most basic form, the computation requires the sequential set-up and production times of each operation for each job. In the gear cutting example, the production time of 44.32 hours is added to the set-up time of 1 hour to give a total of 45.32 hours. However, different items typically require different process sequences to complete them. At any point in time there are orders in the plant (work in process) that have reached various stages of completion, other orders just beginning to be processed, and orders planned for release to the shop in the near future. In addition, some parts may have been scrapped during the process; in other cases, more parts than required may be produced to use leftover material or due to error. All of these factors necessitate a reliable method of collecting data concerning the status of work in process and the work available for processing in each work center. This is discussed further in Chapter 14.

Thus, backward scheduling starts with the due date of an item and works backward operation by operation assigning queue time, operation time, wait time, and move time to the appropriate time period on the basis of the actual lot size and expected queue, operation, wait, and transit times. Figure 13–4 represents graphically the backward schedule of an order for 532 gears described in the item routing file in Table 13–1.

INFINITE LOADING. According to Table 13–3, Order 5 is required for completion on Day 26. Operation 20, the gear cutting operation, requires 45.32 hours. To ensure that the subsequent operations and interoperation times are met, the gear cutting operation must be started in Day 19 and completed by the end of Day 24 (see Figure 13–4). Thus, in infinite loading—Step 4 of the CRP procedure—gear cutting is scheduled to take place during Days 19 through 24, without regard to any orders already scheduled for that work center during the same period. Table 13–3 and Figure 13–5 show the effects of infinite loading. The gear cutting center is overloaded through Day 20.

Figure 13–5   Graphic Representation of Infinite Loading

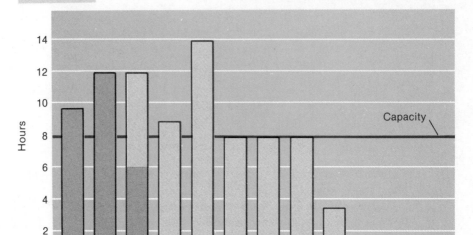

FINITE LOADING. Step 5 of the CRP process is to adjust either the schedule or the capacity so that the operation is feasible or so that the process is loaded consistent with finite resources. Finite loading assigns orders to each resource such as personnel, machine centers, tooling, and energy consumption so that all operations do not require more resources than are available. There are numerous ways that resources may be combined or that the schedule may be adjusted to achieve finite loading. These methods include overtime or hiring more personnel, defining a second shift, subcontracting for parts, substituting available parts from inventory, or filling the order from another plant. Of course, the delivery date of low-priority orders may also be set back, which permits the expediting of orders for important customers.

The output of finite loading is a detailed schedule of each order and each work center that takes into consideration the capacity factors mentioned earlier, the order due dates, and other criteria. These criteria and scheduling concepts and techniques are discussed further in Chapter 14. Table 13–4 and Figure 13–6 illustrate finite loading of the machining of 532 gears in the gear cutting department. Although other options might be possible, in this case the completion date of the gear cutting operation was extended to Day 27, which, considering the following operations, would mean the delivery date would be Day 30. Of course, other scheduling alternatives could have been

Table 13–3 Infinite Load: Gear Cutting

Today's Date: 16

Order No.	Time Required	Order Status*	Past Due	Day							
				17	18	19	20	21	22	23	24
1	15.7	R	1.7	8.0	6.0						
2	12	R	8.0	4.0							
3	7	P			6.0	1.0					
4	6	P					6.0				
5	45.3	P				8.0	8.0	8.0	8.0	8.0	5.3
	86		9.7	12	12	9	14	8	8	8	5.3

*R = released order; P = planned order.

Table 13–4 Finite Load: Gear Cutting

Today's Date: 16
Capacity: 8 Hours Per Day

Order No.	Time Required	Order Status*	Day											
			17	18	19	20	21	22	23	24	25	26	27
1	15.7	R	8.0	7.7									
2	12	R		.3	8.0	3.7							
3	7	P				4.3	2.7						
4	6	P					5.3	.7					
5	45.3	P						7.3	8.0	8.0	8.0	8.0	6.0
	86.0		8	8	8	8	8	8	8	8	8	8	6.0

*R = released order; P = planned order.

Figure 13–6   Graphic Representation of Finite Loading

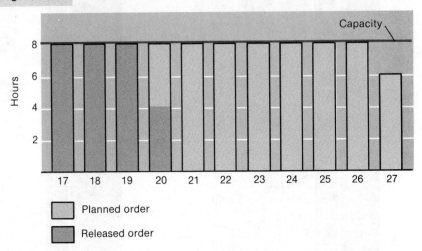

□ Planned order

■ Released order

selected to complete the job on time, but the cost might have increased as a result.

INPUT/OUTPUT PLANNING AND CONTROL

Input/output(I/O) planning and control is an integrated process; as might be expected, it involves input/output planning and input/output control. I/O planning involves planning the input to and output from each work center for each time period. Work in process and the queue (backlog of work) at the entry (gateway) work center and other critical (or bottleneck) work centers are also considered. Additionally, the process also establishes the size of deviations and the difference between planned and actual inputs and outputs that will be considered acceptable. Subsequently, I/O control releases orders to production, measures actual inputs and outputs at each work center, and compares them to the plan. Variations beyond normal limits are analyzed for cause and to determine the appropriate corrective action.

Although it is impossible to fully separate the planning and controlling of inputs and outputs, this chapter emphasizes I/O planning, which is part of short-range planning; Chapter 14 emphasizes I/O control, which is an execution activity.

Continuous Process I/O Planning

The basic concept of I/O planning and control is that ending work in process equals beginning work in process plus input minus output. I/O planning in a continuous process plant is similar to that of a single-operation production process because in a continuous process many successive work cen-

Figure 13–7 Input/Output Relationship of a Continuous Process or Single-Operation Process

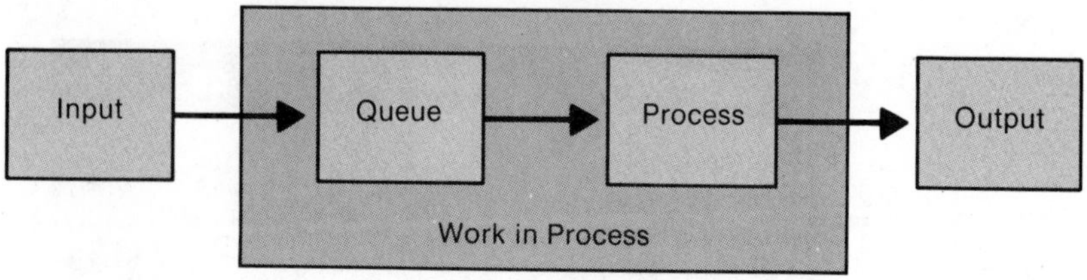

ters would be represented by the "process." This relationship is represented schematically in Figure 13–7.

Because input must be absorbed by output or work in process, it follows that increasing input when operating at full capacity results in increased work in process. Input and output are measured in the same units as capacity requirements, usually labor hours, machine hours, gallons, tons, or just units. Tables 13–5 through 13–8 reveal the impact of I/O planning by illustrating the following four situations:

1. Balancing input and output
2. Increasing input with the plant operating at capacity
3. Increasing input to bring output to capacity
4. Decreasing input to reduce work in process

Table 13–5 exemplifies a planned balance of input and output for Weeks 26 through 29. The work center is operating at capacity, with an output rate of two units per day or ten units per week. There is a material queue (backlog) of two units, and ten units are being processed per week. Thus, the work in process is 12 and the lead time is the weekly capacity plus the beginning queue divided by the production per day, or $(10 + 2)/2 = 6$. Note that if the process is operating at capacity and inputs are equal to outputs, then the work in process and the lead time remain constant.

The situation of increasing input while operating at full capacity is illus-

Table 13–5 Planned Balanced Input/Output
Single Process Production
Input/output balanced; beginning queue—2 units

Week	26	27	28	29
Planned input	10	10	10	10
Planned output	10	10	10	10
Lead time (days)	6	6	6	6
WIP (material)	12	12	12	12

Output rate   2 per day

Table 13–6   Planned Increased Input; No Change in Capacity
Beginning queue—2 units

Week	26	27	28	29
Planned input	10	12	12	12
Planned output	10	10	10	10
Lead time (days)	6	7	8	9
WIP (material)	12	14	16	18

Table 13–7   Planned Increased Input to Bring Operations to Capacity
Beginning queue—0 units

Week	26	27	28	29
Planned input	6	10	12	10
Planned output	6	8	10	10
Lead time (days)	5	5	6	6
WIP (material)	8	10	12	12

trated in Table 13–6. Work in process and lead time increase. In this case, controlling production often becomes more difficult and the operation is probably less efficient.

Table 13–7 illustrates bringing an operation up to capacity. Input is increased, causing the output of the workcenter to increase as well. Note that work in process varies as does the lead time, which is the weekly production plus two units in the queue divided by the daily production, because with an input of ten units there is no queue. In this example, the average weekly queue equals the work in process minus ten units (the process capacity).

Table 13–8 illustrates the decreasing of input to bring work in process within bounds while maintaining capacity. Lead time and work in process both decrease in this example.

Table 13–8   Planned Decreased Input to Reduce Work in Process
Beginning queue—6 units

Week	26	27	28	29
Planned input	10	8	8	10
Planned output	10	10	10	10
Lead time (days)	8	7	6	6
WIP (material)	16	14	12	12

Figure 13–8   Flow Patterns in a Job Shop

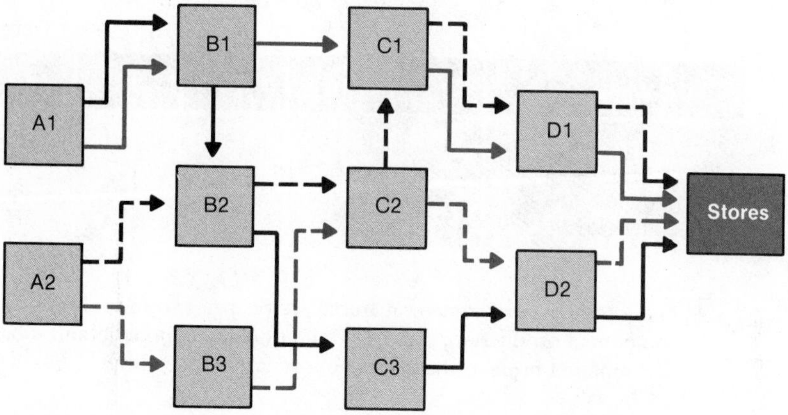

Input/Output Planning and Control for a Job Shop

Input/output planning and control in a job shop is more complicated because orders follow a variety of paths from start to finish. Figure 13–8 illustrates possible flow patterns in a job shop.

Work centers A1 and A2 in Figure 13–8 are frequently called gateway centers; they are the work centers in which work begins. Work centers B1, B2, B3, C1, C2, and C3 are intermediate or downstream centers; and D1 and D2 are the finishing or final work centers.

Queues and work in process at gateway centers are relatively easy to plan by treating them as single process work centers. Input to these work centers should never be greater than output unless one of the following conditions exists:

1. The work center is operating below actual capacity and increased output is desired.
2. An increased queue is required to reduce idle time due to variations in output exceeding the present planned queue.

Input and output at downstream and final work centers is much more difficult to control because of multiple routes and differing priorities. These topics will be discussed further in Chapter 14.

Order Release Planning

If operating properly, MRP has planned the release of orders on the basis of item due dates and normal lead times. The order release system further plans order releases so that

1. In both continuous and repetitive process environments, material and/or components arrive at a rate equal to the rate of the production process and in ample time to avoid disruption.

Table 13–9 Planned Capacity and Order Releases
Gateway work center

Date: Week 14

Week	15	16	17	18	19	20
Capacity (hours)	80	80	80	80	80	80
Cumulative Capacity	80	160	240	320	400	480
Planned load	95	110	60	50	60	100
Cumulative load	95	205	265	315	375	475

2. In a job shop environment, material arrives prior to the release of orders for component production, and the production of components and subassemblies is completed prior to the release of orders for assembly.

The MRP planned order release dates must be revised when capacity planning reveals that the load in the plant will be outside acceptable tolerances during certain periods. If the master schedule is within capacity constraints, the total load over the planning horizon will not exceed total capacity (although loads may exceed capacity in some periods and fall short in other periods). When capacity is constant, load adjustments must be made in underloaded and overloaded periods. This is accomplished by early and late releases of orders. However, orders can be released as planned if capacity can be varied sufficiently through various adjustment techniques.

Table 13–9 illustrates a highly variable load at a gateway work center by period requiring revisions in the planned order releases. Planned order releases must be reduced in Weeks 15, 16, and 20 by approximately 15, 30, and 20 hours, respectively. Excluding overtime or subcontracting, this may be accomplished by moving some orders from Weeks 15 and 16 to Weeks 17 and 18 (i.e., starting them late) and moving orders from Week 20 into Week 19 (i.e., starting them early).

Selection of orders from Weeks 15 and 16 for later release is based on the priority of orders and the anticipated load on the different downstream work centers where capacity is required by the different orders. For example, orders required to replenish a safety stock would be selected for a late start while an order for a component required for an assembly would be started on time. Other things being equal, orders utilizing underloaded downstream work centers would be planned for release prior to orders requiring fully loaded downstream work centers.

SERVICE OPERATIONS CAPACITY PLANNING

The variety of environments in service operations capacity planning is much greater than the variety in manufacturing. However, since many manufacturing organizations also have service functions and departments, manufacturers also face this variety at least in some parts of their operation. In general, these problems are solved using one or some combination of the following approaches:

1. Fixed facility and equipment capacity with sufficient staff available to operate at the maximum capacity—it is anticipated that customers will be turned away or not wait in some cases. Theaters, restaurants, retail stores, dental clinics, and many commercial and professional service organizations operate in this manner.

2. Flexible capacity to meet unpredictable surges in demand—flexibility is obtained by émployee assignments, overtime, and cooperative agreements. Union Electric, a major electric utility in Missouri, obtains the repair capacity to repair damage due to severe storms by overtime (drawing repair crews from unaffected divisions of its 24,000-square-mile territory), assigning construction crew linemen to repair duties, and in severe cases, using repair crews from neighboring power companies such as Illinois Power. In accord with their cooperative agreement, Union Electric repair crews are also available to aid Illinois Power when the situation demands it. The point is that short-range capacity requirements planning consists of a set of procedures for obtaining a dramatic increase in repair capacity through established plans for reallocating flexible resources. Emergency service organizations regularly operate in this manner.

Personnel capacity is usually the constraining factor in planning short-range capacity for services. The work force capacity problem often is complicated by the service organization being open seven days a week for two or three shifts. Service operations must determine the number of staff required in the following situations:

1. When the staff required is independent of the demand within a given range
2. When the staff required varies with the demand

A typical theater requires the same number of ticket sellers, ushers, and concession staff members whether the theater is full or virtually empty, although an extra usher and another clerk for the concession stand may be added if an especially large attendance is expected. For the most part, doctors' offices also have a fixed number of personnel, as do automotive repair centers.

On the other hand, organizations hosting major events, such as college or professional sporting events, concerts, or conferences, must calculate their staffing requirements on the basis of forecasted weather and attendance. Advance sales of tickets are an excellent barometer of actual attendance in most of these cases. The timing (day or evening), expected mix (adults, children, and teenagers), and weather for outdoor events also is used to forecast the sale of beverages, hot dogs, popcorn, and so on.

Staffing of some service operations are subcontracted on a regular basis.

For example, some professional athletic teams, municipal conference centers, and opera houses have contracts with an ushering service. The ushering service is informed of the date and place, the expected crowd, and other critical factors and has the responsibility of obtaining the ushers. The ushering service usually has a core of regulars and an ample supply of part-time workers on call.

CONCLUSIONS

Capacity requirements planning and input/output planning are two principal techniques that link the long- and medium-range capacity planning methods with line execution. CRP identifies the exact volume and timing of requirements in the short run and loads those requirements on the available resources through a schedule. If sufficient capacity is available, then this infinite loading-generated schedule is sufficient; if not, then the schedule must be adjusted through overtime, hiring, subcontracting, maintaining inventories, or delaying deliveries. This adjustment consistent with resource availability is called finite loading.

Once the schedule is established for each work center and each operation of each order, a method of planning for the control of the operation must be developed. This is usually achieved through input/output planning and control. The most desirable schedule is a balance of inputs and outputs, near capacity, for each time period. Realistically, however, this may not be possible. Thus, controlling inputs and outputs to minimize work in process and to keep lead times down will likely improve the flexibility and efficiency of the operation.

QUESTIONS

1. How does CRP relate to the MPS?

2. When is the FAS used?

3. What would cause the RCCP to develop an infeasible schedule?

4. How does CRP improve upon RCCP?

5. List the five steps of the CRP process. Generally, from where does information for each step come?

6. Given the following items of information, in which CRP file would you expect to find them?

   a. Set-up time
   b. Machine hours per shift

  c. Capacity of each source
  d. Efficiency
  e. Scrap rate
  f. Lead time of each source
  g. Planned wait

7. What is the difference between operaton time and interoperation time?

8. What is the difference between infinite and finite loading?

9. How are a continuous process and a single process similar?

10. When should input to a work center be greater than output?

11. How does order release planning differ in continuous process, job shop, and repetitive process environments?

12. What alternatives are available to the operations manager to adjust an infinitely loaded schedule to a finitely loaded schedule?

13. In a service environment, what strategies for capacity planning are available for organizatons to follow?

14. List the general categories into which staffing situations apply for service organizations. Give an example for each category.

PROBLEMS

1. Refer to Figure 13–4. Compute the total time (operational and interoperational times—eight hours for each task) for the following jobs:

Job	Operations	Units
1	10, 30	600
2	20, 30, 40	800
3	10, 20, 30, 40	400

Operation	Set-up Time	Run Time
10	0.25	0.05
20	1.00	0.0833
30	0.10	0.0033
40	0.85	0.0725

Times in minutes

2. Compute the total time for each of the jobs at the top of page 472. Assume that the interoperational time for each task is eight hours.

Job	Operations	Units
1	20, 40, 50	1000
2	10, 20, 30	1200
3	10, 30, 40, 50	950
4	20, 30, 50	1400

Operation	Set-up Time	Run Time
10	.40	.01
20	.80	.06
30	1.50	.1
40	.75	.05
50	.60	.005

3. Determine the capacity time for the following data:

Item	Set-up Time	Requirements	Cycle Time
W	75	4,000	2.5
X	62	8,000	1.875
Y	51	10,000	0.75
Z	25	6,000	0.25

*Times are in minutes

4. Determine the capacity requirements for the following component parts of end item A.

Part	Set-up Time*	Requirement	Cycle Time*
B	25	1000	.1
C	90	50	.25
D	60	6000	1.25
E	250	200	4.0
F	15	180	.8
G	7	750	1.75

*Times in minutes

5. Finite load the following operation on a first come, first served basis. Total capacity per day is nine hours.

Order Number	Arrival Day	Time Required (Hours)
1	3/25	12.6
2	3/25	9.3
3	3/26	18.2
4	3/26	8.3
5	3/26	4.1

6. Load the following operation on a first-come-first-serve basis. Total capacity per day is 7.5 hours. Today's manufacturing calendar date is 121; none of these jobs have been started.

   a. Infinitely load the following orders.
   b. Finitely load the following orders, assuming that no overtime or subcontracting is possible.
   c. Finitely load the orders, given a 20% short term availability of overtime.

Order #	Arrival Date	Time Required (Hours)	Due Date
6028	98	6	135
6029	105	11	124
6030	106	23	125
6031	118	4	127
6032	118	18	126
6033	119	13	130
6034	121	9	132

7. A work center is operating at capacity with an output rate of 500 units per week; the beginning queue is 250 units, and planned input is 500 units. Calculate work in process and lead time.

8. Given the following workcenter data, make the required input/output planning computations and adjustments.

Beginning Queue	6 units	Capacity/day = 3		
Week	**30**	**31**	**32**	**33**
Planned input	12	15	21	15
Planned output	15	12	18	15

   a. Compute the WIP for each week.
   b. Compute the lead time in days for each week.
   c. What would explain the planned output of week 31, of week 32?
   d. Use planned input to reduce WIP to 15 units per week.
   e. Use planned input to stabilize lead time at 6 days.

REFERENCES

Aherns, Roger. "Basics of Capacity Planning and Control." APICS 24th Annual International Conference Proceedings (1981), pp. 232–235.

Belt, Bill. "Integrating Capacity Planning and Capacity Control. " *Production and Inventory Management* (1st quarter) 1976.

Campbell, Kenneth L. "Rough Cut Capacity Planning—What It Is and How to Use It." APICS 25th Annual International Conference Proceedings (1982), pp. 406–409.

Capacity Planning Reprints. Falls Church, Va.: American Production and Inventory Control Society, 1986.

Groover, Mikell P. *Automation, Production Systems, and Computer Integrated Manufacturing.* Englewood Cliffs, N.J.: Prentice Hall, 1987.

Lankford, Ray. "Short Term Planning of Manufacturing Capacity" APICS 21st Annual International Conference Proceedings (1978), pp. 37–68.

Wemmerlov, Urban. *Capacity Management Techniques for Manufacturing Companies with MRP Systems.* Falls Church, Va.: American Production and Inventory Control Society, 1984.

Wight, Oliver W. "Input-Control, A Real Handle on Lead Time." *Production and Inventory Management* (3rd Quarter) 1970.

PART V
EXECUTION AND CONTROL

CHAPTER 14
OPERATIONS ACTIVITY CONTROL

OBJECTIVES

After completing this chapter you should be able to

- Describe how operations activity control closes the planning and control loop

- Describe the major differences between operations activity control in a flow line environment and in a job shop

- Calculate the priority of each item in a group produced on a batch flow line

- Describe the difference between sequencing and scheduling

- Discuss the many common priority scheduling rules and the rationale of each and be able to determine the different priorities of each order in a group based on different rules

- Describe how input/output control can affect work-in-process, lead time, and output, and describe why final workcenter input/output control is important

- Describe a gateway, intermediate, final, downstream, and upstream work center

- Calculate planned or actual work-in-process given beginning work-in-process, planned or actual input, and output.

- Describe how the status of work at downstream work centers can affect sequencing decisions at upstream work centers

- Describe the basic elements of order release and dispatching and how their applications differ in different production environments

- Identify the essential elements of a production activity control system and the typical reports that it produces

476

OUTLINE

Introduction
Manufacturing Flow Lines
    Batch Flow Lines
    Runout Time Scheduling
Job Shop Scheduling
    Scheduling Policies and Objectives
    Late Orders
Service Operations Scheduling
    Seven-Day Scheduling Algorithm
Input/Output Control
    Single Work Center Processes
    Multiple Work Centers
        Gateway Work Center Control
        Downstream Work Center Control
        Final Work Center Control
Order Release
Dispatching
Production Reporting
    Data Collection
    Typical Reports
Conclusions
Questions
Problems
References

INTRODUCTION

The time arrives when plans must be executed. The function of operations activity control (OAC)—often called production activity control (PAC) or shop floor control (SFC) in manufacturing firms—is to have activities performed as planned, to report on operating results, and to revise plans as required to achieve desired results. The principles and concepts of operations activity control have broad applicability. They are useful in manufacturing and service environments, however, since different environments exist in manufacturing organizations and in service organizations, different approaches and techniques are applicable in each environment. This chapter discusses operations activity control in manufacturing and then presents some problems of operations activity control in service organizations.

Figure 14–1 shows the sequence of the various planning and control activities. We are now at the point where material requirements planning and capacity requirements planning have been completed and the detailed purchasing and operations schedules must be determined and released for execution.

Figure 14–1 Operations Activity Control Schematic

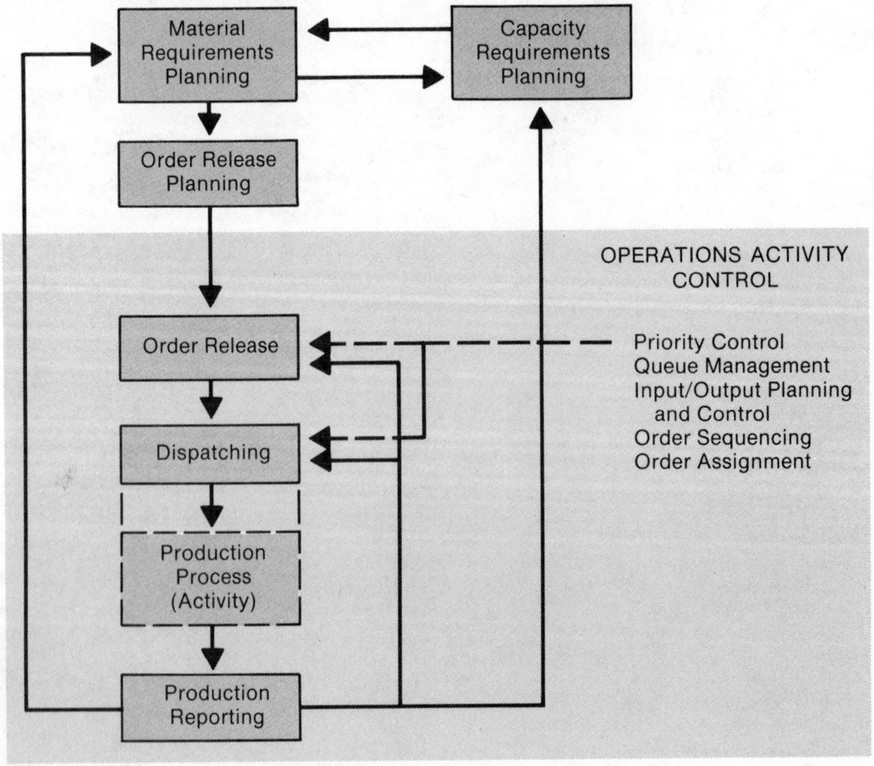

The PAC system also closes the planning and control loop as illustrated in Figure 14–1 by measuring actual output and comparing it to the plan. Although all PAC systems perform the same basic functions, individual systems differ due to different outputs (products), production processes, facility layouts, multiplant or single production facility situations, and the available capacity of personnel and/or equipment.

MANUFACTURING FLOW LINES

Chapter 5 described several different types of production processes or layouts, including continuous and batch flow lines, job shop, and project (fixed position) processes. This section describes scheduling for a flow process. Once the output rate of a flow line has been established, scheduling consists of assuring the proper rate of flow of materials and supplies to the line as well as the scheduling of the appropriate number of personnel for the line. Chapter 9 described the design of the line and organization of the tasks in order to obtain the desired output rate.

Batch Flow Lines

As noted in Chapter 5, a family of items may be produced in batch quantities on the same line with some changes in the setup, a cleaning of the equipment, and changes in incoming materials. (If no time is required for switching from one item in the family to another, then the different items can be mixed in the same run and a mixed model line exists.) Thus, the primary objective is to reduce and eventually eliminate the time required for changing between items in a group. The smaller the changeover time, the greater the scheduling flexibility and the smaller the scheduling problem. Batch flow lines exist in beverage companies, ice cream manufacturers, soap powder packaging facilities, and pharmaceutical plants. Typically, a group of similar items are manufactured on the batch line. The quantity of an item produced depends on that item's production rate and the length of time it is run. Deciding what item to run next and the quantity to be run depends on the following factors.

1. The on-hand (available) quantity of each item
2. The demand rate of each item
3. The time required to change between different items
4. The production rate of each item
5. The sequence, if any, in which items should be run

When the set-up (changeover) times are relatively small and independent of the sequence in which the items are produced, the decision is relatively simple; the item with the smallest runout time is run first. Again, this emphasizes the importance of reducing changeover times.

Table 14–1 Runout Time, Example 1

Item	Inventory	Demand (units per day)	R (in days)	Scheduling Priority
A	80	20	4.0	1
B	100	10	10.0	2
C	150	12	12.5	3
D	60	4	15.0	4

Runout Time Scheduling

Runout time is the days of demand (usage) coverage that is in inventory. For example, if a company uses (or sells) twenty printed circuits, Part No. 101, each day and has eighty of them in stock, the runout time of Part No. 101 is four days. *Runout* time (R) is calculated as follows:

$$R = \frac{\text{units in inventory}}{\text{demand (usage) rate}}$$

Let us look at an example including four items, shown in Table 14–1. The R value of Part B is calculated as follows:

$$R(\text{B}) = \frac{100}{10} = 10.0 \text{ days}$$

If the setup times for the items in the example group are relatively short and the production lot quantities are small due to relatively low demand rates and low setup costs, there is no problem. Sufficient time usually will exist to manufacture all items on schedule. However, let us look at another example of four machined parts made on the same machine, a traditional machine tool with a larger setup time and corresponding larger production quantities (see Table 14–2). The demand (usage) rates are also larger.

Table 14–2 Runout Time, Example 2

Item	Inventory	Demand (units per day)	R (in days)	Economical Production Quantity	Economical Production Time (in days)
A	80	80	1.0	400	2.0
B	150	75	2.0	400	2.0
C	60	30	2.0	300	1.5

This company is in trouble. Some of these items should have been manufactured last week. The purpose of this example is to point out that:

1. Manufacturing engineering should improve (reduce) the setup and thus the production run quantities and time. In this case, computer numerically controlled (CNC) machine that can shift from one part to another with little or no setup time may be appropriate. Lack of flexibility may be more costlly than providing it.
2. Proper order release decisions are as important as the quantity decision.
3. The planner must consider the expected order release dates and capacity requirements for all items produced in a work center.

Order quantity and order release decisions are more complicated when more than one group is run on the same equipment, capacity is limited, or the items in a group must be run in a particular sequence, (e.g., first Item A, then B, C, etc.) to achieve minimum changeover (setup) times. For a further discussion of these problems see Chapter 8 of Fogarty and Hoffmann (1983).

JOB SHOP SCHEDULING

The physical layout of a job shop usually groups equipment performing similar functions in the same area. Typically there are many different orders being processed in the plant at the same time and relatively few have the same routing (the department-by-department path through the plant). *Scheduling* is the assignment of starting and completion times to orders (jobs); it frequently includes the times when orders are to arrive in and leave each department. Sequencing is the assignment of the sequence in which orders are to be processed (e.g., do Order C first, then B, followed by D, etc.). However, in practice and in the literature, scheduling frequently refers to both the time schedule and the sequence of orders or jobs. The selection of a scheduling system, approach, or technique depends on the objectives of the schedule and the criteria by which its results will be measured. Thus, we examine scheduling objectives and criteria next.

Scheduling Policies and Objectives

Management policies and objectives are the basis for scheduling decisions. However, the operations manager may define the scheduling objectives in various ways, including the following: minimize average lateness of orders, minimize maximum lateness, minimize manufacturing lead time (minimum average flow time), minimize work-in-process, and maximize utilization of bottleneck work centers. Achievement of these objectives depends on more than scheduling (planning) and control, however. The flexibility—or lack of it—of the manufacturing equipment and processes also affect scheduling options. The importance of methods analysis, facility layout, setup reduction, and the development of manufacturing cells cannot be overemphasized. Fortunately, most of the objectives are mutually supportive; for example, reducing manufacturing lead time reduces work-in-process and increases the probability of meeting due dates. In addition, scheduling the proper orders to achieve maximum utilization of bottleneck work centers also will often support the other objectives.

Many methods (sometimes called priority rules) exist for establishing the priority of orders. The priority, often expressed numerically, is used to determine the sequence in which the orders should be processed. The rules described in the following section are probably the most common but many variations and combinations of these methods exist. However, the list in Table 14–3 provides a good overview of basic rules and their objectives.

The example given in Table 14–4 is based on data concerning four orders in a manufacturing plant in central Illinois. It shows the scheduling priorities that resulted from each of the previously described priority rules. All orders were in the same department, which we call Department 7.

Slack time (ST) and the critical ratio (CR) were calculated as described in Table 14–3.

ST = Due date
  $-$present date $-$ total operation (setup + run time) remaining.

Thus for Order A,

$$ST = 130 - 125 - 3.0 = 2.0$$

CR = (Due date $-$ present date)/manufacturing lead time remaining

Thus for Order D,

$$CR = (138 - 125)/9.0 = 1.44$$

Applying each of the priority rules, except FCFS, to the four orders gives the following processing sequences:

> SOT (Shortest Operation Time) B, A, C, D
> STPT (Shortest Total Processing Time) A, C, B, D
> EDD (Earliest Due Date) A, B, C, D
> FO (Fewest Operations) D, A, C, B
> ST (Slack Time Remaining) A, B, D, C
> CR (Critical Ratio) B, A, C, D

Although the selection of any four orders at a given time in a specific department will produce results different from those in the example, the above results are not unusual. Different rules produce different sequences but certain patterns tend to appear in most. For example, orders A and B are each scheduled first or second by most rules. One factor that also should be

Table 14–3 Common Priority Decision Rules

Rule	Objective
FCFS—First Come, First Served	Run the orders in the sequence in which they arrive at the work center. This "fairness" rule is especially appropriate in service organizations where most customers often either need or desire the completion of the service as soon as possible.
SPT, SOT—Shortest Processing (Operation) Time	Run the orders in the inverse order of the time required to process them (smallest time first) in the department. This rule usually results in the lowest work-in-process, the lowest average job completion (manufacturing lead time), and average job lateness. Unless this rule is combined with a due date or slack time rule, jobs (orders) with long processing times can be extremely late.
STPT—Shortest Total Processing Time	Run the orders in the inverse order of the total processing time remaining. The rationale of this rule is similar to the preceding one. It accomplishes similar objectives when most jobs follow a common process.
EDD—Earliest Due Date	Run orders with the earliest due date first. This rule works well when processing times are approximately the same.
FO—Fewest Operations	Run first the orders with the fewest operations remaining. The logic of this rule is that fewer operations involve less queue time and, as a result, the rule reduces average work-in-process, manufacturing lead time, and average lateness. However, jobs with a relatively large number of operations can take excessively long if another rule is not combined with this one.
ST—Slack Time	Run first the order with the smallest slack time and continue the sequence in the ascending order of their slack times. Slack time equals the due date minus the remaining processing time (setup plus run time). This rule supports the achievement of due date objectives. The slack time remaining per operation is a variation of this rule.
CR—Critical Ratio	For orders not already late (overdue), run first those orders with the lowest critical ratio. The critical ratio equals the due date minus the present date divided by the normal manufacturing lead time remaining.

considered is the status of the work center to which each order goes next. There would be little point in scheduling Order A first if its next operation was in a workcenter overloaded with higher priority orders.

An advantage of the SOT rule is that the data required to use it is readily available to the immediate supervisor. However, due date data may not be, and the other rules require calculations and considerably more data. Particularly

Table 14–4 Scheduling Priority, Department 7, Day 125

Order	Due Date	Current Operation Time	Total Operation Time Remaining	Manufacturing Lead Time Remaining	Number of Operations Remaining	Slack Time	Critical Ratio
A	130	1.5	3.0	6.0	3	2.0	.83
B	132	1.0	4.5	9.5	5	2.5	.74
C	136	2.0	4.0	8.0	4	7.0	1.38
D	138	3.5	7.0	9.0	2	6.0	1.44

Note: All times are in days

with a large number of orders, this usually requires a computerized shop floor control system.

Late Orders

Late orders are of special interest because management is interested in minimizing their lateness. The concept of slack time, the time ahead of or behind schedule, can be used to aid in these decisions. However, slack time may be computed by several different methods; manufacturing lead time remaining and processing time remaining are the two most widely used. The manufacturing lead time remaining method computes the number of days ahead or behind schedule by subtracting the manufacturing lead time remaining from the actual lead time remaining. The priority is then computed based on the number of days behind or ahead of schedule. Alternatively, the processing time remaining computes the priority, based on the number of days behind or ahead of schedule by subtracting the processing time remaining from the actual time remaining. These computations are shown in Tables 14–5 and 14–6.

When queue and move time make up a large but variable portion of man-

Table 14–5 Priority of Overdue Orders—Manufacturing Lead Time Remaining

Order	Date Due**	Actual Time Remaining	Manufacturing Lead Time Remaining	Days Behind or Ahead of Schedule	Priority
A*	40	5	2	+3	5
B	35	0	10	−10	3
C	35	0	8	−8	4
D	25	−10	4	−14	2
E	25	−10	8	−18	1

*Not Overdue
**Present Date is Day 35

Table 14–6   Priority of Overdue Orders—Processing Time Remaining

Order	Date Due	Actual Time Remaining	Processing Time Remaining	Days Behind or Ahead of Schedule	Priority Rank
A*	40	5	2	+3	5
B	35	0	4	−4	4
C	35	0	5	−5	3
D	25	−10	1	−11	2
E	25	−10	3	−13	1

*Not Overdue
Present Date is Day 35

ufacturing lead time, and can be compressed by priority sequencing, ranking is improved using days overdue plus process time remaining rather than total lead time remaining. This is illustrated in Table 14–6 which considers the processing time remaining. However, a temporary increase in capacity may be a better solution.

The days behind schedule, when computed using total manufacturing lead time in Table 14–5 indicates that Order B is further behind schedule than Order C and thus has a higher priority. However, a ranking based on processing time remaining gives Order C a higher priority as illustrated in Table 14–6.

SERVICE OPERATIONS SCHEDULING

The labor-intensive nature of many services combined with seven-day weeks and multiple shifts presents scheduling problems not found in the eight-hour, Monday-through-Friday operation. Hospital personnel, police officers, firefighters, bus drivers, retail employees, and telephone operators are occupations for which such scheduling problems exist. Service operations, as well as manufacturing firms operating a seven-day schedule, usually must provide each employee with two consecutive days off and no more than forty hours work per week. Although most employees prefer to have Saturday and Sunday off, a substantial minority have other preferences. As a result, there are many practical ways of handling the seven-day scheduling problem. Practical approaches include the following:

1. Employ personnel to work Saturday and Sunday either as part of their five-day week or as regular part-time employees.
2. Establish personnel requirements and have employees pick their work days on the basis of seniority, on a rotating basis, or using some other criteria. For example, a large midwestern newspaper presents the biweekly personnel requirements in the pressroom to the union representative (shop steward) who is responsible for the assignments. Employees pick their assignments on the basis of seniority. Differential pay for weekends and holidays in such cases

often influences employee choices. Individuals in the same job category also may trade assignments. The advantage to management is that an individual selected by the employees is responsible for the assignments.

3. Allow for self-selection and flexibility when possible. Employees indicate their preferred day off and the manager attempts to fulfill their requests. This is especially true when working hours may conflict with the wedding of a friend, a graduation, or other special occasion. It also is common to allow employees to trade assignments.

Now, let's examine a scheduling algorithm that is useful for obtaining a feasible schedule.

Seven-Day Scheduling Algorithm

The following algorithm provides the minimum number of employees to operate one shift for seven days with each employee having two consecutive days off. It is based on the work of Browne and Tibrewala (1975). An example is used to describe the procedure.

Step 1.— List the number of personnel required on each day of the week to be scheduled. For example, a small general store requires the following number of clerks in the coming week.

	S	M	T	W	Th	F	S
Personnel requirements	3	4	5	4	5	6	7

Step 2.— Find the set of two consecutive days with the minimum total personnel requirements and omit them from the schedule for Worker 1. In the example, the total requirements for Sunday and Monday are seven individuals, less than the total for any other two consecutive days.

	S	M	T	W	Th	F	S
Personnel requirements	3	4	5	4	5	6	7

	S	M	T	W	Th	F	S
Worker 1 assignments			X	X	X	X	X

This step assigns personnel to the five-day set that requires the largest number of personnel. Assigning personnel to the other two days would have generated discontinuities (days without requirements) in later assignments.

Step 3.—Subtract the days assigned from the initial requirements and repeat Step 2.

	S	M	T	W	Th	F	S
Initial requirements	3	4	5	4	5	6	7
Assigned	0	0	−1	−1	−1	−1	−1
Remaining	3	4	4	3	4	5	6

In this case a three-way tie occurs between Sunday-Monday, Tuesday-Wednesday, and Wednesday-Thursday. There are rules to break ties and to assure balance, as follows.

1. *Ties*—When a tie occurs, select the pair farthest from the highest value. Thus, in Step 3, Sunday and Monday were chosen because they are more distant from the coming Saturday than are Tuesday and Wednesday or Wednesday and Thursday. Note that organizations frequently schedule two weeks at a time when Friday through Monday are the highest requirements.
2. *Balance*—To assure balance, the two days selected as the days off should not include a day with the highest requirements.

Continue Steps 2 and 3 until all requirements are filled. The complete schedule is shown in Table 14–7.

Since there is a total of thirty-four days coverage required in the week and each worker is limited to five days work, a minimum of seven workers is required with only four days of work available for one. The solution to the example problem obtains the minimum number of personnel and also the requirement of at least two consecutive days off for each worker. Obtaining the minimum number of workers as well as two consecutive days off for each worker may not be feasible when personnel requirements vary dramatically from day to day. The following is an example of such a situation:

	S	M	T	W	Th	F	S
Personnel requirements	6	3	8	5	2	6	5

One possible solution to the problem is shown in Table 14-8. Note that for Worker 2's assignment the tie after the largest day was arbitrarily selected. Further, Workers 6 and 7 do not get five days of work or two consecutive days off. Certainly other decision rules might be used in these types of situations. Flexibility is the key in managing such situations. It includes assigning workers

Table 14–7   Seven-Day Scheduling Example

	S	M	T	W	Th	F	S		S	M	T	W	Th	F	S
Remaining requirement	3	4	5	4	5	6	7	Worker #1	–	–	x	x	x	x	x
Worker 1	0	0	–1	–1	–1	–1	–1								
Remaining requirement	3	4	4	3	4	5	6	Worker 2	–	–	x	x	x	x	x
Worker 2	0	0	–1	–1	–1	–1	–1								
Remaining requirement	3	4	3	2	3	4	5	Worker 3	x	x	–	–	x	x	x
Worker 3	–1	–1	0	0	–1	–1	–1								
Remaining requirement	2	3	3	2	2	3	4	Worker 4	x	x	x	–	–	x	x
Worker 4	–1	–1	–1	0	0	–1	–1								
Remaining requirement	1	2	2	2	2	2	3	Worker 5	–	–	x	x	x	x	x
Worker 5	0	0	–1	–1	–1	–1	–1								
Remaining requirement	1	2	1	1	1	1	2	Worker 6	x	x	–	–	x	x	x
Worker 6	–1	–1	0	0	–1	–1	–1								
Remaining requirement	0	1	1	1	0	0	1	Worker 7	–	x	x	x	–	–	x
Worker 7	0	–1	–1	–1	0	0	–1								
Remaining requirement	0	0	0	0	0	0	0	Total	3	4	5	4	5	6	7

to other tasks on low-demand days, programs to balance demand, permanent part-time workers, and the relaxation of the two consecutive days off policy for each worker every week.

INPUT/OUTPUT CONTROL

Input/output control is an effective capacity management technique in both manufacturing and service organizations. In Chapter 13 we discussed input/output planning and the relationship of planned input, output, and the work-in-process (the orders in queue plus the orders being processed). In this chapter actual inputs, outputs, and work-in-process are added to the analysis. This enables the planner to determine what action is necessary to achieve

Table 14–8   Seven-Day Scheduling Example

	S	M	T	W	Th	F	S		S	M	T	W	Th	F	S
Remaining requirement	6	3	8	5	2	6	5	Worker #1	x	x	x	–	–	x	x
Worker 1	–1	–1	–1	0	0	–1	–1								
Remaining requirement	5	2	7	5	2	5	4	Worker 2	x	x	x	–	–	x	x
Worker 2	–1	–1	–1	0	0	–1	–1								
Remaining requirement	4	1	6	5	2	4	3	Worker 3	–	–	x	x	x	x	x
Worker 3	0	0	–1	–1	–1	–1	–1								
Remaining requirement	4	1	5	4	1	3	2	Worker 4	x	x	x	x	–	–	x
Worker 4	–1	–1	–1	–1	0	0	–1								
Remaining requirement	3	0	4	3	1	3	1	Worker 5	–	–	x	x	x	x	x
Worker 5	0	0	–1	–1	–1	–1	–1								
Remaining requirement	3	0	3	2	0	2	0	Worker 6	x	–	x	x	–	x	–
Worker 6	–1	0	–1	–1	0	–1	0								
Remaining requirement	2	0	2	1	0	1	0	Worker 7	x	–	x	x	–	x	–
Worker 7	–1	0	–1	–1	0	–1	0								
Remaining requirement	1	0	1	0	0	0	0	Worker 8	x	–	x	–	–	–	–
Worker 8	–1	0	–1	0	0	0	0								
Remaining requirement	0	0	0	0	0	0	0	Total	6	3	8	5	2	6	5

the desired output, work-in-process, and manufacturing lead time objectives. We will examine the case of a single processing center and then the more complicated case of multiple work centers and many orders with different routings.

Single Work Center Processes

Single process work centers are common in many service operations; equipment repair, document copying, typing, and some data processing activities are examples. In addition some manufacturing processes have only one work center or a dominant (bottleneck) work center. Gateway workcenters, continuous and repetitive batch lines, and a uniform routing through a group of work centers also may be treated in many cases as a single processing work center for input/output analyses purposes.

Input/output analysis compares the scheduled order (or task) inputs to the process, and the scheduled outputs to the actual inputs and the actual outputs. This information comes from production schedules and from completed job reports. Further computations can provide the cumulative input deviation, the cumulative output deviation and the planned and the actual work-in-process (WIP). These computations are

$$\text{Input cumulative deviation} = CD_{i-1} - PI_i + AI_i$$

$$\text{Output cumulative deviation} = CD_{i-1} - PO_i + AO_i$$

$$\text{Planned WIP} = WIP_{i-1} + PI_i - PO_i$$

$$\text{Actual WIP} = WIP_{i-1} + AI_i - AO_i$$

where

$$i = \text{The time period}$$

$$PI = \text{Planned input}$$

$$PO = \text{Planned output}$$

$$AI = \text{Actual input}$$

$$AO = \text{Actual output}$$

$$CD = \text{Cumulative deviation}$$

Management can then develop various measures of process performances, including an acceptable level of input and output deviation and acceptable levels of WIP.

Three different situations illustrate first a process in control, second, the use of input/output control to reduce work-in-process, and third, input/output controls under conditions of decreased output.

In the first example, illustrated in Table 14–9, the situation is under control. Actual input and actual output differ little from the plan; the work-in-process is never more than four standard hours of output different from the plan. Typically management will establish an acceptable cumulative deviation, perhaps six hours of work-in-process in this case for example, as possible due to random events.

Table 14–9   Input/Output Control: Situation in Control

	Week				
	26	**27**	**28**	**29**	**30**
Input					
Planned	80	80	80	80	80
Actual	78	82	84	77	81
Cumulative deviation	−2	0	4	1	2
Output					
Planned	80	80	80	80	80
Actual	82	78	82	83	78
Cumulative deviation	2	0	2	5	3
Work-in-Process (end of week)					
Planned (36 at end of week 25)	36	36	36	36	36
Actual (36 at end of week 25)	32	36	38	32	35

Note: All values are in standard hours

Calculations of work-in-process examples are as follows:

$$WIP(i) = (i - 1) + IP(i) - OP(i)$$

$$\text{Planned: } WIP_{26} = 36 + 80 - 80 = 36$$

$$\text{Actual: } WIP_{29} = 38 + 77 - 83 = 32$$

As noted in Table 14–9, the work-in-process at the end of a week equals the beginning work-in-process plus the input minus the output.

The second situation is illustrated in Table 14–10. There, a reduction in input beginning in Week 26 and constant output were planned to reduce work-in-process from forty standard hours to twenty hours. After five weeks,

Table 14–10   Input/Output Control: WIP Reduction

	Week					
	25	**26**	**27**	**28**	**29**	**30**
Input						
Planned		75	75	75	75	80
Actual		75	76	74	77	78
Cumulative deviation		0	1	0	2	0
Output						
Planned		80	80	80	80	80
Actual		82	76	82	81	79
Cumulative deviation		2	−2	0	1	0
Work-in-Process (end of week)						
Planned	40	35	30	25	20	20
Actual	40	33	33	25	21	20

Note: All values are in standard hours

actual results coincide with the plan; this is only possible if twenty hours of work in process will sustain the production rate of two standard hours of output per hour. Once the desired level of work-in-process has been reached, the input must be returned to the output level. This is an example of a management action to make the process more efficient, as measured by WIP.

Table 14–11 illustrates an application of input/output control in an unanticipated situation. Continuing the situation in Table 14–9, an equipment failure during Week 30 has decreased output and the work-in-process has risen to 60 hours. The equipment has been repaired during the weekend. The plan was to work 10 hours overtime in Weeks 31 and 32 increasing output by 25 percent to 100 hours, hold input constant at 80 hours and reduce the work-in-process to 20 hours. However, the equipment performed erratically during Weeks 31 and 32 and output falls short as shown in Table 14–11. First, everything should be done to rectify the equipment problem; but in the meantime planned input and output should be reduced. Maintaining the present input level will only maintain the high work-in-process and hinder production. Planned output should be based on the actual capacity of approximately 1.6 standard hours per clock hour. Thus, as shown in Table 14–11, 60 hours of input, 80 hours of output, 10 hours overtime are planned for Week 33. If the equipment operates properly and produces two standard hours per hour (100 for the week), sufficient work-in-process exists to prevent machine downtime due to lack of work. The principles of input/output control are:

1. The planned output should realistically represent equipment and labor capacity.
2. A planned or actual input greater than the realistic output will increase WIP, hinder production, and increase manufacturing lead times.

Table 14–11 Input/Output Control: Decreased Output

	Week			
	30	31	32	33
Input				
Planned		80	80	60
Actual		80	80	
Cumulative deviation		0	0	
Output				
Planned		100	100	80
Actual		85	76	
Cumulative deviation		−15	−24	
Work-in-Process (end of week)				
Planned	60	40	20	39
Actual	60	55	59	

Note: All values are in standard hours

Figure 14–2 Order Flow Patterns in a Job Shop

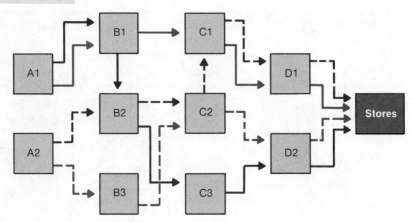

Multiple Work Centers

Work flow through multiple work centers is often represented schematically. Two formats are commonly used, the flow-by-order format and the flow-by-volume format. Figure 14–2 is a schematic representation of four possible order flow patterns in a job shop with ten work centers. Work centers A1 and A2 are gateway work centers. The first operation is performed in one of these two work centers. Work Centers B1, B2, B3, C1, C2, and C3 are intermediate centers, and D1 and D2 are the finishing or final work centers. All work centers except gateway centers also are called downstream work centers. We will examine I/O control at each type of work center. Figure 14–3 is a schematic of the flow patterns Kettner and Bechte (1981) found in a large complex job shop. Although this schematic does not show separate orders, it does use the width of the channels to show the proportional work flow volume between work centers.

One of the primary management control processes for input/output control is the dispatch list or order release, a hard copy or computer screen that lists work orders in priority sequence daily for each work center. Additionally, the dispatch list often contains detailed information on the priority, location, resources, quantity, and capacity requirements of each order by operation. The dispatch list reflects the orders that have been released (or approved) for production.

GATEWAY WORK CENTER CONTROL. Management of the release of orders controls the input, queues, and WIP at gateway work centers. If the work center is running smoothly, output also is controlled. The input to the gateway work centers also influences inputs to downstream work centers. There is little reason to have a long queue at the gateway work center. Keeping

Figure 14–3   Funnel Model of a Job Shop

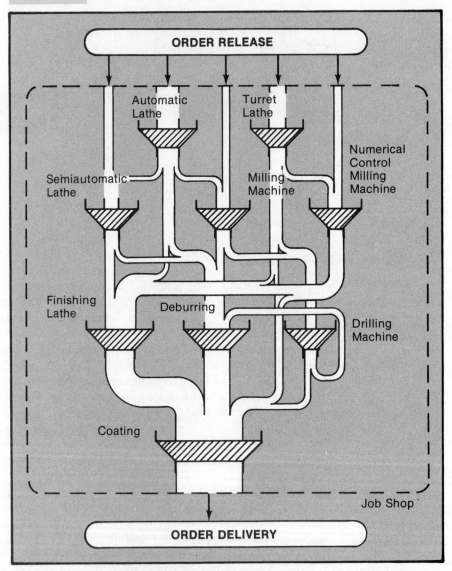

gateway queues at a minimum enables the dispatcher to use the latest available information when establishing order release priorities. It also reduces WIP and expediting.

DOWNSTREAM WORK CENTER CONTROL. The input and queues at downstream work centers are controlled by dispatching (order sequencing) at upstream work centers in the process flow. For example, if Work Center C3 in Figure 14–2 is running short of work, while there is a relatively large queue of high-priority orders at Work Center C2, priority in Work Center B2 should be given to orders going to C3 next. This requires that order release decisions recognize the needs of downstream work centers as well as the gateway work centers, and of course, other factors such as due dates.

FINAL WORK CENTER CONTROL. Output of the final work centers influences shipments, due date performance, billings, accounts receivable, and cash flow. Final output usually is one of the dominant measures of production management performance. Controlling the final work center input is necessary to achieve the desired output. This involves coordinating the flow of parts, items, and subassemblies required in final assemblies. Thus, dispatching must also be concerned with achieving control of the volume and specific items entering the final work centers. In some complex job shops, large-scale computer simulations are used to provide completion-oriented priority control, extending backward from the final work center to gateway operations (Lankford 1978).

ORDER RELEASE

Order release initiates the execution phase of production; it authorizes production and/or purchasing. The planned order becomes a released order (or open order). Placement of a purchase order or the initiation of manufacturing follows shortly. Order release planning (see Chapter 13) may take place until the moment of order release. Authorization of order release is based on priority, the availability of materials and tooling, and the loads specified by I/O planning. Release of an order triggers the release of the following:

1. *Requisitions for material and components required by the order.* If some of these items are not required immediately and have not been allocated previously, they should be allocated now.
2. *Production order documentation to the plant.* This documentation may include a set of both engineering drawings and manufacturing specifications and a manufacturing routing sheet.
3. *Requisitions for tools required in the first week or so of production.* Tooling, including tapes for numerically controlled machines, required in later operations is reserved—if not already reserved—for the appropriate period. Tooling can be included in the master production schedule and the item bill of materials; its availability is thus coordinated with material and equipment availability.

The time required to deliver production order documentation, tooling, and materials to the first operation is included in the normal planned lead time for the order. Once an order has been released, it is added to the dispatch list.

DISPATCHING

Dispatching informs first-line supervision of the released orders, the priority of available tasks, and the sequence in which orders should be run. This information can be transmitted via a hard copy (handwritten, typed, or computer printout) or via video output on a cathode ray tube (CRT); telephone and face-to-face conversation also can be used but do not document the decisions. A dispatch list should be prepared for each work center with the frequency of updating depending on the typical order-processing time. If orders take a day or less to process, dispatch lists usually are prepared daily. If they take a few days, lists may be prepared weekly with midweek revisions handled on an exception basis with on-line processing. In a flow line process environment, a single list indicating the rate of flow (or in a batch flow line, which orders are to be started) will control work on the entire line, which may be viewed as a single work center. Table 14–12 is an example of simple dispatch list information. It identifies the date, the plant, and the work center; it includes the work center capacity and lists the orders, their quantity, their capacity requirements, and their priority. Orders usually are listed in descending priority for a specified period.

The planner determines the final dispatch list ranking of orders on the basis of multiple criteria including a formal priority index such as the critical ratio or scheduled start date, input control at downstream work centers, the availability of tooling, the status of other parts required in the same next assembly, energy consumption patterns, and sequencing and assignment criteria. For example, if the next operations for orders S-4276 and S-4518 were at work centers heavily loaded with high priority orders, while the next operation for Order S-4625 was at an idle work center, then order S-4625 may be processed first in spite of its CR or scheduled start date on this operation. In addition, if energy costs of production are relatively high, scheduling rules may schedule orders to minimize energy consumption peaks (Baker 1979).

Few dispatching decisions can be made in a totally programmed or automatic fashion. A computer can provide valuable assistance by keeping an

Table 14–12 Dispatch List Information

Part Number	Order Number	Quantity	Standard Hours per Unit	Total Standard Hours	CR Priority
9706	S-4276	200	.3	60	.6
B1319	S-4518	100	.8	80	1.0
H4276	S-4625	120	1.5	180	1.3

Plant 02; Date 7/1; Department 27; Work Center M3; Capacity 85 hours accurate record or order status. It can also provide an inquiry capability, responding to the requests of managers and planners concerning the status of any order. However, the dispatcher must exercise judgment in balancing operating costs and customer service when determining the final priority of orders. Often local rules, or heuristics, are developed to simplify and structure scheduling policies.

PRODUCTION REPORTING

Reports describing the actual production status are necessary for control. Dynamic response to changing conditions is possible only if timely, accurate, and adequate information is available. The information must enable management to take meaningful corrective action concerning production schedules.

The process environment influences the design of the production reporting system. Reporting in a continuous process plant may take place on an exception basis with feedback occurring only when the output rate falls below an acceptable level. All reporting systems should have an exception reporting capability informing management whenever machine failure, material shortages, or similar events threaten planned output.

Parts fabrication in a job shop environment requires more data collection for control than continuous processes or repetitive manufacturing of discrete parts. Once a flow process is initiated, it will continue smoothly unless machine failure, employee absenteeism, scrap, a materials shortage, or production inefficiencies occur. Exception reporting usually works well in these circumstances. Flow in a job shop is more complex; order status estimates are less certain. Thus, the processing and movement of orders does not automatically follow their release into the production stream as do orders in a flow process. Control in a job shop usually requires information concerning the following:

1. The release of orders
2. The beginning and completion of operations
3. The movement of orders
4. The availability of processing information, tooling, and material
5. The queues in each work center

Exception reporting is frequently adequate for controlling the availability of information required for processing, tooling, and material. Reporting both the beginning and completion of operations is appropriate when the total operation times are relatively long. For example, if the estimated completion time of processing a lot of parts through a particular operation was four days, reporting initiation of the operation makes sense. On the other hand, if an operation requires only an hour and one-half, reporting its completion should be sufficient.

Figure 14–4   Reporting Ticket

ML605	30				
Part No.	Oper. No.	Quantity	Start	Finish	
95620		29			
Order No.	Operator No.	Dept.	Scrap	Supervisor	

(Some information is preprinted on a form; other information is added by an operator. Frequently a supervisor checks the accuracy of information.)

Data Collection

On-line reporting systems directly report events as they occur usually via a data terminal or other device capable of electronically transmitting the data to a centralized recording station. Such data is called real-time information since the records are updated instantaneously. Whether an organization requires real-time information as provided by on-line processing or whether periodic reporting (by shift, day, or week) is sufficient for the desired control depends on the situation.

In some cases the operator reports the initiation or completion of an operation, order movement, and so forth via a data terminal or by completing an operation reporting form included in the job packet. (Figure 14–4 is an example of a reporting ticket). In other cases the supervisor or timekeeper is responsible for reporting this information.

Typical Reports

The status of WIP, inventory availability, and work center queues and utilization influences order release and dispatching decisions. When an on-line, real-time reporting system exists with inquiry capability, then management, dispatchers, and planners can obtain current status information virtually instantaneously. The response to their inquiry may be presented on a video output device and/or produced on a hard copy output. If on-line capability does not exist, daily status reports are required in most cases. In all cases, periodic summary reports are required to evaluate production performance.

The following information should be available to planners on either a real-time or periodic basis:

1. *Released order status* (see Table 14–13). This report gives the status of every order that has been released physically—dispatched—to the plant including

part number, description, quantity, order release date, order due date, operations completed, order location, quantity scrapped, and quantity good.

2. *Unreleased order status* (see Table 14–14). This report lists all orders whose release is past due. The cause of their delayed release also is noted—for example, long queues of higher priority order at gateway work centers, lack of required tooling, or lack of required material or parts.

3. *Dispatch list—priority scheduling report* (see Table 14–12). This report lists in priority sequence all orders in each department plus those expected to arrive shortly—perhaps in the next day. Standard hours required for processing also are listed.

4. *Weekly I/O by department* (see Table 14–9).

5. *Exception reports.* These should be designed to meet the needs of the organization. Possible exception reports include a scrap report, a rework report, and a late orders report as illustrated in Figure 14–5. A review of scrap reports will reveal if quality problems are recurrent with a particular item, operation, or operator. They also can trigger the release of new orders or a quantity increase on unreleased orders for the same item. The rework report also can alert management to quality problems and unplanned capacity

Figure 14–5   Exception Reports (Examples)

A. Scrap Report (weekly, daily, or by exception)

Order Number	Part Number	Quantity	Operation	Cause
M7240	2784	12	30	Operator error
M6843	6813	5	60	Welding fixture out of alignment

B. Rework Report (Items Requiring Rework)

Order Number	Part Number	Quantity	Operation(s)	Cause
M6927	B8315	30	40 & 50	Eng. change
M7435	B8316	40	40 & 50	Eng. change

C. Late Orders Report (or Delayed orders Report)
Date: 5/7

Order Number	Part Number	Quantity	Due Date	Operation Time Remaining	Queue Time Remaining	Cause
6895	R7516	100	5/7	2	2	Matl. late
6743	C8319	75	5/14	4	3	Scrap
7013	67059	120	5/17	6	6	Machine down
6985	28076	40	5/20	8	8	Tool late

Table 14-13 Released Order Status Report

Date 5/24/83 (275)					Planned			Actual		Location (Work Center)	MLTR*
Part Number	Description	Order Number	Quantity On Order	Quantity Completed	Release Date	Due Date	Release Date	Completion Date			
P865	Pin	952931	80	—	270	290	270	—		17	15
B6803	Bushing	956735	160	—	275	292	270	—		21	10
R6027	Ring gear	959063	40	—	260	294	265	—		9	29

*MLTR—manufacturing lead time remaining (days)

Table 14-14 Unreleased Order Status Report

Date 5/24/83 (275)				Planned[1]			
Part Number	Description	Order Number	Order Type	Quantity	Release Date	Due Date	Cause[2]
SA9502	Value assembly	957021	M	100	270	280	LOC
SA6807	Switch assembly	968052	M	250	265	275	WCOL
ES3750	Gear	968090	P	500	270	290	VOL
B6750	Bracket	970211	M	200	250	280	TNA

[1]Gregorian dates have been converted to shop calendar dates.
[2]Typical codes: LOC—lack of component; WCOL—work center overload; VOL—vendor overloaded; TNA—tooling not available.

requirements. The purpose of the late orders report is to inform management of orders that require expediting and possibly of customers who should be informed of late delivery. If the late orders list is extensive, the possibility of a capacity problem or an unrealistic MPS should be investigated. The late orders report should focus on a number of orders that can be expedited efficiently and that have high priority.

6. *Performance summary report.* The performance summary report should state the number and percentage of orders completed on schedule during a specific period—week or month—and the lateness of a late order. A late orders aging report, similar to an accounts receivable aging report, will reveal the magnitude of any delivery problems. Performance also should be reported in terms of volume—tons, units, feet, etc.—or dollars. The causes of late orders also should be tabulated.

The types of reports possible are many and varied. This chapter has included only some of them. Too many reports diminish the value of each. Different situations require different information and different organization of that information.

CONCLUSIONS

Production activity control is concerned with converting plans into action, reporting the results achieved, and revising plans and actions as required to achieve desired results. Thus, PAC converts plans into action by providing the required direction. This requires the appropriate prior master planning of orders, work force personnel, materials, and capacity requirements.

Order release, dispatching, and progress reporting are the three primary functions of PAC. Dispatching is the activation of orders per original plans, and those dispatching decisions are affected by queue management, I/O control, and priority control principles and techniques that are intertwined and mutually supportive. They are useful in the management of lead time, queue length, work center idle time, and scheduled order completion. Reports on the status of orders, materials, queues, tooling, and work center utilization are essential for control. Many report types with a variety of information are possible. Examining a given situation will reveal which reports and information are required.

QUESTIONS

1. What are the scheduling objectives of manufacturing flow lines, batch flow lines, and runout scheduling?

2. Differentiate scheduling and sequencing.

3. Identify four scheduling objectives.

4. List five priority rules for operations sequencing and give an example where each applies.

5. Identify several factors that make service sector scheduling different from manufacturing scheduling.

6. Give several ways to adjust the rules of work schedules for highly erratic scheduling requirements.

7. Why are the cumulative input and output deviations important?

8. What is a gateway work center? Should such a center be managed like an individual work center?

9. What information do flow-by-order and flow-by-volume work flow schematics depict?

10. How would order release rules be adjusted to consider multiple work centers?

11. When should the production activity control to release orders change them from planned orders to released orders?

12. Why is it advisable to have hard copies of the dispatch list? How often should dispatch lists be prepared?

13. How does dispatching to a line flow differ from dispatching to a job shop?

14. How does production reporting differ in a flow shop versus a job shop?

15. In a job shop, when is exception production reporting appropriate?

PROBLEMS

1. Determine the slack time and critical ratio for each of the orders in the table at the top of page 503. Compute the processing sequence for the orders using the SOT, STP, EDD, FO, ST, and CR techniques.

Scheduling Priority, Department 12, Day 105							
Order	Due Date	Current Operating Time	Total Operating Time Remaining	Mfg. Lead Time Remaining	Number of Operations Remaining	Slack Time	Critical Ratio
A	117	0.5	5.5	9.0	3		
B	112	1.5	6.0	11.0	4		
C	109	1.0	3.0	6.0	2		
D	109	2.0	4.0	6.0	2		

Note: All times are in days

2. The Bensonville Foundry has received orders for five different finished castings. A finished casting must first be molded, then burnished, then plated, and then polished—a four-step operation. The production data for the five jobs is as follows:

Bensonville Foundry—Scheduling Priority—Date 138							
Order	Due Date	Current Operating Time	Total Operating Time Remaining	Mfg. Lead Time Remaining	Number of Operations Remaining	Slack Time	Critical Ratio
210	141	2.1	4.1	− 1.1	3		
211	156	6.0	9.0	9.0	2		
212	171	5.1	16.2	16.8	3		
213	163	6.4	11.4	13.6	4		
214	148	3.2	6.8	3.2	1		

Determine the slack time and critical ratio for each of the orders; compute the processing sequence for these orders using the SOT, STP, EDD, FO, ST, and CR techniques.

3. From the data below determine the priority for sequencing using the manufacturing-lead-time-remaining technique:

Day 67

Order	Due	Actual Time Remaining	Mfg. Lead Time Remaining	Days Behind/ Ahead of Schedule	Priority
A	79	12	9		
B	77	10	8		
C	71	4	7		
D	74	7	8		

4. From the data below determine the priority for sequencing using the processing-time-remaining technique:

Day 67

Order	Date	Actual Time Remaining	Processing Time Remaining	Days Behind/ Ahead of Schedule	Priority
A	79	12	6		
B	77	10	8		
C	71	4	5		
D	74	7	4		

5. From the data below determine the priority for sequencing using the manufacturing-lead-time-remaining technique:

Day 265

Order	Due	Actual Time Remaining	Mfg. Lead Time Remaining	Days Behind/ Ahead of Schedule	Priority
154	289		20		
155	274		14		
156	277		9		
157	274		11		
158	279		17		
158	281		13		

6. From the data below determine the priority for sequencing using the processing-time-remaining technique:

Day 265

Order	Due	Actual Time Remaining	Processing Time Remaining	Days Behind/ Ahead of Schedule	Priority
154	289		20		
155	274		12		
156	277		6		
157	274		10		
158	279		15		
158	281		9		

7. A large department store requires between three and seven salespeople per day in the men's department as shown. Use the seven-day scheduling algorithm to determine how the salespeople should be scheduled while giving them two consecutive days off. How many employees are needed? What is the schedule?

	Sun.	Mon.	Tue.	Wed.	Thur.	Fri.	Sat.
Number of employees	6	3	5	6	5	7	7

8. Edward's All Cloth car wash uses employees to do the final detailing of customer's cars. Although business can vary depending on the weather, the average number of cars per hour over the past twelve weeks is shown below. If employees can detail only eight cars per hour, schedule the labor requirements. Use the seven-day scheduling algorithm.

	Sun.	Mon.	Tue.	Wed.	Thur.	Fri.	Sat.
Number of cars per hour	62	18	24	21	27	56	68

9. Use the following data to answer the questions below:

	Week				
	10	11	12	13	14
Input					
Planned	65	65	65	65	60
Actual	64	67	66	66	61
Outputs					
Planned	65	65	65	65	65
Actual	67	66	66	65	64
Work-in-process (end of week)					
Planned	25	25	25	25	20

   a. What is the actual WIP at the end of Week 12?
   b. What is the cumulative input deviation at the end of Week 13?
   c. What is the cumulative output deviation at the end of Week 14?
   d. What is the actual WIP at the end of Week 14?

10. From the following data

	Week					
	32	33	34	35	36	37
Input						
Planned	25	25	25	25	25	25
Actual	24	23	24	25	24	25
Outputs						
Planned	25	25	25	25	25	25
Actual	23	23	23	24	24	25
Work-in-process (end of week)						
Planned	10	10	10	10	10	10

a. Compute the cumulative input deviation.
b. Compute the cumulative output deviation.
c. Compute the planned WIP.
d. Compute the actual WIP.
e. What is the actual WIP on a weekly basis?

11. Using the data in Problem 10, if an equipment failure occurred during Week 34 and actual output was reduced to 12 units, adjust the plan to keep the process in control. Plant engineering has assured management that the equipment will be operational by the beginning of week 35.

REFERENCES

Baker, Eugene F., "Flow Management the 'Take Charge' Shop Floor Control System." *1979 APICS Conference Proceedings*, pp. 169–174.

Bechte, Wolfgang, "Load Oriented Order Release." *1988 APICS Conference Proceedings*.

Browne, James J. and Rajen K. Tibrewala, "Manpower Scheduling." *Industrial Engineering*. (August, 1975), pp. 22-3.

Fogarty, Donald W. and Thomas R. Hoffmann, *Production and Inventory Management*. Cincinnati: South-Western, 1983.

Kettner, Von Hans and Wolfgang Bechte, "Neue Wege der Fertigungs-steurung durch belastungsorientierte Auftragsfreigabe." *VDI-Z (Society of German Engineers Journal)* Vol. 123, No. 11 (1981), pp. 459-466.

Lankford, Raymond L., "Short-Term Planning of Manufacturing Capacity." *1978 APICS Conference Proceedings*, pp. 37–68.

——— "Scheduling the Job Shop." *1973 APICS Conference Proceedings*, pp. 46–65.

Melnyk, Steven A. and Phillip L. Carter., "Identifying the Principles of Effective Production Activity Control." *1986 APICS Conference Proceedings*, pp. 227–231.

Melnyk, Steven A. et al., *Shop Floor Control*. Homewood, Ill. Dow Jones-Irwin, 1987.

Wasseiler, William L., "Fundamentals of Shop Floor Control." *1980 APICS Conference Proceedings*, pp. 352–354.

Wight, Oliver W., "Input-Output Control, A Real Handle on Lead Time." *Production and Inventory Management*. (3rd quarter, 1970): 9–31.

CHAPTER 15
PROJECT MANAGEMENT (PERT/CPM)

OBJECTIVES

After completing this chapter, you should be able to

- Identify those characteristics that are unique to projects

- Understand how to construct and analyze a network planning diagram

- Use statistical activity times to analyze a PERT network

- Understand the process of crashing a particular expected project completion time, and the constraints of crashing

- Identify the principles of project control

OUTLINE

INTRODUCTION

Project evaluation and review technique (PERT) and critical path method (CPM) have received acclaim and acceptance across the industrial spectrum. The primary reasons for this broad and enthusiastic reception are:

1. The principles underlying the procedure followed in applying these techniques are transparently clear.
2. The techniques provide an integrated approach to project planning, scheduling, and control that does work.
3. Plans and schedules can be developed in the detail warranted by the complexity of the project and by the degree of control desired.
4. The principles and procedures are applicable to projects of all types including such diverse activities as research, engineering design, construction, fabrication of an assembly line, preparation of a dinner, major surgery, the rebuilding of a blast furnace, installation of a new management information system, and the increase of production output by the addition of a second shift.

In manufacturing, these techniques are especially useful in planning and controlling the production of items that are custom designed around basic models to meet the special requirements of individual customers. The production cycle for such items usually includes design and production engineering activities as well as fabrication processes. This situation is common in the production of large equipment items such as material-handling systems, truck bodies for utility companies, and industrial cleaning equipment.

Project management techniques are also helpful in the following types of operations management activities:

1. Short-range planning—crew changes, equipment startups and teardowns
2. Increasing capacity—reducing planned maintenance time
3. Calculating manufacturing lead time—based on critical path of purchasing, fabrication, and assembly
4. Reducing work in process—reducing the critical path of fabrication and assembly.

Project management techniques are also widely applicable in service organizations, where many types of service outputs can be viewed as projects. Examples include the management of a consulting contract, the creation of a television program, and the introduction of a new banking service.

A PROJECT

Certain characteristics distinguish those tasks most suitable for the application of project management techniques. These characteristics include the following:

1. Projects have a definite beginning and end. The building of a new plant, the hiring and training of an additional labor crew, the design and fabrication of

tooling for a new product, the installation of a new (substantially redesigned) information system—all possess this characteristic. Whereas installing a new assembly line and producing the first acceptable lot constitutes a project, running that assembly line for the next month or year is more appropriately viewed as an ongoing, repetitive nonproject activity.

2. Project activities are one-at-a-time activities for the most part, isolated by either time or space. The fabrication of a single, large pressure vessel might be planned and controlled using project management techniques; planning and controlling the fabrication and assembly of ten such vessels at the same facility within the same time requires increased application of the principles and techniques discussed in the chapters concerning medium- and short-range planning.

3. Projects can be subdivided into activities that have definite beginnings and ends; that is, the nature of the process does not require that activities be initiated immediately upon completion of the preceding activity, as is the case in certain refining processes where the next step must begin immediately due to the inability of the material to retain a chemical or physical property for any period without incurring substantial additional expense during a holding phase. Thus, the making of steel, the refining of gasoline, and the production of ice cream are not suited for the application of project management techniques, whereas the launching of a space shot, the construction of a nuclear submarine, and the teardown, cleaning, and restarting of a bottling line are.

4. The activities that must be performed to complete the project have a definite sequential relationship. There are known technological factors that require certain activities to be completed before others and that allow other activities to be performed simultaneously. Thus, each activity can be defined with respect to every other activity as preceding, succeeding, or independent. Two activities that are independent may be performed in any order with respect to each other.

5. An estimate of the time required to complete each activity is available. These times are based on an assumed rate of the use of material, personnel, and equipment. For example, a time estimate to fabricate an assembly fixture is based on the use of personnel and equipment with certain capabilities and the availability of the material and information required for fabrication.

BACKGROUND

PERT was developed jointly by members of Booz, Allen and Hamilton and the Navy's Special Project Office while planning the research, design, fabrication, and testing necessary for the production of the first nuclear submarine. They studied existing project management techniques and found none adequate for such a complex project. Application of PERT to the Polaris submarine project was one of the key factors for it being completed two years prior to the originally scheduled due date.

At about the same time, J. E. Kelley, Jr. of the Univac Division of Remington Rand, and Morgan Walker of DuPont, working independently of the Polaris group, developed CPM as a result of a study concerning the planning and

Figure 15–1   Gantt Chart

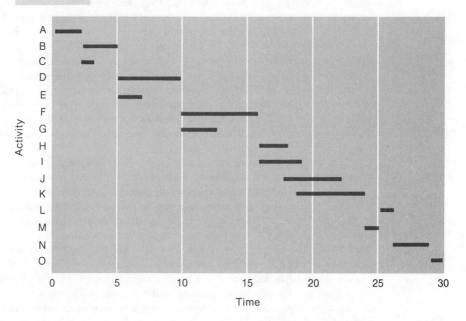

control of chemical plant maintenance. There are many similarities between PERT and CPM in their original form and some essential differences, which we will discuss later. However, real-world applications frequently incorporate features of both techniques in a hybrid fashion as desired by project management.

The forerunner of PERT and CPM was the Gantt chart developed by Henry Gantt around 1910. As illustrated in Figure 15–1 (which is based on activities listed in Table 15–1), the Gantt chart is a graph with time on the horizontal axis and activities on the vertical axis. The following example used to illustrate these techniques has been taken from a real-world situation with minor changes for the sake of simplicity. No changes have been made in essential characteristics.

DEVELOPING A NETWORK PLANNING MODEL

The firm whose activities are described in Table 15–1 and Figure 15–1 produces material-handling systems. Some are standard assemblies fabricated to catalog specifications, while others are custom designed and fabricated to meet customer requirements. The activities described in Table 15–1 are required to complete the fabrication of a specific custom-designed order. Figure 15–1 is a Gantt chart for these activities. We use this situation to illustrate the process of developing a network model.

Table 15–1 Design, Fabrication, and Assembly Planning Data

Symbol	Activity Description	Activities Preceding	Activities Concurrent	Activities Following	Requirements (Weeks)
A	Mechanical design (1)	None	None	B, C	2
B	Mechanical design (2)	A	C	E, D	3
C	Electrical design (1)	A	B, E	D	1
D	Electrical design (2)	B, C	E	F, G	5
E	Mechanical fabrication (1)	B	C, D, F, G	H, I	2
F	Mechanical fabrication (2)	D	E, G	H, I	6
G	Electrical fabrication (1)	D	E, F, I	H	3
H	Electrical fabrication (2)	E, F, G	I	J, K	2
I	Mechanical subassembly (1)	E, F	H, G, J	K	3
J	Mechanical subassembly (2)	H	K, I	M	4
K	Electrical installation (1)	H, I	J	M	5
L	Electrical installation (2)	M	None	N	1
M	Piping installation (1)	J, K	None	L	1
N	Piping installation (2)	L	None	O	3
O	Startup, test, and ship	N	None	None	1

In general, the starting point of each activity corresponds to the finishing point of the activity that directly precedes it. However, if an activity has more than one preceding activity, then care must be taken in preparing a Gantt chart. Perhaps the most critical step, the one in which planning errors occur most frequently in preparing a Gantt chart, is accurately recording the starting points of activities that have more than one preceding activity. For example, Activity H cannot begin until Activities E, F, and G have been completed. The temptation is to chart Activity H immediately upon completion of Activity G, rather than waiting for Activity F, the last of the predecessors, to be completed.

The Gantt chart is a powerful aid in planning relatively simple projects although it does not provide the insight that the network scheduling models such as PERT and CPM do. The Gantt chart does, however, reveal the normal length of the project: thirty weeks in the case of the example in Figure 15–1. The advantages of network scheduling models that incorporate the concepts and techniques of PERT and CPM over the Gantt chart and other similar techniques are as follows:

1. Explicit representation of the sequential relationship between the activities that must be performed to complete the project
2. Ease in determining the critical path; i.e., the longest path (connected sequence of activities) from the beginning to the end of the project
3. Ease in determining the individual activities whose completion on schedule is not critical to completion of the entire project on schedule
4. Ability to determine the impact on project completion of the probability of different activities being completed in less or more time than the most likely time estimate

First, we will develop a network with attributes common to both CPM and PERT, then we will describe those characteristics that differentiate these two techniques. As noted earlier, features of both can be combined in real-world applications as long as the required data and information-processing capabilities are available. The steps in building a network planning model are to (1) obtain the necessary input data, (2) construct the network model, and (3) determine the critical path.

Data Requirements

The necessary input data include a list of the activities that constitute the project, the time required to complete each activity, and the sequential relationships of the activities. The CPM approach uses deterministic (fixed) activity times. The PERT method, as shown later, uses statistical (variable) activity times. Table 15–1 illustrates the input data required to construct a network model. As might be expected, the efficacy of the planning and control decisions that result from the use of the network model are directly affected by the accuracy and completeness of the input data. (Grossly inaccurate or incomplete data lead to inadequate and unrealistic plans.)

It is not unusual to reorganize input data when developing the network. For example, the original data sheet for the material-handling system included all mechanical design activities under one activity. Discussions between planning and engineering representatives working together on development of the network revealed that electrical design activities could begin at a point where mechanical design activities were only partially complete. This led to the decision to divide mechanical design into two activities: mechanical design (1) and mechanical design (2). Developing the network model frequently provides added understanding and improved planning and execution of the project.

Constructing the Network

A network model is formed by connecting the symbols (arrows in this case) representing sequential activities in accordance with the input data. The arrows are connected to numbered nodes (junctions). These nodes represent events—that is, the completion of one activity and the beginning of another. Figure 15–2 includes the various symbols used in activity-on-the-arrow networks. The activity-on-the-node method will be briefly discussed later.

Constructing the network begins with identifying in Table 15–1 the activity (or activities) that has no predecessors and connecting it to the activities that follow it immediately (as illustrated in Figure 15–3). Activity A has no predecessors, and Activities B and C follow it immediately. The next step is to add the arrows for those activities that immediately follow the followers of the initial activity. Table 15–1 reveals that Activity B immediately precedes Activities D and E; and that Activity C is also an immediate predecessor

Figure 15–2   Network Modeling Symbols and Conventions

Figure 15–2   Network Modeling Symbols and Conventions

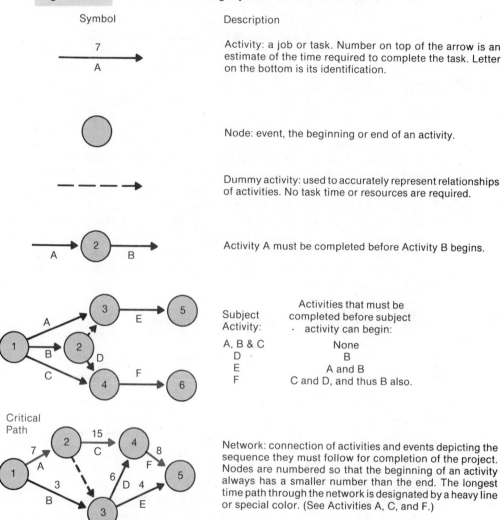

Symbol

Description

Activity: a job or task. Number on top of the arrow is an estimate of the time required to complete the task. Letter on the bottom is its identification.

Node: event, the beginning or end of an activity.

Dummy activity: used to accurately represent relationships of activities. No task time or resources are required.

Activity A must be completed before Activity B begins.

Subject Activity:	Activities that must be completed before subject activity can begin:
A, B & C	None
D	B
E	A and B
F	C and D, and thus B also.

Network: connection of activities and events depicting the sequence they must follow for completion of the project. Nodes are numbered so that the beginning of an activity always has a smaller number than the end. The longest time path through the network is designated by a heavy line or special color. (See Activities A, C, and F.)

of Activity E. These relationships require the use of an additional symbol, a dummy arrow, as illustrated in Figure 15–4.

Dummy activities do not represent a task; they require no time; nor do they use any resources. They are used to represent precedence requirements accurately and to uniquely identify activities. Without the dummy activity, for example, the network in Figure 15–5 might be interpreted to mean that both Activities B and C must be completed before either Activity D or E can begin. This is inaccurate.

Construction of the network follows in this fashion until all activities are

Figure 15–3   Initiation of a Network

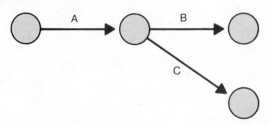

represented. A number is then assigned to each node so that the node at the start (tail) of each activity (arrow) has a smaller number than the node at the finish (head). This rule is important in using computer programs that identify activities by their node numbers (i, j—where i represents the start and j the finish of each arrow) and whose logic is based on i being less than j. For example, Activity A is denoted by (1,2). If one cannot assign the numbers in this manner, there is an inconsistency in the stated precedence relationships and they should be reviewed to determine the error. Note that the dummy activities have also been labeled.

Figure 15–4   Network Development Continued

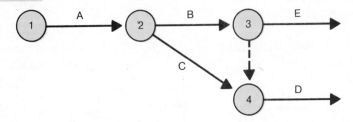

Determining the Critical Path

Complete development of the network per the data contained in Table 15–1 is shown in Figure 15–6. The time estimate for each activity has

Figure 15–5   The Network Without a Dummy Activity
(An Inaccurate Representation)

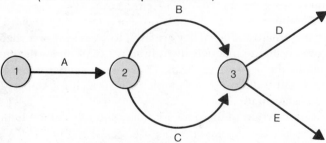

Figure 15-6   Network Model

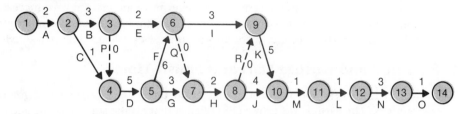

been added on top of each arrow to facilitate determination of the critical path.

Determination of the critical path involves defining each possible path from the start of the project to its finish, then calculating the length of each path, and, finally, determining the longest path. The longest path is the critical path because the completion of activities on this path determines whether or not the project is completed on schedule. On the other hand, if activities not on the critical path fall behind schedule, it is still possible to complete the project on schedule.

Table 15–2 lists the different paths that can be followed from the start to the finish of the project as illustrated by the network model of Figure 15–6. Comparing the lengths of these paths reveals that the critical path consists of Activities A, B, P, D, F, I, K, M, L, N, and O with a length of 30 weeks.

Two other things also are immediately apparent. First, since activities A, M, L, N, and O are on each path, they must be part of the critical path. If the path lengths were being calculated manually, these activities could be omitted until the longest length of the other segments was determined. They would then be added to determine the critical path length. The second obvious conclusion is that even in relatively simple situations, such as this

Table 15–2   Activity Paths in Figure 15–6 and Their Lengths

Number	Description (Activities)	Length (Weeks)
1	A, B, E, I, K, M, L, N, O	21
2	A, B, E, Q, H, R, K, M, L, N, O	20
3	A, B, E, Q, H, J, M, L, N, O	20
4	A, B, P, D, G, H, J, M, L, N, O	25
5	A, B, P, D, G, H, R, K, M, L, N, O	26
6	A, B, P, D, F, Q, H, J, M, L, N, O	28
7	A, B, P, D, F, Q, H, R, K, M, L, N, O	29
8*	A, B, P, D, F, I, K, M, L, N, O	30
9	A, C, D, G, H, J, M, L, N, O	26
10	A, C, D, G, H, R, K, M, L, N, O	23
11	A, C, D, F, Q, H, J, M, L, N, O	26
12	A, C, D, F, Q, H, F, K, M, L, N, O	27
13	A, C, D, F, I, K, M, L, N, O	28

*Critical path

example, there can be many possible paths. As the complexity of the project increases, the calculations required to determine the critical path increase at an even greater rate. Use of a computer program facilitates determination of the critical path and other attributes such as slack (float) time per activity.

Latest and Earliest Start and Finish Times

The earliest and latest start and finish times can be calculated for each activity. The earliest start time (ES) of an activity is the sum of all the activities on the longest path to that activity. It is the earliest time an activity can begin, given that all preceding activities on this path begin as early as possible. Referring to the network in Figure 15–6, the ES for Activity I (6,9) is 16 weeks from the beginning of the project. This is based on the time to complete Activities A, B, P, D, and F, the longest path to Activity I. The earliest finish time (EF) of an activity is equal to its earliest start time plus its activity time. For example, the earliest finish time for Activity I is 19 weeks. The latest finish time (LF) of an activity is equal to the scheduled project completion time minus the time requirements of the longest path from the end of that activity to the completion of the project. For example, the LF for Activity B is 30 − 25, or 5, and the LF for Activity C is also 5. The latest start time (LS) for an activity is the latest time it can be started without delaying completion of the project. The LS of an activity is equal to the scheduled project completion time minus the time requirements of the longest path from the end of that activity to the completion of the project and the activity time. Or, more simply, it is the latest finish time minus activity time. Referring again to the network in Figure 15–6, the LS of Activity B is 30 − 28, where 30 is the length of the critical path and 28 is the time required to complete Activities B, P, D, F, I, K, M, L, N, and O. The ES, EF, LS, and LF of all activities in Figure 15–6 are listed in Table 15–3.

Slack (Float) Time

The term slack describes the amount of delay an activity can experience without affecting project completion. Whenever the desired project completion time is equal to the time requirements of activities on the critical path, as is the case in the example illustrated in Figure 15–6, all activities on the critical path have zero slack.

There are two types of slack, total slack and free slack. Total slack is the amount of time that completion of an activity can slip and the project still be completed on schedule—given that all the other activities are completed on schedule. It is equal to LS − ES, or to LF − EF. Total slack may include free slack and slack shared with another activity. Free slack is defined as the amount of time the completion of an activity can slip and not delay the start of any subsequent activity.

For example, the total slack of Activity G in Figure 15–6 is 4 (17 − 13). Note that one week of Activity G's four weeks of slack is shared with Activity

Table 15–3   Activity, ES, LS, EF, LF, and Slack Times (In Weeks)

Actvity	Duration	ES	LS	EF	LF	Total Slack	Free Slack
A	2	0	0	2	2	0	0
B	3	2	2	5	5	0	0
C	1	2	4	3	5	2	2
D	5	5	5	10	10	0	0
E	2	5	14	7	16	9	9
F	6	10	10	16	16	0	0
G	3	10	14	13	17	4	3
H	2	16	17	18	19	1	0
I	3	16	16	19	19	0	0
J	4	18	20	22	24	2	2
K	5	19	19	24	24	0	0
L	1	25	25	26	26	0	0
M	1	24	24	25	25	0	0
N	3	26	26	29	29	0	0
O	1	29	29	30	30	0	0
P	0	5	5	5	5	0	0
Q	0	16	17	16	17	1	0
R	0	18	19	18	19	1	1

H. If the actual completion of G slips four weeks, H has no slack and must be completed without slippage to reach Node 9 in 19 weeks (the LS of Activity I). If, however, the completion of G slips three weeks or takes place on schedule, then Activity H has one week of slack. Thus, Activity G has four weeks of total slack and three weeks of free slack.

An alternative method of determining the critical path makes use of these concepts of ES and LS. By examining Figure 15-6, the ES for each activity can be computed by moving from left to right through each node, assuming the project starts at time zero. Then the LS for each activity can be computed by moving from right to left assuming the last event takes place at project completion time. The critical path is then noted as the sequence of activities for which the earliest and latest start times are equal—that is, those that have zero slack. This is summarized as follows:

Critical path = Longest path through the network

Earliest start (ES) = Longest path to an activity

Earliest finish (EF) = ES plus activity time

Latest finish (LF) = Project completion time minus
the time of the longest path to project completion

Latest start (LS) = LF minus activity time

Total slack = LS minus ES, or LF minus EF

($LS - ES$ equals $LF - EF$)

Free slack = ES of any subsequent activity minus EF

Calculation of each activity's free and total slack informs project management of those activities whose completion can be delayed (and how much each can be delayed) without affecting project completion and the amount of delay an activity can experience without affecting the ES of another activity. This information is valuable in scheduling project activities in a limited resource or time environment. In some cases, the time from the start of a project to its desired completion date may be greater than the length of the critical path. All activities have slack in such situations. Each activity on the critical path has total slack equal to the difference between the critical path length and the time from the beginning until the desired completion of the project. For example, if the desired completion of the example project was in Week 32 instead of Week 30 and the job was scheduled to begin in Week 0, then all activities would have an additional two weeks of slack.

A sample computer printout for this problem is given in Figure 15–7. The printout gives information for both events and activities. The events are sequentially numbered, and the earliest occurrence and latest occurrence of the event is shown. The event is labeled as critical if the critical path activities pass through it. The activities are indicated with letters, and the precedence relationship is shown by the start and finish nodes. The total slack is computed and, if 0, the activity is identified as critical. Free slack is also indicated.

In summary, the network planning nodes represent the activities of a project according to sequence and duration. They assist in the identification of the critical path and of the amount of total and free slack. Thus, the project manager can identify key milestones toward the completion of a project and the location and amount of available slack in activities that may be completed late without affecting project completion time.

PROGRAM EVALUATION AND REVIEW TECHNIQUE (PERT)

The distinguishing characteristic of PERT is its ability to encompass the inherent uncertainty of estimated activity completion times in certain types of projects. Although one may predict with relative certainty the time requirements of activities performed frequently in the past and with little variation in the time required, the time estimates of activities required to develop new technology or to perform a new and different task are inherently less certain. Thus, it is not surprising that a PERT approach frequently is adopted for research and design projects and that network models without provisions

Figure 15–7   Sample Computer Output

```
                   NORMAL EVENT TIMES
    EVENT   EARLY         LATE
            OCCURRENCE    OCCURRENCE
    1       0             0            CRITICAL
    2       2             2            CRITICAL
    3       5             5            CRITICAL
    4       5             5            CRITICAL
    5       10            10           CRITICAL
    6       16            16           CRITICAL
    7       16            17
    8       18            19
    9       19            19           CRITICAL
    10      24            24           CRITICAL
    11      25            25           CRITICAL
    12      26            26           CRITICAL
    13      29            29           CRITICAL
    14      30            30           CRITICAL
                   NORMAL ACTIVITY TIMES

    ACTIVITY   EVENT        ACTUAL   TOTAL       FREE
               PRECEDENCE            SLACK       SLACK
    A          1 -2         2        CRITICAL    0
    B          2 -3         3        CRITICAL    0
    C          2 -4         1        2           2
    D          4 -5         5        CRITICAL    0
    E          3 -6         2        9           9
    F          5 -6         6        CRITICAL    0
    G          5 -7         3        4           3
    H          7 -8         2        1           0
    I          6 -9         3        CRITICAL    0
    J          8 -10        4        2           2
    K          9 -10        5        CRITICAL    0
    L          11-12        1        CRITICAL    0
    M          10-11        1        CRITICAL    0
    N          12-13        3        CRITICAL    0
    O          13-14        1        CRITICAL    0
    P          3 -4         0        CRITICAL    0
    Q          6 -7         0        1           0
    R          8 -9         0        1           1
    EARLIEST POSSIBLE COMPLETION UNDER NORMAL CONDITIONS IS 30
```

for measuring uncertainty are used in the management of many construction, equipment rebuilding, and assembly projects.

Time Estimates

PERT achieves a probabilistic estimate of project completion by obtaining three estimates for each activity, describing the statistical distribution of possible times for each activity, and determining the standard deviation of each activity time and also of the project completion time. Using PERT, the three time estimates for each activity are

1. The optimistic time (A) (the time required to complete the task if all goes especially well)
2. The pessimistic time (B) (the time required to complete the task if things go wrong)
3. The most likely time (M—the mode) (the time required to complete the task in most cases)

The A and B times are estimated on the basis that the probability of an actual time falling outside their range is about 1 in 100. The expected activity time and its variance calculation are based on the assumption that the distribution of activity times approaches that of a *beta* distribution.

Figure 15–8 illustrates the general shapes of two *beta* distributions. In Curve 1 it is skewed to the right, the B time is a greater distance from the M time than the A time estimate, and the expected time (T_{e_1}) is greater than the M time. Curve 1 reflects the belief that difficulties that will delay the project are most likely to occur. In Curve 2 just the opposite is true.

Curve 2 is skewed to the left, the A time is a greater distance from the M time than the B time and the expected time (T_{e_2}) is less than the M time. Curve 2 reflects a higher probability that everything will go perfectly.

The estimates of the expected activity time (t_e) and measures of its variability (σ^2_t) are as follows:

$$t_e = \frac{A + 4M + B}{6}$$

$$\sigma^2_t = \left(\frac{B - A}{6}\right)^2$$

Figure 15–8   Profiles of Beta Distributions

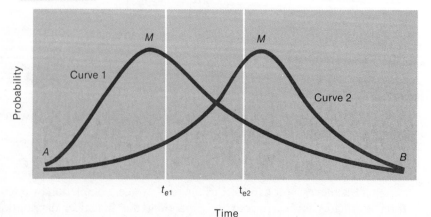

For example, let the three time estimates for Activity K from the earlier example be the following:

$$A = 4$$

$$M = 5$$

$$B = 8$$

Then,

$$t_e = \frac{4 + 20 + 8}{6} = 5.33$$

$$\sigma_t^2 = \left(\frac{8 - 4}{6}\right)^2 = .44$$

$$\sigma_t = \frac{2}{3} = .67$$

These values indicate a distribution of activity times similar to that illustrated in Figure 15–9. Table 15–4 lists the optimistic, most likely, and pessimistic time estimates for the activities listed in table 15-1. These time estimates permit the calculation of expected times and variance estimates for each activity (also contained in Table 15–4).

The expected length of any path through a network is the sum of the expected lengths of the activities on the path. The longest such path is, of course, the critical path. Although the average time estimates of many activities differ slightly from the deterministic estimates given earlier, in this case the critical path is still that path consisting of Activities A, B, P, D, F, I,

Figure 15–9 Distribution of Times for Activity K

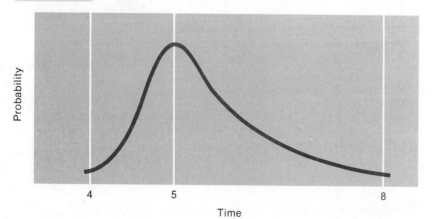

Table 15–4   Three Time Estimates, the Expected Activity Time, and Its Variability

Activity	Time Estimates in Weeks				
	A	M	B	t_e	σ_t^2
A	1.6	2.0	2.4	2.0	.018
B	2.0	3.0	4.6	3.1	.188
C	.9	1.0	2.0	1.15	.034
D	3.0	5.0	7.0	5.0	.444
E	.6	2.0	2.8	1.9	.134
F	4.6	6.0	7.4	6.0	.218
G	2.5	3.0	3.5	3.0	.028
H	2.0	2.0	3.0	2.17	.028
I	2.0	3.0	5.0	3.17	.250
J	2.0	4.0	6.0	4.0	.444
K	4.0	5.0	8.0	5.33	.444
L	1.0	1.0	1.0	1.0	.000
M	.8	1.0	2.0	1.13	.040
N	2.8	3.0	3.6	3.07	.018
O	1.0	1.0	3.0	1.33	.111

K, M, L, N, and O. However, the estimated project (critical path) length is now 31.13 weeks instead of 30 weeks due to the slightly longer average time estimates for Activities B, I, K, M, N, and O. This difference is not uncommon because deterministic estimates of activity times tend to be the M time rather than the expected time, and activity time distributions tend to be skewed to the right. In many cases, the small differences between these two methods of estimating total time and the negligible variances of activity times do not justify the added costs of developing a PERT network. However, in cases with substantial activity time variances or substantial costs associated with late project completion, the development of a PERT network and calculation of the probability of completing the project on schedule justify the added expense.

Project Completion Probability Distribution

Since the time required to complete each activity is a random variable, the expected time to complete the entire project (the sum of critical path expected times) is also a random variable. The variance of the expected time is equal to the sum of the variances of the activities on the critical path. Thus,

$$T_E = \sum_{i=1}^{k} t_{ei}, \qquad \sigma_T^2 = \sum_{i=1}^{k} \sigma_{t_i}^2$$

where:

T_E is the expected time required to complete the project

σ_T^2 is the variance of the distribution of estimated
   project completion time

$\sigma_{t_i}^2$ is the variance of expected activity completion time

t_{ei} is the estimated average element time

i represents activities on the critical path

k is the number of activities on the critical path

   In our example, the critical path consists of Activities A, B, P, D, F, I, K, M, L, N, and O. Using the data contained in Table 15–4, T_E and σ_T^2 can be calculated as follows:

$$T_E = 2.0 + 3.1 + 0 + 5.0 + 6.0 + 3.17 + 5.33 + 1.13 + 1.0 + 3.07 + 1.33$$

$$= 31.13$$

$$\sigma_T^2 = .018 + .188 + 0 + .444 + .218 + .25 + .444 + .04 + 0 + .018 + .111$$

$$= 1.731$$

   Since the standard deviation is equal to the square root of the variance,

$$\sigma_T = (1.731)^{1/2} = 1.316.$$

   Due to what is known in statistics as the central limit theorem, the distribution of a sum of random variables follows a normal, bell-shaped distribution, regardless of the distribution of the components of the sum. This enables us to use the table of areas under the normal curve (Appendix Table A) to calculate the probability of the project being completed within specific time frames.

   To begin with, we know that there is a 50 percent probability that the project will be completed within 31.13 weeks, the expected time, and a 50 percent chance that it will take longer; but what is the probability that it will be completed in 30 weeks or in 35 weeks? To answer this question we must calculate the number of standard deviations a desired completion time is from the average completion time. The following formula is used:

$$Z = \frac{T_D - T_E}{\sigma}$$

where

T_D = the desired completion time

Z = the number of standard deviations separating T_D and T_E

Thus,

$$Z = \frac{30 - 31.13}{1.316} = -.86$$

Appendix Table A shows that the area of the curve from the mean to .86 standard deviations is equal to .3051. Figure 15–10 illustrates the relationship of $T_{D_{30}}$, $T_{D_{35}}$, and T_E, in addition to the probability of their occurrence. In the case of $T_{D_{30}}$, T_D is less than the average; thus the probability represented by the area between T_E and T_D is subtracted from .50 to determine the probability, $P(T_D)$, of completing the project on or before T_D.
Thus,

$$P(T_D \geq 30) = .50 - .3051$$

$$= .1949$$

Figure 15–10   Relationship Between Completion Times, Standard Deviations, and Probabilities

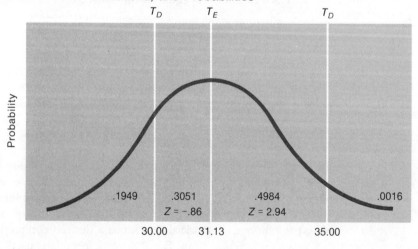

Because $T_{D_{35}}$ is greater than the T_E, the probability represented by the area between T_E and T_D is added to .5 to determine the probability, $P(T_D)$ of completing the project on or before T_D. Performing these calculations when T_D equals 35.0 weeks gives the following:

$$Z = \frac{35 - 31.13}{1.316} = 2.94$$

Referring again to the areas of a standard normal distribution (see Appendix Table A), we find that the area of the curve between the mean and 2.94 standard deviations is .4984. Thus,

$$P(T_D \leq 35.0) = .50 + .4984$$

$$= .9984$$

Our calculations indicate that there is a 99.84 percent probability that the project will be completed within 35 weeks. This is misleading because it assumes a 100 percent probability of completing the activities on all other paths within 35 weeks. Calculating the exact probability of completing a project within a time period greater than T_E is not straightforward. Subtracting the sum of the probabilities of the different paths requiring a time greater than T_D from 1—that is, $1.0 - \Sigma P(T_{E_i} > T_D)$—will give a conservative probability estimate due to the interdependence of the paths. One clear indication that a second path may take the place of the critical path is if a near critical path has a high variance. Simulation (see Chapter 23) may also be used to estimate the probability of T_D when $T_D > T_E$.

In summary, our time estimates and calculations indicate that it is almost certain that the project will be completed within 35 weeks and that there is slightly more than a 19 percent (19.49) probability that the project will be completed within 30 weeks.

THE SCHEDULED ALLOCATION OF RESOURCES

Determination of the critical path network is a necessary planning step prior to scheduling. Decisions concerning which resources, workers, and machines will be assigned to tasks during a given period also are influenced by other factors such as the total resources available, other projects competing for the same resources, penalties for late completion, bonuses for early completion, and the relationship of the time available to the time required for completion of the project. The final schedule must be developed in concert with capacity requirements planning as discussed in Chapter 13.

Up to this point discussions of activity times were predicated on resources being allocated to activities at a normal rate (usually defined as the most efficient rate). However, in most cases management has the additional options of (1) applying additional resources to decrease the duration of an activity—that is, crashing the activity—or (2) reducing the resources to a below-normal rate and increasing the duration of the activity. For example, a contractor responsible for the construction of a building may have determined a 58-week estimated completion time for the building. Two incentives normally would encourage the contractor to finish the project ahead of schedule. First, the contractor must pay fixed overhead costs, such as equipment rental, for each week on the job site. Second, the contract may specify a bonus for each week that the project is completed ahead of schedule. Thus, the contractor is encouraged to bear extra costs for critical path activities to reduce the total time on the project. Note that the incentive only applies to critical path activities. Overtime, expedited shipment or production, and more costly subcontracting would be techniques that the project manager could use to crash the project, but the cost would be greater than normal.

Recognition of the relationship of activity time durations to the allocation of resources was discussed first in literature concerning deterministic CPM models. However, the possibility of allocating resources to alter activity duration also exists in projects managed with the assistance of a PERT model; the distribution of possible activity times merely shifts. (In fact, other parameters in addition to the mean may change; but we will consider only changes in t_e).

Likely scheduling objectives include reduction of the project duration, cost minimization, and smoothing resource requirements over time. The typical real-world project schedule usually requires that some balance be achieved between specific objectives in each of these areas. First, we will examine a case for which resources are unlimited; the project duration must be shortened to a specific length with minimum additional costs.

Figure 15–11 illustrates the most typical relationship of activity times and resources allocation; this is the case in which an activity can be completed in normal time (t_n), at normal cost (C_n), or with the expenditure of additional resources in crash time (t_c), at a crash cost (C_c). It also may be completed in all times between t_c and t_n at the corresponding costs between C_c and C_n. Whether a single approximation of the slope is satisfactory or not depends on the degree of curvature.

In real-world situations, extending the time may either increase the total costs due to drawn-out inefficiencies or the costs may remain essentially the same. For example, if the normal procedure is to have four workers on an assembly, reducing the number to three will increase total costs only if some of the assembly operations are performed more efficiently by four persons working as a team. Increased costs associated with shortened activity times are the result of overtime, additional setup and learning costs when the job is split among more workers, and the use of less skilled workers or less efficient machines.

Figure 15–11   Total Cost Versus Activity Duration

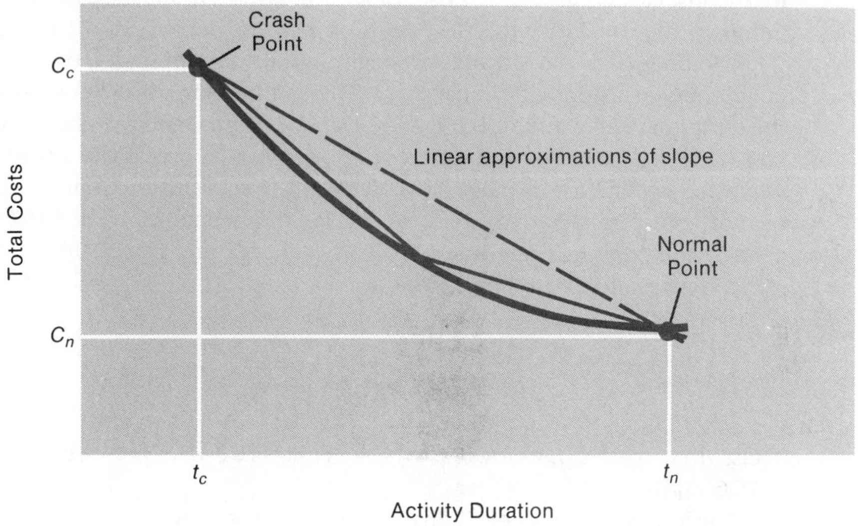

Cost Minimization

Project completion costs usually are at a minimum when resources are expended at the normal, most efficient rate. If, however, the aggregate organizational demand for resources is unusually low at a particular time, surplus resources requiring no additional out-of-pocket expense may be applied to a project even when shortening its length is not a priority. In such a case, the recorded costs of a particular project may increase due to inefficiencies, but total corporate expenditures will not increase and resources will be freed in a later period during which additional demand may materialize. For example, labor may be committed to maintenance ahead of schedule because it is more readily available during the off-season than during peak production.

Shortening Project Length

There are many occasions when it is desirable to complete a project in less than normal time. Bonuses for early completion, penalties for late completion, weather problems anticipated beyond a certain date, a combination of relatively light aggregate demand in proximate periods and heavy demand in later periods, and accelerated revenue generation are some of the possible justifications for attempting to complete a project early.

Resources must be available when required if a modified project schedule is to be implemented successfully. As will be illustrated shortly, analysis of project time-cost tradeoffs will provide the information indicating when these resources are required. Thus, this analysis is initiated on the assumption that such resources are available. If there is competition for such resources, as frequently is the case, time-cost tradeoff analysis results will be one of the inputs to the capacity allocation decision process described in Chapter 5.

The time-cost tradeoff analysis begins with a determination of the approximate time-cost slope of each activity. This is a measure of the cost to shorten the duration of an activity. Table 15–5 lists the normal and the crash times and costs for each activity. All the times included in it approximate actual values, while the cost figures are fictitious. Table 15–5 reveals, for example, that the cost of completing Activity F in six weeks, the normal time, is $15,600; the cost of completing it in three weeks, the crash time, is $20,000. The cost slope is calculated as follows:

$$\text{Cost slope} = \frac{C_c - C_n}{t_n - t_c}$$

Thus, the cost slope for activity F equals $1,467 per week ([20,000 − 15,600]/[6 − 3]).

The following example illustrates how management can use cost slope and related information in resource allocation decisions required during project planning. If management desires to complete the design, fabrication, and assembly of the material-handling system in 27 weeks rather than the normal 30 weeks, additional resources must be allocated to selected activities on the

Table 15–5 Normal and Crash Times and Costs

Activities*	Events	t_n**	t_c***	C_n	C_c	Cost Slope ($ per Week)
A	1–2	2.0	1.5	$ 4,800	$ 5,600	$1,600
B	2–3	3.1	2.6	7,680	8,500	1,640
C	2–4	1.15	.8	3,100	3,600	1,429
D	4–5	5.0	3.0	13,500	18,000	2,250
E	3–6	1.9	.9	4,960	6,000	1,060
F	5–6	6.0	3.0	15,600	20,000	1,467
G	5–7	3.0	2.0	4,200	5,000	800
H	7–8	2.17	1.2	3,025	4,000	938
I	6–9	3.17	1.17	4,100	4,400	150
J	8–10	4.0	2.5	5,200	5,600	267
K	9–10	5.33	3.0	3,730	4,500	330
L	11–12	1.0	.6	700	1,100	1,000
M	10–11	1.13	.8	790	1,000	636
N	12–13	3.07	2.0	2,015	2,400	350
O	13–14	1.33	1.0	2,100	2,700	1,200

*Critical path activities = A, B, D, F, I, K, L, M, N, and O.
**Normal time values are the same as estimated average time (t_e) in Table 15–4.
***Crash times are also averages from a distribution similar to that of t_e

critical path. (Reduction of the duration of activities not on the critical path will not reduce the time required to complete the project.) In some cases, it may be necessary to reallocate resources within the project; in other cases, it may be possible and desirable to obtain additional resources (external to the project).

If internal reallocation is required, additional resources should be sought from those activities where slack is greatest and applied to an activity or activities where they will have the greatest impact. For example, Activity E, mechanical fabrication 1, has nine weeks of slack. If some of the personnel and machines normally assigned to Activity E can be reallocated to Activity F, mechanical fabrication 2, the length of the critical path can be reduced.

Guidelines for applying additional resources to the reduction of the critical path include the following:

1. Additional resources should be applied to critical path activities and also to those noncritical paths whose lengths approach that of the critical path. Resources, where transferable, should be taken from activities that have the greatest amount of total slack. This approach will reduce the likelihood of creating a new critical path.
2. Additional resources should first be applied to activities with the smallest cost slope. This will minimize the costs of reducing the project length.
3. Additional resources should be applied to activities required relatively early in completion of the project. Once opportunities to reduce the project length are foregone, they cannot be regained. Should unplanned difficulties arise in early activities, later opportunities still will be available to compensate for unplanned delays.

Of the activities on the critical path, activity I has the smallest cost slope, $150 per week. The project duration can be reduced two weeks $(3.17 - 1.17)$ merely by investing an additional $300. Yet a total savings of three weeks is required to reduce the project to 27 weeks. Since a two-week reduction is achieved by applying additional resources to Activity I, another one-week reduction must be found. Candidate activities on the critical path, in rank order of their cost slopes, are

Rank	Activity	Cost Slope	Possible Reduction (Weeks)
1	K	$ 330	2.33
2	N	350	1.07
3	M	636	.33
4	L	1,000	.4
5	O	1,200	.33
6	F	1,467	3.0
7	A	1,600	.5
8	B	1,640	.5
9	D	2,250	2.0

Selecting Activity K for the planned application of an additional $330 will reduce the duration of Activity K by one week, but unless activities H or J (which go on in parallel) are reduced, no reduction can be achieved.

Considering that it costs $938 to shorten Activity H by one week, but that Activity H can only be shortened by .97 weeks, it technically should not be considered further. Activity J can be shortened by one week for $267. Thus, the total cost to shorten Activities K and J simultaneously is $330 and $267, or $597.

A less costly alternative could be found. Activity N costs $350 per week to crash and can be crashed for the required one week. However, it is much later in the project completion sequence. Thus, the scheduler has the option of crashing Activities K and J, an earlier and less risky but more costly option, or Activity N, a less costly but possibly more risky alternative.

It is not uncommon for planned shortening of project length to increase the number of activities that are critical. It is also true that many possible options must be examined before selection of the one that best meets management's criteria is found. It is difficult to keep track of all the interactions in evaluating alternatives. However, this resource allocation problem can be formulated and solved as a linear programming problem as discussed in Chapter 22.

Other Cost Slopes

Not all activities possess one of the cost slopes illustrated in Figure 15–12, but many do. Discontinuous cost slopes, for example, can exist in the case of purchased parts that may be delivered in, say, two weeks if shipped by truck or rail and in a day or two if shipped by air express. Nothing in between is possible for practical purposes. Some activities inherently develop very slowly (gestational), and applying additional resources does not affect the time required to complete the activity. Physical growth, aging, fermentation, and some chemical processes cannot be shortened. Knowledge inputs, such as those required by research and design activities, also fall into this category on some occasions, as may product testing and evaluation. Decreasing the

Figure 15–12 Other Cost Slopes

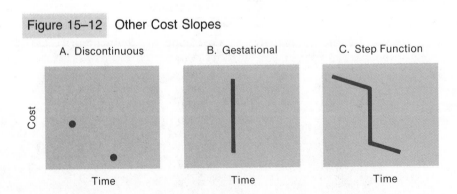

time requirements of such activities beyond a certain point may require an additional capital investment—as illustrated by a step increase in cost—to obtain the required additional personnel or machine capacity. Other cost slopes are also possible. The point is that the costs related to the possible durations of each activity must be analyzed to determine which cost slope adequately represents the cost-time relationship of each activity.

PROJECT CONTROL

The greatest benefit of network models is the improved insight they provide concerning project completion status. For example, activities behind schedule, but with sufficient slack to still complete the project on schedule, do not require the corrective action. However, a behind-schedule activity on the critical path with negative slack would demand corrective action.

Successful project completion requires timely monitoring of work completion and comparison to scheduled completion. Control of projects is based on the same principles that control ongoing, nonproject activities. Although these are covered in other chapters, it is worth repeating some of them here.

1. Plans should be realistic and not reflect an overstated estimate of capacity.
2. Control of the planning activity itself requires:
    a. Management commitment to the objectives of the plan and the availability of the resources
    b. Agreement (preferably in writing) by the appropriate managers and supervisors that the precedence relationships, time estimates, and costs are realistic
3. A performance reporting system with adequate, accurate, and timely information should exist. Most project completion situations are dynamic. Changing conditions and actual performance initiation and completion may change priorities.
4. Procedures should exist for evaluating performance on a regular basis, determining what, if any, corrective action is required, and revising schedules and operating plans accordingly.

Daily or at least weekly reports of performance to date listing revised, early, and late start and finish dates, activity slack, expected project completion, and activities to be initiated in the current period are necessary to implement control.

ACTIVITY ON THE NODE

As mentioned earlier in this chapter, a project can be represented by a network with the activities on the node as well as by the activity-on-the-arrow approach, which we have used to this point. Figure 15–13 is an example of an activity-on-the-node network. It is based on the data contained in Table

Figure 15–13   Activity-on-the-Node Network Model

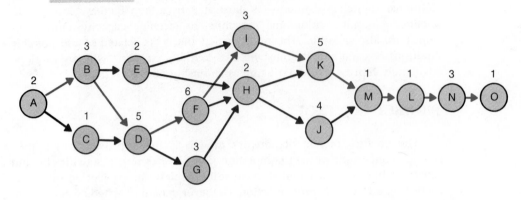

15–1 and is the counterpart of the activity-on-the-arrow network in Figure 15–6.

Examination of Figure 15–13 reveals the advantages of the activity-on-the-node approach. Dummy activities are not required; manual network construction and modification are simpler. At one time there was a scarcity of available computer software packages for activity-on-the-node applications, but that is no longer the case. Either deterministic or probabilistic (PERT type) models can be used with either activity-on-the-arrow or activity-on-the-node representations. Selection between these two approaches depends primarily on local conditions and preferences.

Network models have been widely accepted as valuable aids in planning and controlling project activities. They are especially useful in defining the relative priorities of the tasks that constitute the project, estimating the probability of completing the project within specified time periods, scheduling resources for specific tasks, and determining if task completion times require either a revision of the schedule or a reallocation of resources.

CONCLUSIONS

PERT and CPM are commonly used to assist in the management of projects. Because they show the critical path and the impact of slack, they are an improvement over previously used Gantt charts. The methodology permits numerous variations, including deterministic or statistical data input, activity-on-the-arrow or activity-on-the-node approaches, and crashing to achieve various objectives. Although available computer programs readily solve the algorithm, there is a great deal of judgmental interaction required of the program manager.

Accurate estimation of activity times and the full understanding of the activity interaction is essential. Computations to several decimal positions are highly dependent upon the estimation of activity durations (in the case of

CPM) or of optimistic, realistic, and pessimistic times (in the case of **PERT**). Yet, the very nature of the project as a unique and one-time series of **activities** makes estimation difficult and unreliable. For this reason, the most **important** contribution of the PERT/CPM process is probably to make the **management** decision issues visible to the project manager. The identification of the **critical** and near-critical paths, the computation of slack associated with each **activity**, the evaluation of crashing opportunities and crashing cost scopes all focus the activity planning issues for the project manager. Subsequently, scheduling **and** the allocation or reallocation of resources is much easier.

QUESTIONS

1. Give several reasons for the very positive acceptance of PERT/CPM methods.

2. Identify several applications of PERT/CPM techniques to manufacturing and service operations.

3. Not all tasks are suitable for project management techniques. What characteristics should a task possess for PERT or CPM to be effective?

4. What are the advantages of PERT and CPM in comparison to Gantt charting or other similar techniques?

5. Differentiate between CPM and PERT.

6. What are dummy activities? Why are they necessary?

7. What is the difference between the activity-on-the-arrow and the activity-on-the-node approaches to CPM/PERT?

8. What data are necessary input for both PERT and CPM procedures?

9. What is the critical path? Differentiate critical activities from noncritical activities.

10. How are the earliest start time (ES) and earliest finish time (EF) calculated?

11. What is the latest start time (LS)? How are the latest finish time (LF) and latest start time (LS) calculated?

12. Differentiate total slack from free slack.

13. What purpose is served by calculating each activity's free and total slack times?

14. Describe the data inputs required for the beta distribution PERT problem.

15. What is the effect of high variance on a path that has a great deal of total float time?

16. What is the effect of high variance on a path that has zero total float?

17. When is the added expense of developing a PERT (or statistical approach) rather than a CPM (deterministic) network justified?

18. When considering crashing a project, what guidelines should management follow?

19. What is the impact on management if a particular flow chart has two critical paths (same duration) or if one path is only slightly different (less duration) than the critical path?

PROBLEMS

1. The process for a helicopter engine rebuilding facility can be indentified by the following five activities.

No.	Task	Predecessors	Time (Weeks)
1	Disassemble	—	4
2	Test parts	1	2
3	Remachine some parts	2	5
4	Test machined parts	3	1
5	Reassemble engine	2, 4	3

   a. Prepare a Gantt chart of these activities.
   b. Prepare a CPM flow chart using the activities-on-the-node method.
   c. Compute the durations of the paths. Which is the critical path? How much slack time does the noncritical path have?

2. The Adams Company desires to modify part of its diesel engine manufacturing process. The following six activities, task sequences, and times have been identified below.

No.	Task	Predecessors	Time (Weeks)
1	A	—	3
2	B	A	2
3	C	A	4
4	D	B, C	5
5	E	B, C	4
6	F	D, E	3

a. Prepare a Gantt chart for the above operation.
b. Prepare a CPM flow chart using the activity-on-the-arrow technique. (Note: there will be dummy activities.)
c. Compute the duration of paths: A, B, D, F; A, C, D, F; A, B, E, F; and A, C, E, F. Which is the critical path?
d. Based on the expected time along the critical path, how much total slack does each path have?
e. Compute the earliest start time (ES), latest start time (LS), earliest finish time (EF), latest finish time (LF), total slack, and free slack for each task.

3. Below are ten activities, their precedence requirements, and their times to completion.

No.	Task	Predecessors	Time (Weeks)
1	A	—	3
2	B	—	5
3	C	—	7
4	D	A	8
5	E	B	5
6	F	C	5
7	G	E	4
8	H	F	5
9	I	D	6
10	J	G, H	4

a. Prepare a CPM flow chart using the activity-on-the-arrow method. (Note: activities I and J end at the same node.)
b. Calculate the earliest start (ES) and earliest finish (EF) times for each activity.
c. Calculate the latest start (LS) and latest finish (LF) times for each activity.
d. What is the total slack for each activity?
e. Define the critical path.
f. What is the expected project duration along the critical path?

4. Below are eight activities on the arrow and their durations in weeks.

Activity	Duration (Weeks)
1–2	4
1–3	6
2–4	3
3–5	2
3–4	5
2–5	9
4–6	7
5–6	3

    a. Prepare a CPM flow chart for these activities.
    b. Calculate the earliest start (ES), earliest finish (EF), latest start (LS), and latest finish (LF) times for these activities.
    c. What is the total slack for each activity?
    d. Define the critical path.
    e. What is the expected project duration along the critical path?

5. The following data depict 12 activities on the arrow with their durations in days.

Activity	Duration (Weeks)
1–2	6
1–3	1
1–4	1
2–5	2
3–6	5
4–6	2
4–7	3
3–7	4
2–8	3
5–8	1
6–8	4
7–8	5

    a. Prepare a CPM flow chart for these activities.
    b. Calculate the earliest start (ES), earliest finish (EF), latest start (LS), latest finish (LF), and total slack for these activities.
    c. Define the critical path.
    d. What is the expected project duration along these paths?

6. The normal and crash times and costs for the activities in Problem 3 are below. Calculate the cost slopes in dollars per week and determine which activities should be crashed.

Activity	t_n	t_c	C_n	C_c
A	3	1	$ 2,500	$ 4,500
B	5	4	12,000	15,000
C	7	6	16,000	17,700
D	8	6	4,250	5,575
E	5	4	1,450	2,350
F	5	4	7,850	8,400
G	4	2	22,325	25,300
H	5	3	15,500	17,000
I	6	4	5,500	6,200
J	4	3	3,900	4,550

7. Consider the same activities as in Problem 3. Disregard the individual times, but use optimistic times (A), pessimistic times (B), and most likely times (M), for PERT calculations as follows:

No.	Task	Predecessors	A	M	B
1	A	—	2	3	5
2	B	—	3	5	9
3	C	—	5	7	9
4	D	A	7	8	10
5	E	B	4	5	8
6	F	C	4	5	7
7	G	E	3	4	6
8	H	F	4	5	8
9	I	D	5	6	8
10	J	G, H	3	4	6

a. Calculate the estimated time of completion (t_{ei}) for each task.

b. What is the variance (σ_t^2) for each activity in Problem 7?

c. The critical path is the same as in Problem 3. What is the standard deviation for the project duration?

d. Calculate the probabilities that the project will be completed within the following time frames:

Week

19

20

21

22

23

24

8. A building contractor desires to complete an office building as rapidly as possible. The contractor has done many projects similar to this, so he believes the estimates to be quite accurate.

Task	Description	Duration (Months)	Predecessors
A	Foundation	2	—
B	Steel frame	1	A
C	Floors	3	B
D	Electrical	2	C
E	Plumbing	3	C
F	Roof	1	C
G	HVAC	1	F
H	Exterior	3	D, E, G
I	Interior	4	H

a. Prepare a flow chart for these activities.
b. Compute the times for each path.
c. Which is the critical path?
d. What are the earliest start (ES), earliest finish (EF), latest start (LS), and latest finish (LF) for these activities?

9. It has become imperative that the information in Problem 8 be more fully analyzed because of incentive and penalty clauses negotiated into the contract. The new information for PERT analysis is below.

Task	Description	A	M	B
A	Foundation	1.5	2	3
B	Steel frame	.5	1	3
C	Floors	2.0	3	4.5
D	Electrical	1.0	2	3
E	Plumbing	2.5	3	5
F	Roof	0.25	1	2
G	HVAC	0.75	1	1.75
H	Exterior	2.0	3	5
I	Interior	3.5	4	4.5

a. Calculate the estimated time to completion (t_{ei}) for these activities.
b. What is the project's estimated time to completion along the critical path?
c. Calculate the variances of all the activities in the project.
d. Calculate the critical path variances.
e. What is the standard deviation of the critical path?
f. What are the probabilities of completing the project within the following number of months: 14, 15, 16, 17, and 18.

REFERENCES

Burgess, A. R., and James B. Killebrew. "Variation in Activity Level on a Cyclical Arrow Diagram." *Journal of Industrial Engineering* 13, no. 2 (March–April 1962): 76–83.

Clingen, C. T. "A Modification of Fulkerson's PERT Algorithm." *Operations Research* 12, no. 4 (July–August 1964): 629–631.

Elmaghraby, Salah E. "On Generalized Activity Networks." *Journal of Industrial Engineering* 17, no. 11 (November 1966): 621–631.

Elmaghraby, Salah E. "On the Expected Duration of PERT Type Networks." *Management Science* 13, no. 5 (January 1967): 299–306.

Elmaghraby, Salah E. "The Theory of Networks and Management Science, II." *Management Science* 17, no. 2 (October 1970): 54–71.

Fulkerson, D. R. "Expected Critical Path Lengths in PERT Networks." *Operations Research* 10, no. 6 (November–December 1962): 808–817.

Kelley, James E. "Critical Path Planning and Scheduling, Mathematical Basis." *Operations Research* 9, no. 2 (May–June 1961): 296–320.

Klingel, Jr., A. R. "Bias in PERT Project Completion Time Calculations for a Real Network." *Management Science* 13, no. 4 (1966): 194–201.

Levin, Richard I., and Charles A. Kirkpatrick. *Planning and Control with PERT/CPM.* New York: McGraw-Hill Book Company, 1966.

Levy, Ferdinand K., Gerald L. Thompson, and Jerome D. Weist. "The ABC's of the Critical Path Method." *Harvard Business Review* (September–October 1963): 98–108.

MacCrimmon, Kenneth R., and Charles A. Ryavec. "An Analytical Study of the PERT Assumptions." *Operations Research* (January–February 1964): 16–37.

Malcolm, D. G., et al. "Application of a Technique for Research and Development Program Evaluation." *Operations Research* 7, no. 5 (September–October 1959).

Moder, Joseph J., and Cecil R. Phillips. *Project Management with CPM and PERT*, 2d ed. New York: Litton Educational Publishing, Inc., Van Nostrand Reinhold Company, 1970.

Shaffer, L. R., J. B. Ritter, and W. L. Meyer. *The Critical Path Method.* New York: McGraw-Hill Book Company, 1965.

Van Slyke, Richard M. "Monte Carlo Methods and the PERT Problem." *Operations Research* 11, no. 5 (September–October 1963) 839–860.

Weist, Jerome D. "Heuristic Programs for Decision Making." *Harvard Business Review* (September–October 1966) 129–143.

Weist, Jerome and Ferdinand Levy. *A Management Guide to PERT/CPM*, 2d ed. Englewood Cliffs, N.J.: Prentice-Hall, Inc., 1977.

CHAPTER 16
PURCHASING MANAGEMENT

OBJECTIVES

After completing this chapter, you should be able to

- Explain why purchasing management is important

- Describe the major activities of purchasing and the major categories into which purchases are usually grouped

- List and explain the important factors in a make-or-buy decision

- Describe the purchasing cycle and its phases

- Identify the essential elements and describe the flow of data in a purchasing management information system

- Define and evaluate special types of orders, quantity discounts, and factors affecting order quantities

- Explain the importance of supplier relations and supplier evaluation

- Define value analysis and explain its objectives and process

OUTLINE

INTRODUCTION

Purchased parts and materials constitute 30 to 60 percent of the cost of goods sold in most manufacturing firms. Thus, a small percentage decrease in the cost of purchased items can result in a much larger percentage increase in profits. For example, if the cost of purchased materials is 50 percent of sales and profit is 10 percent of sales, decreasing the cost of those same purchased materials to 48 percent of sales will increase profits by 20 percent, as illustrated in Figure 16–1. Volsky (1981) has reported how Lubriquip saved $140,000 in the cost of purchased items through a formal program focused on several high dollar product groups. Since purchasing also is crucial in achieving product quality and delivery schedules, a study of purchasing policies, procedures, and decisions can be rewarding.

ABC ANALYSIS

One of the first steps in managing purchased items should be the performance of an ABC analysis. Applying the ABC principle to purchasing management involves

1. Classifying items on the basis of relative importance
2. Establishing different management controls for different classifications with the degree of control being commensurate with the ranked importance of each classification

The letters *A, B,* and *C* represent different classifications of descending importance; however, it may be necessary to have more than three classes. Criteria for classification should reflect the difficulty of controlling an item and the impact of the item on costs and profitability.

ABC analysis usually is illustrated using the annual dollar volume criteria. In a typical distribution, 20 percent of purchased items are *A* items, which account for 80 percent of the annual purchasing budget. These items merit the most stringent purchasing controls. Typically, 30 percent of items are *B* items, accounting for 15 percent of the annual dollar volume. Thus, half the items purchased are *C* items, together making up only 5 percent of the budget. For these items, carrying costs are usually low and ordering systems are used that minimize purchasing costs and virtually guarantee against stockouts.

Annual dollar volume is not the only criterion for ranking the value of an item. Other factors used to classify items in an ABC analysis include the following:

1. Unit cost
2. Scarcity of material or capacity used in producing an item

Figure 16–1   Purchasing Costs and Profits as a Percentage
of Sales Income

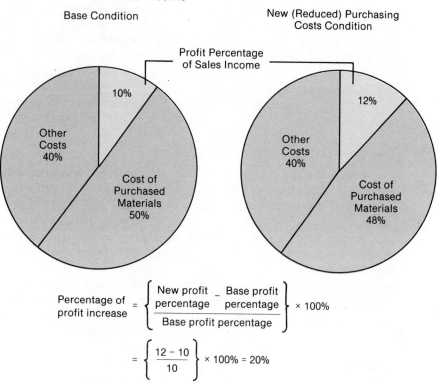

3. Lead time
4. Storage requirements for an item
5. Pilferage risks, shelf life, and other critical attributes
6. Cost of a stock-out
7. Engineering design volatility

   Widespread application of electronic data processing to inventory and purchasing management has had an impact on some applications of ABC analysis. Accurate and timely records now can be maintained economically on all items except for those with very low costs, such as standard rivets, washers, and other pan stock items. For record-keeping purposes, only *A* and *C* items may exist; but record-keeping procedures are only one aspect of inventory and purchasing management. Other planning and control procedures, such as evaluation of forecasts and cycle counting frequencies, still may be influenced by the result of an ABC analysis.

PURCHASES

The purchasing department usually has the task of procuring all the goods and services required by the organization. Thus, its activities account for a greater portion of the cost of sales than the cost of materials alone indicates.

Items purchased fall into the following major categories:

1. Custom equipment and services
2. Standard office, maintenance, and manufacturing supplies and services
3. Materials, components, and supplies consumed in producing a product

Custom Equipment and Services

Process equipment, material-handling equipment, and communications equipment are examples of items frequently designed and fabricated to meet the special needs of the purchaser. Advertising, public relations, market research, engineering, (product) tests, and software development are examples of purchased custom services. An organization purchases these services because it either does not have the capability to produce them efficiently or its internal resources are fully loaded with other tasks. Custom purchases usually begin with a funding request that states the need and justifies the expense. Since the department requesting the service usually possesses greater knowledge of the technical requirements and the supplier's capabilities than the purchasing department, purchasing often plays a supporting role, overseeing the paperwork and advising the technical experts of conditions or factors they might have overlooked. Each case may be different, and purchasing's cognizance of these differences and how they should be handled contractually can reduce misunderstandings and future difficulties. In more complex and costly expenditures, the legal department may take an active role in either developing or approving the final contract.

Standard Supplies and Services

Envelopes, paper clips, paper towels, and light bulbs are a few of the many office and general maintenance supplies purchased. These are C items, commercially available for the most part. Once a reliable source of acceptable quality and cost is found, purchasing is a clerical function interrupted by a periodic, perhaps annual, review of the supplier's performance. Technological changes also may trigger a review. As is the case with most C items, it is better to have extra on hand than to be waiting for an order to arrive. The cost of a stock-out usually is more expensive than carrying an ample safety stock.

Manufacturing supplies such as cutting oil, drill bits, cutting tools, and sandpaper are also C items and should be managed accordingly. Standard hardware items such as rivets, washers, and fasteners (pan stock) are kept in trays or pans on the shop floor readily available for use. Thus, they are managed not by a perpetual record system but by a visual review two-bin system (see Chapter 11).

Manufacturing Material, Components, and Supplies

The bulk of purchasing expenditures are for the material, components, and supplies that become part of the final product. Management of these items and their consumption directly affects the flow of incoming cash, production efficiency, inventory costs, profit, and return on investment. Thus, determination of their order quantities and order timing must be coordinated closely with manufacturing planning. Some organizations have combined the positions of inventory planner and buyer of manufacturing material and components to achieve this coordination.

Many types of equipment have components subject to failure. Since manufacturing equipment and material-handling equipment downtime is very expensive, spare components usually are purchased and stocked. Spare tires, bulbs for overhead projectors, belts, pumps, motors, actuators, and solenoids are examples. The manufacturing and maintenance engineering departments should decide which and how many of each spare component to stock. These decisions should be based on manufacturing engineering estimates of failure rates, impact of a failure on production, and the cost of spares.

PURCHASING MATERIALS AND COMPONENTS

The objectives of purchasing materials and components are to (1) maintain a continuity of supply in keeping with a schedule, (2) provide material and components that meet or exceed a specified level of quality, and (3) obtain the required items at the lowest possible total cost consistent with delivery and quality requirements. These objectives are gained through activities such as the following:

1. Evaluating and approving vendors
2. Requesting quotations
3. Negotiating price and delivery
4. Preparing purchase orders
5. Determining purchase cash commitments
6. Tracking planned and open purchase orders
7. Determining order quantities and order release timing
8. Accurate processing of receipts
9. Handling receipts with discrepancies
10. Monitoring releases against blanket orders, systems, and other special contractual arrangements
11. Analyzing variances in item and vendor prices, deliveries, and quality

Purchasing's role in planning and controlling priorities and capacities is very similar to the role of production activity control (PAC). While PAC closes

Figure 16–2   Relationship of Purchasing to Other Operations
                Management Activities

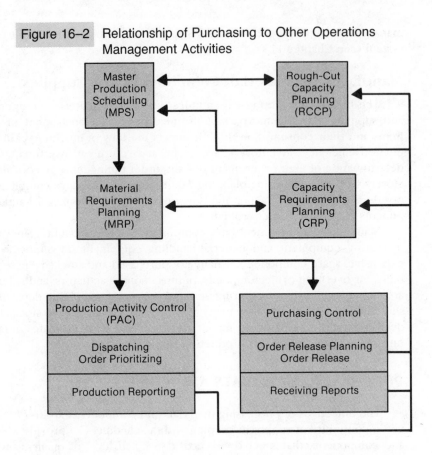

the planning and control loop with respect to shop management, purchasing closes it with respect to vendor management, as illustrated in Figure 16–2.

MAKE-OR-BUY DECISIONS

Make-or-buy decisions—that is, whether to manufacture or purchase supplies—must be made regarding material, components, assemblies, and services. Such decisions occur during long-, medium-, and short-range planning. For example, the management of an automobile manufacturing company may make a long-range decision to purchase an engine rather than build a new engine-manufacturing line. Similarly, a contract may be signed with a consulting firm to develop an integrated CAD/CAM system including a manufacturing control subsystem. At the same time, a one-year contract for part programming may be given to a software house due to the heavy initial programming load. The commitment to use a given amount of shop capacity per month for a product family during the next 12 months is another example of a medium-range make-or-buy decision—in this case, a make decision. In the short range, a local machine shop may be employed to produce some gear blanks rather than to run the lathe department overtime during the next two weeks.

All companies find it necessary to purchase some material and components. Paint, raw material, rivets, bolts, castings, and commercial electronic components are common purchases. Vertical integration is economically feasible only to a point. Factors that make some items readily identifiable as purchase items include:

1. The purchaser's lack of the required technical capability
2. Patents or trade secrets possessed by the supplier
3. Cost advantages of the supplier due to many customers

The make-or-buy decision is not immediately clear with other items. For example, many metal fabricators are faced with the decision of machining special gears themselves or having them machined by a specialized firm (a gear house). Other firms specialize in metal cutting and forming, plastics molding, diecasting, heat treating, and plating. These firms develop expertise in one or two areas and frequently provide a viable alternate source of components or a scarce processing capability. When the potential purchaser possesses a comparable capability, the make-or-buy decision ensues.

Make-or-buy decisions affect a wide variety or services. They extend from services such as design engineering, tool design, advertising, and public relations to more mundane services such as janitorial, lawn care, and printing.

Factors that influence make-or-buy decisions include:

1. Capacity available
2. The marginal costs of the items or skills involved
3. The relative quality
4. Lead time
5. Supplier relations

If a company has the capability but its capacity is fully utilized, overtime may be the only alternative to purchasing. If, on the other hand, both personnel and equipment are not fully utilized and a no-layoff policy exists, the marginal costs of producing an item internally are the costs of material only. To merit consideration, both the internal and external sources of supply must produce adequate quality. If the output of any one source far exceeds minimum quality at no additional cost, it is obviously preferable.

The lead time and the reliability of delivery promises also are important considerations. Many suppliers have a reputation for short lead times and good quality—but at a price. Whereas some suppliers thrive on producing small quantities on short notice at irregular intervals, others require a more stable relationship involving purchase commitments for weeks or months at a lower unit cost. Thus, the supplier's preferred role and the existing purchaser-supplier relationships and commitments influence the make-or-buy decision.

THE PURCHASING CYCLE

The purchase of raw materials and components can be viewed as having three phases: (1) prior to the order, (2) the order itself, and (3) after the order. The time prior to the order purchasing should be concerned with developing, evaluating, and selecting suppliers. Occasionally, engineering will develop requirements for a material or component not available in the marketplace. Purchasing and engineering must work with suppliers, perhaps funding research, in developing such items. Purchasing also should be adding to the list of acceptable suppliers for specific materials and components. Strikes, fires, floods, other calamities, and changes in vendor pricing or manufacturing practices can disrupt a heretofore reliable supplier. The supply chain frequently has many links, and the purchasing office may have to develop contacts with suppliers of their suppliers.

Evaluation of potential suppliers is based on their manufacturing process, product quality, management, financial health, lead time, price, and capacity. The manufacturing process is a major determinant of product characteristics such as appearance, performance, reliability, and life expectancy. Poor management or inadequate financing can lead to a short life span for a supplier and to disruptions of deliveries. Unusually long or unreliable delivery lead times decrease the competitive position of any supplier. An assessment of vendor capacity is necessary to determine what proportion of the requirements the vendor can handle and if additional suppliers are necessary. Supplier evaluations frequently involve a visit to the vendor's facility to examine the production and quality control management systems as well as the manufacturing process. Many organizations have a formal vendor qualification process that must be completed before a supplier's quotations will be accepted.

Supplier development and selection usually is a medium-range planning activity. During the same time period purchasing should participate in establishing the master production schedule (MPS). The purchaser's role is similar to the production planner. Using the production capacity of the vendors and their lead times, the purchaser should confirm that the MPS is realistic in terms of supplier lead time and capacity. An overstated MPS relative to purchase requirements will result in premium costs for overtime and transportation or late deliveries, disrupted production, excess inventory, and perhaps idle work centers.

Whenever possible, purchasing should negotiate for future capacity from vendors furnishing more than one item. This policy gives both supplier and purchaser a long-term commitment for a specific volume of a product family. The relationship remains flexible because the purchaser does not have to specify the quantity or item until required by the supplier's short-range time fence. Burlingame and Warren (1974) reported on such a relationship between Twin Disc Inc. and the Neenah Foundry Company. Carter and Monczka (1978) reported a similar relationship that Steelcase, Inc. has with its supplier of plywood seats and backs and its suppliers of fabric and yarn.

A supplier's ability to adapt to engineering and schedule changes also is important; it is measured by monitoring the vendor's performance. The evaluation of suppliers continues through the control process. Purchasing is primarily an execution activity—as opposed to planning and control—with the dominant elements being order placement and receipt. Thus, we will examine the order placement and receiving phases in detail.

ORDER PLACEMENT

An order can be initiated in several different ways. A periodic review of inventory, an item reaching its order point, or the arrival of the planned order release date in a material requirements planning (MRP) system may reveal the need for additional purchased items and trigger a purchase requisition (see Figure 16–3). A computerized system may generate a purchase requisition automatically on the planned order release date or when the inventory of an item is reduced to or below its order point. The planner-buyer then may edit the requisition before placing the purchase order. This is another situation where ABC analysis may be applied. For example, purchase orders for *A* and *B* items may be reviewed, while those for *C* items are processed automatically. Each requisition is identified by number and usually contains the item number, item name, date, quantity, buyer's name, due date, supplier number, and supplier name. Since there is not a standard requisition form suitable for all companies, this information may vary; for example, the purchase requisition also may include the price and the account to be charged. Requisition control may be achieved by a system capable of reporting purchase requisitions for which purchase orders have not been prepared.

Timing the release of a requisition requires that all segments of lead time be considered. These segments include the planner's time, the buyer's time, the time required by the vendor to process and ship the order, receiving and inspection, and movement to the required work center. If quotations are required prior to order placement, additional time is required. In most cases, however, the price of raw materials and components used repetitively is known prior to the required order release.

Purchasing Contract Arrangements

The *blanket order* is probably the most common contract arrangement between a purchaser and a supplier. It is a contract to purchase a minimum quantity over a period, usually a year. The purchasing department negotiates the initial contract, which may involve a fixed price, a price range, or a price tied to another base (e.g., the cost of labor or raw materials). The minimum and maximum quantities that may be ordered over a given subperiod, say every 30 days, may be specified also. Once a blanket order is contracted, production and inventory control usually may send requisitions directly to the supplier, requesting shipments of specified quantities by given dates.

Figure 16–3   The Purchasing Process: Order Placement and Receipt

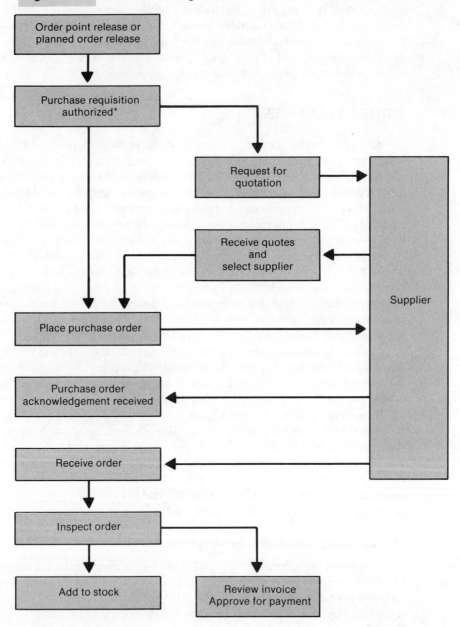

*In many cases, the organization has selected the primary and secondary suppliers in the order planning phase.

Purchasing is involved only in establishing and renegotiating the contract, if necessary.

A *standing order*, sometimes called a supply contract, is a blanket order for an indefinite period. It may specify a given quantity of an item to be shipped at fixed intervals, or it may call for delivery only on receipt of a requisition with the quantity allowed to vary within a given range during specified intervals.

Blanket and standing orders are advantageous to both the buyer and the seller. The buyer receives a price discount because of the quantity commitment and eliminates the cost of repetitive purchase orders. The seller, in turn, receives a guarantee of sales for a relatively long period. Additionally, if the seller's capacity planning suggests it, the seller can produce the required items early without the normal risks of building to stock. These contracts frequently contain provisions governing the notice required for revising or canceling the contract as well as the costs of termination.

As noted earlier, when more than one item produced on the same equipment is purchased from a supplier, the buyer may place an initial blanket order for a supplier's capacity only; later orders will specify which items are to be produced with this capacity. Both parties must agree to the lead time for the orders defining which items are to be produced.

Even when a blanket order does not exist, orders for *B* and *C* items may be placed with the assumption that the catalog or last-quoted price is still applicable. A purchase order acknowledgment sheet or ticket may be made part of the purchase order. The vendor then must use it to inform the purchaser if there have been any changes in price, delivery, or other specifications. The magnitude of the order and the probability of a change or misunderstanding determines if the purchaser will follow up with the supplier until an acknowledgment agreeing to the terms of the purchase order is received.

Systems and distributor contracts were described by Friessnig (1981) as follows:

> *Systems contracts*: Under a systems contract, vendors maintain, at their facilities, backup supplies of materials, and periodically inventory and replenish materials at your facility. A special order form is completed by the supplier which replaces and serves the function of the purchase order, receipt acknowledgment, and the invoice. Hardware, stationery, and operating supplies are typical commodities covered by a systems contract. In the service environment, many retailers establish systems contracts with vendors in such areas as breads, candies, and photographic supplies.
>
> *Distributor contracts*: Under a distributor contract, vendors normally maintain, at their facilities, predetermined quantities of specific materials dedicated for your use. Purchase order releases are made against the master contract.

Just-in-time inventory management procedures have encouraged the use of systems and distributor contracts (see Chapter 20). Such contracts usually require shipment within a given time period (e.g., three days). If the supplier is unable to ship, the purchaser has the right to obtain the merchandise from a second supplier. Often fines for noncompliance are used in these circumstances.

Prerequisite Data

Purchasing activities require that certain data be available to the planner-buyer. This information may be kept on 3-by-5 cards, in notebooks, or, more typically today, in a computer file. A common organization is (1) the item (part) master file, (2) the vendor file, (3) the requisition file, (4) the open purchase order file, including a master file and a detail file, and (5) the purchase history file.

The item master file is used in many activities including MRP, inventory management, and cost estimating. There is much similarity between the part master file of manufactured items (described in Chapter 12) and the master file for purchased items. The item (part) master file contains a record for each purchased item. The data in each record may be divided into general data and supplier data. Typical items in the general data portion include the item number, the item description, value classification, the on-hand quantity, the allocated quantity, available quantity, on-order quantity, lot size quantity, ordering rules, type of demand, and substitute items. The supplier data of the item master file will include the supplier number, address, telephone number, supplier's item number, price, and lead time. The supplier information will be available for each approved supplier. Most item master files contain additional data to meet the needs of a given environment and for use in other activities.

The vendor (supplier) file contains a record for each supplier; each record contains data describing the supplier performance, the location of the supplier, and the principal products obtained from the supplier. Typical data that might be included in such a file include:

1. A number uniquely identifying the supplier
2. The supplier's name
3. The supplier's address
4. The supplier's telephone number
5. The product or products sold by the supplier
6. The total units purchased this year to date—by item
7. The total dollars spent with the supplier this year
8. Information similar to Items 6 and 7 for one or more previous years
9. The percentage of units or lots that have not passed receiving inspection during the present year or last 12 months—sometimes by item
10. A measure of item performance in service
11. A measure of delivery performance, such as average lead time and standard deviation
12. Current price
13. Method of payment

14. Discount schedule
15. Payments due
16. Unfilled (outstanding) purchase orders

It would not be unusual to find additional information in the vendor file; the data items listed, however, are most of those usually required.

The open purchase order file contains a record of each released purchase order. Since two or more items may be ordered on the same purchase order, the purchase order record frequently contains a master (or header) section and a detail section for each item. The master section of the file includes information such as the following:

1. The purchase order number—a unique number usually serially assigned to successive purchase orders
2. Order status—a code indicating whether partial shipments have been received, the total order has been received, the order has been canceled, or the order has been closed
3. Purchase requisition number
4. Purchase requisition date
5. The supplier number
6. The buyer number
7. The number of shipments—a code indicating whether the order is for a single shipment, multiple shipments, a blanket order, a standing order, or any other special arrangement
8. Acknowledgment code—an indication of whether or not an acknowledgment is expected (if one is expected, other data fields are required in the record to reveal the status of the acknowledgment)
9. The total cost of the order
10. Special charges for transportation, special handling or packaging, insurance, expediting, etc.

The purchase order detail file contains information such as the following:

1. The item number (with applicable engineering changes)
2. The item name
3. The item line number on the purchase order
4. The unit of measure
5. The unit price
6. The requisition number
7. The requisition date
8. The quantity ordered
9. Date required
10. Various other dates (e.g., first and latest promised delivery dates, estimated delivery dates, shipping date, and date received)
11. A location code revealing whether the item is at the supplier, in transit, in receiving, in inspection, in material review, or in stores
12. The receiving report number
13. The quantity received
14. The quantity accepted by inspection

Other data concerning the disposition of rejected items by the material review board also may be included.

A separate file, the purchase history file, may exist for closed purchased orders, since they are voluminous and the data they contain are not accessed as often as open order data. The records in this file may be identified by item (part) number, supplier number, and/or purchase order number. It typically includes quotation data, unit price, other costs, terms, relevant dates, quantities, the buyer, scheduled delivery date, actual delivery dates, scrap quantities, deviations from specifications, and rework.

The list of data included in the files just described is not exhaustive. Many other data items may be required to achieve all the goals of purchasing in a given situation.

Requisition Control

Release of a planned order should result in the preparation of the requisition. A computerized system may prepare a purchase order automatically for some inventory items on their planned order release date. Requisitions for selected items, say A items and emergency orders, may be edited and expedited or delayed by the buyer. The system should minimize the time planner-buyers spend on routine activities and allow them to concentrate on the A items, critical because of their cost, delivery problems, or quality problems.

The system must allow the planner-buyer to determine the status of all requisitions. The system should have the capability of listing requisitions of a given or higher priority for which purchase orders have not been prepared. Priority may be based on the age of the requisition, a critical ratio, the order receipt due date, or some combination.

Wight (1974) and Benson (1981) both report on the combination of the traditionally separate roles of the planner and the buyer into one position, the planner-buyer. We have used the term planner-buyer in this text to represent either that situation or the traditional separation of the planner and the buyer. Combining the roles of the planner and buyer into a single position makes sense when a formal order release system generates valid due dates and when contact with each supplier can be maintained by a single planner-buyer.

Supplier Lead Time and Delivery

MRP, capacity requirements planning (CRP), and input/output (I/O) planning and control aid in achieving desired supplier lead time and delivery. Providing suppliers with the planned requirements by period gives them valid priorities and reduces the surprises common when using order point systems. The use of CRP and I/O planning to regulate the flow of orders to a supplier reduces the likelihood that orders will exceed the supplier's production capacity.

Supplier lead times are dynamic; they change as demand for the supplier's products vary, as the supplier increases or decreases capacity, and with the priority the supplier assigns to the purchaser's order. The planner-buyer should be sensitive to changes in the vendor's lead time and update the purchasing information system by revising the lead time in item and vendor records as these changes occur. Providing suppliers with long-term visibility of requirements and valid short-term priorities aids in controlling lead times. Morency (1977) reported on the excellent results by Bausch and Lomb Inc. in controlling supplier lead time and managing supplier capacity through the development of an MPS, MRP, and contract purchasing.

The Purchase Order Quantity

Chapters 11 and 12 included detailed treatments of how to calculate order quantities. Those chapters dealt with, among other topics, the impact of dependent and independent demand and quantity discounts. This section describes a more complex order quantity situation and ranking of quantity discount opportunities. The buyer-planner should ascertain the dominant factor when determining the quantity of an item to be purchased. Supplier packaging, transportation costs, quantity discounts, and production requirements can affect the purchase order quantity.

Let us analyze the following example. The MRP calls for 60 units of a purchased item for each of the next 12 weeks. Estimated requirements beyond that period are also 60 units per week. The company operates 50 weeks a year. The purchaser estimates that the cost of preparing a purchase order is $50. The supplier uses crates holding 150 units and charges an extra $20 for purchases of less than a full crate. The items cost $100 each at the supplier's dock. The supplier offers a 4 percent discount on orders for 600 or more units. The purchaser estimates it costs $100 for the truck to pick up one partial or full crate and deliver it to the plant. Carrying additional crates on the same trip costs an estimated $10 per crate. (Alternate shipping methods are more expensive.) The purchaser uses an inventory carrying cost rate (k) of .30 per year. What is the most economical order quantity?

The lot-for-lot (L4L) order quantity approach results in a weekly order for 60 units. Applying the traditional economic order quantity (EOQ) model without consideration of the transportation costs, partial crate charges, or quantity discount gives an order quantity of 100 units. If we add the flat $100 transportation cost to the order preparation costs, the EOQ model gives an order quantity of 173 units. None of these approaches, however, considers the reduced transportation cost per unit when two or more crates are combined in one shipment; nor do they consider the quantity discount.

The total costs for the different likely order quantities are tabulated in Table 16–1. Total costs include the unit costs, carrying costs, ordering costs, partial crate costs, and transportation costs. These costs are calculated as follows:

Table 16–1 Tabulation of Total Costs per Order Quantity

A. Lot For Lot

Q = 60 units; N = 50

Unit costs = $100 × 3,000	=	$300,000
Carrying costs = .3 × $100 × .02 × 50 × 60/2	=	900
Ordering costs = 50 × $50	=	2,500
Partial crate costs = $20 × 50	=	1,000
Transportation cost = $100 × 50	=	5,000
		$309,400

B. Simple EOQ

Q = 100 units; N = 30

Unit costs = $100 × 3,000	=	$300,000
Carrying costs = .3 × $100 × .03333 × 30 × 100/2	=	1,500
Ordering costs = 30 × $50	=	1,500
Partial crate costs = $20 × 30	=	600
Transportation costs = $100 × 30	=	3,000
		$306,600

C. One Crate

Q = 150 units (one crate); N = 20

Unit costs = $100 × 3,000	=	$300,000
Carrying costs = .3 × $100 × .05 × 20 × 150/2	=	2,250
Ordering costs = 20 × $50	=	1,000
Partial crate costs = none	=	0
Transportation costs = $100 × 20	=	2,000
		$305,250

D. Two Crates

Q = 300 units (two crates); N = 10

Unit costs = $100 × 3,000	=	$300,000
Carrying costs = .3 × $100 × .10 × 10 × 300/2	=	4,500
Ordering Costs = 10 × $50	=	500
Partial crate costs = none	=	0
Transportation costs = $110 × 10	=	1,100
		$306,100

E. Price Break Quantity

Q = 600 units, C = $96; N = 5

Unit costs = $96 × 3,000	=	$288,000
Carrying costs = .3 × $96 × .20 × 5 × 600/2	=	8,640
Ordering costs = 5 × $50	=	250
Partial crate costs = none	=	0
Transportation costs = $130 × 5	=	650
		$297,540

558

Total unit cost = Cost per unit (C) times the annual requirements (R)

$$= CR$$

Carrying cost = the product of the carrying cost rate (k), the cost per unit (C), the order interval $(t-$expressed in years by dividing the number of weeks by 50), the number of orders per year (N), and one-half the order quantity $(Q/2)$

$$= kCtNQ/2$$
(Note: tN equals 1.0 by definition when the period of analysis is one year.)

Ordering cost = the number of orders per year (N) times the preparation cost per order (S)

$$= NS$$

Partial crate cost = the charge per partial crate (C_p) times the number of orders per year (N)

$$= C_p N$$

Transportation cost = the number of shipments per year (N) times the cost of transportation (C_t)

$$= NC_t$$

where

$$C_t = \$100 + \$10(m - 1)$$

$$m = \text{number of crates per shipment}$$

The data in Table 16–1 reveal that the quantity discount is the dominant factor in the lot size decision. Purchasing in order quantities of 600 units results in an annual savings of $7,710 over the next best method. Since average inventory investment computed as $QC/2$, increases from $7,500 to $30,000 when we purchase 600 units rather than 150 in one order, the rate of return, computed as the savings divided by the incremental investment, on our investment equals $7,710/($30,000 − $7,500), or approximately .34. Depending upon the investment opportunities of the firm and the rates of return available, this may be a wise investment.

Quantity Discounts

The unit price of many items varies with the quantity purchased; a lower unit cost exists for larger purchase quantities. Chapter 11 described the process for determining the minimum cost order quantity for individual items with a quantity discount schedule. However, analyzing quantity discounts on only an individual item basis can lead to excessive inventory. Purchasing larger than the basic order quantity may be economically justified for many individual items. Purchasing the larger quantity for all such items can result in overcrowded stockrooms and in an inventory investment exceeding financial resources. The buyer must be able to select the most advantageous discount opportunities given total storage availability and financial capacity.

This selection can be based on a rate of return approach when opportunities concern items whose use is anticipated for the foreseeable future. When the opportunities concern items with different periods of anticipated usage, a present value approach is preferable. Let's examine the rate-of-return approach.

The rate of return approach ranks discount opportunities on the basis of their annual rate of return. Beginning with the highest rate of return opportunity and calculating the cumulative added inventory investment as the next highest rate opportunity is added in rank order sequence, the planner can determine the best selection of opportunities under a given investment constraint.

The annual rate of return on investment (ROI) earned by purchasing a discount quantity equals the annual net savings divided by the increased inventory investment. Annual net savings equal the annual decrease in total unit costs due to the price discount plus the annual ordering cost savings due to the reduced number of orders per year minus the increased inventory carrying costs.

That is, expressed as a mathematical model:

Total savings (TS) = unit cost savings (UCS) + ordering cost savings (OCS)
        $-$ increased inventory carrying costs (ICC)

where

$$UCS = D \times A$$

$$OCS = SA\left(\frac{1}{EOQ} - \frac{1-D}{DOQ}\right)$$

$$ICC = \frac{k}{2}(DOQ - EOQ)$$

D = Discount expressed as a decimal percentage

A = Annual requirements in dollars—without discount

S = Cost of placing order

$$EOQ = \text{Economic order quantity in dollars}$$

$$DOQ = \text{Discount order quantity in dollars}$$

$$k = \text{Annual carrying cost rate}$$

and the rate of return on investment is calculated as follows:

$$ROI = \frac{TS}{(DOQ/2) - (EOQ/2)}$$

Let us calculate the rate of return obtained from the discount for Item 1 in Table 16–2. From the table we have:

$$A = \$54,800$$

$$D = .02$$

$$EOQ = \$3,160$$

$$S = \$32$$

$$k = .35$$

$$DOQ = 5,000$$

$$UCS = D \times A$$

$$= .02 \times \$54,800$$

$$= \$1,096$$

The annual ordering cost savings (OCS) equals the cost of ordering times the decrease in the number of orders per year.

$$OCS = \$32 \times \$54,800\left(\frac{1}{\$3,160} - \frac{1 - .02}{\$5,000}\right)$$

$$= \$211$$

The annual increased inventory carrying costs equal the annual carrying cost rate (given as .35) times the increase in average inventory investment.

$$ICC = .35(\$5,000/2 - \$3,160/2)$$

$$= \$322$$

Total net savings is given by

$$TS = \$1,096 + \$211 - \$322$$

$$= \$985$$

The rate of return on investment equals the total savings divided by the increased inventory investment.

$$ROI = \$985/(\$5,000/2 - \$3,160/2)$$

$$= 1.071 \text{ or } 107.1\%$$

Similar data and the results of similar calculations are recorded in Table 16–2 for each of nine items. The increase in inventory investment due to the larger order size depends on the usage pattern. This example assumes a steady usage rate typical of independent demand, and the increase is estimated as one-half the difference between the normal and discount order quantities. Thus, for Item 1 the increased inventory investment equals $.5(\$5,000 - \$3,160)$, which equals \$920. When those units added to the order quantity to obtain a discount likely will be held for a relatively long period of little or no usage, estimate the increased investment as a higher proportion, say .75, of the difference between the order quantities.

The next step is to list all discount opportunities in rank order with ranks based on the rate of return as illustrated in Table 16–3. These calculations and tabulations aid management in answering questions such as: If a maximum of \$5,000 can be added to inventory, which discounts should be taken? What additional investment is required to obtain all discounts with a rate of return greater than 30 percent? The rates of return, annual discount, and average increase in inventory listed in Table 16–3 in ranking order reveal that the discounts on Items 5, 1, 3, 8, and 2 have a rate of return greater than 30 percent. The data in Table 16–3 also reveal that the discounts on Items 5, 1, and 3 are the best discount opportunities if there is a \$5,000 limit on the added inventory investment for this group of items.

PURCHASING CONTROL

The purchasing department should exercise control over individual purchase orders, purchase commitments, and vendor performances. Control of individual purchase orders begins with the control of the requisitions as described previously.

Purchase Order Control

Purchasing should be able to determine the status of each order including whether it is currently a planned order, a firm planned order, placed,

Table 16–2 Evaluation of Quantity Discounts Rate-of-Return Approach

Item	Annual Requirements (A)	Economic Order Quantity (EOQ)	Discount (D)	Discount Order Quantity (DOQ)	Annual Discount (UCS)	Ordering Cost Savings (OCS)	Increase in Average Inventory	Increase in Carrying Costs	Total Net Savings (TS)	Rate of Return (ROI)
1	$54,800	$3,160	.02	$ 5,000	$1,096	$211	$ 920	$ 322	$ 985	107.1%
2	48,635	2,976	.018	6,000	875	266	1,512	529	612	40.4
3	32,408	2,430	.05	7,500	1,620	294	2,535	887	1,385	54.6
4	28,620	2,282	.052	10,000	1,488	314	3,859	1,351	448	11.6
5	22,987	2,040	.115	5,000	2,643	230	1,480	518	2,355	159.1
6	18,453	1,850	.045	6,000	830	227	2,075	726	331	16.0
7	11,008	1,418	.062	4,500	682	176	1,441	504	354	24.6
8	7,431	1,160	.09	3,000	669	131	920	322	478	52.0
9	1,650	545	.075	1,200	124	54	378	132	46	12.2

Ordering costs (S) equal approximately $32. The carrying cost rate (k) is .35.

Table 16–3 Ranking Discount Opportunities by Rate of Return

Item	Rank	Return	Added Inventory	Cumulative Added Inventory
5	1	159.1	$1,480	$1,480
1	2	107.1	920	2,400
3	3	54.6	2,535	4,935
8	4	52.0	920	5,855
2	5	40.4	1,512	7,367
7	6	24.6	1,441	8,808
6	8	16.0	2,075	10,883
9	9	12.2	378	11,261
4	10	11.6	3,859	15,120

acknowledged, received, or closed. Acknowledgment may be required only if the supplier requests a change in the order price, quantity, or product specification. The purchasing department can request acknowledgments also for orders to new suppliers or for orders with unusual quantities, product specifications, or shipping instructions. The purchasing information system should provide the capability of monitoring acknowledgments and following up on those not received in the prescribed time.

Purchase Commitments

Purchase orders call for deliveries that generate accounts payable and, thus, negative cash flow. Controlling the cash commitments begins with the MPS, MRP, and the resulting planned purchase orders. The planned order release dates, delivery lead times, and payment schedules determine when payment is due. Summing the cash commitments of the planned purchase orders from a given MPS enables management to evaluate the effect of purchases on projected cash requirements. Balancing projected cash requirements with budgeted available cash may require revisions in the MPS and planned purchase order releases. Working capital budgets may necessitate more frequent purchase orders for smaller quantities.

As purchase orders are released, actual cash commitments should be tabulated and compared to planned commitments. If significant variances exist, analysis can determine if they are due to price, quantity, or delivery changes. Accounting and finance can use actual purchase order cash commitments in controlling short-term cash flow.

SUPPLIER RELATIONS

Suppliers are as important to most manufacturers as their own production capability. The customer-supplier relationship affects the quality and cost of the purchaser's product as well as the purchaser's customer service capability.

Relations with suppliers involve or primarily concern the following:

1. Overall strategy
2. Part design
3. Quality
4. Delivery schedule (quantity)
5. Pricing
6. Communications

Overall Strategy

Nakane and Hall (1981) have pointed out that many Japanese firms consider suppliers as relatives. Trust and loyalty dominate the relationship that emphasizes mutual assistance to strengthen the production capabilities of both companies. Such relationships also exist in the United States, although to a much lesser extent. Automobile owners value highly the mechanic on whom they can depend, and companies develop a loyalty to a reliable cleaning service. Such relationships usually provide quality and service resulting in lower total costs than those found in a caveat emptor (let the buyer beware) environment.

Part Design

In some cases, the nature of the item or the relative design engineering strengths of the purchaser and supplier naturally lead to the purchaser providing detailed specifications. In other cases, the purchaser may provide only the interface design requirements (mechanical, electrical, and hydraulic connections, for example) and the general functional requirements. Thus, the supplier performs part of the design function to achieve quality and cost objectives. This is obviously true in the case of commercial items purchased from catalogs. When suppliers and customers view final product quality and cost as common objectives, design modification to achieve these objectives may originate two or more levels below the final product manufacturer. The firm making the mold for a plastic component, for example, may suggest a change in the component's design to the component manufacturer who, in turn, suggests it to the firm assembling the final product. In brief, design improvements and value analysis are not limited to the firm performing the final assembly.

Quality

The consumer does not distinguish between the quality of purchased components and the quality of those items manufactured by the firm from whom the final product is purchased. Both are equally important. When, for example, a solenoid in a dishwasher fails, the consumer holds the dishwasher manufacturer responsible. Thus, many organizations require that the quality control system as well as the manufacturing and financial capability of a potential supplier be approved prior to issuing any purchase orders to the same supplier. Continued improvement in supplier quality is an important result of the cooperative attitude necessary to developing a successful customer-supplier relationship. This attitude is manifested by the purchaser providing technical assistance to overcome production difficulties at the supplier, clearly delineating the critical from the not-so-critical characteristics, and providing immediate feedback of poor quality.

The Schedule

Supplier capacity characteristics are important to the purchaser in any environment. These include

1. Capacity, overall rate of production, and capacity commitments to the purchaser
2. Ability to respond to production rate changes
3. Ability to respond to product mix changes
4. Planning lead times required by the supplier to revise commitments

With this knowledge, the purchaser can avoid making unrealistic demands of the supplier. Purchasers should treat suppliers' schedules in the same manner as they treat their internal master production schedule. Planning fences should be established for things such as delivery requirements, parts fabrication, and material purchases (see Chapter 8). In addition, the purchaser should work with suppliers advising them how to reduce lead time and increase production flexibility.

Pricing

The cost to the purchaser may be based on a competitive bid, a cost-plus contract, a specified percentage of the cost—usually in the case of experimental or development work—or a negotiated figure. Negotiated costs are sometimes based on target costs based in turn on learning curves and competitive factors. The important point is that long-term quality suppliers develop only under profitable conditions, and purchasers survive and prosper only with quality and cost-competitive purchased parts.

Communications

Communications is an important element in supplier relations. In some companies, the planner and buyer is a combined position, thus simplifying communication between planning and the suppliers. Suppliers should be able to contact the purchaser's design engineers and in some cases expect aid in developing or improving manufacturing processes. The point is that surprises should be a rare occurrence; the supplier should be informed of the relative importance of the purchaser's requirements; and the purchaser should have a clear picture of the supplier's capabilities.

ORDER RECEIPT AND RECEIVING

Receiving and purchasing activities are tied together by their very nature. Receiving plays a crucial role in purchasing control. Shipments from suppliers arrive at receiving. Receiving must record the date of arrival; identify the supplier, the item, and the quantity; inspect as required; forward the item to the proper location; and inform purchasing, inventory control, quality control, and accounting of these actions. Because all items may not require a detailed inspection of physical and performance characteristics, purchasing should assure that receiving knows the appropriate inspection procedures for all items. Receiving should confirm that the items are labeled properly and correspond to the purchase order. Receiving then must decide whether to send items directly to a manufacturing work center or to a given storage location. This requires prior instructions from either purchasing or planning. Movement to the wrong location can result in production delays and lost items. Receiving may have a list of critical items that should be expedited through receiving and sent immediately to manufacturing. Also, receiving normally should notify the buyer-planner and manufacturing of their arrival.

Receiving should inform purchasing of partial shipments as well as quantities that exceed the overshipment tolerance. The buyer then can follow up on items still due and decide if the excess quantity should be returned to the supplier. Items that do not meet inspection requirements may be sent to a material review area. Representatives of quality control, engineering, purchasing, manufacturing, and sometimes the supplier then will decide on the disposition of the rejected item. Some may be reworked, others may be accepted as a usable variation, and others will be returned to the vendor.

Just-in-time (JIT) purchasing requires suppliers to deliver components to the purchaser's receiving dock or sometimes directly to the production line as they are required. This approach is used widely in Japan and has been implemented at the Kawasaki Plant in Lincoln, Nebraska as reported by Schonberger, Sutton, and Claunch (1981). Suppliers often are located near the purchaser, usually have a long-term contract (for a year or the production season), and deliver once or twice daily. This approach reduces the purchaser's work in process (see Chapter 20 for a further explanation of the JIT approach).

Purchasing control is the final stage in the preorder, order, and postorder purchasing cycle. Purchasing activities have a substantial impact on material costs, availability, and quality. Effective purchasing can decrease inventory investment, increase customer service, and improve profits dramatically.

VALUE ANALYSIS

The *APICS Dictionary* (Wallace and Dougherty 1987) defines value analysis as "the systematic use of techniques which serve to identify a required function, establish a value for that function, and finally to provide that function at the lowest overall cost. This approach focuses on the functions of an item rather than the methods of producing the present product design." Because of the high cost of purchased items, value analysis is often applied as part of the purchasing function. In this context its objective is to find lower-cost alternative ways of performing the functions of currently purchased items.

Even as a purchasing function, value analysis is often a team project. Although the composition of the team depends on the nature of the organization, it usually includes members from design engineering, marketing, manufacturing engineering, and materials management (purchasing). As specific problems are considered, experts are added from each of these areas and others. Suppliers may be invited to participate, and external consultants can provide valuable assistance.

The purpose of value analysis is to define the function of an item, to determine its cost, and to ascertain its value (what it should cost).

The function should be described simply, such as

Item	Primary Function
Nut	Hold wheel on
Tube	Conduct hydraulic fluid
Knob	Adjust volume
Rivet	Secure strap

Since an item may have a secondary function (e.g., the rivet on a shoulder strap also may be decorative), these functions should be recognized and included in the cost and value analyses. The basic questions are: What does it do? and What should it do? An item's value is the lower of the minimum cost at which its essential functions can be fulfilled and the maximum price the customer will pay for the item. Customers, of course, usually do not buy components; they purchase end products. Thus, the latter measure of value (customer's willingness to pay) is not directly applicable to individual items; however, it is applicable to the total costs of the items in an end product.

Finding alternative items as well as simplifying product design, manufacturing processes and setups, material handling, and distribution practices can reduce costs, capacity requirements, and manufacturing lead time while improving customer service.

CONCLUSIONS

The purchasing department has many responsibilities. Those that relate directly to production and operations management concern order quantities, order release, the cost of purchased items, vendor capacity, the lead time of purchased items, the vendor's flexibility in adjusting to engineering and schedule changes, and vendor delivery performance. Planning and control of vendor deliveries are as crucial to achieving production and operations management objectives as planning and control of production. Techniques useful in controlling production also are useful in controlling vendor deliveries. The purchasing department's role extends across the long-, medium-, and short-range planning horizons. New methods exist for extending capacity planning and control to encompass suppliers' facilities and improve their delivery performance. The just-in-time philosophy has dramatically influenced contemporary purchasing practices and vendor relationships.

QUESTIONS

1. Why would an organization purchase custom equipment and services from an outside vendor when it is capable of producing the desired good or service in-house?

2. When an organization purchases custom equipment and services, what role does the purchasing department usually play?

3. What is ABC analysis? How is it applied to purchasing management?

4. In ABC analysis, what factors may serve as criteria for classifying an item's value?

5. What should be the purchasing department's objectives when purchasing materials and components? How would the purchasing department achieve these objectives?

6. Explain the similarity between purchasing's and production activity control's role in planning and controlling priorities and capacities.

7. Many organizations often face make-or-buy decisions. Identify the factors that may affect these decisions.

8. A critical task of the purchasing department is vendor evaluation. What areas of the potential supplier's operations should be analyzed before being accepted.

9. What is a blanket order? How does it differ from a standing order? What are the advantages of blanket and standing orders?

10. Compare and contrast systems contracts and distributor contracts.

11. When establishing a vendor file, what information should be included?

12. When should the position of planner-buyer be instituted?

13. Why are supplier lead times an important consideration for the purchasing organization?

14. When quantity discount, transition, or other special opportunity lot size analysis indicates a substantial increase in order size, what other factors should the purchasing department examine?

15. In value analysis, what process should be followed to evaluate and compare alternatives?

16. When ranking two or more projects for implementation, what areas should be considered?

PROBLEMS

1. A company's sales last year were $25 million, profit was $5 million and the cost of purchases was $15 million. If the rate of inflation is zero, and sales volume remains the same, how much must the cost of purchased items be reduced to increase profits by 10 percent.

2. A small telecommunications firm markets a fax unit. The company produces 100 units per week, and future forecasts reflect stable demand. One assembly for the unit costs $200, preparation of a purchase order is estimated at $25, and annual carrying costs are 30 percent. The supplier's production schedule size calls for a production run of 400 units. They charge an additional $20 for ordered quantities of less than 400 units. The plant operates 50 weeks each year. Transportation costs per delivery are $100. Calculate the total yearly costs for a lot-for-lot approach and an EOQ technique.

3. Using the data from Problem 2, calculate the total costs if the company were to order a full production run of 400 units and a double production run of 800 units. Also calculate the total costs if the vendor were to offer a 5 percent price break for orders of greater than 1,200 units.

4. The annual requirements in dollars for an assembly needed for production is $37,825. EOQ is $2,705, discount order quantity is $7,000, and the discount percentage is 8 percent. Calculate the annual discount, ordering cost savings, increase in average inventory, increase in carrying costs, net

savings, and rate of return if the organization were to purchase assemblies at the discount order quantity. The order cost is $50 per order, and the carrying cost rate is 25 percent.

5. An item has a two-level discount schedule. The ordering costs are $25, and the carrying cost rate is .30.

Annual Requirements	EOQ	Discount Percent	Discount Order Quantity
$62,400	$4,200 6,000	3% 2%	6,000 9,000

Calculate the annual requirements for the second level, the annual discount, ordering cost savings, increase in average inventory, increase in carrying costs, net savings, and rate of return for each level.

6. The promised delivery lead times for five suppliers and their actual lead times on recent orders are as follows (different materials are supplied):

Supplier	Promised Lead Time (Days)	Actual Lead Time of the Last Ten Shipments (Oldest Orders First)
A	6	9, 7, 6, 9, 5, 9, 8, 9, 10, 10
B	10	12, 12, 11, 10, 10, 9, 10, 11, 10, 9
C	15	14, 15, 13, 17, 17, 16, 14, 15, 13, 15
D	20	20, 18, 19, 22, 22, 21, 24, 24, 26, 28
E	25	30, 29, 31, 29, 28, 30, 28, 31, 32, 28

Evaluate the performance of each supplier. Have any trends developed that may require discussions or negotiations with a supplier?

7. A security hardware manufacturer purchases circuit boards and memory to store information for the processor to call upon when needed. Assume that 1,000 units are produced every month, each with the purchased board and memory. The board costs are $700, purchase order preparation is $50, and carrying costs are 35 percent annually. The supplier mass produces thousands of the boards each week and charges an extra $200 for orders less than 5,000 units. The plant operates 52 weeks each year. Transporation costs per delivery are $100. Calculate the total yearly costs for a lot-for-lot approach and an EOQ technique.

8. Using the data from Problem 7, calculate the total costs if the company were to order 5,000 units. Also calculate the total costs if the vendor were to offer a 10 percent price break for orders of greater than 6,000 units.

REFERENCES

Benson, Randall J. "Can Purchasing Supply Tomorrow's Factory?" APICS 24th Annual International Conference Proceedings (1981), pp. 355–359.

Burlingame, L. James, and R. A. Warren. "Extended Capacity Planning. "APICS 17th Annual International Conference Proceedings (1974), pp. 83–91.

Carter, Philip L., and Robert M. Monczka. "Steelcase, Inc.: MRP in Purchasing." *Case Studies in Materials Requirements Planning.* Washington, D.C.: American Production and Inventory Control Society, 1978, pp. 105–129.

Fogarty, Donald W. and Thomas R. Hoffmann. *Production and Inventory Management.* Cincinnati: South-Western Publishing Co., 1983.

Friessnig, Rudy. "In Line—Real Time Procurement." APICS 24th Annual International Conference Proceedings (1981), pp. 363–365.

Monczka, Robert M., and Phillip L. Carter. "Productivity and Performance Measurement in Purchasing." APICS 19th Annual Conference Proceedings (1976), pp. 6–9.

Morency, Richard R. "A Systems Approach to Vendor Scheduling Under Contract Purchasing." APICS 20th Annual Conference Proceedings (1977), pp. 458–467.

Nakane, Jinichiro, and Robert W. Hall. "Transferring Production Control Methods Between Japan and the United States." APICS 24th Annual International Conference Proceedings (1981), pp. 192–194.

Schonberger, Richard J., Doug Sutton, and Jerry Claunch. "KANBAN (just-in-time) Applications at Kawasaki USA." APICS 24th Annual International Conference Proceedings (1981), pp. 181–191.

Volsky, Sanford L. "Purchasing's Inflation Fighter: The Computer." APICS 24th Annual International Conference Proceedings (1981), pp. 360–362.

Wallace, Thomas F., and John R. Dougherty. *APICS Dictionary.* 6th ed. Washington, D.C.: American Production and Inventory Control Society, 1987.

Wight, Oliver W. *Production and Inventory Management in the Computer Age.* Boston, Mass.: Cahner Books, 1974, pp. 140–144.

CHAPTER 17
DISTRIBUTION MANAGEMENT

OBJECTIVES

After completing this chapter, you should be able to

- Identify the five strategic decisions in distribution management and appreciate the need for integration of these decision areas

- Show the relationship of the distribution system with the production and purchasing systems in different production process environments

- Differentiate pull and push distribution inventory management systems and describe the operation of several varieties of each

- Show the effects of different distribution system inventory costing procedures

OUTLINE

INTRODUCTION

This chapter concerns distribution management and the integration of production management and distribution management. After a product is manufactured or a service-producing environment is created, the emphasis of the organization shifts toward distributing the good or providing the service. The distribution and service process involves many of the same issues as production management; however, the concerns may more directly consider customer convenience and needs.

Time and place have value. The objective of distribution inventory management is to have the right good (i.e., inventory) or service in the right place at the right time at a reasonable cost—that is, to achieve a desired level of customer service at or below a specified cost—which will help establish or maintain a competitive advantage. To achieve this objective, distribution strategies and policies should be part of an integrated organizational strategy encompassing all functional areas. It is particularly important that decisions made by marketing, engineering, finance, and manufacturing be linked systemically because decisions in one area usually affect results in others.

STRATEGIC DECISIONS

Five major strategic decisions dominate distribution management systems. These are

1. Selection of geographic markets
2. Defining the role of the distribution center
3. Designing the distribution system
4. Locating distribution centers
5. Selecting a distribution inventory management system

Although each of these areas is identified as a separate decision, they also must be linked systematically. Locating the distribution centers, for example, must be clearly integrated with other decisions. This discussion will briefly introduce the first four strategic decisions and then will consider in detail the distribution inventory management system, which is of direct and immediate concern to the operations manager because it must interface directly with the production system.

Selection of Geographic Markets

Decisions concerning geographic markets require very close coordination of the operations and the marketing staffs. The marketing staff will be concerned with price, product, place, and promotion, while the operations staff addresses the first three issues in terms of cost, product design, and delivery requirements. The fourth marketing concern, promotion, can have notable effects on production capacity requirements. Thus, the selection of the geographic markets, which is primarily a function of the marketing staff, significantly affects the volume of demand, needed production capacity, and the required capacity of the distribution system.

Often, the selection and definition of geographic markets will be a given to the operations manager. In some cases, the marketing function will be responsible for the distribution system and the operations function will merely deliver the product to a finished goods warehouse. Alternatively, the operations function may be responsible for management of the distribution system through regional and local warehouses. In this latter case, the function may be called materials management. The distribution function may be organized in a variety of different ways; however, it is critical that linkages between the marketing function and the operations function be well established at all levels, and that communications be rapid and accurate.

Role of the Distribution Center

The distribution function usually is associated with a make-to-stock situation; however, it also can be required in a predominantly make-to-order situation. In both situations, distribution centers often perform some fabrication or assembly jobs because those jobs can be accomplished more economically than at the factory. For example, manufacturers of special truck bodies (customized to order) and related equipment such as derricks, aerial devices, and diggers frequently ship the equipment and truck body to the distributor for final assembly.

Many products require some fabrication as part of the installation process. The mounting of equipment and installation of hydraulic, pneumatic, and electrical lines in many cases must be performed at the fixed site or can be performed there less expensively by the distributor than by the manufacturer.

Performing final assembly, finishing, and packaging operations at distribution centers enables direct shipments or bulk shipments from the plant to the distribution point. For example, the direct shipment of a truck chassis from the truck chassis manufacturer to the distributor, rather than through the truck body manufacturer, can save costs as well as time. Additionally, the use of less-expensive bulk shipments can result in considerable savings because the distance from the plant to the distribution point usually is substantially greater than the distance from the distribution center to the customer. Thus, the distribution center may perform the final fabrication or assembly operation in the manufacturing process. In addition, it may serve as a repair and service center, which frequently is a very profitable activity.

Designing the Distribution System

The design of the distribution system includes decisions concerning the number of warehouses, their size, their location, whether they are owned or leased, and methods of transportation. More specific considerations, including building or purchasing of facilities, directly controlling or subcontracting them to a vendor, and purchasing of transportation equipment or signing long-term contracts with carriers, are capacity planning decisions.

Most warehouses and material-handling equipment are used easily by many different organizations with different products. Relatively minor and inexpensive modifications usually are all that is required. Thus, they usually are much easier to purchase or to sell than manufacturing facilities. However, these same conditions encourage the contracting of similar distribution services with a common distributor. The use of the same local bottling and distribution systems by several soft drink companies is an example of these efficiencies.

The nature of the product, the distance, the cost, and time requirements determine the most appropriate mode of transportation. A pipeline is most economical for some liquids and gases sold in large volume at a low unit cost. Shipping very expensive, lightweight items long distance by air is frequently the least costly method because of reduced time and lower carrying costs. The availability of company-owned carriers can generate substantial savings. This is especially true when little competition exists among common (commercial) carriers and when return loads can be picked up at a supplier's facility.

Locating Distribution Centers

Once the distribution system has been designed conceptually, it must be put in place and the current facilities must be adjusted to better meet distribution requirements. These location decisions for distribution centers are the implementation of the previously noted decision, designing the distribution system. Numerous analytical approaches are available to consider the facility location problem (see Chapter 4). These methods can address a variety of distribution system objectives including costs, service items, routing alternatives, and schedules.

In addition to the computational processes of distribution center location, numerous other types of information and constraints are normally imposed on the problem. Efficient access to truck, water, rail, or air routes and the availability and skills of the local work force are almost always prime considerations in location decisions. Another more subtle yet important consideration includes the fit of the distribution center with the needs and requirements of the community. A Chicago machine tools distributor, for example, recently relocated part of its operation to Bloomington, Illinois to take advantage of good highways and better proximity to customers. Another factor, however, was the receptivity of the community to the proposed relocation.

DISTRIBUTION INVENTORY MANAGEMENT SYSTEMS

The fifth strategic decision, selection of the distribution inventory management systems, is almost always related to the production system. In the case of make-to-stock items, the distribution cycle is buffered from the production cycle by stocks at distribution points. Thus, the distribution system is somewhat less directly tied to the production system. In all cases, however, the two systems must be closely tied. Figure 17–1 shows how the inventory management of production and distribution systems are integrated in various types of industries.

The production and distribution inventories of the project, the job shop (make-to-order), the assemble-to-order, and the make-to-stock environments are tied together by the requirements forecasting and allowable lead time relationships. The project, job shop, and assemble-to-order environments all require a direct linkage of the production and distribution systems. Alternatively, the make-to-stock environment buffers the distribution system from the production system by creating inventories. Similarly, the regional distribution system may be buffered from the local distribution system by inventories. These inventories may be in the form of finished goods for direct customer orders or in the form of repair parts to satisfy maintenance requirements.

The different relationships between the production and distribution environments is important because of the effects that a customer order can have on the system. In the make-to-stock environment, the customer order directly affects the warehouse where the order is filled, but it does not have the same impact on the scheduling of assembly, production, or purchasing orders. These are buffered by inventory and smoothed by forecasts. Alternatively, in the project, job shop, and assemble-to-order environments, no finished goods inventory buffers are available; thus, the delivery process must be smoothed

Figure 17–1   Relationship of Production and Distribution Inventories in Various Industries

Type of Industry	Procurement	Produce Components	Assemble Products	Distribution
Project	← ————————— Allowable Lead Time ————————— →			
Job Shop (make to order)	Forecast Raw Materials	← ————— Allowable Lead Time ————— →		
Assemble-to-Order	Forecast Raw Materials and Components		← ——— Allowable Lead Time ——— →	
Make-to-Stock	Forecast Raw Materials, Components, and Products			← Allowable Lead Time →

through the use of lead times for backordering the assembly or for production and procurement actions.

Distribution inventory management systems can be classified as pull or push systems. In a pull system, the warehouse determines its requirements based on a forecast or on customer requirements and orders from the factory; it "pulls" inventory into the warehouse. In a push system, the forecast requirements for all warehouses are summed by period and scheduled production and available inventory is allocated on a prorated basis to the warehouses. The inventory is "pushed" into the warehouses. Actual systems frequently combine features of both push and pull systems.

Pull Systems

The archetype pull system orders without regard for the needs of other warehouses, the inventory available at the central warehouse, or the production schedule. The warehouse controls the ordering system. Traditional pull systems include the order point system, the periodic review system, and the sales replacement system. The base stock system is primarily a pull system, but it may exhibit some push system characteristics.

THE ORDER POINT SYSTEM. The order point system uses the same rationale that was applied to inventory management in Chapter 11. The branch warehouse orders from the main warehouse whenever the quantity in stock at the branch reaches a designated order point. The order point is based on the normal demand during the average time required to obtain the order (replenishment lead time) from the central warehouse plus the safety stock. There is little interaction between the branch warehouse and the central warehouse, which receives the orders without any warning. This system can result in a very erratic demand on the central warehouse. It requires a relatively large safety stock at the central warehouse in addition to the safety stocks at the branch warehouses.

THE PERIODIC REVIEW SYSTEM. With the periodic review system (sometimes called the fixed order interval or the cycle review system), branch warehouse inventory status is determined at a specified interval; the warehouse orders the quantity required to bring inventory to the target level (maximum). Branch warehouse safety stock must be greater in this system than in an order point system since it must cover variations in demand during the cycle as well as during lead time. Traditionally, this method has been used when orders for many items from a single source are combined for economies of purchasing and transportation.

THE SALES REPLACEMENT SYSTEM. Each warehouse periodically (perhaps quarterly) establishes a stocking level for each item based on local demand. Sales at each warehouse are reported to the central warehouse at periods shorter than the normal order interval. Shipments replacing the quantities sold are sent to each warehouse at the end of the replenishment periods. Periods usually are established to obtain economical shipments such as full truck loads. Increased warehouse reporting of sales to the central warehouse decreases the effect of erratic demand on the central warehouse. It enables manufacturing and purchasing to improve the coordination of planned orders with warehouse sales.

ADVANTAGES AND DISADVANTAGES OF PULL SYSTEMS. The advantages of a pull system are that it can operate autonomously and has lower data processing and communication expenses than a push system. However, distributed data processing and computers have decreased these costs substantially. Pull systems also have inherent disadvantages. In a strict pull system, orders are placed with the central warehouse without any knowledge or consideration of the needs of other warehouses. The ordering warehouse usually is unaware of shipping plans that may include the combination of shipments to two or more warehouses or the use of a different size truck or railroad car. Orders also are submitted without regard to available inventory, production schedules, or irregular occurrences (e.g., the addition of a new private label customer).

The result of several local warehouses ordering from a central warehouse may be erratic demand throughout the assembly, production, and purchasing systems. This lack of integration can be very costly. As these deficiencies in pull systems have been recognized, communications between regional warehouses and the central supply have increased and greater control of shipping quantities has been placed at the central supply. Thus, many systems with the basic characteristics of a pull system have taken on some characteristics of push systems.

THE BASE STOCK SYSTEM. Each retail outlet—if company owned—and each warehouse periodically (perhaps quarterly) establishes a stocking level for each item. Sales are reported on a weekly or, preferably, a daily basis to all inventory-holding facilities (see Figure 17–2), rather than reporting them only when ordering. Thus, the regional warehouse, the central warehouse, and the factory are aware of demand trends. This system usually is not subjected to shock waves of unexpected demand. The primary advantage of this system is that it enables manufacturing, the central warehouse, and regional warehouses to plan and react on the basis of actual customer demand rather than the replenishment orders filled at secondary stock points such as regional warehouses. The system reduces the unpredictability of demand on the warehouses and the factory. The total demand for an item across the entire system is usually more stable than demand measured by individual stocking points in the system.

The base stock level at each stocking location equals the forecast demand during replenishment lead time and the interval between sales reports plus the safety stock. The supplying operation—rather than the stocking

Figure 17–2   The Base Stock System Flow of Sales Data, Orders, and Inventory

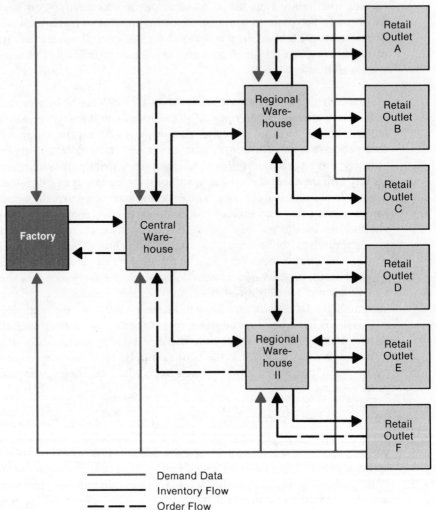

location—initiates replenishment orders on the basis of customer demand and available stock. This system eliminates many of the inherent deficiencies of the classic pull systems by incorporating features now identified with push systems.

Push Systems

Push systems (1) consider total projected requirements (all warehouse and direct sales requirements), inventory available at the regional warehouses and the central warehouse, inventory in transit, and scheduled receipts from the source (plant or supplier) and (2) determine the quantity available for each warehouse and direct factory sales. This allocation is controlled centrally on the basis of such criteria as equal days coverage of demand, shipping schedules, and competitive factors. The central warehouse decides what to send—that is, what to push—to the regional warehouses. This section discusses the distribution requirements planning approach, an extension of material requirements planning, and several variants.

DISTRIBUTION REQUIREMENTS PLANNING (DRP). DRP ties production and distribution planning together by determining aggregate time-phased net requirements at the same point in the material flow as the master schedule (see Figure 17–3).

The master schedule is the link between distribution and manufacturing. Master scheduling uses the distribution requirements, the inventory on hand, and the production planning strategy and constraints to determine the master production schedule (MPS).

Figure 17–3   Information Flows in Distribution and Production Planning

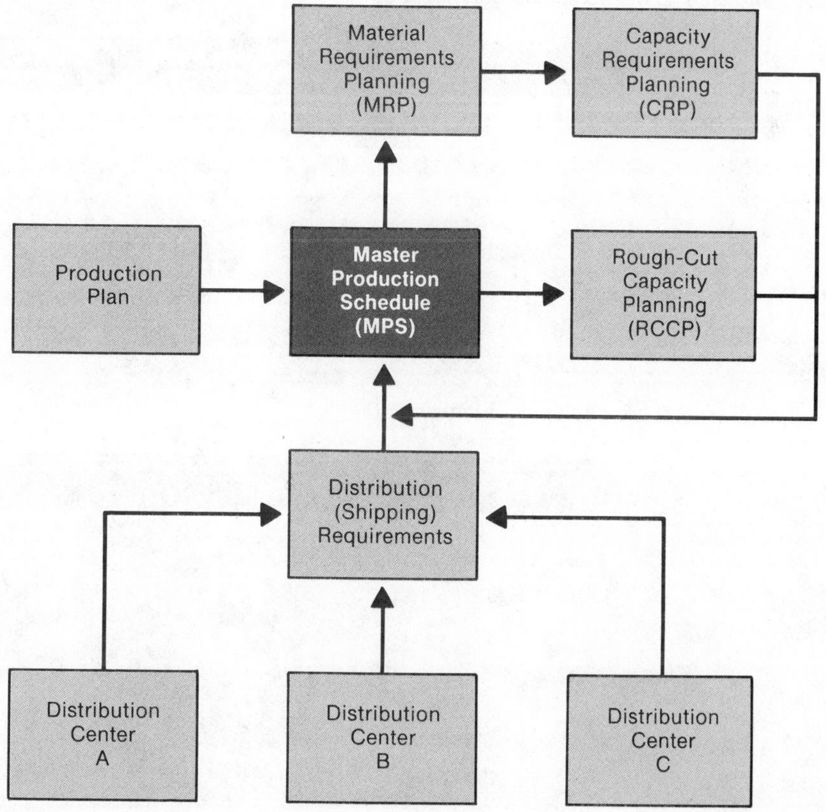

Table 17–1 illustrates the distribution requirements plans of Distribution Centers A, B, and C. Distribution Center A, for example, has a forecast of 50 units for each of the first four weeks and 100 units for each of the last four weeks. Due to space limitations, the example uses only eight weeks; a typical

Table 17–1 Distribution Requirements Planning for Distribution Centers A, B, and C

Distribution Center A	Current Week	Week 1	2	3	4	5	6	7	8
Forecast		50	50	50	50	100	100	100	100
In transit				200		200		200	
Planned receipts					200		200		200
Projected on hand	150	100	50	0	150	50	150	50	150
Planned shipments			200		200		200		

On hand: 150; lead time: 2 wks; shipping quantity: 200

Distribution Center B	Current Week	Week 1	2	3	4	5	6	7	8
Forecast		100	100	100	100	100	100	100	100
In transit			250		250			250	
Planned receipts				250		250			250
Projected on hand	200	100	0	150	50	200	100	0	150
Planned shipments		250		250			250		

On hand: 200; lead time: 2 wks; shipping quantity: 250

Distribution Center C	Current Week	Week 1	2	3	4	5	6	7	8
Forecast		200	200	200	200	150	150	100	150
In transit									
Planned receipts		400		400		400			400
Projected on hand	50	250	50	250	50	300	150	50	300
Planned shipments			400		400			400	

On hand: 50; lead time: 1 wk; shipping quantity: 200

distribution requirements plan would cover 12 months. An examination of Table 17–1 reveals that shipment receipts are planned for Distribution Center A in Weeks 4, 6, and 8 to prevent a stock-out. Note that neither safety stock nor safety lead time is planned in any of the distribution centers. A two-week delivery lead time means that shipments to Distribution Center A from the central warehouse (or, in this case, the plant) must be planned for Weeks 2, 4, and 6. Planned shipments and receipts for Distribution Centers B and C are determined in a similar manner.

DRP logic works as follows:

1. Subtract the forecast requirements from the sum of inventory on hand and in transit to determine the period in which the inventory on hand will be less than zero or, if safety stock is used, less than the safety stock.
2. Order a planned shipment receipt in the period determined in Step 1. (The shipping order quantity may be fixed or determined by a number of factors described later.)
3. Calculate the planned shipping period by subtracting the planned replenishment lead time from the planned shipment receipt period.
4. Add the planned shipment receipt to the projected on-hand balance at the distribution center and return to Step 1 continuing the process to the end of the planning horizon.

Table 17–2 summarizes the requirements for all the distribution centers. Tables 17–3 and 17–4 show two master schedules illustrating different possible methods of meeting these requirements. Master Schedule A in Table 17–3 has an MPS with a lot-for-lot production and no planned safety stock. Master Schedule B in Table 17–4 has an MPS with level production—350 units in each week—and no planned safety stock. Manufacturing lead time is one week in both cases. If other requirements existed, they would be added to the distribution requirements summary in Table 17–2 and incorporated into the shipping requirements in Tables 17–3 and 17–4.

Relatively smooth demand at the distribution centers can result in lumpy aggregate demand at the plant. This lumpiness is particularly apparent in Table 17–3, the lot-for-lot schedule. However, with a small amount of average inventory on hand and no safety stock, the plant can satisfy all distribution center requirements with no stock-outs, although inventory does drop to fifty units. Other scheduling strategies could be used, and some safety stock would normally be maintained. In this manner, DRP provides the planner with excellent forward visibility of future needs. The master production schedule integrates the aggregate distribution requirements and the scheduling of production.

MERCHANDISING ENVIRONMENT. In a merchandising environment, a simplified model would show a central purchaser using several suppliers to fulfill the distribution requirements of several retail centers. In this case, the master production schedule is replaced by the master purchase schedule as illus-

Table 17-2   Distribution Requirements Summary

Distribution Center	Current Week	Week						
		1	2	3	4	5	6	7
A			200		200		200	
B		250		250			250	
C			400		400			400
Total	–	250	600	250	600	0	450	400

Table 17-3   Master Schedule A

	Current Week	Week						
		1	2	3	4	5	6	7
Shipping requirements	0	250	600	250	600	0	450	400
MPS receipt	0	250	600	250	600	0	450	400
Projected on hand	50	50	50	50	50	50	50	50
MPS release	250	600	250	600	0	450	400	?

Lot-for-lot Production; Safety Stock: 50 Lead Time: 1 week

Table 17-4   Master Schedule B

	Current Week	Week						
		1	2	3	4	5	6	7
Shipping requirements		250	600	250	600	0	450	400
MPS receipt	0	350	350	350	350	350	350	350
Projected on hand	350	450	200	300	50	400	300	250
MPS release	350	350	350	350	350	350	350	350

Level Production; Safety Stock: 0 Lead Time: 1 week

trated in Figure 17–4. This enables the firm to keep its requirements visible to suppliers for their production planning and master schedules.

ALLOCATION AND PUSH SYSTEMS. The latest ship date is a common criteria for assigning priorities to warehouse shipments. The latest ship date is the day projected stock at a given warehouse will reach zero, minus the normal

Figure 17–4   Information Flows in a Merchandising Environment

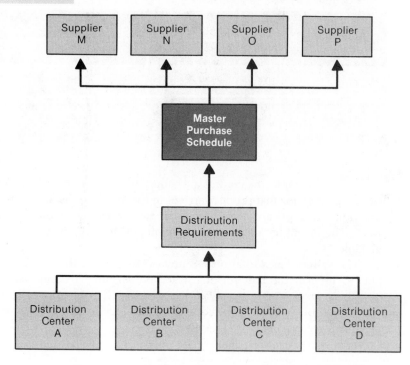

replenishment lead time of that warehouse. If, for example, the stock of Item 927 at Warehouse H is projected to reach zero on Day 85 and the replenishment lead time is eight days, the latest ship date is Day 77.

Up to this point, we have addressed only the distribution of individual items, however, combining many items in one shipment (a joint shipment) is common. In a joint shipment, the fixed cost of shipping, often a major expense, is spread across many items with only a minor per-unit shipping cost. This is analogous to major and minor setups in production and to combined purchase orders. The economies result from full carloads and reduced paperwork per item. The quantity of an item sent to a given warehouse may be limited by truck or train car capacities and the requirements for other items. In such cases, a good practice is to ship equal run-out quantities of each item. Thus, the warehouse can be expected to run out of several items at approximately the same time and to initiate a new multiple-item order.

We also have assumed that the central warehouse has sufficient stock of an item to meet the requirements of all branch warehouses. When this is not the case, a reasonable approach is to send an equal run-out quantity to each warehouse. These quantities, sometimes called fair shares, will provide each warehouse with coverage for the same number of days of projected sales.

Table 17–5   Warehouse Distribution Requirements

Warehouse	On Hand	Requirements per Week					Daily Usage
		1	2	3	4	5	
Minneapolis	10	25	25	25	25	25	5
Atlanta	20	30	30	30	30	30	6
Denver	18	20	20	20	20	20	4
Pittsburgh	10	15	15	15	15	15	3
Total	58	90	90	90	90	90	18

Let, for example, the central warehouse have 140 units of Product A as the latest ship date for that product arrives in the Minneapolis branch warehouse. Additional receipts are not expected at the central warehouse for at least a week. The inventory and the requirements of the four warehouses are given in Table 17–5.

The system has a total of 198 units; 140 units at the central warehouse plus 58 units at the four regional warehouses. Since 18 units are used each day, there is an 11-day supply in the system. The objective is to ship each warehouse the quantity required to bring its stock to an 11-day supply. These quantities are calculated as follows:

$$TS = \frac{\sum I_i}{\sum d_i}$$

$$R_i = TS \times d_i$$

and

$$Q_i = R_i - I_i$$

where

TS = Time supply in days

I_i = Inventory on hand in Warehouse i

d_i = Daily demand for Warehouse i

R_i = Requirements for Warehouse i during run-out period

Q_i = Shipping quantity for Warehouse i

In the example,

$$TS = \frac{10 + 20 + 18 + 10 + 140}{18} = 11 \text{ days}$$

$$R_1(\text{Minneapolis}) = 11 \times 5 = 55$$

$$Q_1 = 55 - 10 = 45.$$

The quantities for the other warehouses are calculated in the same manner. The shipping quantities are

Warehouse	Quantity Allocated
Minneapolis	45
Atlanta	46
Denver	26
Pittsburgh	23
Total	140

Thus, the 140 units have been allocated to provide coverage for an equal time period in all warehouses. The central warehouse ships 45 units to the Minneapolis warehouse. If carriers are not leaving for some warehouses before the arrival of additional receipts, their respective fair shares may be sent to the other warehouses. The space available on a carrier is assigned on the basis of the relative priority of the items vying for shipment. This is similar to the technique Porter (1979) calls the Force-Balance method and to the allocation procedure described in American Software's *Inventory Management Systems* (Newberry 1978). Newberry and Bhame (1981) have pointed out the need to tie distribution to demand forecasting using forced consensus on a bottom-up, top-down basis. A push allocation system works especially well when there are regular shipments to branch warehouses (e.g., every week or two) or when shipping costs do not require the shipment of relatively large quantities. Push allocation can combine the projection of branch warehouse and central supply requirements by period. Research and analyses of distribution systems have increased in the last few years; DRP and push allocation systems have resulted. We can look forward to further developments and refinements.

MULTIECHELON INVENTORIES AND HOLDING COSTS.   The existence of two or more inventory-holding locations creates a costing problem. Conventional inventory-costing approaches would suggest identifying the inventory on hand, with possibly an accounting for in-transit inventories. Then the appropriate per-period holding cost would be applied to the inventory estimate to compute the cost of carrying inventory. Recall from Chapter 11 that the cost of carrying inventory was the denominator of the EOQ formula and was part of the basis for inventory costing using various procedures.

This approach to costing inventories does not recognize that inventories in a multiechelon system are dynamic—that is, the quantity of a particular item that passes through an echelon may vary notably from the static count of items at the end of the period. For example, in a one-month period, a specific item may have been ordered, passed through all echelons of the distribution system, and been delivered to the customer. Such an item would not appear as an inventory holding using the conventional computational procedure.

To resolve this problem with the static process of computing inventory costs, the multiechelon inventory cost computation approach has been developed. Echelon inventory is defined as the number of items currently held at a stocking point or the number of items that have passed through the stocking point during the accounting period. The rationale for the concept of echelon inventory is that the activities necessary to pass the item through the stocking point require holding costs to be incurred (e.g., costs resulting from security, internal placement and movement, identification and control, and administrative management).

These costs, which are borne at each echelon are not as great as those at the plant. Thus, the echelon holding cost rate of a particular stocking location is defined as the incremental cost of stocking the item at the particular echelon rather than at the higher level. A key point is that the conventional and echelon methods give the same total inventory-holding costs when costs for all levels are computed. However, the economic order quantities are very different, with the echelon method providing for more inventory at lower levels. Thus, the echelon method provides more inventory closer to the customer, but at the same holding cost. A simple example is shown in Table 17–6.

In this example, conventional computations are accomplished using the given inventory-holding rates and average inventories for the upper and lower echelons. The echelon method computations assume that the lower holding rate is the incremental cost per item of carrying inventory at the lower level. Additionally, the average echelon inventory rates, which are given, assume that all items at the lower echelon have passed through the upper echelon. For the EOQ computations, annual demands of 1,000 and setup costs of $400 and $100 are assumed for the upper and lower echelons, respectively. This example shows that the echelon method will place greater inventories closer to the customer with the same total holding costs. Research in this area has been done by Clark and Scarf (1960) and by Muckstadt and Thomas (1980).

SHIPPING QUANTITIES. It is important to remember that practical aspects of the environment will always be major determinants of shipping quantities. We already have discussed the fair share allocation to warehouses if sufficient inventories are not available. Other practical factors that influence shipping quantities are the desirability of full carload or truckload shipments, weight and cube (volume) constraints, and pallet size consideration. Because the total inventory cost curve is generally inelastic in the vicinity of the computed economic order quantity, large adjustments of the shipment size to

Table 17–6 Comparison of Conventional and Echelon Inventory
Management Systems

Conventional Method

Level	Holding Rate	Average Inventory (Units)	Holding Cost	EOQ
Upper	$10	150	$10(150) = $1,500	$\sqrt{\frac{2(1,000)400}{10}} = 283$
Lower	$15	100	$15(100) = $1,500	$\sqrt{\frac{2(1,000)100}{15}} = 115$
Total			$3,000	

Echelon Method

Level	Holding Rate	Average Inventory (Units)	Holding Cost	EOQ
Upper	$10	250	$10(250) = $2,500	$\sqrt{\frac{2(1,000)400}{10}} = 283$
Lower	$ 5	100	$5(100) = $ 500	$\sqrt{\frac{2(1,000)100}{5}} = 200$
Total			$3,000	

accommodate such practical considerations result in little change in the total distribution inventory cost (see Chapter 11).

CONCLUSIONS

Distribution management is crucial in achieving customer service objectives. The trend in distribution inventory management is toward systems that provide planners with visibility of future requirements and substantially reduce unexpected demands. This chapter has identified the five strategic decisions in distribution system management and detailed the management of distribution inventory management systems.

The linkages of the distribution inventory vary depending upon the project, job shop (make-to-order), assemble-to-order, or make-to-stock environment. These linkages are important because distribution efficiency results from the integration of lead times and requirements forecasting. Two general methods address the management of distribution inventories—pull systems and push systems. Improved information technology and lower costs have increased the adoption of push systems in the past few years.

Through distribution requirements planning, the distribution system is increasingly viewed as an extension of the internal materials requirement planning system and its outgrowth, the manufacturing resources planning (MRP II) system. By calculating all warehouse requirements and scheduling production against this calculation and by distributing families of items based on common usage rates, distribution costs can be reduced. Close control of shipping assures high customer service at a reasonable cost.

QUESTIONS

1. What is the objective of distribution management? Describe how a current good or service achieves this objective.

2. List the five strategies of distribution management. Select a product that demonstrates each of these five strategic decisions.

3. How do the four Ps of marketing relate to operations management?

4. Give an example where the operations manager is not responsible for distribution systems.

5. Why are warehouses and distribution centers easier to purchase or sell than manufacturing facilities. Give an example of such a situation.

6. How are production processes and distribution inventory systems interrelated?

7. For the following production environments, demonstrate how process and distribution inventories are related.
   a. An electronic parts assembler
   b. A refrigerator manufacturer
   c. A custom cabinetmaker
   d. A rug dealer
   e. An office building contractor

8. Differentiate the pull distribution system from the push system.

9. Name three traditional pull systems. What is a disadvantage of each?

10. Give two advantages and two disadvantages of the pull system.

11. Describe the base stock system. What advantages does this system have?

12. How is DRP related to MRP?

13. Given the following products, recommend a distribution system.

    a. Distribute soft drinks to vending machines at 50 locations in a large city.

    b. Distribute newspapers to delivery companies for street distribution by vendors.

    c. Distribute replacement parts such as batteries or windshield wiper blades to local garages.

    d. Distribute power mowers to company-owned and company-operated retail outlets.

14. What is the latest ship date? In what way is the use of the latest ship date helpful to distribution management?

15. The fair share method of allocating inventory is used under what circumstances?

16. Why don't static inventory management approaches correctly reflect requirements of a dynamic system?

17. Suggest several factors that would affect inventory holding rates other than EOQ or similar mechanical computations. Why do these variances from the exact EOQ not make much difference in total cost?

PROBLEMS

1. From the following data, develop a master production schedule (production is lot-for-lot, safety stock is 20 units, and lead time is 1 week):

Distribution Requirements Summary					
		Week			
Distribution Center	Current Week	*1*	*2*	*3*	*4*
A		20		15	
B			30	20	
C		15	10		20

2. Given the requirements from a distribution requirements summary for an organization at the top of page 594, compute the MPS, projected on-hand inventory, and MPS release for a lot-for-lot system with a safety stock of 100 units, and a lead time of 1 week.

Distribution Requirements Summary							
Distribution Center	Current Week	Week					
		1	2	3	4	5	6
1		125			200		100
2			250			150	
3			250			200	
4		125		150			200

3. Use the data from Problem 2; however, production is no longer lot-for-lot, it is a fixed weekly quantity of 300 units with no safety stock. The initial on-hand inventory is 250 units. Compute the MPS receipt, projected on-hand inventory, and MPS release.

4. A central warehouse has 99 units on hand. A railroad strike has prohibited additional deliveries to the central warehouse.

Warehouse Distribution Requirements						
Warehouse	On Hand	Requirements per Week				Daily Usage
		1	2	3	4	
A	15	20	20	20	20	4
B	10	15	15	15	15	3
C	20	25	25	25	25	5
Totals	45	60	60	60	60	12

a. Determine how many days supply is currently available throughout the system.
b. Ship each warehouse the quantity required to bring its stock to the available number of days calculated in Part a above.

5. The central warehouse in New York has 1000 units on hand. An embargo has prohibited imports from the country producing the product. There are other countries producing it but until contracts can be negotiated and signed, shipments will be halted.

Warehouse Distribution Requirements								
	On Hand	**Requirements per Week**						**Daily Usage**
Warehouse		**1**	**2**	**3**	**4**	**5**	**6**	
Toledo	168	125	125	125	125	125	125	25
Cincinnati	194	170	170	170	170	170	170	34
Cleveland	214	200	200	200	200	200	200	40
Dayton	120	100	100	100	100	100	100	20
Louisville	89	90	90	90	90	90	90	18
Pittsburgh	140	190	190	190	190	190	190	38

  a. Determine how many days supply is currently available throughout the system.
  b. Ship each warehouse the quantity required to bring its stock to the available number of days calculated in Part a above.

6. Using the conventional method, determine the holding costs and EOQ for upper and lower levels. Annual demand is 15,000 units; set-up costs are $500 and $100. Compare the results with those of the echelon method.

Level	Holding Rate	Average Inventory (units)
Upper	$25	1,250
Lower	$35	750

7. From the data below, calculate holding costs and EOQ using the conventional and echelon methods. Annual demand and set-up costs are the same as in Problem 6.

Level	Holding Rate	Average Inventory (units)
Upper	$25	2,000
Lower	$10	750

REFERENCES

Clark, A. J., and H. Scarf. "Optimal Policies for a Multi-Echelon Inventory Problem." *Management Science* 6, no. 4 (July 1960): 475–490.

McLeavey, D. W., and S. L. Narasimhan. *Production Planning and Inventory Control.* Boston: Allyn and Bacon, Inc., 1985.

Muckstadt, J. A., and L. J. Thomas. "Are Multi-Echelon Inventory Methods Worth Implementing in Systems with Low-Demand-Rate Items?" *Management Science* 26, no. 5 (May 1980): 483–494.

Newberry, Thomas L., ed. *Inventory Management Systems.* Atlanta: American Software, 1978, pp. 8–1, 8–2.

———, and Carl D. Bhame. "How Management Should Use and Interact with Sales Forecasts." *Inventories and Production Management* 1, no. 3 (July–August 1981): 4–11.

Porter Robert W. "Centralized Inventory Management in the Multilevel Distribution Network," APICS 22nd Annual International Conference Proceedings (1979), pp. 81–82.

CHAPTER 18
QUALITY ASSURANCE AND CONTROL

OBJECTIVES

After completing this chapter, you should be able to

- Define quality and understand its characteristics

- Identify the costs of quality and cost tradeoffs

- Understand interfaces of the quality control system and the objectives of the four quality control subsystems

- Use statistical quality control procedures to measure quality under various designs

- Understand how to implement a quality control inspection plan

OUTLINE

Introduction
    The Costs of Quality
    Quality Assurance
The Quality Control System
    Interfaces with Other Systems
    The Quality Specification and Design Subsystem
    Process Quality Planning and Control Subsystem
        The Process
        Methods of Measurement
        Equipment and Devices
        Personnel
        Measurement and Documentation
        Disposition
    Material Quality Planning and Control Subsystem
        Supplier Approval Procedures
        Supplier's Procedures
        Informing Suppliers
        Measurement, Documentation, and Control
        Supplier Evaluation
    Product Performance Subsystem
        Product Performance
        Reliability
        Maintainability and Serviceability
        Product Liability Exposure
        Corrective Action
    Special Quality Study Projects
Statistical Quality Control
    Control Charts
    Acceptance Sampling
    Operating Characteristic Curves
    Rectifying Inspection
    Multiple Sampling
Conclusions
Questions
Problems
References

INTRODUCTION

Quality is something that we are all familiar with yet it seems to have a nebulous meaning that is hard to pin down in practice. In some instances, the differences in perception of quality are due to such individual characteristics as taste or color. In other situations, a product or service may be unacceptable because of the user's expectations, whether they are realistic or not. Perhaps the best definition of quality is "fitness for use." The user or consumer is the ultimate judge of whether or not a service or product meets a need or performs satisfactorily.

The consumer's perception of quality is usually predicated on several characteristics. First, the consumer is concerned with the absolute criteria of design quality, which may be the result of engineering specifications. Second, the user is concerned with whether or not the design quality is adhered to. This characteristic is usually called conformance quality. In addition, the consumer may be interested in reliability and/or maintainability of the service or product. These latter aspects may really be particular forms of design and conformance quality.

Quality characteristics have been grouped into five classes by Juran (1980):

1. *Structural*: Length, frequency, viscosity, strength, etc.
2. *Sensory*: Taste, beauty, appearance
3. *Time-oriented*: Reliability, maintainability, availability
4. *Commercial*: Warranty, guarantees
5. *Ethical*: Courtesy, honesty, integrity

These characteristics determine the real and perceived quality of goods and services. If a product is of the appropriate length and strength but is unreliable, it may be viewed as being of poor quality. Similarly, a service that is delivered courteously but has poor structural characteristics (a polite waiter serving a bad-tasting meal) is also of poor quality.

What is the right quality for a producer? Each enterprise must examine its market and determine an appropriate quality standard. For instance, the quality standards for a five-star restaurant may be different from those of a fast-food chain, but there is a market for both. Thus, the first quality decision a firm faces is to select an appropriate design quality. A firm may very well compete on the basis of any of the characteristics cited previously: it may have the strongest, the best looking, the most reliable, or the most courteously delivered product. It need not be best in all areas and, indeed, need not be superior in any area if it addresses an appropriate market need. However, no matter what its design quality, people expect it to adhere to that design—that is, to have conformance quality.

The decision on design quality is not just an engineering design choice. It is a fundamental corporate strategy decision that should involve marketing, finance, and operations as well as engineering. It directly addresses what market segment a firm is going to compete in and impacts the ability of the company to produce the product or service. This in turn impacts the capital requirements and cash flows of the organization. This is one of the fundamental decisions of the firm, and yet it has often been overlooked in establishing corporate policy. In a study by the Strategy Planning Institute (Mertz 1977), it was found that firms with high-quality products and services were also the most profitable. Those firms also had the largest share of the market and benefited most from general market growth. Thus, it is possible to build market share through high quality rather than low price.

The Costs of Quality

High conformance quality would seem to be costly. But, Harold S. Geneen, former chairman of ITT, says, "Quality is not only right, it is free. And it is not only free, it is the most profitable product line we have." (Crosby 1979). The reasoning behind this is that the true costs of producing less than quality goods or services are the costs of doing things wrong, such as scrap, rework, and service costs. Usually, firms only consider the direct costs of quality, such as inspection or higher cost materials. However, the true costs of quality include both quality control costs and failure costs. Control costs involve both the prevention of defects, which is designed into the product or service and into the production process, and the appraisal or inspection to determine conformance quality. Prevention costs are those expenses involved in establishing the initial design quality and carrying out preventive actions during product creation (e.g., performing marketing research directed at customer quality needs, establishing product specifications, training workers, and performing process capability studies and planning, vendor evaluation and selection, quality audits, and preventive maintenance). Appraisal costs are those incurred in determining whether the product or service conforms to requirements. They include expenses associated with inspection and testing of incoming materials, work-in-process control, finished goods monitoring, and the establishment of procedures for carrying out inspection (e.g., training, manuals, and laboratories).

The costs that are so often overlooked are the failure costs, both internal and external. Scrap, rework, redesign, downtime, broken equipment, reduced yields, and downgrading a product to sell at a lower price are all examples of internal hidden costs of poor quality. They are reflected not only in obvious direct labor costs, but also in the indirect effects of reducing output for a given level of inputs—that is, reduced productivity. The amount of effort required to rectify errors results in many companies having to make substantial investments in additional equipment to increase their capacity so as to be able to handle this added work load. Scrapping returned merchandise, allowing discounts for below specification products, making warranty repairs or refunds, and losing credibility with the customer all give rise to quality costs incurred in dealing with external quality failure. The point is that the cost of poor quality often exceeds the cost of good quality.

In order to have a successful quality assurance and control program, it is essential that a firm measure all the aspects of the cost of quality. It is important to remember that expenditures for prevention and appraisal may easily offset the costs of failure. A typical experience is illustrated in Figure 18–1, which shows that while control costs are an increasing percentage of the costs of quality, total costs decrease up to a point because of the significant reduction in failure costs. Through judicious spending on prevention and appraisal, it is possible to reduce the cost of failures.

Proper allocation of the dollars spent on control is also important. Proper process design can help reduce the number of defective items produced. Correct selection of equipment used to make the product may significantly affect product quality. Overstraining an operator or machine may not only cause human or equipment failure, but also may result in faulty products being produced. Overloads or improper use of equipment may quickly put the equipment out of adjustment or alignment, which also reduces quality. Thus, process design engineers should be aware of the quality capabilities or production tolerances of equipment in order to avoid specifying processes that will inherently produce defective parts. For example, the inherent ability

Figure 18–1 The Costs of Controlling Quality

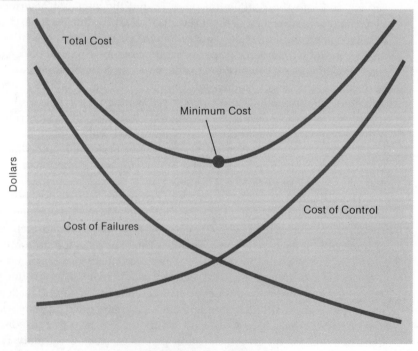

AMOUNT OF INSPECTION

to hold tight tolerances varies from hundredths of an inch for ordinary lathes to thousandths of an inch for honing and lapping operations.

Similarly, training workers in correct methods and instilling a philosophy of good quality in all employees can reduce failures. The zero defects concept is such a method. It is based on the idea that poor quality is the result of mistakes that can be caused by two things: (1) lack of knowledge and (2) lack of attention (Crosby 1979). The former can be remedied through education, but the latter is an attitude problem. The quality expectations of individuals can be changed if the concept of zero defects is made a performance standard for everyone. Zero defects programs can be applied in traditional production operations as well as in all facets of the business operation, including engineering, sales, data processing, accounting, financing, and advertising.

In the 1960s some U.S. firms developed zero defects programs to motivate workers to be more quality conscious. While they were sometimes successful, they often failed to have any lasting impact. Perhaps that was because as a program the effort had a beginning date and an ending date. As Crosby (1979, p. 234) has said, "Success is a journey, not a destination." Today the concept of zero defects has been revived and instead of being a one-shot program, the ideas have become an ongoing process of quality consciousness.

It is not the carelessness or lack of capability on the part of workers that is the primary cause of poor quality. In fact, of all controllable errors, 80 percent are management controllable and only 20 percent are operator controllable (Juran and Gryna 1980). That is, errors in process design and equipment selection, maintenance programs, operator training, and similar tasks that are management controlled are the major source of errors.

The appropriate focus for improving quality and reducing its cost is for top management to be committed to prevention by instilling the concept that quality must be a way of life not just a program to deal with a temporary problem. If management thinks that workers don't care, then they probably won't.

Quality Assurance

Quality assurance is the title given to those management activities and systems required to provide assurance that the overall quality control task is being carried out. The quality assurance system is the aggregate quality management system. It interfaces with other general management systems performing similar functions relative to the organization's financial, personnel, facilities, and marketing policies and capabilities. Its goals are to

1. Establish quality level policy objectives and monitor the achievement of those objectives on an aggregate basis
2. Establish organizational quality control budgets and monitor performance with respect to those budgets
3. Evaluate and approve the quality control management system relative to its effectiveness, adequacy, and costs

4. Interface with those departments handling legal and insurance matters to involve their cooperation in the development and implementation of a product liability control system as an integral part of the quality control subsystems

THE QUALITY CONTROL SYSTEM

The quality control system should (1) define specific product and service quality level requirements, (2) determine the relationship of design and process characteristics to output quality and related process requirements, (3) determine methods, personnel, and equipment for measuring quality, (4) measure and record the quality achieved, and (5) trigger corrective processes when actual quality varies from the acceptable quality.

Four integrated subsystems can be used to achieve these objectives. They are

1. Quality specification and design subsystem
2. Process quality planning and control subsystem
3. Material quality planning and control subsystem
4. Product performance subsystem

In addition, special quality control project studies exist concomitantly with these subsystems. Before examining these subsystems, the interfaces of the quality control system with other subsystems will be discussed.

Interfaces with Other Systems

Specification of quality requirements begins in market research, continues as part of the product design activity, and culminates in the quality specification and design subsystem output. That output delineates the specific product or service attributes that affect quality and must be measured.

Market research, or some group fulfilling that function, discovers or determines a need that exists and the relationship of customer acceptance to possible quality levels of the product or service fulfilling that need. This relationship of quality and customer acceptance is translated into a quality level—that is, an expected sales relationship.

The broad outline of the product design takes shape during the initial stages of market research and is fully developed in product design, a collaborative effort of design personnel, marketing personnel, those responsible for producing the product or providing the service, and those responsible for output quality. Resolution of the final design follows an examination of constraints on quality due to the organization's capability to produce the quality and an examination of the relationship of the costs of achieving specific quality levels, the resulting production costs, and profit.

The Quality Specification and Design Subsystem

The activities of this subsystem are an integral part of the product design activities. Its objectives are to determine that the designed output

1. Will meet the customer's need
2. Will operate under end use conditions
3. Can be produced or provided given the organization's capabilities
4. Will function with a specified level of reliability, where reliability is defined in terms of minimum mean time between failure (MTBF)
5. Will require less than a specified amount of maintenance hours and material costs per operating hour
6. Can be repaired within a certain time frame a specific proportion of the time (e.g., repairs can be accomplished within one hour 95 percent of the time)
7. Embodies all reasonable measures to protect the consumer from bodily or economic harm due to product malfunctioning or customer misuse

Product and service liability always has been a prime concern of most organizations. A deep and sincere interest in providing services and products that fulfill the need of the customer and do not cause harm through failure, misapplication, or misuse is not new. However, the need for product liability planning and control is more important today because customers possess a greater awareness of their ability to obtain redress for bodily or economic harm.

The primary purpose of product liability planning is to protect the consumer from injury and damage; its secondary purpose is to generate evidence that the organization has taken all the necessary and reasonable steps in product design, fabrication, inspection, and testing to protect the welfare of the consumer. Such documentation places management in an excellent position to defend itself against liability litigation.

Liability planning and control is also important in the service sector. The present interest in medical malpractice litigation and insurance attests to the need for management interest in service liability control.

There has been, and in some organizations there continues to be, an unfortunate tendency to isolate product liability due to its legal and insurance ramifications. The growing social and economic importance of these aspects demands integration of product liability planning and control in the quality control subsystems. The objectives of product liability and control are to

1. Determine those attributes or characteristics that, if not held within specifications, can contribute to failure under normal usage and possible injury to the consumer
2. Design the product or service so that when it is built or provided per design the probability of failure is less than some specified rate
3. Test units, fabricated to design, for failure under normal and extreme operating conditions, and make any changes in the design or manufacturing process required to achieve performance objectives

4. Determine what characteristics must be inspected and what tests must be run on fabricated units to assure that design and production process standards have been met prior to releasing the units for sale
5. Clearly inform the customer of the
   a. Proper use of the product and the conditions under which use is dangerous and unadvisable
   b. Maintenance required to sustain safe use
6. Document the product liability planning and control system and procedures as well as the result of all tests and inspections

Determining that the design of a proposed product or service (1) will fulfill the customer's need, (2) can be produced by the organization, and (3) will meet serviceability, maintenance, and product liability objectives requires that the design itself be scrutinized and appropriate performance tests and measurements be made on experimental, prototype, and pilot models.

A classification system based on the relationship of each characteristic to performance, reliability, safety, and so forth should be developed. One possible classification system uses three classes of defects: critical, major, and minor. The critical category is reserved for characteristics that if not met could lead to personal injury. The failure of automobile brakes and an electrical shortage in a hair dryer are excellent examples of critical characteristics. A major characteristic is a noncritical characteristic, but one that is required for the product or service to fulfill its function. A minor defect is one that does not substantially alter the performance characteristics of the product. Blemishes on a white sidewall of a tire illustrate a minor defect, while a defective picture tube is an illustration of a major defect.

These three levels constitute one possible way of classifying quality characteristics. Specific conditions may warrant a finer distinction among classes, which could be achieved by increasing the number of levels to four or five. It should be noted that the nature of a product greatly influences the classification of a characteristic. For example, the finish on a piece of furniture is certainly a major characteristic, while the exterior finish of an automobile battery casing is a minor item. This list of items to be measured is an input to the other quality control subsystems and is a determinant of what quality control processes, test results, and inspection results are documented.

Process Quality Planning and Control Subsystem

This subsystem concerns the what, where, when, and who of quality control during operations. It frequently involves major expenditures for personnel, equipment, and inspection and testing activities. The objectives of this subsystem are to

1. Determine the process attributes and characteristics to be measured
2. Determine the methods of measurement and develop detailed instructions describing the measurement process

3. Determine, procure, maintain, and control the equipment and devices required to make the necessary measurements
4. Determine, select, and train the personnel required to implement the quality control procedures
5. Measure and record operational quality in terms of the number of defects, seriousness of defects, and causes
6. Provide corrective action procedures for out-of-control situations
7. Decide the disposition of quality deficiencies

THE PROCESS. In the production of most products or services, there are certain processes and materials that have a greater effect than others on the quality of the end product or service. For example, the nature of material, the alignment, and the physical finish and dimensions of the read/write heads of a floppy disk drive are more critical than the material, finish, and physical dimensions of the case surrounding the drive.

METHODS OF MEASUREMENT. Just how measurements are to be taken and whether 100 percent inspection or a statistical sampling plan should be implemented are the types of decisions that must be made before documenting these decisions by standard quality control procedures. As an illustration, testing of the metallurgic properties of the metal being poured plus a check of the physical dimensions is sufficient for many castings. In other cases, x-ray methods may be required to demonstrate the lack of casting irregularities and guarantee the strength of the casting; or a sampling inspection procedure may provide sufficient guarantee of the desired quality level when it is not possible to test every unit or when the cost of 100 percent inspection is not justified. For example, not every round of ammunition produced can be tested for explosive and ballistic characteristics. Statistical inspection decisions are examined in greater detail in the discussion of statistical quality control.

Two traditional yet effective methods of process inspection in a production setting are first-part inspection and patrol inspection. First-part inspection involves the detailed inspection of the first part, or a pilot lot of the first parts, produced by a process. This procedure increases the probability that the proper equipment, tooling, material, and process are being used and that improper processing will be discovered before an entire production lot is scrapped. Patrol inspection consists of an inspection of a process on a random basis. First-part and patrol inspections are performed by either the supervisor, the operator, or the inspector. Conditions such as the caliber of the operator, the nature of the attribute measured, and the organization's success or lack thereof in following one of these approaches determine which inspection method is followed. Application of the concepts of first-part inspection and patrol inspection are found in many settings. Two types of inspection procedures may be used: (1) variables inspection or (2) attribute inspection. In the former, each dimension or characteristic is measured; thus length, hardness, surface finish, and other characteristics can be expressed numerically. In attribute inspection only a determination of whether or not the characteristic is within tolerable limits is ascertained. So-called go–no go gauges are used, and simply a yes or no answer is the result. Attribute inspection is generally less expensive and less time consuming than variables inspection.

EQUIPMENT AND DEVICES.   General-purpose equipment includes items ranging from relatively inexpensive micrometers and thermometers, to special-purpose inspection gauges, fixtures, and testing devices, to elaborate facilities such as automobile test tracks and bombing ranges. Judicious selection of such equipment in most situations requires the same level of knowledge and experience as selection of a measurement method. Selecting, procuring, maintaining, and controlling these items of equipment is a major task in many organizations; frequently it is a special field of study itself and is a determining factor in the efficacy of process quality control.

PERSONNEL.   Briefly, individuals must be selected and trained to carry out the measuring process. The capability necessary and the number of individuals required must be determined and the personnel recruited, selected, and trained for implementation of measuring procedures. Development of the skills of quality control personnel is a continuous process as products, processes, equipment, and procedures evolve.

MEASUREMENT AND DOCUMENTATION.   Product quality must be measured on both a quantitative and qualitative basis, and the measurements must be recorded. Quantification of the qualitative aspects occurs when defects are classified into categories such as critical, major, and minor, which were described earlier. A classification such as this is one of the inputs to the organization's aggregate measure of quality.

Products or services that do not meet the desired quality standards generate two types of required corrective actions: (1) the disposition of the defective product or service and (2) an analysis of the cause of the deficiency.

DISPOSITION.   Defective products fall into three categories: (1) defective units are beyond being reworked and must be scrapped, (2) they can be reworked to meet specifications, or (3) they can be modified to meet all the functional requirements but still not meet the standard blueprint specifications. Those latter units are approved on a variance basis; many organizations establish a material review board, consisting of engineering, manufacturing, quality control, marketing, and a customer's representative, to review proposed rework of defective parts that are outside standard blueprint specifications. Approval by all the members must be received before rework can proceed.

Material Quality Planning and Control Subsystem

Purchased raw materials, components, and supplies have a substantial impact on the output product quality of most organizations. Controlling product output quality demands that the quality of inputs be controlled. For example, in a health care institution, these items range from blood plasma to disposable cups; bacterial contamination of any of one item can immobilize the institution.

The objectives of the material quality planning and control subsystem are to

1. Establish procedures whereby a supplier's capability in terms of facilities, personnel, and methods to produce required quality are certified and specific suppliers are approved
2. Develop procedures that suppliers must follow in controlling and documenting quality
3. Inform suppliers of quality requirements
4. Measure, record, and control the quality of purchased material
5. Evaluate and control the quality performance of individual vendors

This subsystem thrusts the primary responsibility for producing and controlling quality on the supplier, with the purchaser providing support and exercising final control. Since contracts, agreements, and arrangements usually are made by purchasing, this system and much of the required information flows through purchasing with its knowledge and commitment.

SUPPLIER APPROVAL PROCEDURES. The capability and reliability of all suppliers must be carefully evaluated. Weeks and months can be lost due to the failure of low-bidding, fast-talking suppliers to deliver the required quality. Capability evaluation teams with representatives from manufacturing, engineering, and quality control, following established procedures, usually can distinguish between potential suppliers with sufficient capability and those who have little probability of delivering the desired quality. Establishing and implementing procedures for determining the conditions when such an evaluation is necessary and when and how such an investigation should be conducted are wise investments.

SUPPLIER'S PROCEDURES. Transferring the responsibility for incoming material quality to the supplier frequently involves specifying the tests and inspections that must be made and recorded prior to shipment. Documents certifying these tests and their results usually must be delivered with the material if that material is to be accepted.

INFORMING SUPPLIERS. Prospective suppliers must know the capability evaluation requirements that must be met before they qualify as a supplier. Approved suppliers, those who have met the capability evaluation requirements for a specific group of products, must be informed of the quality requirements of any product for which they hope to obtain a contract as well as the relative importance of these requirements. They must know exactly what is expected of them.

MEASUREMENT, DOCUMENTATION, AND CONTROL. Incoming material quality must be measured, documented, and controlled in a manner similar to the measurement, documentation, and control of products and services produced by the organization itself. Disposition of quality problems associated with incoming material also is handled similarly to the disposition of problems with internally produced output, including the utilization of the material review board when necessary.

SUPPLIER EVALUATION. The quality performance of individual suppliers must be controlled after they have passed the capability requirements inspection and have been approved by the evaluation team. This control is obtained through further testing and inspection procedures and the results obtained. Tabulation of the incoming inspection results by supplier should be maintained as should records of those performance failures after purchase that are attributable to poor supplier quality. These results are incorporated in the measurement of organizational aggregate quality. This is discussed further in the next section.

Product Performance Subsystem

Performance of the product or service is what quality control is all about. Does the product do the job? How well? How long will it do the job? If management does not have the answers to these and related questions, it does not know what the quality of its output is.

The product performance subsystem measures output quality. Its objectives are to

1. Measure performance in terms of end-use objectives, warranties, and guarantees
2. Measure reliability
3. Measure maintainability and serviceability
4. Measure product liability exposure
5. Trigger corrective action when actual results fall below the acceptable range

This subsystem must extend beyond the confines of the organization to achieve these objectives. Many organizations do an excellent job of measuring the performance of products before they leave the plant, but they fail to follow up with adequate measures of product or service performance experiences by the customer.

PRODUCT PERFORMANCE. Many products undergo severe performance testing prior to full-scale production. Transportation vehicles, medicines, therapeutic devices, and educational processes usually undergo such tests. Although some are required to meet legal requirements, all are run to verify that the output does meet performance requirements. Performance tests, even if exhaustive, rarely can reveal all the bugs in the design and in the process.

Continuous testing during production and observation of failures during use are required to evaluate output performance completely.

RELIABILITY.   Performance without frequent interruption due to failure is necessary for longstanding consumer acceptance. Reliability is measured in terms of the mean time between failure (MTBF) or in terms of the proportion of times a unit will perform when called upon. The probability of a car starting is a good example of the latter.

MAINTAINABILITY AND SERVICEABILITY.   What maintenance is required on a regular basis? How much does it cost? How long does it take? Answers to these questions influence the consumer's decision to purchase and to make recommendations to fellow consumers. Objectives must be established and results measured.

The relative ease or difficulty of making scheduled and emergency repairs depends on product design, parts availability, and availability of capable service personnel. Design determines maintenance requirements such as lubrication, cleaning or replacing filters, and adding fluid as well as the ease with which these routine maintenance activities and emergency repairs can be made. Design also determines how accessible these items are. Replacing spark plugs in one model of a well-known car required that the entire engine be removed to reach one of the plugs, a classic example of poor serviceability design.

PRODUCT LIABILITY EXPOSURE.   Certain types of failure can bring bodily injury to the user and subject others to economic losses. Whenever these failures can be attributable to poor design, inadequate processes, or sloppy execution of a process or service, the producer is exposed to liability litigation. Measurement of this exposure is based on the results of in-house performance testing and analysis of field failures. Complete elimination of such exposure is theoretically impossible; however, judicious planning, testing, and adequate documentation that all reasonable steps have been taken to protect the consumer will minimize exposure. Liability control should be an ongoing activity rather than a periodic fireworks display.

CORRECTIVE ACTION.   When product performance, reliability, maintainability, serviceability, or product liability exposure do not fall within acceptable limits, the system should initiate analysis of the cause automatically. Investigation of process and product deficiencies frequently is conducted by an ad hoc task force organized specifically for that project.

Special Quality Study Projects

Quality control is a dynamic field; concepts, techniques, and supporting equipment are evolving and improving constantly. Keeping abreast of these changes and evaluating their potential applications in the organization is imperative if the quality control function is to maintain its competitive effectiveness. Quality study projects arise from the need to resolve existing quality problems and the need for sustained improvement in quality control methods, equipment, personnel, and systems. These quality control studies frequently are interwoven with product design and process design studies aimed at improving output performance and reducing costs.

In some cases the cause of a quality problem frequently is immediately apparent as operator error, improper material, or tool failure. In other cases the cause is not immediately apparent. This is especially true when a product repeatedly fails in use after having passed all the process and product inspection requirements. Recurrent quality problems should lead to project investigation of the situation. This analysis may conclude that the basic cause of the problem is poor engineering design, improper tooling, improper production or assembly processes, inadequate inspection, improper use by the customer, or some combination of these. Some quality problems may be attributed to marketing and top management when an insufficient time period has been provided for design or testing.

STATISTICAL QUALITY CONTROL

Besides the managerial aspects of quality, statistical and mathematical aspects of inspection, control, and management of quality are important for quality assurance. Since 100 percent inspection and testing may not be feasible, so-called identical parts are not truly the same in all respects, and production processes will vary, statistical methods have been applied to quality control and enforcement.

Control Charts

Although interchangeable parts may look and act alike, they are not truly identical. Refined measuring devices will ascertain that there are differences from part to part. The differences may be quite small; nevertheless, as production proceeds, sizes and other physical properties will vary in a random fashion. In addition, random sampling variation will occur. These small differences between sample characteristics are expected to occur and their range of variation can be predicted by statistics. As long as the observed variation in production is within this predictable range, the process is said to be in control.

Variation may also be caused by some unusual condition. When the process produces parts outside of the range of variation expected from chance causes, the process is said to be out of control and an assignable cause must be sought. In order to keep track of these variations, to prevent the production of defective items, and/or to promote the production of extraordinarily good items, a control chart is used. The control chart shows the limits within which sampling variation alone may occur; statistics, such as means or ranges of small samples, are plotted and compared with the limits.

A statistical theorem, the central limit theorem, states that when small samples are involved, the means of those samples will tend to be distributed according to the properties of a normal distribution, regardless of the distribution of the population from which the samples were taken. Furthermore, that normal distribution will have the same mean as the mean of the population from which the samples were taken. Since the properties of the normal or bell-shaped distribution are well known, it is relatively easy to establish the expected limits for the control charts.

The standard deviation (denoted by the Greek letter sigma, σ) is a measure of the variability of a process. The population standard deviation, the actual variability of the process, is defined as

$$\sigma = \sqrt{\frac{\sum_{i=1}^{n}(X_i - \mu)^2}{N}}$$

where

$$X_i = \text{Individual members of the population}$$

$$\mu = \text{Population mean}$$

$$N = \text{Number of members of the population}$$

Since the population standard deviation may not be known, the sample standard deviation, s, is used as an estimate of it. It is calculated as follows:

$$s = \sqrt{\frac{\sum_{i=1}^{n}(X_i - \overline{X})^2}{n - 1}}$$

where

$$X_i = \text{Individual members of the sample}$$

$$\overline{X} = \text{Sample mean}$$

$$n = \text{Sample size}$$

The mean of the distribution of sample means ($\mu_{\overline{X}}$) equals μ, and the standard deviation of the sample distribution (σ_s) equals $\sigma/\sqrt{n}$. Since the sample means are distributed normally, about 68 percent of the sample means will be within one standard deviation of the sample distribution from the mean, and 99.74 percent of the samples will be within three standard deviations of the sample distribution from the mean.

In order to control processes in which inspection of variables is involved, two charts are necessary—one to detect unusual variation in the mean and the other to monitor changes in the process variability. These are the $\overline{X}$ (X bar) and range (R) charts, respectively. Frequently these charts are set up not on the basis of the goals desired, but rather on the basis of what the process is actually doing. Since the limits on the $\overline{X}$ chart are a function of the variability of the universe from which the samples are being taken, it is necessary to set up the R chart first in order to make sure that the variability is in control.

The R chart has a central line at the average range of the samples taken so far. From a knowledge of the theoretical properties of the distribution of the range, upper and lower control limits can be established. Whenever a plotted point falls outside the control limits, the operation is said to be out of control and action is initiated to find the assignable cause. However, the operation may actually be correct, but an extreme sampling value may be the problem. Searching for an assignable cause, when none actually exists, is an error. If the limits were set far apart, in terms of multiples of the standard deviation, this would reduce the likelihood of trying to find a cause when none existed. But at the same time it would increase the likelihood of not detecting shifts in the process. In other words, widely set limits would increase the chance of making a different type of error—that is, not searching for an assignable cause when in fact a shift has taken place. Ideally the costs of searching versus not detecting shifts should be considered in setting up limits. Generally, however, these are not known and the expedient way is to set limits at plus or minus three standard deviations.

Perhaps the best way to comprehend this procedure is to follow through on an example. In Table 18–1 the data are given for the diameter of a connecting shaft. For the past week, five samples per day consisting of seven items in each sample have been taken. For each sample or group the mean and range have been calculated as shown in the last two columns in Table 18–1. The central line on the R chart is simply the average range over the 25 samples ($\overline{R} = .0216$). From a knowledge of the statistical properties of the distribution of the range it is possible to construct a table of factors for establishing the upper and lower control limits on the R chart. Complete tables of control chart factors can be found in most texts on statistical quality control (Duncan 1974). A set of these factors is given in Table 18–2. The lower control limit (LCL) is set at $D_3\overline{R}$, and the upper control limit (UCL) is set at $D_4\overline{R}$. In this case, since the samples are of size seven, the LCL equals .076 × .0216 or .0016; the UCL equals 1.924 × .0216 or .0416. The chart is then set up as in Figure 18–2, and the 25 values are plotted.

Since none of the R values is outside the control limits, we can proceed to set up the $\overline{X}$ chart. The central line is the grand average of the means of the

Table 18–1 Raw Data and Averages for Setting Up Control Charts on a Process

Day	Sample Number	Shaft Diameter X_i							$\bar{X}$	R
1	1	.628	.630	.637	.615	.625	.625	.631	.6273	.022
	2	.616	.626	.622	.630	.626	.630	.616	.6237	.014
	3	.626	.605	.624	.623	.634	.621	.622	.6221	.029
	4	.617	.629	.632	.626	.615	.623	.614	.6223	.018
	5	.623	.621	.632	.626	.618	.625	.628	.6247	.014
2	1	.627	.635	.636	.614	.621	.619	.615	.6238	.022
	2	.630	.611	.616	.628	.627	.618	.612	.6203	.019
	3	.610	.635	.629	.622	.616	.617	.607	.6194	.028
	4	.621	.630	.631	.625	.623	.615	.622	.6238	.016
	5	.611	.625	.625	.629	.623	.613	.617	.6204	.028
3	1	.627	.627	.624	.623	.638	.616	.631	.6266	.021
	2	.623	.631	.630	.616	.631	.633	.625	.6270	.017
	3	.625	.624	.636	.618	.621	.619	.642	.6264	.024
	4	.618	.634	.619	.627	.623	.642	.619	.6260	.024
	5	.620	.630	.628	.621	.639	.618	.631	.6267	.021
4	1	.618	.616	.632	.634	.617	.614	.615	.6208	.020
	2	.614	.630	.635	.623	.629	.623	.626	.6257	.021
	3	.619	.634	.626	.609	.632	.631	.614	.6236	.026
	4	.630	.616	.613	.632	.623	.620	.625	.6227	.019
	5	.623	.638	.627	.624	.619	.631	.611	.6247	.029
5	1	.614	.633	.639	.615	.624	.620	.618	.6233	.024
	2	.622	.630	.613	.626	.614	.624	.629	.6226	.017
	3	.615	.619	.625	.617	.638	.620	.622	.6223	.023
	4	.616	.629	.612	.631	.631	.630	.611	.6228	.020
	5	.629	.619	.622	.613	.622	.626	.638	.6241	.025

$\bar{\bar{X}} = .6237 \quad \bar{R} = .0216$

Source: Tables 18–1, 18–3, Figures 18–2, 18–3, and 18–4 are from *Production: Management and Manufacturing Systems*, Second Edition, by Thomas R. Hoffmann. ©1971 by Wadsworth Publishing Company, Inc. Reprinted by permission of Wadsworth Publishing Company, Belmont, California 94002.

Table 18–2 Factors for Computing Control Chart Limits

Number of Observations in Sample n	Factors for X̄ Chart A₂	Factors for R Chart	
		D₃	D₄
2	1.880	0	3.268
3	1.023	0	2.574
4	.729	0	2.282
5	.577	0	2.114
6	.483	0	2.004
7	.419	.076	1.924
8	.373	.136	1.864
9	.337	.184	1.816
10	.308	.223	1.777
11	.285	.256	1.744
12	.266	.284	1.717
13	.249	.308	1.692
14	.235	.329	1.671
15	.223	.348	1.652

samples, $\overline{\overline{X}}$, which in this case is .6237. The control limits are set at $\overline{\overline{X}}$ plus or minus three standard deviations of the mean. Using the range as an estimator of the standard deviation and incorporating all of the statistical manipulations into one number (A_2), the lower control limit is $\overline{\overline{X}} - A_2\overline{R}$ and the UCL is $\overline{\overline{X}} + A_2\overline{R}$, or .6147 and .6327, respectively. Values for A_2 are also tabulated in Table 18–2. Constructing the $\overline{X}$ chart and plotting the data (see Figure 18–3), we find that all the sample values are also in control. If either the range values or the $\overline{X}$ values had been out of control, it would be necessary to track down the assignable cause before actually using the charts to control future production. Revision of these charts will be necessary in the future if any consistent improvement is detected, such as decreased variability.

When attribute inspection is being employed, it is necessary to use only

Figure 18–2 An R Chart from Table 18–1 Data

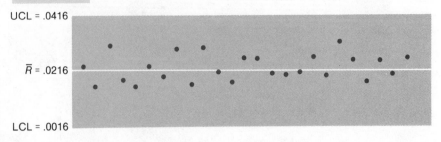

UCL = .0416

$\overline{R}$ = .0216

LCL = .0016

Figure 18–3   An $\bar{X}$ Chart from Table 18–1 Data

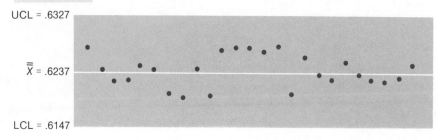

UCL = .6327

$\bar{\bar{X}}$ = .6237

LCL = .6147

one chart, a p chart. This is because the standard deviation about the mean number of defectives is a function of the mean and not independent as in the case of variables inspection. Considering the data in Table 18–3, the average percent defective ($\bar{p}$) is .0756 and the control limits are at $\bar{p} \pm 3\sigma_p$, where

$$\sigma_p = \sqrt{\frac{\bar{p}(1 - \bar{p})}{n}} = .038$$

and n is the sample size, in this case 50. Plotting the data results in a chart such as the one given in Figure 18–4, where the UCL is .1896 and the LCL is 0.

Table 18–3   Data for a p Chart

Date	Number of Defectives*	Percent Defective	Date	Number of Defectives	Percent Defective
Aug. 12	2	.04	Sept. 1	1	.02
13	1	.02	2	8	.16
16	1	.02	3	3	.06
17	7	.14	7	1	.02
18	2	.04	8	8	.16
19	9	.18	9	3	.06
20	7	.14	10	5	.10
23	2	.04	13	4	.08
24	1	.01	14	2	.04
25	5	.10	15	2	.04
26	5	.10	16	3	.06
27	4	.08			
30	6	.12			
31	3	.06			

*Constant sample size of 50.

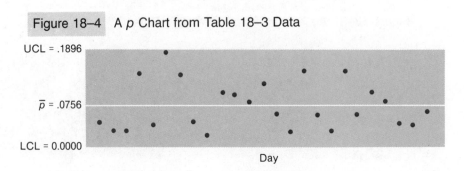

Figure 18–4   A *p* Chart from Table 18–3 Data

Acceptance Sampling

The most basic form of sampling inspection is acceptance sampling. In this technique the inspector examines a sample from a lot of material and, on the basis of the number of defective items in the sample and pre-established criteria, either accepts or rejects the lot. On accepted lots no further tests of the items not in the sample are needed; neither is the remainder of the rejected lots examined. Thus, the inspector does not determine the actual quality of the lots, nor is there a direct influence on product quality. Indirectly, when acceptance sampling is used internally, between departments, workers may become more quality conscious and thus improve their output. Rectifying inspection, described later, does result in improved quality for lots that leave an inspection station.

To a statistician, acceptance sampling is a form of applied hypothesis testing. A statement is made about what quality the lots should be; sampling error limits are established on the basis of the sampling distribution and associated probabilities; a sample is taken; and the quality statement and the lot are either accepted or rejected, depending upon whether the sample's characteristics are within the limits. Because of the specialized nature of the sampling distributions and the frequency with which these quality control techniques are applied, the statistical procedures have been simplified and standardized.

A typical acceptance sampling plan specifies the sample size, (n) and the maximum number of defective items in the sample that can be tolerated without rejecting the entire lot. This allowable number is termed the acceptance number, (c). For example, $n = 27$ and $c = 2$ means that out of a lot a sample of 27 is taken. If the number of defective items is 2 or less, accept the lot; if 3 or more are found, reject the lot.

What is the appropriate sampling plan for a given situation? A plan should be selected or designed so that material of good quality will have a low probability of being rejected and material of poor quality will have a low probability of being accepted. Rejection of good material is called a Type I error. The probability of making such a mistake is termed the producer risk, because it is the producer who suffers from having a lot rejected as being below quality standards simply because the few defective items in the lot clustered in the sample. The probability of Type I error is usually denoted by the Greek letter alpha (α). Generally α is taken as 5 percent, and the definition of good material, say a lot that is 1 percent defective, is called the acceptable quality level (AQL). The AQL is the maximum percent defective considered acceptable.

The sampling plan should also be designed so that material of poor quality has a low probability of being accepted. Acceptance of poor material is called a Type II error, and its probability of occurrence is designated by the Greek letter beta (β). This type of error is associated with the consumer's risk, since the consumer suffers if the lot is bad but is accepted as good because only a few of the defectives happened to be found in the sample. Generally β is taken as 10 percent, and a high percentage, say 8 percent defective, is defined as poor quality. This definition of poor is embodied in the lot tolerance percent defective (LTPD). Given α, the AQL, β, and the LTPD, it is possible to design a sampling plan that meets these characteristics and requirements.

Although the relationship of the variables is quite complex, several common-sense interpretations are possible. For example, in most situations, if all other variables are held constant and either the α risk is reduced or the AQL is increased, then the sample size and the acceptance number or count are increased. Correspondingly, for most practical situations, if the β risk is reduced or the LTPD is reduced, then the sample size and the count are increased. These changes in sample size and acceptance number generally hold in the relevant range of values that are commonly used for α, β, AQL, and LTPD. Table 18–4 shows 12 very commonly used plans with α, β, AQL, and LTPD values given and the approximate sample size (n) and acceptance number (c) computed.

In most cases, computer programs will be used to compute exact sampling plans. Such programs will either compute the historical or sample standard deviation then, given α, β, AQL, and LTPD assumptions, identify the

Table 18–4 Commonly Used Risk and Defect Plans

Plan	α	AQL	β	LTPD	n	c
1	.10	.01	.20	.10	18	1
2	.10	.03	.20	.10	45	3
3	.05	.01	.20	.10	25	1
4	.05	.01	.10	.10	40	1
5	.05	.01	.10	.08	55	2
6	.05	.02	.10	.10	60	3
7	.05	.01	.10	.08	80	2
8	.05	.02	.10	.08	96	4
9	.05	.01	.10	.05	120	3
10	.01	.01	.10	.05	200	6
11	.05	.02	.10	.05	250	9
12	.01	.01	.05	.03	700	14

sample size and acceptance number or sample mean (see, for example, Banks, Spoerer, and Collins 1986, or Pantumsinchai, Hassan, and Gupta 1983). These programs can offer numerous compromise alternatives. Ultimately, the operations manager must select a sampling plan that considers the cost of sampling, the cost of poor quality, and the risk and cost of making Type I and Type II errors.

Operating Characteristic Curves

One way of looking at this selection problem is in terms of the operating characteristic (OC) curve for the plan. This curve, which is uniquely determined for each value of n and c, shows the probability of accepting a lot as a function of the actual percentage defective in the lot. In other words, it shows the ability of a plan to discriminate between good and bad lots. Some typical OC curves are shown in Figure 18–5. Note that as the value of c decreases while n stays constant, the curve becomes more steep. Figure 18–6 shows what happens when c is held constant and n is varied. In this latter case, the plans become more discriminating as n increases, but this is at the cost of more inspection. The relationship between α, the AQL, β, and the LTPD can be seen in Figure 18–7 for a given OC curve. Calculation of an OC curve is straightforward, but much calculation may be involved. Since it is assumed

Figure 18–5 OC Curves for Typical Sampling Plans

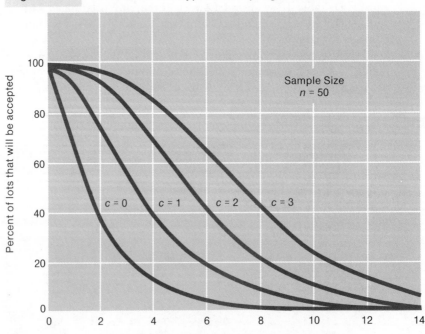

Product quality in percent defective (100 p)

Figure 18–6   OC Curves for $c = 2$ and Various Values of n

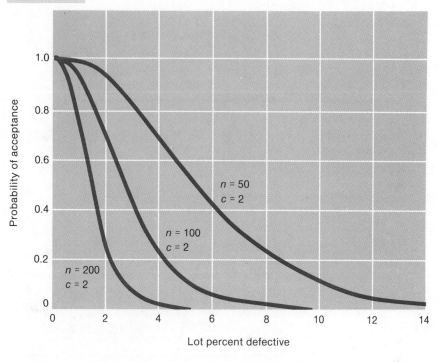

that the samples are always small in relationship to the entire lot, the properties of the binomial distribution are appropriate. The general equation for
the probability (P) of finding exactly d defective items in a sample of size n
when the lot is p fraction defective is given as

$$P(d/n) = \frac{n!}{d!(n-d)!} p^d (1-p)^{n-d}$$

Since for a given sampling plan you will accept a lot if there are c or fewer
defectives found, it is necessary to calculate the probability of getting exactly
0 defectives, 1 defective, 2 defectives, and so on up to c defectives and then
to add these probabilities together. For example, consider the following plan:

$$n = 50$$

$$c = 1.$$

If a lot were 4 percent defective (i.e., $p = .04$), what would be the probability
of accepting it? To find out, we proceed as follows:

Figure 18–7   Relationship of AQL, α, LTPD, and β

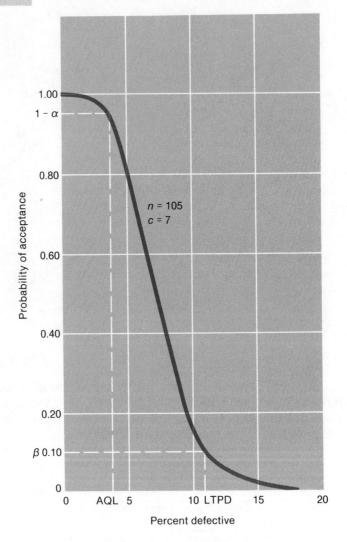

$$P(1 \text{ or fewer defective items}) = P(0/50) + P(1/50)$$

$$P(\text{acceptance}) = \frac{50!}{0!(50-0)!}.04^0(1-.04)^{50-0}$$

$$+ \frac{50!}{1!(50-1)!}.04^1(1-.04)^{50-1}$$

$$= \frac{50!}{0!50!}.04^0(.96)^{50} + \frac{50!}{1!49!}.04^1(.96)^{49}$$

$$= .96^{50} + 50(.04).96^{49}$$

$$= .1299 + .2706$$

$$= .4005$$

By repeating this procedure for many different values of p, we can construct the OC curve for this sampling plan.

Rectifying Inspection

If 100 percent of all rejected lots are inspected so that all the defective items are removed and are replaced by good parts, this is called rectifying inspection. As a result of the procedure, the quality of the lots passing the inspection station will be upgraded and the average outgoing quality (AOQ) will be affected.

Using the following terminology:

$p = $ Fraction defective in incoming lots

$S = $ Lot size

$n = $ Number of items in sample

$c = $ Acceptance number

$P_a = $ Probability of such a lot being accepted

The inspection procedure involves examining n items from each lot and replacing any defective items found in the sample with acceptable ones. If the lot is rejected, all the remaining items are inspected and all defectives in the lot are replaced. But if the lot is accepted—that is, if c or fewer defectives are found in the sample—then the $S - n$ items in the remainder of the lot are not inspected. However, since the lots are actually p percent defective, there are $p \times (S - n)$ defectives in the uninspected portion of the lot. This situation in which defective items are allowed to pass will happen P_a of the time.

Consider a numeric example as follows:

$$p = .03$$

$$S = 1,450$$

$$n = 50$$

$$c = 1$$

We are going to inspect 1,000 such lots. Let L be the number of lots to be inspected.

From an OC curve or by calculation, we find that lots that are 3 percent defective will be accepted 55.7 percent of the time. Thus, of the 1,000 lots inspected, 557 will be accepted without further inspection beyond the sample of 50. In each of these lots there are 1,400 noninspected items, and since the 3 percent defectives are evenly distributed, there would be .03 × 1,400, or 42, defective items left in each accepted lot. For the 443 lots rejected there will be no defective items in each lot, but for the 557 lots accepted, there will be a total of 557 × 42 or 23,394 defective items in the combined total of 1,000 lots, which contain a total of 1,450,000 parts. Therefore, the average outgoing quality is 23,394 ÷ 1450 × 1000, or .01613. The procedure we just followed can be expressed by the formula:

$$AOQ = \frac{P_a p (S - n) L}{SL} \text{ or } \frac{P_a p (S - n)}{S}$$

Since n is generally much smaller than S, it is approximately true that the AOQ is simply the product of P_a and p, which, it should be noted, are the ordinate and abscissa of the OC curve.

For a particular sampling plan, if p is small, then the probability of acceptance is high and the AOQ is low because the incoming quality is good; most lots are passed with small improvement in quality. If p is high, few lots pass and most of the bad parts are caught in the rectifying inspection; defectives are then replaced with good parts, reducing the number of defectives in the outgoing lots; hence the AOQ is also low when the incoming quality is poor. By examining a plan's OC curve and making use of the approximation

$$AOQ = pP_a$$

it can be seen that the AOQ is a maximum for some mediocre quality level (see Figure 18–8). But the fact that there is some maximum AOQ for every plan is very significant. This limiting value, the average outgoing quality limit (AOQL), implies that no matter how poor or how good the incoming quality may be, the outgoing quality will be no worse than the AOQL of the plan being used in the rectifying inspection process.

The fraction defective (P_m) at which the AOQL will occur can be found by reference to the approximate x value in Table 18–5 and use of the following formula:

$$P_m = \frac{x}{n}$$

Figure 18–8   AOQ After Screening of Rejected Inspection Lots

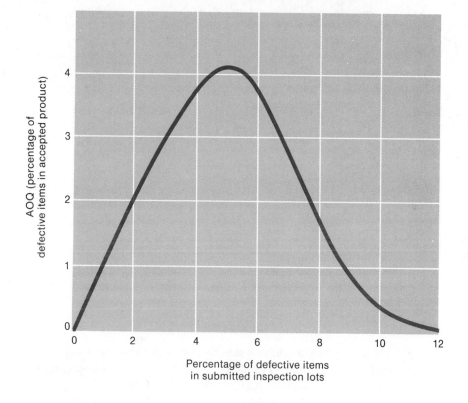

Single Sampling Plan		
Sample Size	Acceptance Number	Rejection Number
225	14	15

For example, in the plan shown in Figure 18–8 with $c = 14$ and $n = 225$:

$$P_m = \frac{11.15}{225} = .0496$$

The AOQL itself is obtained from the y value in Table 18–5 and the following relationship:

$$AOQL = \frac{y}{n}$$

Table 18–5   Values of *x* and *y* for Given Values of *c*

Given c	x	y	Given c	x	y	Given c	x	y
0	1.00	0.3679	10	8.05	6.528	20	15.92	13.89
1	1.62	0.8400	11	8.82	7.233	21	16.73	14.66
2	2.27	1.371	12	9.59	7.948	22	17.54	15.43
3	2.95	1.942	13	10.37	8.670	23	18.35	16.20
4	3.64	2.544	14	11.15	9.398	24	19.17	16.98
5	4.35	3.168	15	11.93	10.13	25	19.99	17.76
6	5.07	3.812	16	12.72	10.88	26	20.81	18.54
7	5.80	4.472	17	13.52	11.62	27	21.63	19.33
8	6.55	5.146	18	14.31	12.37	28	22.46	20.12
9	7.30	5.831	19	15.12	13.13	29	23.29	20.91
10	8.05	6.528	20	15.92	13.89	30	24.11	21.70

Source: Sampling Inspection Tables, Harold F. Dodge and Harry G. Romig (New York: John Wiley & Sons, Inc., 1959), p. 39.

In this case,

$$AOQL = \frac{9.398}{225} = .0418$$

In designing an appropriate rectifying inspection plan, it is best to consider minimizing the cost of inspection while attaining the desired AOQL. As a measure of this objective we can use an average total inspection (ATI) figure.

$$ATI = n + (1 - P_a)(S - n)$$

This is simply a mathematical description of the average number of items that will be inspected. We can minimize this value only for a given process average (p), since P_a will vary for a given plan as a function of p.

To minimize the ATI, note the following relationship.

$$n = \frac{yS}{S(AOQL) + y}$$

Because of the relationships between these variables, it is necessary to use trial-and-error procedures with this equation in order to find a minimum ATI value.

For example, consider a plan for which you want an AOQL of .015 and for which the process average is .01 with lots of 5,000 items. Starting with a *c* of 2, *y* is found to be 1.371 (see Table 18–5). Substituting in the previous equation:

$$n = \frac{1.371(5,000)}{5,000(.015) + 1.371} = 90$$

Computing P_a for $c = 2$, $n = 90$, and $p = .01$, we find it equals 94 percent. Thus,

$$ATI = 90 + (1 - .94)(5,000 - 90) = 385$$

Similarly, trying other values of c, the following table can be constructed:

c	n	ATI
4	164	295
5	203	285
6	242	299

Values of c larger than 5 would result in larger ATIs; therefore, the plan that minimizes the ATI in this case is $n = 203$, $c = 5$.

While this procedure can give rather precise answers, actual selection of plans is greatly simplified by reference to prepared tables. (See, for example, Dodge and Romig 1959.) By aiming for either a given LTPD or AOQL and knowing the general characteristics of the process you are monitoring, an appropriate plan can be selected from the tables to minimize the average amount of inspection.

Multiple Sampling

Since one of the prime virtues of statistical quality control is cost reduction in the inspection process, several other sampling procedures have been developed to help reduce inspection costs still further. The first of these modifications is double sampling. In this method, a sample of size n_1 is taken, and if the number of defectives in the sample is less than c_1, the lot is accepted. If the number of bad parts is greater than c_2, the lot is rejected. If the defective parts number between c_1 and c_2, then a second sample is taken before a decision to accept or reject is made. The second sample of size n_2 is examined. If the combined defectives in both samples exceed c_2, the lot is rejected; if not, it is accepted.

The advantage of double sampling becomes apparent when comparing equivalent single and double sampling plans—that is, plans that have the same OC curve. If lots submitted for inspection are either very bad or very good, it frequently will be possible to make a decision on the basis of the first sample of size n_1. Since it is always true that n_1 is smaller than the corresponding single sampling plan n, less inspection is involved. Unfortunately, if the incoming quality is mediocre, the sample of size n_2 will likely have to be taken; and $n_1 + n_2$ is larger than the single sampling plan sample size. This relationship can be seen in Figure 18–9 in which the average amount of inspection for equivalent double sampling and single sampling plans are plotted against incoming quality.

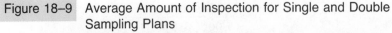

Figure 18–9 Average Amount of Inspection for Single and Double Sampling Plans

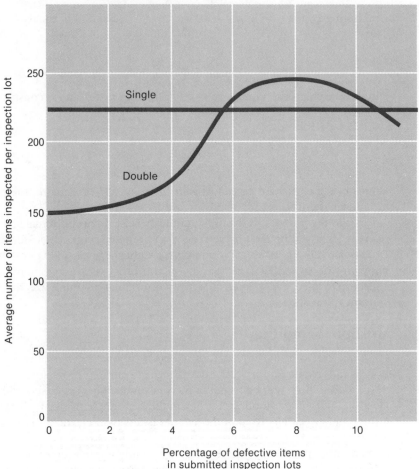

To extend the concept even further, sequential sampling plans have been developed in which one item at a time is inspected in sequence, and on the basis of the cumulative results a decision is made to accept, reject, or continue inspecting. As inspection proceeds, it is possible to calculate a sequential probability ratio (SPR). This ratio of the probability of having found this many or this few defective items in this cumulative sample size if the lot is bad (of LTPD quality) to the probability of this result if the lot is good (of AQL quality). Taking into account α and β, it is possible to establish acceptance and rejection numbers or to plot their equivalents as in Figure 18–10.

Since it is sometimes inconvenient to sample items one at a time, multiple

Figure 18–10   Sequential Sampling Chart

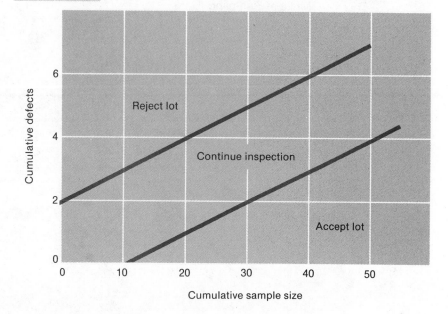

sampling plans have been developed in which small groups of items are inspected and handled in a manner similar to sequential sampling of single items. Here again, by comparing equivalent single, double, and multiple plans, inspection can be reduced still further as is shown in Figure 18–11. A disadvantage of these types of plans is their complexity; multiple values or tables must be kept in mind. Because of this, though in theory they are superior, in practice they are less used.

CONCLUSIONS

Increasingly, operations managers realize the need to define quality with regard to a specific product, develop an assessment of the costs of quality, and organize a quality assurance system. This process, which must be considered in relation to systems in other functional areas, consists of four differentiated subsystems. Numerous objectives in each of these subsystems provide checks that can be used to assess existing quality control programs or to set up and develop new programs. These activities are used to define the design quality.

Statistical quality control measurements evaluate conformance of the product with the design. Various techniques consider quality attributes and variables using large and small samples. By designing a sampling plan under these various conditions to achieve desired quality outcomes, the operations manager can assure that the product has conformance quality.

Figure 18–11 Average Amount of Inspection for Single, Double, and Multiple Sampling Plans

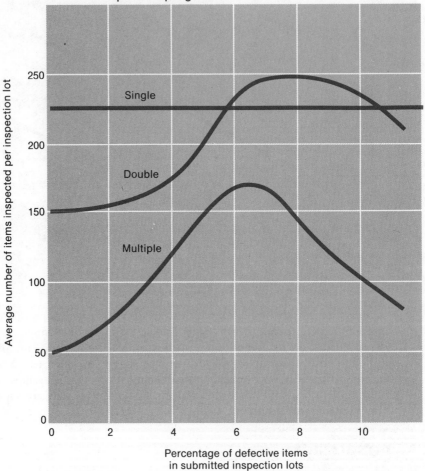

QUESTIONS

1. Explain the concept of appropriate quality.

2. Differentiate design quality and conformance quality.

3. Identify five classes of quality. Within each class identify a particular characteristic and give an example.

4. Compare and contrast prevention costs and appraisal costs.

5. What are failure costs? Give examples of internal and external failure costs.

6. Use a diagram to demonstrate the tradeoff of quality costs. Show appraisal, prevention, and failure costs.

7. Describe several aspects of a zero defects program.

8. Briefly summarize the objectives of a quality assurance department.

9. What are the four integrated subsystems of the quality control system? Give an example of one way that each subsystem could affect quality.

10. What is the purpose of product liability planning and control? How does it interface with quality control?

11. Using the three-class system for rating the importance of product or service characteristics described in the text, classify the critical, major, and minor attributes for the following: childrens' clothing, a lawn mower, and weed killer.

12. For the following products and services, define the process quality planning and control subsystem with regard to the process, measurement, equipment, personnel, and disposition of deficiencies:

   a. A hair cut
   b. A metal file cabinet
   c. A power lawnmower
   d. An electric lightbulb

13. For the following products and services, define the material quality planning and control subsystem with regard to supplier approval, informing suppliers, measurement, and evaluation:

   a. Supplier of delivered pizza
   b. Supplier of ready-mix concrete for a building foundation
   c. Supplier of lumber stock for furniture
   d. Supplier of packaging for cosmetics

14. For the following products and services, define the product performance subsystem with regard to performance, reliability, maintainability, and liability exposure:

   a. A child's dart game
   b. A nationally distributed, over-the-counter pharmaceutical
   c. A suitcase
   d. An automatic toll station

15. In your own words, state the meaning of the central limit theorem.

16. In your own words, what is the meaning of the standard deviation? How is it related to quality control?

17. Differentiate the conditions under which sampling with control charts would be used from those for which acceptance sampling would be used.

18. How are first-part and patrol inspection integrated?

19. What are the functions of a material review board? Who would participate on the board?

20. What are the objectives of the product performance subsystem?

21. When is 100 percent inspection (census) of products infeasible? When would such an inspection be appropriate?

PROBLEMS

1. What are the range and mean for the following observations?
   22, 21, 23, 12, 22

2. For the following observations, determine the range and mean for each sample.

Group	Observations
1	22, 21, 23, 12, 22
2	23, 21, 20, 22, 22
3	22, 22, 20, 21, 22
4	23, 23, 22, 22, 22
5	22, 21, 20, 22, 23

3. For the data above, calculate $\overline{\overline{X}}$ and $\overline{R}$.

4. Calculate the UCL and LCL of an R chart for the data in Problem 2, using the factors given in Table 18–2.

5. Create an R chart and plot the data exhibited in Problem 2. Are all values within the control limits?

6. From the data above, calculate the UCL and LCL limits and create an $\overline{X}$ chart using the factors given in Table 18–2.

7. A shoe manufacturer has received complaints that shoes have been shipped with improper stitching to some customers. The manufacturer inspects a sample of 100 shoes from 10 lots with the following results:

Lot Number	Number Defective
1	4
2	6
3	2
4	7
5	0
6	1
7	6
8	0
9	9
10	2

   a. Calculate p-bar for this sampling.
   b. Determine the UCL and LCL for this sampling.
   c. Plot the data on a p chart. Is the operation in control?

8. A poultry products wholesaler desires to assure that a truckload of egg cases contains little breakage. The supplier sets a lot tolerance percent defective (LTPD) of cases containing broken eggs at 10 percent, but the wholesaler (buyer) desires an AQL of 3 percent. The supplier establishes a 0.20 risk of error of the sample and the buyer a 0.10 risk of error. What should be the sample size and count to reject the lot?

9. If the AQL were 0.02 in Problem 8, estimate the sample size and count.

10. A large toy store receives Contendo games in boxes. Management desires to assure that the boxes are not damaged. The distributor establishes a LTPD of 5 percent damaged boxes, with a 10 percent risk of sampling error. The toy store establishes an AQL of 2 percent defects, with a 5 percent risk of error. Specify the plan.

11. Referring to Problem 10, identify two alternative plans that maintain the same producer risks and defect value, and changes those values for the buyer, which would reduce the sample size. Describe the risks of each.

12. For lot sizes of 5,000 with a process average of .01 defective, compute the appropriate sample size n and the probability of accepting the sample, P_a, for an acceptance number c of 3 and a desired AOQL of .015. Find the average total inspection, ATI, for this sampling plan.

13. For the lot size, process average, and AOQL in Problem 12, find n, P_a, and the ATI for $c = 6$. Compare these results with the results of the example on pages 626–627 to verify the minimum ATI.

14. The owner of a large greenhouse is concerned about the quality level of flats of plants being sent to various retail outlets around the country. She has observed a number of dead plants in a few flats of plants and has decided to determine if her plant shipments are within an acceptable range of quality. For the next 10 days, she observed 5 shipments of 100 flats each. Data of flats containing dead plants are below. Develop R and X-bar control charts, and compute the central value as well as the upper and lower control limits for each.

Group	Observations of Flats with Dead Plants				
	Shipment 1	Shipment 2	Shipment 3	Shipment 4	Shipment 5
1	7	6	5	2	4
2	4	0	2	1	7
3	3	7	2	9	1
4	4	3	7	5	3
5	4	5	2	8	0
6	1	4	6	4	0
7	5	3	2	6	7
8	3	7	5	3	3
9	6	5	1	5	3
10	0	4	8	3	2

15. A bicycle tire manufacturer has been notified from retail outlets that many tires are being shipped in defective boxes. Quality control was instructed to determine if the operation was in control. For the following 10 days they observed 10 lots each day. The mean and range of those observations are given below. Develop R and X-bar control charts; compute the central value, UCL, and LCL for each.

Group	Mean	Range
1	1.50	4.00
2	2.00	5.00
3	1.60	5.00
4	1.10	4.00
5	1.30	3.00
6	1.20	4.00
7	1.50	5.00
8	0.90	3.00
9	0.80	2.00
10	1.20	3.00

REFERENCES

Banks, Jerry, J. P. Spoerer, and R. Lee Collins. *IBM PC Applications for the Industrial Engineer and Manager.* Englewood Cliffs, N.J.: Reston, 1986.

Crosby, Philip B. *Quality is Free.* New York: McGraw-Hill, 1979.

Dodge, Harold F. and Harry G. Romig. *Sampling Inspection Tables* 2nd ed. New York: Wiley, 1959.

Duncan, A. J. *Quality Control and Industrial Statistics,* 4th ed. Homewood, Ill: Irwin, 1974.

Juran, J. M., and Frank M. Gryna, Jr. *Quality Planning and Analysis,* 2nd ed. New York: McGraw-Hill, 1980.

Mertz, Orville. "Quality's Role in ROI." *Quality Progress* (October 1977) p. iv.

Pantumsinchai, Pricha, M. Zia Hassan and Ishwar D. Gupta. *BASIC Programs for Production & Operations Management.* Englewood Cliffs, N.J.: Prentice Hall, 1983.

CHAPTER 19
STRATEGY AND POLICY

OBJECTIVES

After completing this chapter, you should be able to

- Understand the dimensions of the strategy formulation and policy development process

- Know the contributions and limitations of evaluating tradeoffs in strategy formulation and understand the pitfalls of tradeoff analysis

- Appreciate the reasons for a "macro" overview perspective of operations strategy and how such a perspective helps the operations manager to address the requirements of the job

- Identify several strategic overview perspective decisions that operations managers must address, and some of the key information considerations in that perspective

- Know the dimensions of operations policy and how those dimensions relate to the execution and control of a production operation.

OUTLINE

INTRODUCTION

Possibly the single most important aspect of an operation manager's job is to integrate individual production activities as a smoothly functioning operation. This synergy, or harmonious fit of the parts, reduces the waste and increases the productivity of the operation. Operations strategy formulation and policy development provide a method to achieve this integration and to improve effectiveness of operations. However, productivity improvement is a subtle and indirect process. As Skinner (1986) points out, there is a paradox in constantly working toward greater productivity by improving direct labor efficiency or materials utilization. The difficulty of this approach is that it focuses excessively on direct labor efficiency and ignores other ways to use manufacturing as a strategic resource or as the basis for a coherent strategy. Such short-sighted productivity programs often result in other wastes and little or no productivity gains, perhaps even productivity losses. The operations manager should consider quality, lead times, service, rate of product introduction, on-time delivery, and adjustable capacity if a successful strategy is to be developed.

Reconsider, for a moment, the definition of operations management and the dimensions of operations management decisions that were originally presented in Chapter 1. The definition follows and the decision dimensions, originally given in Table 1–1, are repeated in Table 19–1.

> Operations management is the continuous process of effectively using management functions to integrate resources efficiently in an effort to achieve operations goals.

The Relationship of Strategy and Policy

These four dimensions of operations management decisions have been individually discussed in Parts One through Five of this book. They are relevant to the strategy formulation and policy development process because they

Table 19–1   The Dimensions of Operations Management Decisions

Time Period Affected	Resource Managed	Decision Area Affected	Management Function
Long Range Medium Range Short Range Present	Facilities Equipment Materials Labor Information Capital Energy	Capacity Materials Quality Process Personnel	Planning Execution Control Organization Staffing

express core day-to-day, short- medium- and long-range strategic concerns of the operations manager. They suggest that the operations manager must, by definition, be a strategist and must implement strategy through the execution and control of organizational policies. Operations strategy can be defined as

> the present pattern of integrated resource commitments in various decision areas, and planned improvements to that pattern.

This definition of operations strategy directly links strategy to the overall definition of management through the idea of integrating resources efficiently. Operations policy can be defined as

> a guide, based on operations strategy, for execution and control which suggests limits or values, thus aiding decision makers to ensure continuity, consistency, and integration of operations.

Because strategy formulation and policy development are so closely linked, they are often called the strategy formulation and policy development process.

The Six-Step Strategy Formulation and Policy Development Process

The formulation of an operations strategy and communication of that strategy as policy involves six sequential, interactive, and cyclical steps.

1. *Identify corporate strategy requirements*—Define the demands and constraints of the corporate strategy on the operations function.
2. *Specify the evaluation criteria and strategy variables*—Evaluate operations by the general criteria of cost, quality, flexibility, and delivery. Additionally, numerous variables contribute to those criteria.
3. *Generalize to a strategic overview perspective*—Assess the criteria and variables as contributors to key strategic operations management issues. This is the effectiveness measure or doing the right job.
4. *Define strategy alternatives and make decision*—Define alternatives and make a decision that prioritizes or redefines operations activities according to the evaluative criteria. This is the efficiency measure or doing the job right.
5. *Develop policy*—Create the necessary policy guidance.
6. *Manage execution and control processes*—Execute and control the policy as necessary to assure compliance.

The first two steps of the strategy formulation and policy development process—corporate strategy requirements and evaluation criteria—concern strategy formulation. The second two steps—identify contributors and define alternatives and make decisions—are decision-making processes. The last two steps—develop policy and manage execution and control—are considered in the policy development section.

STRATEGY FORMULATION

Corporate strategy involves evaluation of threats and opportunities (T & O) in the external environment and weaknesses and strengths (W & S) of the firm's internal capabilities. This TOWS analysis (Steiner and Miner 1977) gives a clear picture of the competitive domain or niche of the firm and the specific distinctive competence of the production function. The operation should be the best source when measured by one, or possibly two, of the four evaluation criteria (cost, quality, flexibility, or delivery).

Porter (1980) defines three strategic alternatives for the corporation: cost leadership (low-cost, standardized, off-the-shelf products), product differentiation (high-quality, flexible products), and market focus (meeting special needs of a particular market, i.e., delivery, customization). These corporate strategies translate easily to the four evaluation criteria.

Corporate strategy must be sufficiently defined and should aspire to competence in one or possibly two of the evaluation criteria. This focusing of the factory by defining the evaluation criteria (Skinner 1974) is a very important part of the corporate and operations strategy interface. In generic terms, a corporate strategy of XYZ Company might be stated:

> The strategy of the XYZ Company is to increase market share by 1 to 2 percent per year over the next five years through stable growth of present standardized product markets and through improved response to customer demand. This strategy will require an aggressive customer-oriented marketing posture, a broad reevaluation of production methods, some increase in personnel, particularly technical specialists, and close attention to control potentially increasing costs.

This corporate strategy suggests the general direction of the company and is a basis for more detailed strategy development by marketing, operations, human resources, and finance managers. The operations manager must now address the strategy variables.

Strategy Variables and the Evaluation Criteria

The strategic requirements of the operations manager are both uncontrollable and controllable. Because the operations manager has little choice but to comply with uncontrollable requirements, such as the legal requirements of health and safety, industrial relations, and pollution and product safety, those issues are not pursued as a topic of general operations strategy formulation. However, the controllable areas of operations strategy formulation, which include production costs, product quality, process flexibility, and delivery, are very important to the operations manager for two reasons. First, they establish the primary criteria for evaluating operations performance. These are the effectiveness measures—that is, they determine whether the operations manager is doing the right job. Secondly, the controllable areas permit identification of some of the tradeoffs and development of a strategic

Table 19–2   Criteria for Evaluating Operations Efficiency

Criteria	Tradeoff	Strategy Question
Production cost	1. Dollar value of resources (including materials and labor) 2. Prorated sunk costs (including facilities and equipment)	Should the firm produce using a labor-intense or an equipment-intense method?
Product quality	1. Internal reject rate (including scrap, rework, and production seconds) 2. External failure rate (including warrantee work and customer returns and dissatisfaction)	Where should the firm bear the cost of quality—internally or externally?
Customer delivery	1. On-time, on-specification delivery rate 2. Product backordering to respond to customer orders	Should the firm deliver goods from inventories with high responsiveness or by backordering?
Process flexibility	1. Learn and adopt new technologies 2. Learn stable skills and produce	At what rate should the firm adopt new technology or flexibly mix different products in the same process?

overview perspective. Examples of tradeoffs associated with the criteria are noted in Table 19–2.

These evaluative criteria are generally mutually exclusive. If operations is to compete as a low-cost producer, for example, then high process flexibility, responsive product delivery, and high quality are generally precluded because they are usually more costly. Note that recent developments in manufacturing processes have permitted the production of a high-quality product for relatively low costs in some cases. However, in general, higher quality, greater process flexibility, and improved product delivery result in higher costs, which must ultimately be regained by selling more units or increasing unit price. The operations manager should aspire to a clear distinctive competence in only one of the four criteria, with a possible secondary competence. In addition to the evaluation criteria, however, operations strategy must consider the dimensions of operations decision making.

Strategy Variables and the Dimensions of Operations Decision Making

Table 19–1 identifies the four dimensions of operations decision making as time, resource, decision area, and management function.

TIME DIMENSION. Tradeoff decisions must integrate varying time periods, including the long, medium, and short range, and the present. Of course, in the present, the operations manager's primary concern is to keep the production activity functioning. However, the tradeoff considerations between the present and the future are subtle. For example, the postponement of preventive maintenance due in the present period would permit reporting of lower operating costs in the present quarter. However, such as strategy of trading tomorrow for today can be disastrous (Banks and Wheelwright 1979). The operations strategy must effectively integrate the appropriate long-range, medium-range, and short-range considerations with present goals.

RESOURCE DIMENSION.   In a similar manner, the tradeoff decision may involve different combinations of the productive resources noted in Table 19–1. Alternatives include varying combinations of labor-intense or technology-intense processes and capital input (e.g., expenditures for facilities or equipment). For example, a road may be built through a labor-intense strategy employing many workers with crude hand tools. Earlier civilizations relied on such strategies in the absence of alternatives. Modern construction firms would build that same road using a capital-intensive strategy of heavy equipment and fewer laborers. For the operations manager, the key questions are whether the resource is available and at what cost. Through this tradeoff decision process, an operations manager would select various combinations of resources (facilities, equipment, material, human, knowledge, and capital) to integrate and achieve an efficient resource mix.

DECISION AREA DIMENSION.   Tradeoff decisions can also involve capacity, process, inventory, quality, and human resources. For example, the chase or level tradeoff considers the costs of producing to varying demands by adjusting the work force or leveling production and meeting demand through inventory. The level strategy requires more inventory and less capacity, while the chase strategy requires more capacity and relatively less inventory. Similarly, there is a tradeoff between fixed costs of production, associated with such capacity variables as facilities and equipment and the variable costs associated with personnel.

MANAGEMENT FUNCTION DIMENSION.   The fourth decision dimension is the management function. Management must assess its own time commitment to the management functional activities of planning, organization, staffing, execution, and control. The visibility of these five functions, and the manager's commitment to each, makes a statement to the organization and, as a personal leadership activity, is an important part of the operations strategy. For example, the operations manager may intensely schedule planning activities for one week but subsequently schedule other management functions.

The Multidimensional Strategy Tradeoff

These examples of strategy tradeoffs weigh two alternatives and select one or the other, or a combination, as the desired strategy. However, there may be several more specific variables that must be integrated into the operation manager's decisions. Table 19–3 suggests some of the common two-variable tradeoff decisions.

Each tradeoff has implications for cost, quality, flexibility, delivery, and the dimensions of operations decisions. Additionally, each tradeoff has potential impacts on other decisions. For this reason, operations strategy might be realistically viewed as a multidimensional tradeoff of a large number of simultaneous considerations. Operations strategy develops these multiple tradeoffs

Table 19–3   Common Operations Management Tradeoffs and Strategy Criteria

Strategy Area	Variable 1	Variable 2	Common Name
Competance	Build part	Buy part	Make–Buy
	Short-range performance	Long-range growth	Trading tommorow for today
Capacity	Fixed costs	Variable costs	Breakeven analysis
	Build capacity with demand	Build capacity before or after demand	Capacity timing
Facilities	Lease facilities	Own facilities	Lease–Own
	Many facilities	Few facilities	Centralized– Diverse
Process	Line flow production	Process flow production group technology	Process strategy
	Make to order	Make to stock	Customization
	Carrying cost	Setup cost	Economic lot size
	Level production	Chase production	Chase–Level
	Labor intense	Capital, facility, equipment intense	Resource allocation
	Cost of preventative maintenance	Cost of production failure	Maintenance strategy
Materials	Carrying cost	Order cost	Economic order quantity
	Hold inventory	Stockout/Backorder	Safety stock
Quality	Quality of design	Quality of inspection	Product quality
	Reject rate	Warranty, rework rates	Service quality
	Proactive quality	Reactive quality	Quality strategy
	Direct ship to customer	Warehousing, break-bulk, distribution/service centers	Customer service
	Standardized product	Customized product	Customer response
Personnel	Cost of safety program	Cost of accidents	Safety strategy
	Overtime	Hiring	Employment
Research	Immediate production measurement	Long-term process development	Research goals

to integrate the diverse and often contradictory aspects of the operations environment.

Operations research has proposed a variety of computational procedures that permit optimization of a multiple variable tradeoff. Linear programming algorithms consider more than 100 variables and a greater number of constraints through the simplex algorithm. That algorithm has been applied to an aggregate planning tradeoff program, which includes such variables as number of hires and fires per period, overtime requirements, personnel costs, inventory holding and setup costs, unit backorder costs per period, and variable quantities demanded over multiple periods (Pantumsinchai, Hassan, and Gupta 1983). The program provides an optimal (minimum cost) aggregate plan. Such operations research models are used to simultaneously consider the operations variables. However, this use is presently limited by several factors:

1. Management may not understand or fully trust complex mathematical algorithms.
2. The optimization is mechanically accurate but dependent upon input values, which may not be as accurate. Minor input errors could possibly cause major output variances.
3. The models do not include some important variables, among them: maintenance, safety, and, perhaps most importantly, top management commitment.

This discussion of the integration of strategic tradeoffs represents, in a very limited sense, the experience that operations managers gain over a lifetime career of watching the variables and tradeoffs. The depth of these experiences and the complexity of the multivariate interaction cannot be replicated by a mechanical process. Because the tradeoff approach defines a very limited approximate model of the real world and because it specifically does not incorporate a strategic overview perspective, overdependence on the tradeoffs may lead to numerous pitfalls. Recalling Skinner's (1986) comments on the productivity paradox, emphasis of tradeoffs may lead to few productivity improvements because it accepts conditions as given rather than as challenges for improvements. Experienced operations managers tend to try to reduce the impact of the tradeoffs and then assess the issues from a strategic overview perspective.

Reducing the Necessity for Tradeoffs

These tradeoffs have been developed over the years and are considered by many to be an inherent basis for the operations decision maker. Recent efforts, however, have attempted to avoid or minimize the pitfalls of tradeoffs. By accepting the conditions that necessitate the tradeoff, it is argued, operations managers implicitly confirm the higher costs imposed by the tradeoff alternatives. This is viewed as a very serious pitfall because it hides these costs from consideration.

However, by reducing or eliminating the conditions that necessitated the tradeoff, the impact and cost of the tradeoff are reduced. Probably the most widely understood examples are the reduction of process setup costs through careful planning and engineering and the reduction of order processing costs through more efficient communication and information-handling methods. The use of robotic technology, flexible manufacturing cells, and manufacturing information systems all have made the reduced setup times possible. Similarly, the use of credit cards and toll-free telephone numbers for customer ordering have reduced purchasing costs, particularly for small businesses. These methods have clearly diminished the effect of the economic order quantity (EOQ) and economic lot size (ELS) tradeoffs, and thus reduced the total cost of inventory. By addressing the setup or order cost tradeoff and reducing inventory total costs, operations managers are able to realize further efficiencies, including higher inventory turns, greater flexibility to respond to changing customer requirements, reduced delivery times, and, arguably, improved quality.

The advent of overnight package services, courier services, and standardized delivery costs and methods have reduced the distribution costs and time for many types of goods. Suppliers are able to promise delivery within a maximum of two or three days and ship directly to the customer from a single national distribution point. This eliminates the costs of regional warehouses, particularly for lightweight, low-cost, easily shippable items such as repair parts or office supplies. Again, the improved delivery methods have reduced costs, permitting greater flexibility of inventory management and, arguably, improved quality.

Thus, the tradeoff approach to operations strategy formulation may cause the operations manager to be unaware of potential cost reductions in the very variables that imposed the tradeoff. But an even more serious pitfall of the tradeoff approach is that it focuses the attention of the operations manager on details rather than on a strategic overview perspective. Even so, the tradeoff and reduction of the necessity for tradeoffs are inherent in many strategy considerations and in the strategic overview perspective.

THE STRATEGY DECISION-MAKING PROCESS

In an effort to focus on a macro, or strategic scale, overview perspective of the operations management function, operations managers concentrate on several key considerations, which in their experience and in their businesses are central. Once these considerations are identified, the operations manager should develop several strategy alternatives. Each alternative can be objectively costed, the nonmeasurable variables can be summarized subjectively, and a decision can be made.

The Strategic Perspective Issues

The strategic perspective can be broadly focused on eight operations management issues: (1) structural integration, (2) capacity management, (3) facilities evaluation, (4) process technology, (5) materials management, (6) quality assurance, (7) human resources management, and (8) technology research. However, before any of these areas is considered, the operations manager should set aside unnecessary processes or information. The first step is to simplify; then the analysis can proceed with fewer encumbrances (Mather 1986).

STRUCTURAL INTEGRATION—WHAT IS THE DISTINCTIVE COMPETENCE? All organizations must decide what transformation processes they are going to perform and which they are going to purchase. These make-or-buy decisions are also known as process positioning. For example, a brewer may brew and bottle or can beer and also produce its own beer can. A completely vertically integrated brewery also would own and operate the aluminum plant to make the cans and the mines to obtain the raw material.

Such extreme vertical integration, however, is usually precluded because the different processes require substantially different technical capabilities and management approaches. In addition, one organization seldom has sufficient demand to permit efficient operation of a raw material–processing facility. However, vertical integration does make sense when efficient operation of two producers or sequential producers in the product chain operate at roughly the same volume. Vertical integration of suppliers is called upstream or backward integration, while integration of distribution and merchandising is called downstream or forward integration. Although the technology of manufacturing cans is different from that of brewing beer, the repetitive production of cans has many similarities to the packaging of beer and is frequently handled successfully by the same firm.

The motivation to integrate upstream is often to gain control of a critical material or supply or to obtain profits of the supplier. However, the disadvantages can be many. The process technology of a supplier may be different from that of the purchaser, the scale of operations required for efficiency may be considerably different, or competitors of the supplier may develop process or product advances that make their items more attractive, causing capital requirements or the span of general management to increase. For example, although a large automobile company may have enough demand to operate a steel mill, running a rubber plantation to supply raw materials for tires would probably be stretching the span of management. Similarly, a restaurant may bake its own pies or bread, but operating an orchard, flour mill, or wheat farm would rarely make sense.

Vertical integration concerns more than just the material or goods chain. Upstream vertical integration may concern process design, equipment design and assembly, product design, facility design and construction, acquisition of personnel, data capture, and management information system development. Long before college and university nursing programs, hospitals had developed their own nursing education for secondary school graduates. This use of upstream integration in the personnel chain provided control over the quality of incoming personnel and assured a stable supply.

Additionally, many organizations develop their own computerized information systems. McDonnell Douglas and Boeing both began by developing computerized information systems for their own use and then went into the software and management information systems business. However, most small- and medium-sized firms purchase technical expertise in product and process information system design from specialists, even though they may possess considerable technical ability. Restaurants, hospitals, pharmaceutical companies, banks, investment management organizations, and real estate firms, for example, all purchase data and information concerning economic, social, political, and technological trends and developments as well as very specific information and advice concerning process, product, and service improvements. Additionally, many large service organizations have entire staffs devoted to facility design, construction management, information systems implementation, and training, which are all examples of upstream integration.

Downstream integration begins with the establishment of a marketing arm, including distribution, warehousing, and retail outlets. This guarantees access to the market, permits greater flexibility in pricing, and gains the profits of retailing. However, downstream integration requires higher operating costs as warehouses, finished goods, and retail outlets are added. Again, the span of top management is increased as additional personnel and facilities are added.

Downstream integration also applies to more than marketing and distribution. In manufacturing it can include providing user education and training materials and programs; maintenance, repair, and equipment upgrade; and brokerage services for the used equipment market. For example, the Fellows Gear Machine Company overhauls its gear-cutting machines and also maintains a record by serial number of the location of each machine it has sold and the refurbishment performed on each. University career placement services and alumni relations efforts, and the Pioneers Club for retirees of Southwestern Bell Telephone Company, are examples of downstream human resource integration.

Until 1960, firms vertically integrated primarily by purchasing suppliers and developing component manufacturing capacity. However, the advent of excellent manufacturing capabilities in countries with relatively low wages dramatically reversed that trend. For example, U.S. computer companies now use both purchased and manufactured sources for the same part in an assembly operation. Similarly, while many firms are growing larger through mergers and acquisitions, large firms are purchasing more items from smaller firms with fewer labor restrictions. For example, a labor agreement of a large firm may require one operator per machine, whereas a smaller firm with a different contract may be able to have one operator run two or more machines.

CAPACITY MANAGEMENT—HOW MUCH OUTPUT PER PERIOD? Capacity management decisions deal primarily with the output rate and timing, but they are also highly dependent upon the type of process technology selected. The availability of capacity means the availability of facilities, equipment, human resources, materials, and components and supplier capacity. Thus, capacity decisions affect requirements for long-range investment capital, working capital, direct labor, management personnel, and supporting services such as materials management, engineering, data processing, and maintenance. Execution of decisions and subsequent control activities of implementation, either to increase or decrease capacity, affect all other decision areas as well as all resources managed.

With regard to timing, there are three basic capacity choices. An organization may build capacity prior to demand, concurrent with demand, or after demand has developed. A strategy of capturing market share or dominating a new technology early in the product life cycle, in pursuit of the higher profit margins usually available then, is an example of building capacity prior to demand. Chrysler Corporation's development of manufacturing capacity prior to the introduction of the minivan was such a commitment. Such decisions require identification of resources for facilities, equipment, and engineering in anticipation of demand; however, dramatic changes in process technologies, the environment, and public taste, as well as unexpected actions of competitors, can destroy the profitability of a capacity decision to preempt the market. Changes in oil prices, political upheaval in a source country for scarce raw materials, development of computer-controlled machinery, the use of laser technology in manufacturing processes, and increased public preferences for seafood rather than red meat are examples of recent developments that have affected capacity decisions. Thus, the strategy of building capacity ahead of demand is risky but potentially very profitable.

Another timing option is to implement capacity to match forecasted demand as it develops in an established market. The selection of this option precludes the opportunity to dominate a developing area of knowledge; however, it avoids the associated costs. Simultaneously, there is the risk that the firm will be frozen out of the technology by a more aggressive competitor. However, if the product environment is not tremendously dynamic or the market is not particularly attractive to a competitor, this capacity timing decision may be quite viable. This policy of matching capacity to relatively likely (high probability) demand balances the risks of unused capacity and market share losses.

The third capacity timing option is to plan to build capacity after the development of demand. Many firms enter a business only after demand has been clearly defined. The relocation of a fixed facility, for example, is such a significant undertaking that a potential host community must be able to show clear sales demand prior to being considered. Similarly, restaurants and gasoline stations do extensive surveys to determine the potential customer demand prior to making a location commitment. This policy incurs the risk of losing sales, market share, and technology leadership advantages, but it reduces the risk of unused capacity.

These risks can be hedged in a variety of ways. Joint ventures, such as the Alaska pipeline, spread the costs of a very high risk capacity development among several competitors. Additionally, purchase agreements may be designed to buy a supplier's capacity, without specifying the exact product or delivery dates until required by resource lead times. Additionally, subcontracting is widely used to increase capacity with relatively short notice. The use of purchasing methods and subcontracting practices permits capacity increases without a long-range investment in facilities. Similarly, the use of part-time or temporary service employees applies this same rationale to human resource capacity.

FACILITIES EVALUATION—WHERE TO PRODUCE. Facilities decisions concern the size, location, and number of plants, warehouses, distribution centers, service centers, and retail outlets. Geographic marketing plans and operations output rates influence these decisions. Service organizations such as banks, franchised restaurants, eye care centers, motels, car rental agencies, and small fast-print shops all must decide the number, location, and size of facilities. In addition, they must decide what, if any, processing and purchasing will be done by the individual service center and which activities will be centralized. Economies of scale, transportation costs, and environmental conditions affect these decisions.

Economies of Scale. Manufacturing and service productivity is directly related to facility size. Economy of scale refers to the phenomena that as the size of a facility and its output increase, the cost per unit of output decreases. This is due to the relationship of the output volume to the total of fixed and variable costs and to output costs per unit. For example, the capital invested in an oven for a restaurant, a copy machine for an office, or an x-ray machine for a hospital is the same whether one unit or a thousand units are processed per month. In addition, the economic benefits of repetitive flow of discrete parts and continuous production of bulk commodities require a minimum output volume to justify the equipment and personnel required.

Production of larger quantities over a reasonable time period also produces economies due to the learning curve (see Chapter 10). Frequent performance of the same activity provides the opportunity for employees to increase their skill in performing tasks required, to make improvements in tooling and methods, and to improve the design of the product or the service. For example, an appliance service center that repairs a few hundred of a particular appliance per month normally will be more efficient in repairing that unit than an equally competent center that repairs only two or three of the same item per month.

However, increases in facility size and output volume do not always result in lower unit costs. The productivity of a facility can decrease as its size increases due to the increased administrative task of managing a larger facility. In a relatively small plant or service center, the manager can observe and know individual workers and customers. As the facility size increases, direct observations are replaced by administrative layers, formal reporting systems, and physical distance. As the number and layers of managers grow, communication and coordination difficulties increase. Thus, at certain production volumes, overhead costs may increase at a greater rate than the production output. Economies of scale sometimes may be sought by increasing the number of different products produced in a facility; the rationale is that the increased volume, even of different though related products, will decrease overhead cost per unit. Many, including Drucker (1968, 1974), Skinner (1969), and Hayes and Wheelwright (1979) have noted that such additions frequently increase overhead costs due to the dissimilarities in the knowledge, equipment, and skills required by new products. The additional tasks will increase the overhead and decrease the capacity to perform the original tasks.

Transportation Costs and Environmental Factors.   Service facilities normally will locate for customer convenience. However, other environmental factors such as security, growth potential, and colocation with other related services (e.g., in shopping centers) are important in locating service organizations.

Alternatively, manufacturing organizations are usually not located for customer convenience. Transportation costs make an important contribution to the decision; and, since raw materials usually are less costly to transport than finished goods, manufacturing plants are often located closer to markets than to sources of raw materials. Access to major highways, railways, air routes and hubs, and water transportion are important contributors to a facility evaluation for a manufacturing site. Environmental conditions such as an adequate skilled labor supply, a favorable labor-management environment, the availability of services desired by employees, climate, and local cost of living are among the many factors that contribute to facility evaluation.

Facility evaluation, in its strategic sense, considers the economies of scale of production to determine the number and size of the facilities desired; transportation costs and various environmental factors are then assessed. These issues are closely related to process technology, because they require consideration of the immediate labor and resource availability.

PROCESS TECHNOLOGY—HOW TO PRODUCE.   First, it is essential to note that excellence of operations management is no substitute for product knowledge. If, for example, a manufacturer of cheese really does not know how to make good cheese, the best operations management in the world will not save the organization. An organization must know and understand its primary process. Efficiently administered hospitals facilitate good patient care, but the appropriate therapy properly applied is a necessity. The specification of the exact process technology requires careful planning. An automobile can be manufactured using high-speed assembly lines (like most Chevrolets), job shop methods (like Ferraris), or a fixed process (like many of the later assembly operations of luxury cars). Success requires a very careful selection and integration of the appropriate technologies. For example, a line flow process may be used to build a component that feeds a job shop assembly. That product is then installed at a fixed site where further work is done to complete the job. Modular housing units are produced in this manner.

As a result of advances in information handling, the traditional process methods are increasingly being integrated and redefined. New processes are evolving very rapidly. Figure 19–1 identifies a number of these emerging processes differentiated by volume and variety of production.

Variable production lines are similar to traditional line flow systems except that the variable line can accommodate a limited range of different product configurations and designs. For example, the line could be varied among several different models of automobile or a number of different models of diesel engine. At the other extreme, computer integrated manufacturing

Figure 19–1 Process Methods Defined by Quantity and Variety

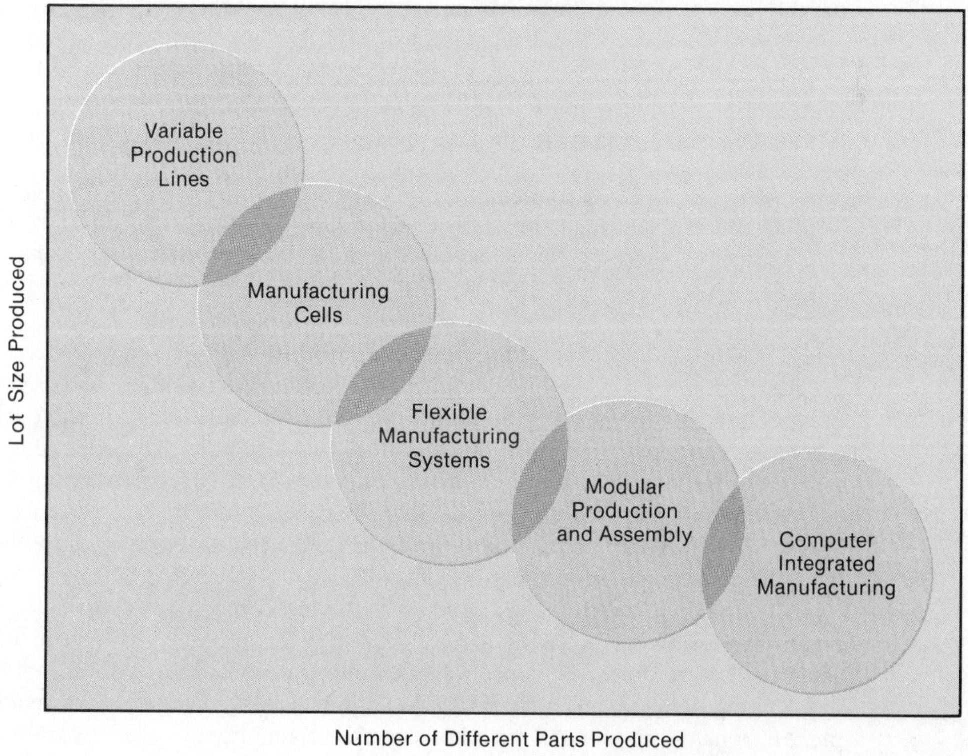

Number of Different Parts Produced

(CIM) permits lot sizes as small as one to be produced using a great variety of operations. Thus, many different parts can be produced in very small lot sizes. CIM can be compared to a fixed process in that it can produce separate lots of one product. Manufacturing cells (MC), flexible manufacturing systems (FMS), and modular production and assembly are comparable to the traditional job shop. These emerging process methods each move toward efficient lot sizing, achieving shorter setups and smaller volumes with greater variety of products.

The implications of these developments for management are that they permit notable increases in manufacturing efficiency and flexibility. This technology permits the development of product lines that are highly customized but that only require reprogramming or program changing, not retooling. The advent of lasers as a multifunction tool, permitting cutting, drilling, welding, and other operations by one tool, further emphasizes manufacturing efficiency and flexibility. The strategic implications of process flexibility and the efficiencies of data and material-handling technology have yet to be fully realized; however, certainly those impacts will affect structural integration, capacity management, facilities evaluation, and materials management.

MATERIALS MANAGEMENT—HOW TO CONTROL RESOURCES.   Operations capacity, process technology, and materials management decisions are inextricably interwoven. Strategy and policy decisions include

1. Integrating inventory, process, and capacity to meet demand
2. Establishing policies for selecting and evaluating suppliers
3. Positioning inventory to provide appropriate stockages where they are needed
4. Selecting methods of controlling the flow of materials and orders, for example, determining the type of items to be included on the master schedule
5. Selecting the criteria for measuring the efficiency of production, planning, purchasing, and inventory management

It was not too long ago that a customer had to wait a week or more for eyeglasses after being fitted. Today, there are optical centers that can provide prescription glasses within an hour. This is a good example of competitive factors leading to reduced manufacturing and service lead time. The reduced lead time requires flexible capacity, improved manufacturing processes, and different production planning and inventory management information systems. It also requires physical proximity of the fitting and eyeglass-grinding activities, which is an example of vertical integration.

The ability to meet delivery requirements can be achieved through (1) higher inventories of finished goods or modular assemblies for which the final assembly is very quick, (2) a process technology designed to respond rapidly to changing demand. (3) a combination of inventory and process. For example, McDonald's restaurants inventory cooked hamburgers in anticipation of short-term demand, while Burger King holds raw materials and uses a flow process to broil hamburgers to order.

Interest in materials management has grown dramatically in the last quarter century. The increased cost of capital, worldwide competition, and the availability of less-expensive and improved information-processing capabilities have nourished this increased interest in materials management. Organizations have invested heavily in data processing equipment, professional staff, and employee training to improve production planning and inventory management. The results of this effort have been extensive long-range improvements in product quality and decreased delivery time and inventory investment.

The process technology, product positioning, product structure, organizational goals, structure and capabilities, and relevant costs and benefits determine the methods and systems appropriate for an organization. However, many competitive organizations are able to achieve inventory turns of 25 or more per year, with no loss of customer service. As inventories move faster through the production process, accurate data systems and procedures are necessary to assure control and delivery to tight customer order schedules.

QUALITY ASSURANCE AND CUSTOMER RESPONSE—HOW TO DESIGN, TEST, AND DELIVER THE PRODUCT. The degree to which a product or service fulfills the need and expectations of a customer is its quality. Thus, quality encompasses a wide range of output service or product attributes, including dependability, availability, reliability, appearance, and others (see Chapter 18). Quality is individually defined for each product. The actual quality achieved depends upon many things including the product/service design, the process technology, quality of materials, and perhaps most importantly— on the execution and control of the production activity. Operations management strategies require an explicit definition of the quality desired. For example, a postsecondary educational institution that trains technicians would have different operations policies than one that prepares students for a scientific research career. Both would presumably be interested in quality graduates, but their process designs and quality measurements would differ. In a similar manner, an organization designing and manufacturing one-of-a-kind high-fashion dresses would have marketing, design, processing, and materials management strategies and processes that are different from a firm that manufactures military uniforms. The point is that the quality should be consistently defined with respect to the requirements of the market.

The ability to fulfill the needs of customers includes not only providing products and services that meet customer quality requirements, but also having them available when and where the customer desires them. Meeting reasonable delivery expectations of customers affects an organization's sales, market share, and profits. Insurance companies frequently emphasize their ability to settle claims within 24 hours; air freight companies compete on their ability to deliver overnight, automotive repair centers such as muffler replacement centers stress their ability to install new mufflers within an hour; and manufacturing firms have competed on the ability to meet wholesale delivery requirements to other manufacturers or retail requirements of the public.

HUMAN RESOURCES MANAGEMENT—ENVIRONMENT AND CONTROLS. Managing the personnel function traditionally was called personnel management or industrial relations to distinguish it from other functions such as marketing, finance, and engineering. It typically dealt with planning and control of payroll, benefits, recruiting, hiring, and layoff budgets. The planning of staffing requirements is frequently performed in conjunction with other functional areas of the organization. More recently, numerous variables of human resources data, including compensation, performance, training, and job information, have been computerized for easy access by functional human resources areas. This automation of the human resources information facilitates personnel administration enormously; however, true human resource management is more than that.

Human resources management recognizes the intrinsic value, needs, and resourcefulness of the employee, provides an environment that nurtures and rewards that resourcefulness, and taps it for the benefit of the employee and for the productivity of the organization. True human resources management efforts recognize that human resources are the single most important asset of an organization, and that management's top priority is to create an environment in which human resources can be productive. Historically, other resources have been more important. Land for agriculture and river transportation routes were the most important asset through the eighteenth century. Subsequently, capital provided the key to organizing transportation, shipping, and insurance firms that linked colonial empires and developing nations. Human labor was the critical resource early in this century; however, today it is the information and the people who have it that provide the key productive resource. Thus, human resources management engenders a spirit of cooperation, mutual trust, and goals; it rejects the adversarial model of many traditional labor-management relationships. The major elements of human resources management are:

1. Recognition of basic human needs and creation of an environment to support those needs
2. Determination of staffing needs by skill and profession under different marketing and production plans and for identifying employees who best fit those needs
3. Evaluation of employee capabilities, skills, potential, interest and development opportunities
4. Provision of rewards to recognize employee interests, objectives, based on both group and individual performance

Ouchi (1981), Peters and Waterman (1982), and other authors have presented many specific examples of this approach in American industry.

RESEARCH IN OPERATIONS MANAGEMENT—HOW TO MEASURE THE SYSTEM.
For the most part, organizations that do perform research have focused on
market research and product design research. Few organizations have a coherent operations management research strategy that contains explicit statements
of research goals and allocates resources to both projects with established
priorities and to open-ended projects.

Many managers are too busy coping with day-to-day problems to improve
and install better management methods. Operations management should
include systematic approaches for (1) establishing research needs (decision
areas where improved approaches are needed), (2) evaluating and selecting
explicit research goals and objectives, (3) allocating resources to operations
management research, and (4) managing (planning, controlling and evaluating) that research.

Formal production operations research programs will minimize the panic-
driven major expenditures of money and energy for a panacea often offered
but seldom found in the apparent wonder drug approaches. Although many
of these approaches can be very helpful in appropriate situations, not only
must the therapy be appropriate for the disease, but the organization must
have the necessary knowledge and experience to use the therapeutic method.
This seldom occurs by chance, but is an outcome of thorough research and
understanding of the situation.

At the simplest level of research, analysis of operations decisions is essential to improving productivity. An operations manager should regularly use
information about the production process to conduct both formal and informal research. For example, the computation of various management performance indicators (e.g., inventory turns, delivery performance, the scrap rate,
production efficiency, capacity utilization, profit per job, etc.), when compared with competitor organizations or evaluated over time, may suggest
areas of further productivity emphasis.

However, most larger firms should also be conducting research to
improve the production method, the composition of the materials, the storage and shipping methods, or the labor-technology interfaces. For example,
the Western Electric Company of AT&T did extensive research in the purifi-
cation and recrystallization of silicon (beach sand) in the early 1960s. Large
pressure vessels were used to heat sand in a catalyst solution until the sand
melted and recrystallized as very pure rocks. These rocks were then cut into
chips, which were used in early touch-tone telephone equipment and switching systems. This manufacturing research provided the basis for development
of the technologies that are currently used to manufacture computer chips.
Most larger firms conduct scientific or laboratory research to develop pure
theory, followed by production operations research to apply those findings
and develop large-scale economic production methods. Today, manufacturers must continually push the findings of laboratory research into full-scale
manufacturing processes to remain competitive.

The strategic overview perspective permits the operations manager to focus the multiplicity of tradeoffs and variables into some six to eight considerations. Note that Table 19–3 was based on the tradeoffs that are incorporated in the strategic overview considerations. The variables provide the information; but, to avoid the pitfalls of the productivity paradox, the operations manager should simplify the situation, reduce the impact of the tradeoffs, and generalize to a strategic overview perspective.

Alternatives and Decision Making

The strategic considerations should suggest several alternative methods of achieving the strategy objective. These alternatives should be specified as accurately as possible and then costed with objective variables and evaluated with subjective variables. The elaboration of alternatives permits the operations manager to consider all of the impacts, advantages, and disadvantages of each. Ultimately, the operations manager must decide on one alternative, often the one that allows the greatest amount of internal consistency.

INTERNAL CONSISTENCY—HOW TO INTEGRATE AND CONTROL. Explicit development of alternatives pertaining to these strategic considerations of operations management have at least three major benefits. First, they enable management to verify internal consistency, minimizing internal friction and improving productivity. Second, they provide a comparative basis for evaluation by technical managers and higher staff. Third, they provide the basis for examining decisions made over six months or a year and for evaluating their degree of correspondence with the overall organizational strategy and policy.

For example, if an organizational strategy is to excel at delivery (taking less time than competitors to fill an order), it should have some combination of excess capacity and flexible equipment and perhaps higher inventory levels than a competitor whose strategic niche was based on price and not delivery. The organization should analyze several specific alternative setups of their operation to determine how to achieve their primary objective—that is, delivery time—with minimum negative effects on the costs, quality, and flexibility. This decision likely would involve capacity, inventory, shipping methods, and other variables.

Thus, the decision-making process for the operations manager includes evaluating specific tradeoffs. However, the operations manager's time would probably be better spent evaluating, integrating, and controlling the eight areas considered here (structural integration, capacity management, facilities evaluation, process technology, materials management, quality assurance, human resources management, and research in operations management).

These considerations are generally strategic in scope and medium or long range in effect.

AN APPLICATION OF ALTERNATIVE DEVELOPMENT AND DECISION MAKING. The following example is designed to give a very general description of the alternative-development and decision-making process. To focus a strategic tradeoff decision, these alternatives can then be compared in terms of the defined efficiency criteria and the most appropriate alternative should be selected.

For example, given the corporate strategy of the XYZ Company (see p. 642), the operations manager needs to maintain the current assembly process, yet find ways to improve customer delivery and flexibility. A review of Table 19–3 suggests that process strategy, customization, maintenance, employment policies, customer response, and customer services tradeoffs are relevant. Of these, several newly developed approaches to process technology, group technology, and the plant within a plant, seem worth further consideration. Objective and subjective variables and tradeoffs are defined and three possible alternatives are developed (see Table 19–4).

In this situation, Alternative 1 is not the best option according to any of the criteria; however, Alternative 2 is best in cost, flexibility, and quality, and Alternative 3 is best in delivery. The corporate distinctive competence, as suggested in the strategy, is delivery, with a secondary emphasis on cost. Thus,

Table 19–4 A Strategic Decision Using Defined Alternatives

	Average Monthly Plant Operating Costs (millions)[1]		
	Alternative 1 Single Automated Line	*Alternative 2 5 Group Technology Cells*	*Alternative 3 Plant Within a Plant*
Personnel[2]	$2.50	$4.50	$3.24
Capital equipment[3]	4.00	2.00	3.00
Inventory	.50	.10	.35
Quality costs[4]	.15	.02	.07
Total measurable costs	$7.15	$6.62	$6.66
Delivery rating[5]	3	2	1
Flexibility rating[5]	3	1	2

[1]Overhead and cost of materials (except scrap rate) are constant across alternatives; thus they are not included here.
[2]Personnel costs are:
  Alternative 1 (1,000 employees @ 2,500.00/mo) = $2,500,000
  Alternative 2 (1,500 employees @ 3,000.00/mo) = $4,500,000
  Alternative 3 (1,200 employees @ 2,700.00/mo) = $3,240,000
[3]Capital equipment costs are:
  Alternative 1 ($240 million over 5 years) = $4,000,000 per month
  Alternative 2 ($120 million over 5 years) = $2,000,000 per month
  Alternative 3 ($180 million over 5 years) = $3,000,000 per month
  Installation costs are assumed to be equal.
[4]Quality costs include estimates of scrap, rework, warrantee, refund, and loss of customer good will.
[5]Subjective variables are rated on a scale of 1 to 3, where 1 = best.

in this example, the operations manager must evaluate Alternatives 2 and 3 in terms of whether the improvement of one ranked position of delivery of Alternative 3 over Alternative 2 is worth the difference in costs. Of course, the operations manager should carefully consider the accuracy of all input information in this decision, because minor variance of the input could notably change the outcomes of this analysis.

The development and testing of alternatives in this manner is facilitated by simulation techniques. A simulation is a mechanical or computer model that represents some part of the production process. Simulations are often used to evaluate the impact of changes in the flow of an operation (e.g., a revised assembly line or a new service layout). Simulation can identify the costs of different alternatives or assess the average number of substandard outcomes by conducting a large number of trial events. These trial events are used by the operations manager to consider different possible costs (for example, different interest rates in computing the cost of capital improvements). The operations manager can then estimate the cost of capital under various conditions, such as a best case, a most likely case, and a worst case.

Another application of simulations is to debug an operation by running many simulations of a schedule so as to find the situations in which parts will not arrive on time or equipment will break down. The simulation helps the operations manager to evaluate decision alternatives, but it may generate errors in representing these outcomes because of imperfect input information.

As a final step in decision making, the operations manager should reconsider the distinctive competence and focus of the operations function. The strategic overview perspective permits the operations manager to identify and evaluate all of the input variables to a decision. This analysis may include specific tradeoffs, but generally it is more helpful if it takes a strategic overview perspective of the organization. Additionally, the analysis may be assisted by graphic or computer analyses of varying types; however, to date, there is no substitute for professional experience. After the strategic decision is completed, the operations manager moves to the next step of the process—that is, the development of an operations policy.

POLICY COMMUNICATION AND IMPLEMENTATION

The formulation of operations strategy and decision making with regard to strategic alternatives, either pertaining to the entire operation or to a portion of operation activities, are the first and second stages of the strategy formulation and policy development process. Appropriate policy vehicles must then be put in place to assure that employees are aware of the strategy and that they understand how various parts fit together. If the strategy and decision-making efforts are not followed by policy development, then the time and effort of the operations manager and staff in those processes are essentially wasted.

Operations policies function in varying dimensions not only to execute and control the development of management strategy, but also to provide strategy information to the user employees. Operations policy may, for example, be written or verbal, it may be permanent or periodic, it may be very broad and general in nature or quite specific. In this section, operations policy is initially defined, the characteristics and dimensions of the operations policy are developed, and the implementation of policy alternatives is discussed.

The Dimensions of Operations Policy

Recall that operations policy was defined as

> a guide, based on operations strategy, for execution and control, which suggests limits or values, thus aiding decision makers to ensure continuity, consistency, and integration of operations.

Based on operations strategy. Initially, operations policy must be based upon the strategic overview perspective. It must reflect the essentials of efficient resource integration as developed in the strategy dimensions and formulation and the decision analysis steps.

Guide for execution and control. Policy is action oriented. As a guide for action, it is the principle link between the identified organizational goals and day-to-day organizational activities.

Limits or values. Policy specifies a prescribed range of acceptable actions and the value systems that drive those actions, and thus assures that delegated authority and practices will remain within acceptable limits. Policy, however, simultaneously permits individual freedom of action.

Continuity, consistency and integration. Policy establishes a framework within which specific questions can be assessed by decision makers and decided upon. This framework expresses the evaluation criteria for continuity or success of the organization and the processes for achieving integration of diverse parts and consistency of organizational performance.

Well-constructed policies, like the strategies upon which they are founded, must incorporate these definitional characteristics. Additionally, the design of an operations policy must consider four dimensions to assure that the policy is appropriate for the situation.

1. Scope—Functional level or breadth of application
2. Formality—Degree of structure, procedure, or standardization
3. Explicitness—Exactitude or vagueness of definition
4. Personal—Ethical or professional code of the individual manager.

SCOPE—LEVEL AND BREADTH. The scope of a policy may vary according to the breadth of organizational function or according to the organizational level where it applies. Considering organizational functions, a policy may apply to one or several functions or to the entire organization. For example, a work break policy may apply only to one shop or to several activities within the operations function. Alternately, jury duty or sick leave policies are normally applicable to employees in all functional areas at a particular level.

Policies may also be applied at varying levels of the organization. Some policies are relevant only at corporate headquarters, others are designed for the corporate divisions, and still others are meant for individual operating units (production plants or service centers). Once established at a particular level, some general policies are applicable at all lower levels. For example, work hours (shift schedules or flexitime policies) are likely to be different from one level of the organization to another. However, legal overtime provisions are applicable to nonexempt employees at all levels and all functions. Thus, policies may apply to single or multiple levels, to single or multiple functions of the organization, or to a range of each dimension. These dimensions and examples are identified in Figure 19–2.

FORMALITY. Like the scope of a policy, the amount of formality of a policy can vary. Highly formal documents, such as a corporate master plan or budget documents, are typed, written in formal terms or formats, and approved as shown by the signature of a designated individual. Such documents are often

Figure 19–2   The Scope of a Policy

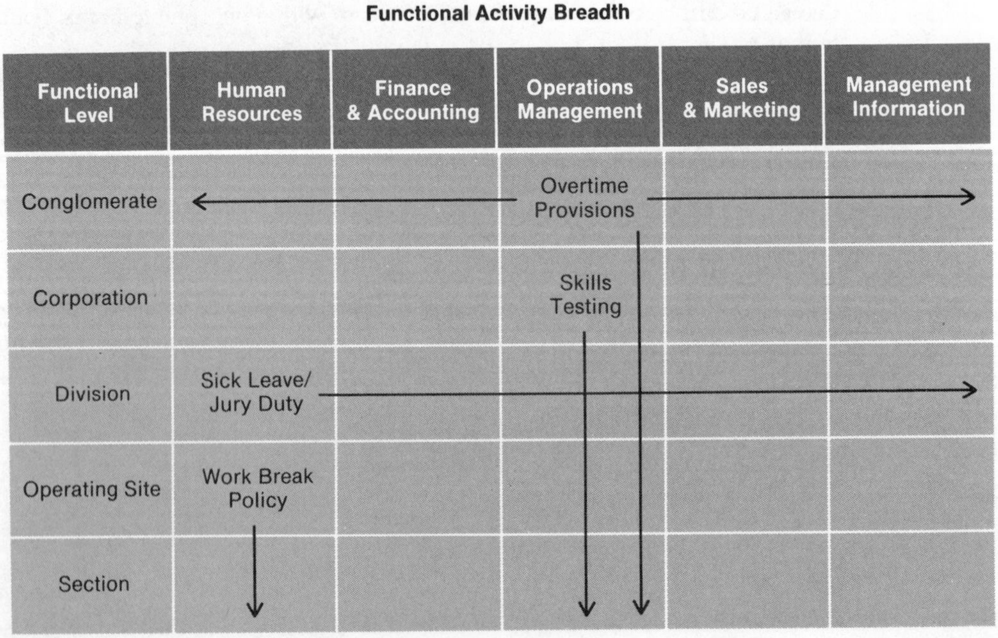

Functional Activity Breadth

Functional Level	Human Resources	Finance & Accounting	Operations Management	Sales & Marketing	Management Information
Conglomerate	←		Overtime Provisions		→
Corporation			Skills Testing		
Division	Sick Leave/ Jury Duty				→
Operating Site	Work Break Policy				
Section	↓		↓	↓	

standardized and identify responsibility to assure immediacy and clarity of communication in situations in which mistakes may be costly or embarrassing or the process may be subject to abuse. Work hour policies, purchase orders, and overtime approvals are examples of formal policy documents.

Other policies, which are not as likely to be questioned or which have lesser impacts, are less formal. Examples might be found in plant security or safety posters, which may have the typed statement "by order of the plant manager." Internal office administration policies are normally typed but may not be signed, and certainly are rarely signed by top management. Some policies may be entirely verbal. The division of responsibilities between members of a work team is an example. The level of formality of a policy is often related to the length of time that the policy is expected to be needed or to whether the policy covers a specific situation or a common occurrence. Short duration and exceptional situations are more likely to be covered by informal levels of policy. The varying levels of formality permit definition of a policy hierarchy as shown in Table 19–5.

EXPLICITNESS. Explicitness is a third dimension of operations policy. A policy may be explicitly defined or extremely vague, depending upon the circumstances. A policy of no smoking in the laboratory is very explicit, probably based on the safety hazards of open flames in the vicinity of chemicals; but a policy statement of long-range organizational objectives may be very nebulous, and purposely so, for several reasons. Turbulence of technology or the market or a substantial conflict among the viewpoints of senior executives may result in a vaguely stated long-range policy. Differing policy explicitness permits varying amounts of perceived freedom of action, which potentially motivates innovation, conflict reduction, structuring, and numerous other behavioral impacts of the policy. Those effects are shown on Figure 19–3.

Policies that are either too explicit or too vague are viewed as permitting

Table 19–5 The Policy Hierarchy

Formality	Type Method	Example of Possible Use
Formal	Master plan	Contingency and future operations
↑	Budget documents	Financial guidance and priorities
	Policy directives	General-purpose communication
	Procedural guides	Technical or highly specific purposes
	Standing operating procedures	Sequential or standardized processes
↓	Operating schedules	Periodic job requirements
	Company rules	Basic personal and job behavior
Informal	Verbal directions	Adjustment, fine tuning of formal guidance

Figure 19–3   Policy Explicitness

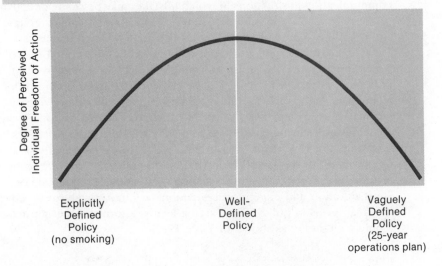

limited freedom of action. The no-smoking policy is very explicit and permits little freedom of action. However, a very vague policy, such as the 25-year operations plan, will also constrain action. Because individuals fear the effects of inaccurately interpreting a vague policy, such policies may lead to inaction or, at a minimum, to group conferencing to evaluate and approve an action. A well-defined policy permits latitude of action and does not constrain individuals by excessive vagueness or explicitness of definition.

PERSONAL LEADERSHIP AND POWER. Policy is often designed to differentiate one section or manager from another or to recognize the inherent uniqueness of particular activities, managers, or individuals. It is sometimes applied by an individual operations managers to establish a personal, ethical, or professional code or standard upon an activity or to give a stamp of recognition and individuality. These approaches are often applied to areas that have limited effects, such as correspondence formats, personal time scheduling, meeting formats, and the like; but they are essential elements of an effective operations management policy. To establish personal leadership, the operations manager may draw upon one or several of the following four power bases.

1. *Traditional*—By making traditional practices into a policy, the operations manager appeals to the need for stability and avoidance of turbulence. This technique is often used in simple, stable organizations.
2. *Rational*—Policy that appeals to logic through formalized, often mathematical, computations is often found in highly dynamic organizations.

3. *Fiat*—Policy may be established by direction when a calamity occurs or the organization is threatened. There just is not time for long discussions; immediate action is possible only if the operations manager directs policy.
4. *Group Norms*—A policy that represents the needs or desires of the group is often the basis for power found in highly complex organizations or technologically interactive environments.

Thus, policy is the means of communicating a strategy and may be varied to fit the situation according to the four dimensions of scope, formality, explicitness, and type of personal leadership policy and power base that is most appropriate to the situation. Like strategy formulation and decision analysis, policy development must be interwoven and integrated as a multidimensional fabric of the organization.

Implementation and Control of Operations Policy

After the operations manager has developed the policy, the policy implementation phase must follow. Returning to the definition of management, the implementation of policy is a continuous process that involves all of the management functions—planning, execution, staffing, organization, and control. In some situations, the strategy formulation and policy development can be accomplished in one cycle. There is no reassessment except to ensure that the policy is being followed. Such one-time efforts may be possible in very stable situations.

However, strategy and policy, particularly when they involve substantive issues and turbulent environments, are normally quite dynamic. They must be reassessed on a regular basis, sometimes once per week, per month, or per quarter. As such, the strategy formulation and policy development process involves all of the management functions. For example, *planning* policy involves selection of the most effective approach, given the four dimensions. *Execution* involves specifying the formal responsibilities to a particular section of the organization for actions pertaining to the policy. *Staffing* and *organization* ensure that there are sufficient personnel with appropriate skills in a designated structure to execute the policy with minimal guidance and to *control* the incidences of failure to comply with the policy. Policy development provides management with the opportunity to proactively anticipate environmental changes and address employee concerns. Too often the operations policies of an organization are outdated. Although management has done much of the strategy formulation and may have completed the decision analysis, the policy formulation and implementation activities have not been maintained.

Ironically, operations managers often explain that they are too busy with execution or controlling activities to worry about strategy formulation and policy development. In such cases, they may be executing or controlling the wrong process, measured by the wrong criteria. There is a good chance that they are not effective (doing the right job) or efficient (doing the job right), and it is certain that no one knows what they are doing. Strategy formulation and policy development are so closely linked to effective management practices that the process cannot be disregarded. The effective operations manager looks for the best fit in formulating a strategic overview and in deciding upon the best alternative and then develops the policy using the communication methods and policy characteristics consistent with the situation. The management functions of planning, organizing, staffing, executing, and controlling are central functions to assure the relevance of and adherence to policy.

CONCLUSIONS

In conclusion, the operations strategy and policy provide the operations manager with a strategy conceptualization, decision-making, and execution and control process. Through policy and strategy, the operations manager can address primarily medium- and long-range goals and directions of the organization and establish and manage the means through which those goals are measured and achieved. Of central importance in the strategy formulation and policy development process is the maintenance of consistency.

Operations strategy and policy have been shown to affect every sphere and dimension of operations management. The level of strategic analysis may be very specific—that is, the operations manager may deal with specific trade-offs between strategic variables. However, a generally more efficient use of the operations manager's time involves commitment to a strategic overview perspective of some six to eight considerations and, on that basis, a commitment to providing an integrated, consistent, and continuous policy. In that sense, the strategy and policy area provides the operations manager with a very powerful tool for integrating change.

QUESTIONS

1. Define the following terms:
   a. Management
   b. Strategy
   c. Policy
   d. Variable
   e. Strategic Overview Perspective

2. Considering a strategy and policy perspective, differentiate between efficiency and effectiveness.

3. How are strategy formulation and policy development related?

4. Briefly trace the six step strategy formulation and policy development process as it might be applied in the following examples. Apply your own experience to make these examples more explicit.

   a. High school—classroom size and facility adequacy
   b. College—admission management area
   c. High tech manufacturing—research in process technology
   d. Newspaper—creation of a new insert
   e. Retailer—new line of clothing

5. What is meant by focusing the factory? Why is it important?

6. In what way do the different dimensions of operations decision-making assist in the formulation of strategy?

7. Tradeoff analysis has been widely used as a contributor to strategy. What are some of the contributions and limitations of this approach?

8. Why does management tend to distrust the use of operations research?

9. Write a corporate-level strategy for the following types of organizations:

   a. The local symphony orchestra and society
   b. A manufacturer of injection-molded parts made primarily for the appliance industry
   c. A company that develops, designs, and manufactures medical instrumentation
   d. A toy company specializing in the design and manufacture of wooden long-life toys
   e. An organization providing supplies to the forestry industry
   f. An organization specializing in emergency repair of marine engines throughout the world

10. Diagram a tradeoff involving human resources management.

11. List several characteristics and elements of management decision making that constitute strategy formulation.

12. Identify several conflicting tradeoff decisions. Show why the variables are conflicting.

13. Develop three alternatives for each of the organizations listed in Question 4.

14. The consultant to a construction company informs management that a meaningful plan of activities and the allocation of resources are neces-

sary for controlling project costs and completion. The general foreman says that planning is a waste of time; materials arrive late, the weather determines what can be done, and the workers (crafts) always seem to be working on a higher-priority project. How would you respond if you were the consultant?

15. Choose two of the organizations listed in Question 4 and list likely political, social, or economic developments in the next five to ten years that should be considered when developing plans for these organizations. Describe how these developments will influence objectives, activities, and decisions in the organization that you selected.

16. A relatively small company in southwestern Illinois has developed an excellent reputation for their ability to handle railway equipment after a train accident. They also have developed competence in designing and manufacturing large wrecker trucks used in this process. Prepare what you think is a reasonable statement of organizational strategies.

17. Identify the criteria for evaluating vertical integration opportunities.

18. The president of a New Jersey company that manufactures rubber bands believes that the company should purchase a rubber plantation and also establish a chain of office supply centers. The president is impressed with the advantages of vertical integration. Evaluate these moves on the basis of your general knowledge. State why you believe each is either a good or a poor idea.

19. Describe three examples of backward integration and three examples of forward integration.

20. For forward and backward integration, give an example that normally would be justified and another that would violate good management principles.

21. What are the three basic choices in capacity timing?

 a. How do these decisions relate to pricing policies?
 b. What are the risks associated with different alternatives?

22. Describe capacity decisions concerning personnel including direct labor, engineering design, information systems, marketing, transportation, distribution, and after-sales service.

23. Describe what is meant by economy of scale and give an example. Describe the pitfalls of following this goal blindly.

24. Describe how diseconomies of scale can occur. Give two examples, one from a service organization and another from a manufacturing organization.

25. Assume you are the CEO of a local organization that repairs garage doors (e.g., springs, automatic openers, and tracks) and sells and installs new doors.

 a. Describe explicit measures of quality that the organization might employ.
 b. Describe how quality objectives affect capacity, equipment, facility, and inventory decisions.

26. Fast-food restaurants are not the only industry in which reduced product/service delivery lead time has dramatically changed the industry. Name at least three other industries.

27. Pick an organization for which you or a friend have worked for on a full time or part-time basis, and describe the major elements of their human resource management program. Suggest policy changes that will benefit both the organization and the employees. Explicitly state the benefits to each and when they would be obtained.

28. A well-known student of American business contends that the fast-food restaurants perform a valuable service to human resource management for industries. To what do you think this person is referring?

29. A firm designs and manufactures inflated rubber seat cushions and mattresses for bedridden and handicapped individuals. The firm has a research department. What type of research do you think they would conduct? What type of research might they be conducting concerning operations management?

30. List the eight major areas in which operations management strategy and policy decisions are made. Give an example of each.

31. Identify the dimensions of organizational policy. Describe one approach to each dimension.

32. What are the four power bases for the development of a personal leadership policy? Give appropriate examples.

33. Given Figure 19–2, show where policies in the following area should be applied by breadth and level:

 a. Cutting machine safety rules
 b. Fire and emergency procedures

    c. Raw materials purchasing policies

    d. Office supply purchases

    e. Expenditure approval authorities by dollar amounts

34. How might office policy help subordinate managers to make day-to-day decisions?

35. When would a formal policy be appropriate? List three examples.

36. When would an informal policy be appropriate? List three examples.

37. What effects can explicitness have on policy? List three situations for which each of the following levels of explicitness would be appropriate:

    a. Explicitly defined policy

    b. Well defined policy

    c. Vaguely defined policy

REFERENCES

Banks, Robert L., and Steven C. Wheelwright, "Operations vs. Strategy: Trading Today for Tomorrow." *Harvard Business Review* (May–June 1979).

Drucker, Peter F. *The Age of Discontinuity.* New York: Harper & Row Publishers, Inc. , 1968.

Drucker, Peter F. *Management: Tasks, Responsibilities, Practices.* New York: Harper & Row, Publishers, Inc. , 1974., p. 775.

Ghoshal, Sumantra. "Global Strategy: An Organizing Framework." *Strategic Management Journal* (1987):425–440.

Hayes, Robert H., and Roger W. Schmenner. "How Should You Organize Manufacturing." *Harvard Business Review* (January–February 1978).

Hayes, Robert H., and Steven C. Wheelwright. "Link Manufacturing Prices and Product Life Cycles." *Harvard Business Review* (January–February 1979).

Hayes, Robert H., and Steven C. Wheelwright. *Restoring Our Competitive Edge: Competing Through Manufacturing.* New York: John Wiley & Sons, 1984.

Jelinek, Mariann, and Joel D. Goldhar. "The Interface between Strategy and Manufacturing Technology." *Columbia Journal of World Business* (Spring 1983): 26–36.

Mather, Hal. "Factory of the Future: Getting from Here to There." *Target* (Fall 1986):11–14.

Pantumsinchai, Pricha, M. Zia Hassan; and Ishwar D. Gupta. *BASIC Programs for Production and Operations Management.* Englewood Cliffs, N.J.: Prentice-Hall, Inc., 1983.

Peters, Thomas J., and Robert H. Waterman, Jr. *In Search of Excellence.* New York: Harper & Row, Publishers, Inc., 1982.

Porter, Michael E. *Competitive Strategy: Techniques for Analyzing Industries and Competitors.* New York: Free Press, 1980.

Ouchi, William. *Theory* Z. Reading, Mass.: Addison-Wesley Publishing Co, 1981.

Skinner, Wickham. "Manufacturing—Missing Link in Corporate Strategy." *Harvard Business Review* (May–June 1969).

Skinner, Wickham. "The Focused Factory." *Harvard Business Review* (May–June 1974).

Skinner, Wickham. *Manufacturing: The Formidable Competitive Weapon.* New York: John Wiley & Sons, 1985.

Skinner, Wickham. "The Productivity Paradox." *Management Review* (1986): 41–45.

Steiner, George A. , and John B. Miner. *Management Policy and Strategy.* New York: MacMillan, 1977.

Stogdill, Ralph M. *Individual Behavior and Group Achievement.* London: Oxford University Press, 1959.

Stobaugh, Robert, and Piero Telesio. "Match Manufacturing Policies and Product Strategy." *Harvard Business Review* (March–April 1983): 113–120.

CHAPTER 20
JIT, TQC, AND ENHANCED SCHEDULING

OBJECTIVES

After completing this chapter, you should be able to

- Appreciate the need for operations process excellence

- Explain why a philosophy of excellence in manufacturing and services must be developed before just-in-time, total quality control, or enhanced scheduling methods are possible

- Describe the methods and potential contribution of just-in-time inventory management to improved process control

- Describe the methods of total quality control and explain how to implement total quality control programs

- Define the concept of enhanced scheduling, and explain how three approaches achieve specific schedule enhancements

- Develop a philosophy of excellence in operations management

OUTLINE

INTRODUCTION—THE PHILOSOPHY OF EXCELLENCE

Several contemporary developments have challenged traditional methods of managing operations processes. Just-in-time (JIT) inventory management, total quality control (TQC), and scheduling efficiency through enhanced scheduling technologies (EST) have been shown to notably improve process efficiency over traditional methods because of faster throughput and better resource management. Although the results are not always conclusive, the success of the methods have encouraged many firms to implement or consider implementing JIT and related techniques (Celley et al. 1986).

Although the planning and implementation of these techniques takes much time and effort, many projects can result in notable cost savings. For example, a survey of 66 JIT implementations (Dilworth 1987) found performance improvement resulting from process changes, reduction of organizational layers, increased teamwork, and lower inventory levels. Similar results were reported by Cincinnati Milacron—Electronic Systems Division, which achieved a 27 percent space savings, a 68 percent overall inventory reduction, a lot size reduction of 50 percent, and an increased productivity level of 36 percent in roughly 18 months. At the same time, the cost of quality decreased from 19 percent of the cost of goods to 14 percent as a statistical process control system was implemented (Powell 1987).

Many of these contemporary ideas are popularly associated with Japanese manufacturing methods; however, most are just good operations management practices of long standing and are quite international. The Japanese took operations management principles seriously and have applied them diligently. However, in *In Search of Excellence*, Peters and Waterman (1982) document numerous examples of American development of these contemporary methods, including the 48-hour guaranteed worldwide service parts delivery policy of Caterpillar Tractor. Similarly, numerous European firms have adapted or internally developed these technologies (Wildemann 1987). Contemporary process control methods have been developed out of necessity by many international firms in pursuit of competitive excellence.

JIT, TQC, and EST appear to challenge many traditional practices of manufacturing and service operations, such as maximum equipment utilization, economic order quantities, large lot sizes, and some aspects of materials requirement planning, distribution management, line balancing, queuing theory, operations scheduling, quality control, and maintenance management, among others. However, careful analysis shows that, in most cases, these contemporary techniques are highly consistent with the basic logic of traditional methods. As such, JIT, TQC, and EST collectively represent a substantive growth in our knowledge of how to better manage production processes.

The Variables of Operations Process Excellence

A limitation of traditional operations control techniques is that they often consider or optimize only one aspect of the production process at a time. For example, the economic order quantity or economic lot size methods optimize the purchase or lot size based on the order (setup) cost and the carrying cost. However, this optimization is accomplished without regard to other factors of the manufacturing process, notably customer satisfaction—which includes cost, quality and delivery—or scheduling, which concerns the flow, efficiency, and flexibility of the production process.

The contemporary approach to process management contends that the goals of inventory management, customer satisfaction, and scheduling efficiency are not mutually exclusive. Rather, goals in these three areas may be pursued in such a way that decisions are mutually supportive of two or more criteria. If the process is managed as a whole and incorporates the four evaluative criteria (cost, quality, flexibility, and delivery) then improved operations process performance will result.

The Essence of a New Philosophy

This chapter will describe several specific ways to improve process control through integration of inventory, quality, and scheduling. At the core is the development of a new philosophy of operations management. The philosophy is a necessary precondition to the implementation of process improvements; it must be in place before further work with inventory, quality, or scheduling can be successful. The philosophy is characterized by several elements usually not found in traditional operations philosophies. Figure 20–1 identifies these elements and establishes a framework that will be used for the further discussion of JIT, TQC, and EST. The elements of the management philosophy outlined in Figure 20–1 are described in the paragraphs that follow.

Integration of Internal and External Environments. Teamwork is the key. Individual performance, often respected in traditional environments, may lead to conflict and wasted effort. Effective group interaction and communication lead to improved performance within small production cells, among departments, and externally with suppliers and distributors. Close integration of suppliers and distributors creates a greater awareness of environmental factors and a stronger customer-market orientation of the production process.

Spirit of Continuous Improvement—Quality, Productivity. There is no fixed work standard; employee teams are expected to work together to continuously improve a product or service. Employees are not expected to work harder, but smarter, and in closer, more synergistic linkages—for example, exploiting learning curve improvements. Employees at all levels are encouraged to understand the production process and to develop new methods, more effective communication, and greater efficiency. Striving for continuous improvement makes a significant impact on quality and productivity.

Emphasis on Job Flow. Traditional methods manage system capacity rather than the process flow and throughput. These methods often involve costly but inflexible equipment to achieve short operation (run) times. Additionally, traditional methods generally require large lots, high work in pro-

Figure 20–1 A Framework for Operations Excellence

```
┌─────────────────────────────────────┐
│        MANAGEMENT PHILOSOPHY         │
│                                      │
│   Integration of internal and       │
│      external environments           │
│   Spirit of continuous improvement   │
│   Emphasis on job flow               │
│   Emphasis on process                │
│   Information management at all      │
│      levels — employee involvement   │
└─────────────────────────────────────┘
```

| JIT | TQC | EST |

Inputs → Transformation Process → Outputs

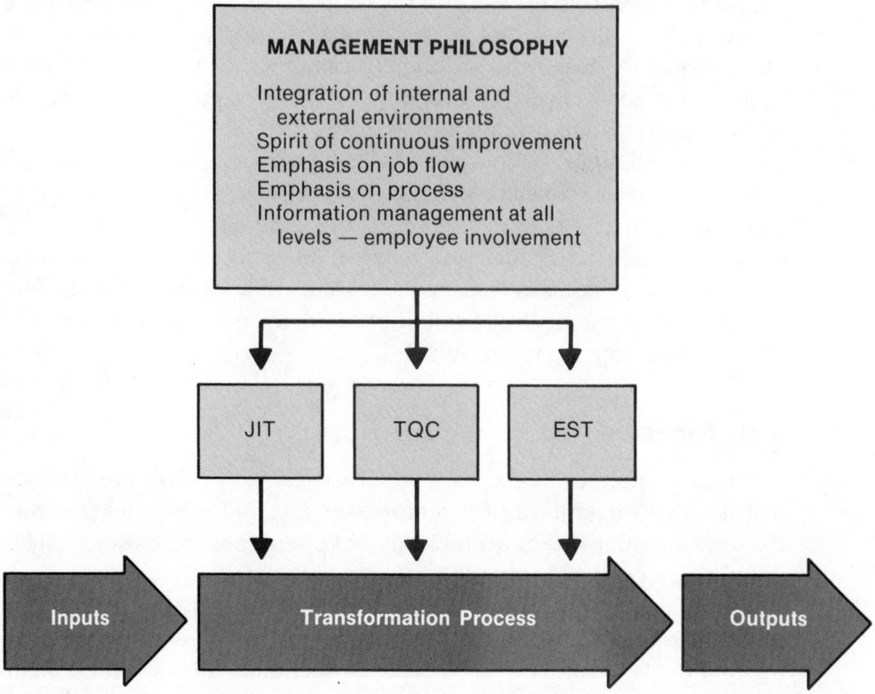

cess, and long manufacturing lead times (throughput times) to benefit from the high setup and start-up costs. Alternatively, the contemporary emphasis is on smoothness and rapidity of process flow, reduction of waste, rapid throughput of necessary production, and short setup and operation times. This is sometimes called the chain of demand.

Emphasis on Process. The production process, as well as the product, is important to operations excellence. If the process is well managed, it will produce the desired products efficiently. A defective product often is the symptom of a process disorder; the process is a major cause of quality defects, wasteful inflexibility, costly inventories, and long manufacturing lead times.

Information Management at All Levels—Employee Involvement. All employees must know and share production goals. The tools of inventory planning, quality control, and scheduling management must be understood and implemented at the lowest level of production and consistently and clearly managed at the highest level. If line employees are given the knowledge, responsibility, and authority to act independently, then multiple layers of staff and supervision can be reduced. Shop reports, identification of supplier requirements, component delivery times, machine utilization, maintenance records, and other daily process information all should be established and managed at the lowest possible operational level. Simultaneously, management must define and consistently integrate operational details in the overall production philosophies and systems.

Intercultural Transfer

In Japan, manufacturing process excellence was achieved in part because the cultural and environmental conditions there facilitated their growth. Thus, these questions arise: Can such methods be transferred from one environment to another? If so, what are the necessary conditions?

Compared with the United States, for example, availability of land and resources are major constraints to manufacturing in Japan. Due to general unavailability of land, it is not as easy for Japanese manufacturing plants to expand; this encourages smaller, more flexible production facilities. The land constraints also mean that suppliers in Japan are not as widely distributed geographically as they are in the United States. Additionally, substantial amounts of many natural resources, including petroleum, iron, coal, and bauxite, are imported, which discourages production waste. Further, Japan's manufacturers had to be export oriented to pay for imported resources, which limited product variability and encouraged modularization (Plenert and Best 1986).

Additionally, numerous cultural variations and their organizational impact have been identified in several studies of Japanese industry (Hatvany and Pucik 1981; Ouchi 1982; Pascale and Athos 1981). The holistic concern for people and the collective, homogeneous value system of the densely populated islands have encouraged emphasis on lifetime employment, slow and thorough evaluation and promotion processes, nonspecialized (non–functionally oriented) career paths, participative decision making, and a collective sense of responsibility. The cultural reality suggests that American labor will be less homogeneous and less team oriented than their Japanese counterparts. Thus, in most cases strict imitation of Japanese practices probably will not work well.

There are numerous instances of successful application of JIT and related management techniques in the United States. Harley Davidson (Willis 1986, Gelb 1985), Hewlett Packard (Riopel 1986), General Motors (Rohan 1985), and John Deere (Quinlan 1982) are only a few of the many companies that have successfully implemented these techniques. However, success has not come easily in all cases (Hutchins 1986). The process of adjusting the organization to the new philosophies is often very difficult. For example, Harley Davidson initially used a 35-page, highly legalistic supplier contract before scaling back to a less formal, two-page document. JIT cannot be just an extension of "old practices"; it requires a totally new approach.

A survey of foreign suppliers to the U.S. automobile industry found notable improvements resulting from the implementation of JIT and similar techniques; however, that study also noted quality, paperwork, commitment, and similar cultural difficulties. Numerous cultural factors affect JIT implementation and ensure that JIT will vary from country to country. Certainly, labor structure, cultural values, geographic diversity, and widespread computeriza-tion will affect American implementations (Celley et al. 1986). Operations managers must carefully weigh the cultural and environmental contribution to the success of a particular technique and select those that fit the specific operations environment and needs of the firm.

Thus, a new philosophy of the management of operations has developed. This philosophy requires extensive communication and involvement both among workers and with the external environment; concern with process efficiency, quality, and productivity; and flexibility of equipment and labor. In some production environments, competitive conditions require acceptance of these new techniques and pursuit of a philosophy of excellence, and many more manufacturing and service environments are adjusting toward these approaches. In most situations, however, the establishment of a philosophy of excellence is a required precondition to the successful implementation of a JIT, TQC, or enhanced scheduling effort. The philosophy is often so closely related to the implementation that it is considered a part of JIT, TQC, or enhanced scheduling.

JIT—JUST-IN-TIME INVENTORY MANAGEMENT

Althought the JIT approach to manufacturing was used at the Ford Motor Company's Dearborn plant early in this century, the reawakening of interest initially focused on Japan in the 1960s. The economic recovery from World War II and the cultural and environmental conditions combined to encourage a philosophy consistent with the development of JIT. As JIT practices took hold, inventories were reduced, lot sizes were decreased, and deliveries were more frequent. The improved throughput rates and lower inventory costs resulted in rather notable operations efficiencies.

Traditional manufacturing organizations use large inventories to increase the efficiency of the production process. Large inventories are held so that production orders are not delayed due to lack of raw materials or components, so that there is work in process for labor, so that long setup times to achieve short operation times are economically justified, and so that there are finished goods inventories for customer deliveries. Machines and facilities are operated for long production runs at close to capacity and inventories are used as buffers to minimize the effects of idle labor and machines, machine failures, and scrap.

Unfortunately, large inventories do not solve production problems; they only conceal them. A widely used illustration of this dilemma involves the water flow of a river. Three dams represent various impediments to product flow and create pools of inventory behind them. These inventory pools are created to assure a constant and dependable product flow and to overcome process limitations in product throughput, process deviations, and economic order quantities. JIT reduces and eliminates the factors, such as queue time and long setups that cause the dams in production, thus permitting greater throughput or faster flow of the product. This analogy is depicted in Figure 20–2.

Beyond this somewhat simple analogy, however, is the fact that when inventory carrying costs are high, as they were during the early 1970s, operations managers should look for ways to decrease inventory levels. However, when the costs of carrying inventory decrease, as they have during the 1980s, at first consideration, there would appear to be less incentive to reduce inventories. However, that is not the case since there are many hidden benefits of lower inventories, such as quality improvements, scheduling efficiencies, reduced manufacturing lead time, improved delivery performance, and an improved competitive position.

Considered another way, the question is whether you should manage inventory as a push (supply) system, by providing all of the inventory that could possibly be used, or, as a pull (demand) system, responding only to

Figure 20–2   The Water Flow Analogy

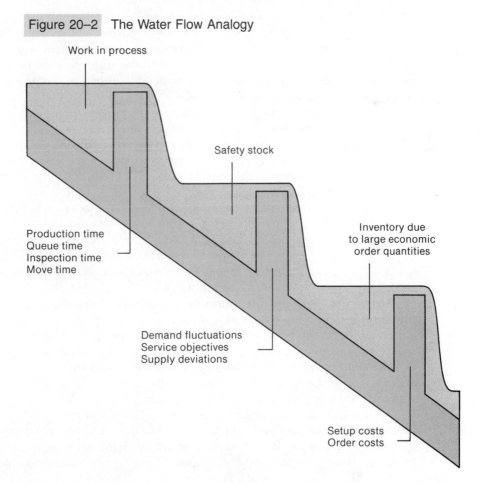

specific inventory demands as they are required by production and ultimately by the customer. With a push inventory management system, quality defects, scheduling irregularities, and other problems are covered by the excess inventory, and scheduling systems are set up to optimize capacity rather than flow. With pull inventory management, quality must be high and scheduling must be flexible, responsive, and without bottlenecks. Management decisions pertaining to the three process variables—inventory, customer-required quality, and scheduling—are highly interrelated.

The Definition of JIT

> JIT embodies a philosophy of excellence to establish demand-pulled inventory practices that produce to design specifications at a rapid but smoothed delivery rate with zero idle inventories, zero unnecessary leadtimes, and increased employee involvement in the process.

The important aspects of this definition are discussed in the paragraphs that follow. Note that this is a rather abstract or pure definition. Many firms are applying some of the concepts and adjusting others consistent with their operational environment to work toward a JIT inventory system. Of course, JIT must embody the philosophy of excellence, described in the preceding section, as a precondition for its success.

Produce to the Demand Pull. In a pure JIT process, products are not manufactured unless there is a clearly defined order; however, JIT is also applicable to the work in process of a make to stock environment. Component parts are produced as they are required for finished goods, and finished goods inventory is closely controlled (make to stock). JIT assumes that production costs are best recovered by rapid delivery of the product. Additionally, capacity is viewed as a sunk cost; it is not a consideration in operations process decisions.

Produce to the Design Specifications. Very tightly enforced quality control processes ensure that the product is exactly as specified by the product design or customer requirements. JIT implies a zero defects quality control effort—that is, total quality control (TQC).

Produce to a Rapid but Smoothed Delivery Rate. The production process is smoothed so that there is little wasted energy or delay. Products move rapidly, though consistently, through the process. To hold an order that requires a minimum lot size for production efficiency would mean sacrificing delivery time (and possibly a loss of business); this would be unacceptable under JIT. Reduction of setup times reduces the minimum economic lot size, with the ideal being an economic lot size of one.

Zero Idle Inventory Holdings and Zero Unnecessary Lead Times. Inventories are not produced until they are demanded by the next step of the production process or to meet minimal finished good stock requirements. Production lead times are carefully computed from average process and transportation times. In a JIT system, employers would prefer that an employee sit and do nothing rather than produce a part that was not immediately required. In practice, this time often is used for equipment cleaning and maintenance, methods improvements, and similar activities. Although the firm must bear the cost of unproductive labor, it does not bear the additional costs of energy and machine wear in production, changes in product specification, material costs, or potential confusion due to high inventories. This rapid and smooth flow suggests zero idle inventory and zero unnecessary lead time.

Encouraging Employee Involvement. Direct employee involvement is the only way that the myriad of process control details and process improvements can be handled. This gives employees an opportunity for personal development and growth. For this reason, JIT often requires extensive employee training, thorough communication within the plant, and extensive interaction with suppliers. Employee flexibility and involvement with larger segments of the production process are also usually required. This is a time-consuming long-range process that requires the employee's commitment. Thus, JIT encourages management methods that allow for employee development.

The Characteristics And Tools Of JIT

The philosophical approach of a JIT system is very different from traditional process control approaches. To achieve a successful JIT implementation, a number of different characteristics of the manufacturing process must be considered and monitored by management. These characteristics and tools, several of which are unique to JIT implementations, are listed in Table 20–1 and discussed in the following paragraphs.

Small inventories. Large inventories are regarded as a costly liability. Companies with a JIT system report that inventory turns (a relative measure of inventory investment, frequently the rate of annual cost of sales to inventory investment) may increase from two or three turns per year to 25 or more turns per year under JIT. That is, if annual sales were $100 million and the

Table 20–1 The Characteristics and Tools of JIT

JIT Characteristics	JIT Tools
Small inventories	Modular product design
Fast setups	Good housekeeping
Small lots	Visible information
Frequent delivery	displays
Flexible labor	Kanban
Flexible equipment	
Consensus management	
Integrated technical	
support and vendors	

initial inventories were $25 million, the firm would turn inventory four times per year. Reducing inventories to $4 million with the same sales level would give 25 turns, an often-reported improvement under JIT.

Fast setups. Internal setups (those within the machine and made when the machine is not producing) are minimized and are designed for rapid replacement. External setups (those that the operator can change while the machine is running) are often designed to be accomplished as part of the machine production cycle. These techniques reduce overall setup times, which are critical because if setup times can be reduced the lot size necessary to economically cover that setup cost can also be reduced.

Small lots. As setup times are reduced, lot sizes also can be reduced. Under JIT, lot sizes should be sufficient only to satisfy immediate production needs with no excess. The ideal is a lot size of one unit of production.

Frequent delivery. Suppliers often make three or four deliveries per day, which usually go directly to the production line not to a warehouse. Of course, this requires greater care in scheduling and higher transportation costs, but it reduces space and handling requirements.

Flexible labor. Line workers have more responsibility to identify what must be done and the authority to take immediate action. This may mean, for example, that a small, flexible team of workers in a group technology layout is responsible for all aspects of production and delivery of a particular job.

Flexible equipment. Equipment is designed for maximum flexibility, both in rapidity of processing and quick adjustment to multiple functions. Computer-controlled equipment and common mountings for different parts are often used to permit rapid adjustment from one function to another. Thus, setup time is minimized, which is an essential component of flexible manufacturing.

Consensus management. Management processes are geared toward consensus rather than edict. Complex, highly detail-oriented, and persuasive management processes are necessary to form a labor-management-supplier team that interacts successfully.

Integrated technical support and vendors. Both technical support (purchasing, inventory management, quality control) and suppliers are fully integrated in the operation. Suppliers often take turns providing more frequent, less than truck-load-sized deliveries.

The tools of JIT include modular product design, good housekeeping, visible information displays, and the kanban. Modular product design is often used in JIT to permit greater product variety with fewer component parts. The use of common connectors, standardized bolt hole locations, integrated gear design, and common component dimensions, permits modules to be assembled into a great number of different end products. For example, a lift truck can be assembled from three engines (gas, propane, electric), three wheel configurations (three wheel-single rear wheel, three wheel-single front wheel, four wheel), with or without a driver's cab, and with two tire options (cement surface only or dirt and gravel). Thus, while the plant builds a total of 10 modules $(3 + 3 + 2 + 2)$, the product has 36 possible configurations $(3 \times 3 \times 2 \times 2)$. Modular design permits increased product variety with standardized production modules and facilitates product modification and upgrade, while holding inventories down.

Good housekeeping is normally associated with any well-managed operation; under JIT, however, it becomes an obsession. Good housekeeping means simply that the number of impediments to job flow on the shop floor is minimized. Excess dirt or paperwork, extra jobs on the shop floor, additional and complex actions, or poorly maintained equipment are all disruptive to the smoothness and speed of job flow, which is so critical to JIT. Thus, unnecessary clutter is eliminated, and required items are carefully defined and controlled.

Visible information displays are important both to good housekeeping and to employee decision making. For example, a diesel engine manufacturing plant, which intermixes many different types of engines on the same assembly line, identifies each engine with a color-coded shop order form. As the engine moves along the assembly line, employees must know ahead of time which module (carburetor, piston, oil pan, etc.) to assemble on the specific engine. The solution is to place the order form, with color-coded areas signifying particular options, prominently on the front of the engine block, where it can be seen by workers in down-flow positions. Other examples include numbered display panels used to notify restaurant service personnel when food is ready for delivery to customers, and video displays in airports that identify for passengers the appropriate arrival and departure gates and baggage claim docks. In service applications, the information system is often available directly to the customer. For example, toll-free numbers are widely used by many service organizations to provide reservations, ordering, product information, maintenance, and other services more directly to customers.

The Kanban

The kanban is an example of a tool that has developed rather uniquely in Japan. Kanban, in Japanese, means card or visible representation. The card is a mechanical means to require inventory movement based on need, although the card itself is not required for the functioning of the kanban logic. For example, in its simplest form the inventory management of the grill emblem of an automobile might involve two wooden cases, each with compartments to hold six grill emblems. The system starts when a case is emptied at the assembly department. The case is returned to the production department and exchanged for a full case. The arrival of the empty case at the production department authorizes and initiates the production of enough emblems to fill the case. The steps of the kanban operation (see Figure 20–3) are as follows:

1. Case 1 is used at the assembly department. When it is empty, it is moved to the production department and Case 2 is used by the assembly department.

Figure 20–3 Kanban Movement

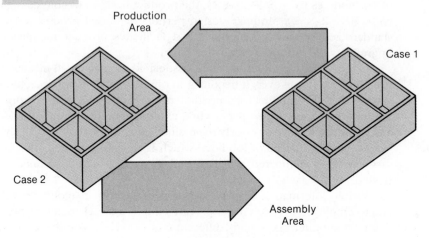

2. Case 2 is filled at the production department. When it is filled with six emblems, it is ready for use by the assembly department.

In this simple example, the component case itself is sufficient to assure that parts are produced as they are needed by the assembly line. A full case is called forward to the assembly line as needed, and the returning empty case is the signal to produce more; there is no separate control of the parts. However, if the components were costly or purchased from a supplier, the firm might desire to use a card on each case to control the inventory used. A computer card, or other machine-readable format, could be used to indicate authorization to produce the part or authorization to withdraw the part from storage; thus, the terms production kanban and withdrawal kanban are used.

The timing of the assembly process would dictate the number of individual component compartments in each case, the number of cases to use, and the exact rules of case movement during the production process. If the production rate varies, the number of cases and kanban cards can be decreased or increased. Safety stock and production lead time are thus incorporated in the kanban logic. Computation of the number of kanban cards and containers is as follows:

$$K = \frac{\text{Average demand over lead time + Safety stock}}{\text{Container volume}}$$

or

$$K = \frac{D(W + P + T)(1 + S)}{Q}$$

where:

K = Number of kanban cards or containers needed

D = Demand for the part per hour

W = Waiting time per container in hours (average)

P = Processing time per container in hours (average)

T = Transportation average time in hours (used only with external purchases)

Q = Quantity of parts in container

S = Safety factor (probably .1 for internally produced components)

For example, if demand for the part was 250 units per hour, the container quantity was 25, the average production time was 9 minutes (.15 hours), and the average wait in a holding area was 12 minutes (.2 hours), the following computations suggest that approximately four kanban containers should be used, or

$$K = \frac{250(.20 + .15 + 0)(1 + .10)}{25} = 3.85 \cong 4$$

In this simple example, the case defines the lot size of 25. The size of case could be varied for greater convenience (if the components were lighter or heavier, for example). Rules of case movement might be that one case at a time is moved forward to the assembly area as needed, and any empty case is immediately returned and filled.

When the system was originally set up, it might initially use a high safety factor, requiring a larger number of cases. But, as experience is gained (the learning curve effect), the safety factor could be reduced and the number of kanbans decreased. Alternatively, the case might be redesigned to hold a larger number of parts, thus reducing the number of cases and movement required; if the items were handled individually, the Q value would be 1. As variance in process times or changes in demand occur, the system becomes self-regulating. An employee will make parts only when an empty case or card authorizes them. If there is no requirement for parts, the employee is expected to do preventive maintenance, assist another employee, or just stop working.

Supplier shipments are handled in exactly the same manner, except that they include an external transportation time and probably a larger safety factor. Depending upon the reliability of the suppliers, a safety factor of .25 or higher may be appropriate. Needless to say, proximity of the supplier is important in JIT external purchasing operations; it is not uncommon to find suppliers grouped in industrial complexes close to their demand. In the prior example, if the transportation time were 15 minutes (.25 hours) and the safety factor were .30, then the total number of kanban cases required would be:

$$K = \frac{250(.20 + .15 + .25)(1 + .30)}{25} = 7.8 \cong 8$$

A protective container might be designed to transport two cases from the supplier to the assembly line, and appropriate rules might be formulated of how much and when to move. Whether the kanban uses elaborate information systems or just a simple case depends upon the complexity of the process and the value and complexity of the product.

JIT in Services

In this discussion, the JIT system has been described in a manufacturing context, where inventory reduction has been the primary savings from increased throughput. Although a JIT implementation is not generally associated with services, there are numerous applications of JIT principles in service organizations. The visible displays to assist service personnel in restaurants have been mentioned. Additionally, the fast-food industry has made an enormous change in the technology of preparing and serving food. Self-service salad bars, standardized and modularized menu items, precooking for high demand periods, and functionalized packaging all have helped move fast-food restaurants from the traditional hamburger snack to a full line of breakfast, lunch, and dinner meals (Gorman 1987).

More traditional restaurants are competing with the fast-food industry by guaranteeing service within five or ten minutes or the meal is free. This guarantee is particularly popular with the luncheon menu but is increasingly used for breakfast and dinner. By moving patrons more rapidly through fixed seating (capacity), the restaurant is able to achieve a greater turnover of the tables and thus greater volume on fixed capacity. Additionally, the traditional restaurants are responding with full-time standardized menus. In some markets, deliveries of individual meal packets are provided from food processing centers once or several times per day in carefully sized shipping containers that become refrigerator inserts. Partial cooking, combined with microwave final preparation, reduces customer waiting times.

In a mail-order warehouse, large amounts of inventory cause the same problems. Large inventories require greater storage, cause confusion, and cost money. Thus, the emphasis is on rapid flow and throughput of inventory. For this reason, many mail-order shipping warehouses are highly automated and will guarantee shipment of a telephone order within 24 or 30 hours.

Another example is an office supply retail store that uses a kanban system to manage boxes of continuous feed computer paper. At the store, there are two boxes each of seven different types of paper (different widths, different numbers of manifold copies, etc.), or a total inventory of fourteen boxes of computer paper. Whenever a box is sold, a colored sticker is pulled off the box and is the basis for a telephone order for next-day delivery. Past and forecast demand patterns reveal that there is little probability of more than two calls for a particular type of paper within 24 hours, but stockage levels (the number of kanban stickers) could be increased if necessary. Of course, this inventory management system could be run with a bar code reader and computerized inventory control software, but for a small office supply store the stickers are simple and inexpensive. The delivery can be frequent because many line inventory items at the store are handled in the same manner through one distributor, which of course services many such office supply stores. The distributor carries eight to ten days of stock and is replenished weekly for most items.

In all services, the identification of the fixed capacity constraint and the adaption of methods to signal utilization and the requirement to further produce or order can be found. Accurate system capacity and utilization information can notably enhance product flow through the service process. The only requirement is to carefully evaluate the service production process and identify the necessary signals.

The Relationship of JIT to Traditional Operations Logic

Conceptually, JIT seems to violate several of the traditional concepts of manufacturing, the most obvious of which are the maximum utilization of equipment and the economic order quantity (EOQ) and economic lot size (ELS) formulas. Recall that those formulas define an optimal purchase order quantity or production lot size based on the tradeoff between two variables: (1) order (setup) costs and (2) carrying costs. This typical EOQ/ELS relationship was discussed in Chapter 11 and is shown here as the black curves in Figure 20–4.

However, if the order or setup times, and thus order (setup) cost, could be decreased, the order (setup) cost curve would shift downward and to the left. The optimum EOQ/ELS would simultaneously decrease. For example, decreased setup times (and costs) could be achieved by mounting die pairs on hinged arms, which would permit rapid, one-motion mold changing. Times could also be reduced if major portions of the setup were redesigned as an external setup rather than an internal setup, permitting much of the next setup to be made as the machine was finishing a prior job. These changes would shift the cost of the order (setup) to the left (from cost 1 to cost 2), which would reduce the optimum EOQ/ELS, as shown as the blue curves

Figure 20–4 Economic Order Quantities Reduction Through JIT

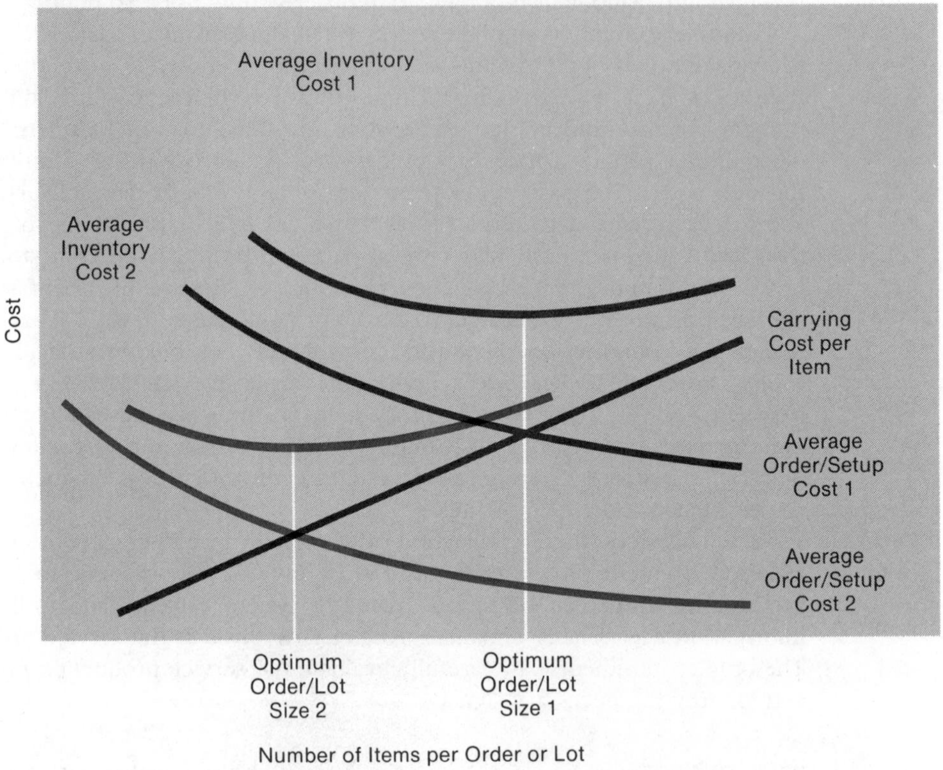

Average Inventory
Cost 1

Average
Inventory
Cost 2

Cost

Carrying
Cost per
Item

Average
Order/Setup
Cost 1

Average
Order/Setup
Cost 2

Optimum
Order/Lot
Size 2

Optimum
Order/Lot
Size 1

Number of Items per Order or Lot

in Figure 20–4. The JIT optimum then is approached more closely by the optimum order/lot size 2. Ideally, a JIT system would reduce setup costs to the point that the optimal lot size is one. Thus, given faster and less costly setups, JIT is fully consistent with the EOQ/ELS logic.

Other possible contradictions of traditional practices should be noted. Increased numbers of deliveries, particularly in less than truckload lots, would appear to be less efficient. However, if several suppliers agree to share mutual deliveries, delivery costs under JIT can actually be decreased. Careful evaluation and selection of those parts for JIT deliveries might use A-B-C analysis. Class A consists of high dollar value materials, or bulky parts and should be considered for daily delivery and careful management. Class C consists of low dollar value parts and requires deliveries at less frequent intervals. This type of analysis, defining classes by dollar value, bulk, density of use, or other factors, is consistent with the Pareto concept of varying intensity of management according to the value of the good (Ansari and Heckel 1987).

As suppliers increasingly move toward the efficiencies of JIT demand chains, they can realize further efficiencies. Although supplier relations and interfaces would seem to be more complicated due to increased supplier interaction, they may be simplified because of a reduction in the number of suppliers. According to a study by O'Neal (1987), this changing philosophy of supplier relations is reflected by a 150 percent increase in single-source supplier policies, combined with a greater frequency of interaction with suppliers, particularly in the purchasing, materials management, and quality sections. Thus, JIT leads to a narrowing of traditionally diverse supplier relationships.

JIT Implementation

JIT requires very careful planning and integration for success. For example, the material-as-needed (MAN) program at Harley Davidson developed only after the concept had been tested in a pilot program. As the MAN program developed, the following elements were accomplished:

1. Setup reduction
2. Focus flow production
3. Lead time reduction
4. Inventory reduction
5. Stable and consistent schedule
6. Employee involvement
7. Containerization
8. Part control—MAN cards
9. Statistical process control
10. Preventive maintenance
11. Strong line organization
12. Supplier programs

The implementation at one Harley Davidson plant involved all 250 employees. In two months they were able to change from a single-product assembly line to a mixed-model line. The final assembly line uses a repeated family sequence that generates a continuous and stable requirement for component parts each day (Gelb 1985).

Different circumstances suggest different approaches to JIT implementation. The following list (Voss 1987) shows the sequential steps that were used by Japanese managers to implement JIT in a British firm. These steps should not be regarded as a recipe for JIT implementation. However, they are representative of the types of management activities necessary and their approximate sequence. In this regard, each JIT implementation is different; JIT can be described as a very heterogeneous process.

1. *Clean house*. Establish cleanliness, orderliness, tidiness, and clarity.
2. *Eliminate obvious waste*. Identify and resolve practices that create unnecessary scrap, unevenness, and unreasonableness.
3. *Manage detail*. Train managers in the types of information to manage and the techniques used to manage it.

4. *Develop teamwork.* Create committees, quality circles, or other vehicles for employee-management interaction.
5. *Install preventive maintenance.* Identify critical machines and maintenance requirements and periods.
6. *Install statistical process control.* Identify critical quality measurements and the mean and variances.
7. *Train employees.* Gain employee involvement in and support for the new methods.
8. *Develop production flow.* Identify and time the demand chain; reduce setups.
9. *Simplify handling.* Develop containers, storage locations, and material-handling techniques.
10. *Establish performance objectives.* Establish tentative work standards, but ones that management and labor are encouraged to improve upon.
11. *Structural simplification.* Reorganize the technology structure and simplify reporting procedures, information processing, and work rules.

One particularly promising method of implementing a JIT system is short cycle management (SCM). This technique, which has also been called short cycle scheduling (SCS) and short interval scheduling (SIS) involves gradual reduction of the production cycle. Of course, this reduction encourages development of smaller lot sizes, faster set ups, and other just-in-time efficiencies. A derivative of SCM is synchronous scheduling, which applies the JIT logic to synchronize the production of several or many parts.

JIT applications have been widely accepted in varying types of processes (e.g., continuous flow, assembly and batch operations, and job shops) and in various functional areas (e.g., purchasing, services, manufacturing, and distribution) (Schonberger, 1987). Certainly JIT is attractive in many types of businesses; but it is important to note some of the limits of a JIT system and to recall the costs of JIT (commitment, education, and communication). JIT would probably not be appropriate if a long-range management commitment were not possible, if employee acceptance would be difficult and employee training costs and turnover high, if production processes were simple or inventory costs were low, or if operating in a custom-order product environment. Most American firms are gradually and cautiously moving toward JIT practices, adapting specific aspects of JIT philosophies and inventory management practices as they fit the development directions and strategies of the firm. In a sense, JIT implementation is a rather eclectic process. Distribution distances, cultural values, automation, and the multitude of highly competitive suppliers limit the direct application in America of techniques that have been developed in different environments overseas.

TQC—TOTAL QUALITY CONTROL MANAGEMENT

The second, and highly related, approach in the pursuit of production process excellence is total quality control (TQC). The traditional production environment separated production and quality functions. The typical operations manager was responsible for purchasing materials or components, scheduling production, and shipping output. The typical quality control section inspected that output, often at the end of the production run, and rejected those parts that did not meet design specifications. This approach may create a disruptive dichotomy between operations and quality control— operation's goal is to fill orders and ship a product, while quality control's goal might be viewed as impeding that flow. More importantly, the traditional approach violates a basic tenet of quality control: "You can't inspect quality into a product; you have to build it in."

Traditional quality control practices involved computing an inspection sample size, examining the sample, and then accepting or rejecting the lot based on that sample. Given the sample size and lot size, the probability that the sample actually represented the state of the population was computed and the associated risks of error were evaluated. Thus, traditional quality control separated the good from the bad with some risk of error. The difficulty with this traditional approach is that there is a cost associated with the bad products or services, even though they are accurately identified by the quality control evaluations. The costs of scrap, storage, retesting, product downgrading, and rework represent costs of internal failure. If the quality control sampling is in error, there would be further costs of the error, including warranty replacements, allowances, and customer ill will.

On the other hand, total quality control operates under the assumption that it is cheaper to commit time and money to defect prevention than to waste it in rework, scrap, and replacement. In a number of cases, the total costs of internal and external failure for an uninterrupted production run have been found to be greater than the costs of stopping the run, identifying and fixing the process defect, and running the process to the quality specification. Numerous slogans have been used to represent the principles and emphases of TQC programs.

Slogan	Principle
"Let's have a zero defects day"	Defects are not tolerated.
"If you can't do it right the first time, when will you have time to do it right?"	Quality is controlled at the source. If necessary, production is stopped and the defective product and the process are corrected.
"Quality is everyone's job."	Quality is an end in itself; it should be internalized by all employees.

TQC concepts were first suggested by American W. Edwards Deming, while he was serving as a consultant to several Japanese firms in the 1950s. Subsequently, it was proposed in America by A. V. Feigenbaum (1961). Fourteen points proposed by Deming (1985) are as follows:

1. Achieve constancy of purpose in the company.
2. Learn a new philosophy.

3. Require statistical evidence of process control on incoming critical parts.
4. Requiring statistical evidence of process control from vendors will require reduction in the number of vendors.
5. Use statistical methods to recognize the sources of trouble.
6. Institute modern aids to training on the job.
7. Improve supervision.
8. Drive out fear.
9. Break down barriers to communication between departments.
10. Eliminate numerical goals, slogans, pictures, and posters, that urge people to increase productivity. Numerical goals have a negative effect through frustration.
11. Look carefully at work standards. Assure that they help people do a better job.
12. Teach employees to use statistical methods.
13. Train people in new skills.
14. Start at the top. Top management must push every day for total quality control.

The Definition of TQC

The fourteen points emphasized top management's key role in defining and teaching the necessity of quality. Quality is viewed as the responsibility of each employee along the entire chain of production from input suppliers to distributors. Enhanced communication along this chain and use of statistical methods are required. Deming's fourteen points provide the foundation for the definition of TQC today. Put simply, the definition of TQC is

a philosophy of zero defects, which assigns quality responsibility at the source of production by (1) training in and using established statistical techniques to identify and anticipate quality failure and (2) by improving equipment reliability through monitoring and preventive maintenance.

TQC departs from traditional quality control methods in several ways. Statistical process control and preventive maintenance anticipate production failure. Quality assessment of every item, rather than inference based on a sample, and quality assurance at the source, rather than after production, differentiate TQC programs from traditional quality control.

The Characteristics and Tools of TQC

The characteristics of TQC include: (1) census evaluation/zero defects, (2) quality at the source, (3) equipment reliability/reduced redundancy, and (4) reduced scrap and waste.

Census Evaluation/Zero Defects. Every component and every process is evaluated for quality during the production process. A census (100 percent sampling) assures zero defects. Often quality control jigs, or measuring devices, are set up such that when a part is produced, it is moved from the producing equipment through the jig to the next workstation. If the piece fails that quality check, the equipment is checked and adjusted and the part is reworked until it passes; then the piece is sent to the next station.

Quality at the Source. Quality is inherent in the production process; it is the responsibility of the producing organization or individual. Often TQC operations will not inspect incoming parts or material because certified suppliers have provided quality inspection results for each lot. In addition to integrating the responsibility for quality with the production, quality at the source attempts to identify defects as they are produced and save the costs of further work on defective parts.

Equipment Reliability/Reduced Redundancy. Assurance of proper equipment functioning through various programs, such as preventive or statistical maintenance, is necessary for total quality control. When a quality defect occurs, the *process* is first examined and corrected, then the *product* is fixed. Because equipment reliability is assured, the need for redundant backup equipment is reduced.

Reduced Waste and Scrap. Wasted materials cost money. End pieces (lumber at a housing construction site) and scrap (production breakage or defects) have been carried as inventory, transported, and worked on through various steps of production. Scrap and waste require greater safety stocks and make production scheduling more difficult, thus, reducing scrap or waste results in savings.

Several tools are used to support these TQC objectives; they include statistical process control, stop-line prerogatives, preventive maintenance, and fishbone analysis.

Statistical Process Control. Statistical process control measures each critical variable of each unit of production and establishes process averages. In one statistical process control application, the deviation of each observation from the average is computed, and the process is considered out of control if any measures fall outside of the control limits (often set at three standard deviations from the mean). In a second approach, the process is considered out of control if more than five or six sequential observations fall on the same side of the mean or move in a clearly ascending or descending pattern. This second approach permits the anticipation of process-generated defects and the correction of the process before product defects occur.

Stop-Line Prerogative. A stop button or stop signal is mounted at every workstation; it permits any line employee to stop the entire production process. This is used when a quality deficiency is encountered. The stop button, sometimes accompanied by a horn and flashing red lights, permits engineers and supervisors to immediately respond to and fix a problem anywhere in the facility.

Preventive and Statistical Maintenance. Preventive and statistical maintenance procedures are increasingly used for critical equipment or parts. For example, helicopter engines require very thorough maintenance schedules, including periodic analysis of the oil for metal flakes (indicating wear) and regular engine rebuilds. Similarly, equipment failure in TQC systems would stop production of the item and potentially cause delays in subsequent work activities. Thus, preventive maintenance checks and periodic complete maintenance evaluations are built directly into the production schedule.

Fishbone Analysis. Unlike the first three tools of TQC, the fourth tool, the fishbone analysis and the fishbone chart, is a departure from traditional quality control tools. It was developed by Dr. Kaoru Ishikawa, one of Japan's foremost authorities on quality. The chart resembles a fishbone with the primary bones representing the major quality contributors and secondary bones representing lesser quality contributors. The chart is prepared by employees who work directly with the production process and is helpful in analyzing the reasons for quality defects.

Figure 20–5 shows an example of a fishbone analysis for a company that makes the adhesives and paper for release products. Release products are labels or stickers that are sold fixed to a carrier but are pulled from the carrier and stuck to another object. Preprinted price stickers or mailing labels are examples of release products. Quality control for the release product is critical because the label must have a weak enough adhesive to pull from the carrier (backing paper) without tearing the label, yet be strong enough to adhere to the recipient object surface. This measure of adhesiveness is called the release value.

The fishbone chart shows four principle contributors to defective release values: strength of the label paper, strength of the release adhesive, coating of the carrier paper, and surface of the recipient object (i.e., envelope or paper on which the labels are placed). Once the quality problem has been isolated to one of the four principle contributors to defective release values, possible secondary reasons are pursued by the analysis. For example, if the strength of the release adhesive were found faulty, secondary reasons would be evaluated (e.g., humidity, temperature, speed of application rollers, chemical formulation of the adhesive, electron dryer mechanism, and consistency of the mixture). The fishbone chart is very useful in quality diagnosis of complex processes because it encourages a logical analysis to sequentially isolate quality problems.

TQC Implementation

Like JIT, a TQC program should not be undertaken lightly; it should be part of a long-range plan and commitment of the organization. The success of a TQC program is directly related to the carefulness of its planning and implementation. To develop a TQC program, management should take a series of steps.

Create a Quality Culture. Without a culture, and the underlying philosophy of quality, TQC will fail. The culture is the basis for employee acceptance

Figure 20–5   The Fishbone Chart for Release Products

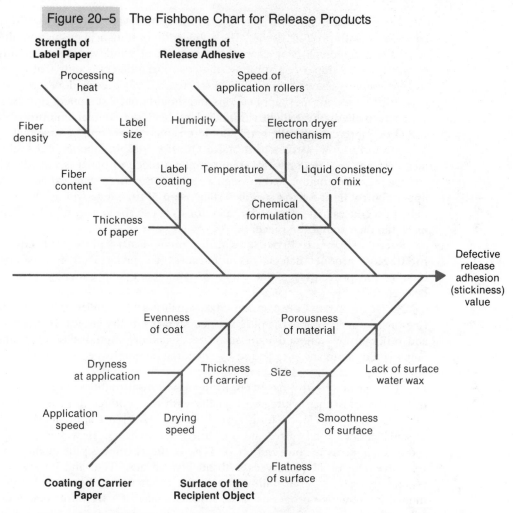

of and faith in the program. Without that culture the necessary responsibility for and self-correction of errors will not develop.

Costing the Program. The costs of quality should be carefully studied, including both the costs of defects and of defect prevention. Budgeting for the cost of quality early in the process is important. The budget should not separate quality control from production. Rather, the mechanism of quality assurance and the costs should be built into every job standard. Training in quality evaluation methods should be provided to every employee and should be budgeted as a cost of quality.

Evaluate 100 percent of Production. The evaluation should use statistical techniques, but it should not be bound by them. Management should carefully select a number of quality criteria, then develop checks to ensure compliance with product design. The application of statistical evaluation ultimately is judgmental. For example, if a piece of window glass is slightly thicker than the upper control limit, the cost of the defect is only that materials are being wasted. That should be corrected, but the window glass can probably be used for most applications and should not be scrapped. However, a window pane that was slightly thinner than the lower control limit probably would be more easily broken and should be sold as a second or scrapped.

Use Simple Measures and Make Quality Visible. Simple and visible measures are best understood. For example, a piece of metal is milled to a specific measure, then passed through a jig set at the three standard deviation upper control limit for the specified dimension. If the piece will not fit, or is tight, procedures may require the operator to check the setting of the milling machine, then remill the piece.

Spend Time on Process Maintenance—Both Labor and Equipment. Most product defects occur because of a process error. Personnel training and preventive maintenance of equipment help eliminate process defects.

Insist on Total Compliance. Make quality a blue collar responsibility (e.g., make quality part of the performance rating). Quality circles, TQC teams, and other group interactive formats are essentially methods of providing employee training and interaction by encouraging employee involvement.

Total quality control has been distinguished from traditional quality control processes in that it integrates quality with the production process. TQC methods were developed from several of the traditional approaches, such as statistical process control and preventive maintenance. However, perhaps the most important contribution of TQC is the reemphasis of quality and reinvolvement of all employees with quality. Because TQC and JIT systems require the same overall philosophy or environment and because they are mutually interactive programs, TQC is usually part of a JIT implementation. Without the overall climate or constancy of purpose (Deming 1985), TQC is not possible. JIT is dependent upon high quality, and TQC is dependent upon the frequent inspections during the process, which are easier under JIT. JIT and TQC systems are mutually supportive methods of controlling the manufacturing process (Schonberger 1982*b*; Masaracchia 1987).

EST—ENHANCED SCHEDULE TECHNOLOGIES

The third part of the contemporary process management approach, enhanced schedule technologies (EST), addresses possible variations in a JIT schedule due to uncontrollable circumstances. JIT inventory management strives for a stable product flow through the production process and a consistent, if not fixed product lead time. Similarly, TQC attempts to eliminate product defects and equipment breakdown. Those techniques address inventory management and quality control very effectively; however, should they fail and should stock-outs or defects occur, production would be stopped for all subsequent operations.

Thus, the EST approach to excellence of operations process management is used to smooth process scheduling and to minimize the effects of potential stoppages. Simply stated, these enhanced scheduling technologies use process simulation techniques to identify potential production bottlenecks. These bottlenecks may be resolved in many ways, but a practical solution is to plan a small amount of inventory directly after the probable bottleneck, preventing the bottleneck from interrupting subsequent processes.

The Definition and Characteristics of EST

To pursue the water analogy of Figure 20–2, flow through a JIT process can be seen as the movement of a shallow but fast-moving stream through a series of rapids. Although JIT attempts to smooth the flow, there are still some small pools that result from sequencing and lot-sizing bottlenecks. The EST approach is used to identify the bottlenecks (quiet pools) that occur and to smooth the flow of production through those bottlenecks by creating small buffer inventories. EST techniques are defined as

> the use of computer simulation techniques to enhance scheduling flows, by finding efficient order sequences and lot sizes, given a finite process capacity.

This definition suggests the following characteristics of EST.

Simulation Techniques. Certain critical characteristics of the production process are identified and measured, and the operations process is modeled using a computer program. Several simulations of the process are run, which permits the identification of efficiencies or bottlenecks. The analyst can then adjust the model to search for an enhanced flow.

Enhanced Schedules. The simulation process can provide an improved, and sometimes optimal, scheduling solution by reducing or eliminating bottlenecks.

Efficient Lot Sizes. In EST techniques, lot-sizing efficiency can be improved in two ways. The first approach is to separately compute production and transfer lot sizes, based on such factors as average setup, production, and movement times. The second approach addresses probabilities of bottlenecks due to defects, breakdowns, or process imbalances. Thus, production and transfer lot sizes may be adjusted to minimize these inefficiencies.

Finite Capacity. The simulation process permits the definition of the capacity of each workstation or each production step. Multistep processes will often have one or a few bottlenecks, which constrain the total throughput of the process and limit the input to every other step or workstation. The identification of these capacity constraints permits process adjustment, for example, by creating an additional work center or by dividing the activities of the bottleneck work center among two work centers.

Generally, these scheduling simulations model a production flow, identify efficiencies and bottlenecks, and permit simulated manipulation by adjusting both the definition of the model (number of workstations, processing times, etc.) and the definition of the flow between workstations.

The current tools of EST include OPT, XCELL+ , and Q-Control, which are proprietary software products. Because these products are quite widely used, and because they address EST scheduling, they are discussed here.

OPT—Optimized Production Technology

OPT, which was developed by Moshe Goldratt, uses four modules to evaluate data inputs: (1) The buildnet module, (2) the serve module, (3) the split module, and (4) the brain module. The *buildnet* module permits the user to create a model of the process by defining inputs of current inventory, bills of materials, routings, and demands; then it runs an error check of the model. The *serve* module provides a load profile of the system and computes the average utilization of each manufacturing process. The average utilization rate of each process is rank ordered permitting identification of bottlenecks. The *split* module sorts all operations into those affected by the bottleneck and those not affected. Finally, the *brain*, or OPT, module uses a proprietary algorithm to find a good (though, despite the name, not necessarily optimal) scheduling solution using finite capacity and forward scheduling logic (Vollmann 1986).

The process is iterative because as the four programs are run errors may be identified (e.g., more than 100 percent utilization of a resource); these errors will have to be corrected and the program restarted. The program output identifies suggested sequences, buffer stocks, and batch sizes. The output provides a statement of materials required for the planning horizon and a detailed product flow and production schedule for each workstation.

XCELL+ Factory Modeling System

The XCELL+ Factory Modeling System was developed by Richard Conway and his associates (Conway et al. 1987) at Cornell University. XCELL+ creates a logical model of production flows by defining the manufacturing process as five elements: work centers, receiving areas, shipping areas, buffers, and maintenance facilities. These elements are linked together in process flows. The variables of the production process, such as capacities, setup times, process times, quality reject rates, and maintenance constraints, are depicted in the model and graphically represented on the screen. Rather elaborate production systems of up to 60 work centers and 240 processes can be defined. Once the network is established, simulations can be run to test the particular layout and schedule for smoothness of flow.

The simulations trace, at various speeds for ease of viewing on the screen, the process flow through the net and provide plots of utilization and efficiency. Gantt charts show the status of each workstation (busy; idle—no material; idle—waiting for input 1; idle—waiting for input 2; blocked—can't output; undergoing maintenance; or waiting for maintenance); and computations are provided of the efficiency of each workstation. On the basis of these simulations, additional workstations, adjusted processing times, or other smoothing methods can be used to balance the process. XCELL+ includes conveyor linkages, specified routings, temporary storage locations on the shop floor, and optimally routed patterns, though not optimal production scheduling.

Q-Control—Waiting Line Evaluation

Q-Control is also a proprietary scheduling system, developed by William Sandman in the late 1970s (Sandman 1980). The program identifies the workstation where large amounts of queue time develop—that is, where jobs are waiting for equipment or labor to be available to process them. The longer the queue at a workstation, the more the disruption of the process flow and the greater the bottleneck.

The software is run each night and simulates the next day's plant operations; it has the objective of identifying and minimizing the effect of bottlenecks. The proprietary algorithm balances job requirements against both equipment capacity and existing work in process in a unique approach called dual balancing. Although Q-Control was designed to reduce work in process, it has also had the effect of reducing by one half the order completion times and shop days of work time per order, and roughly doubling the turns of work in process. (Sandman 1980).

EST Implementation

Although these EST techniques offer tremendous scheduling enhancements, particularly in complex production systems, there are some difficulties that should be noted:

1. The methodologies all are dependent upon an accurate description and timing of each step of the production process. Although most would agree that the production process can be described and modeled, measurement and timing of the process may be more difficult and is certainly costly.
2. The methodologies all require extensive data entry and regular system maintenance and interaction. Each of these software systems is sufficiently complex so as to be unsuitable for direct use on the plant floor by line employees. It would require technical staff personnel.
3. None of these methodologies incorporate cost evaluation (e.g., overhead, equipment, labor, scrap, or rework costs). They schedule only for flow efficiency without regard to the differing costs or priorities of different jobs. Costs are assumed to be equal.

Implementation of EST techniques such as OPT, XCELL+, and Q-Control will probably be most effective with small lot sizes and differentiated production. They are able to smooth the typically lumpy flow of a job shop and move it toward the efficiencies of repetitive manufacturing. EST techniques may be easier to implement than JIT and TQC methods because the software is run, a best schedule is identified, and the schedule is implemented by production activity control. The programs do require extensive technical and programmer involvement, but they probably will require less training effort for nontechnical employees.

However, the use of these technologies may aggravate the perception that the schedule is generated by a black box. Behavioral or cost constraints are not permitted by any of the software programs, which might encourage programmers to attempt to adjust available input variables to accommodate these limitations. Thus, the proposed schedule may not be realistic or easily explainable, and for that reason, it may not be accepted on the shop floor. Implementation of EST will require a general understanding by all employees, certainly an appreciation of the overall philosophy, initial testing of the software, and a recognition that some variables of the process just cannot be modeled.

EST techniques start with a traditional or JIT-derived shop schedule and improve the smoothness of work flow. By creating a model of the process, the EST approach simulates the performance of numerous different scheduling alternatives to find an enhanced, though not necessarily optimal, schedule. EST methods are derived from the traditional scheduling approaches, including lot sizing and simulation, but are different from traditional approaches because of the emphasis on flow.

CONCLUSIONS

The process management methods noted in this chapter address three very different areas of manufacturing process excellence. Each of the three approaches necessitates a philosophy of integrating suppliers and distributors, an emphasis on job flow, and a spirit of continuous improvement. The JIT system further evaluates inventories and the ensuing effects on setups, lot sizes, and deliveries; TQC deals with cost-effective quality management; and the various EST methods use simulation to smooth production process flows. Figure 20–6, which completes the framework begun in Figure 20–1, summarizes the three approaches and indicates that they originate in the same management philosophy and contribute to the same result—improved process management.

Inventory management, quality control, and process scheduling, which have traditionally been considered as separate and sometimes mutually exclusive objectives of manufacturing, have been shown to be at least partially integratable. JIT and TQC methods are highly interdependent, and the EST

Figure 20–6   A Framework for Operations Excellence

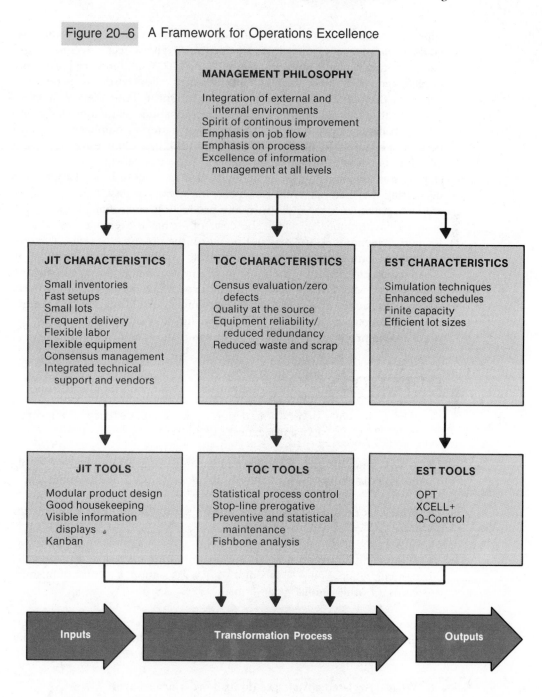

approach has demonstrated an ability to effectively control what otherwise could be a very lumpy flow. As the programs take effect, inventory sizes decrease, and quality improves. Both JIT and TQC methods require more management effort and training, but ultimately they cost less. Scheduling efficiency through EST can further enhance the throughput of the system.

Note that the differences between traditional and contemporary methods of managing operations processes are a matter of emphasis and must be driven by the overall philosophy of the firm. Few firms today represent pure traditional or entirely contemporary approaches. Most firms have used a step-by-step approach for implementation and are presently working toward decreasing the material cycle times and improving quality. However, there are circumstances, defined both by the production environment and by the financial environment, in which the costs of further movement toward contemporary techniques just may not be worth the potential benefits. The cost of implementation must be weighed against expected improvements in an iterative implementation technique. Make a minor change, see what happens, and then consider further options. Initial experiences of user firms are very positive. The achievement of these improvements would suggest that the traditional tradeoffs among inventory, quality, and scheduling efficiency are not necessary; improvements in each can be simultaneously achieved.

QUESTIONS

1. Why is the philosophical foundation of process excellence so important to JIT, TQC, and EST approaches?

2. Why is it necessary to establish a philosophy to integrate external suppliers and distributors prior to establishing a JIT, TQC, or EST approach?

3. Why is worker involvement a necessary precondition to JIT implementation?

4. How might inventories of an ice cream parlor be reduced using a JIT system? What about the inventories of a gas station, a printer of business cards, or other similar small firms?

5. Considering customer buying patterns at the ice cream parlor, are there limits to inventory reduction and JIT applicability? What about such limitations at the gas station, the printer, or other similar small firms?

6. What JIT-related advantages do mail-order firms have?

7. Give several reasons why unions might be hesitant to fully endorse the contemporary approaches to process management.

8. Considering that the Common Market has permitted many European nations to integrate productive systems across national and cultural boundaries, what effects would this development potentially have on JIT implementation?

9. Describe a familiar production process (three or four steps) in terms of the waterflow analogy. (e.g., construction of an interstate highway bridge or toll booth, building a bicycle frame.)

10. Compute the number of kanbans required for each of the following operations:

Item	Hourly Demand D	Average Waiting Time (minutes) W	Average Processing Time (minutes) P	Average Transport Time (minutes) T	Quantity Q	Safety Factor S
Auto door handle	75	15	12	0	15	.1
Computer keyboard	100	10	20	30	20	.2
Television tube	200	10	30	40	6	.25
Fish meal for dinner	10	10	3	30	10	.25
Sewing machine in store	.25	10	10	48	1	.25
Precooked hamburgers	60	3	5	0	1	.1

11. Considering Figure 20–4, if, as setup times decreased, carrying costs (defined as the daily management time required for an item) increased at a greater rate, what would be the effect on total inventory costs and the optimal lot size? Would a JIT system work in such a situation?

12. Propose five specific actions that you would consider to implement JIT in a retail clothing store, a video tape and computer software retailer, a metal fabrication job shop, a housing development construction site, or your own business.

13. Develop a fishbone chart for a university course registration process, a garden hose manufacturer, a business card printer, or a playing card manufacturer.

14. Describe why JIT and TQC approaches are interdependent.

15. Why are EST methods not necessarily optimal?

16. Why might EST methods be tough to implement? What characteristics would make them easier to implement?

REFERENCES

Ansari, A., and Heckel, Jim. "JIT Purchasing: Impact of Freight and Inventory Costs." *Journal of Purchasing and Materials Management* (Summer 1987): 24.

Ansari A., and Modarress, Batoul. "Just-In-Time Purchasing: Problems and Solutions." *Journal of Purchasing and Materials Management* (Summer 1986): 11.

Celley, Albert F., et al. "Implementation of JIT in the United States". *Journal of Purchasing and Materials Management* (Winter 1986): 9.

Conway, Richard, et al. *User's Guide to XCELL+ Factory Modeling System.* Redwood City, Calif.: The Scientific Press, 1987.

Deming, W. Edwards. "The Roots of Quality Control in Japan: An Interview with W. Edwards Deming." *Pacific Basin Quarterly* (Spring/Summer 1985).

Dilworth, James D. *Information Systems for JIT Manufacturing.* Wheeling, Ill.: Association for Manufacturing Excellence, 1987.

Feigenbaum, A. V. *Total Quality Control: Engineering and Management.* New York: McGraw-Hill, 1961.

Gelb, Thomas A. "The Material as Needed Program at Harley-Davidson" *Proceedings of the 1985 Annual Conference of the Association for Manufacturing Excellence*, pp. 49–64.

Goddard, Walt. "Kanban versus MRP II—Which is Best for You?" *Modern Materials Handling*, November 5, 1982, p. 41.

Gorman, John. "Fast-food Push Puts Time on Diner's Side." *Chicago Tribune*, August 23, 1987.

Green, Donald R. "Direct Pegging, MRP/JIT Bridge." *P&IM Review* (April 1987).

Gunn, Thomas G. *Manufacturing for Competitive Advantage: Becoming a World Class Manufacturer.* Cambridge, Mass.: Ballinger, 1987.

Hall, Robert W. "Measuring Progress: Management Essential." *Target* (Summer 1987): 5–13.

Hall, Robert W. *Zero Inventories.* Homewood, Ill.: Dow Jones–Irwin, 1983.

Hatvany, Nina, and Vladimir Pucik. "An Integrated Management System: Lessons from the Japanese Experience." *Academy of Management Review* (July 1981): 470.

Hutchins, Dexter. "Having a Hard Time with Just-in-Time." *Fortune*, 9 June, 1986, p. 64.

Lundrigan, Robert. "What Is This Thing Called OPT?" *Production and Inventory Management* (Second Quarter 1986): 2.

Masaracchia, Philip. "TQC–The 'Quality' Component of J-I-T." *P&IM Review* (April 1987): 44.

Meleton, Marcus P. Jr. "OPT—Fantasy or Breakthrough?" *Production and Inventory Management* (Second Quarter 1986): 13.

O'Neal, Charles R. "The Buyer-Seller Linkage in a Just-In-Time Environment." *Journal of Purchasing and Materials Management* (Spring 1987): 7.

Ouchi, William G. "Theory Z: An Elaboration of Methodology and Findings." *Journal of Contemporary Business*, 2, no. 2, (1982): 27–41.

Pascale, Richard T., and Anthony G. Athos. *The Art of Japanese Management*. New York: Simon & Schuster, 1981.

Peters, Thomas J., and Robert H. Waterman. *In Search of Excellence*. New York: Harper & Row, 1982.

Plenert, Gerhard, and Thomas E. Best. "MRP, JIT, and OPT: What's 'Best'?" *Production and Inventory Management* (Second Quarter 1986): 22–29.

Powell, Cash. "Workshop Report: Cincinnati Milacron-Electronics System Division." *Target*. (Summer 1987): 28–33.

Quinlan, J. "'Just-in-Time' at the Tractor Works." *Material Handling Engineering* (June 1982): 62–65.

Riopel, Robert J. "JIT: Evolutionary Revolution." *Manufacturing Systems* (July 1986): 44.

Rohan, Thomas M. "The Empire Strikes Back." *Industry Week* April 15, 1985, pp. 40–48.

Sandman, William E. *How to Win Productivity in Manufacturing*. Dresher, Pa.: Yellow Book of Pennsylvania, 1980.

Sandras, William A. Jr. "JIT/TQC Changes in Thinking for Information Systems." *P&IM Review* (April 1987): 33.

Schonberger, Richard J. *Japanese Manufacturing Techniques: Nine Hidden Lessons in Simplicity*. New York: Free Press, 1982*a*.

Schonberger, Richard J. "Some Observations on the Advantages and Implementation Issues of Just-in-Time Production Systems." *Journal of Operations Management*, 3, no. 1 (November 1982*b*): 5.

Schonberger, Richard J. *World Class Manufacturing Casebook: Implementing JIT and TQC*. New York: Free Press, 1987.

Vollmann, Thomas E. "OPT as an Enhancement to MRP II." *Production and Inventory Management* (Second Quarter 1986): 38.

Voss, Chris. "International Perspectives on Just-In-Time Manufacturing." Symposium presented at the annual meeting of the National Academy of Management, New Orleans, August 1987.

Wildemann, Horst. "JIT Progress in West Germany." *Target* (Summer 1987): 23–27.

Willis, Rod. "Harley Davidson Comes Roaring Back." *Management Review* (March 1986): 20–27.

PART VII
TECHNICAL SUPPLEMENTS

CHAPTER 21
FINANCIAL ANALYSIS

OBJECTIVES

After completing this chapter, you should be able to

- Explain the concept of the time value of money and why it is important in evaluating decision alternatives that have costs or cash inflows in different time periods

- Compute the present value of a single sum or a series of cash flows to be received in the future

- Explain the rationale behind depreciation and illustrate several methods for computing depreciation

- Explain break-even analysis, including its assumptions and limitations, and demonstrate its relevance to the operations manager

- Calculate the break-even point and the profit coefficient and demonstrate how each is useful in analyzing the outcome of operations management decisions

OUTLINE

INTRODUCTION

Successful operations management decision making often requires a working knowledge of certain tools of financial analysis. In large organizations, major financial decisions are usually made by managers in other functional areas, such as the treasurer's office or the credit department. However, virtually all decisions in any organization have financial implications. The operations manager must be aware of basic financial relationships in order to recognize these implications. Furthermore, in smaller organizations, operations managers may be directly involved in financial decisions.

Three financial concepts are introduced in this chapter. The time value of money is one of the most important considerations in any decision involving future cash flows. Depreciation is important in decisions involving fixed investments. And break-even analysis is useful in evaluating current operations and fixed investments. Many readers already will be familiar with these tools. For those who are not, this chapter is intended to provide a brief overview. A more complete discussion can be found in any financial management text (see, for example, Neveu 1989 or Brealy and Myers 1984).

THE TIME VALUE OF MONEY

A given amount of money in hand today has more value to an individual or an organization than the same sum to be received at some time in the future. This concept is known as the time value of money. Money in hand today can be used to purchase needed items today, or it can earn interest until needed. If money is needed today it can be borrowed, but it takes a larger sum to pay back the loan with interest in the future. Business organizations must be able to provide investors with an increase in the value of their investments. To do this they must consider the time value of money in any decision that involves money at more than one point in time. For most operations managers in business organizations, almost all decisions fall in this category.

Compounding a Single Amount

A sum of money in hand now increases in value over time if it is lent or deposited in an interest-bearing account. Simply stated, one dollar invested at an annual interest rate of i percent will be worth $1 + i$ dollars a year from now. Let

i = Annual rate of interest (a decimal value)

t = Number of annual interest periods

An amount A invested now will have a future value of $FV_{i,t}(A)$ in t years if invested at rate i. That is,

$$FV_{i,t}(A) = A(1 + i)^t$$

For example, $100 invested at 10 percent for two years will be worth

$$FV_{10\%,2}(\$100) = \$100(1 + .10)^2 = \$121$$

Discounting a Single Amount

An important analytical technique that can help evaluate future events realistically is the concept of present value. A dollar in hand today is worth more than one dollar that will be forthcoming in the future. The present dollar can be used to buy a useful article, it can be invested and receive interest, or it can be used to pay outstanding bills and thus avoid interest charges. Just how much more it is worth now may depend upon a number of factors, not least of which are the alternative uses to which it could be put at present. In financial considerations, the best alternative use (say, the highest interest rate at which a sum could be invested) determines the discount rate—that is, the interest rate used to compute the present value of a future sum.

At a discount rate of i percent, a dollar received one year hence is worth only $1/(1 + i)$ dollars today. The present value $PV_{i,t}(A)$ of an amount, A, to be received t years from now is

$$PV_{i,t}(A) = \frac{A}{(1 + i)^t}$$

If $100 is to be received in two years, discounted at 10 percent, it has a present value of

$$PV_{10\%,2}(\$100) = \frac{\$100}{(1 + .10)^2} = \$82.64$$

Compounding an Annuity

An annuity is specified income payable at specified intervals for a fixed period. For example, suppose that a payment P is to be deposited into an account at the end of each year for a period of t years and will receive interest at rate i. How much will the account be worth at the end of t years? The amount[1] is referred to as the future value of an annuity with annual payment P compounded at interest rate i for t years, $FVA_{i,t}(P)$, which is equal to

$$FVA_{i,t}(P) = P\frac{(1 + i)^t - 1}{i}$$

For example, if we deposit \$100 into an account at the end of each year for five years, and the account pays 10 percent interest, the value of the account at the end of the five years will be

$$FVA_{10\%,5}(\$100) = \$100\frac{(1 + .10)^5 - 1}{.10} = \$610.51$$

In contrast to depositing a known amount at the end of each year and determining how much it will compound to in t years, it is possible to

---

[1]This equation is determined using the steps that follow. Since each amount A will earn interest from when it is first deposited until the end of year t,

$$FVA_{i,t}(P) = P(1 + i)^{t-1} + P(1 + i)^{t-2} + \ldots + P(1 + i) + P$$

$$= P[(1 + i)^{t-1} + (1 + i)^{t-2} + \ldots + (1 + i) + 1]$$

To get a simple expression for the sum in brackets, let

$$X = (1 + i)^{t-1} + (1 + i)^{t-2} + \ldots + (1 + i) + 1$$

Now multiply each side of the equation by $(1 + i)$:

$$X(1 + i) = (1 + i)^t + (1 + i)^{t-1} + \ldots + (1 + i)^2 + (1 + i)$$

Note that the right-hand side of the equation is the original series, X, plus a term $(1 + i)^t$ and minus one. Thus,

$$X(1 + i) = X + (1 + i)^t - 1$$

Grouping X terms,

$$X(1 + i) - X = (1 + i)^t - 1$$

or

$$X(1 + i - 1) = (1 + i)^t - 1$$

or

$$iX = (1 + i)^t - 1$$

Hence,

$$X = \frac{(1 + i)^t - 1}{i}$$

and therefore

$$FVA_{i,t}(P) = P\frac{(1 + i)^t - 1}{i}$$

determine what annual deposit will be required to yield a given amount at the end of t years. This is known as a sinking fund. The sinking fund payment required to accumulate an amount A in t years, $SFP_{i,t}(A)$, is

$$SFP_{i,t}(A) = A\frac{i}{(1 + i)^t - 1}$$

To accumulate \$500 in five years, the amount that must be deposited at the end of each year into an account that pays 10 percent is

$$SFP_{10\%,5}(\$500) = \$500\frac{.10}{(1 + .10)^5 - 1} = \$81.90$$

Discounting an Annuity

Suppose now that someone agrees to pay you P dollars at the end of each year for t years and interest is earned at a rate i. This amount[2] is referred

---

[2]This equation is determined using the steps that follow. Each payment is discounted from the time you receive it:

$$PVA_{i,t}(P) = \frac{P}{(1 + i)} + \frac{P}{(1 + i)^2} + \frac{P}{(1 + i)^3} + \ldots + \frac{P}{(1 + i)^t}$$

$$PVA_{i,t}(P) = P[(1 + i)^{-1} + (1 + i)^{-2} + (1 + i)^{-3} + \ldots + (1 + i)^{-t}]$$

As in Footnote 1, let

$$Y = (1 + i)^{-1} + (1 + i)^{-2} + (1 + i)^{-3} + \ldots + (1 + i)^{-t}$$

Multiply both sides by $(1 + i)$:

$$(1 + i)Y = 1 + (1 + i)^{-1} + (1 + i)^{-2} + (1 + i)^{-3} + \ldots + (1 + i)^{-t+1}$$

Now the relationship of these two equations can be noted as in Footnote 1 or, equivalently, the former can be subtracted from the latter:

$$
\begin{aligned}
(1 + i)Y &= 1 + (1 + i)^{-1} + (1 + i)^{-2} + \ldots + (1 + i)^{-t+1} \\
-Y &= \quad\; -(1 + i)^{-1} - (1 + i)^{-2} - \ldots - (1 + i)^{-t+1} - (1 + i)^{-t} \\
\hline
(1 + i)Y - Y &= \qquad\qquad\qquad\qquad\qquad\qquad\qquad\qquad -(1 + i)^{-t}
\end{aligned}
$$

Simplifying,

$$iY = 1 - (1 + i)^{-t}$$

or

$$Y = \frac{1 - (1 + i)^{-t}}{i}$$

and, by multiplying the numerator and denominator by $(1 + i)^t$ and returning to the original equation,

$$PVA_{i,t}(P) = P\frac{(1 + i)^t - 1}{i(1 + i)^t}$$

to as the present value of the annuity or $PVA_{i,t}(P)$. It would be calculated as follows:

$$PVA_{i,t}(P) = P\frac{(1 + i)^t - 1}{i(1 + i)^t}$$

If you are to receive $100 at the end of each year for five years, the present value of all the payments, discounted at 10 percent, is

$$PVA_{10\%,5}(\$100) = \$100\frac{(1 + .10)^5 - 1}{.10(1 + .10)^5} = \$379.08$$

The converse of this is the capital recovery payment, $CRP_{i,t}(A)$, which is the payment one must make annually to repay an amount A received today. That is,

$$CRP_{i,t}(A) = A\frac{i(1 + i)^t}{(1 + i)^t - 1}$$

Suppose you borrow $500 today at 10 percent and must pay it back in five equal annual payments beginning one year from today. The payment would be

$$CRP_{10\%,5}(\$500) = \$500\frac{.10(1 + .10)^5}{(1 + .10)^5 - 1} = \$131.90$$

Continuous Compounding and Discounting

For each of the previous equations, if payments were made or received n times per year, then the interest rate per period would be i/n, but the number of payments in t years would be nt. In this case the compounding factor would be

$$FV_{i/n, nt}(A) = A(1 + i/n)^{nt}$$

Now as n approaches infinity, that is, when we have continuous compounding or discounting, the expression $(1 + i/n)^{nt}$ approaches its limit, e^{it}, where e is the base for natural logarithms. (See Appendix E for values of e^x.) For example, $100 continuously compounded at 10 percent for one year would yield

$$\$100\, e^{.10} = \$110.52,$$

Table 21–1   Summary of Compound Interest
Factor Formulas

Type	Discrete	Continuous
Single payment Future value	$(1 + i)^t$	e^{it}
Single payment Present value	$\dfrac{1}{(1 + i)^t}$	e^{-it}
Sinking fund payment	$\dfrac{i}{(1 + i)^t - 1}$	$\dfrac{i}{e^{it} - 1}$
Capital recovery payment	$\dfrac{i(1 + i)^t}{(1 + i)^t - 1}$	$\dfrac{ie^{it}}{e^{it} - 1}$
Future value of an annuity	$\dfrac{(1 + i)^t - 1}{i}$	$\dfrac{e^{it} - 1}{i}$
Present value of an annuity	$\dfrac{(1 + i)^t - 1}{i(1 + i)^t}$	$\dfrac{e^{it} - 1}{ie^{it}}$

which is more than the $110 that would result if the interest is compounded only once, at the end of the year. Banks sometimes compound continuously in order to increase the effective yield on deposits. For example, in the case illustrated here, a bank might advertise 10.52 percent effective yield on a deposit with a nominal interest rate of 10 percent.

Table 21–1 gives the interest factors for all the formulas discussed and also gives the continuous versions. Each of the factors should be multiplied by the appropriate amount or payment to determine the desired present or future value or payment.

DEPRECIATION

Machines and buildings wear out, and their values decrease day by day; eventually they must be replaced. This gradual loss in value is termed depreciation. This verbal model of the way in which capital equipment is slowly consumed is indisputable, but the exact mathematical manner in which it occurs is arguable. Possible patterns of depreciation are shown in Figure 21–1.

When an organization purchases a capital asset it makes an investment. Capital investment is not an expense even though there is a cash outflow, because the cash is merely exchanged for an asset of equal value. However, expense is incurred as the asset wears out and decreases in value. Methods of accounting for this depreciation are necessary for two reasons: (1) to compute taxes and (2) to accurately state the value of the assets of the

Figure 21–1 Patterns of Depreciation

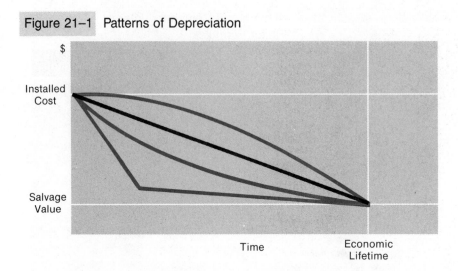

organization. It is not necessary that an organization use the same method of computing depreciation for these two purposes.

The U.S. Internal Revenue Service (IRS) allows depreciation as a tax-deductible expense; it is not included in profit. This is because the asset was originally purchased with profits that have already been taxed. Setting aside some of the organization's revenues as depreciation allows the recovery of that investment. If all the revenues set aside as depreciation were accumulated during the life of an asset they could be used to replace the asset when it is fully depreciated. For accounting purposes, some rule must be used to compute depreciation; a number of such rules have been used for both tax computation and asset valuation. The IRS currently specifies the method to be used for tax computation for most assets.

One of the key factors in determining depreciation is the expected useful life of the equipment. This factor is complicated by obsolescence—that is, the decrease in value of the existing equipment because of new developments external to the item itself. Obsolescence may be gradual, as in men's clothing, or sudden, as in women's clothing. Often it cannot be predicted, and so the useful life may suddenly be cut short. One reason industry is constantly trying to shorten the allowed useful life is to hasten recovery of capital in order to be prepared for sudden obsolescence.

The most common and basic model for depreciation is the straight-line method. In this case the annual depreciation is a constant dollar amount calculated as the installed cost minus the salvage value divided by the useful life.

$$D = \frac{C - S}{N}$$

where

$$D = \text{Depreciation charge per year}$$

$$C = \text{Initial cost}$$

$$S = \text{Salvage value}$$

$$N = \text{Life in years}$$

A fast write-off is also often attempted in order to build up quickly a cash reserve for other uses while waiting to spend it on a replacement. Two ways to do this are the declining-balance and the sum-of-the-digits techniques.

Under the declining-balance method, a constant percentage of the remaining depreciated value is written off each year. When this percentage is twice the value computed from a straight-line assumption, this is referred to as the double-declining-balance method. For example, if a piece of equipment initially cost $10,000 and has a useful life of ten years, then the declining-balance factor could be no larger than $2 \times 1/10$. The depreciation schedule for the first three years would be as follows:

$$D_1 = .2 \times 10,000 = \$2,000$$

$$D_2 = .2 \times (10,000 - 2,000) = \$1,600$$

$$D_3 = .2 \times (10,000 - 2,000 - 1,600) = \$1,280$$

Each year the amount written off is less, but initially the amounts exceed the $10,000/10$ that would be written off by the straight-line method. The value at the end of the year (V_n) can be shown as follows for a $10,000 initial cost (C) and a depreciation factor (f) of .2.

$$V_1 = 10,000 - 10,000(.2)$$

$$= 10,000(1 - .2)$$

$$V_2 = 10,000(1 - .2) - 10,000(1 - .2)(.2)$$

$$= 10,000(1 - .2)(1 - .2)$$

$$= 10,000(1 - .2)^2$$

$$V_3 = 10,000(1 - .2)^2 - 10,000(1 - .2)^2(.2)$$

$$= 10,000(1 - .2)^3$$

Or in general,

$$V_n = C(1 - f)^n$$

This depreciation is continued until the remaining value is equal to the salvage value.

Another alternative model used in depreciation is called the sum-of-the-digits method because the depreciation factor depends upon the sum of the digits up to the useful life. If a piece of equipment had a useful life of five years, then the denominator of the factor would be: $1 + 2 + 3 + 4 + 5 = 15$. The numerators would be obtained by using these digits in reverse order.

$$D_1 = \frac{5}{15} \times \text{ (initial cost } - \text{ salvage value)}$$

$$D_2 = \frac{4}{15} \times \text{ (initial cost } - \text{ salvage value)}$$

$$D_3 = \frac{3}{15} \times \text{ (initial cost } - \text{ salvage value)}$$

For a comparison of these three methods applied to an asset with an initial investment of $12,000 and a $2,000 salvage value at the end of its ten-year useful life, see Figure 21–2.

The tax laws of 1981 and 1986 established a set of depreciation schedules known as the Accelerated Cost Recovery System (ACRS). The ACRS arbitrarily establishes for tax purposes the depreciable lifetimes of assets according to

Figure 21–2 Comparison of Three Depreciation Models

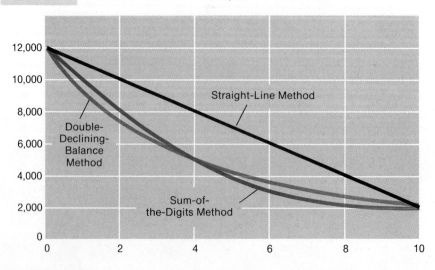

categories that are defined in the law. These lifetimes are generally shorter than the actual economic lifetimes of the assets, thus depreciation for tax purposes is accelerated. The amount of depreciation to be taken each year over the lifetime is also specified for each category. The ACRS is the only accelerated method that may be used to compute depreciation for tax purposes, but the straight-line method may still be used. The other methods may also be used for other accounting purposes.

BREAK-EVEN ANALYSIS

One of the basic tools of financial analysis is the break-even chart. This concept describes two relationships: (1) that the total cost of producing a product for sale is the sum of certain fixed costs—that is, expenses independent of volume and variable costs that are a function of the number of items produced and (2) that total income is equal to the product of the selling price and the number of units sold. This is a simplification, since certain fixed costs may be constant and variable costs and revenue may be linear only within a particular range of volume. However, the model describes how almost all costs and revenues are determined.

The corresponding graphic model, the break-even chart of Figure 21–3, shows the point at which a process just recovers its costs—that is, where it breaks even. The break-even point (BEP) occurs at the point at which the sales revenue just equals the total cost.

Examining the chart, we can project down from the point where the two lines intersect and determine the break-even quantity. A more precise statement of the cost function that is illustrated by the graph is

$$C = B + AV$$

Figure 21–3   Break-Even Chart

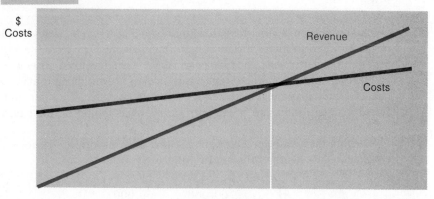

Number of BEP Units

where

$$C = \text{Total cost of production}$$

$$B = \text{Fixed costs}$$

$$A = \text{Variable cost per unit produced}$$

$$V = \text{Volume}$$

Letting R = total revenue and P = selling price per unit, then

$$R = PV$$

These two equations are very explicit: both the cost and revenue are described as linear relationships. However, they may be applicable only within a specified range. Inclusion of more general relationships—that is, quadratic or noncontinuous—can be formulated as mathematical models, but the resulting equations would be more complex than the ones shown here.

This mathematical model can be manipulated easily to reveal various properties of the cost-price relationship. For example, the break-even point occurs where cost and revenue are equal—that is, where $C = R$.

$$C = R$$

$$B + AV = PV$$

$$B = PV - AV = V(P - A)$$

or

$$V_{BEP} = \frac{B}{P - A}$$

An advantage of a mathematical model is that it can be easily manipulated or transformed to focus attention on other variables. For example, consider a firm that currently sells door locks for \$2.75 each, has fixed costs of \$60,000, and has variable costs of \$1.50 per unit. Because of anticipated manufacturing changes, they may be able to reduce variable costs to \$1.30 per unit. If they are to maintain the same break-even point, what should be their new selling price?

Letting the subscript E denote existing and subscript N denote new, the volume at the existing break-even point is

$$V = \frac{B}{P_E - A_E} = \frac{60,000}{2.75 - 1.50} = \frac{60,000}{1.25} = 48,000 \text{ units}$$

For the new situation at the break-even point,

$$R = C$$

$$P_N V = B + A_N V$$

$$P_N = \frac{B + A_N V}{V} = \frac{B}{V} + A_N$$

$$P_N = \frac{60,000}{48,000} + 1.30$$

$$= 1.25 + 1.30 = \$2.55$$

In general, if the break-even point is to remain constant, then

$$P_N = P_E + (A_N - A_E)$$

In the example, this means:

$$P_N = \$2.75 + 1.30 - 1.50 = \$2.55.$$

Thus, for the break-even point to remain constant, the new price must equal the existing price plus the difference between the new and existing variable costs.

Another interesting relationship that arises in examining the way profits vary with sales level is the profit coefficient (P_c), defined as follows:

$$P_c = \frac{\text{Fixed costs}}{\text{BEP volume in dollars}}$$

$$= \frac{B}{\$V_{BEP}} = \frac{B}{P(\frac{B}{P-A})}$$

$$= \frac{P - A}{P}$$

This is a useful figure in determining profits for any sales level. Recalling that profits equal revenue minus costs,

$$\text{Profit} = R - C$$

$$= PV - (B + AV)$$

$$= V(P - A) - B$$

Multiplying and dividing the first term on the right by P, we get

$$\text{Profit} = \frac{VP(P - A)}{P} - B$$

or since VP equals revenue and $(P - A)/P$ equals the profit coefficient, then

$$\text{Profit} = (\text{Revenue} \times \text{Profit coefficient}) - \text{Fixed costs}$$

This equation can also be solved for the profit coefficient resulting in an alternative definition:

$$\text{Profit coefficient} = \frac{\text{Profits} + \text{Fixed costs}}{\text{Sales revenue}}$$

Consider the problem of TIM Co., which currently has a sales volume of $250,000, fixed costs of $120,000, and a profit of $60,000 at this level of sales. Through installation of some new equipment, they can reduce variable costs per unit by 15 percent but will increase fixed costs by 7 percent. Anticipating a 10 percent increase in sales, how much will their profits change? First, their profit coefficient is

$$P_c = \frac{\text{Profits} + \text{Fixed costs}}{\text{Sales revenue}}$$

$$= \frac{\$60,000 + \$120,000}{\$250,000} = .72$$

If there is a 10 percent increase in sales with no reduction in cost parameters, their new profits will be

$$\text{Profits} = RP_c - B$$

$$\text{Profits} = (\$250,000)(1.1)(.72) - \$120,000$$

$$= \$198,000 - \$120,000$$

$$= \$77,000$$

Therefore, the change in profits at a 10 percent increase in sales and through altered costs can be calculated as follows:

$$\text{Profit increase} = .15(\$77,000) - .07(\$120,000)$$

$$= \$11,550 - \$8,400 = \$3,150$$

This same break-even approach can be used to compare alternative processes. The lock company in our earlier example is considering the purchase of a new assembly line that will raise fixed costs to $80,000 and reduce variable costs to $1.25. For a selling price of $2.50, what must be the sales volume in order for the new facility to be more profitable?

$$C_E = 60,000 + 1.5V;$$

$$C_N = 80,000 + 1.25V;$$

$$R = 2.50V$$

Since the revenue is constant, profits are a function of costs only. Therefore, by setting the existing cost formula equal to the new cost equation, we can solve for the point at which the new installation will become less costly than the existing facility. To see this more clearly, examine the corresponding schematic model in Figure 21–4.

Figure 21–4   Cost-Volume Relationships for Alternative
Production Processes

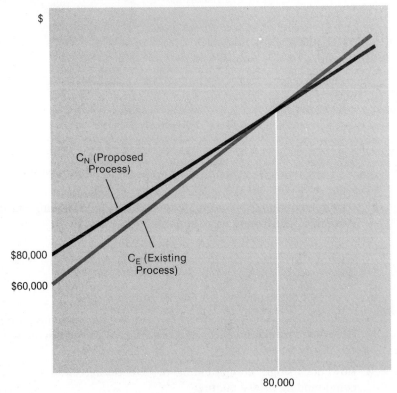

$$C_E = C_N$$

$$60,000 + 1.50V = 80,000 + 1.25V$$

$$.25V = 80,000 - 60,000 = 20,000$$

$$V = 20,000/.25 = 80,000$$

CONCLUSIONS

In all for-profit businesses and many other organizations the operations function is inextricably linked to the financial function. It is operations that produces the product that generates revenue. While operations managers may not make purely financial decisions, they provide input to other managers who do make those decisions. And virtually all operations decisions have some impact on the finances of the organization. For this reason, operations managers must be familiar with some of the tools of financial analysis. This chapter provides an overview of three of those tools: the time value of money, depreciation, and break-even analysis.

QUESTIONS

1. Name the three major methods of financial analysis used by operations managers.

2. Describe the concept of the time value of money.

3. Why is it important to evaluate future cost using discounting?

4. How is compounding or discounting a single amount different from compounding or discounting an annuity?

5. What is the difference between an annuity and a sinking fund?

6. What is the logic of discounting an annuity?

7. How is the capital recovery payment related to the discounted annuity?

8. How does single compounding or discounting differ from continuous compounding or discounting?

9. Why is it necessary to compute the cost of depreciation?

10. Why is it advantageous for business to push for reduced useful lives of assets?

11. What is the accelerated cost recovery system?

12. What two relationships are involved in break-even analysis?

PROBLEMS

1. If $200 is invested at 8 percent interest for four years, what will it be worth?

2. If $1,000 is invested at 12 percent for seven years, how much will it be worth?

3. What is the present value of $1,000, deliverable in five years at 10 percent?

4. If you were absolutely rational, would you rather have $2,000 today or $3,100 in five years? An annual interest rate of 9 percent is expected.

5. If a student makes a deposit of $2,000 of earnings from a summer job once per year for four years, can the student pay the expected first year college expenses of $10,000? The interest rate is 8 percent. How much is the student short or ahead of the $10,000 goal?

6. If $50 were placed in a savings account each month for three years at an annual rate of 12 percent, what is the value of the account? Note: there are no withdrawals from the account.

7. If 5 percent of an employee's annual salary of $22,500 is taken at the end of each year and retained in a company thrift account that pays 9 percent annually, how much is in the account at the end of five years?

8. To accumulate $1,200 in four years, how much must be paid into an account today if the account bears 6 percent interest?

9. How much must be deposited annually in a savings account at 7 percent to pay an expected $11,000 college bill four years from now?

10. If you are to receive $300 at the end of each year for four years, discounted at 8 percent, what is the present value of all payments?

11. What is the annual payment if you borrow $3,000 for a car and must repay the amount in five equal annual installments at 10 percent interest?

12. If a bank offered 8 percent continuously compounded interest, how much is a $300 deposit worth after three years?

13. What is the value of a student's bank account if deposits of $2,000 were made annually for four years at 8 percent continuously compounded? Compare this answer with that of Problem 5.

14. If $5,000 must be paid off in four years, what annual payment must be made, given a 12 percent continuously compounded interest rate?

15. What is the present value of a $2,000 annual payment over five years, given an interest rate of 8 percent continuously compounded?

16. How large an annual contribution must be made to repay $7,000 received today if the interest rate of 10 percent is continuously compounded?

17. If a milling machine costs $30,000 and the salvage value is expected to be $10,000 in ten years, compute the annual depreciation for the first three years using:

    a. The straight-line method
    b. A double-declining-balance method
    c. The sum-of-the-digits technique

18. What is the break-even volume for a product with fixed costs of $20,000, variable cost of $0.40 and a selling price of $1.00?

19. A firm expects to decrease manufacturing costs from $12.50 to $11.80 per unit. If fixed costs are $15,000 and the price of the item is $20.00, what is the current break-even point? What would be the new break-even point? If the firm desires to maintain the same breakeven point, what is the new selling price?

20. SRA Inc. currently has annual profits of $150,000 on a sales volume of $1,000,000 and a fixed cost of $250,000. They are considering purchasing a new system that would provide faster delivery. The equipment reduces variable cost by 20 percent but increases fixed cost by 10 percent. If sales volume is constant, by how much do profits change? If sales increase by 5 percent in the first year due to the more rapid deliveries, what would profits be?

21. The Roberts Machine Tool Company presently has fixed costs of $130,000 and variable costs of $2.30 each, for a product that sells for

$4.25. If new equipment is purchased for $30,000, raising fixed costs to $160,000 but reducing variable costs to $1.95, what sales volume is required for the new facility to be more profitable?

REFERENCES

Brealy, R., and S. Myers. *Principles of Corporate Finance*, 2d ed. New York: McGraw-Hill Book Company, 1984.

Neveu, R. P. *Fundamentals of Managerial Finance*, 3d ed. Cincinnati: South-Western Publishing Co., 1989.

CHAPTER 22
MATHEMATICAL PROGRAMMING

OBJECTIVES

After completing this chapter, you should be able to

- Define mathematical programming and differentiate linear programming and goal programming

- Describe the characteristics of a situation or problem that make linear programming an appropriate analytical technique

- Set up the objective function and constraints of a variety of problems for solution using linear programming

- Solve simple linear programming problems graphically and using the simplex technique

- Explain goal programming, and set up and solve simple goal programming problems

OUTLINE

INTRODUCTION

The techniques referred to as mathematical programming include methods to solve linear, nonlinear, integer, geometric, goal, stochastic, 0-1, and mixed integer problems as well as the transportation problem, the assignment problem, and others. Each of these techniques and their associated solution procedures involves a model of some process or situation and the determination of a best or optimal (maximum or minimum) solution (in terms of profits, costs, or other measure or measures of merit) through the proper allocation of limited resources.

The fundamental concepts were developed in the 1940s and 1950s and have been elaborated upon ever since. Generally, many practical problems involve prodigious amounts of computation; hence, the rise in usefulness of mathematical programming has paralleled the growth in computers. Many texts are devoted exclusively to one or more of these techniques, and lengthy users' manuals exist for standard computer packages. Our purpose here is only to acquaint or refresh the reader with the basic models and solution techniques, particularly as they are found in applications related to production and operations management. Such applications include optimal blending of raw materials into a final product, aggregate planning, optimal critical path method (CPM) schedules, capital budgeting, and other resource-constrained, complex problems.

LINEAR PROGRAMMING AND THE SIMPLEX SOLUTION TECHNIQUE

At the heart of linear programming (LP) is a model of the real world expressed in linear equations; that is, all variables are to the first power (e.g., X, Y, etc., not X^2, nor products like XY). Furthermore, none of the variables can take on negative values, and they must be continuously divisible—that is, they can take on values such as 0.5 or 3.167 as well as 4. Finally, there is no uncertainty in the coefficients or values in the model. (The various other mathematical programming techniques either relax these conditions to obtain more realistic models—such as, nonlinear and stochastic programming—or impose additional conditions to handle real-world situations more accurately (such as integer and goal programming). The solution procedures are generally more complex as a result.) While these conditions (linearity, nonnegativity, continuity, and certainty) may seem restrictive in developing models, they have proved not to be a hindrance in many settings.

The general form of a linear programming problem is a set of linear relationships defining the tradeoffs for each resource that is to be allocated and a single objective function that gives the contribution of each decision variable. Mathematically that might resemble the following:

Constraints	$5X + 6Y \le 27.75$
or	$4X + 2Y \le 13$
Requirements	$3.6X + 8.1Y \ge 23$
Objective	Maximize $1.8X + 2Y$

(Note: The nonnegativity constraint is usually not shown explicitly, nor is it required, since the solution procedure guarantees its existence.)

In a problem such as this (one having only two variables), the system of equations can be easily graphed and the solution obtained by inspection. Few real-world problems are this simple, but the graph can illustrate the innate features of any mathematical programming problem so it is worth examining briefly before going on to a purely mathematical procedure, the simplex technique.

Graphical Representation and Solution

The first equation, $5X + 6Y \le 27.75$, represents an area (technically a half plane) bounded by and including the line $5X + 6Y = 27.75$. Note that the inequality ($\le$) is what distinguishes the line from the area bounded by the line. Since both X and Y must be positive, the area is further confined to that bounded by the X and Y axes (the first quadrant). This is shown in Figure 22–1. We can now add the constraint $4X + 2Y \le 13$, which, since any feasible solution must simultaneously satisfy both constraints, effectively

Figure 22–1 Area Bounded by $5X + 6Y = 27.75$ and the X and Y Axes

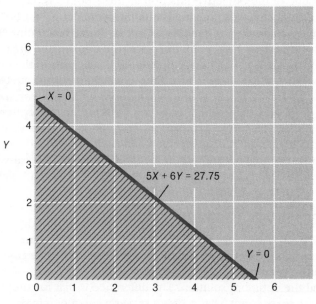

chops off a corner of the first area (see Figure 22–2). Finally, the requirement that $3.6X + 8.1Y \geq 23$ confines the solution space to the area previously defined lying above $3.6X + 8.1Y = 23$ is illustrated in Figure 22–3.

The objective is to maximize the value of $1.8X + 2Y$. This equation defines a family of straight lines all parallel to each other and so having the same slope $(-1.8 \div 2.0)$. Our task is to find the one positioned to have the largest sum and still intersect the solution space. In Figure 22–4 several have been drawn that intersect the feasible region at various places. Perhaps it is not obvious (but maybe it is after a little study) that the optimal solution will always lie on a corner (vertex) of the constrained space or on an edge connecting two corners and not on a line through the middle of the area. This is one of the important discoveries of the theory of linear programming. It means that instead of having to search the entire area defined by the constraints we need only look at the corners in order to find the optimal solution. There are an infinite number of points in the area, but there is only a finite number of corners (four in our example). Purely mathematical techniques are simply organized methods of examining, either implicitly or explicitly, these corners.

In our example the four candidates for possible optimal solutions are at the following points:

X	Y
0	2.839
0	4.625
1.607	3.286
2.353	1.794

The value of the objective function at these points is 5.679, 9.25, 9.465, and 7.823, respectively. Thus, the optimum occurs at $X = 1.607$ and $Y = 3.286$ as can be confirmed graphically as the most extreme point (from the origin) at which the line $1.8X + 2Y$ intersects the constrained area.

Perhaps it is worth noting that, if the coefficients of the objective function had a ratio of less than 5 to 6 (the coefficients of the first constraints), for example, 1.6 to 2, the optimum would be at $X = 0, Y = 4.625$. If the ratio rose to greater than 4 to 2 (e.g., 1.8 to .8), then the optimum would be at $X = 2.353, Y = 1.794$. This sort of analysis of the structure of the problem and the impact of changes to the coefficients is referred to as postoptimality or sensitivity analysis and is commonly done when the real-world coefficients have some uncertainty about them or when they could be altered.

The Simplex Solution Technique

For problems having many variables, graphic solution procedures are inadequate, so algebraic techniques are required. The basic rule of action, however, remains the same: examine the extreme points of the solution space to find the optimum solution. The difference is that for simplex problems the solution space is not a flat area but rather a volume or hypercube; the corners,

Figure 22–2   Area Further Bounded by $4X + 2Y \leq 13$

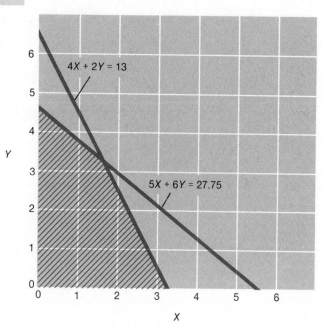

Figure 22–3   Area with all Constraints in Place

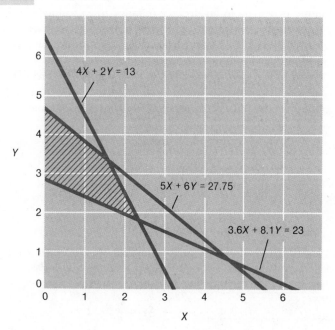

Figure 22–4   Constrained Area with Intersecting Lines

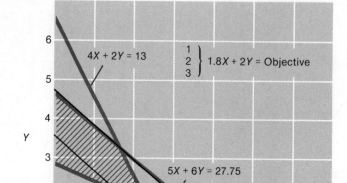

therefore, can be referred to as vertices. Furthermore, the algebraic simplex technique proceeds in an orderly manner to examine the vertices in such a way that each one does not have to be explicitly examined. The mathematics ensures that variables stay positive, that the optimum will be found, and that the procedure will then terminate.

The first step in applying the simplex procedure is to convert the inequality constraints into equalities by introducing additional variables. We can illustrate the process with our previous two-variable example. Thus,

$$5X + 6Y \leq 27.75$$

becomes

$$5X + 6Y + S_1 = 27.75.$$

Where S_1 takes on whatever slack value is necessary for given X and Y values in order that the sum will equal 27.75 exactly. Similarly,

$$4X + 2Y + S_2 = 13.$$

But, if we only included a slack variable in the third equation,

$$3.6X + 8.1Y \geq 23$$

to yield

$$3.6X + 8.1Y + S_3 = 23$$

then S_3 would have to be negative, which would violate the nonnegativity constraint. To rectify that we introduce an artificial variable with a positive coefficient and a slack variable with a negative coefficient. For example,

$$3.6X + 8.1Y + A_3 - S_3 = 23$$

Now we must incorporate these additional variables into the objective function. Since the slack variables contribute nothing to the cost or profit, their coefficients are zero. The artificial variable, on the other hand, is just that, and while the simplex procedure needs it to get started, we do not want it in the final solution. To accomplish that we simply assign it a large negative profit coefficient, often referred to as "big M" where M is a very large number. Thus the objective is to maximize

$$1.8X + 2Y + 0S_1 + 0S_2 - MA_3 + 0S_3$$

Subject to

$$
\begin{aligned}
5X + 6Y \quad + S_1 \qquad\qquad\qquad &= 27.75 \\
4X + 2Y \qquad\quad + S_2 \qquad\qquad &= 13 \\
3.6X + 8.1Y \qquad\qquad\quad + A_3 - S_3 &= 23
\end{aligned}
$$

For convenience this can be converted to matrix form by just writing down the numeric values and remembering that those in the first column apply to X, the second column to Y, and so forth.

Objective	1.8	2	0	0	$-M$	0	
Subject to	5	6	1	0	0	0	27.75
	4	2	0	1	0	0	13
	3.6	8.1	0	0	1	-1	23

For an initial solution, we can assume both X and Y are 0 and let $S_1 = 27.75$, $S_2 = 13$, $A_3 = 23$, and $S_3 = 0$. That choice for X and Y does not yield a good objective value, but the equations are satisfied and we have an initial feasible solution. In order to keep track of everything we will establish the following format (or tableau as it is sometimes called):

C_j		1.8	2	0	0	$-M$	0	
		X	Y	S_1	S_2	A_3	S_3	Solution quantities
0	S_1	5	6	1	0	0	0	27.75
0	S_2	4	2	0	1	0	0	13
$-M$	A_3	3.6	8.1	0	0	1	-1	23
Z_j		$-3.6M$	$-8.1M$	0	0	$-M$	M	$-23M$
$C_j - Z_j$		$1.8 + 3.6M$	$2 + 8.1M$	0	0	0	$-M$	

The C_j row (j is the column number) at the top contains the coefficients of the objective function; the C_j column at the left contains the objective coefficients of the variables in the solution (whose names appear in the second column). The values in the Z_j row are the sum of the products of the C_j column of coefficients with the jth column of coefficients in the body of the table; e.g., $Z_1 = 0 \times 5 + 0 \times 4 + 3.6(-M) = -3.6M$. The $C_j - Z_j$ row is used to determine which variable to next bring into the solution in order to get the greatest improvement in the objective function. To do this, we look for the largest positive value $(2 + 8.1M)$ and find it under Column Y. This is referred to as the key column. Next we see which variable must go out when Y comes in. To do this we compute the ratio of the solution quantities (in the right-hand column) to their respective coefficients in the key column and identify the smallest of these which is nonnegative. In our case the ratios are: $27.75 \div 6 = 4.625$, $13 \div 2 = 6.5$, and $23 \div 8.1 = 2.83$. The smallest of these is the last one, so Row 3 is the key row. This means that we are going to bring into our solution Y in place of A_3. While the basic process is very similar to the usual Gaussian elimination procedure normally used in solving simultaneous equations, it is convenient here to compute the new table of coefficients with the following formula:

$$\text{New value} = \text{Old value} - \frac{\begin{array}{c}\text{Corresponding value} \\ \text{in key row}\end{array} \times \begin{array}{c}\text{Corresponding value} \\ \text{in key column}\end{array}}{\text{Key number}}$$

where the key number is the number at the intersection of the key row and key column (8.1 in our example). Thus, the new value in the X column, first row (the one with S_1 in it) is computed as

$$\text{New value} = 5 - \frac{3.6 \times 6}{8.1} = 2.333.$$

The new tableau is thus computed as follows:

C_j		1.8	2	0	0	-M	0	
		X	Y	S_1	S_2	A_3	S_3	Solution quantities
0	S_1	2.333	0	1	0	-.741	.741	10.713
0	S_2	3.111	0	0	1	-.247	.247	7.321
2	Y	.444	1	0	0	.123	-.123	2.840
Z_j		.888	2	0	0	.246	-.246	5.680
$C_j - Z_j$		.912	0	0	0	-.246 - M	.246	

Repeating this procedure, we find the largest value is .912 in the column headed by X and the key row is the S_2 one with a ratio of $7.321 \div 3.111$. The new matrix is tabulated, then, as follows:

C_j		1.8	2.0	0	0	-M	0	
		X	Y	S_1	S_2	A_3	S_3	Solution quantities
0	S_1	0	0	1	-.750	-.556	.556	5.222
1.8	X	1	0	0	.321	-.079	.079	2.353
2	Y	0	1	0	-.143	.159	-.159	1.794
Z_j		1.8	2	0	.292	.176	-.176	7.823
$C_j - Z_j$		0	0	0	-.292	-.176 - M	.176	

Repeating once again, the largest $C_j - Z_j$ is .176 under the column headed S_3, and the smallest ratio is $5.222 \div .556$ for the row labeled S_1. The next matrix is thus:

C_j		1.8	2.0	0	0	-M	0	
		X	Y	S_1	S_2	A_3	S_3	Solution quantities
0	S_3	0	0	1.800	-1.350	-1.00	1	9.400
1.8	X	1	0	-1.43	.429	0	0	1.607
2	Y	0	1	.286	-.357	0	0	3.286
Z_j		1.8	2	.314	.057	0	0	9.465
$C_j - Z_j$		0	0	-.314	-.057	-M	0	

Examination of this $C_j - Z_j$ row shows that none of the values is positive and, therefore, no further improvement in the objective function can be made. The optimal solution values are therefore $X = 1.607$ and $Y = 3.286$, which yield the optimal objective function value of 9.465. This is, of course, the same solution we found earlier by graphical means. The advantage of the algebraic simplex technique is that a great deal more information can be obtained from this final matrix, and we are not limited to just two (or three) variables as we are for graphical presentations.

While extensive development of postoptimality or sensitivity analysis is beyond the scope of this text, an indication of some of the additional insights that can be gained from this technique is seen by looking at the meaning of the $C_j - Z_j$ row values. These are the so-called shadow costs (or shadow prices) and give the marginal change that would occur in the objective function for each unit of a variable that would enter the solution. For example, looking at the second tableau (see page 737), we observed a shadow cost of .912 for variable X. This means that the objective function will increase by .912 for each unit of X we bring into the solution. Because of the constraints we could only bring in $7.321 \div 3.111$ units, and hence the objective function increased by .912 times 2.353, or 2.146. This is confirmed as $7.823 - 5.680$, the difference between the objective function values for the successive solutions (slight difference in last digit is due to rounding). Similar computations allow one to state the range of values for each constraint under which the solution will not change or to predict the sensitivity of the solution to possible changes in the cost or price coefficients.

Obviously the amount of computation for this procedure is quite large; hence, computer programs have been developed to minimize the computational burden. Because of the availability of these programs, the difficulty in applying linear programming is not in solving such problems, it is in formulating—that is, stating—the problems in linear equations and in subsequently interpreting the results. The following section describes several such formulations.

EXAMPLE FORMULATIONS OF PRACTICAL PROBLEMS

As pointed out earlier, the basic practicality of LP is in its ability to model complex real-world situations. Problems, therefore, in operations management can be confronted with greater confidence by the decision maker using LP. The constant competitive conditions prevailing in business, industry, and government necessitate the use of tools that help in the decision-making process. Many have found LP to be such a tool.

The Linear Programming Aggregate Planning Problem

The first example of the use of linear programming is found in the area of aggregate planning. The problem is to schedule varying levels of production over some planning horizon so as to minimize costs. Simple to very complex formulations of the problem have been developed. The following will illustrate a possible formulation of this situation.

D_i = Predicted demand in Period i

i = 1, 2, or 3 (For a 3-period time horizon)

P_i = Scheduled regular time production output in Period i

P_i^* = Maximum regular time production output that can be scheduled in Period i

O_i = Overtime output scheduled in Period i

O_i^* = Maximum overtime output that can be scheduled in Period i

r = Regular time cost per unit

s = Overtime cost per unit

c = Inventory carrying charge per unit per period

h_i = Cost of increasing production by one unit of output (hiring cost)

f_i = Cost of reducing production by one unit of output (firing cost)

I_i = Increase in production level in Period i

R_i = Reduction in production level in Period i

For each time period:

$$P_i \leq P_i^*, \text{ and}$$

$$O_i \leq O_i^*$$

The inventory constraints are as follows:

$$P_1 + O_1 \geq D_1$$

This assumes that the initial inventory is 0. The inventory at the end of Period 1 will be:

$$P_1 + O_1 - D_1$$

and so for Period 2 demand:

$$P_1 + O_1 - D_1 + P_2 + O_2 \geq D_2$$

Rearranging terms we next obtain:

$$P_1 + P_2 + O_1 + O_2 \geq D_1 + D_2, \text{ or}$$

$$\sum_{k=1}^{2} P_i + \sum_{i=1}^{2} O_i \geq \sum_{i=1}^{2} D_1$$

This can be extended easily by analogy to Period 3 as:

$$\sum_{i=1}^{3} P_i + \sum_{i=1}^{3} O_i \geq \sum_{i=1}^{3} D_i$$

Next we examine the hiring and firing constraints. These, respectively, are simply:

$$I_i \geq P_i - P_{i-1}, \text{ and}$$

$$R_i \geq P_{i-1} - P_i$$

or by rearranging terms we have the following:

$$I_i - P_i + P_{i-1} \geq 0, \text{ and}$$

$$R_i + P_i - P_{i-1} \geq 0$$

and, specifically for Period 1,

$$I_1 - P_1 \geq -P_0, \text{ and } R_1 + P_1 \geq P_0$$

So much for the constraints. Our objective is to minimize costs—costs of production, costs due to work force level changes, and inventory carrying costs. For the first period,

$$(rP_1 + sO_1) + (bI_1 + fR_1) + c(P_1 + O_1 - D_1)$$

In the second period there are similar production and change costs, and the inventory costs are

$$c(P_1 + O_1 - D_1 + P_2 + O_2 - D_2)$$

The third period is a simple extension of these. The total cost can then be summarized as

$$r\sum_{i=1}^{3} P_i + s\sum_{i=1}^{3} O_i + b\sum_{i=1}^{3} I_i + f\sum_{i=1}^{3} R_i + c\sum_{i=1}^{3} \sum_{i=1}^{i} (P_j + O_j - D_j)$$

As an example consider the following case:

Month	D_i	P_i^*	O_i^*
1	3,400	3,200	900
2	4,500	3,200	900
3	3,750	3,000	700

$r = \$17$ per unit $f = \$12$ per unit
$s = \$25$ per unit $c = \$4$ per unit
$b = \$30$ per unit $P_0 = 3,000$

The constraint equations are thus:

$$P_1 \leq 3,200$$

$$P_2 \leq 3,200$$

$$P_3 \leq 3,000$$

$$O_1 \leq 900$$

$$O_2 \leq 900$$

$$O_3 \leq 700$$

$$P_1 + O_1 \geq 3,400$$

$$P_1 + P_2 + O_1 + O_2 \geq 7,900$$

$$P_1 + P_2 + P_3 + O_1 + O_2 + O_3 \geq 11,650$$

$$I_1 - P_1 \geq -3,000, \text{ or } P_1 - I_1 \leq 3,000$$

$$I_2 - P_2 + P_1 \geq 0$$

$$I_3 - P_3 + P_2 \geq 0$$

$$R_1 + P_1 \geq 3,000$$

$$R_2 + P_2 - P_1 \geq 0$$

$$R_3 - P_3 - P_2 \geq 0$$

The objective function is

$$17 \sum_{i=1}^{3} P_i + 25 \sum_{i=1}^{3} O_i + 30 \sum_{i=1}^{3} I_i + 12 \sum_{i=1}^{3} R_i + 4 \sum_{i=1}^{3} \sum_{i=1}^{i} \left(P_j + O_j - D_j \right)$$

The solution, obtained with a standard LP computer program, is

Month	P_i	O_i	I_i	R_i
1	3,075	900	75	0
2	3,075	900	0	0
3	3,000	700	0	75

Examination of the solution shows that not all regular time capacity is used in the first two periods, and yet overtime is used fully. At first glance this may seem wrong, but not when the cost of hiring is recognized. It is common for companies to resort to overtime or subcontracting when hiring costs are substantial.

This formulation of the aggregate planning problem is not very complex relatively. Other concepts such as subcontracting, underutilization of the work force (without firing, that is, insufficient utilization), and back orders or shortages might be included (Shore 1973).

The Feed Mix Problem

Another classic linear programming problem is typified by the feed mix problem. (It could also arise in determining the optimal ingredients in grass seed manufacture, cereal making, or sausage formulation.)

Suppose the Super Chicken Production Company can purchase and mix one or more of three different grains, each containing different amounts of four nutritional elements. The production manager specifies that any feed mix for the chickens must meet certain minimal nutritional requirements and at the same time be as low in cost as possible. Grains can be bought and mixed on a weekly basis at known prices to meet known total nutritional requirements during that week.

The following table summarizes the production manager's requirements and options.

Nutritional Ingredient	Contribution/Unit Weight			Minimum Total Requirements
	Grain 1	Grain 2	Grain 3	
A	1	0	1	1,200
B	3	2	.5	4,000
C	5	7	9	5,500
D	0	3	4	750
Cost/Unit Weight	$30	$37	$45	

Use the following symbols:

$$X_1 = \text{Amount of Grain 1 to include in mix}$$

$$X_2 = \text{Amount of Grain 2 to include in mix}$$

$$X_3 = \text{Amount of Grain 3 to include in mix}$$

The requirements are as follows:

$$\text{For Nutritional Ingredient A: } X_1 + X_3 \geq 1,200$$

$$\text{For Nutritional Ingredient B: } 3X_1 + 2X_2 + .5X_3 \geq 4,000$$

$$\text{For Nutritional Ingredient C: } 5X_1 + 7X_2 + 9X_3 \geq 5,500$$

$$\text{For Nutritional Ingredient D: } 3X_2 + 4X_3 \geq \quad 750$$

These must be satisfied while minimizing

$$30X_1 + 37X_2 + 45X_3$$

The solution to this problem is to use 1,180.64 units of Grain 1; 224.19 units of Grain 2; and 19.36 units of Grain 3, at a total cost of $44,385.48 for the entire feed mix.

The Fluid Blending Problem

A variation on this problem is the fluid blending problem. This problem was one of the first ever formulated as a linear programming problem, and variations of it are in wide use today in refineries, foundries, and chemical plants. The problem is similar to the feed mix problem; however, a set of output blends are to be derived from a set of inputs. Let

$$X_{ij} = \text{Number of gallons of Input } i \text{ to be used in Output Blend } j$$

Assuming two inputs are to be blended into three outputs, the first constraints are

$$X_{11} + X_{12} + X_{13} \leq S_1 \text{ (the available supply of Input 1), and}$$

$$X_{21} + X_{22} + X_{23} \leq S_2$$

The second set of constraints relates to the demand (D_j) for each output and is as follows:

$$X_{11} + X_{21} \geq D_1$$

$$X_{12} + X_{22} \geq D_2$$

$$X_{13} + X_{23} \geq D_3$$

Suppose further that each Input Chemical i contains a critical constituent (a), the proportion of which in each input is a_i. A constraint is that Output 1 must have at least a fraction of r_{a1} of that constituent. These proportions can be related as

$$\frac{a_1 X_{11} + a_2 X_{21}}{X_{11} + X_{21}} \geq r_{a1}$$

This equation can be rewritten as

$$a_1 X_{11} + a_2 X_{21} \geq r_a X_{11} + r_a X_{21}$$

Combining terms to get a simple linear equation we have

$$(a_1 - r_{a1})X_{11} + (a_2 - r_{a1})X_{21} \geq 0.$$

Similarly, Output 2 must have at least a proportion r_{a2} of constituent a. The corresponding equation is formulated as follows:

$$\frac{a_1 X_{12} + a_2 X_{22}}{X_{12} + X_{22}} \geq r_{a2}, \text{ or}$$

$$(a_1 - r_{a2})X_{12} + (a_2 - r_{a2})X_{22} \geq 0.$$

For Output 3 we have the following:

$$(a_1 - r_{a3})X_{13} + (a_2 - r_{a3})X_{23} \geq 0.$$

A second critical constituent (b) might be constrained to be no more than proportions r_{b1}, r_{b2}, and r_{b3} in their respective outputs. This results in similar equations, which are given next.

$$\frac{b_1 X_{11} + b_2 X_{21}}{X_{11} + X_{21}} \leq r_{b1}, \text{ or}$$

$$(b_1 - r_{b1})X_{11} + (b_2 - r_{b1})X_{21} \leq 0$$

For the other two products,

$$(b_1 - r_{b2})X_{12} + (b_2 - r_{b2})X_{22} \leq 0$$

$$(b_1 - r_{b3})X_{13} + (b_2 - r_{b2})X_{13} \leq 0$$

Assuming that Output 1 sells for $\$O_1$, per gallon, Output 2 for $\$O_2$ per gallon, and Output 3 for $\$O_3$ per gallon, and that Inputs 1 and 2 cost $\$I_1$, and $\$I_2$, respectively, the objective is to maximize profits; namely,

$$(O_1 - I_1)X_{11} + (O_1 - I_2)X_{21} + (O_2 - I_1)X_{12} + (O_2 - I_2)X_{22}$$

$$+ (O_3 - I_1)X_{13} + (O_3 - I_2)X_{23}$$

As an example, suppose we have available 12,000 gallons of Input 1 and 8,000 of Input 2. Fluid 1 is 20 percent phosphorous, and Fluid 2 is 15 percent phosphorous. Fluid 1 is also 75 percent inert ingredients, and Fluid 2 is 80 percent inert ingredients. We wish to make 5,000 gallons of each of three outputs. The first is to be at least 17 percent phosphorous and not more than 77 percent inert ingredients. For the second, the figures are 18 percent and 76 percent, and for the third the figures are 19 percent and 78 percent. Output 1 sells for $20 per gallon, Output 2 for $17 per gallon, and Output 3 for $22 per gallon. Inputs 1 and 2 cost $12 and $15 per gallon, respectively.

The set of equations would be as follows:

$$X_{11} + X_{12} + X_{13} \leq 12,000$$

$$X_{21} + X_{22} + X_{23} \leq 18,000$$

$$X_{11} + X_{21} \geq 5,000$$

$$X_{12} + X_{22} \geq 5,000$$

$$X_{13} + X_{23} \geq 5,000$$

$$.03X_{11} - .02X_{21} \geq 0$$

$$.02X_{12} - .03X_{22} \geq 0$$

$$.01X_{13} - .04X_{23} \geq 0$$

$$-.02X_{11} - .03X_{21} \leq 0$$

$$-.01X_{12} + .04X_{22} \leq 0$$

$$-.03X_{13} + .02X_{23} \leq 0$$

The objective is to maximize

$$8X_{11} + 5X_{12} + 10X_{13} + 5X_{21} + 2X_{22} + 7X_{23}$$

The optimal solution uses all of Fluid 1 ($X_{11} = 3,000$, $X_{12} = 4,000$, and $X_{13} = 5,000$) and 5,250 gallons of Fluid 2 ($X_{21} = 2,000$, $X_{22} = 1,000$, and $X_{23} = 1,250$) and achieves a profit of \$114,750. Note that only Output 3 is produced above its minimum requirement of 5,000 gallons.

The Project Duration Reduction Problem

In Chapter 15 the problem of reducing project duration was introduced and examined. As was described, the analysis and determination of which activities to crash and by how much is quite complicated. It is difficult to enumerate all the possibilities; the number of them is quite large. If we assume, as we did in the example in Chapter 15, pages 529–532, that the cost slope is linear between normal and crash times then this problem can be formulated as a linear programming problem.

Consider Figure 22–5, a revision of Figure 15–11. The i and j refer to event numbers, and C_{ij} would thus be the cost of the activity that lies between Event i and j. The t_{ij} are the activity times. C_{ij}^{c} is the crash cost, t_{ij}^{c} is the crash time, C_{ij}^{n} is the normal cost, and t_{ij}^{n} is the normal time.

The slope (b_{ij}) of the cost tradeoff line is

$$b_{ij} = \frac{C_{ij}^{c} - C_{ij}^{n}}{t_{ij}^{n} - t_{ij}^{c}}$$

and hence the cost (C_{ij}) is as follows:

$$C_{ij} = a_{ij} - b_{ij}t_{ij}$$

The objective function is to minimize the sum of the C_{ij}'s within the constraints of not reducing the t_{ij}'s below their minimums (crash times) while remaining within the precedence relationships of the activities. This can be expressed as follows:

$$\text{minimize} \sum_{ij} C_{ij} = \text{minimize} \sum_{ij} (a_{ij} - b_{ij}t_{ij}), \text{ or}$$

$$\text{minimize} \sum_{ij} -b_{ij}t_{ij}, \text{ or}$$

$$\text{maximize} \sum_{ij} b_{ij}t_{ij}$$

Figure 22–5 Activity Cost Versus Activity Duration

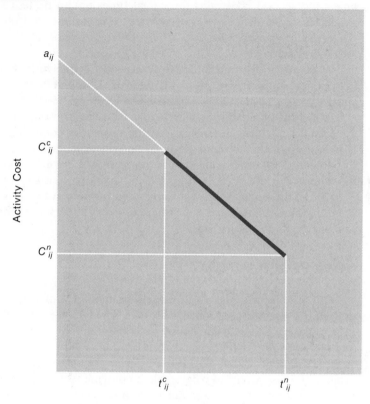

subject to:

1. $\quad\quad\quad\quad t_{ij} \le t_{ij}^{n}$
2. $\quad\quad\quad\quad t_{ij} \ge t_{ij}^{c}$
3. $\quad x_i + t_{ij} - x_j \le 0$
4. $\quad\quad\quad x_e - x_1 \le T$

where:

x_i = Time of occurrence of Event i

x_e = Ending event and $T_c < T < T_n$

T_c = Total time if all activities are crashed and T_n is the total normal time

The first equation constrains the actual times not to exceed the normal times; the second constrains the actual times not to be less than the crash times. The third defines the precedence relationships, and the fourth equation sets the elapsed time goal. There is one equation of Types 1, 2, and 3 for each activity.

When the problem in Table 15–5, page 530, is thus formulated and solved, the optimal solution is to crash Activities I, J, K, and N to 2.17, 3.27, 3.27, and 2.0 weeks, respectively, at a cost of $1,409.91.

If, instead of aiming for a particular date to finish on, a bonus is offered for each week ahead of normal that the project is completed, then a slight modification of the previous formulation will yield an optimum solution. To the objective function add $-Bx_e$, (where B is the weekly bonus, and x_e is the time of the last event). Also, replace Equation 4 with $x_1 = 0$. In this same example, if the bonus is $500 a week, then it only pays to crash to Week 28, since the incremental cost of crashing one more week exceeds $500. (Only Activities I, K, and N are crashed.)

GOAL PROGRAMMING

One of the criticisms of linear programming is that there is room for only one objective function; hence, the several objectives that a decision maker may have need to be expressible in a common measure (like dollars). Another difficulty arises because the constraints may not actually be as rigid as the solution procedure suggests. For example, a firm may wish to maximize profit, but it also wants to have stable employment, a diversified product line, and minimal pollution. These goals are not easily nor naturally transformed into dollar measures, nor are they easily set as constraints while the profit equation is maximized.

An alternative linear equation approach to this type of problem is goal programming (GP). To use this procedure, it is necessary to consider both the structural, or technological constraints (raw material and machine-hour availability, for example), and objectives. For each constraint, possible deviations are stated, and for each objective, a target level is set. The objective is to minimize stated constraint deviations and variations from the target levels. The GP procedure provides a methodology for minimizing these deviations and for dealing with them in the rank order specified while not violating the technological constraints.

To see how this works, reconsider the LP problem stated earlier as

$$5X + 6Y \leq 27.75$$

$$4X + 2Y \leq 13$$

$$3.6X + 8.1Y \geq 23$$

with the objective of maximizing

$$1.8X + 2Y$$

Deviations below the goal are symbolized by

$$d_n^-$$

and those above by

$$d_n^+$$

Assume that the problem has the same constraints, but our goals are, first, to make just as much X and Y and, second, to maximize profit. The constraints are restated as follows:

$$5X + 6Y + d_1^- = 27.75$$

$$4X + 2Y + d_2^- = 13$$

$$3.6X + 8.1Y - d_3^+ = 23$$

Note how these were constructed. Our less-than constraints allow a negative deviation (akin to the slack in an ordinary LP problem), and the greater-than constraint allows the subtraction of a positive deviation (a surplus). Our profit goal is added by setting some reasonably large value for the profit and allowing a negative deviation, such as the following:

$$1.8X + 2Y + d_4^- = 20$$

Now the equal production goal is constructed by allowing the difference between X and Y to be either positive or negative.

$$X - Y + d_5^- - d_5^+ = 0$$

Our objectives can then be stated as:

Priority 1: minimize $d_5^- + d_5^+$, and

Priority 2: minimize d_4^-

Before considering variations on this problem formulation, the mechanics of the solution procedure should be examined. Begin by setting up a matrix similar to our original LP matrix (see Figure 22–6). There are several differ-

Figure 22–6　Initial Goal Programming Matrix

$P=$		0	0	0	0	0	P_0	P_2	P_1	P_1	
	Basis	X	Y	d_1^-	d_2^-	d_3^+	A_3	d_4^-	d_5^-	d_5^+	RHS
0	d_1^-	5	6	1							27.75
0	d_2^-	4	2		1						13.0
P_0	A_3	3.6	8.1			−1	1				23.0　←
P_2	d_4^-	1.8	2					1			20.0
P_1	d_5^-	1	−1						1	−1	0.0
$C_j - Z_j$　P_2		−1.8	−2								−20.0
P_1		−1	1							2	0.0
P_0		−3.6	−8.1								−23.0

ences between Figure 22–6 and the matrix in the simplex solution. Across the top, in place of the costs (C_j's) are the priority levels (P_n's). Note particularly that for the inequality $3.6X + 8.1Y \geq 23$, on page 748, where an artificial variable is required in order to create a nonnegative basis (i.e., in a greater-than constraint), a priority of P_0 is established instead of the big M used in the LP simplex calculation. Below the matrix, in place of a single $C_j - Z_j$ row there are now several rows, one for each priority level and, by convention, they are ordered downward in increasing levels of importance. The entries are computed in a manner similar to the LP simplex. For the column head X:

$$C_j - Z_j = 0 - (5 \times 0 + 4 \times 0 + 3.6 \times P_0 + 1.8 \times P_2 + 1 \times P_1) = -3.6P_0 - 1.8P_2 - P_1$$

These coefficients are then entered in their respective rows of the $C_j - Z_j$ priority levels.

　　Selecting a variable to enter the solution proceeds as in the LP simplex, but with a slight modification. Start with the highest priority and select the most negative element. Continue working with that level until all its entries are zero or positive and then move to the next lower level and examine its entries. Select the most negative in that level, so long as no positive, nonzero $C_j - Z_j$ exists in that column for a priority level already examined. Continue in this stepwise manner through all levels of priority.

　　The criterion for which variable leaves the solution is the same as in the LP simplex—that is, divide the RHS column entries by their respective positive

Figure 22–7   First Iteration Result

		0	0	0	0	0	P_2	P_2	P_1	P_1	
		X	Y	d_1^-	d_2^-	d_3^-	A_3	d_4^-	d_5^-	d_5^+	RHS
0	d_1^-	2.333		1		.741	−.741				10.713
0	d_2^-	3.111			1	.247	−.247				7.321
0	Y	.444	1			−.123	.123				2.840
P_2	d_4^-	.911				.247	−.247	1			14.321
P_1	d_5^-	1.444				−.123	.123		1	−1	2.840 ←
$C_j - Z_j$	P_2	−.911				−.247	.247				−14.321
	P_1	−1.444				.123	−.123			2	−2.84
	P_0						1				0

coefficients in the selected entry variable column and choose the smallest. The remainder of the simplex computations are as illustrated previously.

Figure 22–7 shows the result of the first iteration. The entries in $C_j - Z_j$ for P_0 are all positive or zero so move on to the P_1 row. The most negative of these is in the column headed X, and the smallest ratio is $2.840 \div 1.444$ in the row labeled d_5^-; so X replaces d_5^-. Note that even if the $-.123$ in the column headed A_3 were the most negative, it could not have been chosen because of the plus one in the row below it.

Figure 22–8 shows the next iteration. Since all P_1 entries are zero or positive, move to P_2; and find we can improve P_2 by bringing in d_3^+ in place of d_2^- (as shown in Figure 22–9). Now the entry in the column headed d_5^- cannot be brought into the solution because to do so would reduce achievement of goal P_1. Since all other entries in Row P_2 are positive, this represents the optimal solution; that is,

$$X = Y = 2.167$$

P_2 misses being achieved by 11.767, for a net profit of $20 - 11.767$, or 8.233.

Some Considerations and Limitations

There are some considerations and limitations to GP. We still have linear equations and continuous variables. (Some research is being done on integer versions of GP.) Within any priority level the deviations must be commen-

Figure 22-8   Second Goal Programming Iteration

		X	Y	d_1^-	d_2^-	d_3^+	A_3	d_4^-	d_5^-	d_5^+	RHS
0	d_1^-			1		.940	-.940		-1.615	1.615	6.126
0	d_2^-				1	.513	-.513		-2.154	2.154	1.205
0	Y		1			-.085	.085		-.308	.308	1.966
P_2	d_4^-					.325	-.325	1	-.631	.631	12.530
0	X	1				-.085	.085		.692	-.692	1.966
$C_j - Z_j$	P_2					-.325	.325		.631	-.631	-12.53
	P_1								1	1	0
	P_0						1				0

surable—that is, dollars or pounds or hours—but different levels may be in different dimensions. It is possible to give different weights to the various deviations within a level—that is, we could weight a negative deviation with a factor of two and a positive deviation with a one if we were more concerned

Figure 22-9   Final Solutions Matrix

		X	Y	d_1^-	d_2^-	d_3^+	A_3	d_4^-	d_5^-	d_5^+	RHS
0	d_1^-			1	-1.833				2.333	2.333	3.917
0	d_3^+				1.950	1	-1		-4.200	4.200	2.350
0	Y		1		-.167				-.667	.667	2.167
P_2	d_4^-				-.633			1	.733	-.733	11.767
0	X	1			.167				.333	-.333	2.167
$C_j - Z_j$	P_2				.633				-.733	.733	-11.767
	P_1								1	1	0
	P_0					1					

with the former. Postoptimality analysis is more complicated for GP than for LP.

Because GP opens up a broader way of looking at problems, it lends itself to finding solutions to sets of problems in a what-if mode. Interchanging the order of goals 1 and 2 in this previous example results in a quite different solution—namely, the same solution as the plain LP formulation achieved. In more complex problems involving more goals it is likely that the decision maker will want to explore a variety of goal structures and to consider the sensitivity of the solutions to any structural changes as well.

A Goal Programming Formulation of a Manufacturing Mix Problem

A standard linear programming illustration is the product mix problem, which is illustrated as follows. Among the many products a plant has, there are two that tend to cause a bottleneck in their conflicting use of manufacturing resources. They are motors and compressors. The motors require 2.25 hours of machining, while the compressors require 1.5 hours each. The finishing operation requires 1.5 hours for each motor and 3 hours for each compressor. Storage is 1.5 cubic meters for each. Machining is limited to 13,500 hours, finishing is limited to 18,750 hours, and storage is confined to 11,250 cubic meters. The profit contribution of motors is $30 each; for compressors it is $50 each.

To determine how many motors and compressors to make in order to maximize profit, let X_M be the production quantity of motors and X_C be the same for compressors. The problem can be formulated as follows:

$$\text{Maximize } 30X_M + 50X_C$$
$$\text{Subject to } 2.25X_M + 1.5X_C \le 13,500$$

$$1.5X_M + 3\ \ X_C \le 18,750$$

$$1.5X_M + 1.5X_C \le 11,250$$

The calculation is straightforward and results in producing 2,500 motors and 5,000 compressors.

Suppose, however, we have some additional objectives; for example, to maximize sales, to limit in-process inventory, to allow limited overtime, or to restrict cash tied up in receivables. These can be incorporated if the preceding problem is changed to allow a GP approach.

First, assume that we want to sell at least 3,000 of each product. In-process inventory of $200 is required for each motor, and for each compressor $375 is required. The technological constraints of the linear programming formulation can be transformed as follows:

$$2.25X_M + 1.5X_C + d_1^- - d_1^+ = 13,500$$

$$1.5X_M + 3X_C + d_2^- - d_2^+ = 18,750$$

$$1.5X_M + 1.5X_C + d_3^- - d_3^+ = 11,250$$

If the limit on in-process inventory is $2 million, then

$$200X_M + 375X_C + d_4^- - d_4^+ = 2,000,000$$

For the sales goals,

$$X_M + d_5^- = 3,000, \text{ and}$$

$$X_C + d_6^- - d_6^+ = 3,000$$

The profit goal is contained in the following:

$$30X_M + 50X_C + d_7^- - d_7^+ = 300,000$$

Next, rank the conflicting goals. A possible ordering is listed here.

Priority 1: Minimize d_4^+ Priority 3: Minimize d_7^+ .

Priority 2: Minimize $d_5^- - d_6^-$ Priority 4: Minimize $d_1^- + d_2^- + d_3^-$

In order, minimize the excess in-process inventory, make your sales goals, make your profit goal (if possible), and try not to exceed plant capacity.

The optimal solution is to make 4,375 motors and 3,000 compressors. Goals 1 and 2 are met, but profit is only $281,250, and capacity in both finishing and storage are exceeded.

If we interchange Goals 1 and 4, then the optimal solution is to make 3,000 motors and 4,750 compressors. This does not exceed plant capacity, and it does meet sales goals; however, in-process inventory goes up to $2,381,250. In compensation for this 19 percent increase in inventory there is also a 16 percent increase in profits to $327,500. Whether this is acceptable or not depends upon financial constraints, but it certainly is worth exploring.

The other linear programming problems that were formulated could also be transformed into GP problems and conflicting goals considered.

CONCLUSIONS

The techniques of mathematical programming are varied. The essence of mathematical programming is the creation of a mathematical model and rigorous manipulation of the model to secure an optimum solution to a real-world problem. Since mathematical programming is designed to deal with complex problems having many variables, the models are often complex, albeit less complex than the real world. Since the modeling process always involves extraction of the important from the complex, there is always some sort of simplification. In some problems this may involve too much simplification; however, if the appropriate technique—linear programming, stochastic, or goal programming—is chosen the process and solution should at least shed light and provide information even though the solution is not optimal in the real world.

QUESTIONS

1. Identify four assumptions of the basic linear programming model.

2. In what ways are linear programming assumptions relaxed to permit more realistic models?

3. Why is it helpful that the solution to a linear programming problem may only be found at the intersection of constraints?

4. How is the nonnegativity constraint relevant in the geographical solution? Why is it often not shown in maximization problems?

5. Given a feasible area, how does the analyst determine which corner is optimal?

6. What information is provided by the slack (surplus) variable?

7. When and why are slack variables added to constraint equations in the simplex solution technique?

8. Which constraints are normally found in the aggregate planning application of the linear programming problem?

9. Identify several different examples in which linear programming can be applied to a mixing application.

PROBLEMS

1. Peninsula Tennis Company makes two different brands of tennis racket. The organization desires to maximize profits. Their graphite racket has a profit of $27, while their aluminum racket has a profit of $22. Each week, however, there are only 500 hours available in the forming department,

250 hours in stringing, and 200 hours in packaging and shipping. It takes 3 hours, 1.5 hours, and 1 hour, respectively in these departments, to produce the graphite racket. The aluminum racket takes 1.5 hours, 2 hours, and 1 hour, respectively, in these departments. In developing a linear program to determine the best product mix,

a. Write the objective function.
b. Write the constraint for forming.
c. Write the constraint for stringing.
d. Write the constraint for packaging and shipping.
e. Solve for the optimal values using the graphical method.

2. From the following data:

$$\text{Max } 12X_1 + 18X_2$$

s.t.

$$15X_1 + 10X_2 \leq 250$$

$$8X_1 + 5X_2 \leq 100$$

$$6X_1 + 12X_2 \leq 150$$

$$X_1 + X_2 \leq 12$$

$$X_1, X_2 \geq 0$$

a. Graph the constraints.
b. Identify the feasible area for solutions.
c. Which of the above constraints border the feasible area?
d. Identify which constraints determine the optimal solution.
e. Solve for the optimal values of X_1, X_2.
f. What is the optimal profit value?

3. From the following data:

$$\text{Min } 7X_1 + 9X_2$$

s.t.

$$12X_1 + 9X_2 \leq 196$$

$$7X_1 + 12X_2 \geq 49$$

$$2X_1 + 8X_2 \geq 50$$

$$X_1, X_2 \geq 0$$

a. Graph the constraints.
b. Identify the feasible area for solutions.
c. Identify which constraints bound the feasible area.
d. Identify which constraints determine the optimal solution.
e. Solve for the optimal values of X_1, X_2.
f. What is the optimal (least-cost) value?

4. A doll manufacturer desires to maximize profits on two doll products. Doll 1 contributes $15 to profitability, and doll 2 contributes $10. Dolls must be processed by shaping, assembly, and painting, which are done by Departments A, B, and C, respectively. The departments must spend the following amounts of time on each of the two dolls and have the indicated time available:

	Doll 1	Doll 2	Total Time Available
Department A	3	0	180
Department B	0	5	200
Department C	4	6	360

a. Write the objective function and constraints.
b. Graph the constraints.
c. Identify the feasible area for solutions.
d. Identify which constraints bound the feasible area.
e. Identify which constraints determine the optimal solution.
f. Solve for the optimal values for X_1, X_2.
g. What is the optimal profit value?

5. Solve Problem 4 using a computer software program or the simplex technique.

a. Identify the optimum profit and contribution of Doll X_1, and Doll X_2.
b. What resources are not fully used? If those assets are transferable, where should they be reallocated?
c. What would be the revised total profit if all surplus resources were reallocated?

6. Product A has a profit of $3.50 per unit, Product B, a profit of $2.50 per unit. The resources required for products A and B are:

	Product	
	A	B
Wood—board feet	3	4
Pipe—linear feet	2	1
Plastic—cubic feet	5	3

Currently on hand, there are 700 board feet of wood, 1,200 linear feet of pipe, and 900 cubic feet of plastic. Determine the production that would maximize profit with available resources.

    a. Formulate the objective function and the constraints.
    b. Graph the constraints.
    c. Identify the feasible area for solutions.
    d. Determine which constraints bound the feasible area.
    e. Solve for the optimal values of X_1, X_2.
    f. What is the optimal profit value?

7. Using the following data:

$$\text{Min. } 153X_1 + 220X_2$$

s.t.

$$0.5X_1 + 0.6X_2 \leq 45$$

$$20.0X_1 + 9.0X_2 \leq 1,220$$

$$4.0X_1 + 3.0X_2 \geq 196$$

$$13.0X_1 + 19.0X_2 \geq 741$$

$$X_1, X_2 \geq 0$$

    a. Graph the constraints.
    b. Solve for the optimal values of X_1, X_2.
    c. What is the optimal (least-cost) value?

8. Three products, X, Y, and Z, require processing on machines A, B, and C. The machines have respectively 200, 400, and 500 hours available weekly. Product X requires 1 hour, 2 hours, and 4 hours on machines A, B, and C, respectively. Product Y requires 2 hours, 3 hours, and 1 hour, respectively, on machines A, B, and C; and product Z requires 5 hours, 3 hours, and 4 hours, respectively, on machines A, B, and C. Each unit of product X yields $10 profit, each unit of Y yields $12, and each unit of Z yields $5 of profit. The solution to this problem at the top of page 759 has been generated using a computer.

    a. Formulate the objective function and constraints of the problem.
    b. What is the maximum profit? How much does each product contribute to that profit?
    c. In a price war, by how much could you reduce your profits on each product individually without affecting machine utilization?
    d. Which machine has unused time and, if transferable, where would you transfer it? Why?

Variable	Variable Value	Original Coefficient	Coefficient Sensitivity
X1	114.28	10	0
X2	42.85	12	0
X3	0	5	26.72

Constraint Number	Original RHS	Slack or Surplus	Shadow Price
1	200	0	5.43
2	400	42.85	0
3	500	0	1.15

Objective function value: 1,657.15

SENSITIVITY ANALYSIS

Objective Function Coefficients			
Variable	Lower Limit	Original Coefficient	Upper Limit
X1	6.0	10	48
X2	2.5	12	20
X3	No limit	5	31.71

Right Hand Side			
Constraint Number	Lower Limit	Original Value	Upper Limit
1	125	200	230
2	357.14	400	No limit
3	100	500	800

9. The following table describes the various qualities of corn grain:

Grain Quality	Corn Grain 1	Corn Grain 2	Corn Grain 3	Total Requirements
Moisture content	7	5	2	≥ 4
Nutritional value	22	27	28	≥ 25
Percent broken kernels	10	12	6	≤ 9
Cost	$2.95	$3.13	$3.50	

a. Determine the objective function and the constraint formulas.
b. Use a computer software program or the simplex technique to solve for the mix that produces the least cost per bushel.
c. The available quantities are 8,000, 3,000, and 6,000 bushels for Grains 1, 2, and 3, respectively. If a customer wants 14,000 bushels of this mixture,

1. Are there enough bushels of the various qualities on hand for delivery?
2. How many bushels of each grain are necessary to meet this demand?
3. What is the total cost?

d. Analyze the slack and shadow price variables.

10. The Car Tool Company produces two types of wrenches that provide equal profit ($10 each) to the organization. They have been producing equal quantities of each. Manufacturing limits are as follows:

Model	Setup hours/unit	Casting hours/unit	Finishing hours/unit	Assembly hours/unit
Open end	2.5	8.25	3.0	0.5
Adjustable	0.5	8.75	1.0	1.0
Hours available	22,826	91,304	34,239	22,826

a. If they continue with their equal quantity rule, how much should they make to maximize profit?
b. If they alter their quantities to maximize profit, how many of each should they produce?
c. Because of a machine failure, casting capacity is reduced to 69,943 hours. How does this affect the solutions to a and b?

11. Profits for two products A and B are equal ($250). The following table shows the time requirements for these products in their three work centers:

	Cutting hours/unit	Sanding hours/unit	Assembly hours/unit
Product A	5.25	1.75	5.25
Product B	3.00	3.00	7.00
Hours available	48,870	23,750	61,670

In order to maintain a constant work force level, all the assembly capacity must be used exactly. At the same time, management wants to minimize overtime in cutting and sanding, maximize profits, and produce at least 9,000 units of Product A and 3,000 units of Product B.

a. If the goals are as stated here, what is the optimal solution?

b. If Goal 4 is placed above all the others, without changing their order, what is the solution?

12. For the following aggregate planning data, what should be the production each month and how much inventory will be held each period? What will be the total cost?

Month	Demand	Maximum Production	
		Regular	Overtime
1	4,275	3,700	900
2	4,760	4,000	1,000
3	5,545	4,500	1,100
4	4,438	4,000	1,000

$r = \$14$ per unit $f = \$15$ per unit
$s = \$21$ per unit $c = \$3$ per unit
$h = \$35$ per unit $P_0 = 3,500$

13. Each day, a gasoline dealer mixes products from three refineries to create a regular and premium unleaded fuel. Refineries 1, 2, and 3 have 18,000, 16,000, and 12,000 barrels of fuel available, respectively, with 88, 90, and 94 octane. The distributor requires 22,000 barrels of regular and 14,000 barrels of premium fuel. Regular fuel has a minimum octane level of 89, premium a minimum of 92 octane. Refinery 1, 2, and 3 inputs cost $18, $22, and $24 per barrel. Regular and premium fuels will sell for $31 and $33 per barrel through the distributor's channels.

a. Determine the objective function to maximize profit for the distributor, and the constraints.

b. Use a computer software program to find the profit maximization of the dealer.

c. Analyze the shadow and slack variables.

REFERENCES

Hillier, Frederick, and Gerald Lieberman. *Introduction to Operations Research*, 2d ed. San Francisco: Holden Day, 1974.

Lee, Sang M. *Goal Programming for Decision Analysis.* Pennsauken, N.J.: Auerbach Publishers Inc., 1972.

Plane, Donald, and Gary Kochenberger. *Operations Research for Managerial Decisions.* Homewood, Ill.: Richard D. Irwin, 1972.

Shore, Barry. *Operations Management.* New York: McGraw-Hill, 1973.

Wagner, Harvey. *Operations Research*, 2d ed. Englewood Cliffs, N.J.: Prentice-Hall, 1974.

CHAPTER 23
SIMULATION

OBJECTIVES

After completing this chapter, you should be able to

- Define simulation and differentiate between simulation and analytical models

- Describe the general procedure for conducting a simulation

- Explain the rationale for using simulation

- Set up and run a simple simulation model using a random number table

- Identify situations in which simulation would be appropriate, and describe the benefits and shortcomings of its application

OUTLINE

INTRODUCTION

Simulation is the process of designing a model of a decision situation and experimenting with the model to evaluate alternative decisions. In the broadest sense, the various mathematical, graphical, and tabular models discussed throughout this text are all simulation models in that they are representations of reality used to evaluate possible decisions. The term, however, is usually applied more narrowly to stochastic or Monte Carlo simulation. Stochastic simulation is different from analytical modeling approaches, such as economic order quantity (EOQ) and mathematical programming models, in that it does not solve for an optimal solution. Instead it runs a mathematical or logical model of the situation and determines by trial and error which values of the decision variables result in satisfactory, if not the best, operating results.

In any situation there are certain variables that management controls. Order quantity, safety stock, the number of operators, the schedule, and order priority rules are examples of these variables. Stochastic simulation, based on the laws of probability, enables management to evaluate the possible values, and combinations of values, of these variables in terms of the results achieved. A simulation model enables management to answer what-if questions such as the following:

1. If a maintenance worker is added, will the savings due to decreased machine downtime be greater than the additional labor costs?
2. What effect will a 10 percent increase in safety stock have on stock-outs?
3. What effect will a planned 20 percent reduction in queue length have on work in process and idle time?

The exact values of some events such as demand, lead time, and machine failure in any period cannot be predicted with certainty, but the probability distribution of each can be known. In many situations the sequence of events may not be predictable. Periods of high demand, for example, may be intermingled with periods of low demand. Stochastic simulation is especially beneficial when events are nondeterministic but probabilistic or when the exact sequence of events cannot be predicted.

PROCEDURE AND RATIONALE

The procedure for creating a simulation is based upon building a logical representation of a system, recognizing the input variables and their statistical variations, exercising the model to make it behave like the real world it represents, and observing the consequences. The specific steps are as follows:

1. Describe the decision to be studied and its objective (for example, determining the level of safety stock that minimizes the sum of stock-out and inventory holding costs under stochastic demand conditions).
2. Construct a model that replicates reality and permits measurement of the objective function under different conditions.

3. Determine the frequency distribution of the uncontrollable events. Determination of more than one frequency distribution is necessary if more than one event is probabilistic.
4. Convert the frequency distribution(s) to cumulative probability distribution(s). The data may be fit to a theoretical distribution (e.g., Poisson) or to an anticipated actual distribution.
5. Establish the initial conditions.
6. Generate (obtain) sets of random numbers, one set for each event to be simulated.
7. For each random number, determine the corresponding value of the event (input) of concern.
8. Insert these values in the model measuring the decision effectiveness and compute the results.
9. Repeat Steps 5, 6, and 7 many times, at least 100, for each of the alternatives. Determination of the exact number of repetitions required to achieve a statistical confidence in the results of the simulation is beyond the scope of this book.
10. Apply controls. Compare the parameters (mean and variance) of the simulated events to the actual distribution parameters.
11. Select the particular course of action that achieves the best results on the basis of the preselected criteria and that is within control limits.
12. Repeat Steps 6 through 11 using a new set of random numbers and compare results.
13. Select the course of action that consistently produces the best results.

Two results of the procedure constitute its rationale: (1) the event values occur with the same relative frequency in the simulation as they do in reality and (2) the numerous repetitions of the procedure include the many possible sequential combinations and yield their measure of effectiveness. The probability of occurrence of each sequence is the same as it is in reality. For example, if in the real world there is a 5 percent probability that one machine will fail during an eight-hour period, simulated history will have one failure per eight-hour day approximately 5 percent of the time. If, in addition, an eight-hour period with only one failure can be followed by an eight-hour period with either a small number of failures, a relatively large number of failures, or an average number of failures, then simulation will include each possible sequential pattern in the proportion that it occurs in the real world. Analytical solution approaches cannot adequately represent this combination of probabilistic events and a wide variety of possible sequential combinations with widely varying effects on outcomes.

BUILDING A SIMULATION MODEL

Each situation must be studied, and a model must be developed for it. When a decision criterion, such as minimizing total costs or maximizing rate of return, has been selected, the designer of the simulation experiment must determine which variables influence the result and how they influence it. This requires that the designer possess adequate knowledge of and an insight into the real-world situation. Without this knowledge and insight it is unlikely that the model will adequately represent the real world. For example, the designer must decide whether to include the possibility of machine failure.

After the model has been developed, it must be validated. The model validation process begins with the usual questions: Does the model appear accurate? Does it provide reasonable answers? Does it have face validity? Do others familiar with the real-world situation agree that the model is representative and the results reasonable? If the model is run using historical data and the results are compared with actual results, does actual receipt of a specific number of orders and hours per order result in the same costs predicted by the model?

Simulation Example Using a Random Number Table

Consider the case of an organization, or a department within an organization, that receives a different number of orders each day, and those orders vary in the time required for processing. The company is interested in determining how many machines it should have to minimize the combined cost of machine idle time and order-waiting time. The company knows the cost of machine idle time, the cost of order waiting time, and the probability distributions of the number of orders each day and of the number of hours required to process an order. The number of machines that will result in minimum total variable costs cannot be determined analytically because such approaches do not consider the sequential pattern of the hours required for processing. A stochastic simulation includes these sequential patterns.

This problem can be couched in a maintenance setting. Machine failure and repair time can be the probabilistic events rather than orders received and the time required for processing. Furthermore, our example can be expanded to include priority of processing rules such as first-come, first-served; a ratio of delivery time to lead time; and order profit. A first-come, first-served priority rule is used to keep the example simple.

The minimization of total variable costs—idle machine cost plus order-waiting cost—is the objective function. The company has calculated these costs as $3.00 per hour for idle machine time and $5.00 per hour for back orders. Therefore, the measure of effectiveness is as follows:

$$\text{Total variable costs} = (\$3 \times \text{idle machine hours}) + (\$5 \times \text{hours for back orders each day})$$

(Note: The model oversimplifies reality for purposes of illustration. The cost figures are hypothetical.) The determination of such costs is a crucial step in any model-building procedure. The number of machines that minimizes these costs is the optimal number of machines (Steps 1 and 2).

The next step is to describe the frequency distribution of the probabilistic events. There are two such events: (1) the number of orders per day and (2) the number of machine hours required per order; therefore, two frequency distributions are required. The frequency distributions for these inputs, based on historical data, and their cumulative probability distributions are shown in Figure 23–1 (Steps 3 and 4).

Figure 23–1   Cumulative Probability Distributions

A. Number of Orders

No. of Orders	Prob.	Cum. Prob.
0	.10	.10
1	.15	.25
2	.25	.50
3	.30	.80
4	.15	.95
5	.05	1.00

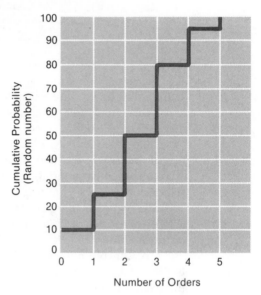

B. Number of Hours per Order

Hours/ Order	Prob.	Cum. Prob.
5	.05	.05
10	.05	.10
15	.10	.20
20	.10	.30
25	.20	.50
30	.25	.75
35	.15	.90
40	.10	1.00

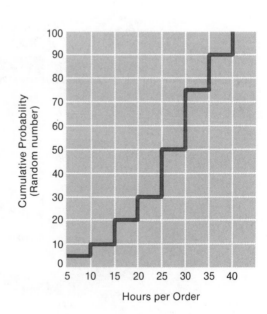

Table 23–1 Determination of the Number of Orders

Day	Random Number	Number of Orders
1	26	2
2	78	3
3	57	3
4	58	3
5	23	1

The initial conditions (in this case, the backlog of orders and machine status) must be set. The example has an arbitrary initial setting of no backlog and all machines idle. Considerable study is required in most situations to determine realistic initial conditions (Step 5).

Tables 23–1 and 23–2 list the random numbers that determined the number of orders per day and the number of hours per order. These numbers were obtained by going to a random number table (see Appendix Table B), selecting an arbitrary starting point and taking that number and as many consecutive two-digit numbers as are needed. Table 23–3 lists the summarized activity of the five days simulated in the one trial of this example. For the sake of brevity, only one trial of five days is made (Steps 6 and 7).

A reasonable number of machines with which to begin the experiment is the number required for the average number of order hours per day. In the example, the average number of orders per day (see Table 23–1) is 2.4 and the average hours per order is 26 (see Table 23–2); thus, the average

Table 23–2 Determination of the Number of Hours Per Order

Order Number	Random Number	Hours per Order
1	85	35
2	75	30
3	74	30
4	28	20
5	40	25
6	69	30
7	60	30
8	11	15
9	74	30
10	15	15
11	04	5
12	21	20
13	97	40
14	66	30
15	42	25

Table 23–3   Trial One—Simulated Activity

TVC = Cost of idle time (CI) + cost of waiting time (CW)
CI = $3 an hour of machine idle time
CW = $5 an hour of orders held over each day

A. Using 8 Machines—64 Hours of Available Machine Time per Day

Day	Order Hours Received	Total Order Hours to be Processed	Hours Idle	Hours Back Ordered	CI	CW
1	65	65	0	1	0	5
2	75	76	0	12	0	60
3	75	87	0	23	0	115
4	50	73	0	9	0	45
5	20	29	35	0	$105	0

$105 + 225 = $330 TVC

B. Using 9 Machines—72 Hours of Available Machine Time per Day

Day	Order Hours Received	Total Order Hours to be Processed	Hours Idle	Hours Back Ordered	CI	CW
1	65	65	7	0	21	0
2	75	75	0	3	0	15
3	75	78	0	6	0	30
4	50	56	16	0	48	0
5	20	20	52	0	156	0

$225 + $45 = $270 TVC

C. Using 10 Machines—80 Hours of Available Machine Time per Day

Similar calculations render TVC = $345

number of order hours per day is 62.4 (2.4 × 26). Eight machines, providing 64 hours of available machine time per day, is a rational starting point. Total variable costs (TVC) are determined for operating with eight, nine, and ten machines (see Table 23–3).

The TVC of operating with nine machines is less expensive than operating with eight or ten machines. Since the cost curve is smooth and well behaved, a minimum at this point indicates that the TVCs with seven and eleven machines must be higher. Therefore, it is not necessary to calculate the TVC for seven or eleven machines (Step 8).

The following is a brief explanation of how the first few days' simulation was run using eight machines. All others were performed in essentially the same manner.

1. The random numbers listed in Tables 23–1 and 23–2 were obtained from a table of random numbers. The table was entered at two different points: one to obtain the random numbers for the number of orders per day and another to obtain the random numbers for the number of hours per order.
2. To determine the number of orders per day, the first random number, 26, is compared to the cumulative probability distribution (see Figure 23–1) and found to correspond to two orders, since 26 is greater than 25 and less than 50. In the same manner 78 corresponds to three orders for the second day (50 < 78 < 80).
3. The number of hours per order are determined in the same manner using the second set of random numbers and the cumulative distribution for the hours per order (see Figure 23–1).
4. Thus, on the first day of simulation, two orders arrive requiring 35 and 30 machine hours, respectively, which is one hour more than capacity. Thus, one order hour is back ordered at a cost of $5. The backlog initial condition was set at zero (see Table 23–3).
5. Three orders arrive on the second day requiring 75 (30 + 20 + 25) machine hours. Adding these to the one-hour backorder from Day 1 brings the total processing requirement to 76 hours—12 more than capacity—for a cost of $60 (see Table 23–3).
6. The simulated inputs and costs for all other days are determined in the same manner.

Simulation Using Computers

The computer's speed and accuracy has made the application of simulation to industrial problems practical. A computer cannot construct a model of the real world, nor can it select the settings of controlled variables for the experiment. It cannot evaluate assumptions or estimate the extent the future will conform to the past unless given specific instruction how to do so. The designer still performs these vital functions. However, the computer can generate or select random numbers and perform extensive calculations very quickly. Moreover, computer software designed to facilitate simulation is readily available for a variety of applications.

As a further example of a simulation problem consider the following situation. A production process manufactures about 12 units per day—specifically, that is 12 units 80 percent of the time, 11 units 10 percent of the time, and 13 units 10 percent of the time. Orders are received according to the following distribution:

Number of Orders per Day	Frequency
5	.10
6	.15
7	.25
8	.35
9	.15

Each order can be for one or more units. The distribution of order size is as follows:

Units per Order	Frequency
1	.5
2	.3
3	.2

Some units not sold can be saved on a given day to satisfy demand the following day, but because of perishability we cannot save them a second day.

The company is considering expanding sales and wants to see what it has to do to production to handle various sales increases. The principal concern is with the service level. The new sales levels to be examined are for the following distributions:

Number of Orders per Day	Frequency
6	.10
7	.10
8	.35
9	.30
10	.15

Units per Order	Frequency
1	.2
2	.5
3	.3

The cases to be considered are (1) no increase in number of orders, but increased units per order; (2) increased orders, but no increase in size of orders; and (3) increase in both orders and size of orders. To begin, production will be left as is, or it will be increased by two units per day.

Using a computer, first simulate the current situation to see whether the simulated results resemble current practice. (This test of the accuracy or validity of the simulation model is sometimes termed face validity.) After all, if we cannot simulate the current situation, we cannot have any confidence in our simulation of predicted situations.

Table 23–4 summarizes some of the simulation runs. Note that service drops from 94 percent to 83 percent with no change in production but an increase in orders. To compensate for the increased orders, production must be raised by two units each day to reach a satisfactory 97 percent service level. But with increased units per order as well, production must be increased further to 17 units each day, on average, in order to have a 95 percent service level.

Sensitivity Analysis

After the initial solution of the problem is obtained, a sensitivity analysis is advisable. Such analysis evaluates the impact of changes in the parameters. For instance, would the optimum number of machines in the first example still be nine if the cost of idle time were $3.50 instead of $3.00, or if the cost of backordering were $5.25 instead of $5.00, or if processing time were reduced by 10 percent across the board because of increased operating efficiencies, or if the number of orders turned out to be 15 percent higher than anticipated? This analysis is performed by running the simulation with one or more of these factors changed to the alternate possibility and by calculating the resulting costs.

Such an analysis enables us to evaluate how sensitive the decision is to variations in real-world conditions. If changes similar to those described above have little or no effect on the decision, the situation is described as being insensitive relative to those factors. Each decision situation must be examined to determine its sensitivity to changes in specific parameters.

SIMULATION IN PRACTICE

Although simulation is widely used in production and operations management, it has limitations. It is especially valuable in situations for which

Table 23–4 Service Level Changes as a Function of Demand and Production Changes

Demand Conditions	MPL*	Service Level
Current level	12	94%
Increased orders	12	83%
	14	97%
Increased orders and units per order	12	66%
	14	78%
	17	95%

*Mean production level (units per day)

models can be specified but for which critical input variables are probabilistic. It is important that the operations manager be able to recognize appropriate applications of simulation and understand the advantages and limitations of its use.

Benefits of Simulation

Simulation is relatively inexpensive; the cost of simulating a production system and using the model to experiment with different policies (for example, different scheduling priority systems) is much lower than experimenting with the system in reality. Simulation (building a model of the system, manipulating that model, and operating with different policies in effect) also provides those involved with a better understanding of the situation. It is an excellent training device, since the individuals involved get a feel for the interaction of the controlled variables and their impact on decision results.

Pitfalls and Safeguards

Most mathematical models of real-world systems greatly oversimplify. As the simple model is modified to achieve greater correspondence with reality, the mathematical complexities increase at a much greater rate than the model's correspondence to reality. For instance, note that the first example does not consider the possibility of machine failure. Inclusion of that factor could have been accomplished with the addition of a third probability distribution defining the probability of machine failures. Although it was omitted to keep the example simple, its inclusion would be desirable if machine failures were relatively common.

In addition, there is the slight possibility that nonrepresentative inputs might be generated by simulation. In one run of only 100 repetitions, there is always the possibility that the average random number, and therefore the average event value, may be considerably above or below the expected .50 value. Should this occur, the simulation results could be misleading. Running the simulation four or five times substantially reduces the possibility of nonrepresentative event values. Each run must be made with a unique set of random numbers. The average measure of effectiveness value of these runs is used to evaluate the effect of the specific values of the controlled variables (number of machines in the example) being compared.

The values in Table 23–4 are the result of having replicated each run three times, which was deemed sufficient because the service levels differed only slightly between runs.

Some Applications

William Lee and Curtis McLaughlin (1974) reported on the development and implementation of a simulation model of the aggregate material management function in an $11 million firm. They evaluated decisions concerning work force size and stability, overtime, inventory fluctuations, and cash flow over given operating ranges of demand and capacity.

David A. Collier (1980) studied the interaction of single stage lot size models (EOQ, lot-for-lot, period order quantity, etc.) in a material requirements planning system. He examined various combinations of these rules among the levels in a product structure. His work is typical of the research going on in this area. An earlier paper on this same subject (Goodman, Hardy, and Biggs 1977) uses a different, quite elaborate model and examines these rules for various performance criteria.

Frederick C. Weston, Jr. (1980), looked at EOQ, reorder point, and exponential smoothing interactions in an elementary setting. He demonstrated, among other things, that the results of this type of system may be quite contrary to generally accepted theory.

CONCLUSIONS

Stochastic simulation is a synthetic method of dynamically representing a decision system over time and evaluating feasible alternate values of controlled variables. It is quicker and less expensive than trial and error in the real world. It is especially useful when the complexity of a situation prevents application of an analytical model. Stochastic simulation works because (1) simulated event values occur with the same frequency as they do in the real world and (2) sequential combinations of event values have the same probability of occurrence as they do in the real world. The use of the computer with its capacity to accurately handle a large quantity of data through many mathematical steps in a relatively short period of time has been a boon to the utilization of stochastic simulation, and the development of special simulation programming software has reduced the cost.

The design of the simulation model and the experiment is the cornerstone of the process. Critical assumptions are always necessary: Will the future conform to the past? If historical data are not to be used, can a standard probability distribution be used to generate inputs? Inaccurate assumptions and sloppy experiments can generate misleading answers. Stochastic simulation is no panacea, but it is a valuable tool when applied properly.

QUESTIONS

1. Do simulation techniques generally give optimal results?

2. Which sort of variables are evaluated using stochastic simulation? Give several examples.

3. What is a simulation and what does it do?

4. What is the rationale for simulation? Why is simulation considered to give representative results of the real world?

5. What action may be taken to determine how accurately the simulation will represent a real-world situation?

6. What variables would you include in a simulation to determine whether an auto-repair garage should add another maintenance bay?

7. What are the advantages of simulation?

8. What are the disadvantages of simulation?

9. Why might a 100 iteration simulation misrepresent the real-world average? How might this condition be avoided?

10. Describe an application of simulation to a general problem type with which you are familiar.

11. What assumptions are critical for the accuracy of the stochastic simulation?

PROBLEMS

Note: most simulations would require $\geq$ 100 iterations to assure stability. Recognizing that manual methods will likely be used by some students, these problems call for only 5 to 10 iterations. If computer software programs are used, 100 or more iterations would be appropriate.

1. The cumulative probability of the number of telephone calls per five minutes in a telephone reservation system of a major airline is given below.

Number of Calls	Cumulative Probability
1	0.05
2	0.15
3	0.35
4	0.65
5	0.85
6	0.95
$\geq$ 7	1.00

a. Use the random number table to determine the number of calls that will occur in a five-minute period.

b. Determine the average number of calls in a five-minute period (five iterations).

2. Given the probability of receiving calls during a five-minute period in Problem 1, the probabilities stated below give the length of each call.

Length of Calls	Cumulative Probability
1 minute	0.03
2 minutes	0.12
3 minutes	0.45
4 minutes	0.70
5 minutes	0.85
6 minutes	0.95
> 6 minutes	1.00

a. Conduct a simulation of one five-minute period to determine how many reservation clerks you would require.
b. Determine, in five iterations, the average total minutes that are required to answer all calls in the five minute period.
c. On the basis of b above, recommend the number of reservation clerks.

3. In a machine tool operation, completion and delivery of a component is affected by faulty materials and operator error. Additionally, a work stoppage may be caused by late deliveries of bar stock and the unavailability of the forklift to carry away pallets of finished product. Given the following simple probabilities, simulate the delivery of this component.

Raw Materials Availability	Raw Materials Quality	Operator Fault	Fork Lift Availability
Yes 0.83	Good 0.90	No 0.87	Yes 0.80
No 0.17	Bad 0.10	Yes 0.13	No 0.20

a. Perform ten iterations. What is the probability that the product will be delivered?
b. Given the probabilities and an infinite number of trials, what is the probability that a quality component will be delivered?
c. If an operator training program were conducted to reduce operator faults to 0.10, conduct ten simulations to determine how sensitive the process is to this change.
d. If operator fault is reduced to 0.10, given the probabilities and an infinite number of trials, what is the probability that a quality component will be delivered?

4. The number of vehicles that enter a toll plaza per minute between three and five o'clock on weekdays has been validated at the following cumulative distribution.

Number of Vehicles	Cumulative Distribution
1	0.02
2	0.09
3	0.21
4	0.43
5	0.67
6	0.84
7	0.96
≥ 8	1.00

   a. Use the random number table to find the number of vehicles that will enter this toll plaza during ten different one-minute periods.

   b. What is the average number of vehicles per minute?

   c. If each toll booth can handle an average of two vehicles per minute, use ten iterations to evaluate the flow of vehicles. How many booths would you recommend?

5. The vehicles that enter the toll plaza in Problem 4 are either cars with discount tokens, cars paying cash, campers, or trucks. They enter the plaza in the indicated proportion and pay the indicated toll. Conduct a simulation of vehicles entering the plaza for five minutes.

Type of Vehicle	Toll	Cumulative Probability
Car/discount token	$0.40	0.65
Car/cash	0.50	0.85
Campers	0.80	0.93
Trucks	1.25	1.00

   a. What types of vehicles enter the plaza?

   b. What is the average per-minute receipt?

   c. What is the minimum and maximum per-minute receipt?

   d. Assuming that the distributions are correct, if you did 100 simulations or more, would this be a good model?

6. In Problem 4 above, if each toll booth could accommodate three vehicles per minute, use ten iterations to evaluate the flow of vehicles. What is the effect on the number of booths that you would have open?

7. The Speedy Pizza Company delivers pizza in a ten mile radius. Delivery truck utilization depends on the number of orders for delivery each hour and the round trip time of each delivery. Use the data at the top of page 778 for the necessary evaluations:

Number of Orders per Hour		Round Trip Time for Each Delivery	
Orders	Cumulative Probability	Time (Minutes)	Cumulative Probability
3	0	10	.14
4	.05	20	.37
5	.14	30	.74
6	.38	40	1.00
7	.61		
8	.88		
9	1.00		

a. Conduct an evaluation of one hour of a particular evening. How many trucks should the company have?

b. Conduct an evaluation of five one-hour periods on one evening. How many trucks should the company have?

8. On-time completion of jobs at a work center is dependent upon the number of machinists who report for work and the number of machines that are functional each day. Those probabilities follow.

Workers		Machines	
Number	Cumulative Probability	Number	Cumulative Probability
5	.65	6	.61
4	.80	5	.73
3	.88	4	.85
2	.92	3	.91
1	.99	2	.97
0	1.00	1	.99
		0	1.00

a. Conduct five simulations. How many employee-machine pairs are available each day?

b. Conduct ten simulations. What is the frequency that at least five labor-machine teams are available? Four teams? Three teams? Two teams?

9. A company leases one forklift that costs $100 a day regardless of whether it is used or not. On some days there are enough orders, both incoming and outgoing, to keep two or three forklifts busy. They are rented at $150 a day as needed. The demand is as follows:

Number Needed	Percentage of Days
0	5
1	50
2	30
3	15

Simulate 30 days to estimate whether or not the company should lease a second forklift.

10. A common maintenance/inventory problem involves group replacement. For example, if one of several similar components fails in a given machine, should all be replaced in order to save subsequent downtime? The answer depends on service life (SL), repair time, and costs. The following table gives the service time distribution for an electronic tube in a machine. Each machine contains three tubes.

SL	Probability of SL or Less
6,000	.05
8,000	.50
10,000	.75
12,000	.85
14,000	.93
16,000	.98
18,000	1.00

The cost of each tube is $50. The cost to replace one, two, or three tubes is $100 plus a variable cost of $10 per tube replaced. Simulate the breakdown of the tubes in a machine for a period of 120,000 hours, and determine which of the following policies is lowest cost.

a. Replace only the tube that fails.
b. Replace all tubes if any one fails.
c. Replace failed tubes plus any that have been in service over 8,000 hours.

REFERENCES

Collier, David A. "The Interaction of Single-Stage Lot Size Models in a Material Requirements Planning System," *Production and Inventory Management* 21, no. 4 (1980): 11–20.

Goodman, Stephen H. , Stanley T. Hardy, and Joseph R. Biggs. "Lot Sizing Rules in a Hierarchical Multistage Inventory System." *Production and Inventory Management* 18, no. 1 (1977): 104–116.

Lee, William and Curtis McLaughlin. "Corporate Simulation Models for Aggregate Materials Management," *Production and Inventory Management* 15, no. 1 (1974): 55–67.

Weston, Frederick C. Jr. "A Simulation Approach to Examining Traditional EOQ/EOP and Single Order Exponential Smoothing Efficiency Adopting a Small Business Perspective." *Production and Inventory Management*, 21, no. 2 (1980): 67–83.

CHAPTER 24
WAITING LINE THEORY

OBJECTIVES

After completing this chapter, you should be able to

- Identify the characteristics of a waiting line or queueing problem

- Describe ways that queueing theory can be useful to operations managers in waiting line applications

- Recognize a variety of queue disciplines and service facility arrangements

- Understand the structure of queueing problems and describe the types of data necessary to solve them

- Analyze simple, well-defined waiting line problems

OUTLINE

INTRODUCTION

Customers must frequently wait for service, whether it is waiting at a teller's window in a bank, at the grocery checkout counter, at a toll station, at a tool crib, or at an emergency room. Items being processed and departments in both service and manufacturing organizations also wait for services. Students wait in registration lines; patients wait for x-rays; orders wait for the availability of a chef; parts wait for the availability of a machine or an assembly workstation; departments wait for maintenance and delivery services. Waiting line concepts and models are useful for analyzing these situations. (Waiting lines also are known as queues.) They are used for solving staffing problems (e.g., the number of maintenance workers to hire), and for making facility decisions (e.g., the number of loading docks, toll stations, or machines necessary). Thus, waiting line, or queueing, theory provides excellent tools for analyzing many operations management decision situations in both manufacturing and services. For example, they can tell us the waiting times of customers, the average number of customers in the queue, and the optimum number of service facilities.

Both analytical models and simulation methods are useful for analyzing waiting line situations. Analytical models usually require straightforward information that requires less data processing. However, analytical models require that the situation being analyzed fits the model specification. For example, a model may be based on customers joining the waiting line (arrivals) at a constant average rate with each arrival independent of previous arrivals. Arrivals in the actual situation must follow this pattern for the model to be useful. When a situation does not meet the specifications of available models, as is frequently the case, then simulation is more appropriate.

This chapter describes analytical methods; Chapter 23 describes simulation.

WAITING LINE TERMINOLOGY

Common terminology and symbols exist to describe waiting line situations and models:

λ = Mean arrival rate of customers (the expected number or average number of arrivals per time period)—for example, 2 arrivals per minute, 120 arrivals per hour, or 960 arrivals per shift

$1/\lambda$ = Expected interarrival time (time between successive arrivals)—for example, an average interarrival time of .5 minutes (an average of 2 arrivals per minute)

μ = Mean service rate capacity (the expected number or average number of customers processed or serviced per time period)—for example,

2.5 customers per minute, 150 customers per hour, or 1,200 customers per shift, which does not mean that 1,200 customers will be served, only that the capacity exists

$1/\mu$ = Expected service time (average time required to process a customer, for example, .4 minutes or 24 seconds)

ρ = $\lambda/(\mu s)$ utilization factor for a service facility (proportion of time that the facility is servicing customers)

s = Number of service channels

L = Expected number of units in the queuing system, including those being serviced

L_q = Expected waiting line length (not including units being serviced)

W = Expected time in the system (time required for service plus W_q)

W_q = Expected time in the waiting line

P_0 = Probability of no units in the system

P_n = Probability of n units in the system

A few relationships are the same for all waiting line situations; thus one model is applicable to all situations. These relationships are as follows:

$$\rho = \frac{\lambda}{s\mu}$$

$$L = \lambda W \text{ or } W = \frac{L}{\lambda}$$

$$L_q = \lambda W_q \text{ or } W_q = \frac{L_q}{\lambda}$$

WAITING LINE CHARACTERISTICS

Determining the characteristics of a situation is the first step in analyzing a waiting line problem. Those characteristics are

1. The customer population
2. The arrival pattern

3. The queue
4. The service facility
5. The service time

The Customer Population

For analysis purposes, arrivals may come from a finite population or from one that is infinite. For example, there is an infinite number of customers who might arrive at a highway toll station, at a hospital emergency room, or at the order entry workstation in a company. (The orders usually arrive at the order entry desk via the telephone or the mail.) On the other hand, a company may have a finite number of delivery trucks, say seven, that may call (arrive) for repair. The essential difference between a finite and an infinite population is that the arrival of a unit from a finite population reduces the probability of the arrival of a second unit. With an infinite customer population the arrival of a customer does not change the probability of another arrival. A population size of 30 customers frequently is used as the somewhat arbitrary dividing line between finite and infinite populations. This is because when the population is 30 or more, analysis using models applicable to finite populations produce virtually the same results as models applicable to infinite populations. When in doubt, it is best to use both approaches and compare the results. In addition, when the queue and service times are relatively short and the probability of the serviced customer (item) immediately requiring service again is high, a small number of customers may constitute an infinite population. For example, for all practical purposes the population is infinite in the case of 15 identical pieces of sensitive electronic equipment when the service merely requires that the reset button be pushed, sufficient attendants are available to achieve virtually no waiting time, and an immediately following interference or vibration may require another reset.

Arrival Rates

Arrival rates are described by either the probability distribution of arrivals per unit of time (e.g., an average of two arrivals every minute), or by the interarrival time probability distribution (e.g., a .10 probability of an arrival within one minute, a .30 probability of an arrival within two minutes, etc.).

When arrivals from an infinite population occur at random but with a steady (constant) average and are independent (the number of arrivals in one period does not affect the number in the next), the probability of arrival is described by a Poisson distribution, given by the following model:

$$P(n, T) = \frac{e^{-\lambda T}(\lambda T)^n}{n!}$$

where

$$P(n, T) = \text{Probability of } n \text{ arrivals in time } T$$

$$\lambda = \text{Mean arrival rate per unit of time}$$

$$T = \text{Time period}$$

$$n = \text{Number of arrivals in time } T$$

$$e = 2.71828\dots, \text{ the base of natural logarithms}$$

For example, if arrivals from an infinite population are independent and occur at random every two minutes on the average, then the probability of one arrival in one minute is calculated as follows (obtain the value of e^{-2T} from Appendix E):

$$P(1,1) = \frac{e^{-2\times1}(2 \times 1)^1}{1!} = .13534 \times 2 = .27068$$

The probability of three arrivals in four minutes is obtained as follows:

$$P(3,4) = \frac{e^{-2\times4}(2 \times 4)^3}{3!} = \frac{.00034 \times 512}{3 \times 2 \times 1} = .0290$$

On the other hand, in the same situation (infinite population, random arrivals, and a steady average arrival rate), the interarrival time has an exponential probability distribution. The probability of an arrival in time t is very low when t is quite small and grows exponentially as t increases until the probability approaches 1.0. For example, a machine that fails every 800 hours on the average has a very low probability of failing within ten hours but a high probability of failing once in 1,600 hours of operation. (Notice that a failure is the arrival of a call for service.) The model for determining the probability of an arrival within a given time period is

$$P(T < t) = 1 - e^{-\lambda T}$$

where

$$P(T < t) = \text{The probability that the time between two arrivals } (T) \text{ will be less than } t$$

$$\lambda = \text{The mean arrival rate}$$

$$e = 2.71828\dots, \text{ the base of the natural logarithms}$$

For example, if on average an arrival occurs once every 800 hours ($\lambda = 1 \div 800$) calculate the probability of an arrival within 80 hours.

$$P(T \leq 80) = 1 - e^{-1/800\times80} = 1 - e^{-.10} = 1 - .90484 = .09516$$

Given the same situation, calculate the probability of an arrival within 1,600 hours.

$$P(T \leq 1,600) = 1 - e^{-1/800 \times 1,600} = 1 - e^{-2} = 1 - .13534 = .86466$$

Arrivals may follow many distributions: they may be constant, with no variance, when coming from a machine-controlled process; some may fit an Erlang distribution, which is described by Saaty (1983); others may not correspond to any standard distribution and must be analyzed by simulation.

The Queue

Three attributes of the queue influence the behavior of a waiting line system and should be recognized in the analysis. They are

1. The maximum length of the line
2. The behavior of arrivals
3. The queue discipline

LINE LENGTH. The length of many lines is not limited (e.g., the number of mail orders received in a week). In other cases, physical limits prevent arrivals from entering the line. For example, there may be a limited number of spaces at a garage to hold vehicles awaiting repair. Other examples of limited queue length space motivating arrivals to seek service at another facility—or to be sent there—include hospital emergency rooms and restaurants. When an emergency room in a metropolitan area is loaded with serious cases, it may direct ambulances to nearby hospitals.

BEHAVIOR OF ARRIVALS. In some cases it is clearly the customer's behavior that limits the queue length and not the line's physical limits. For example, one customer will stand and wait when all chairs are occupied in a barber shop but another will not. Some customers, a percentage that frequently can be measured, will not wait three days for maintenance service, 45 minutes in a restaurant even if lounge seats are available, or three weeks for delivery of an automobile; they will go to competitors. Customers may enter the queue, stay awhile, lose patience, and leave. Most of the basic waiting line models assume no physical limits on the queue length and assume that customers are willing to enter the line and wait. The analyst should verify the validity of these assumptions before applying a model in a given situation. When these conditions do not exist, a more advanced model or simulation should be used.

QUEUE DISCIPLINE. The priority rule or rules for determining the order in which customers in the waiting line are served is the queue discipline. First come, first served (FCFS) is the most common in service industries and is the assumption of elementary waiting line models. There are many other possibilities including: shortest processing time, need of the customer (e.g., life or death), and favored customer. Priority rules are discussed in greater detail in Chapter 14. The queue discipline affects the expected wait of a given customer and the number of customers in the queue.

The Service Facility

The structure of the service facility and the distribution of service times are essential characteristics in the analysis of a waiting line. The structure consists of the number of channels and the number of stages. Figure 24–1 shows these possibilities.

Other structures also are possible. For example, multiphase systems may have a single channel as the first phase and two or more channels in the sec-

Figure 24–1   Service Facility Structures

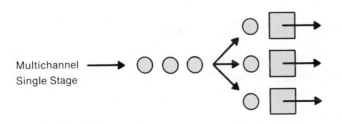

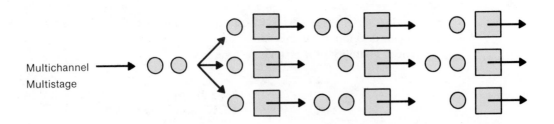

ond phase. Such structures are not uncommon in manufacturing, banking, and restaurants. Such situations may be analyzed using simulation, by developing an advanced model, or by finding in the literature an advanced model that fits the situation.

Service Times

Service times are similar to arrival times in that the times of different processes conform to many different statistical distributions. They may be constant with the service, always requiring the same amount of time. Constant times occur when the service operation is provided by a machine; it may exist for practical purposes when an operator-controlled process takes virtually the same time for each performance.

When service time is random, it usually is approximated by an exponential distribution. However, many service activities have minimum times for completion that prevent them from conforming to an exponential distribution. For example, the average time to tune up an engine may be 30 minutes, with the minimum being 20 minutes. However, the actual distribution of times may correspond reasonably well to an exponential distribution if we include those times when (1) the work can't be performed due to a lack of parts, (2) a more serious problem is discovered after 10 minutes and the customer decides to postpone the service, and (3) a less serious problem is discovered (a loose sparkplug wire) and the repair is not required.

Let's examine some elementary situations and basic models. Unless otherwise noted, the population source will be infinite and queue discipline will be first come, first served.

SINGLE CHANNEL (SERVER) MODELS

Many waiting line situations (problems) have a single server. Examples that apply the appropriate set of models to a few of these cases are discussed below.

Single Channel, Poisson Arrivals, and Exponential Service

A company that sells and services copying machines in Springfield, Missouri has one service technician. A call for service arrives every two hours on the average, and the average total time (transit time plus service time) required to service the calls is 1 hour and 15 minutes. The following models have been developed for this situation.

The probability of n arrivals in time period T,

$$P(n, T) = \frac{e^{-\lambda T}(\lambda T)^n}{n!}$$

The probability of an arrival with a given time period,

$$P(T \le t) = 1 - e^{-\lambda t}$$

The probability that n or more units (customers) are in the system,

$$P_n = \left(\frac{\lambda}{\mu}\right)^n \left(1 - \frac{\lambda}{\mu}\right)$$

For this situation,

$$\lambda = 1/(2 \text{ hours}) = .5 \text{ units (arrivals) per hour}$$

$$\mu = 1.25 \text{ customers or units served per hour (average capacity)}$$

The probability of the service technician being able to respond immediately to a call for service equals the probability of no units in the system. Thus,

$$P_0 = \left(\frac{\lambda}{\mu}\right)^0 \left(1 - \frac{\lambda}{\mu}\right) = \left(\frac{.5}{1.25}\right)^0 \left(1 - \frac{.5}{1.25}\right) = 1 \times (1 - .4) = .6$$

and the probability of waiting, a delay, is obtained from

$$P_w = 1 - P_0 = 1 - \left(\frac{\lambda}{\mu}\right)^0 \left(1 - \frac{\lambda}{\mu}\right) = \frac{\lambda}{\mu} = \rho = \frac{.5}{1.25} = .4$$

Other values of interest are calculated as follows:
The average (expected) units in the system,

$$L = \frac{\lambda}{\mu - \lambda} = \frac{.5}{1.25 - .5} = .67 \text{ units}$$

The expected time in the queue plus servicing,

$$W = L/\lambda = .67/.5 = 1.33 \text{ hours.}$$

The expected waiting line length,

$$L_q = \frac{\lambda^2}{\mu(\mu - \lambda)} = \frac{.5 \times .5}{1.25(1.25 - .5)} = .26 \text{ units}$$

The expected time in the queue,

$$W_q = \frac{L_q}{\lambda} = \frac{.26}{.5} = .52 \text{ hours}$$

Single Channel, Poisson Arrivals, and Constant Service

Either arrival times or service times can be constant. If both are constant, the arrival time must be less than the service time or the waiting line will grow to an infinite length. An example with constant service, poisson arrivals, single server, an infinite population, and a first come, first served queue discipline is given here.

Each vehicle in a large metropolitan fleet undergoes automatic testing and diagnosis every 5,000 to 6,000 miles. The test involves driving the vehicle into position, hooking it up, running the test, obtaining the computer printout, logging test results on the vehicle log, and driving the vehicle out. For practical purposes, the test takes a constant 15 minutes, equaling four units per hour, and the variance approximates zero. Vehicles arrive for service every 18 minutes on average with arrivals following a Poisson distribution. Thus,

$$\mu = 4$$

$$\lambda = 3.33$$

$$\rho = .833$$

$$P_0 = 1 - \rho = 1 - .833 = .167$$

$$L_q = \frac{\rho^2}{2(1 - \rho)} = \frac{(.833)^2}{2(1 - .833)} = 2.08 \text{ vehicles}$$

$$L = L_q + \rho = 2.08 + .833 = 2.91 \text{ vehicles}$$

$$W = \frac{L}{\lambda} = \frac{2.91}{3.33} = .873 \text{ hours}$$

$$W_q = \frac{L_q}{\lambda} = \frac{2.08}{3.33} = .624 \text{ hours}$$

It is interesting to note that if the service times were exponentially distributed rather than constant and all other factors were the same, the length of the waiting line, L_q, would be twice as large and the length of the wait, W_q, would be twice as long.

MULTIPLE CHANNEL MODELS

What if management of the copy machine company decides to add another service technician to reduce the waiting time of customers? How much will the waiting time be reduced? Recall that arrivals had a Poisson distribution and service times had an exponential distribution.

The performance characteristics of this situation are given by the following models (relationships) where s is the number of servers.

$$\rho = \frac{\lambda}{s\mu}$$

$$P_0 = \left[\sum_{n=0}^{s-1} \frac{(\lambda/\mu)^n}{n!} + \frac{(\lambda/\mu)^s}{s!\left(1 - \frac{\lambda}{\mu s}\right)} \right]^{-1}$$

$$P_n = P_0 \left[\frac{(\lambda/\mu)^n}{n!} \right] \text{ for } 1 \leq n \leq s$$

$$P_n = P_0 \left[\frac{(\lambda/\mu)^n}{s!(s)^{n-s}} \right] \text{ for } n \geq s$$

$$L_q = \frac{P_0(\lambda/\mu)^s}{s!(1 - \rho)^2}$$

$$L = L_q + \frac{\lambda}{\mu}$$

$$W_q = \frac{L_q}{\lambda}$$

$$W = W_q + \frac{1}{\mu}$$

Thus, adding a second server ($s = 2$) in our example gives the following results:

$$\lambda = .5$$

$$\mu = 1.25$$

$$s = 2$$

$$\frac{\lambda}{\mu} = .4$$

$$\rho = .2$$

$$P_0 = \left[\frac{(.4)^0}{0!} + \frac{(.4)^1}{1!} + \frac{(.4)^2}{2!}\left(1 - \frac{.5}{2 \times 1.25}\right)^{-1} \right]^{-1}$$

Remember that by definition zero factorial (0!) equals one.

$$P_0 = \left[1 + .4 + .08(1 - .2)^{-1}\right]^{-1} = \left[1.4 + .1\right]^{-1} = .666$$

$$P_1 = .666[.4] = .267$$

The probability of a customer waiting is equivalent to the probability of 2 or more units being in the system, which equals 1.0 minus the sum of the probability of no units and the probability of 1 unit in the system.

$$P_{n>1} = 1.0 - (.667 + .267) = .066$$

Other measures of performance are

$$L_q = \frac{.666(.4)^2.2}{2(1 - .2)^2} = \frac{.0213}{1.28} = .017 \text{ units}$$

$$L = .017 + .4 = .417 \text{ units}$$

$$W_q = \frac{.017}{.4} = .0425 \text{ hours}$$

$$W = .0425 + \frac{1}{1.25} = .8425 \text{ hours}$$

Thus, the addition of another service technician reduces the probability of a customer waiting from .4 to .066, the average wait from .52 hours to .0425 hours, and the average waiting line length from .26 units to .017 units. Management compares these benefits to the cost of hiring another technician and judges whether the change is cost effective.

CONCLUSIONS

Queueing theory is a valuable decision tool for the operations manager. Waiting lines, or queues, occur in a wide variety of manufacturing and service situations. On the shop floor, queueing analysis often can make scheduling and production activity control more efficient, especially when process times are random but have a well-defined distribution. In service industries, queueing models are often used to describe the arrival and servicing of customers.

This chapter is not intended to present a complete analysis of waiting lines. More specialized sources are available for a wide variety of problems. It is important, however, that the operations manager recognize waiting line situations and understand the value of queueing analysis. The first step in such an analysis is identifying the structure and characteristics of the situation. Then data should be collected, tabulated, and plotted; and distributions of variables such as arrival rates and servicing times should be identified. Only then can appropriate analytical or simulation models be applied.

QUESTIONS

1. Describe three service applications of waiting line theory.

2. Describe three manufacturing applications of waiting line theory.

3. What is the difference between the assumptions of finite and infinite customer populations? Give an example of each. When is a finite population large enough to be an infinite population for waiting line theory purposes?

4. In what ways can arrival rates be described? In what ways can service rates be described?

5. Describe the possible waiting line characteristics of customers waiting at a bank for tellers, a small local grocery store, and an interstate gas station.

6. Define appropriate length of the queue, behavior of arrivals, and queue discipline that might be expected in

 a. A hospital emergency room
 b. A restaurant
 c. A rock concert ticket booth

7. Give an example of each of the following types of service facilities.

 a. Single channel/single stage
 b. Single channel/multistage
 c. Multichannel/single stage
 d. Multichannel/multistage

PROBLEMS

Unless otherwise stated, the following problem situations have an infinite customer population, independent random arrivals, single channel–single stage service, first come–first served queue discipline with patient customers, and random service times.

 1. Given λ equals three customers per hour and μ equals five customers per hour, determine W, L, W_q, and L_q.

2. If λ = five ships per day and μ equals nine ships per day for a canal lock operation, what is the probability that there are:

   a. No ships waiting or being serviced?
   b. One ship waiting or being serviced?
   c. Two ships waiting or being serviced?
   d. Three ships waiting or being serviced?
   e. Two or more ships waiting or being serviced?

3. If there is only one porter during the early morning hours at an expensive hotel where guests do not carry their own luggage, a guest arrives every 15 minutes and can be shown to the room in an average of 10 minutes,

   a. What is the probability that another employee would have to help the porter?
   b. Determine L.
   c. Determine W.
   d. Determine L_q.
   e. Determine W_q.

4. Using the data from Problem 3, use the constant service assumptions to determine the probabilities. Compare the results.

5. Given exponential service and Poisson arrivals, the local gas station has only one lane for full service. Ten customers per hour arrive, and it takes an average of four minutes each to service them.

   a. What is the probability of no cars in the system?
   b. What is the probability of one car in the system?
   c. What is the probability of two cars in the system?
   d. What is the probability of three cars in the system?
   e. Determine L.
   f. Determine W.
   g. Determine L_q.
   h. Determine W_q.

6. Using the data from Problem 5, what is the probability that

   a. There are less than two cars in the system?
   b. There are greater than three cars in the system?

7. An overseas telephone switching station receives an average of five calls per minute. There are 96 outgoing circuits, and calls last an average of 12 minutes.

   a. Determine λ and μ.
   b. What is the probability that all circuits will be busy?

8. Customers arrive at a bank at the rate of one per minute and wait in a large queueing area for the first available teller. Four teller stations are always open and each can serve customers at the average rate of one customer every three minutes.

   a. What is the probability that four or more people will be waiting in the queue?
   b. If no more than six persons are willing to wait, what is the probability that customers will be lost?

9. The Metropolitan Yacht Club offers a motor ferry service from the club wharf to anchored yachts. If on a typical Saturday morning, the average frequencey of requests for service is one every six minutes and the average round-trip delivery time is 20 minutes,

   a. How many ferries should be in operation to assure that there would always be less than a 15-minute wait for service?
   b. If there were five ferries available, what is the probability of having two or more groups waiting?

10. At the local gas station, there is one pump for regular gas and one pump for premium. At the self-service rate, one customer can be served every four minutes at each pump. Hourly arrival averages during the days of the week between the hours of 4 P.M. and 6 P.M. are indicated below.

Day	Regular Customers	Premium Customers
Monday	8	5
Tuesday	6	3
Wednesday	2	1
Thursday	8	5
Friday	12	10
Saturday	9	7
Sunday	3	4

   a. Assuming Poisson arrival and exponential service, compute the following for Friday and regular gas:

      1. The pump utilization
      2. The average number of customers in line
      3. The average number of customers in the system
      4. The average waiting time in line
      5. The average waiting time in the system

   b. Define and evaluate the problem for another time period.

REFERENCES

Cooper, R. B. *Introduction to Queueing Theory.* 2nd ed. New York: Elsevier, 1980.

Gross, D., and C. M. Harris. *Fundamentals of Queueing Theory.* New York: Wiley, 1974.

Page, E. G. *Queueing Theory in Operations Research.* New York: Crane-Russak, 1972.

Saaty, T. L. *Elements of Queueing Theory.* New York: Dover, 1983.

APPENDIX TABLES

TABLE A

Areas Under the Normal Curve

TABLE B

Random Number Table

TABLE C

Unit Learning Curve Values

TABLE D

Cumulative Learning Curve Values

TABLE E

Values of e^x and e^{-x}

Table A   Areas Under the Normal Curve

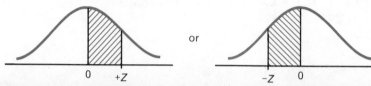

Z	.00	.01	.02	.03	.04	.05	.06	.07	.08	.09
0.0	.0000	.0040	.0080	.0120	.0160	.0199	.0239	.0279	.0319	.0359
0.1	.0398	.0438	.0478	.0517	.0557	.0596	.0636	.0675	.0714	.0753
0.2	.0793	.0832	.0871	.0910	.0948	.0987	.1026	.1064	.1103	.1141
0.3	.1179	.1217	.1255	.1293	.1331	.1368	.1406	.1443	.1480	.1517
0.4	.1554	.1591	.1628	.1664	.1700	.1736	.1772	.1808	.1844	.1879
0.5	.1915	.1950	.1985	.2019	.2054	.2088	.2123	.2157	.2190	.2224
0.6	.2257	.2291	.2324	.2357	.2389	.2422	.2454	.2486	.2517	.2549
0.7	.2580	.2611	.2642	.2673	.2704	.2734	.2764	.2794	.2823	.2852
0.8	.2881	.2910	.2939	.2967	.2995	.3023	.3051	.3078	.3106	.3233
0.9	.3159	.3186	.3212	.3238	.3264	.3289	.3315	.3340	.3365	.3389
1.0	.3413	.3438	.3461	.3485	.3508	.3531	.3554	.3577	.3599	.3621
1.1	.3643	.3665	.3686	.3708	.3729	.3749	.3770	.3790	.3810	.3830
1.2	.3849	.3869	.3888	.3907	.3925	.3944	.3962	.3980	.3997	.4015
1.3	.4032	.4049	.4066	.4082	.4099	.4115	.4131	.4147	.4162	.4177
1.4	.4192	.4207	.4222	.4236	.4251	.4265	.4279	.4292	.4306	.4319
1.5	.4332	.4345	.4357	.4370	.4382	.4394	.4406	.4418	.4429	.4441
1.6	.4452	.4463	.4474	.4484	.4495	.4505	.4515	.4525	.4535	.4545
1.7	.4554	.4564	.4573	.4582	.4591	.4599	.4608	.4616	.4625	.4633
1.8	.4641	.4649	.4656	.4664	.4671	.4678	.4686	.4693	.4699	.4706
1.9	.4713	.4719	.4726	.4732	.4738	.4744	.4750	.4758	.4761	.4767
2.0	.4772	.4778	.4783	.4788	.4793	.4798	.4803	.4808	.4812	.4817
2.1	.4821	.4826	.4830	.4834	.4838	.4842	.4846	.4850	.4854	.4857
2.2	.4861	.4864	.4868	.4871	.4875	.4878	.4881	.4884	.4887	.4890
2.3	.4893	.4896	.4898	.4901	.4904	.4906	.4909	.4911	.4913	.4916
2.4	.4918	.4920	.4922	.4925	.4927	.4929	.4931	.4932	.4934	.4936
2.5	.4938	.4940	.4941	.4943	.4945	.4946	.4948	.4949	.4951	.4952
2.6	.4953	.4955	.4956	.4957	.4959	.4960	.4961	.4962	.4963	.4964
2.7	.4965	.4966	.4967	.4968	.4969	.4970	.4971	.4972	.4973	.4974
2.8	.4974	.4975	.4976	.4977	.4977	.4978	.4979	.4979	.4980	.4881
2.9	.4981	.4982	.4982	.4983	.4984	.4984	.4985	.4985	.4986	.4986
3.0	.4986	.4987	.4987	.4988	.4988	.4988	.4989	.4989	.4989	.4990

Table B   Random Number Table

6663	0696	6964	6935	3077	6821	8774	1951	9228	9856
8558	8714	9132	3207	6221	8776	9366	5563	6306	2010
8666	5692	0397	7806	3527	5242	3519	8278	9806	9540
4535	3457	0319	6396	0550	8496	8441	2896	5307	2865
7709	0209	1590	1558	7418	6382	7624	8286	4225	7145
7472	0681	9746	4704	5439	7495	4156	4548	4468	7801
5792	0245	8544	2190	6749	6243	9089	5974	4484	8669
5370	4385	9413	4132	8888	9775	8511	6520	1789	0816
4914	1801	9257	3701	3520	0823	5915	5341	2583	0113
6227	8568	1319	0681	8898	9335	3506	4813	5271	5912
7077	0878	1730	0093	9731	6123	6100	0389	0522	7478
8044	7232	7466	0349	3467	0174	1140	5425	2912	7088
4280	3474	3963	5364	7381	8144	7645	5116	0300	6762
8821	4375	9853	9138	0596	6294	3415	4358	2713	8343
8523	5591	3956	3516	8472	2884	8550	3524	3919	3967
6558	3999	0480	3046	8285	1693	2330	7610	2674	3679
1806	3227	9710	8548	5003	6345	6815	9612	3378	5091
9256	0103	1347	8074	4534	0373	9885	1182	0795	7094
6128	2383	9223	4459	8974	4525	0441	7379	0677	6135
4913	6686	4453	0223	7344	6333	8080	1075	5077	2590
3491	9060	0496	5251	2385	3425	7426	0827	7816	3100
1530	7750	1800	5491	4713	3572	8914	3287	3518	4166
5894	9256	1529	4922	7235	9046	5771	3954	6794	1984
7107	7293	5387	9880	4642	6092	4389	3820	4119	5821
5337	8973	0322	7474	5526	7386	3476	0762	9613	8789
9644	9317	7214	9388	5131	7891	6504	8672	4880	1557
3820	4209	4876	6906	9257	4447	8541	5250	8272	9513
7142	7821	9281	0016	4180	2971	7259	3844	3801	5372
3342	0965	3189	7217	0428	6227	8967	1417	4771	0157
7599	6804	3587	7765	9790	5331	8654	5337	8883	1268
5905	5242	3262	2409	1039	8727	2752	3265	1110	6722
9016	0268	2134	8633	9959	8970	2688	9149	8124	3244
3508	3038	3095	6480	3089	7948	7897	4792	9288	5206
9393	2211	6921	8622	2688	7890	1363	1282	9525	5299
8151	0355	0688	3432	8580	9888	2402	0000	1307	1611
6730	6635	9948	3730	5977	6089	6678	7734	1086	1435
1834	3191	4042	7264	9511	0549	4267	2888	9166	1935
9028	7539	3215	9958	7826	7569	0633	4506	0807	5650
6556	7547	1155	1975	7882	5929	1493	7455	4865	2179
4285	8922	8721	3307	6236	6329	5228	7599	6689	1946

From *Production: Management and Manufacturing Systems*, 2d ed., by Thomas R. Hoffmann. © 1971 by Wadsworth Publishing Company, Inc. Reprinted by permission of Wadsworth Publishing Company, Belmont, California 94002.

Table C   Unit Learning Curve Values

| Units | Improvement Ratios | | | | | | | |
	60%	65%	70%	75%	80%	85%	90%	95%
1	1.0000	1.0000	1.0000	1.0000	1.0000	1.0000	1.0000	1.0000
2	0.6000	0.6500	0.7000	0.7500	0.8000	0.8500	0.9000	0.9500
3	0.4450	0.5052	0.5682	0.6338	0.7021	0.7729	0.8462	0.9219
4	0.3600	0.4225	0.4900	0.5625	0.6400	0.7225	0.8100	0.9025
5	0.3054	0.3678	0.4368	0.5127	0.5956	0.6857	0.7830	0.8877
6	0.2670	0.3284	0.3977	0.4754	0.5617	0.6570	0.7616	0.8758
7	0.2383	0.2984	0.3674	0.4459	0.5345	0.6337	0.7439	0.8659
8	0.2160	0.2746	0.3430	0.4219	0.5120	0.6141	0.7290	0.8574
9	0.1980	0.2552	0.3228	0.4017	0.4930	0.5974	0.7161	0.8499
10	0.1832	0.2391	0.3058	0.3846	0.4765	0.5828	0.7047	0.8433
12	0.1602	0.2135	0.2784	0.3565	0.4493	0.5584	0.6854	0.8320
14	0.1430	0.1940	0.2572	0.3344	0.4276	0.5386	0.6696	0.8226
16	0.1296	0.1785	0.2401	0.3164	0.4096	0.5220	0.6561	0.8145
18	0.1188	0.1659	0.2260	0.3013	0.3944	0.5078	0.6445	0.8074
20	0.1099	0.1554	0.2141	0.2884	0.3812	0.4954	0.6342	0.8012
22	0.1025	0.1465	0.2038	0.2772	0.3697	0.4844	0.6251	0.7955
24	0.0961	0.1387	0.1949	0.2674	0.3595	0.4747	0.6169	0.7904
25	0.0933	0.1353	0.1908	0.2629	0.3548	0.4701	0.6131	0.7880
30	0.0815	0.1208	0.1737	0.2437	0.3346	0.4505	0.5963	0.7775
35	0.0728	0.1097	0.1605	0.2286	0.3184	0.4345	0.5825	0.7687
40	0.0660	0.1010	0.1498	0.2163	0.3050	0.4211	0.5708	0.7611
45	0.0605	0.0939	0.1410	0.2060	0.2936	0.4096	0.5607	0.7545
50	0.0560	0.0879	0.1336	0.1972	0.2838	0.3996	0.5518	0.7486

60	0.7386	0.5367	0.3829	0.2676	0.1828	0.1216	0.0785	0.0489
70	0.7302	0.5243	0.3693	0.2547	0.1715	0.1123	0.0713	0.0437
80	0.7231	0.5137	0.3579	0.2440	0.1622	0.1049	0.0657	0.0396
90	0.7168	0.5046	0.3482	0.2349	0.1545	0.0987	0.0610	0.0363
100	0.7112	0.4966	0.3397	0.2271	0.1479	0.0935	0.0572	0.0336
120	0.7017	0.4830	0.3255	0.2141	0.1371	0.0851	0.0510	0.0294
140	0.6937	0.4718	0.3139	0.2038	0.1287	0.0786	0.0464	0.0262
160	0.6869	0.4623	0.3042	0.1952	0.1217	0.0734	0.0427	0.0237
180	0.6809	0.4541	0.2959	0.1879	0.1159	0.0691	0.0397	0.0218
200	0.6757	0.4469	0.2887	0.1816	0.1109	0.0655	0.0371	0.0201
250	0.6646	0.4320	0.2740	0.1691	0.1011	0.0584	0.0323	0.0171
300	0.6557	0.4202	0.2625	0.1594	0.0937	0.0531	0.0289	0.0149
350	0.6482	0.4105	0.2532	0.1517	0.0879	0.0491	0.0262	0.0133
400	0.6419	0.4022	0.2454	0.1453	0.0832	0.0458	0.0241	0.0121
450	0.6363	0.3951	0.2387	0.1399	0.0792	0.0431	0.0224	0.0111
500	0.6314	0.3888	0.2329	0.1352	0.0758	0.0408	0.0210	0.0103
600	0.6229	0.3782	0.2232	0.1275	0.0703	0.0372	0.0188	0.0090
700	0.6158	0.3694	0.2152	0.1214	0.0659	0.0344	0.0171	0.0080
800	0.6098	0.3620	0.2086	0.1163	0.0624	0.0321	0.0157	0.0073
900	0.6045	0.3556	0.2029	0.1119	0.0594	0.0302	0.0146	0.0067
1000	0.5998	0.3499	0.1980	0.1082	0.0569	0.0286	0.0137	0.0062
1200	0.5918	0.3404	0.1897	0.1020	0.0527	0.0260	0.0122	0.0054
1400	0.5850	0.3325	0.1830	0.0971	0.0495	0.0240	0.0111	0.0048
1600	0.5793	0.3258	0.1773	0.0930	0.0468	0.0225	0.0102	0.0044
1800	0.5743	0.3200	0.1725	0.0895	0.0466	0.0211	0.0095	0.0040
2000	0.5698	0.3149	0.1683	0.0866	0.0427	0.0200	0.0089	0.0037
2500	0.5605	0.3044	0.1597	0.0806	0.0389	0.0178	0.0077	0.0031
3000	0.5330	0.2961	0.1530	0.0760	0.0360	0.0162	0.0069	0.0027

Table D Cumulative Learning Curve Values

Units	Improvement Ratios							
	60%	65%	70%	75%	80%	85%	90%	95%
1	1.000	1.000	1.000	1.000	1.000	1.000	1.000	1.000
2	1.600	1.650	1.700	1.750	1.800	1.850	1.900	1.950
3	2.045	2.155	2.268	2.384	2.502	2.623	2.746	2.872
4	2.405	2.578	.2758	2.946	3.142	3.345	3.556	3.774
5	2.710	2.946	3.195	3.459	3.738	4.031	4.339	4.662
6	2.977	3.274	3.593	3.934	4.299	4.688	5.101	5.538
7	3.216	3.572	3.960	4.380	4.834	5.322	5.845	6.404
8	3.432	3.847	4.303	4.802	5.346	5.936	6.574	7.261
9	3.630	4.102	4.626	5.204	5.839	6.533	7.290	8.111
10	3.813	4.341	4.931	5.589	6.315	7.116	7.994	8.955
12	4.144	4.780	5.501	6.315	7.227	8.244	9.374	10.62
14	4.438	5.177	6.026	6.994	8.092	9.331	10.72	12.27
16	4.704	5.541	6.514	7.635	8.920	10.38	12.04	13.91
18	4.946	5.879	6.972	8.245	9.716	11.41	13.33	15.52
20	5.171	6.195	7.407	8.828	10.48	12.40	14.61	17.13
22	5.379	6.492	7.819	9.388	11.23	13.38	15.86	18.72
24	5.574	6.773	8.213	9.928	11.95	14.33	17.10	20.31
25	5.668	6.909	8.404	10.19	12.31	14.80	17.71	21.10
30	6.097	7.540	9.305	11.45	14.02	17.09	20.73	25.00
35	6.478	8.109	10.13	12.72	15.64	19.29	23.67	28.86
40	6.821	8.631	10.90	13.72	17.19	21.43	26.54	32.68
45	7.134	9.114	11.62	14.77	18.68	23.50	29.37	36.47
50	7.422	9.565	12.31	15.78	20.12	25.51	32.14	40.22

60	7.941	10.39	13.57	17.67	22.87	29.41	37.57	47.65
70	8.401	11.13	14.74	19.43	25.47	33.17	42.87	54.99
80	8.814	11.82	15.82	21.09	27.96	36.80	48.05	62.25
90	9.191	12.45	16.83	22.67	30.35	40.32	53.14	69.45
100	9.539	13.03	17.79	24.18	32.65	43.75	58.14	76.59
120	10.16	14.11	19.57	27.02	37.05	50.39	67.93	90.71
140	10.72	15.08	21.20	29.67	41.22	56.78	77.46	104.7
160	11.21	15.97	22.72	32.17	45.20	62.95	86.80	118.5
180	11.67	16.79	24.14	34.54	49.03	68.95	95.96	132.1
200	12.09	17.55	25.48	36.80	52.72	74.79	105.0	145.7
250	13.01	19.28	28.56	42.08	61.47	88.83	126.9	179.2
300	13.81	20.81	31.34	46.94	69.66	102.2	148.2	212.2
350	14.51	22.18	33.89	51.48	77.43	115.1	169.0	244.8
400	15.14	23.44	36.26	55.75	84.85	127.6	189.3	277.0
450	15.72	24.60	38.48	59.80	91.97	139.7	209.2	309.0
500	16.26	25.68	40.58	63.68	98.85	151.5	228.8	340.6
600	17.21	27.67	44.47	70.97	112.0	174.2	267.1	403.3
700	18.06	29.45	48.04	77.77	124.4	196.1	304.5	465.3
800	18.82	31.09	51.36	84.18	136.3	217.3	341.0	526.5
900	19.51	32.60	54.46	90.26	147.7	237.9	376.9	587.2
1000	20.15	34.01	57.40	96.07	158.7	257.9	412.2	647.4
1200	21.30	36.59	62.85	107.0	179.7	296.6	481.2	766.6
1400	22.32	38.92	67.85	117.2	199.6	333.9	548.4	884.2
1600	23.23	41.04	72.49	126.8	218.6	369.9	614.2	1001
1800	24.06	43.00	76.85	135.9	236.8	404.9	678.8	1116
2000	24.83	44.84	80.96	144.7	254.4	438.9	742.3	1230
2500	26.53	48.97	90.39	165.0	296.1	520.8	897.0	1513
3000	27.99	52.62	98.90	183.7	335.2	598.9	1047	1791

Table E Values of e^x and e^{-x}

x	e^x	e^{-x}	x	e^x	e^{-x}
0.0	1.0000	1.00000	3.0	20.086	0.04979
0.1	1.1052	0.90484	3.1	22.198	0.04505
0.2	1.2214	0.81873	3.2	24.533	0.04076
0.3	1.3499	0.74082	3.3	27.113	0.03688
0.4	1.4918	0.67032	3.4	29.964	0.03337
0.5	1.6487	0.60653	3.5	33.115	0.03020
0.6	1.8221	0.54881	3.6	36.598	0.02732
0.7	2.0138	0.49659	3.7	40.447	0.02472
0.8	2.2255	0.44933	3.8	44.701	0.02237
0.9	2.4596	0.40657	3.9	49.402	0.02024
1.0	2.7183	0.36788	4.0	54.598	0.01832
1.1	3.0042	0.33287	4.1	60.340	0.01657
1.2	3.3201	0.30119	4.2	66.686	0.01500
1.3	3.6693	0.27253	4.3	73.700	0.01357
1.4	4.0552	0.24660	4.4	81.451	0.01228
1.5	4.4817	0.22313	4.5	90.017	0.01111
1.6	4.9530	0.20190	4.6	99.484	0.01005
1.7	5.4739	0.18268	4.7	109.947	0.00910
1.8	6.0496	0.16530	4.8	121.510	0.00823
1.9	6.6859	0.14957	4.9	134.290	0.00745
2.0	7.3891	0.13534	5.0	148.413	0.00674
2.1	8.1662	0.12246	5.5	244.692	0.00409
2.2	9.0250	0.11080	6.0	403.429	0.00248
2.3	9.9742	0.10026	6.5	665.142	0.00150
2.4	11.0232	0.09072	7.0	1096.633	0.00091
2.5	12.1825	0.08208	7.5	1808.042	0.00055
2.6	13.4637	0.07427	8.0	2980.958	0.00034
2.7	14.8797	0.06721	8.5	4914.769	0.00020
2.8	16.4446	0.06081	9.0	8103.084	0.00012
2.9	18.1741	0.05502	10.0	22026.466	0.00005

AUTHOR INDEX

SUBJECT INDEX